Chinese Religiosities

Chinese Religiosities

Afflictions of Modernity and State Formation

EDITED BY MAYFAIR MEI-HUI YANG

Global, Area, and International Archive
University of California Press

BERKELEY   LOS ANGELES   LONDON

The Global, Area, and International Archive (GAIA) is an initiative
of International and Area Studies, University of California, Berkeley,
in partnership with the University of California Press, the California
Digital Library, and international research programs across the UC
system. GAIA volumes, which are published in both print and open-
access digital editions, represent the best traditions of regional studies,
reconfigured through fresh global, transnational, and thematic
perspectives.

University of California Press, one of the most distinguished university
presses in the United States, enriches lives around the world by
advancing scholarship in the humanities, social sciences, and natural
sciences. Its activities are supported by the UC Press Foundation and
by philanthropic contributions from individuals and institutions. For
more information, visit www.ucpress.edu.

University of California Press
Berkeley and Los Angeles, California

University of California Press, Ltd.
London, England

Library of Congress Cataloging-in-Publication Data

International Conference on Religion, Modernity, and the State in
China and Taiwan (2005 : University of California, Santa Barbara)
    Chinese religiosities : afflictions of modernity and state formation /
edited by Mayfair Mei-hui Yang.
        p.   cm. (Global, area, and international archive)
    Includes bibliographical references (p.   ) and index.
    ISBN: 978-0-520-09864-0 (pbk. : alk. paper)
    1. China—Religion—20th century.   2. Religion and state—China—
20th century.   3. China—Civilization—20th century.   I. Yang,
Mayfair Mei-hui. II. Title.
BL1803.I58   2008
200.951'0904—dc22   2008024032

Contents

Acknowledgments

Most of the essays in this volume were first presented at the International Conference on Religion, Modernity, and the State in China and Taiwan, held at the University of California, Santa Barbara, October 28–30, 2005. This volume could not have been produced without the funding of two key grant agencies that supported the international conference: the Chiang Ching-kuo Foundation and the University of California Pacific Rim Program. The editor and contributors wish to extend our sincere appreciation to these two agencies for their support. We would also like to thank the UCSB Interdisciplinary Humanities Center for providing a conference site and logistical support. Warm appreciation is extended as well to Professor Tu Kuo-ch'ing and his Taiwan Studies Center at UCSB for additional financial support of scholars presenting papers on the religious situation in Taiwan.

The editor also wishes to express appreciation to the following participants at the UCSB conference who presented papers, offered valuable comments and suggestions, and posed challenging questions: Peter van der Veer, Kenneth Dean, Robert Weller, Bill Powell, Julia Huang, Adam Chau, Dan Smyer Yu, Chen Hsi-yuan, Dominic Sachsenmeir, Liu Xun, Kuo Cheng-tian, Fan Lizhu, Christian Jochim, and Charlotte Furth. We are also indebted to Nathan MacBrien at the Division of International and Area Studies at the University of California, Berkeley, for his unflagging support of our volume, for putting up with delays, and for allowing Chinese characters in the body of the text. An anonymous reader provided very useful comments and suggestions for each essay, which are greatly appreciated. Many thanks also go to Pan Shiying for her tireless efforts and detailed work on the Chinese- and Western-language bibliographies and on the formatting of the manuscript. Gratitude is also extended to He Hongguang for his valuable work on the index and in proofreading. Last but not least, Mayfair Yang would like to extend loving thanks to Philip Myers and Kai Keyang Zhang for their patience and family support.

Introduction

Mayfair Mei-hui Yang 楊美惠

At a conference at the University of California, Berkeley, in 2004, I gave a paper on the revival of popular religion based on my fieldwork in rural Wenzhou, on the southeastern coast of China (M. Yang n.d.).[1] Afterward, a U.S.-trained Chinese scholar with an academic position in the U.S, but born and raised in China, asked why I was studying religion when it has never been very important in China and the Chinese people have always been pragmatic and secular, even in imperial times. This was a view familiar to me from the 1980s, in conversations with intellectuals and even with working-class people during two-and-a-half years of living in Beijing. It is symptomatic of the cultural amnesia that has beset China, rendering many Chinese unaware of the vast modern efforts to demonize and eradicate the rich religious life that was long an integral part of China.

The Chinese sociologist C. K. Yang wrote that both Western sinologists and China's own modern cultural elites, including the journalist-reformer Liang Qichao (1873–1929) and philosopher-essayist Hu Shi (1891–1962), held that religion was not an important feature of Chinese culture, and that what religious life there was, such as Buddhism and Christianity, had been introduced from foreign lands (C. K. Yang 1961; Liang 1981a). Yang explained that Western sinologists overlooked the richness of Chinese religious life because they focused on agnostic elite Confucianism and did not pay attention to popular religion. Chinese intellectuals, for their part, denied Chinese religion out of their sense of national humiliation and their need for "emphasizing the dignity of Chinese civilization in the face of the political and economic superiority of the nationalistically oriented Western world" (C. K. Yang 1961:6). Extending his insight, I suggest that the denial of Chinese religion among educated Chinese may have something to do with their internalization of three world orientations introduced from the

1

modern West: (1) a century of Western missionary contempt for Chinese "idol worship" and "superstitions," (2) a sense of the superiority of science and modern rationality in the nationalist cause of China's self-strengthening, and (3) social evolutionist doctrines that arranged different cultures and religious systems of the world into a hierarchical progression whose teleological end was Western-style civilization. Indeed, under the pressures of a Western Protestant and secular outlook, even Confucianism, whose ancient texts were all about ritual practice, was deritualized and made over into a disembodied philosophy and moral system to accord with modern notions of civilized culture.

This volume seeks not only to document the empirical changes that Chinese religious life underwent in modernity, which for China coincided with the twentieth century, but also to reflect upon, evaluate, and critique these changes. We need to ask: what were the self-understandings and historical discourses that propelled these changes in Chinese society, and what historical conditions gave rise to these discourses and collective actions? This collection of essays by historians, anthropologists, sociologists, and religious studies scholars provides a historical background to the vicissitudes of Chinese religious life in the twentieth century, a period of cataclysmic social change, warfare, trauma, and poverty, as well as economic growth at the end of the century. The essays published here document different phases of the transformation, persecution, decline, and resurgence of religious life in China and Taiwan, offering points of comparison with other periods in Chinese history as well as with other places in the world. The twentieth century in China was an unprecedented era, when ambitious social engineering almost succeeded in bringing a sudden end to cultural heritages accumulated over millennia. These momentous changes are too dramatic to merely document; their historical triggering mechanisms, discursive rationales, and political strategies must also be analyzed. The contributors to this volume seek new understandings and evaluations of the social consequences of radical state secularization in China, and an alternative approach to Chinese religious culture.

MODERNITY, SECULARIZATION, AND ÉTATIZATION: AN INTERTWINED PROCESS

The term "modernity," as employed by contributors to this book, both encapsulates and distances itself from the notion of "modernization." In this book's approach to modernity, the various socio-historical changes implied by "modernization" are acknowledged, such as urbanization, industrialization, technological innovations, modern medicine, mass media, mass education and mass political participation, the decline of aristocracies and social hierarchy, the prominence of nation-states, secularization, and the increasing commodification of goods and human labor. However, the contributors to this volume depart from the naïvely positive and teleological connotations of "modernization" as human progress, liberation, and "enlightenment." Whereas Western liberal modernization theories celebrated the modern and sought to root out the stubborn obstacles that traditional culture posed to achieving economic development, the adoption of the term "modernity" here signals a more sober, reflective, and critical stance that seeks to highlight the reconfiguration of power relations with the world's entrance into the modern age.

While "modernization" focuses on material and social changes, the notion of "modernity" in this book emphasizes the new knowledge and discourses that fueled these changes and that have been constitutive of modernity and power. Thus the European Enlightenment of the eighteenth century had a major impact on twentieth-century China. Beginning in the late nineteenth century, Confucian reformist thinkers such as Kang Youwei, Tan Sitong, Yan Fu, and Liang Qichao attempted to expand traditional religious cosmology to accommodate the new Western knowledge of evolutionism that radically altered such basic categories as time, space, and the human role in the cosmos. In the process, they transformed a Confucian cosmology that privileged the power of divine forces, to which the ethical sage must attune his efforts at moral self-cultivation, into a more naturalized cosmology, which gave more primacy to teleological direction and human will, rationality, and action (Furth 1998). Hence at the height of European imperialism, "the reformers' accounts of imperialism were more self-critical than anti-Western" (Furth 1998:37), and they basically accepted Europe as the epitome of civilization (*wenming*). This self-critical spirit, in which China's venerable Confucian culture and religious traditions were found to be "backward," was radicalized in the nationalism of the May Fourth Movement of the 1920s (Schwarz 1986; Chow 1960).[2] Here the freedom of the individual person was upheld in the attack on the authority of patriarchal kinship, gods, elders, and ancestors; significantly, however, this "liberated" individual was at the same time vigorously subsumed to the collective interest of the nation-state and later, to the Revolution and the Party. The centrality of knowledge and discourse in modernity is underscored by the fact that it was the educated class who spearheaded so many modern social movements in China, including the Communist Revolution, and by the importance of such means of disseminating knowledge and discourse as the mass media (newspapers, books, novels, journals, film, and radio), public education, and state propaganda.

In most places around the world, the embracing of Enlightenment knowledge and evolutionism was accompanied by a disparagement of traditional religious orientations. Indeed, it may be said that traditional religious culture usually served as the foil against which modern knowledge was able to ascend. The process of secularization is usually understood as the process whereby traditional religious orientations, rituals, and institutions lose their grip on social life, no longer seem viable in modern urban, industrial, and commercial society, and gradually decline.[3] Secularization can also mean that religious impulses retreat from modern institutions, which become functionally specialized (e.g., political organizations, educational institutions, social welfare agencies, and economic enterprises), so that religion is henceforth exercised only in the private sphere or in specialized religious organizations. This process of secularization was thought of as natural, necessary, and inevitable, given the skepticism and empiricism of modern science and the material accomplishments of modern technology, the emphasis on individual achievement, and the rationalization necessary for efficiency. This volume suggests that although secularization seems to be intrinsic to the initial or early experience of modernity, we cannot assume that the process of modernity will assume a secular mold indefinitely.

Increasingly, over the past two decades, the secularization thesis and its teleology have been criticized for failing to account for the continued viability and persistence of religious orientations in the modern world.[4] Rather than realizing the promises of modernity, secularization may have contributed to the multiple ills of modernity. Some of the troubles of modernity—spiritual impoverishment amid material overproduction, radical class polarization, rural poverty and urban ghettos, uprooted communities, blind industrial and economic growth without regard to social or natural consequences, the plundering of the natural environment, and, above all, the expansion and penetration of state power—may have something to do with secularization and the severing of cultures from their historical embeddedness in religious, ritual, and cosmological systems. Furthermore, the secularization thesis fails to account for the dramatic religious resurgence evident in diverse places around the world. These places include Iran, whose Islamic Revolution shocked the world in 1979; India, where the Hindutva movement burned down the Babri Mosque at Ayodhya in 1992 and captured a political party; the Middle East, Malaysia,

Indonesia, Turkey, and Pakistan, where Islamist movements have corroded secularist state projects and educated women have chosen to readopt the veil; the U.S., where the growing strength of the Christian Right was palpably felt in the 2000 and 2004 presidential elections; and, most recently, Burma and Tibet, where Buddhist monks and nuns joined public opposition to secular military forces in 2007 and 2008. As José Casanova (1994) has observed, Western Europe may be one of the few exceptions in the world to the resurgence of religion in the public sphere.

Outside the West, many secularizing experiences show that they must be understood in terms of the colonial and postcolonial historical contexts in which modernity unfolded, since secularization was part of the colonial process and engendered anti-colonial reactions (Asad 2003; van der Veer 2001; Comaroff & Comaroff 1997). In many colonial places, native religions were suppressed, first by Western (or Japanese) colonizers and missionaries, and then by the nationalist and postcolonial elites in state modernization drives. We have witnessed a resurgence of religious forces in recent years, in which traditional religions are transformed by their engagements with modern conditions, even as they often invoke their archaic and authentic qualities (Nandy 1998; Chatterjee 1998; Mankekar 1999). Thus it is not surprising that critiques of the liberal secularization thesis have been especially forthcoming from scholars of postcolonialism, since secularization has often had devastating consequences for the self-determination and formation of native civil societies (Asad 2003; Bhargava 1998; Chatterjee 1986, 1998; Duara 1995a; Nandy 1998; Esposito & Tamimi 2000; Jakobsen & Pellegrini 2000; Mahmood 2005; Chakrabarty 2000a).

Whereas the more dramatic and vociferous forms of religious resurgence around the world have taken the form of political movements that seek to challenge or even take over the secular state, religious revival in post-Mao China has been marked by quiescence and accommodation with the state. Despite the fact that, in China's long imperial history, many sectarian and millenarian religious movements propelled peasant rebellions to topple and found new dynasties (see David Palmer in this volume), there has been virtually no politically inclined religious movement in China since the Taiping Rebellion (1850–64) and Boxer Rebellion of 1900, except for Tibet and a tiny Uyghur separatist movement (see Dru Gladney in this volume). Although Falungong (Practice of the Wheel of the Law), the body-cultivation movement guided by syncretistic Buddhist-Daoist teachings that blossomed across urban and north China in the 1990s, did possess implicit political messages, it was only after its practitioners encountered harsh state persecution in 1999 that the movement adopted a strident anti-state stance.[5] This relative absence of religious rebellion or fundamentalism may be related to the sheer intensity and systematicity of twentieth-century state secularization drives in China and the deep penetration of modernist and nationalist sentiments, which have caused Chinese religious cultures to lose confidence in traditional cosmologies or become preoccupied with defensive struggles of sheer survival. Thus, in contemporary China, unlike religious resurgences elsewhere in the world, fundamentalism and religious violence have not been a major problem. Rather, state violence against various religious groups has been the dominant theme.

This collection of essays sets itself apart, on the one hand, from the Western liberal paradigm of secularization as a natural process of modernity, and on the other hand, from the dominant Chinese intellectual approach to religion since the May Fourth Movement, when educated Chinese turned against traditional religious culture as a shameful hindrance to modernization. In the liberal paradigm, secularization (or the marginalization of religious practices and institutions from the power structures of society) is regarded as a natural outcome of modernity and capitalism, since this-worldly competition, production, and consumption cannot coexist with other-worldly religious orientations. The essays in this volume suggest that we may need to reverse this assumption for places where modernity, with its Western forms, did not evolve from within their own cultures but was introduced or imposed from outside. Instead of modernity and capitalism leading naturally to secularization in these places, secularization may have emerged only *after* the state forcibly paved the way by means of state secularization campaigns.

Throughout the book, attention is focused on the agency of the modern Chinese state-in-formation, since it can be documented that the decline of religious life in China coincides with the renewal and expansion of the modern state. This volume takes as its starting point the proposition that secularization in China, and perhaps elsewhere in the world, was carefully and sometimes violently engineered in that complex process of "étatization" that gave birth to, and enabled the growth and expansion of, the modern state. The essays assembled here show in different ways that in Chinese modernity there has been a crucial connection and working out of the troubled relationship between religious life and the self-strengthening of the state. It follows that intellectual paradigms such as the secularization thesis and the nationalist disparaging of traditional religion construct a knowledge system that directly benefits the modern state. Thus for scholars to continue to embrace secularism in the context of China's traumatic and painful twentieth century, without reflection or reexamination, is to be complicit with one of the greatest state expansions in modern world history.

This volume is a response to Talal Asad's call (2003) for a reversal of the way anthropology and other disciplines have always studied religion, myths, and rituals as things needing explanation; thus it aims to contribute to a new field of "the anthropology of secularisms." In the course of human history, it has not been religions that have been remarkable but modernity and its insistence on secularization. This is why we need to critically examine modernity's underlying reasons and consequences for human life on the planet.

As Janet Jakobsen and Ann Pellegrini (2000) point out, we need to recognize the plurality of secularization processes and secular ideologies in the modern world. What made Chinese secularization different from the Western experience was the fact that it was a top-down process engineered by the educated elites and the modern state, and that it was part of a nationalist and centralizing process whereby local communities and their deity cults were shorn of their identities and autonomy. At least two genealogies can be traced for this secularization experience: (1) the structure of religio-political authority in China's past, and (2) the semi-colonial history of China's entry into modernity. Confucian religious and moral-political discourse, along with its elaborate system of state sacrificial rituals, was the dominant religious tradition in imperial China because it suffused the state. Anthony Yu (2005) has shown that the sovereign power of the Confucian imperial state contrasted with the institutional weakness of Buddhism, Daoism, and sectarian and popular religions, so that the latter seldom possessed anything comparable to the autonomy and authority of the Church in Europe.[6] This historical legacy may help explain the rapidity with which the flexible polytheistic system of dispersed and differentiated local and regional ritual territorialities of imperial times was swallowed up into a modern monolithic and centralized nation-state territoriality.

Although China was never fully colonized by Western powers, the urgency of foreign imperialist threats to Chinese sovereignty from Western, Japanese, and Russian powers, and the desperate desire for state-strengthening, were essential ingredients contributing to the violent and totalizing nature of the modern secularization process in China. In contrast to many other colonies of the West, Chinese nationalist elites eagerly embraced all the modern discourses that the West had to offer: Enlightenment, social evolutionism, Protestantism, and scientific atheism. The Protestant-informed categories of "religion" and "super-stition" produced a new definition of "civilization" (*wenmin*) modeled on Western science and progress, and distant from the old Confucian notions of the cultured and cultivated sage. At the same time, these categories were indispensable tools in the relentless disenchantment of social life.

Although they did not explicitly employ the terms "secularization" or "secularism," Marxist theorists and the various state socialist societies they inspired comprised an alternative secularizing force and discourse to Western liberalism. Marxist evolutionary theory also inscribed the historical necessity of revolutionary progress toward a communist stage of equal distribution and productive abundance through "materialist" rather than spiritual means. It regarded the peasant class as backward-looking and religion as "the sigh of the oppressed" and "opium of the people," whose abolition would not only relieve the peasants of their "illusory happiness" but be a step toward their attainment of "real happiness" (Marx 1970). Since Marxist class theory understood religion to be "the expression of real suffering and a protest against real suffering" (Marx 1970), as well as an instrument of domination by the ruling class, it also assumed that after the class struggle and revolutionary victory, the need for religion would naturally subside. In the various state socialist societies, the revolutionary state took pains to reeducate the masses to give up their superstitions and embrace "atheism." At the same time, socialist states took control of religious institutions, their land and properties, and either eliminated the religious clergy or absorbed them into civil servant bureaucracies (Lane 1981; Grant 1995; Sorokowski 1989:22; Sapiets 1989; Husband 2000; MacInnis 1972, 1989).

Neither the Marxist nor the liberal understanding of religion and modernity, both of which had a powerful influence in twentieth-century China, was able to see the beneficial role of religious life. Liberal secularization theory presented a depoliticized "natural history" of religion in modernity, in which the decline of religion was but the natural outcome of the structures and needs of economic development and modernization. And although Marxism was quite aware of the political role of religion, as a legitimation device for the old ruling class or as the voice of class suffering or popular protest, it did not foresee that the elimination of religious culture from the people would be a key enabling factor for a new kind of secular state domination and penetration. Community rituals were thought to be pointless and superstitious, and their roles in integrating communities, forging local identities, and maintaining local autonomy from the state (Duara 1988a) were all unappreciated. What both Chinese and Western historians have recently discovered about lineages, monasteries, and temple associations in late imperial China—namely, their important role as social welfare and charitable organizations that collected donations from the rich and gave relief to the poor, especially in times of natural disaster and social crisis (Li S. 2005; Brook 1993; Wang 1997; Duara 1988a; Zheng 1995:37; J. Smith 1999; Zhang 2005)—was clearly not understood in the twentieth-century decimation of Chinese religious organizations. Buddhism's teachings on the interconnectedness of all forms of living beings and the fleetingness of human life, and the emphasis on living in harmony with nature found in Daoism and Chinese geomancy (*fengshui*), were forgotten in the Faustian pursuit of industrial production. Such catastrophic events as the great famine after the Great Leap Forward, deforestation, and, since the 1980s, accelerated air pollution in cities, water pollution, and pervasive degradation of the natural environment can all be linked to the loss of traditional Chinese religious environmentalism (Cai 2007). Even as traditional Chinese medicine was preserved by the modern state as Chinese "science," its genealogy and embeddedness in Daoist religious practices of health, longevity, immortality, and ritual cultivation of the body was willfully forgotten. Similarly, the Chinese Marxist glorification of peasant rebellions always left out the crucial religious and apocalyptic inspirations for the struggles of the poor and oppressed, and the age-old need for human actions to conform with shifting cosmological patterns.

One of the consequences of modernity is that we tend to think of religion and state politics as two separate categories, each with its separate institutions, imaginaries, and practices, and forget that throughout most of human history they were intimately linked and mutually embedded. The sovereign powers of past state orders all had their ritual capitals, court and state rituals, and cosmologies that embedded earthly political orders in the realms of the sacred transcendant (Geertz 1980; Zito 1997; K. C. Chang 1983; Carrasco 2000). Indeed, secularization does not merely affect the social realm but entails the sundering of this deep connection of the political and the sacred, and the expansion of the political sphere at the expense of the religious sphere. Neither liberal nor Marxist theory has been able to confront the profound and intricate imbrication of religious power with premodern state orders, much less the wrenching experience of modernity's attempt to pull them asunder. The incompleteness, or perhaps the impossibility, of this rupture between the sacred/religious and the political order—what Claude Lefort suggested might be the "permanence of the theological-political" (1988)—has been demonstrated again and again in modernity. We have seen this "permanence" in the various leader-cults of the modern world, from the Meiji emperor at the dawn of Japanese modernity to the quasi-religious energies generated by the cults of Hitler, Stalin, Hirohito, and Mao Zedong. Walter Benjamin observed that, in the "age of mechanical reproduction" (photography and film), art which has for millennia been embedded in religious ritual and exuded a sacred "aura" loses that aura, becoming alienated from its function as magical technology and is transformed into an object increasingly used in mass politics (1969:224). Thus art moves from the religious to the political sphere. For Benjamin, the "cult value" of art finds "a last refuge" and "ultimate entrenchment" in the "human countenance," seen in the obsession with portraiture in early photography, where "aura emanates . . . in the fleeting expression of a human face" (1969:226). In modernity's leadership cults around the world, we see the stubborn tenacity of modern sovereign power's "aura," in which portraits of the national leader are ubiquitous in the social landscape, as in the powerful cult of Mao (M. Yang 1994a).

In the course of human history, the violent birth or rebirth of so many new state orders was not just a political event but also a religious one. State Shinto launched the modern Japanese state, and more recently we are seeing how militant religious movements ranging from Islamism to Hindutva to fundamentalist Christianity are trying to reclaim from secularism not only the public sphere but the modern state itself. At the same time, there have been modern religious movements, ranging from Tibetan and Burmese Buddhism to the Polish Catholic Church and Latin American Liberation Theology, that have pushed in a different direction of contesting state sovereignty. Whether establishing or resisting the state, these modern attempts to reconnect the political and religious spheres have often had explosive and violent results. In this "return of the repressed," we can see that the story of modernity and secularization remains an unfinished tale. Thus it is only by abandoning the "natural history" narrative of modernization or revolution, and linking the vicissitudes of religions to the birth pains and growth traumas of the modern state, that we can see secularization and religious resurgence as different phases of a single troubled and unfinished process in the modern history of the state. Only then can we begin to address the urgent question of how to divert the ever-present power of religious energies away from the militant and expansionist projects of modern nation-states and toward projects of recovering the lost ground of local communities, public spheres, and national and global civil societies.

"RELIGION," "SUPERSTITION," AND TECTONIC SHIFTS IN THE MODERN CHINESE STATE ORDER

Like most societies before modern times, Chinese culture got along without the notion of religion and without distinguishing the religious from other aspects of social life (Schipper 1993:2–3). Religious traditions were designated by the term *jiao* (教, "teachings")—as in *fojiao* for Buddhism, *daojiao* for Daoism, and *Hui jiao* for Islam—but there was no universal or generic category of religion to designate human relations with the supernatural realm. Historians and other scholars of modern China inform us that the pregnant linked terms *zongjiao* (宗教, "religion") and *mixin* (迷信, "superstition") were introduced to China from the West via Japan at the very end of the nineteenth century and gained increasing life and potency in the early twentieth century (Goossaert 2005b, 2006b; Nedostup 2001; Cohen 1993; L. Liu 1995; Chen X. 2002). The modern Chinese term *zongjiao* was rendered from the Japanese term *shukyo*, which made use of classical Chinese characters, or *kanji*; thus their readoption into China has earned them the label of "return graphic loans" by Lydia Liu (1995:33; Nedostup 2001:22–26). *Zongjiao* in classical Chinese was originally associated with Buddhism, appearing in usage from the Six Dynasties period (220–589 C.E.) onward. The compound referred to the specific teachings of a sect, or school of thought (Chen X. 2002:45–54), and did not possess the full meaning of what we mean by religion in modern times—namely, a distinct religious system in contrast to secular life and differentiated from other religious systems. In modern times, the compound was first used in an 1869 maritime trade treaty between Japan and Germany to translate the German *religionsubung* and the English phrase "exercise of religion" (Chen X. 2002:48; Nedostup 2001:23). Writing in 1913, the British missionary and later professor of Chinese at Oxford University W. E. Soothill noted, "The Chinese, recognizing this deficiency [namely, that they had no word corresponding to the Western concept; their word usually so translated 'does not mean either religion or a church in our sense of those terms'] and feeling the need of a term meaning a religion, have recently adopted the term Tsung-Chiao from the Japanese, who had adapted it to suit their own need for a term to cover the Western idea of religion" (Soothill 1923:6; cited in W. C. Smith 1962:58). The term *zongjiao* was rapidly popularized through the 1902 writings of the late Qing reformer and scholar Liang Qichao (Bastid-Bruguiere 1998; Nedostup 2001:24–27). From the first uses of this term in China, the notion of religion was closely linked with the notion of Christianity, and they were often taken to refer to one and the same thing, with the consequence that throughout the twentieth century in China, ideas of religion implicitly took Christianity, and more specifically Protestantism, as the standard and quintessential model of religion.

Similarly, the neologism *mixin* is a modern category, and can be translated as "misguided belief." My digital search of the vast *Siku Quanshu*, the eighteenth- century compilation of officially approved texts of the whole Qing empire, revealed no use of the term *mixin*.[7] According to the authoritative *Hanyu da cidian* (Luo 2001), the compound *mixin* only started to appear as a term in late Qing texts. Classical Chinese since ancient times had the term *mi*, which had various meanings of "indistinct or blurred," "confused," "infatuated with," and "lost."[8] These older usages of *mi* did not oppose categories of the false illusory supernatural world against true empirical reality, or religion against science and rationality, as did the late Qing, early Republican notion of *mixin*. The term *mixin* was taken from the modern Japanese *meishin*, which first appeared in Japanese writing in 1889 (Nedostup 2001:26). In 1902, the reformist intellectual Liang Qichao was one of the first Chinese to publicly disseminate the distinction between religion and superstition, by emphasizing that religion can be useful in modern society if its moral teachings are retained but its superstitions destroyed (Liang 1981b; Nedostup 2001:27; Bastid-Bruguiere 1998). Although Liang briefly flirted with the idea of modern China adopting a state religion such as Confucianism, he expressed contempt for things like magical Daoism, which he thought did not merit the status of religion and had only done damage to Chinese civilization (Liang 1981a).

In her book on the cultural translation of foreign ideas in early twentieth-century China, Lydia Liu makes the point that "translingual practices" are not merely the linguistic translation of one language into another; rather, they are the very medium in and through which cultural and political power relations are negotiated and implemented, and in the modern era there was a deep asymmetry in the power relations between China and the West (L. Liu 1995). The slippages, distortions, enhancements, and accommodations of meaning that occur as a guest language enters a host language are produced as the host reappropriates the alien form and inscribes new values to fit it into its own environment and to meet the needs of the time. The guest language may simultaneously serve as a vehicle through which a foreign discursive power becomes embodied within a host culture, lodged deeply in something as pedestrian, unconscious, and everyday as language. These power tensions and realignments could be observed quite clearly when the Western relational terms of "religion" and "superstition" entered Chinese linguistic usage. First of all, the notion of "religion" was itself quite new in the West, and the term "superstition" had taken on new political significance after the Protestant Reformation and the Enlightenment, which had an ambivalent relationship with an older Roman Catholicism. When these terms were introduced into Japan, they were positioned and shaped by the political exigencies of the Meiji Restoration there, which sought to promote State Shinto and emperor worship and weaken the political hold of Buddhist and sectarian traditions (Hardacre 1989; Ketelaar 1990). Later, when these terms entered the Chinese vocabulary, they were swept up into the national elite efforts to reform traditional culture and promote a new nationalism in order to counter the threats posed by European and Japanese imperialism.

According to Wilfred Cantwell Smith, the modern English notion of "religion" derives from ancient Roman times, from the Latin term *religio*. However, the sense we give to the term "religion" today—that of an integrated body of beliefs, moral teachings, and practices organized into an observable discreet social institution, with its own history and particular geography—is of very recent vintage, dating only to the nineteenth century in the West. Originally, the Latin term was used only as an adjective, to designate an awesome higher power or a taboo (W. C. Smith 1962:20–21). Among Renaissance humanists and Protestant Reformers, the term came to describe an inner piety of individual worshippers. Later, the European Enlightenment, the religious clashes in the seventeenth and eighteenth centuries, and European encounters with far-flung exotic religious life around the world shaped the word's modern meaning and added the semantic layer of a discreet category of "religion in general," as opposed to economic, political, or artistic life. Thus Smith makes the important argument that for most of human history people have been religious without needing the notion of religion, and that "the rise of the concept of 'religion' is in some ways correlated with a decline in the practice of religion itself" (W. C. Smith 1962:19). Yet whereas in Europe "religion" was a term that emerged into consciousness alongside the gradual decline or transformation of religious life, in China the introduction of this term facilitated an active and purposive suppression of religious life. This suppression was undertaken without benefit of detailed examinations of just how Chinese religious practices might work differently from Christian ones, or how they operated and played beneficial roles in a Chinese social order.

Up until the sixteenth and seventeenth centuries, there were many points of similarity in the religious life of ordinary European and Chinese people, but the Protestant Reformation involved a purging of the magical in European Christianity, especially in Protestant areas (Thomas 1971; H. Geertz 1975).[9] An austere and rationalized Protestantism sought to expel older "idolatrous" traditions of magic, exorcism, miracles, divination, ghosts and devils, witchcraft, religious charms, and even worship of the saints and the Virgin Mary, all of which were part of Catholic practice. Liturgical services were also drastically scaled down in Protestantism. These older elements in Catholicism were then regarded as "superstitions" that needed to be eliminated to prevent them from corrupting "true" religion, harking back to the early Judeo-Christian invention of mono-theism and its anti-pagan discourse (Tambiah 1990). Nineteenth-century Protestant missionary accounts of Chinese religions frequently expressed horror and disgust at the "idolatry" and dizzying array of polytheistic gods to whom the Chinese kowtowed in what the Protestants considered to be servile obeisance (Reinders 2004; Roberts 1992). Indeed, missionaries in China often paraphrased biblical passages such as Psalm 115, which points out the inanimate nature of idols:

> Their idols are silver and gold, the work of men's hands.
> They have mouths, but do not speak; eyes, but do not see.
> They have ears, but do not hear; noses, but do not smell.
> They have hands, but do not feel; feet, but do not walk;
>   and they do not make a sound in their throat.
> Those who make them are like them; so are all who trust in them.
>   (NORTON, ed. 2005:786; quoted in Reinders 2004:9)

In the writings of the anti-ritualistic Protestants, Chinese "ritual was con-sistently described as useless, degraded, empty, and ridiculous . . . China was perceived as uniquely engulfed in ritual" (Reinders 2004:96). Thus Chinese religious practices were easily slotted into existing Protestant polemics against Catholic ritualism and "superstition."

In nineteenth-century Europe, carried along by the momentum of evolutionary theories, this Protestant "religion" versus "superstition" dynamic was transformed into the "religion" versus "magic" binarism of early sociology and anthropology (Tambiah 1990). The evolutionist distinc-tion between religion, which was privileged as more advanced, and magic, which was considered the product of more primitive societies and the folk religions of the European past, became an important issue for nineteenth-century social science thinkers such as James Frazer and Edward B. Tylor. For sociologist Emile Durkheim, the difference between magic and reli-gion lay in the fact that magic answered only to individual needs and its specialist practitioners had no social organization, whereas religion was "a unified system of beliefs and practices relative to sacred things, . . . which unite into one single moral community called a Church, all those who adhere to them" (1995:39–44). For anthropologist Bronislaw Malinowski, the difference between magic and religion lay in the "extreme simplicity" of magic, which he regarded as an early "pseudo-science" of spells and ritual techniques seeking intervention in nature, while religion possessed more complex tenets, cosmologies, myths, and gods, and promoted harmony with the environment, courage in times of crisis, and equanimity at the prospect of death (1992:87–90). Thus an older Protestant distinction between religion and superstition was preserved in the new, supposedly secular social-evolutionist theories, which privileged religion over magic as the more advanced form.

At first, China seemed quite capable of holding its own in the face of the dual intrusion of Protestant and evolutionary discourses. Taiwan scholar Chen Xiyuan (Chen Hsi-Yuan) has shown how the Qing imperial government official Peng Guangyu, who was invited to represent Confucianism at the First World Congress of Religions in Chicago in 1893, resisted the Western tendency to relativize Confucianism and relegate it to the category of "religion," or *zongjiao* (H. Chen 2005). Peng argued that Confucianism was not a religion, for it had superceded religion long before, when it displaced ancient Chinese shamanism (*wu*), which shared many features with Christianity: worship of God, prophecy and revelation, priests and missionaries. Instead, Peng sought to relativize both "religion" and Christianity to the status of Chinese secondary "teachings" (*jiao*) such as Buddhism, Daoism, and Islam, which in the imperial Chinese order revolved around the primary "teaching" (*jiao*), or "sun," of Confucianism.

Very rapidly, however, the confidence of nineteenth-century Chinese imperial authorities in the superiority of Confucian civilization gave way to a new respect for Western science, technology, and culture. In the new Copernican universe of early twentieth-century Chinese reformers, nationalists, and revolutionaries, all religions of the world, including the old universal imperial Confucian cosmology, were made to revolve around the new sun of Science. Their embrace of the Western terminology of "religion" and "superstition" emphasized the Western Enlightenment sense of religion as being opposed to science and rationality, the post-Reformation sense of superstition as the idolatrous and magical corruption of a true authentic religion, and the evolutionist sense of superstitions as primitive precursors of religion. From the Japanese Meiji-era context of usage, Chinese nationalists kept the pejorative sense of "religion" as a sectarian tradition opposed both to modern education and to the establishment of a new national imperial authority and "state doctrine," or *kokkyo* (Ketelaar 1990:41; Nedostup 2001).

The Guangxu emperor's edict of 1898 decreed that all temples of the empire, with the exception of sites for state sacrifices, be taken by local officials and converted into schools and state offices. Vincent Goossaert (2006) has persuasively argued that this edict of the Hundred Days Reform Movement (Wuxu Bianfa) was the first turning point in China from an older Confucian anti-clerical (i.e., anti-Buddhist and anti-Daoist) movement, familiar in late imperial times, to a new modern anti-superstition movement.[10] What was new about this movement and its language was its harsh iconoclasm, its support of state-strengthening, and its attacks on China's myriad local-community territorial cult organizations. Territorial cults had always been exempt from late imperial state crackdowns on sectarian and heterodox cults (*xiejiao, yinsi*). Now, instead of the former language of preserving state orthodoxy (*zhengjiao*) against heterodoxy (*xiejiao*), in which the imperial state positioned itself inside a religious cosmology while championing the orthodox religious stance, this edict took the unprecedented position of standing outside a religious worldview altogether to promote modern science and education. Although internal court intrigue led to the abrogation of this edict, in subsequent years local officials across the empire seized local temples and ritual sites, destroyed icons of gods inside them, and converted them into schools, local state offices, or sources of revenue for the expanding state.

The fact that this first salvo against superstition originated from within the state in 1898 shows that the primary agent of secularization in modern China was, and is, the state. Much like the Protestant Reformation, which was a bridge between a religious medieval society and a modern secular society, state Confucianism in China, which had always had secular tendencies, led the way to Chinese secularization in the last years of the Qing dynasty. This leadership by scholar-officials and the new intelligentsia of Chinese secularization challenges the traditional Marxist understanding of religion and modernity. Here, neither the old imperial ruling class nor the new nationalist ruling class were vested in preserving religion to bolster its legitimacy or to give numbing opium to the people. Instead, they were in the forefront of seeking to "enlighten" the people and liberate them from the shackles of religion and superstition to strengthen the nation. Similarly, it was not the people who demanded that the state secularize and rationalize itself, and divest itself of its ancient ritual apparatuses of state sacrifice and ceremonies, patronage of Buddhist and Daoist temples, and state canonization of gods. The turn against ritual, religion, and superstition came from within the ranks of the state and new intellectual elites themselves, propelled by external threats to China's national sovereignty. Thus the situation of Chinese religious culture in modernity must be approached with a Foucauldian skepticism about Enlightenment notions of "liberation," and remain alert to how new modes of power are deployed through the very process of "liberation" (Foucault 1978, 1982). Rather than being the natural byproduct of modernization pressures, the fortunes of Chinese religious life must be understood as part of the internal transformation of the state order—that is, as the effects of radical measures in the self-strengthening of the state. As the state shed its ancient religious and ritual apparatuses, the category of religion came to be positioned outside it, as a target that helped the state define itself and strengthen its leadership role in modernity.

Early on in the Republican era, five world religions came to be recognized in China as enjoying the "freedom of religion"—Catholicism, Protestantism, Islam, Buddhism, and Daoism (Goossaert 2005b)—and these five legitimate religions are still the same in the era of the People's Republic today. Yet the multitude of local community temples and territorial cult associations formed around gods, goddesses, and immortals, along with sectarian traditions, many of which were undergoing transformation into what Prasenjit Duara has called modern "redemptive societies" (Duara 2003), were all placed into the category of "superstitions" to be purged from the social body. Other popular forms of religious life, such as geomancy (*fengshui*), exorcism, divination, spirit possession and shamanistic travel, and the placating of ghosts and demons, were also lumped into this category. The reason probably derives from the nationalist elites' unthinking adoption of Christianity as the model for what a legitimate religion should look like: a church-like organization, an organized clergy and ordination system, a textual history, theological doctrines and scriptures, and so forth.

The distinction between religion and superstition continues to have a strong hold today in China. In my fieldwork in rural Wenzhou from 1991 to 2005, local elders who manage deity temple associations and sit on lineage and festival organizational committees often asked me how to distinguish between religion and superstition, precisely because they are frequently accused by local government officials of fomenting superstition yet feel that what they are doing is beneficial to the community. Indeed, to get around the problem of being banned as "superstition," most deity temples there sought to register with local governments as Daoist organizations and started learning Daoist rituals, which are more legitimate in official eyes.

The distinction has become so entrenched in state logic that in 2001, when I interviewed an official at the Religious Affairs Bureau of the State Council in Beijing and asked about deity temples, ancestor rituals, ghost festivals, divination, and geomancy, he informed me that his office only dealt with "the five religions, not superstitions." He suggested I go to the Ministry of Civil Affairs (Minzhengbu) or the Ministry of Public Security because superstitions were handled by these bureaucracies.

Given the destructive effects of the categories of religion and superstition in modern China, and the problems of imposing the Western/Protestant category of "religion" onto the unique features and organizational forms of Chinese religious practices, the title of this volume is "Chinese Religiosities." Here Wilfred Cantwell Smith's observation is relevant: that "human history might prove more intelligible if we learned to think of religion and the religions as adjectives rather than as nouns—that is, as secondary to persons or things rather than as things in themselves" (W. C. Smith 1962:20). The term "religiosity" takes the adjective "religious" and makes it a noun. In adopting this term in our title, I wish to avoid two damaging distinctions that the old term "religion" implies and activates: (1) the distinction between religion and superstition, and (2) the distinction between inner (individual) faith and collective religious institution.

At the beginning of the twenty-first century, we are trying to operate in a more decentered global order that does not privilege the West as the single model of modernity, so we no longer have the nineteenth-century European need to distinguish between religion and superstition. We have seen how this distinction excluded and denigrated not only non-Western religiosities in relation to Christianity but also the religiosities of the lower classes, and of rural and uneducated people in relation to urban educated people. In the Daoist tradition, this distinction is especially inappropriate because of the intertwined histories of philosophical and textual Daoism, alchemical and body-cultivation technologies, the complex pantheon of gods, goddesses, and immortals, herbal and talismanic healing techniques, and a transcendental cosmology. Being at once magical technology, textual philosophy, self-cultivation, medical practice, and collective rituals, Daoism defies the distinction between magic/superstition and religion, and between religion and science. It can only be hoped that contemporary Chinese intellectuals and official policies will soon shed this foreign, nineteenth-century distinction between religion and superstition.

The reason to avoid the second distinction, between individual piety or faith and religious institution, is, again, that it privileges the Protestant emphasis on religious interiority, whereas many other religious traditions prioritize ritual performance and collectivity over individual faith. In English usage, the term "religiosity" is often employed to designate the religious feeling or experience of individual believers, harking back to the Reformation notion of *religio* as the inner piety of individual worshippers. By adopting the term "religiosity" in place of the old term "religion," we contribute to erasing this distinction, which, though important in Christianity, is often unnecessary or even misleading when applied to other religious traditions. Since this distinction is often predicated on a deep mind-body division that seems central to Christianity, it does not work well for Chinese religiosities, which are organized around ritual performance and do not uphold the mind-body division.

ICONOCLASM, EVOLUTIONISM, AND THE CHINESE COMMUNIST REVOLUTION

After the Confucian scholar-official reformers of the late Qing, the 1919 May Fourth Movement, often called the "Chinese Enlightenment," of educated urban elites gave further impetus to anti-superstitious ventures. The deepening of Chinese intellectual convictions about the value of Western science and social evolutionism meant that the tenor of May Fourth discourse was much more radical and iconoclastic than before. Although the dismissal of traditional Chinese religiosities originated among Westerners, the new Chinese intelligentsia exerted full agency and creatively adapted Western Orientalist discourse to their nationalist discourse. Major intellectuals, including Chen Duxiu, Hu Shih, and Cai Yuanpei, castigated popular religion for its backwardness. In an article published in the influential journal *New Youth* (新青年), entitled "On the Smashing of Idols" (*Ouxiang pohuai lun*), Marxist Chen Duxiu held forth in a long diatribe that echoed Protestant missionary discourse:

> These idols made of clay and carved in wood are really useless things; but just because someone respects them, worships them, burns incense and kowtows to them, and says they have magical efficacy (*lingyan*), ignorant villagers become superstitious of these manmade idols and believe that they really possess the power to reward good deeds and punish evil. . . . All religions are idols that cheat people; Amitabha Buddha is a cheat and a liar, Jehovah is a cheat and a liar, and so is the Jade Emperor. All the gods, buddhas, immortals, and ghosts that are revered by religionists are useless and cheating idols, and they should all be smashed! (Chen D. 1918b:99)

In the same article, Chen unexpectedly goes on to declare in an anarchist vein that the state (*guojia*) is also an idol that domestically upholds the power of the aristocratic and propertied classes, and that promotes international competition between states, thus posing an obstacle to achieving world peace and the state of Great Unity (*datong*) for humankind. However, Chen's call to smash the state was ignored in the twentieth century; only his slogan to smash religious idols was heeded.

Armed with May Fourth convictions, schoolteachers, professors, and students trudged patriotically into the countryside to ransack temples and forcibly convert the rural people to modernity. These forays, however, were small in scale compared to the more systematic destruction of religious sites carried out by the modern state. Prasenjit Duara has shown that after the collapse of the Qing dynasty in 1911, the new Republic conducted several anti-superstition campaigns in which soldiers, officials, and local gentry captured local temples and smashed idols (Duara 1991, 1995). The captured temples provided offices and revenue sources for the expanding local governments, as well as classrooms for new schools. In the 1920s, Mao Zedong observed with approval the smashing of temple gods and the appropriation of temple buildings and property by local peasant associations and the Guomindang local government in rural Hunan Province (Mao 1965). So great was religious destruction throughout China that by the 1940s it is estimated that well over half the temples that had existed at the time of the emperor's edict in 1898 had been seized, destroyed, or diverted from their religious uses (Goossaert 2006:308). Most of the remaining temples met their fate after the Communist Revolution of 1949, especially during Land Reform (1949–51), the Great Leap Forward campaign (1958–60), and the devastating "Smash the Four Olds" (破四舊) campaign (1966–69) of the Cultural Revolution.

Given the ferocity and destructiveness of the anti-religious movements in twentieth-century China—perhaps the most dramatic and systematic in the modern world, and certainly in China's own three-thousand-year history—it is incumbent upon us to examine the compelling reasons and discursive rationales for them. These can be summed up in three words: scientism, evolutionism, and nationalism. Danny Kwok has shown how "scientism," or the doctrine "which places all reality within a natural order and deems all aspects of this order, be they biological, social, physical, or psychological, to be knowable only by the methods of science" (Kwok 1965:21), held sway among May Fourth Chinese intellectuals of the 1910s and 1920s, intensifying into "science-worship" in the 1930s, and thereafter. The doctrine or ideology of science was far more important than the actual practice of science, due to the newness of science at that time, the lack of financial and institutional resources, and the paucity of trained scientists, which meant that very few scientific experiments were carried out in China. Indeed, most of the vociferous proponents of science had little training in scientific methods and tended to equate science with social science and social evolutionism (Kwok 1965:81). What science gave these intellectuals was an authoritative weapon in their relentless attacks against all things traditional in Chinese culture. The skepticism and hypothesis-making spirit of science were often forgotten in the new dogmatic faith in science. At about the same time that Einstein's General Theory of Relativity (1907–15) and Heisenberg's Uncertainty Principle (1927) and quantum mechanics emerged, Chinese scientism was promoting the old Newtonian world, with its rigid universal and absolute laws and nineteenth-century determinism and foundationalism, to an axiomatic Truth for the explanation of all reality. The doctrine of materialism, in which all phenomena of the universe, including human culture, ethics, and religious and spiritual matters, are reducible to material aspects of nature and move according to predictable scientific laws, had special appeal.[11]

Ever since Yan Fu translated Thomas Huxley's *Evolution and Ethics* into Chinese in 1898, and Herbert Spencer's *A Study of Sociology* in 1902 (Wright 2001; Furth 1998), Western nineteenth-century social evolutionism has had a profound effect on the thinking of China's nationalist intellectuals. Given the dire situation of China—beset by corruption and ineffectualness at court, military and economic humiliations suffered at the hands of the European, American, and Japanese powers, the danger these powers posed of dividing up the Chinese empire among themselves, and the miserable poverty and lack of education of the mass of the people—it is not surprising that social evolutionism gave Chinese educated elites a persuasive discourse with which to address their situation. The Chinese interpretation of social evolutionist theories was that, in the "struggle for existence" among races and the competition among nations, China was overburdened by its long history and old thinking, and hence not "fit" to compete. The Chinese race was in danger of extinction, both physically and culturally. Although China had an ancient civilization and was far more developed than the primitive peoples of the world, who remained without writing, agriculture, and philosophy, China lacked the scientific spirit that was necessary for the "survival of the fittest" in the modern world. Instead, to most intellectuals of the time, the Chinese people were lost in a stupor of religion and superstition.

In 1919, the journal *New Youth* published a translation of one chapter from the popular book *The Wonders of Life,* written by German evolutionary biologist Ernst Haeckel (1905, 1919), some of whose ideas later were to prove attractive and useful to the Nazis.[12] The translator wrote in the preface that he had decided to publish this translation because he was fed up with Chinese "spiritualism"—the "City Gods, Earth Gods, the Four Generals, the 'original Dao,'" and so forth. He wanted to make people aware that the Chinese thinking of his day was equivalent to that of the European Middle Ages, and that only "materialism" (*weiwu de yiyuan-lun*) could provide medicine for China. Haeckel's chapter was typical in its nineteenth-century opposition of science and religion/superstition, construction of a hierarchy of races of the world, and sense of European superiority. Haeckel asserted that "superstition and unreason are the worst enemies of the human race, while science and reason are its greatest friends. Hence it is our duty and task to attack the belief in miracles wherever we find it, in the interest of the race" (Haeckel 1905:56; 1919:108–9). He outlined an evolutionary history of religions in which the lowest stage of "savages" (the Veddahs of Ceylon, Andaman Islanders, Bushmen, Australian negroes, Hottentots, etc.) worshipped "fetishes," whereas the next stage of "barbarians" (who possessed agriculture and cattle) had progressed to "animism," worshipping gods in the forms of men and animals and holding notions of the immortal soul. Finally, with the highest stage of "civilization," religion evolves with the subordination of all the gods to a chief god, until the achievement of "monotheism," the Reformation, and then modern science (Haeckel 1905:59; 1919:129). Never mind that the invention of monotheism actually took place when the Jews were a stateless tribal people; for Haeckel, monotheism and post-Reformation Christianity were evolutionarily the highest and most civilized religious forms, until science displaced religion.

Given the deep influence of such evolutionist thinking on the ranks of educated Chinese, it is not surprising that those who entered officialdom should vigorously pursue state anti-superstition campaigns, and that those who did not become officials should support them. Evolutionist thought, with its unconscious post-Reformation influences and its denigration of magic, animism, and polytheistic systems of multiple gods as "lower stages" of human evolution, also helps explain the contempt that Liang Qichao and other Chinese elites had for popular Daoism, folk religion, and shamanism in China, with their multitudes of gods, goddesses, and immortals.

The categories of "savagery, barbarism, and civilization" were common tropes in nineteenth-century Western thought. In 1877, Lewis Henry

Morgan had already published his classic *Ancient Society, or Researches in the Lines of Human Progress from Savagery through Barbarism to Civilization*. This was a book with far-reaching consequences, not only in the history of anthropology as a discipline but in China after the Communist Revolution, because Karl Marx and Friedrich Engels had been inspired by Morgan's work. Morgan argued that there was a single line of evolutionary progression of technological, kinship, marriage, and property systems, and that these systems were coordinated with one another, forming three great stages of evolution through which all human societies passed at different times. Morgan was attracted to the communal property system of the Iroquois and other "savage" peoples, and his discovery of what he called "the gens" (clans) as forms of social organization was a breakthrough. However, his description of the beginnings of the state (what he called "nations") was limited mainly to the examples of Greece and Rome, which explains why he defined civilization as the invention of the phonetic alphabet and the keeping of written records.

Both Marx and Engels were greatly excited by Morgan's writing, especially his materialist focus on the history of human technologies and their transformation of social organization. One can easily see how Engels modeled his classic *The Origin of the Family, Private Property, and the State*, first published in 1884, on Morgan's book. This is a book of historical materialism, in which the simple technology of hunting-and-gathering societies produces an egalitarian sexual division of labor and "primitive communism" without private property, while the advent of pastoral livelihoods gives rise to the first patriarchal private property of domesticated animal herds. Following Morgan, Engels accords the state a diminutive origin and function: merely to guarantee the domination of the owners of private property, whether slave owners, feudal lords, or modern capitalists. Both Morgan's and Engel's books were translated into Chinese and widely read by educated Chinese after the Chinese Communist Revolution of 1949.

In the Soviet Union, Joseph Stalin went on to write "Dialectical and Historical Materialism" in 1938, outlining the evolutionary history of humankind. Stalin's book in which this essay appeared became a standard text for Communists the world over, and was required reading for all Chinese Communist Party members in the 1950s (Stalin 1972:300). In Stalin's synthesis of Morgan and Engels, human history is summed up in five stages, or "modes of production": primitive communal, slave, feudal, capitalist, and socialist. Unlike in the Soviet Union, there was never a Khrushchevian denunciation of Stalinism in China, and many of Stalin's ideas, especially this five-stage theory, held sway well into the 1980s. Thus Marxist knowledge, which generally underestimated state power and presumed that class structure issued from impersonal technological and economic forces, took root in a land where, since ancient times, an archaic state had exerted inordinate power over not only the peasantry but the aristocracy, landed gentry, merchants, trade, and the markets as well. The doctrine of historical materialism took over a land where the ancient invention of bronze technology in the Shang dynasty was applied *not* to economic subsistence but to two technologies that launched the birth of the state: bronze ritual vessels and weapons of war (K. C. Chang 1983). Presiding over a modern China that witnessed perhaps the greatest expansion of the state in modern history, Marxism did not help people recognize that the new class structure of socialist society was a political product of the state rather than a product of an independent market economy.

In American anthropology, Morgan's ethnocentrism and "unilineal evolutionism," in which all cultures of the world are presumed to follow a single trajectory of development modeled after the history of Europe, have largely been discredited. In the notion of "multilinear evolution," different cultures follow many different paths of evolution, in accordance with their changing ecological environment and cultural diffusion from other cultures (Steward 1955).[13] In 1950s China, however, the narratives of social evolution propounded by Morgan, Engels, and Stalin were to enjoy the double status of unquestioned scientific Truth and unchallengeable Communist Party doctrine.[14] Marxist evolutionism had a tremendous impact on postrevolutionary minority studies and policy in China, as well as on Chinese archaeology (Wang M. 2004; Gladney 1996). In the 1950s, state-sponsored ethnographic studies were carried out on diverse minority groups living in China's border areas, documenting their languages, subsistence techniques, marriage systems, social organization, folklore, and customs. These studies were often haunted by an obsession with evolutionary classification that is the legacy of Morgan, and usually imposed Stalin's five-stage schema as well. There were many discussions and debates on whether a certain minority group should be classified as "primitive communism" (*yuanshi gongchan zhuyi*) or as at the stage of "slavery" (*nuli shehui*), and these designations had consequences for the shape of state policies for each minority. Similarly, archaeological excavations and studies of ancient China were ruled by questions such as: at which point did ancient China shift from primitive communism to slavery, and from slavery to feudalism? The peculiar provincial history of Europe, whereby a centralized Roman empire ("slavery") dissolved into petty kingdoms in the medieval period ("feudalism"), became the universal and necessary history of all humankind. Although the term "feudalism," which describes dispersed and decentralized polities, is more appropriate for medieval Europe and Japan, the whole two-thousand-year history of the Chinese imperial period from the Qin empire to the Qing dynasty was taken as the "feudal era," despite the fact that China has had a highly centralized state since 221 B.C.E. and experienced a commercial revolution in the Song dynasty that commodified land, property, and labor at least a thousand years ago. It was only in the late 1980s that Chinese archaeology started taking political risks to break away from the straitjacket of nineteenth-century evolutionary discourse (Tong 1989).

After the Communist Revolution, since Buddhism and Daoism were labeled major institutions of "feudalism," the relationships of the Buddhist *sangha* and Daoist priesthood with lay communities were regarded as "exploitative." The military incorporation of Tibet in 1959 was fueled by the conviction that the Chinese people were "liberating" Tibetans from the "slave system" that served the exploitative class of aristocracy and Buddhist monks. Indeed, the strong religiosity of Tibetan culture was taken as a mark of their "backwardness," and this view continues to be dominant in China today. José Cabezón's chapter in this volume lays out vividly the great contrast between the conscious conservatism and anti-modernist stance of the monastic community in Tibet and the hyper-modernism of Chinese state culture, a legacy of unilineal evolutionism.

During Land Reform in the early 1950s, monastic and temple corporate landholdings in most areas of the country were seized, thus ending the tenant farmer rents that had provided Buddhist and Daoist monks and nuns with their subsistence, and local communities with their religious festivals. In many places, there was inadequate preparation of the clergy for their new life as rural laborers, leading to dire hunger at monasteries (Welch 1972:42–67). Ancestral corporate land owned by local lineages, whose proceeds were used to pay for sacrificial rituals to the ancestors, upkeep of ancestor halls, widows, and orphans, and the education of promising lineage boys, were also confiscated during Land Reform. Although Morgan, Marx, and Engels admired the communalism of primitive societies, in the actual implementation of their ideas in China there was seldom any recognition of the communal, corporate, and redistributive nature of temple, monastic, and lineage wealth and landholdings. In the course of agricultural collectivization in Communist China, the thinking was not in support of local autonomy but aimed at creating ever-larger units of production that were fully integrated into the state administrative hierarchies and chains of command descending from Beijing (Zhou 1996). Thus rural collectivization eliminated the old system of ritual territoriality whereby local community identities were installed through rituals to local deities, Earth Gods, City Gods, and lineage ancestors.

Much has been written about the destruction of religious sites and sacred objects, the persecution of religious leaders and followers, and the prohibitions on public religious rituals after the Communist Revolution, so I will not belabor the issue here.[15] I am mainly concerned with showing that the destruction of religious life did not start with the Communists, although the period of the "Smash the Four Olds" campaign in the Cultural Revolution was the most severe religious decimation and persecution in the twentieth century. The Chinese Constitution of 1954 guaranteed its people the "freedom of religion," despite the fact that the Communist Party doctrine of "atheism" and its strong adherence to evolutionist thinking meant that after 1949, this constitutional right was seldom available in actual practice. In the French Revolution, the de-Christianization campaign—which included nationalization of Catholic Church lands, defrocking of priests and nuns, abolition of independent Church income, prohibition of public Catholic ceremonies and festivals, and destruction of religious objects and churches—lasted only six years, from 1793 to 1799 (Desan 1990). In Communist China, in contrast, the anti-religious terror lasted more than three decades, and this does not include the previous four decades of Republican-era anti-superstition movements. From 1949 until the 1980s in China, monks, nuns, ritual specialists, shamans, and devout lay practitioners in all the different religious traditions were harassed and terrorized, made to undergo "thought reform" (*sixiang gaizao*), imprisoned, sent to labor camps, forced to marry against their will, and even tortured and executed by overzealous local cadres or ordinary thugs who took matters into their own hands. In the early 1950s, great numbers of members of sectarian or redemptive societies, such as the Yiguandao (Way of Pervading Unity)s, were executed as "counterrevolutionaries" (David Palmer in this volume; DuBois 2005b). Conditions did vary from one place or period to another, and there were pockets in China where local cadres gave more latitude to religious activities.

Before the radical extremes of the Cultural Revolution, the Communist Party had a more gradualist approach to weaning the Chinese people away from religious life. The Religious Affairs Bureau was set up in 1954 under the State Council in Beijing, with lower branch offices at provincial and local levels to oversee the implementation of religious policy. Several national religious organizations were established to serve as a bridge between various religious communities and the party-state: the Buddhist Association of China was established in 1953, the National Daoist Association in 1957, the Three-Self Patriotic Movement (for Protestants) in 1954, the Chinese Catholic Patriotic Association in 1957, and the China Islamic Association in 1953. These entities were to facilitate the downward movement of Party directives to local religious leaders and to channel up concerns from the grassroots to Party leaders. All these government associations published their own journals and held annual national meetings. However, during the Cultural Revolution, even these government religious agencies were unacceptable for a society bent on atheism, and they were all disbanded, along with their journals. They were only revived after the promulgation of "Document 19" by the Central Committee of the Chinese Communist Party in 1982, which admitted "leftist errors" in past dealings with religious life and called on Party cadres throughout the country to allow religious activities and to return places of worship to their congregations (MacInnis 1989:7–26). Since Document 19, the various "patriotic" religious organizations have played increasingly expanded roles in managing the astounding groundswell of popular religious revival throughout China in the post-Mao era. These state religious organs are charged both with protecting the rights of religious groups and with constraining what has often been regarded as the unruly growth and expansion of religious activity in the post-Mao Reform era.

The religious revival in China since the 1980s has been truly impressive, and English-language studies of this phenomenon have barely kept pace with new developments.[16] Historically famous Buddhist and Daoist temples and monasteries across the country have opened their doors to dense crowds of tourists and worshippers, who have flooded their coffers with entrance fees and donations. About forty Buddhist academies across the country now recruit and train aspiring young monks and nuns, and Buddhist and Daoist ordination ceremonies have been reinvented. With much controversy in Buddhist circles, some Buddhist centers, such as Shaolin Monastery in Henan Province, birthplace of Chan Buddhism, even resemble profitable commercial corporations; their monks, with MBA degrees, jet around and engage more in accounting and promoting tourism than in meditation (Anonymous 2006). Meanwhile, myriad rural areas and small towns all over China have revived the old system of ritual territoriality as an expression of local community identity, through the worship of tutelary deities and community rituals (Chau 2006; M. Yang 2004; Dean 1993).

At the same time, this revival is carefully managed and monitored by state authorities at all levels. All religious groups must register with the state and accept the authority of one of the relevant five official state patriotic religious organizations. This means that some groups can never receive official approval, their petitions for permits to build a religious building of worship are not granted, and they must lead an "underground" (*dixia*) existence. Unregistered underground religious groups are still subject to state persecution, and places of worship built without government permits—whether temples, churches, or mosques—continue to be seized, dismantled, or even blown up with dynamite (M. Yang 2004; French 2006). In other areas, where the local authorities are willing to look the other way, underground religious organizations carry out their activities in the open.

The recent "Regulations on Religious Affairs," promulgated by the State Council in Beijing in March 2005 (Guojia Zongjiaoju 2004), contains new provisions that bode well for the continued development of religious activities in China. The "Regulations" explicitly permit religious bodies to publish and disseminate religious literature (Article 7), establish religious schools (Article 8), send members abroad for religious study (Article 10), conduct large-scale religious activities (and processions) outside of religious sites, after government approval (Article 22), operate public undertakings and keep the proceeds for religious expenditures (Article 34), accept donations from individuals and organizations, both domestic and foreign (Article 35), and enjoy tax exemption or reduction (Article 36). They also expressly forbid any organization or individual from encroaching upon, damaging, or confiscating the legal property of a religious body (Article 30). It is not clear whether the state exempts itself from Article 30, but this clause opens the way for local groups to raise legal objections to seizure of their religious sites.

With the leadership of Hu Jintao and Wen Jiaobao since 2002, a shift in Party ideology from rapid growth of the "socialist market economy" and the "Four Modernizations" to the construction of a new "harmonious society" (和諧社会) has occurred, with subtle gestures toward a new state Confucianism. China may well have embarked on a new path of state-led reconstruction of institutional religious life, in which the state is no longer content merely to monitor and control the grassroots upsurge of religiosity but is assuming an active, leading role in managing, guiding, and rebuilding the various bodies of religious clergy, theological doctrines, and institutional religious structures. One indication of this new direction was the First World Buddhist Forum (世界佛教論壇), held in April 2006 in Hangzhou, China, sponsored by the Buddhist Association of China and the new Religious Cultural Communication Association of China. Never in modern history had China sponsored such a large-scale religious conference, which gathered a thousand Buddhist monks and scholars from thirty-seven countries and was covered by major media outlets in China. According to Chinese Buddhist scholar Xuan Fang, the theme of the conference, "A harmonious world begins from the mind/heart" (和諧世界, 從心開始), was pathbreaking in the history of the People's Republic, since we cannot imagine this sort of "idealist" slogan in past Communist Party orthodoxy (Xuan 2007). Another indicator of the path of state-led religious reconstruction is that Chinese central government agencies have quietly established a one-semester training program for high-level clerics of the five officially recognized religions at People's University in Beijing. The rationale for the state-sponsored training of religious leaders was that, due to past destruction of religious organizations, the "religious quality" (宗教素质) of many clergy in China was unsatisfactory: their educational levels were too low, they lacked managerial skills, and above all, many did not have sufficient understanding of their own religious history, doctrines, rituals, and theologies. Thus they need to learn how to communicate with and earn the respect of their lay constituencies and worshippers.

RELIGIOUS RENEWAL, TAIWAN, AND TRANSNATIONAL CHINESE RELIGIOSITY

We now know that, during the tumultuous first three decades of the twentieth century, there was a groundswell of effort by popular religious communities, as well as educated religious people, to reform and adapt traditional religiosities to the pressing needs of modernity in China. Working with Japanese surveys conducted in China in the 1920s and 1930s, Prasenjit Duara (2003) has shown how a plethora of new religious movements, or "redemptive societies," were established, adapting late imperial traditions of sectarian, millenarian, and syncretistic movements, often with a new global, universalistic outlook. With membership often in the millions, redemptive societies such as the Hongwanzihui (Red Swastika Society), Daodehui (Morality Society), Tongshanshe (Fellowship of Goodness), Zailijiao (Teaching of the Abiding Principle), and Yiguandao (Way of Pervading Unity) dispensed charity and provided work to the destitute; taught moral self-transformation and abstinence; built hospitals, orphanages, and drug rehabilitation centers; lectured against materialism, alcohol, and opium; and promoted Asian spiritual regeneration and self-cultivation in the face of Western materialism. Thomas DuBois (2005b) has found that in many rural north Chinese villages, membership in these new religious societies was much larger than for Buddhist organizations. These redemptive societies mixed traditional Buddhist, Daoist, or sectarian religiosity and iconography with modern organizational structures and outlooks of universalism, and even science. Their universalism and lack of interest in observing the territorial boundaries of nationalist desires earned them the suspicion and active persecution of both the Guomindang and Communist states. It would seem that both modern states felt greatly threatened by the powerful religious effervescence that these societies could produce among their enthusiastic followers, and by their ability to tap into cosmic sources for salvationist projects that spilled over and across nation-state boundaries.

At the same time, many educated people in urban areas resisted the tide of May Fourth secular modernity and thought deeply about religious approaches to modern life. They looked for ways of instilling new life into moribund religious traditions and reforming them to address the conditions of modernity. The important Buddhist reformist monk Taixu (太虛, 1890–1947) was a leader in this effort; his philosophy of "this-worldly Buddhism" (人間佛教) sought to counterbalance the traditional Buddhist focus on transcending our fleeting human existence with an interest in how to properly conduct oneself in this temporal life through charitable works (Welch 1968). In the Daoist world, Chen Yingning (陳櫻寧, 1880–1969) sought to promote a new approach to the ancient self- and body-cultivation techniques of inner alchemy (*neidan*) by emphasizing the materiality of body, breath, and cosmos, a departure from the traditional discourse of the Void, or Emptiness (*xu*). Liu Xun's (2006) research shows how, concerned with the physical health of individual Chinese bodies and the body of the nation, Chen Yingning tried to reconcile the considerable ancient Daoist knowledge of body cultivation and discipline with modern science and medicine. Such Buddhist and Daoist leaders led growing religious movements in urban areas. Faced with direct threats to their religious institutions, Buddhist, Daoist, and Muslim leaders started to form modern national-level organizations so as to coordinate their defense against state seizure of religious land and property (Vincent Goossaert in this volume). At the same time, Christian churches and congregations were increasingly led and organized by native Chinese Christian leaders, and the National Christian Council founded in 1922 was under Chinese rather than missionary leadership (Ryan Dunch in this volume).

Unfortunately, these early twentieth-century movements of religious transformation and reform were never allowed to reach full fruition. Religious reform and adaptation to the conditions of modernity were hampered and interrupted by the turmoil of the brutal Japanese invasion and the civil war between the Guomindang and Communists. Rebecca Nedostup's chapter examines how, in its early years on the Mainland, the Guomindang state was a nationalist modernizing state and just as hostile to traditional religiosity as the Communists were. However, the Guomindang lacked the tight and disciplined organization, the ideological zeal, and the totalizing and revolutionary social engineering project of its Communist rival. After the Communist Revolution, state persecution put a violent end to the various efforts to adapt Chinese religiosities to modern life. While China during the Maoist period (1949–79) closed its doors to the outside world and entered a paroxysm of class struggle, political reeducation, and collective labor, some very interesting and understudied religious developments were taking place in a Chinese cultural enclave offshore, on the island of Taiwan.

After the Guomindang retreated to Taiwan in 1947–49, its treatment of religious culture in Taiwan was much milder than what occurred on the Mainland in the Maoist era (Katz 2003; Qu H. 1997; Chen Y. 1987). The Guomindang did not seek the eradication of religion but the registration of religious organizations with the government and the curtailment of traditional religiosity in public culture. Taiwanese popular religion and its village and neighborhood deity cults, festivals, and pilgrimages did present a challenge to the Guomindang, who feared that it represented a Taiwanese nativism opposed to the Guomindang's elite Confucianism. Thus both the Guomindang public school system and the state media promoted a new form of state Confucianism that emphasized patriotism in the public sphere and filial piety in the family. During the four decades of martial law (1947–87), there were some cases of state persecution, such as the suppression of the Yiguandao (Way of Pervading Unity) and Zhanglaohui (Elders Society, Presbyterian Church). Groups that cultivated good ties with officialdom were able to grow and prosper, whereas those that did not properly register with the authorities or cultivate good relations often suffered state harassment (Liu H. 1991; Lee F. 2009). Although the Guomindang continued to scale down public rituals and religious festivals such as the Ghost Festival of the seventh lunar month, and to oppose "wasteful" ritual expenditures (Weller 1987), it allowed considerable latitude to most religious organizations to select their own leaders and plan their own activities. Thus all kinds of Chinese religiosities, syncretic groups, and new religions have found a home in Taiwan. Surprisingly, the island's economic prosperity and high-tech industries since the 1970s—and the population's increasing educational levels, urbanization, and cosmopolitanism—have not dampened Taiwanese religiosity. In a survey of 4,000 adults throughout the island in the 1980s, 65 percent described themselves as followers of Buddhism, Daoism, or popular religion (Qu 1997:4). Between 1930 and 1981, the number of Buddhist, Daoist, and deity temples in Taiwan almost doubled from 3,661 to 5,531; by 2001, there were 9,707 registered with the state (Katz 2003:90), and by 2006, there were 11,573 large registered temples (Zhonghua Mingguo Neizhengbu 2007). These figures do not include the myriad small, family-run storefront temples that have blossomed in recent years throughout the island. Today it is common to find storefront deity temples sharing the same urban block as 7-Eleven chain-stores on a busy commercial street full of automobile traffic. This is what I found in the summer of 2000 in the city of Taizhong (Taichung), when I attended a lively family-run temple festival for the goddess Mazu, complete with ritual procession, sacrificial animals, and opera performances for the deity. One minute the owner-manager of the storefront temple was bemoaning the recent fall in value of Taiwan stocks; the next minute he was rolling around on the ground, foaming at the mouth, possessed by a god who was speaking through him!

It was in postwar Taiwan (as well as Hong Kong, Singapore, and Chinese communities of Southeast Asia) that the unfinished projects of reform and adaptation of Chinese religiosity to the conditions of modernity found a place to continue. In his detailed study of various schools and associations of Daoist inner alchemy and body-cultivation practices from the 1950s to 1970s in Taiwan, Daoist scholar Lee Fengmao (2009) has written a forgotten chapter of Taiwan religious history. He has found that many groups which sought to reform and adapt Daoist culture to modern urban life moved from the Mainland to Taiwan along with the Guomindang retreat. In Taiwan they appealed to the growing middle and professional classes, many of whose members were trained in modern Western science and technology, and at the same time wished to reconcile Daoist alchemical principles of self-cultivation with modern scientific and medical knowledge. Many followers of the reformist Buddhist monk Taixu also moved to Taiwan, and today Taiwan is home to a plethora of dynamic Buddhist sects and organizations that are this-worldly in orientation, and that are extending their activities of moral edification and religious charity on a transnational scale (J. Huang 2005). Richard Madsen's chapter in this volume charts the postwar growth of some major Buddhist and Daoist

Figure I.I.   Spirit medium Liu Youmian (with author Mayfair Yang on left) and sacrificial offerings of animals, to celebrate the third anniversary of Liu's storefront temple of the maritime goddess Mazu in Taizhong (Taichung), Taiwan, July 26, 2000. Photo by bystander.

organizations in Taiwan, and examines their experience of religious rationalization and their role in building Taiwan civil society.

As travel and business between Mainland China and Taiwan become ever more frequent, many Taiwan religious groups have started to connect with, and exert subtle influences on, religious life back on the Mainland. There have been many religious delegations, pilgrimages, and charitable aid and temple-building donations moving from Taiwan and Southeast Asia to China. Many deity cults and religious groups in Taiwan have gone to their deity's native place on the Mainland to worship and donate money for new temples and poverty relief. My own chapter in this volume charts the parallel movements of Taiwan capitalist television media and religious pilgrimage to Mainland China, subverting the political boundaries of modern state territoriality. At the same time, there has been an increasing outward movement on the part of Mainland religious entities to make religious connections abroad. Mainland Buddhist and Daoist delegations have visited their counterparts in Taiwan, Hong Kong, Singapore, Japan, and Southeast Asia, and individual monks and nuns have also been able to spend time abroad, undergoing religious study at other Asian monasteries or performing rituals for overseas Chinese communities in Southeast Asia. Chinese pilgrims have started to travel to the ancient sites of Lumbini and Bodhgaya, the origins of Buddhism in the Ganges Valley of northern India, and many lay Chinese Buddhists seek the religious counsel and training of Tibetan Buddhist lamas. Chinese Muslims have also been allowed to make the hajj pilgrimage to Mecca, and many Chinese imams have contact with religious centers in the Middle East. Although religious proselytizing by foreigners is prohibited in the People's Republic, there is growing contact between Chinese Christians and American and Korean Christian organizations. In Yunnan Province, the Dai ethnic minority is sending monks and nuns for training at Theravada Buddhist centers in Thailand. Some Mainland Chinese who have emigrated to Western countries have also discovered Christianity, or rediscovered Chinese Buddhism or Daoism while abroad. These are all clear signs that, along with the increasing globalization of the Chinese economy, a globalization of Chinese religiosities is occurring as well.

ORGANIZATION OF THIS VOLUME

The essays in this volume are divided into four parts, arranged according to four broad themes of state culture and religiosity in modern China. The two chapters in Part I, by Prasenjit Duara and Ya-pei Kuo, deal with the possibilities and potentialities of a historical moment before the anti-religious forces fully took root in China, when religious and ritual orientations were still considered a viable and important part of the task of constructing national identity. Both chapters examine what Duara calls the "traffic" between religious and secular orders, at a time when modern Chinese discourse had not yet hardened into the dominant Western secular model for a strict separation between the religious and the secular.

Duara's chapter asks why the new Chinese nation-state in the early twentieth century developed a strong anti-religious character, whereas ethnic identity among the Peranakan overseas Chinese in the Dutch Indies, who were in contact with the same reformers and revolutionaries on the Mainland, developed a strong religious character. A syncretic Confucian-Buddhist-Daoist orientation informed the construction of modern Peranakan Chinese ethnic identity. Duara suggests that China's semi-colonial status prevented the "traffic" between religious and secular orders in the construction of a modern Chinese national identity. In the relative absence of direct or prolonged colonial occupation in China, the colonial imposition of European or Christian definitions of civilization was weak, so Chinese nationalism was not forced to retreat to traditional Chinese religiosity in order to contest or resist an alien colonial identity. In the full colonial context of the Dutch Indies, however, the modernizing Peranakan Chinese turned to older nativist religious resources to assert their Chinese identity and citizenship rights against both Western colonial and Islamic domination.

Ya-pei Kuo's chapter examines a significant transformation in the two-thousand-year tradition of the imperial state cult in the last years of the Qing dynasty, before the Chinese state was fully secularized and disencumbered of its ancient ritual system of governance. The veneration of Confucius was elevated by the imperial court from the status of middle sacrifice to that of grand sacrifice in 1906, and all modern-style state schools throughout China were required to observe rituals to Confucius. These ritual innovations have usually been interpreted by scholars as an example of a backward-looking "last stand of Chinese conservatism" in the face of modern pressures for change. However, Kuo's novel understanding is that these measures sought to transform imperial subjects into modern citizens through a new kind of ritual government and education, combined with a subtle downgrading of the ritual power of the emperor. New governing devices, such as the national school system and nationalist ideology, signified the beginning of modern state-formation in Chinese history. The Xinzheng (New Policies) reforms set themselves apart from later secular revolutionary regimes and offered a unique vision for China's political modernity by grounding their project of nation-building on traditional symbolic culture. These two chapters by Duara and Kuo prompt us to reflect on how Chinese history might have unfolded had the path of radical state secularization not been pursued and, instead, a ritual and religious approach to modernity, national identity, and citizenship been allowed to take its course.

The five chapters grouped in Part II explore how modernizing state discourses and state actions have radically changed the contours and structures of religious life at different points in the twentieth century. Rebecca Nedostup explores the difficulties encountered by the Guomindang state in the 1930s, when it sought to replace an ancient imperial state system of ritual government on the one hand, and the strong popular tradition of religious festivals based on the lunar calendar and local ritual identities on the other. Guomindang secularization campaigns targeted the lunar calendar as the "staff headquarters of superstition," promoting the "national" (i.e., combined Republican and Gregorian) calendar as a way of unifying all citizens in a shared national temporality. While banning or downgrading traditional ritual festivals like the Ghost Festival, the Guomindang also felt the need to invent its own new sacred civic ceremonies, much as the French Revolution had. However, as Nedostup suggests, these new national secular rituals lacked the emotional depth of traditional festivals; stressing content (nationalist messages) rather than ritual form (which had been noisy, "fun," ritually extravagant, and locally organized), they failed to win over the populace. In this competition between the new "affective regime" of the modern state and the older system of popular religious rituals, Nedostup sees the potential for hybrid civic rituals that could have addressed the popular yearning for public expressions of the suffering and death associated with the war and national insecurity. She shows that in Guomindang hands, ritual lost the structuring power it had possessed in the old emperor system—namely, that of mediating between the earth and the cosmic order—and became merely a legitimating symbol.

The two chapters by David Palmer and Benjamin Penny make connections between conditions of religious life in modernity and ancient religious traditions in imperial Chinese history. Palmer traces a recurring streak of what I would call "state hysteria" in state discourse through the two-thousand-year history of the imperial state down to the present day. Since ancient times, the Chinese state has violently suppressed sectarian and millenarian religious movements and associations that did not meet Confucian standards of orthodoxy and that it feared would lead to peasant rebellions. The modern persecution of popular mass "redemptive societies"—the descendants of imperial sectarian movements—first by the Republican and then by the Communist state, follows a line of continuity from the early Ming (fourteenth-century) suppression of popular religion. Palmer presents a detailed analysis of the shifting state vocabulary and discourse surrounding state efforts to identify and suppress such movements in the twentieth century, and makes a radical argument that state condemnations of Falungong in the 1990s are a departure from fifty years of modern state discourse predicated on scientism and anti-superstition. The resuscitation of the imperial state term *xiejiao*, or "evil cult," harks back to ancient Chinese state doctrines against heretical movements while incorporating new global, Western social science and psychological notions of modern "cults" and "new religions." What is emphasized now in Chinese state discourse is not "science" or "superstition" but these new movements' efforts to destabilize the social order, while "religion" is regarded as a benign preserver of order.

The chapter by Benjamin Penny traces a persistent "cultural unconscious" that informs the contemporary struggle between the Chinese

Communist state and Falungong, a religious body-cultivation movement that was officially banned in 1999. Trained in the sinology of ancient Chinese religions, Penny brings his knowledge of popular Buddhist, Daoist, and sectarian religious discourse in imperial times to his discussion of a contemporary phenomenon understood in the West merely as a human rights issue. Through close textual analysis, Penny uncovers the theological rationales of Falungong and shows how they are contemporary emanations of deep unconscious cultural categories and assumptions of orthodoxy, sovereignty, salvation, and relations between human and spirit realms. He suggests that, in contrast to the Communist state's understanding of Falungong as an organization motivated by the desire to challenge state sovereignty, this religious group merely wished the state to recognize and accept it as an orthodox national religious orientation that will loyally serve the interests of the nation. Failing to win state recognition, Falungong has retrieved an ancient discourse of divine retribution: when state officials violate their sacred trust with unjust behavior, Heaven sends down natural catastrophes and imbalances in nature and the cosmos.

Ryan Dunch's chapter examines the asymmetrical dialogue between Chinese Protestant theologians and Communist Party theoreticians and policy-makers in the Reform era since 1978. Since the 1920s, Chinese Protestant thinkers have had to counter the charge that they are unpatriotic and linked with Western imperialism, and this engagement with Communist Party discourse is the latest response. Despite the fact that the terms and parameters of this dialogue are clearly set by the Party, Dunch suggests that Protestant theologians have been able to make some inroads in Party policy toward religion. For example, in the 1980s, Protestant theologians took on the conservative Party position that religion was "the opium of the people" and therefore of no benefit to socialist modernization. They also challenged the idea that religion would inevitably die out in socialist society. Although Party theoreticians never formally acknowledged these points, there has been unofficial recognition of these arguments, as reflected in relaxation and other changes in official policies toward religious practice.

The modern history and diversity of Chinese Muslims form the subject of Dru Gladney's chapter. Gladney traces the historical waves of different Islamic teachings that have influenced Chinese Muslims, from the traditionalist and sinified Gedimu Islam to Sufism in the late seventeenth century, Wahhabi-inspired Yihewani (Chinese for the Ikhwan al-Muslimin, or Ikhwan Muslim Brotherhood) in the nineteenth century, and the more recent rise of fundamentalist Salafiyya Islam in Northwest China since the 1980s. Besides their adherence to different Islamic teachings, what also creates great diversity among Chinese Muslims is the history of their incorporation into the Chinese empire and their assimilation into Han Chinese culture. The Hui people are descended from Middle Eastern travelers and merchants who have lived alongside Han people for centuries, and are therefore the closest to Han Chinese of all Chinese Muslims and generally accommodationist toward the Chinese state. At the other extreme are the Uyghur Muslims of Xinjiang Province, who were only formally incorporated into the Chinese empire in the late Qing dynasty. In the course of state secularization drives in the twentieth century, what aided Chinese Muslims in holding on to their religious culture was their status as ethnic minorities, along with the state's concern for good foreign relations with Middle Eastern countries.

The three chapters in Part III deal with religious institutions and changes in the structural organization of religious life in modern China. The chapter by Vincent Goossaert traces the modern Chinese invention of "church-like" religious associations in the first years of the new Republican state. They formed unifying bureaucracies for Buddhist, Daoist, Confucian, and Muslim traditions at the national level. In the history of Chinese civilization, there were never any empirewide religious associations that represented the interests of a religious community, its clergy and laypeople, to the imperial state. Temples, monasteries, and mosques had autonomy of self-governance and were all localized according to lineages descended from a religious founder. Goossaert finds that the influence of Christian thought and practice among modern Chinese elites and national leaders led to a fashioning of religious structure along the model of Christian churches. These new associations sought to purge themselves of the "superstitious" local village cult systems and rituals of popular religion. Although their efforts were short-lived due to the interruptions of war, they laid down the basic structural foundations for later periods, such as the People's Republic.

Ji Zhe's chapter takes up the Western theory of secularization and shows how such themes as "separation of church and state," "deinstitutionalization and privatization of religion," and the "public versus private sphere of religion," which have been taken as universal, are based on the history of the Christian West and fail to account for the modern transformation of Buddhism in China. With Chinese Buddhism, modernity has accomplished a process of institutionalization never before experienced in the history of China. In China, state secularization demanded that religious forces unify and institutionalize themselves into formal and rational organizations at the national level. Buddhist leaders in the early twentieth century sought to gather into a unified force across local interests and divisions in order to counter the modern state expropriation of Buddhist properties (temples, monasteries, and landholdings). Later, the Communist state relied on formal Buddhist associations to exert its control over Buddhists across the country. Originally intended as mediums of state control and surveillance, in the post-Mao era Buddhist associations have paradoxically provided an essential structural foundation for the representation of Buddhist interests in negotiation with the state.

Tibetan Buddhism's ancient monastic institutions form the subject of José Cabezón's chapter. Tibetan culture is highly religious; monks and nuns are greatly respected, and before China's military incorporation of Tibet into the Chinese nation-state in 1959, a significant proportion of its population pursued a monastic life. Cabezón outlines two fundamentally opposed worldviews: (1) Tibetan Buddhism's traditionalist religious culture and its relativizing of temporal life as a fleeting moment in endless reincarnation; and (2) the Chinese Communist state's embracing of secular modernism, nationalism, productivism, and material life. Cabezón shows how the clash between these worldviews came to a head over the Chinese state control of Tibetan Buddhist monasteries. Before 1959, the combined population of the three largest and most prestigious monasteries (Drepung, Sera, Ganden) was about 25,000–28,000 monks and nuns. Due to strict state controls, by the mid-1990s, the monastic population in these three places numbered less than 2,500 combined. Cabezón examines the various strategies by which the Chinese state controls and disciplines Tibetan monastic orders, and how it has sought to reshape and reindoctrinate the Tibetan clergy. This is the only chapter in the collection that provides explicit suggestions to Chinese policy-makers, to increase Tibetan monastic autonomy.

Part IV looks outward from Mainland China to Taiwan, which may serve as a harbinger of future developments in China. Richard Madsen's chapter takes up Max Weber's thesis on the rationalization of religion into a this-worldly ethical system and finds that, in the context of such a highly urbanized, cosmopolitan, commercialized, educated, and high-tech place as Taiwan, Weber is both right and wrong. Weber was wrong to assume that only Protestantism possessed the rational-ethical features of religiosity that were conducive to modernity, but he was right in that the religious organizations that have been most successful in Taiwan bear many of these rational-ethical features—namely, emphasis on individual internal religious orientation, rationalization of complex liturgical systems, and a focus on doing good works in this life. In Taiwan, the educated professional middle class continues to pursue a religious orientation to life. Moreover, despite the fact that the Guomindang privileged Christian organizations and discouraged native Chinese religious heritage, Madsen finds that Buddhism and Daoism have the fastest-growing constituencies among the Taiwan middle class. Madsen examines four reformed religious organizations—the Ciji Gongdehui (Buddhist Compassionate Relief Association), Foguangshan (Buddha's Light Mountain), Fagushan (Dharma Drum Mountain), and Xingtiangong (Enacting Heaven's Business Temple)—and finds them to be thoroughly globalized, with modern organizations and financing structures, and catering to individual inner cultivation as well as engaging in charitable social works.

Finally, my own chapter explores the complex interactions of three different spatial systems: modern nation-state territoriality; Chinese popular religion's ritual spatiality; and satellite television's transnational footprints, which transgress the space of nation-state territorial broadcast systems. More specifically, I look at the strange alliance of capitalist media (in this case, Taiwan satellite television) and popular religion (the Mazu goddess pilgrimage from Taiwan to the Mainland): both are committed to enlarging their space of operations by expanding to Mainland China. China wishes to strengthen its nation-state territory by incorporating Taiwan, while pro-independence forces in Taiwan wish to construct a separate and autonomous space of nation-state. Both nation-state territorialities are threatened by the border transgressions of religious pilgrimage across the Taiwan Strait. The forces of Taiwan religious pilgrimage find a strange ally in the capitalist media, which broadcasts the crossing of political boundaries by the pilgrimage. However, the spatiality of the Mazu goddess cult is configured quite differently from both nation-state and capitalist media: temples trace matrilineal descent from an originary mother temple on the Mainland. Thus, a premodern ritual spatiality has been preserved in the Taiwan Mazu cult that challenges two masculine spatial structures of modernity: the nation-state and capitalist media.

PART I

Religious Approaches to Citizenship

*The Traffic between Religious Orders
and the Secular National Order*

1 Religion and Citizenship in China and the Diaspora

Prasenjit Duara 杜贊奇

Why is it that religion is foregrounded in the knowledge of some societies, whereas in others—most notably, China—it emerges as largely irrelevant to developments, particularly to modern history? One could posit various explanations that incorporate the power (or powerlessness) of institutionalized religion in relation to the state, but here I want to explore a different track. I want to show that the energies, needs, and ideals that are frequently understood under the rubric of religion become reorganized and channeled into different institutions and practices that we have come to call secular—and that at the same time, what we now call religion is reconstituted by "secular" forces. In other words, what we call "religious" may in some societies be organized and perceived as being in the "secular" domain, and vice versa.

Reacting to the perceived or alleged claims of Christianity (itself undergoing reformulation) as the spiritual ideology of the modern era, Chinese and Japanese groups began to create their own new distinctions among ritual, religion, superstition, and secularism—distinctions that also circulated in the East Asian region as a whole. In the first part of this essay, I look at several cases of this reconstitution and circulation, such as the Confucian religion movement; the New Life Movement (Xin Shenghuo Yundong) of the Guomindang; and the adaptation (and nonadaptation) of popular redemptive societies in China, such as the Yiguandao (Way of Pervading Unity) and the recent Falungong (Practice of the Wheel of the Law), among others. Although the transmutation (or traffic) of religious ideas into political ideas has been noted since Fichte and Weber, the reverse process is key to understanding the dynamics of the religious and the secular, especially in China.

In the second part of this essay, I focus on the religious ideas of the

Peranakan Chinese in the Dutch Indies in the first half of this century. This case is analytically interesting because although the elite of this group were affected by many of the same ideas current in very early twentieth-century China—notably, the Confucian religion movement—by the 1920s they had developed in a different direction. I argue here that the social and discursive circumstances of living in a colonial society generated a divergence from the Chinese path, and in some ways caused the religion of the Peranakan Chinese to resemble the reformist religions of other colonial societies, such as India. These historical circumstances not only fostered the expression of identity in the language of religion but generated a different grammar for the social ensemble as well.

TERMS AND CONCEPTS

The history of secularism is now well known. The ascendancy of the European absolutist state, which put an end to the Religious Wars in the sixteenth century, was based on the relegation of conscience, or the inner moral person, to a private sphere of the mind, not to the public *actions* of citizens. As citizens, individuals were subject to the political authority of the state. Thus was produced the difference between inner devotion and morality versus outer politicality (Koselleck 1988). The history of secularism in Europe is, then, the process whereby the absolutist and its successor, the nation-state, institutionalized this separation through a three-hundred-year period of state-building and identity-formation. Talal Asad has argued further that the very idea of religion itself is a modern Western invention. Western states delineated and reified a separate sphere as "religion." Even the church became prepared to follow this distinction, and it tended increasingly to characterize religion in terms of the motivations and subjective states of individual believers (Asad 1993:39).[1] In this way, religion became increasingly associated with a new view of human subjectivity.

Asad has shown how this modern Western reification was transmitted to the rest of the world as the natural expression of religion. At the same time, however, the institutionalization of this bifurcation of "religion" and the secular was inseparable from the circulation of the nation-state form across the world in the twentieth century. Given that nation-states were founded on ideals of science, progress, popular sovereignty, and freedom, these states themselves became cosmologically and practically committed to the creation of religion as a distinct and contained sphere. Whereas in most pre-national states what we anachronistically (following Asad) call "religion"—whether in terms of institutions or cosmology—was fused with the polity, modern nation-states seek to keep them apart. For instance, Article 36 of the 1982 Constitution of the People's Republic of China says that the state may not compel or discriminate against people's religious beliefs; it also specifies that "no one may make use of religion to engage in activities that disrupt public order, impair the health of citizens, or interfere with the educational system of the state." Although there are, of course, significant differences, the U.S. Constitution institutes a similar separation: the First Amendment declares that "Congress shall make no law respecting an establishment of religion, or prohibiting the free exercise thereof."

But the relegation of moral authority and authenticity—often embedded in religious presuppositions—to the private sphere could not, even in Western societies, be fully sustained. Indeed, as we shall note below, the bifurcation was tendential and not fully legislated upon until the early twentieth century. Reinhart Koselleck points to a different kind of incompleteness, one that was a form of resistance. Enlightenment thought would try to counter the separation through the eighteenth century by asserting the superiority of nonpolitical moral authenticity, for instance, among Freemasons and Republican thinkers who sought to reembed this authenticity in political institutions. The moral authenticity of such groups derived from a combination of religious ideas (as residue or transformation of Christian conscience) and Enlightenment ideas of natural innocence associated with Rousseau and others. In doing so, Enlightenment proponents concealed their own politicality (opposing the state) under the ideal of moral superiority or utopianism (Koselleck 1988:80–85). Thus, from the beginning, the institutionalized differentiation between religion and secularism was accompanied both by the conscious challenge to this separation and by the prereflexive traffic between the two. The thrust of this essay is to explore the prereflexive or nonovert challenge to this separation.[2]

Behind the apparently stable division between religion and secularism expressed at a constitutional or institutional level, a busy traffic between "religious" and "secular" ideas and practices has taken place through the twentieth century. By introducing the idea of "traffic," I want to grasp and go beyond the modern state's constitutional strategy of containing and regulating what it has designated as religion. Both the state, by means of its legal, classificatory, and coercive powers, and social groups are constantly breaching this separation and remaking religion and the secular sphere. One of the factors enabling this breach is actually the lack of definition of religion itself in most national constitutions and international law (Gunn 2003:190–191). This underspecification enables the changing content of the meaning of religion.

The vehicles of the traffic I consider here are the practices and ideas of subject-formation whereby citizens and religious subjects are created. In the twentieth century, the term "citizenship" has come to refer to rights and obligations of the individual to the political community—typically, the nation-state. The legal content of citizenship has, of course, changed over the course of the century, and the relationship of rights to obligations has also varied across space. Thus social rights came to be included later in the century, and the obligations of the citizen in pre–World War II East Asia (國民, *guomin, kokumin*) tended to overwhelm his or her rights. What I refer to here is less the legal definition of citizenship than its normative foundations in practices of subject-formation.

While the nation-state has historically been founded on nonreligious or nonsectarian sources of sovereignty, it has nonetheless found the resources of faith, ritual, myth, and religious loyalty too valuable simply to abandon. Similarly, popular conceptions of the religious subject have found political ideas of nationalism and citizenship irresistible for the legitimacy and power that they confer. Subject-formation in the era of nation-states is a vast topic, but the relationship between religious and national subjectivity has yet to be explored in depth.[3] Both forms of subjectivity involve consolidating the values of morality and authenticity as well as the practice of discipline and reflexivity, often to the advantage of the nation-state. But these practices—such as *qigong* practices in contemporary China, which are often inseparable from their older cosmologies—may embed goals and activities that subvert the power and ideals of the nation.

Finally, I am concerned with the circulation of "global models of religious citizenship," or the simultaneous reformulation of the consciousness of citizens and religious subjects across the world. From the late nineteenth century on, it was Christian missionaries associated with imperialist powers in Asia who provided the dominant models of the religious citizen. They brought lessons from their own societies of ways for the religious subject to adapt—and, indeed, contribute—to the growth of nationalism and imperialism in the West. After the turn of the century, however, the emergence of what came to be known as "world religions"—including the revamped and reformed Buddhism, Confucianism, Hinduism, and Islam—adapted older practices and disciplines to reposition the subject in relation to the faith and nation-states. Thus religion and secularism were formed by two types of circulations: by global and regional circulations, and by circulation between the constantly reconstituting spheres of religion and the secular themselves.

CHANNELING RELIGION IN MODERN CHINA

By the late nineteenth and early twentieth centuries, when the secular-religious differentiation spread among emergent and new nations as a central feature of modernity, the Chinese state and literati sought to adapt it in the context of available historical resources. There were four relevant features to what we might retrospectively see as the domain of religion in late imperial China.

The first was the imperial state cult and orthodoxy. This included reverence of Confucius and Confucian doctrines but was by no means exhausted by them. The sacrifices and reverences (祭祀, *jisi*) performed by the emperor, as the supreme priestly figure, to Heaven and deities such as Guandi, the God of War (and Loyalty), were reproduced through the state cult of sacrifices by bureaucrats and village leaders all the way down to the tutelary deity (*tudi*) of the village. This is the territorial-ascriptive and bureaucratic model of religion, which combines *jisi* and *jiao* (教, *teachings*).

The second feature was the realm of village or community religion, which tended to be seen in early accounts as continuous with the state cult (Wolf 1978). More recently, Stephan Feuchtwang and others have argued that the differences between the two were both organizationally and cosmologically significant. Popular religion conceived of the cosmos as more personalized and violent than did the state cult, with threatening and rewarding forces operating through mythic efficacy (Feuchtwang 2001:74–84). It was this realm of community religion that became the target of modernizing reformers and radicals from the early twentieth century on. Although the conflict between intellectuals and community religion has been studied for China, I explore this encounter in the Dutch Indies, where community religion has been curiously folded into the project of modern identity-building.

The third element includes the licensed religions of Buddhism and Daoism. The institutionalized forms of these religions had a relatively marginal role in the lives of ordinary people by the late Qing. Thus, for instance, Buddhist monks were mainly called on to perform funerary rites, while Daoists carried out various other ritual services, including magical and prophesying performances. However, communal religion frequently absorbed rites and ideas from these religions, and many monks and priests operating at this popular level were not recognized or properly ordained by institutionalized Buddhism or Daoism.

The fourth and final element, operating sometimes within the framework of the local versions of the state cult but often outside it, consisted of the hundreds, if not thousands, of popular religious societies or sects (會道門, *huidaomen*), many of which were informed by the syncretism of the three religions (*sanjiao;* Confucianism, Buddhism, and Daoism). I have identified many of these as redemptive societies because they frequently entailed a program to "save the world" (救世, *jiushi*) and the self. Among them were the White Lotus, the Yiguandao, and many others. Their redemptive message drew on a rich vein of late imperial gentry syncretism (*sanjiaoheyi*) that first gained popularity in the late Ming period (the late sixteenth and the seventeenth century). This movement, which involved the Confucian gentry as well as Daoist and Buddhist leaders, was inspired by Wang Yangming's commitment to the moral self-transformation of ordinary people, and urged the extinguishing of worldly desires and engagement in moral action (Chow 1994:21–25).

What was the relationship between the imperial state and these popular religious societies? Licensed religions were reasonably well controlled, but the growth of syncretic redemptive religions in the early modern period, fueled by commercialization and mobility, had a complex relationship with the state. On the one hand, there was persecution because the *jiushi* ideal imagined a different world—despite, or perhaps because of, the popular interpretation of Confucianism as world-redeeming—and also occasionally involved an apocalyptic vision of transformation. On the other hand, these redemptive societies often shared a public transcript and some cosmological ideas about Heaven, so that superscription, camouflage, and other types of accommodation could be negotiated. Guandi, as I have argued elsewhere, served as a perfect medium for the articulation of such an accommodative strategy (Duara 1988b).

It is fruitful to study the Chinese case together with the Japanese one, because there was considerable traffic between the understandings of the two, both before and after the turn of the twentieth century. The two countries often responded to similar problems and drew from some common cultural resources. Like China, Tokugawa Japan had a similar mold of state cult based on Confucian ideas of Heaven; Shinto rites and control of Buddhist temple structures shored up the authority of the shogunate. The Tokugawa sought to make local temples the organs of state control of religion. Households were ordered to register at a Buddhist temple, and thus although Buddhist sects were in a sense favored, they were also kept under strict observation (Shimazono 2004:77). Similarly, the control of licensed Buddhism (especially in the early nineteenth century) often led to its ritualism and to the emergence of redemptive and syncretic new religions (such as those based on the Lotus Sutra), which were often persecuted but also accommodated if they operated within certain limits.

In China, as in Japan (and as in Korea and Vietnam), there was a departure from this older mold in the transition to becoming a nation-state. In the first place, at the turn of the century the idea of national or state rites, was seen by both China and Japan as a necessary desideratum of a nation-state. Although the ideas of freedom of religious belief and the separation of church and state had emerged even before the American and French revolutions, many European states continued to have state or national churches; it was not until 1905, for example, that the French National Assembly passed a law separating church and state, which according to some authorities still did not entail a full separation (McIntire 2002:153). Moreover, both China and Japan were threatened by Christian conversions, and although the Meiji state declared the freedom of religious worship, State Shinto was developed as a response to Christian and Buddhist conversion. Chinese reformers at the turn of the century were, additionally, convinced by powerful missionaries, such as Robert Morrison and Timothy Richards, that the secret to modernity lay in science and the church. During the late Qing reforms—in particular, the education reforms that followed the Boxer Rebellion of 1900—the government therefore introduced the notion that the Chinese classics were the equivalent of the branch of knowledge that the world called "religion" (宗教, *zongjiao*). In 1906, it also elevated reverence of Confucius to the same level as reverence of Heaven, a proposition that the earlier Qing emperors would no doubt have rejected on the grounds that it diminished the emperor's authority as the Son of Heaven.

Thus it is clear that both the Japanese and the Chinese models of a state religion merged modern nation-state paradigms with an East Asian historical model of the state as having monopoly access to Heaven through rites and sacrifices (*jisi*). Was there something historically distinctive about the sacrifice- and rite-performing state? Indeed, one might suggest that these rites and sacrifices cannot be seen as "religion," and Shinto priests and bureaucrats certainly opposed the classification of State Shinto as religion (Hardacre 1989:49). Rather, these rites and sacrifices represented the ritual authority underpinning state power that was part of the inherited cosmology of the East Asian state—authority that came to be resignified less in cosmological than in symbolic terms. What exactly these models of state ritualism sought to achieve—in terms of citizenship—is worthy of understanding. Here I want to suggest, in a most preliminary way, that the *jisi* model adapted the imperial Chinese conception of the ritual synchronization of the polity as the performance of power. The bureaucratization, standardization, and synchronization of Shinto shrine worship throughout the nation (and empire) were accompanied by the pedagogy of the Three Great Teachings, which incorporated the campaign for conscription, national taxation, and compulsory education (Hardacre 1989:32–33, 43–55).

If the state cult continued to be associated with the modified *jisi* and was not necessarily perceived to represent religion, was there a need, from the point of view of the state, for the new idea of religion in China? Although I have yet to conduct a systematic survey, Chinese literati at the end of the century seem to have been conflicted by this question. Prima facie, there is no reason to think that the literati ever considered Confucianism a religion in the Jesuit sense. Indeed, the new Republic of 1912 abandoned the education of the Confucian classics in primary schools. But a non-state movement, led most notably by Kang Youwei and his followers, famously tried to develop Confucius into a religious figure. This is known as the movement to establish Confucianism as a national religion (孔教會, Kongjiaohui), which developed during the first fifteen years or so of the twentieth century.

This movement sought to attain a certain model of citizenship that drew upon current understandings of Christianity. In response to those who urged that a national religion was incompatible with religious freedom, Kang Youwei pointed to the many European countries (England, Germany, Denmark, etc.) that supported national churches. Kang sought to model Kongjiao explicitly on the current practices and organization of Christianity. He proposed sacrifices to Confucius and Heaven by officials, and by establishing Confucius associations all over the country, he sought to institutionalize Confucian preachings and Sunday worship, a Confucian calendar (like the Christian system of dating), and the celebration of Confucius's birthday. In these ways, the Kongjiao movement sought to absorb what it conceived to be the power of Christianity while rejecting the content of Christian beliefs. At the same time, by establishing Confucianism as a "national religion," Kang and his followers clearly sought to create a national tradition that was suitable for the creation of a national citizenry (see Ya-pei Kuo's chapter in this volume).

The president of the Republic, Yuan Shikai, was not averse to the reverence of Confucius, but he was ultimately opposed to the effort to establish it as a national religion. Scholars have speculated about possible reasons for his opposition, such as the dangers of alienating the Christian missionaries and powers, and of further alienating the Buddhist regions of Tibet and Mongolia and the Muslim west, which already lacked a sense of belonging to the Republic. In 1914, however, Yuan revived the synchronized sacrifices and reverences to Heaven and Confucius (and the consolidation of the Yue Fei/Guandi temples). But he was careful to declare that reverence of the sages was not a religious act. Like the Meiji state, the Republic was making a distinction between state rituals drawn from history (*jisi*) and the notion of "religion," which citizens were free to choose (Mori 2004:6).

As the second decade of the century came to a close, the growth of radicalism within China, which dovetailed with secularizing international developments such as the Russian Revolution and the disestablishment of national churches, made the movement for a national religion increasingly unviable within the intellectual circles of Chinese society. Indeed, the May Fourth Movement was premised not merely on anti-Confucianism but on an unremitting hostility to religion. The Confucian religion movement became increasingly obscured, and many of its advocates, such as Zheng Xiaoxu, began to declare it a Confucius learning movement (Mori 2004:8–9). At the same time, the religious interpretation of Confucianism, or the effort to see it as a part of a redemptive faith, became more developed in the new syncretic redemptive societies, such as the Morality Society (道德會, Daodehui), that flourished during this period.

Finally, among state initiatives, I consider here the New Life Movement initiated in 1934 by Jiang Jieshi (Chiang Kai-shek). Modeled significantly on the YMCA movement, it sought to synthesize historical ideals of Confucianism with spiritual notions of citizenship.[4] As Jiang's wife, Madame Jiang Jieshi (born Song Meiling 宋美齡, the daughter of a Christian entrepreneur adopted by missionaries), described it, the movement sought to draw upon Confucian ideals of spiritual and moral renovation (*gexin*) as the inner counterpart to outer political and economic reform. As Jiang himself put it, "Today we all recognize the important place of the Confucian ideals of *li, yi, lian, chi* (propriety, justice, honesty, and shame/modesty) in revolutionary nation-building (*geming jianguo*)" (Jiang J. 1976:84). Founded initially to rehabilitate the communist-dominated region of Jiangxi that the Guomindang had ravaged, the campaign was extended to the entire country, calling on ideals of self-discipline and moral regulation to produce a new citizenry dedicated to the collective. Its ideal of mobilization included the total transformation of the individual through reform of customs and everyday practices relating to personal hygiene and moral improvement.

Madame Jiang, however, modeled the movement on Christian and YMCA activities, and quoted missionary observations in her English-language publications, as in the following passage:

The suppression of the communist-bandits and the work of the New Life Movement are proving to be the first stage of a long battle against ignorance, dirt, carelessness, unsuitable dwellings, and the corruption that has for so long cost so much in human suffering. Like the program of Christ this movement is concerned with the poor, the oppressed, the sick, and the little children who have never been given a chance to enjoy life. Out of it will come a strong and united China, which will command the respect of the world, and that new China, like the very old one, will be based firmly upon the four cardinal virtues, with the addition of those desirable elements which go to make a modern world. (Chiang, Mme. 1935:73).

Confucianism here is cast as the moral and spiritual foundation for building new citizens, but in the process it has been significantly recast along the idea of contemporary Christian engagement. It is instructive that neither the New Life Movement nor the Confucian religion movement emphasized the ethic of *xiao* (filial piety), which had been central to historical Confucianism. Moreover, Jiang Jeishi is known to have emphasized *chi* (shame, or, in this context, national shame) for China's humiliation, which he interpreted as something he and the Chinese people had to endure until the time was ripe to avenge the nation. Indeed, Jiang, who began to systematically read the Bible in 1934, admired Jesus especially for being able to endure great humiliation through his spirit of forbearance, sacrifice, and struggle (G. Huang 2005).

The flourishing of very large numbers of redemptive societies despite persecution in late imperial China paralleled the flourishing of the so-called New Religions in Japan during the nineteenth century, which were also deeply salvationist and somewhat syncretic. Shimazono (2004) estimates that from the late nineteenth through the twentieth centuries, these New Religions, such as the Tenrikyō, Ōmotokyō, Hitonomichi, Reiyūkai, and others, commanded followings representing 15–20 percent of the population. Although in many ways they adapted to modernist and nationalist discourses, several of them were still severely persecuted by the state during the 1920s and 1930s (Garon 1997:60–71).

In China, the earlier ambivalence, involving proscription on the one hand and accommodation on the other, was complicated by the rocky history of the Republic. When the government was dominated by Yuan Shikai and subsequently by the warlords, the redemptive societies actually flourished, and many of them were able to adapt to the demands of the new age. Thus the Daoyuan (School of the Way), the Daodehui, and others expanded their syncretic vision of the three religions into the five religions, including Islam and Christianity. Indeed, this twentieth-century syncretism was mobilized to adapt to modern discourses. Organized with charters and bylaws, and armed with a strong this-worldly orientation and rhetoric of worldly redemption, these societies re-created themselves on the global model of religious citizenship. Nowhere is this clearer than in the case of the Hongwanzihui (Red Swastika Society), whose name was and could be understood in Buddhist terms (in China the swastika was a symbol of eternity), but which was also unmistakably an Eastern equivalent of the Red Cross Society. This society also had branches in Paris, London, and Tokyo and numbered professors of Esperanto among its members (Suemitsu 1932:292–305, 354).

Many of these organizations responded to the needs for setting up schools and reform programs. Thus the Zailijiao (Teaching of the Abiding Principle) was famous for its program of inner discipline to reform opium and other drug addicts, while other such groups undertook engineering projects to benefit the public infrastructure. Perhaps their participation in a modern discourse is revealed most clearly by their allegiance to that most fundamentally modern discourse: evolutionism, or the linear History of progress. Many of their arguments and propositions were framed by this discourse of evolutionary History. They argued that human evolution (*jinhua*) would stall and turn even more destructive if the present trend toward hedonistic materialism (exemplified by the West) was not countered by moral and spiritual regeneration (Takizawa 1937:67). Thus their spiritualism was dedicated to restoring humanity's evolution to perfection.

After the ascendancy of the Guomindang, these groups were initially banned once again and attacked in the anti-superstition movement of the early years. The ban was later lifted on some of these groups, such as the Daoyuan, but they remained widely mistrusted and controlled. Indeed, the Red Swastika Society was permitted to operate as a legal entity separate from the Daoyuan (they were rejoined under the Japanese occupation). Under the Guomindang, the state implemented not a twofold division of secular versus religious, but a threefold division between secular, religious, and superstitious spheres. In the simple act of defining the "religious," the state developed the capacity to produce or conduce qualities compatible with its model of citizenship and state- and nation-building, while excluding most of those it could not control as "superstitious" and thus illegal (Duara 2003:109–10).

To be sure, state redefinitions were scarcely the only means whereby religious groups developed models of subjecthood compatible with citizenship. Chinese Buddhist groups under Taixu and many of the redemptive societies were aware of models of this-worldly engagement and even took part in the project of nation-building (Tuttle 2005:121–24). But the process in China was much less developed than that in Japan. In Japan, new models of progressive history and Enlightenment civilization became inseparable from nationalism and imperialism, and Buddhism was more than once actively complicit in the wartime slaughter of populations in Asia.

One of the boldest attempts by the state to transform the Chinese redemptive societies took place in Manchukuo (1932–45). In part because the puppet state required the support of the redemptive societies—certainly more than did either the Chinese or Japanese regimes—it sought to bring them into the public sphere and out of the illegal status that most of these groups had under the Guomindang. The model explicitly identified by the Manchukuo regime was that of Christianity, which leaders such as Tachibana Shiraki saw as having been successfully molded by Western states into civic organizations contributing to the state- and nation-building project (Duara 2003:112–16).

Elsewhere I have discussed at some length the changing subjectivity of women in the Morality Society (Daodehui) as it was brought into the realm of "civic religion" (Duara 2003, chap. 4). The narratives of these women are replete with the tension of having to simultaneously live up to what they believed to be the core moral-religious beliefs of the Daodehui and lead a modern life. For example, a recently married woman accepted the foreordained nature of the daughter-in-law to be like that of water: to serve all in the family with devotion (be filial to her in-laws, help her husband attain a Buddhist nation, and be kind to her children) and to rid herself of vain desire. At the same time, women could follow men in devoting themselves to the public good. Indeed, once a wife had satisfactorily served her in-laws, it was incumbent upon her in the next phase to serve the world (Manzhouguo 1936, no. 4:134–35). In these narratives, many women sought new roles by combining the opportunities of citizenship in the puppet state with their religious faith and duties. Nevertheless, the Manchukuo state was unable to bring many of these redemptive and sectarian societies into its public sphere, in part because, in accord with their religious ideals, these groups continued their resistance to the puppet state.

CONFUCIUS IN THE SOUTH SEAS

Thus far we have discussed the traffic between religion and secular citizenship within East Asia. Here I will discuss the case of the Chinese Peranakans of the Dutch Indies during the first part of the twentieth century. The Peranakan case not only illustrates these themes further, it introduces the traffic between religion and national and ethnic identity-formation. Lying, as it were, at the intersection of two different regional systems—the independent if politically subordinate East Asian region, and the dependent European colonial region—the Peranakan community allows us to observe the imbrication of different sets of circulatory ideas and practices. Thus we may also be able to identify the particularity of the secular-religious differentiation in modern China.

The Indies Peranakans trace their origins to Chinese trader-immigrants to the Indies some five centuries ago, who created what G. W. Skinner has called "creole cultures" (or a third culture) in Southeast Asian societies. At the upper levels, these merchant communities interacted—often as bureaucrats and advisors—with the royal court and aristocracies in local society. At the lower levels, too, Chinese traders frequently married local women and spoke the local languages or the lingua franca.

Whereas in the noncolonial parts of Southeast Asia, such as Thailand and Cambodia, the Chinese tended over several generations to assimilate with the local populations, in the colonial societies of British Malaya, the Dutch Indies, and the Spanish Philippines, colonial policies of segregation from both Europeans and indigenous people tended to stabilize the creole culture among these earlier immigrants. These creole communities became important economic and managerial intermediaries between the colonial power and native population on the one hand, and between the colonial power and new Chinese immigrants in the later part of the nineteenth century on the other. In many cases, these communities were blamed for the ills of the colonial system as such, by serving as its most proximate instrument of exploitation (Skinner 1996:50–63).

The wave of new immigrants from China, known as the *sinkeh* in Malaya and *totok* in the Indies, transformed the status of the creole communities in the colonies. In the Philippines, the mestizo who had earlier sided with the natives against the Spanish were largely assimilated into the Filipino population. In Malaya, the Baba Peranakans tended to assimilate with *sinkeh;* only the Indies Peranakans, for a host of historical reasons, remained distinctive. Today they still account for about 3 percent of the population of Indonesia. The Indies Peranakans spoke bazaar Malay, the lingua franca of urban Indies, and wrote their literature in this market Malay, as opposed to the Chinese written by *totoks* and the court Malay favored by the Indonesian elites (Suryadinata 1993b:101–3). In 1920, less than a third of all Chinese in Indonesia used Chinese as their main language or everyday speech. Even in the 1930s, about 80 percent were born in

Indonesia, and 80 percent of those had fathers born in Indonesia (Mackie & Coppell 1976:6–7).

The survival and evolution of Peranakan identity had to do with their particular relationships with the Dutch colonial state and with China and the new Chinese. But the identity itself was significantly expressed in the language and practices of religion, which marked them off not only from their local neighbors but, in interesting ways, from other Chinese as well. Initially, at the turn of the century, it was the Peranakans who sought to take the lead in the re-sinicization (or perhaps simply sinicization) project. As Chinese nationalist organizer Hu Hanmin noted, in 1908 there were few Peranakans who knew their Chinese names or had anything Chinese about them save the queue, ironically a symbol, particularly for the revolutionary nationalist, of the subordination of Chinese to the Manchus (Hu H. 1964:459). Kwee Tek Hoay added that they knew their homeland not by its name of *Zhonghua* but by the pejorative Western appellation, *Tjina* (Kwee 1936–39:11).

The early Peranakan sinicizers were responding in part to the efforts of Chinese nationalists seeking to mobilize their wealth and identities, but the initiative also came simultaneously from local and regional efforts at mobilization. The connections between Peranakans in various parts of Southeast Asia, facilitated by the new media of newspapers and magazines as well as by the wave of new arrivals from China, led to a new consciousness of China and Chineseness. For instance, the Confucian texts *The Great Learning* and *Doctrine of the Mean* were translated into Malay in 1900. In the Dutch Indies, this consciousness among the Peranakan elite became institutionalized in the Tiong Hoa Hwe Koan, or THHK (中華會館, Zhonghua Huiguan or Chinese Association). The THHK was formed in 1900 by "awakened" Peranakan leaders to propagate the Confucian religion, support Chinese education, and reform the customs of the Chinese (Kwee 1936–39:17).

During this early period, the most influential Chinese nationalist group in Southeast Asia was the reform party led by Kang Youwei and Liang Qichao. The emergence of national consciousness among Peranakan leaders coincided with the failure of the Hundred Days Reform (Wuxu Bianfa) and the subsequent Boxer Rebellion, which was regarded as disastrous. Consequently, reform of Chinese customs and the introduction of modern education in Chinese, English, or Dutch were high on the agenda of the THHK. But of equal if not greater significance for them was the propagation of the "Confucian religion." The goal of the reformers was "to create a religion or a moral system that was pure for use as a guide and a source of improvement in their social lives. . . . [Reforms were to be undertaken] insofar as possible in keeping with those principles of the prophet Confucius so necessary to civilized conduct" (Kwee 1936–39:6, emphasis added). Indeed, as D.E. Willmott observed in his 1960 study, interest in religion among the Chinese in Indonesia had grown steadily until then (Willmott 1960:188). There the urge to reform customs among the Chinese elites led not to the decline of religion, as it did in among intellectuals in China itself, but to new articulations of faith and practice as well as to the spread of Christianity.

The reasons that religion became more rather than less influential in the Dutch Indies, in contrast to the situation in China, seem to be rather clear. In the Indies, religion represented a desideratum of a modern community (as part of a rational and deistic civilization), and became closely tied to the problem of national and civilizational identity as well. Compare this Confucian movement to Kang Youwei's in China. Indeed, the two movements were closely related. The founders of the THHK were profoundly influenced by Kang's ideas and programs. The Confucian school was expected to meet twice a month, on the first and fifteenth days, and to hear sermons and explanations of Confucian texts in the manner of its counterpart in China, although the Indies Peranakans were also self-consciously following the example of the missionary schools (Kwee 1936–39:15). In 1903, Kang Youwei gave several lectures to throngs of listeners at the THHK center in Batavia. He served as their advisor, and the THHK leaders even asked him to adjudicate a dispute over religious protocol (discussed below).

Yet, as noted above, Kang's Confucian religion movement disappeared into the Confucian learning movement and into the suppressed redemptive societies. The reasons were connected both to the rise of the anti-religious May Fourth Movement and to Kang's inability to secure state support. I suggested earlier that the Guomindang's New Life Movement can be seen as the Confucian religion movement's secular successor. But while the New Life Movement participated in the traffic by fashioning itself as the traditional conscience of the new citizen, it neither saw itself as a religion nor represented a source of moral authority separate from or transcending the authority of the state. Moreover, the social and political environment in which Kang sought to cultivate the Confucian religion movement did not necessitate a strong identitarian movement to distinguish the self from powerful rejecting or assimilating Other(s) in religious terms.

It is true that Kang responded to the pressures of Christianity and the imperialist discourse of civilization. But if we can distinguish analytically, for the moment, between the effort to create a religion perceived as a requirement of moral citizenship and what was primarily an identitarian movement, then I believe the balance, for Kang, lay in the former. Certainly, the powerful anti-Christian and anti-religious movement launched by the intelligentsia in the 1920s revealed that they did not seek their alternative source of identity in the recognized religions.

In the colonial environment of the Dutch Indies, the balance was reversed, in that the Confucian movement as religion was perceived to be essential to the challenge of identity. This challenge came not only from Christianity's hegemonic presence in the colonial environment, where the rulers identified Christianity with civilized religion, but also from Islam, which claimed to represent the majority of the population and was identified with the "religions of the book" (i.e., Judaism, Christianity, and Islam). Islam had competitive claims to civilization, particularly when monotheism and anti-idolatry were assumed to be the norms, or perhaps the rules, of the game of civilized religion. In these ways, among Peranakans the Confucian Association (THHK) and the Three-in-One Society, or Sam Kauw Hwee (三教會, Sanjiaohui), resembled other non-Islamic colonial religious renewal or reform movements, such as modern Buddhism in Sri Lanka or Burma and Vedanta Hinduism in British India.

Confucian religion in the Dutch Indies tended to become an ideology of nationalism and had to play a role larger than that of either a civic conscience or a privatized religion. This ideology had to both sanction reform and create an authentic foundation for Chinese identity. But if reform and change eroded the authentic, they threatened identity. This is, of course, a classic aporia of nationalist ideology, and haunted the Peranakans no less than anyone else.

Like Kang Youwei and the reformers in China, the THHK also identified Confucianism with education and reform. Modern educational opportunities were a key demand of the Peranakan community, as the best means to improve their situation. Denied Dutch education, the THHK launched Chinese schools to improve its members' educational opportunities. This was initially quite successful and had the effect of pressuring the Dutch to introduce Dutch education for Chinese as early as 1905. Ironically, if not entirely unpredictably, this had the further effect of reducing enrollment in the THHK Chinese schools, and the educational enterprise of the THHK was widely regarded as a failure—though because it had been designed to pressure the Dutch, its failure was also its success. At the same time, that "success" reinforced the Dutch or non-Chinese orientation of the Peranakans (Mackie & Coppel 1976:9).

The reform of "superstitious and burdensome customs," especially in the areas of funerals and marriages, was of great concern to the THHK. The Peranakan writer, dramatist, reformer, and founder of the Sam Kauw Hwee, Kwee Tek Hoay (1886–1952), wrote a history of the THHK entitled *The Origins of the Modern Chinese Movement in Indonesia*. He spent a good third of the book documenting the efforts of the awakened leaders to expunge everything "false" and reform the impure customs, superstitious beliefs, and offerings to idols and shrines among the Indies Chinese,who were far away "from the ancestral rites, temple ceremonies and other customs of the Chinese tradition." His story of the THHK is an exciting and heroic tale about the reformers, who battle victoriously against the forces of the official cultural authority of the Peranakan community, located in the kapitan's office. This was the office of the Chinese official in Batavia, which managed ceremonies and festivities and ran a traditional school (*yixue*) that taught Chinese characters, although rather lackadaisically (Kwee 1936–39:17–18, 62–63).

After gaining control of the community leadership in the early 1900s, the THHK leaders went about reforming the festivities. During the ceremony of the rites for wandering ghosts in the seventh lunar month, a contest had developed where contestants raced to grab ritual objects at the top of raised platforms. This appeared to be somewhat violent and turbulent, but it was a festive occasion. The reformers simply stopped the flow of money to sponsor the event (Kwee 1936–39:31). They also used the power of the purse to limit the activities of the priest who prayed for the community at the altars of the many gods. They paid the priest 25 *gulden* and asked him to ignore the gods not provided for in his fees! They also prohibited gambling and other competitions at the festivities (Kwee 1936–39:32).

Kwee's narrative turns somewhat tragic at this point because, as he admits, the reform of customs was not popular. A good part of the blame was assigned to the Peranakan women, who were from a Muslim background, uneducated and conservative. On the one hand, this had led to the adulteration of pure Chinese traditions with indigenous elements. Thus prayers were offered not only on lunar holidays of the Chinese calendar but also on Mohammed's birthday. Wedding and funeral customs were burdensome and full of superstitions involving offerings at shrines and temples. On the other hand, the women's lack of education contributed to a blind conservatism. For example, the women and traditionalists insisted on ritual mourning and wailing as a necessary expression of filial piety. Yet Kwee found evidence in the *Xiaojing (Classic of Filial Piety)* that Confucius had been opposed to ritual mourning: "Children who are truly filial do not pretend to weep at a parent's funeral" (Kwee 1936–39:36). The THHK provided an alternative marriage ceremony similar to a civil ceremony. However, it did not have many takers and performed only about six ceremonies over many years. It appears true, as Kwee claimed, that many of the marriage-custom reforms penetrated the Peranakan community anyway, but it is not clear that they were seen as redounding to Confucian or even Chinese ideas (Kwee 1936–39:33–52).

The limited success of Confucianism as a reformist religion among Peranakans eventually caused many of the new Peranakan Confucianists to move away from their religious radicalism. In the early stages, the THHK had been both monotheistic and iconoclastic. During his visit, Kang Youwei was approached to resolve a dispute among THHK members about whether the THHK hall and school should allow portraits at the altars of Confucius and Zhu Xi (Chu Hsi, 1130–1200 C.E.). Kang had no objection at all to the idea and rebuked those opposed to the images. Pointing his finger at them, he said, "You are like the historical figure that prohibited people from worshipping Confucius because it cost too much. As a result, people who felt spiritually deprived prayed at all sorts of temples." According to Kwee, the objectors later persuaded Kang that an altar in the THHK building would make it difficult to prevent people from coming to pray for favors, wealth, and so on. It would become just another temple in Batavia (Kwee 1936–39:24–26).

In the early 1930s, reformers like Kwee began to turn to a more syncretic faith that was simultaneously more catholic and tolerant as well as abstract and interiorized. The Sam Kauw Hwee (Sanjiaohui), also called Tridharma, was the Peranakan equivalent of the Chinese three-in-one syncretic society that combined elements of Confucianism, Buddhism, and Daoism. The Sam Kauw Hwee was established in 1934 and soon became more popular than the Confucian Association (THHK), establishing thirty branches all over Indonesia by 1955. Tridharma accepted popular religiosity and gods, or Toapekong, into the Chinese pantheon, and emphasized the common goals of all religions:

> Taoism showed mankind the path leading to the solitary state beside the First Source called *Tao* (Tao or Dao); Buddhism taught how a person might come to be alone with *Wet* (Law), truth or Dharma, and in this way reach Nirvana; and Confucianism showed how to live in accordance with the True Way and, in this way, become *Seng Djen* (*Shengren*, a superior man). (Suryadinata 1993a:50).

Although their methods differed, their aims were the same: to reach perfect happiness. Indeed, Kwee was also influenced by Hinduism (and, as we shall see, Islam); themes of spirituality and reincarnation recur in his literary works.

Like the modern Vedantist thinkers—Vivekananda and Ramakrishna—in colonial India, Kwee created a two-leveled religiosity. In it, one could entertain many different religious practices and even the worship of gods. But these were only means to achieve the same one God. One might say that Sam Kauw Hwee permitted the reformists to accept icons and popular practices but to remain monotheists in an abstract way. This monotheism responded both to the emerging power of Islam and to the modern interiorization of faith.[5] Tridharma posited the existence of an ultimate God who was often called Tian (Heaven) and was sometimes identified with Allah. On the ninth day of the seventh month, the Chinese always prayed to the God, Allah. They worshiped the wide and endless sky (*tian*), "because only the sky itself can portray or represent the greatness of God." According to an observer of Tridharma in the 1950s, the society emphasized "ceremonial devotion to the ancestors and to the Supreme God, Tuhan Allah. The idea is not to ask for special favors but to purify oneself and offer honor and praise. Magic is considered superstition for the spiritually illiterate" (Willmott 1960:250). Kwee attempted to show that, despite the plentitude of gods and practices, the focus of Tridharma is a single goal and a single God beyond all manifestations: Tian (Allah and Jesus). For him, the Toapekong (gods) were like angels or helpers of God who could help people find their way to God.

Kwee's religious journey from radical Confucian religiosity to the abstraction that equated Allah with Heaven may be read as a code to the layered complexities of Peranakan history in the twentieth century. Turning away from the alienating moralism of the modernizing Confucian elite, Kwee created the syncretic Sam Kauw Hwee, which seems to have been an effort to encompass and systematize what already existed in the culture. This cultural base was and is necessary for the identity of the Chinese community—mainly the Peranakans—who make their home in Indonesia but have not lost their idea of themselves as Chinese. Indeed, the turn to Tridharma coincided with a turn away from the China orientation of the THHK, which became more and more marginal to Indies Peranakans in the mid-twentieth century.

But if Tridharma was the organizational means of maintaining lines of communication with the popular base—a role of religion that presumably became unnecessary in Republican China—it also came to represent a form of religiosity that could address the perceived requirements of a global religion. Tridharma's emphasis on a supreme deity was accompanied by

Figure 1.1.   Tridharma (Sam Kauw Hwee, or Three-in-One Society) devotees in modern Indonesia.

advocacy of personal righteousness and public service. Organizationally, the Sam Kauw Hwee units were modeled on the Christian church, with Sunday activities, pastors, charities, counseling, and the like. Sermons were given on topics such as Mencius and the idea of democracy, Atma and Atman, karma, and reincarnation. Tridharma's leaders, such as the charismatic Bhikhu Jinarakhita (trained originally as an engineer in Holland), espoused Eastern spiritualism and decried Western materialism (Willmott 1960:250–253). It is perhaps true that Kwee Tek Hoay and the Sam Kauw Hwee never succeeded in synthesizing the duality between popular religion and the interiorized God. But more important for us is to grasp how both positions were necessary for Kwee and many Peranakan leaders. The Sam Kauw Hwee allows the Peranakans to have their gods and the one God as well; to have culture and Culture. It encompasses popular Chinese culture and represents a true religion, and is thus the source of both identity and reform.

But what of interiorization? How did the differentiation of church and state, devised in a remote place, come to mean something to Kwee? We can gain some insight into the role that interiorized religion played in Kwee's self-perception from an essay he wrote in 1928 (Suryadinata 1993a:39). After the establishment of Guomindang power in China under Jiang

Jieshi, Kwee wrote a sharp essay denouncing the nationalist clamor urging Chinese to return to China and fully embrace the national project in the motherland. After outlining the hardships that returning Chinese—particularly Peranakans, who did not read Chinese—had experienced, he pressed for self-reliance. Kwee argued that overseas Chinese could best help China by going out into the world and becoming successful. The territory of China had no mystique for him: "If his heart remains Chinese his thoughts and sympathies will remain with the fatherland. Remember, a Peranakan Chinese of Trinidad who cannot read Chinese like Eugene Chen is worth more than a million indigenous inhabitants of China of the caliber of a Chang Tso Lin" (Kwee 1997:26).[6]

Kwee reinforces his case for an interior—or nonterritorial—sense of Chineseness by comparing it with religion. Many people, he says, believe that salvation or benefit will come from devotion to Buddha, Christ, or Mohammed, or by building and repairing temples to Toapekung: "In truth the salvation or damnation of a man depends upon his own deeds. . . . The gods only point the way. This is because the destiny of every man is in his own hands. . . . The blessing of eternal salvation can only be gained by striving for it within oneself." Similarly, Kwee urges, the Chinese in Indonesia ought to look within themselves, depend on their own abilities, improve their position in this country, and accommodate themselves "in a group of various races" (Kwee 1997:46–47). In the end, his Chineseness itself becomes modeled on the principle of religious interiorization. Just as the advent of secularism demanded the interiorization of faith and devotion, so, too, did a minority seek to prepare itself for a nationalist society by delineating the inner self that could adapt in another's nation.

CONCLUSIONS

The Indies Peranakans and Mainland Chinese began to diverge significantly in their need and uses for religion. I have suggested here that in the post–May Fourth period, intellectual elites and political regimes in China had little need for religious conceptions and practices, either to root their identity in or to help in mobilizing moral and other historical resources. Elsewhere, drawing on Lin Yusheng, I have argued that this powerful antireligious face of the Chinese Enlightenment emerged with the breakdown after 1911 of the mode of integration of Chinese elites with culture and morality that had been dependent on the universal emperorship. I have also argued that the absence of a direct colonial power built on a different and allegedly superior cultural foundation obviated the need to construct an oppositional cultural identity based on tradition or religion (Duara 1995, chap. 7). The case study of Peranakan religiosity is, I believe, further proof of this claim.

However, even if religious identity was not necessary for Chinese elites, the quest for unity of the moral and the political, for realization of the authentic values of a people or culture in the body politic, continues to express itself in several different ways. We have tracked the failure of the Confucian religion movement and its transformation into a secular move-ment of moral transformation in the New Life Movement. In Taiwan, the Guomindang government continued to promote Confucian moral educa-tion and ritual patronage as nonreligious foundations of the nation's cul-ture (Jochim 2003). More recently, the new Confucian movement has also been interesting the People's Republic of China (PRC) government, which is seeking alternatives to communist ideology; observe, for instance, the new Confucius Institutes which it has been setting up abroad to resemble the Goethe and Cervantes institutes. But perhaps the most dramatic expression of the quest to realize moral authenticity in the body politic was the Cultural Revolution. The absolutism and the passion it generated breached whatever institutional boundaries and zones of autonomy had remained in PRC society.

Another consequence of the twentieth-century Chinese elites' hostility toward religion was that it was forced to suppress, with repeated failures, most aspects of popular culture that were inseparably fused with "religion" and, worse, with superstition. The way Peranakan elites ultimately came to terms with popular culture gives us clues as to how an alternative relation-ship might evolve on the Mainland. Moreover, the impulses, needs, and yearnings behind the redemptive societies, which were mostly suppressed after the consolidation of Communist power, seem to have resurfaced in contemporary Chinese society. Tied as they are to older cosmologies unit-ing the cosmos, the community, and the body, these groups, whether they be the Falungong or the Yiguandao, inevitably run afoul of the state when they enter the public sphere. As the liberalization of the Taiwanese polity after 1986 shows, expanding the space of religion remains the best way to channel the impulse for transcendence.

2   Redeploying Confucius

The Imperial State Dreams of the Nation,
1902–1911

Ya-pei Kuo 郭亞珮

Few periods in Chinese history were more tumultuous than the seventeen years from 1895 to 1911. In every aspect of social, political, and cultural life, the advent of global modernity fueled drastic changes. The momentum of these changes started in the mid-nineteenth century. After the Opium Wars, Euro-American and Japanese powers of colonial expansion increasingly encroached on the Manchu empire of the Qing with demands for political and territorial concessions, trade expansion, and the right to spread foreign culture and religion in China. Armed with treaties from their home countries signed under duress by the Qing government, Western missionaries, merchants, and diplomats came to China with their respective agendas. Together, they presented a world of new technology, social practices, and radically new concepts to the Chinese, altering Chinese cosmology and the Chinese perception of the world and themselves, and transforming the whole Chinese way of life.

The Xinzheng (新政, New Policies) program of political reforms, initiated by the Qing dynasty's highest authorities in 1902, was part and parcel of this time of change. On the surface, the project stood for the Qing state's response to the social and cultural tumult by exerting leadership in guiding its subjects out of the turbulence and confusion. The reform government purported to embrace the new knowledge and technology in order to fortify and preserve the old values and orientation, and it upheld the famous axiom "Chinese learning for the essence, Western learning for the application" (中學為體, 西學為用; *zhongxue wei ti, xixue wei yong*). The logic of this formula held that modernization should strengthen, rather than alter, the foundations of Chinese culture. In reality, the Xinzheng program soon became a total overhaul of government organization and state apparatus. In 1906, when the Qing promulgated a plan to transform the imperial system into a constitutional monarchy, it transpired that the reforms had become a full acknowledgment of the force of the new. The most enduring institution in Chinese history, the dynastic empire, was to be replaced with an openly imported system.

The Xinzheng program was a government-orchestrated effort to implement a new vision of modernity in China. Many historians have interpreted this effort as a desperate strategy of regime survival at the expense of virtually all of its institutional heritage. Yet even those who hold this opinion do not deny the project's formidable legacy. The thorough revamping of government structure, the compilation of new legal code, and the creation of Western-style schools all departed sharply from the past model and laid the structural foundation for later state formation (Reynolds 1993; MacKinnon 1983). And many of the Xinzheng initiatives introduced what Michel Foucault famously identified as modern political technologies for social discipline and engineering. Institutions such as the prison, the educational system, and the police force were inaugurated, and would become permanent features of the Chinese state apparatus from this point onward (Dikötter 2002; Bailey 1990; MacKinnon 1975). Through these devices, the Xinzheng reforms established a new regime of statecraft and envisioned a modern state that would be both expansive and extractive. Although the collapse of the Qing dynasty in 1911 abruptly forestalled the full implementation of these reforms, the new vision provided the blueprint for later phases of state formation.

The most radical departure of the Xinzheng program from the past was an overt embracing of nationalism. The monarchical empire expressly attempted to engineer its own transformation into a nation-state of mass citizenry. In stretching "the short, tight skin of the nation over the gigantic body of the empire," the motive behind the Xinzheng program was indeed what Benedict Anderson calls an "official nationalism" that aimed to "combine naturalization with retention of dynastic power" (1991:86) by appropriating the image of the nation into the empire's self-representation.[1] However, in contrast to the European examples on which Anderson bases his analysis, the Qing government's deployment of the nation was not "an anticipatory strategy adopted by dominant groups who are threatened with marginalization or exclusion from an emerging nationally-imagined community" (Anderson 1991:101). In 1902, print capitalism and the imagined community barely existed in China. Still, the imperial state shifted its claims to legitimacy to a focus on the representation of China as a nation. The Xinzheng reforms were in this sense the imperial state's systematic reinvention of political symbolism and ritual scheme, an attempt to infuse a shared sense of national time and space into people's lives. Through ritual planning, these reforms wrote the script to enact China's new identity as a nation.

In the following pages, I explore the historical significance of ritual reinvention undertaken by the Qing court and the rise of official nationalism during the Xinzheng reforms. The focal point of this exploration is the reform government's promotion of the worship of Confucius (孔子, Kongzi). Early in the reforms, the Qing state designated the worship of Confucius as the principal component of school rituals in modern schools throughout China. Later, the Manchu authorities further elevated Confucius from the middle to the highest rank in the three-tier system of the state cult. Historians have viewed this as indicative of a backward-looking conservatism of the Qing authorities at the time (Levenson 1965, vol. 2:3–21; R. Smith 1990:285; Yuan 2001:94–202). By situating the promotion of the worship in the context of an emerging official nationalism, I argue that during this brief interlude of the Qing court's reform of state ritual, Confucius was remodeled from one of many great sages and sage-emperors of timeless truth in the imperium into a new image of the nation. By synchronizing and integrating the ritual bodies of both the emperor and the people in front of this new symbol of the nation, the reform government subtly authored a new ritual scheme that signified a united, homogeneous nation. This radical departure from imperial precedents undermined the imperial throne's paramount ritual status. At the same time, the state retained a total power over the composition of ritual and the disciplining of ritual bodies. This ritual innovation, while shifting the center of the imperial order from the sacred body of the emperor to a Confucian image of the nation, enabled the long imperial tradition of ritual government to continue into the new era of nationalism.

By focusing on the imperial state's historical role in instituting nationalism, this essay joins other scholarship in rethinking the putative dichotomy between "nation-state" and "empire" (Duara 2003; DuBois 2005a). Until recent years, this conceptual dichotomy had been one of the cornerstones in understanding the history of nationalism. Benedict Anderson's indictment of official nationalism is a fine example. For Anderson, official nationalism could only be the empire's "conjuring trick" and defense mechanism because nationalism was fundamentally contradictory to how the empire functioned. Nationalism was the historical antithesis of the empire, and official nationalism under the empire could mean nothing but inconsistency. In the China field, the dichotomy has been equally influential. Joseph Levenson (1965) was a prominent representative of using the dichotomy to explain the historical rupture between modern China and its imperial past. Although in many ways the China field has moved beyond Levenson's stance, the heuristic incompatibility between the empire and the nation-state is still one of the most powerful paradigms that inform our understanding of modern China.

The Qing state's efforts at self-transformations proved that the heuristic contrast between nation-state and empire was not absolute. Indeed, to appropriate the model of nation-state meant surrendering a number of imperial claims. Here the dichotomy is indisputable. As Chang Hao has pointed out, the cosmology that underpinned the dynastic empire was under severe challenge by modern scientific knowledge at the end of the nineteenth century. The collapse of this cosmology triggered a "crisis of orientation" among the elites of the empire (H. Chang 1987:5–8). The Xinzheng government's active reforms could be viewed as a response to this crisis. In all official documents of this period, the state noticeably stops using cosmological references to buttress its political authority. But the evidence needed to prove that the Qing state acted out of weakness is lacking. After 1900, the state showed tremendous determination and swiftness in planning the reforms. To account for this willingness to shift the grounds of political legitimacy, one needs to go beyond the "nation-state versus empire" paradigm.

Here some recent theoretical discussions about the continuum between the colonial and postcolonial states may be useful. Postcolonial scholars have argued that, in projecting power imaginaries, the nation-state often drew on the same knowledge of governing techniques as the imperial state (Chatterjee 1986, 1993; Mbembe 2005); the two also shared the same objective of the "structural effect" (Mitchell 1991a). According to this line of analysis, both the colonial state of the empire and the postcolonial state of the nation seek to maximize their governing power by inscribing themselves into the structure of the subjects'/citizens' social lives. Through deploying categories and concepts, they come to govern not as an external force of coercion and restriction but as an internal force of classification and production (Mitchell 1991b). This recognition of a continuum in statecraft has inspired scholars to reassess the putative rupture between modern Chinese states and their imperial predecessor. In his recent article on the discourse of "religion" in East and Southeast Asia, for example, Thomas DuBois draws attention to the precolonial states' appetite for religious control and argues that the real impact of European hegemony "was to integrate the preexistent concerns into larger discourses, transforming them in the process" (2005a:113).

Historians of premodern China have increasingly noted the late imperial state's political aspiration in social engineering. The Ming and Qing
states both expressed political interests in building an empirewide network
of schools down to the most local and individual levels (Schneewind 2006;
A. Leung 1994).They also viewed it as their primary mission to "guide"
subjects into proper ritual behavior and to stamp out deviations from state-
sanctioned orthodoxy and orthopraxy. These precedents prove that the
appetite for social programming predated the modern era, and thus help
explain the swiftness of the Qing state's embrace of some of the practices
of the nation-state. Nationalism placed the imperial state on the moral
high ground and endowed it with a renewed sense of political legitimacy.
It also provided a novel device for controlling political and cultural capital.
In the name of nation-building, the state expanded its governing power
to unprecedented areas. The declaration of the Confucian classics as the
"national religion" in 1904 (Zhang, Rong, & Zhang 1904a) thus coincided
with aggressive policies to confiscate properties of religious establishments
and dismantle local temple communities (Thompson 1996; Goossaert 2005).
By the same token, the creation of a national school system in 1902–4
ran parallel with state-controlled programs of textbook censorship, the
imposition of school uniforms, and pedagogical standardization. The old
institutions of local community schools became targets of state reform and
came to be regarded as obsolete institutions of the past (Borthwick 1983).

The Xinzheng reforms can thus be understood as a historical process
whereby the imperial will sought to appropriate the construct of nation
for its own reification, a process through which the imperial episteme tried
to infuse new life into itself in the modern era. This imperial episteme
used official nationalism for its own perpetuation. It took control of the
process of imagining the nation by actively authoring a new symbolic
and ritual schema. The state, as the true enactor of the nation, wrote itself
into the structure of the collective life of the nation. Contrary to Benedict
Anderson's formulation, the Chinese state created the imagery of the
nation, rather than being created after the national imaginary. Thus state
power in China was not constrained by the nation and did not have to
answer to the imagined community. Despite its espousal of nationalism,
the reform government of the late Qing remained a "nationless state." As
John Fitzgerald has pointed out, in modern China's dual process of state-
building and nation-building, "the state was not just the midwife at the
birth of the nation, but in fact its sire" (1996:58): the successive political
regimes continuously redrew the imagery of the nation according to their
respective assertions of legitimacy. In this process, the nation was "the

desideratum of state-building" (Fitzgerald 1996:59); its attributes reflected the wish of the unitary state, rather than the characteristics of a preexistent entity. Although Fitzgerald's comment was primarily addressing the nation-state formations under the Nationalist and Communist regimes, the reform government of the late Qing also illustrates this phenomenon. The decade of the Xinzheng reforms, in this sense, constitutes a key moment for assessing the legacy of the Chinese empire for the process of nation-state formation in the twentieth century.

CONFUCIUS WORSHIP AND RITUAL GOVERNMENT

Confucius had been worshipped in China since antiquity. The earliest record of imperial worship of the sage dates to the early Han dynasty, at the end of the third century B.C.E. The first state temple dedicated to Confucius was built in the fifth century C.E., during a time of political fragmentation. The cult became a component of the imperial ritual after the reunification in 589 C.E. Along with the establishment of government schools during the Tang and Song, the cult of Confucius spread throughout the empire. During the Ming and Qing, the worship of Confucius was an integral part of the imperial state cult and occupied a stable place in the imperial pantheon (T. Wilson 2002a; Huang J. 2003a).

The system of state cult was one of the most significant institutions that grounded political legitimacy of the empire in the cosmic order. To offer sacrifices and obeisance to Heaven and Earth, and to reward, honor, and command various deities and spirits, were the exclusive prerogatives of the emperor, the Son of Heaven (天子, tianzi). The state cult, more than other imperial rituals, placed the emperor at the center of human communication with the world of gods and spirits, and thus signified the emperorship's cosmic significance.

In addition to reiterating the religious claim, the state cult was a central part of ritual government, the distinctive Chinese approach to statecraft. In China's long history of political thought and practice, ritual (禮, li) occupied a special place.[2] Throughout imperial history, "the scrupulous and pious performance of sacrifices and rites remain[ed] one of the criteria in terms of which the ruler's virtue [was] measured" (B. Schwartz 1985:48). It was the outer manifestation of the moral quality of the ruler. Ritual was also associated with the civilizing mission of the empire. As a social, political, and religious apparatus all in one, ritual was deemed to have the power to shape the interiority of the individual and to harmonize society at large (Yang 1994:226–27; Chow 1994; McDermott 1999). Since the Mandate of Heaven (天命, *tianming*), which gave the Son of Heaven the authority to rule, entailed "a moral responsibility for sustaining the normative social order" and required the political authority to serve as "headquarters of spiritual and ethical initiative" (B. Schwartz 1975:59–60), ritual became the primary device of governing. Through ritual encoding and observance, the state set behavioral norms and moral examples for its subjects, and defined the social-political order without coercion.

Ritual government implied a particular conception of power. Those who placed themselves in a proper relation to the universe were thought to gain access to the inner process of behavioral and moral-spiritual formation in both individual subjects and the social order. The state cult must be understood as an expression of this approach to government and a confirmation of the imperial state's political authority. This claim of authority allowed the state to issue ritual codes and standardize ceremonies, rites, and etiquettes for officials, the court, and the common people. The state-sanctioned knowledge of ritual, in turn, placed the empire within a network of norms and structured it into a hierarchical order (R. Smith 1990). The imperial state's fixation with ritual encoding and performance was not a simple effort of disguising power. As James Laidlaw argues in his critique of Clifford Geertz's symbolist approach, ritual in the world of imperial Chinese politics aimed much higher than the theatrical effect of power evocation. Chinese state rituals initiated, animated, and constituted imperial power itself (Laidlaw 1999).[3]

Although many have referred to the imperial state cult as Confucian,[4] Confucius did not enjoy a particularly glorious career in the state cult. While the imperial state had never been negligent in paying homage to the spirit of the sage, the ritual acknowledgement of Confucius's cultural status had not been consistently grand and prominent. Since the seventh century, the worship of Confucius had been of the rank of "middle sacrifice" (中祀, *zhongsi*) in the three-tiered hierarchy of imperial sacrifices. During the Qing, "grand sacrifice" (大祀, *dasi*) included those to Heaven (*Tian*), Earth (*Di*), the Spirits of Land-and-Grain (*Sheji*), and the imperial ancestors, or Spirits of Former Emperors (*Xiandi*). A step below that, middle sacrifices were offered to the emperors of previous dynasties (*Lidai Diwang*), the Sun, the Moon, and the God of Agriculture (*Shennong*). At the lowest level, that of "miscellaneous sacrifices" (群祀, *qunsi*), the objects of worship were the God of War (*Guandi*), Spirits of Former Physicians (*Xianyi*), the God of Fire (*Huoshen*), the Dragon God (*Longshen*), and other spirits and deities (Feuchtwang 1977:586).

In this hierarchy, Confucius was accorded the highest honor given to a human unrelated to an imperial line. Yet his cult status was arguably in constant decline throughout the Qing. As more and more human worthies, as well as folk deities and spirits, were incorporated and upgraded within the state cult, Confucius worship seemed less significant. In 1853, for example, the God of War was promoted to the level of middle sacrifice and for the first time worshiped by an emperor in person. In 1856, the God of Literature (*Wenchang*) was accorded the same rank (Liu J. 1935:9119–20). By the middle of the nineteenth century, Confucius had to share the state's ritual attention with more icons of the same rank; his ritual status in the imperial state cult was by no means preeminent.

If the sacrificial status of Confucius does not seem to match the late imperial state's ideological indebtedness to the sage, it forms a useful site for interrogating the tension between the Confucian literati and the impe-rial throne. Although the widespread worship of Confucius, independent of imperial patronage, has not been extensively researched, there is no doubt that by the period in question Confucius had become the symbol of the literati's collective identity. The worship of Confucius spread among literati, and the sage emerged as the patron deity for those devoted to the classics.[5] In this vein, state patronage may be seen as following the same state strategy of what Prasenjit Duara calls "superscription" that occurred with other human deities. According to Duara, by incorporating popular worship of a given figure into the state cult, the state defined permissible interpretations without resorting to total suppression. At the same time, it positioned itself as "the patron of patrons" and thereby drew on the symbolic power of the icon in question for its own legitimacy and author-ity. The state cult of Confucius was by definition a subtle means of social control and cultural cooptation; it was never meant as a celebration of the cultural stature of the sage himself (Duara 1988b).

As a flexible strategy, superscription allows for interpretive con-testation—after all, the state could contain but could not eradicate the cultural vitality and fluid dynamism of the symbol. Unlike the cults of Heaven, Earth, Land-and-Grain, and imperial ancestors, which could only be addressed directly from the throne, the worship of Confucius was of the status of "general worship" (*tongsi*) and was widely practiced among different social strata with few restrictions. As a state cult, worship was routinely conducted at Confucius temples (孔廟, *Kongmiao*) or temples of civil culture (文廟, *wenmiao*) attached to the government schools at the imperial, provincial, prefectural, and county capitals. Outside the official network of educational institutions, regional academies (書院, *shuyuan*) had also become an important locus of worship since the Song.[6] Other than collecting books and providing discussion and teaching forums, worshipping the sage was one of the main imperatives for the *shuyuan* movement in the thirteenth century (Chan 1987). After the Ming, the worship of Confucius spread with the expansion of local literacy and community schools in China (A. Leung 1994).

The cult was anything but uniform. Strict in the government schools, everywhere else it varied in its rites and its meaning. *Shuyuan* sometimes participated in the empirewide state cult of Confucius, but only with government permission; along with literacy and community schools, they insisted on separate performance of worship. Some schools stipulated worship on the first and fifteenth days of every month, while others required it only at the beginning of the term. In some cases, a simplified rite was performed daily (Qu & Tang 1991, vol. 1:326, 339, 345, 356, 360; Borthwick 1983:29–30; Shu 1945:43–45; Hu S. 1933:59). The state and the increasingly educated populace both worshipped Confucius, but each attached different meanings to doing so. The same worship could signify imperial authority, express the scholarly elite's collective identity, or constitute a rite of passage into literacy. The meaning of Confucius worship was never monolithic and static. Together, these interpretive perspectives of the worship made the Confucius shrine a site of contestation.

This contestation between the state-sanctioned orthodoxy/orthopraxy and the alternative interpretations and practices required the imperial state's most vigilant management, since the contestation did have the potential to challenge the imperial state's cultural authority and undermine its political legitimacy. To maintain control, the imperial state periodically attempted aggressive interventions. In 1369, for example, the founding emperor of the Ming dynasty (1368–1644), Hongwu (1328–98), in a despotic assertion of power over the bureaucracy, abolished the state cult of Confucius and issued a proscription of the cult outside the sage's hometown in Qufu, Shandong. This proscription was quickly reversed and the state cult of Confucius reinstated, yet efforts to control the cult's cultural meaning continued throughout the history of the Ming dynasty (Huang J. 2003b). Although different interpretations were normally tolerated by the state, the imperial desire for total control never completely died out.

LATE QING CHANGES IN RITUAL GOVERNMENT

The advent of official nationalism at the turn of the twentieth century did not signal the weakening of imperial control. Rather, the Xinzheng reforms were meant to be a doubling process: the matrix of the old ritual contest was dismantled, while a system of modern institutions was established to serve as the new platform for ritual government.

After the Boxer Uprising and the ensuing political turmoil in 1900–1901, Zhang Zhidong (張之洞, 1837–1909) and Liu Kunyi (劉坤一, 1830–1902), two powerful regional officials of Han ethnicity, initiated the Xinzheng reforms with a proposal for a six-level educational structure in place of the examination-oriented imperial school system. The new structure would incorporate the whole nation into a network of modern schools. In the original 1901 proposal, Zhang and Liu (1962) justified the scheme of educational reforms for its effectiveness in producing "men of talent" (人才, *rencai*). By emphasizing *rencai*, Zhang and Liu invoked the traditional utilitarian view of education as the process of producing high-quality civil servants and state bureaucrats. *Rencai* was for the use of the state and implied an elitist view of education. The system would focus on educating the most talented men for the country.

Despite this traditionalist overtone in the educational reform, what is historically significant is that the major advocates of the new-style schools soon revised their position and shifted their attention to elementary education. In 1902, when Zhang Zhidong drew up the actual program for the education reform, he claimed that "to generate men of ability for the state's employment is of secondary significance" (Zhang Z. 1962: 57.13a [3935]). The most urgent task of educational reform was in the area of primary schools. Yuan Shikai (袁世凱, 1859–1916) echoed Zhang's opinion in a 1904 memorial that openly called for abolition of civil service examinations: "The new-style schools were not exclusively for the provision of talent, but mainly for enlightening the minds of the people" (Zhu S., comp. 1958 [1909]:5390). Thus the education of the mass of the people was now the primary purpose of educational reform.

To enlighten the minds of the people entailed a two-pronged approach. The new-style schools would teach Western subjects, such as geography, math, and biology, and impart modern knowledge and skills that citizens would need to secure a livelihood. Education would therefore produce economically independent and intellectually modern-minded people to strengthen the nation. Equally important for the Xinzheng program of enlightenment was the objective of personality transformation. The educational reformers almost unanimously envisioned modern education as a tool for promoting patriotism and political loyalty. In his educational plan, Zhang Zhidong enumerated three guidelines for primary education nationwide: (1) moral cultivation that would make the people know right from wrong; (2) patriotism that would make the people know the importance of defending their nation; and (3) the development of skill training that would give the people the means to become economically self-reliant (Zhang Z. 1962 [1902]:57.13a [3935]). It is noteworthy that two of the three qualities that Zhang underscored were moral traits. The new-style school system was about character formation as much as imparting knowledge.

Prevalent in the official discourse of education was the neologism *guomin* (國民, literally, "the nation's people"). This loanword from Japanese (*kokumin*) functioned at this time as the equivalent to the Western notion of a "national" or "citizen." Zhang Zhidong popularized the term by calling the elementary level of schooling "national education" (國民教育, *guomin jiaoyu*; Zhang Z. 1962 [1902]:57.13a [3935]). Yuan Shikai, in his famous memorial of 1904, also used the term when referring to the elementary school system (Zhu S., comp. 1958 [1909]:5390). To enlighten the people was to transform them from imperial subjects of the emperor into national citizens, a political task that concerned not only the leading intellectuals but state officials as well (Zarrow 1997:16).[7]

For the purpose of citizen formation, the reformers specifically selected several areas of study and gave them a prominent place in school curriculums. In both 1902 and 1904, the imperial guidelines for new schools listed moral cultivation (修身, *xiushen*) or ethics (倫理, *lunli*) first among all the subjects to be taught at all levels. The regulations also stipulated that teachers use classroom time to explicate previous moral examples and Confucian teachings. After ethics, the next conspicuous subject on the list of requirements was classical studies (讀經, *du jing*). The 1904 regulations specified the number of classroom hours only for lessons in this subject (Baily 1990:32).

This emphasis on classical studies was meant to foster patriotism. The *Outline of Educational Principles* of 1904 devoted one long paragraph to explaining the significance of classical learning at the elementary and middle school levels:

> The Classics are China's religion (宗教, *zongjiao*). If schools do not teach the Classics, then the way of Yao, Shun, Yu, Tang, King Wen, King Wu, the Duke of Zhou, and Confucius—in short, the "three cardinal principles and five constant virtues" (三綱五常, *sangang wuchang*)—would be left to perish. China would then be unable to establish itself as a nation. This is so because learning without a foundation would be no learning; political order without foundation would be no political order. Lacking a foundation, love for one's nation

and for one's compatriots would change. [That being the case,] how
could there be any hope for wealth and power? (Zhang, Rong, & Zhang
1904a:212)

Two points deserve our special attention. First, the *Outline* celebrated the
Confucian classics exclusively because of their association with the essence
of the nation. Their value no longer derived from any specific moral doctrines. Rather, the classics defined China and therefore deserved a special
place in the new educational system. Second, the classics and Confucian
ethics, as the epitome of the nation's spirit, became tools for instilling
patriotism. Uniquely Chinese, they helped fasten the people's affection to
the nation and thus facilitated the formation of citizens' moral character.
Overall, classical learning was not only given a new meaning but also
treated as a vehicle for nation-building.

Much like the curricular emphasis on classical learning, Confucius
worship was inserted into the core of the new schools' ritual. As will be
discused below, both the 1902 and 1904 regulations called for worship at
all levels of schools (Zhang, Rong, & Zhang 1904b:381–82). This movement to rally China's future citizens around the image of the sage reached
a new height after the establishment of the Board of Learning (學部,
Xuebu) in late 1905. In March 1906, at the urging of the newly established
board, the court promulgated five virtues as the guidelines for national
education: loyalty to the monarch, reverence for Confucius, public spirit,
martial spirit, and pragmatic spirit (Xuebu 1906a:634–35). In the memorial
proposing these guidelines, Confucius was exalted as the fount of Chinese
language, history, custom, and religion—the quintessence of Chinese
culture.

This exaltation paved the way for the request issued by the Board
of Learning to elevate the state cult of Confucius. In its memorial of
November 1906, the board claimed that one of the five educational guidelines, reverence for Confucius, encompassed all the other virtues. If the
court really wished to enact the educational guidelines, the time had come
to elevate the state cult of Confucius from a middle sacrifice to a grand
sacrifice. Such an action would help elucidate the country's cultural roots
and consolidate the citizens' understanding of their identities during a
time of drastic changes (Xuebu 1906b). This proposal won the imperial
authorities' quick endorsement. In 1906, Confucius joined Heaven, Earth,
Land-and-Grain, and the imperial ancestors and ascended to the highest
level of state sacrifice and obeisance.

Rather than an act of defending the traditional order, the 1906 elevation of Confucius represented a rupture in the history of the state cult. The grand sacrifices, as Angela Zito has convincingly shown, were not a random collection of four different rites of worship. They gathered together the cultural and religious symbols that informed the foundation of imperial rule. Heaven and Earth were the highest forces of the cosmic and moral order. Land-and-Grain stood for the economic basis of the empire. The imperial ancestors had founded and perpetuated the dynastic rule. Since the founding the Qing, these four rites of sacrifice had been bound together to form a class of their own, remaining unaltered for more than two-and-a-half centuries. The performance of these rites took the emperor's ritual body to the four cardinal directions around the capital in accordance with the changing seasons. Sacrifice to this highest level of deities signified the emperor's unique role of unifying human and superhuman realms, and his ability to mediate and bring together the natural, human, and supernatural forces. The grand sacrifices formed the sacred protocol and codification of imperial rulership (Zito 1997).

Confucius's presence in the group tipped the constellation off its semiotic balance. Unlike the other four, Confucius did not represent the cardinal forces of the cosmos, nor was he an integral part of the dynasty's historical mandate. Even after being elevated to the top of the imperial pantheon, Confucius retained his identity as a human in official representations. As an emblematic act signifying the cultural unity of the nation, Confucius worship served a political function that was historically unprecedented. Its presence introduced a new element into the self-contained world of imperial symbolism, and signaled a change in the conception of rulership.

In the wake of the 1906 elevation of Confucius worship, Cao Yuanzhong (1865–1923), an editor in the Bureau for Studying Rites (Lixue Guan), wrote an essay to discuss the ritual implications of this change. Cao pointed out that in the Hall of Esoteric Transmission (傳心殿, Chuan Xin Dian) the emperor was now obliged to offer sacrifices in person to Confucius with three kneelings and nine prostrations. But that would be inappropriate, since the other figures represented in the hall were merely emperors of the previous dynasties (*Lidai Diwang*), who were accorded only middle sacrifices. Performing the rite according to the scale of grand sacrifice in the Hall of Esoteric Transmission would mean honoring the emperors of previous dynasties with the same obeisance as the emperor's own imperial ancestors. This constituted a violation of the principles of status distinction, since the emperor must give priority to his own ancestors over those of other dynastic clans. To avoid such a patent impropriety, Cao suggested that for the Hall of Esoteric Transmission, the rite would have to be reconsidered and revised (Cao 1916).

Cao's appeal for ritual coherence did not resonate with the changing sentiments and concerns in high officialdom. Few took his question seriously. Not only was there no discussion of the specific ritual revision that Cao suggested, but ruling group in general exhibited no inclination to trouble itself about ritual propriety. This indifference toward ritual matters stood in marked contrast to the attitude of the eighteenth century, when the Qing reached its peak of theoretical maturity and aesthetic elaboration in ritual semiotics. Even those straightforward ritual changes called for by the court were not implemented with any sense of urgency. Not until 1910 was there a serious effort to bring the Confucius Temple in the imperial capital into line with its new status (Jin et al. 1934:812–15). This neglect of what would have been grave concerns of ritual propriety in former times confirms Marianne Bastid's diagnosis that "the ritual thinking had lost its grip on the spirit of the lettered and the functionaries at the turn of the twentieth century" (1997b:173).

This indifference coincided with a persistent effort to dismantle the Board of Rites (禮部, Libu) during the Xinzheng reforms. For the better part of imperial history, the Board of Rites had been no less than the third most important board of the government's administrative arm. Its primary responsibility was ensuring ritual orderliness throughout the empire. It supervised court rituals, issued the ritual calendar, and handled all aspects of the state cult. In addition, the Board of Rites administered the civil service examinations and the tributary system that maintained a diplomatic equilibrium between China and the surrounding kingdoms and states. However, the modernization of the empire's political apparatus during the Xinzheng decade witnessed a quick reduction in the administrative significance of this venerable institution. The abolition of the civil service examinations in 1905 eliminated one of its most significant responsibilities; the Board of Rites was no longer involved in the empire's routine operation of recruitment. The imperial practice of granting official recognition to local cults and incorporating them into the state cult, another major function of the board, ceased at about the same time (Sawada 1982). Meanwhile, in preparation for the transition to a constitutional monarchy, the Qing state initiated a government restructuring in 1905. Newly created government divisions, such as the Board of Learning, quietly shattered the administrative power of the Board of Rites. For example, tributary affairs were reclassified as diplomatic affairs and lost their cultural association with ritual. They were thus removed from the Board of Rites's jurisdiction. The newly founded navy and army took over the design and management of military rituals. The Board of Learning similarly came to be in charge of school rituals, including the sacrificial rite to Confucius at new-style schools (Zhu S., comp. 1958 [1909]:5514–15).

Indeed, the very survival of the Board of Rites became an issue. In 1905 the Office of Political Affairs proposed abolishing the board and replacing it with the Board of Learning (Zhu S., comp. 1958 [1909]:2167–70). Although the proposal was not adopted, the question of the Board of Rites' place in the government's new structure remained open for debate. In 1906, the board went through substantial downsizing and consolidation in response to the accusations that it had become superfluous. The only duties it retained were recording court ceremonies, organizing official banquets, supervising the state sacrifices, and conferring imperial honors on individuals of great civil or moral excellence (Zhu S., comp. 1958 [1909]:2343–44). The board lost its administrative significance and became a clerical office for ceremonial references and history. Finally, in 1911, in the last effort at governmental restructuring, the Board of Rites was abolished.

All this was more than a mere reshuffling of managerial responsibilities. It signaled changes in the conception of ritual and ritual government. Moved to a new office, old rituals were renovated. When the work of coordinating foreign affairs was relabeled as diplomacy, it subscribed to a different principle that was, at least nominally, based on the equality of all nations in the world. New military rituals for the navy and army would heighten military morale and discipline, rather than reinforcing the imperial hierarchy. Governmental restructuring instituted new categories of public management and a new notion of what constituted the legitimate business of the state. Ritual lost its conspicuous centrality in the new conception of state affairs.

A NEW RITUAL WORLD OF THE NATION

No longer the matrix of political power, ritual remained a significant political concern throughout the Xinzheng modernizing and nation-building process. For its mission of citizen formation through national education, the state had to rely on ritual for the new purpose of inculcating civic virtues.

The 1904 school regulations stipulated three kinds of ritual occasions in the school calendar and gave Confucius worship a prominent place in them. The first kind celebrated the birthdays of the empress dowager, the emperor, and Confucius. Shangding (上丁), the first *ding* days of the second and eighth months of spring and autumn,[8] which were the designated dates for the imperial state's cult of Confucius, belonged to this category. The second category was special days on the school calendar, such as the beginning and the end of a semester, and the day of commencement. The third category of occasions followed the national calendar, and included the lunar New Year and the first day of the month, when sacrifices were customarily offered to Confucius at schools (Zhang, Rong, & Zhang 1904b:381–82).

No matter the occasion, the rites were rather similar. The school officials, as well as the students, wore formal school uniforms and performed the "three kneelings and nine prostrations" (sangui jiukou) either to the empress dowager or the emperor's "dragon tablet of longevity" (wansui longpai) or to the spirit tablet of Confucius. For school events of the second category, the rite was performed to both the tablet of longevity and Confucius's spirit tablet together. During the monthly and yearly routine sacrifices, only Confucius was honored. After the kneelings and prostrations, school administrators and teachers would stand on the east side of the room, face the west, and receive the students' bows or kowtows. For events of the first category, the regulations further state, "If there is a banquet and speeches are offered by school administrators or students, the appropriate topic would be respect for Confucius's teachings or love for the Qing state" (Zhang, Rong, & Zhang 1904b:381–82).

In the ritual regulations, references to traditional symbolism were abundant. It takes no ritual expert to see that kneeling and prostration, the gestures of absolute obeisance, signified the supreme nature of their object. A bit more knowledge, and one appreciates that "the east" was the honorary position customarily reserved for the teacher and that the traditional ritual calendar was closely followed. Both the timing and the form of rite at new-style schools matched earlier practices of educational rites. Hattori Unokichi (1867–1939), who was teaching in Beijing during the reforms, maintained that the rite of Confucius worship at new-style schools was adopted from the home schools of late imperial times (1926:117).

Despite the ostensible continuity, ritual performance at new-style schools was not simply a repetition of earlier practices. One of the most noticeable differences was the secularization of the rituals. As Thomas A. Wilson has argued, although the image of Confucius was of important symbolic meaning in Chinese society, the worship itself had always had a religious dimension. To worship was "a technical activity requiring exacting ritual mastery aimed at achieving concrete results," namely, nourishing the spirit with a sacrificial feast (T. Wilson 2002b:258–59). Ritual guidelines for the imperial state cult and for *shuyuan* academies had paid meticulous attention to religious technicalities: the length of abstention before worship; the exact kind, number, and arrangement of vessels and sacrifices; and the procedures proper. The physical, albeit invisible, presence of the spirit was always assumed during the rite. In this sense, the worship was squarely grounded in the world of Chinese religion. The realms of the living and the dead coexisted in the same space, and the gap between them could only be bridged through the accurate execution of sacrificial liturgies.

Such concerns with religious technicality were missing in the planning of new-style school rituals. In the worship of Confucius, the offering of sacrifices ceased to be the vital crux of the rite. The regulations meticulously stipulated the performance of the participants but had little to say about the sacrificial details, such as the timing of movements, the vessels employed, and the kind of the offerings presented. The communication between the worshipped and the worshippers—the assumed objective of any sacrificial rites—received short shrift. Even the wording of the regulations betrayed a loss of religious sensibility. After the sacrificial celebration on Confucius's birthday, for example, an entertaining banquet was assumed to ensue. Ostensibly, this practice of feasting at the end of the rite continued the religious custom of distributing the sacrificial food, and thus the blessing, among all participants. Yet the official regulations used only the most common term, "banquet" (宴會, *yanhui*), for the feast, and made no reference to the act of sharing sacrificial food (分胙, *fenzuo*, or 餕餘, *yunyu*). The word choice stripped the custom of its religious connotation. School worship of Confucius in this sense followed the prototype of modern civic ritual, whose meaning completed itself in the very act of collective assembly. The 1904 school regulations carefully stipulated the clothing, actions, and movements of the participants, and focused the liturgical attention exclusively on the choreography of rite.[9]

The second major departure from earlier ritual practice involved the new emphasis on the collectivity. The late imperial rites of Confucius worship were never standardized, but there was always a clear demarcation between the state cult of Confucius and other forms of worship. This demarcation marked off the imperial prerogatives in rituals, which theoretically could not extend beyond the imperium. The state cult was thus extremely exclusive: only the emperor, or his legitimate delegate, was the primary worshipper of Confucius. Only members and potential members (degree holders) of the imperium were permitted to take part. Because the cult of Confucius belonged to the category of general worship, local magistrates would mimic the emperor's sacrificial movements at provincial and prefectural capitals' school temples. Still, the participants were limited to the local elites with imperial degrees.

All the sacrifices carried out by officials, even at the local level, underlined imperial hierarchy. Both civil and martial officials were required to attend, and their spatial positioning during the rite reflected their rank and title. Those who were not qualified for government positions, including students enrolled in the official schools, were by and large excluded. The primary worshipper, the highest-ranking official, was at center stage: a guide (*zan*) would announce to participants his every move. During the rite, he was very often the only moving body that completed the ritual action, offering sacrifices and wine while the others looked on. Only upon the completion of these prescribed actions did the crowd join in, prostrating themselves and kowtowing en masse (Su'erna et al., comps. 1968 [1774]:28; Liu K. 1870, juan 1:1a–7b, juan 4:1a–3a).[10]

The calendrical separation also distinguished the state cult from the general cult. Traditionally, the first *ding* days in spring and autumn were the reserved dates for the state sacrifices to the sage. These dates belonged to the imperial calendar that prescribed the Son of Heaven's and the imperium's ritual schedule. Therefore, the learning communities at government schools were often excluded from the procedure. These members of the student body performed their rites according to the cycle of community life: at the beginning of the terms, on the birthday of the sage, or every day. A quick survey of the regulations of Qing communal and charitable schools confirms that schools without official affiliation almost never scheduled even the simplest rites for students on the *ding* days. Outside the government schools, only the most prominent *shuyuan* academies that had received official funding and imperial sponsorship participated in the *ding* day sacrifices (Qu & Tang 1991:242). Even then, a government official, rather than the school head, had to serve as the primary worshipper. A cultural consensus existed that reserved the *ding* days as the exclusive prerogative of the imperial state for worship of the sage. Everyone else sacrificed and kowtowed on other days.

The demarcation between the state cult and the worship of Confucius by various schools disappeared in the planning of the new-style school rituals. The new regulations ignored the ritual boundaries and invited the future citizens of the nation into the previously forbidden realm of the imperial prerogative. School pupils without imperial degrees were allowed, for the first time, to join the emperor's ritual actions of the state cult. Moreover, even on the special *ding* days, students formed the main body of worshippers. The new guidelines made no ritual distinction between the designated primary worshipper and the auxiliary audience. In performing the rite, students lined up behind the superintendent of the school and bowed in unison to the spirit tablet of the sage. All the participants acted as a single ritual body. The rite concealed, rather than accentuated, differences in generation, age, and social background; this was a single, undifferentiated body of citizens.

State officials' presence was no longer required as the role of the primary worshipper withered away. The students' ritual performance was not only collective but unmediated; each participant enacted the rite and established an individualized and direct relationship to the icon. This direct relationship between the worshippers and the worshipped was another novel aspect of the new ritual. No longer relying on the primary worshipper for completing the ritual act, each student formed a nexus of communication and/or communion with the worshipped icon. The new ritual was premised on, and meant to solidify, the assumed rapport between the citizen and the imagery of the nation.

The retreat of a visible state from the schools' Confucius altars did not mean the relinquishment of power but only a different form of the state exercise of power, however. The 1904 regulations instituted a unified ritual act throughout the nation. Central planning stripped the school rituals of their previous flavor of local variability and eliminated the ritual autonomy of individual schools. It wove each school's ritual activity into a larger imaginary of collectivity, so that the national choreography of rite became a signifier of the imagined national community. Through ritual, the reform government initiated the construction of "national time" and "national space" in modern Chinese history. School pupils across the nation performed the rite according to the same calendar. This ritual synchronization created a novel sense of simultaneity and facilitated the imagination of a shared time. Because the territorial stretch of the new schools was coterminous with national boundaries, the ritual scheme also marked out the geographic extent of the nation and thus delineated its shared space. Furthermore, the standardized rite of worship as part of the program of civic education demarcated from the rest of the populace the true citizens of the nation, who had the experience of modern schooling and presumably shared a national consciousness. Participation in the national scheme of ritual symbolically qualified each person as a member of an imagined nation and made him or her a national citizen of China. No longer inserting itself between the people and the cosmic order at large, the state exerted power by instituting the terms in which its citizens imagined their collective identity and their socio-political environment.

Ostensibly, the elevation of Confucius worship did not change much of the imperial rituals. The emperor, or his designated delegate, continued the worship of Confucius twice a year in Beijing's Confucius Temple. Despite slight moderations, this worship consisted of the same ritual actions that the Qing emperors had performed for hundreds of years. However, there was indeed something new in the whole picture. In comparison with his worship of Heaven, Earth, Land-and-Grain, and the previous emperors of the dynasty, the emperor had a different relationship with the newly elevated icon of Confucius. The emperor could not claim personal rapport with the spirit receiving his offering, nor could he claim the performance of the ritual as his sole prerogative. His ritual role no longer hinged on his claim of divinity. Rather, in the new ritual scheme, the emperor performed the grand sacrifice "as one body" with the citizens. The unprecedented synchronization of the emperor's and the citizens' ritual bodies signified a new ritual order that accentuated the internal cohesion of the nation, rather than the barriers between them. This new ritual order stripped the emperor of his absolute supremacy in ritual matters and reduced him to a symbol of the national collective. As the head of state, he was now the embodiment of the national will, and no longer the will that transcended the national collectivity.

CONCLUSION

The ascendance of this new ritual order not only marked the advent of official nationalism in China but also ushered in a new script of state power. By elevating the figure of Confucius and gradually allowing it to displace and relativize the body of the emperor, the Xinzheng reforms engineered a shift from a monarchical court order anchored in a sacred cosmology to a flattened national formation. In the name of the nation, the state legitimately restructured the social space and encompassed the formally unreachable areas of daily life into its administration. The Xinzheng program, in this sense, was driven by the imperial state's will in appropriating the imported category of "nation" for a new script of power. Although the program only lasted a decade, this script of power was largely inherited by later political regimes. It was the most significant legacy of the late Qing reforms.

PART II

State Discourse and the Transformation of Religious Communities

3 Ritual Competition and the Modernizing Nation-State

Rebecca Nedostup 張倩雯

It is National Day, 1930, and cadres of the Chinese Nationalist Party (Guomindang, or GMD) are trying for the third year in a row to force the public to adopt the "national" (i.e., combined Republican and Gregorian) calendar.[1] It is, they argue, a marker of modernity, of China's entry into the world, of a unified, strong, and scientific nation. The old calendar—based on the movements of the moon and sun and a variety of other cycles, and full of dangerous festivals—is, in contrast, the epitome of backwardness. Its harm ranges far beyond the symbolic, however. An official propaganda slogan explains why, using a striking metaphor:

> Superstition is an obstacle to the progress of the National Revolution, and the old calendar is the staff headquarters of superstition (迷信的參謀本部, *mixin de canmou benbu*)! If we want to complete our revolutionary tasks, we must wipe away the old calendar and bring about the new! (Zhongguo Guomindang Zhongyang Xuanchuanbu 1930:5)

The calendar was not merely a reckoning of time, then, or even representative of a view of history and humankind's place in it. It was an active historical agent in itself—significantly, in China's war-torn early twentieth century, a militarized one. The calendar as "staff headquarters of superstition" conjures up vivid images—one imagines each lunar holiday as a general one who is marshalling his troops of retrograde customs to battle against the Nationalists' Revolutionary Army.

This evocative slogan reveals more than the Nationalists' fondness for military metaphors and organizational techniques, marked though that was. Like their revolutionary forbears in France and Russia, the Nationalists saw the reshaping of time as the basis for their new political world and the prerequisite for modernity. They foresaw a struggle, however, because Chinese governments had attempted to change the calendar for at least two dozen years. To the Nationalists—influenced by a generation of cultural critics, radical students, and even religious reformers who since the beginning of the twentieth century had come to term much of Chinese religion "superstition"—the confluence of public assembly and religious practice that formed the cyclical temple festival was an especially dangerous combatant in that fight. Temple festivals required not only eradication but replacement with a government-led civic ceremonial that would better define the pursuits and aspirations of the modern Chinese citizen.

NATIONALISM, RELIGION, AND RITUAL WORLDS

Over recent decades, evidence has mounted that a basic equation of secular modernity—nationalism replaces religion—has failed to come to completion. Thus far, however, it seems that we have not fully articulated a vocabulary to clarify the exact nature of this failure, or explain the complexities of the contest between state nationalism and religious expressions in a way that accounts for essential differences between the two. During the late 1920s and 1930s, officials of the Chinese Nationalist Party and its government sought to reshape the temporal and spatial landscape by banning temple festivals and holidays of the lunar calendar and replacing them with civic ceremonies of their own design. In exploring the effects of their attempts on the local community of the capital, Nanjing, and on the national scheme to remake Chinese society, I argue that viewing this interaction as a *ritual competition* generated by the GMD's conviction of the existence of two opposing "affective regimes"—the world of superstition and the world of nationalist modernity—allows us to see both the rhetorical claims of state-sponsored secularization and how these claims fall short.

An examination of the competition between new national rituals and older popular or community rituals will serve to dispel one of the more persistent misapplications of nomenclature to nationalist mythmaking and ceremony: that the confluence of civic rite and religious rhetoric or imagery necessarily translates into the existence of "civil," "national" or "political religion," or the "sacralization of the nation." In this respect Mona Ozouf's concluding statements in her tour-de-force exploration of the new festivals of the French Revolution have been highly influential: namely, that the valorization of humankind and antiquity throughout these observances stemmed from a general "need for the sacred" in the absence of fading church power. Turning to a more concrete formulation, she continues, "a society instituting itself must sacralize the very deed of institution" (Ozouf 1988:276). As important as Ozouf's point about the self-narrativizing of revolutionary states is—and it should not be discarded—it is not clear what is necessarily *sacred* (rather than ideal or mythologizing) about the efforts of the revolutionaries. How, exactly, is sacredness a zero-sum game?

Such an equation seems to have tempted many observers of twentieth-century nationalism as well; the totalitarian movements in particular have earned the appellation "political religion." Influenced by functionalist interpretations of religion, scholars have looked for the transcendent in Soviet ideology (Lane 1981) or for "faith, myth, ritual and communion" in Bolshevism, Fascism, and Nazism (Gentile 1996:158), and concluded that the results constituted sacral claims, or something close to them—hence the application of hybrid terminology. Yet it strikes me that the insistence upon calling the results "religion"—that is, declaring them to be a coherent and transcendent whole—rather than being content with naming the constituent parts for what they are (founding myths, cults of personality, civic rituals, and so on) hints too strongly at an underlying wish to delineate false, irrational, or authoritarian political ideology from that which more properly belongs to the sphere of freely debated political ideas. It also suggests a nominalism that conflates religious vocabulary or metaphors that a ruling authority might use with the achievement of the thing itself.

In his essay "Religion, Nation-State, Secularism," Talal Asad provides a useful approach to the problem via the intellectual and political histories of nationalism and religion. He uses as one starting point Clifford Geertz's claims for an equal centrality of sacred symbols to politics in all eras (Asad 1999:183).[2] In Asad's view, this results in a kind of blurring:

> Notions of sanctity, spirituality, and communal solidarity are invoked in various ways to claim authority in national politics (sovereignty, the law, national glories and sufferings, the rights of the citizen and so on). Critics often point to the words in which these notions are conveyed as signs of religion. But the evidence is not decisive. I suggest we need to attend more closely to the historical form of concepts and not to what we take as signs of an essential phenomenon. (Asad 1999:183–84)

For Asad, the key historical transformation is the emergence of the concept of secularism. In nineteenth-century England, for instance, secularism coupled with the notion of society "made it possible for the state to oversee and facilitate an original task by redefining religion's competence: the unceasing material and moral transformation of its entire national population regardless of their diverse 'religious' allegiances" (Asad 1999:185). Thus the operation of nationalism rests on the very concept of secularism. Equally importantly, so does the modern notion of religion. Therefore, Asad concludes, we may note how nationalism draws on "preexisting languages and practices," but to call the result "religion" is to miss the significance of this essential transformation and to fail to understand how rites, symbols, and so forth have been altered in the process (Asad 1999:185–87).

In places such as China, it is in fact very easy to see the unfolding of the historical development that Asad describes, since the importation of the vocabulary of secularism and its production of the modern category of religion followed shortly upon the rise of modern nationalism. As the chapters by Vincent Goossaert and Ya-pei Kuo in this volume explain, at the turn of the twentieth century, political and intellectual figures who were intimately involved in the project of reimagining the Chinese state also facilitated the importation of the neologisms "religion" (*zongjiao*) and "superstition" (*mixin*), reshaping the categorization of Chinese religion and its connection to political authority. Of the numerous and widespread repercussions, the effect of particular concern here is the radical redefinition of the place of ritual in politics and community. Though the religion-superstition formulation bore some trace linkages with imperial-era categories such as "orthodoxy" (正教, *zhengjiao*) versus "heterodoxy" (邪教, *xiejiao*) or "illicit cults (or temples)" (淫祠, *yinci*, or 淫祀, *yinsi*), in its very premise it abandoned the basis of Confucian righteousness and moral emperorship upon which they stood in favor of claims to universal scientific truth.

Furthermore, the rise of (Protestant) Christianity as the model of "religion" and modernity had profound implications for the perception of ritual. Webb Keane (2002) has observed that Protestant missions have become key vehicles of a "representational economy" of modernity for non-elites as well as elites around the world, prominent characteristics of which include a suspicion of elaborate liturgical display and a concern for the correspondence of speech, act, and intention—in other words, "sincerity."

Once such ideas began to take hold in China, they undermined the meaning and purpose of imperial ritual. Qing officials could contemplate elevating Confucius worship to the astonishing detriment of imperial sacrifice (as Ya-pei Kuo shows in her chapter) precisely because the concept of the nation and the meaning of its attached symbols began to supersede the ritual act itself, which had formerly balanced the universe in a way that only an emperor could achieve. GMD ceremonies carried this change to its logical extreme, detaching Confucius entirely from the framework of the imperial-era ritual calendar and removing him from the center of the Chinese nation. Instead, he became simply one in a potentially endless list of "culture heroes" and "revolutionary martyrs" whose significance lay in their symbolic content rather than in the generic rites performed around them. Indeed, the very nature of these modern political rituals lay in their transparency and "sincerity." With the erasure of the imperial cosmology, the state no longer served as a fulcrum point between Heaven and Earth. Under such circumstances of extreme change, it is impossible to speak of the superficial invoking of national symbols and figures from China's distant past or revolutionary present as evidence of a nation made sacred.

AFFECTIVE REGIMES AND THE GENESIS
OF RITUAL COMPETITION

The change in underlying ideology by no means effected an immediate transformation of ritual, social, or cultural systems, of course. Yet confidence in such a rupture generated in the minds of Nationalist modernizers a sense of ongoing competition of "affective regimes," a vision of two coherent worlds locked in struggle for the hearts-and-minds of the Chinese people. This in turn led to real-time competition for ritual, social, and political power. It was the conviction that such affective regimes existed—and that new ones could be erected, just as a nation's infrastructure could be built and its economy planned—that drove Sun Zhongshan's (Sun Yat-sen's) concept of "psychological construction" (心理建設, *xinli jianshe*), and above all his proclamation that "to make revolution, we must transform hearts-and-minds" (*geming xian gexin*). Such ideas formed the ideological basis of the campaign against superstition.

They also brought a self-conscious break with the past—what Prasenjit Duara has termed the "end-of-history syndrome," which engendered the belief that "to remake the people as the foundation of national sovereignty was the most urgent task of the day" (Duara 1995b:92). Thus the affective regimes the Nationalists envisioned were ideal constructs. The "old" world of superstitious associations, full of danger, unscrupulous behavior, and irrational fervor, was believed to be as coherent a sphere as the "new" arena of citizenship and faith in the party and nation. Certainty about the necessity of this divide shaped cultural rhetoric, religious policy, and the party-state's creation of its own ritual rejoinders. The artificial contest between old and new calendars, for example, particularly depended on self-conscious temporal breaks and the construction of a ritual world focused on the nation-state, and on the portrayal of temple festivals (廟會, *miaohui*, or 賽會, *saihui*) as primarily economic (and therefore harmful) enterprises.

No single consistent realm of religious associations can be said to have corresponded to "superstition," as even the one example of the Republican Ghost Festival observances described below makes clear. Less obvious, but just as important, is the fact that the imagined affective regime of GMD nationalism itself contained a great deal of internal contradiction and ambivalence. Nationalist civic ceremony and government-authored rituals drew upon a recent past and uncomfortably persistent present of mass politics and revolutionary fervor. Even those GMD leaders, such as Jiang Jieshi (Chiang Kai-shek), who prized social order above all else struggled with the inherent contradiction between mobilization and control. As the country fell into national crisis after the 1931 Japanese invasion of Manchuria, Jiang and others sought in civic ceremonies a means to both unify the country and atone for the spilled blood of revolutionary martyrs, yet struggled to do so in a secularized fashion.

However artificial the affective regimes imagined by the GMD might have been, they had tangible consequences. They engendered competition between local religious observances and the civic ceremonies of the new state, and thrust local religious communities into competition with the state for resources of economic and political power. The Nationalist universe rested on the creation of a mobilized and disciplined citizenry operating according to a rationalized and nationalized sense of time. Yet as the GMD's difficulty in achieving univocality even over the course of ten short years will show, ritual competition can generate blurring of boundaries and unexpected consequences rather than unequivocal "victory" for either side.

RATIONALIZING TIME AND MIND

The Nationalist conception of competing affective regimes stemmed from the conviction that progressive time, moral symbolism, and carefully mobilized collective action would effect in the Chinese people the proper psychological preparation for citizenship, and, by extension, enable the construction of the Chinese nation. This belief was shared by radical activists who accompanied army units during the Northern Expedition to wrest control of the country from regional militarists, by members of local party branches in Jiangsu and other key areas, by conservative government officials allied with or critical of Jiang Jieshi, and even by the protégés of the militarists brought into the national government in deals of convenience. The result was not always full policy agreement or smooth interaction in local politics, though the broad influence of the religion-superstition formulation was nonetheless striking.

Nationalist discussions of the problem of superstition were marked by a considerable amount of anxiety about the construction of a psychologically sound collective to guarantee not only the physical survival of the nation but also its status in the international arena. Such fears reached back to the strand of the "end of nation" (*wangguo*) discourse from the late Qing and May Fourth eras, which blamed China's cultural disintegration and weakness in the face of imperialism on ignorance and superstition. By the late 1920s, the Nationalists had inherited an intellectual influence that drew from the new disciplines of sociology and social psychology, that insisted on linear and progressive history, and that—despite the violent political break with the Communists—still bore the mark of Marxian materialist analysis. In their pamphlet outlining the motivations and techniques for the anti-superstition campaign, for example, the party Department of Propaganda deployed faddish scientific vocabulary in expressing fears for the national character. Achieving their goal, the department authors explained, meant eliminating "the old thinking and old controls caused by the morbid psychology of our people"—namely, "lacking any faith in one's abilities, [being] weak-willed, and relying on selfish calculation" (Zhongguo Guomindang Zhongyang Zhixing, ed. 1929). This was the condition of superstition, and it was not merely a complaint suffered by individual persons but a malady plaguing society.

Almost by definition, the breadth of the local, national, international, and universal fears and claims of the GMD anti-superstition campaign is nowhere more apparent than in the effort to reorder time. When the Nanjing government had been founded, the renewal of the Gregorian-based calendar, now enshrined as the "national calendar" (國曆, *guoli*), had stood at the very center of "transforming hearts-and-minds." This task was a core element of fulfilling Sun Zhongshan's revolutionary legacy, for he had, in an act heavy with symbolic value, put China on the new calendar on the same day in 1912 that he declared the founding of the Republic.[3] Thus it was only fitting that Sun's self-appointed heirs linked the recovery of both lost enterprises. "The goal of the Chinese revolution," began the party's 1930 pamphlet on the calendar, "is realizing [Sun's ideology,] the Three Principles of the People":

> To complete [his] revolutionary plan, we must wipe away all the bad customs that are obstructing revolution—especially the superstitious and that which does not accord with science. Every day that the old calendar is not abolished and the national calendar is not put into

effect, how will bad customs and evil superstition be erased? Tutelary government and the work of revolution cannot be realized. The Party Leader's saying that "until we clean up the old garbage, we cannot bring in new rule" was no empty talk! (Zhongguo Guomindang Zhongyang Xuanchuanbu 1930:5)

Thus the calendar had historic specificity as well as universal meaning.

First, reclaiming lost "national" time had the happy effect of bringing the clock back to zero, constructing a "memory" based on the moment that Sun declared the birth of both the Republic and a new era from a city that was once again the capital. The new calendar, which, though "in accordance with the world," began with 1912 as its Year One, would tie the reconstituted Chinese nation to Nanjing, to the Republican government, and to the Nationalist party in time and space. This was meant to supersede conflicts over the actual locus of political power, disagreements about the proper form that the national calendar should take, and even more distant truths, such as the fact that Sun Zhongshan was hardly the original advocate of the solar-based calendar in China.[4] The calls to renew Sun's task two-and-a-half decades later can be seen as a similar effort to cast a spotlight back on Nanjing and the "father of the nation" as sources of GMD legitimacy.

Next, the effort to reenforce use of the "national calendar" also reflected internationally focused anxiety and a "productivist" social materialism. The first Nationalist Minister of Interior, Xue Dubi—an ally of the reforming Christian militarist Feng Yuxiang—played the national humiliation card early on. "The Party Leader [Sun] first made this change to show both China and the outside world [our] revolutionary spirit, and demonstrate the new people's farsightedness and independence," he wrote. Because of the decay that had taken place in the interim, however, the change had been only a superficial one among officials, and had not penetrated the minds of the masses. Xue warned that if the reform was not quickly brought to bear, "we will not be able to guard against arousing the laughter of other nations, or bringing the national body (*guoti*) into conflict; moreover, our revolutionary principles will be overturned" (Neizheng Gongbao, June 1, 1928, 1:2 [VII:1]).[5] But for the authors of the Department of Propaganda pamphlet, the national calendar did more than bring China into line with the rest of the world; it allowed China to free itself from the world's grasp. This "most useful and advanced calendrical system in the world" in fact offered a tool for China's emergence from semi-colonialism (Zhongguo Guomindang Zhongyang Xuanchuanbu 1930). Economic rebuilding, for instance, could only take place once the accounting practices of the country's businesses and farms were brought into accord with both the nation and the world powers.

More than any other revolutionary project, the national calendar was viewed as the linchpin between spiritual construction and physical enterprise that would allow the work of nation-building to occur. Complaining about those who took the calendar issue lightly, a 1929 Department of Propaganda internal report argued that by wiping out the old instrument of superstition and supernatural authority, "this party can take a social consciousness that falls back on 'there's no way out' and 'rely on what Heaven has fated,' and turn it into a consciousness of 'people's rights,' 'self-rule,' 'there is a way,' 'hard work and struggle,' and 'make your own fate'" (Zhongguo Guomindang Zhongyang Weiyuanhui Dangshi 1930a, vol. 1:72). This psychological aspect of the old and new affective regimes determined all the other aspects, for without a rewired social consciousness, the Chinese people could never be ready to receive "political tutelage" (*xunzheng*, the process by which the party would teach the people the necessary principles of constitutional representation). The calendar did not simply measure time but shaped human pursuits: this is how it served as the "staff headquarters of superstition." Pasting door gods on entryways, hanging *nianhua* (woodblock prints) of spring-welcoming oxen on the lunar New Year, or playing amidst the lights during the Lantern Festival—all were remnants of the era of sages and emperors. Celebrating gods' birthdays promoted an "idolatrous outlook," one aided and abetted by clergy who depended on income from temple festivals. Eliminating all of these was the only way to bring about a complete transformation of civic consciousness (Zhongguo Guomindang Zhongyang Weiyuanhui Dangshi 1930a, vol. 1:30–31, 34–35).

Thus shifting calendars and attacking old holidays allowed the nascent Nationalist state, as Ozouf has written of French calendrical rewriting, simultaneously to commemorate the memory of the revolution and "to clear away the undergrowth in the forest of customs, for reasons stemming from a sense of order" (1988:162). To a certain degree, Foucault's observations about the need of the modern state to enforce conformity to disciplinary, linear time—with its attendant coded social roles—so as to enhance readiness for war, or at least to promote civil order, seem eerily relevant (1977:149–50, 159–62, 168–69). The objection, after all, was not simply to lunar reckoning but to the numerous cycles to which the "old calendar" was attached, be they agricultural (the twenty-four solar periods), derived from the stem-and-branch system, or otherwise related to religious or personal markers. Furthermore, the concern lay entirely with public manifestations of the calendar, so that the state could stake its claim to universal power.[6] Yet the application of Foucault's analysis of modern governmentality deserves modification for the context of imperialism and the international transmission of ideas. He argues that the development of disciplinary time coincided, in the eighteenth century, with the rise of a view of state-to-state relations that envisioned politics as war. I would argue that this context had changed in vital ways for a country such as China in the early twentieth century. It was not nation-states on (theoretically) equal footing but the unequal power relations of the colonial system and the collapse of the imperial ethos-state that formed the background against which new ideas about time, ritual, and religion became coupled with political power and economic authority. Politics and linear time, therefore, were as much about liberation as about war and social order. The rhetoric of revolution and the promise of self-determination fostered a tension at the very center of the transition between times. Just how much of the "thicket of custom" could be cleared away without sacrificing national character and undermining the necessary compact between a revolutionary government and its citizens?

DEFINING AND ELIMINATING TEMPLE FESTIVALS

At first, party activists engaged wholeheartedly in the battle of affective regimes (between the world of superstition and the world of nationalist modernity). As Nationalist army units and party cadres began inserting themselves into the Jiangsu countryside in the summer of 1928, they took the opportunity to prohibit prominent religious festivals, often just as the events were set to take place (*Zhongyang Ribao*, July 27, 1928, 3:2; August 19, 1928, 3:1). Authorities in cities such as Nanjing, Shanghai, and Guangzhou followed suit over the course of the following year, taking particular aim at the Ghost Festival of the seventh lunar month, especially the events of the fifteenth day, *Zhongyuan jie*, also commonly referred to by the name of the Buddhist rite associated with it, *Yulanpenhui* or *Yulanbanghui* (*Zhongyang Ribao*, August 11, 1929; Poon 2004:214). General bans followed; when those failed, the national government reissued calls for vigilance during the height of the moralistic New Life Movement (Xin Shenghuo Yundong) in the mid-1930s.

As with the calendrical reform movement overall, the impetus was both specific to the political situation and driven by worldview. In many ways such bans fit into the general drive to establish public order early in the regime, which was particularly strong in the central provinces. In both rural and urban Jiangsu, for example, real and alleged threats from intra-party dissension, underground Chinese Communist Party (CCP) activity, secret society uprisings, "bandit" attacks, and labor and student protests spurred the "party purge," the "rural purge," and a surge in urban policing. Even before the massive popular reaction to the invasion of Manchuria, for example, the Nanjing police issued regulations declaring that all marches and rallies must be approved, registered, and enacted on specified routes between the hours of 8 A.M. and 5 P.M. (Anonymous 1933).

In examining the evidence from Jiangsu during the early 1930s, it is therefore not surprising to see a correspondence between places receiving the tightest political monitoring and those where temple festival prohibitions were reported to be in effect. Ministry of Interior customs surveys reveal bans in counties where the party branches were particularly strong, such as Rugao and Liyang, or where urban activists drew close, such as Nanhui, near Shanghai (Zhongguo Di'er Lishi Dang'an Guan Cang 1932a, 1932b, 1932c). In Suzhou, powerful local business, gentry, and religious institutions fell afoul of a radical party branch, with the result that at least until 1931, zealous bans on the Ghost Festival and other lunar holidays had succeeded (Gu Y. 1931:62–63).

On one level, then, temple festivals were simply one type of unsupervised gathering that posed a general threat to order. On another level, however, they presented particular obstacles to Nationalist goals of social engineering. Like the old calendar more generally, they fostered a "lack of faith in oneself." They also encouraged the formation of social groupings that threatened the Nationalist reordering of the nation. Explications of GMD rural policy, for example, drew direct links between the party's eradication of religious processions and temple plays and its future ability to build self-government organizations in the countryside (Zhongguo Guomindang Zhongyang Zhixing, ed. 1930:104–5).

Another line of thinking cast temple festivals as primarily economic events. In the context of anti-superstition discourse, this emerged as a reading of festivals as a means for greedy clergy and local elites to extract hard-earned money from the deluded poor. Sometimes this message was linked with the Nationalists' own symbolic regime via the myth-history of Sun Zhongshan's youthful efforts to combat superstition. One elementary school textbook described the effects of temple festivals in Sun's hometown:

> Every year the village held a temple procession. They took out the statue of the god and paraded it. The people of the village were very pious.

> But in the end, it was only the people who took care of the temple
> who made a lot of money. The people of the village were still poor and
> still suffered. They got nothing out of it at all. (Lü 1936:5–6)

The last sentence was accompanied by an illustration showing monks
and temple managers counting strings of cash while a pinched-faced
man stands by, watching his savings flow away. Such arguments fit into
a common theme in textbooks and anti-superstition propaganda that
contested the notion of the "efficacy" (*ling*) of the gods, arguing that
human efforts and productivity alone constituted true efficacy. Although
high- and low-ranking GMD officials also floated other intriguing interpretations of temple festivals—including the possibility that they could
be freed of their superstitious content and revived as purely trading or
uplifting moral events (Zhongguo Guomindang Zhongyang Weiyuanhui
Dangshi 1930b:43–44; Chen G. 1951:83, and 1991:201)—the overriding
official sense held that that their true nature was delusion and chicanery.
Case in point: the Ghost Festival.

NANJING'S GHOSTS: "HOT AND NOISY"?

Why did the Ghost Festival come in for such opprobrium? Police and party
branches in Zhenjiang, Nanjing, and Guangzhou all sought to curtail it in
1928 and 1929 (*Zhongyang Ribao*, August 19, 1928, 3:1 and August 11, 1929,
2:3; on Guangzhou, see Poon 2004:214). The Ministry of Interior issued a
nationwide ban in 1934. In fact the Ghost Festival is the only festival consistently targeted by name during this period. Robert Weller has shown
that ever since the imperial era, government officials had found numerous
reasons to disapprove of ghost ritual (Weller 1987:75–85, 134–42; see also
1994:169–71). The Nationalists added to these their own specific politics.
They heaped rationalist scorn first on the central act of believing in ghosts
and second, on making offerings to them (Poon 2004:214). Both stages of
the ban on the Ghost Festival coincided with a nationwide drive to prohibit the manufacture and sale of spirit money and other "superstitious
products." Expenditures during the seventh month on these items and on
food offerings, firecrackers, lanterns, and so on were second perhaps only
to money spent at New Year's. At the time of the initial wave of activism,
the Frugality Movement (Jieyue Yundong) had gained steam within the
party, influenced not only by concerns over China's poverty and fragile
economy as well as the related native goods campaign, but also by the
military ethics promoted by leaders such as Jiang Jieshi and Xue Dubi's

patron Feng Yuxiang (*Neizheng Gongbao*, May 1928, 1:1, [IVa:14–16]; Anonymous 1930).

Offerings to ghosts, placed in this light, constituted not only an affront to rationality but a drain on the national economy. A 1928 pamphlet issued by the Ministry of Education, under the long-standing critic of religion Cai Yuanpei, explains the ultimate effect:

> To set fire to a few pieces of paper copper, gold, and silver money, or some paper houses, and [think that] as every piece of paper is consumed it really turns into gold, or copper, or a house—where in the world is this possible? Those who insist on believing this only end up taking the money earned by their own sweat and blood and putting it in the pockets of monks and priests. (Anonymous 1928)

Thus far, the GMD attack on the Ghost Festival fit into the general pattern of their overall critique of Chinese religious practice, wherein disapproval of excessive ritual expenditure and undue clerical power—themselves nothing particularly new in elite discourse in China—was reworked into a rationalist framework centered on the nation-state and its economy. In this schema, *no* ritual could be as effective as productivity was for self, community, or nation. To see more clearly just how the Nationalists' view of the Ghost Festival emerged from or enhanced this pattern—and to see where it departed from the disdain for or fear of such observances that government officials and elites of the imperial era could show—a closer look at how both the festival and the ban operated in the GMD capital is necessary.

The term "temple festivals," of course, masked what were in fact multifocal and multivalent occurrences. And above all others, the "Ghost Festival" was open to numerous levels of meaning among its various events. The wide repertoire of Ghost Month activities that had developed in south and south central China by late imperial times corresponded to an equally wide range of elite and government attitudes: from patronage of Mulian opera as a means of status-climbing in Huizhou (Guo Q. 2005) to official fear and loathing of violent mass "ghost-robbing" ceremonies in late nineteenth-century Taiwan and coastal Fujian (Weller 1987:75–77). Descriptions of seventh month observances in early twentieth-century Nanjing do not point at anything especially violent, though certainly what Weller terms the "hot and noisy" aspect of ghost ritual comes through. In fact, it was precisely the typical diversity of household, neighborhood, temple-based, and citywide rituals that bothered the Nationalist police and party authorities.

Accounts of 1920s Nanjing describe streets periodically filled through-out the month with offerings to hungry ghosts put out by both residents and businesses, who might also invite Buddhist or Daoist clergy for reci-tations (Hu P. 1978:145–48; Chen & Du 1932, vol. 3:52). Pan Zongding, the author of *Nanjing suishi ji*, wrote that during this time Nanjing's public spaces were populated not only by the usual ritual-supervising clerics but by beggars (*lianhuanaozhe*) who circulated songs that, he sniffed, were "half full of rumor" about the identity of specific local ghosts (Pan 1929:12a).[7]

At the midpoint and end of the month, visitors flocked to the temple of Dizang Bodhisattva (Skt. Kshitigarbha, J. Jizō) at Qingliangshan in the western part of town. By this point in its history, it was its role in the activities of the seventh month that gave the Qingliang Dizang shrine a place in the Nanjing religious landscape, for it was not among the large or particularly well-known temples in the city (Ye & Liu 1935:312–20; Zhu X. 1935:244; Nanjing Shizhengfu Mishuchu, ed. 1933:14). Pilgrims flooded halls holding images of Dizang and the Jade Emperor; the scholar-official Hu Pu'an vividly describes the rest of the Ghost Month scene:

> From the beginning of the month on, the worshippers spill outside the temple walls. Another surge comes after the twenty-fifth. The sweat pours off one like rain, and visitors circulate like ants. Tea booths are set up in every corner to serve as spots for burning incense and resting. The dazzle of the decorations and the grandeur of the setup compete with each other to catch the eye. Only at the end of the month, when it is said that the mountain gate [to the underworld] closes, does the activity start to diminish. (Hu P. 1978:8)

The resthouses ("tea booths," *chapeng*) in fact included both sheds for ven-dors of locally famous tea and "Dizang tents" (*Dizang peng*) for visiting spirit-images from smaller temples.[8] These structures, as a 1932 guide to Nanjing remarked, attracted crowds of "women and old folk, plus people in every kind of strange attitude of prostration and mortification (*shao bai xiang shao rou xiang*); but most are there to seek the health of their fam-ily members and to redeem their vows" (Chen & Du 1932, vol. 3:51).[9] The fervent activity of an otherwise unremarkable temple stood in contrast to other sites within the city, such as the Jiming Temple in the north, a place whose festivals continued to frustrate the city government but whose his-toric eminence and continued social prominence in Nanjing were beyond dispute.

Finally, Nanjing residents commemorated Ghost Month along the

Qinhuai River and the Green Stream (Qingxi), which traced their ways through the heart of the city. In localized versions of rituals held elsewhere in China, monks conducted prayers (*daochang*) and crowds made "offerings to the river orphans" (*zhai he gu*, with paper lanterns) and sent off paper "Dharma boats" depicting Dizang and other figures from the Mulian story. Nanjing residents gathered in especially large numbers at the naval yard and former fortress of the Qing naval official Huang Yisheng, on the bank of the Qinhuai facing Mouchou Lake (Ye & Liu 1935:1152–53; Chen & Du 1932, vol. 3:52; Pan 1929:12b).

The potential offenses to modernized urban social order that these activities could pose were numerous. Describing the reasons for the ban, the city government of reformist mayor Liu Jiwen loftily wrote, "The Yulanbang Festival occurs as summer turns to fall. Ignorant people follow it in a swarm, squandering money with no benefit to society" (Nanjing Tebie Shizhengfu Mishuchu Bianyi Gubian, ed. 1930:160).[10] As the image of the "swarm" hints, the perceived injury to social order reached beyond ritual expense, as the proclamations of the city Bureau of Social Affairs (Shehui Ju) and police department—the main authorities charged with enacting the ban—made clear. Social Affairs officials stated that the occasion was the kind where "danger could easily arise" (Zhongguo Di'er Lishi Dang'an Guan Cang 1929), and the Capital Police Department issued a public declaration that

> This sort of ritual-holding (醮, *jiao*) and festivals for spirits recklessly stirs up the gullible; not only is it a source of financial waste, but it can readily start trouble. This city is the place of the national capital—all eyes are turned here, both domestically and from abroad. Now, as we are rewriting the script of politics, all bad habits must be uprooted, so as to erect a model. (*Zhongyang Ribao*, August 11, 1929, 2:3; *Minsheng Bao*, August 11, 1929, 5)

Thus the Ghost Festival took on special significance in the city undergoing ambitious urban planning as the showcase of the Nationalist regime, under the scrutiny of the world as well as the of the GMD's local rivals. As with numerous other aspects of the anti-superstition campaign that intersected with economic and ritual activity in public space (such as the bans on fortune-tellers and spirit mediums or on the trade in spirit money and amulets), the police took primary responsibility for the 1929 Ghost Festival prohibition—a task which in Nanjing held not simply local but national significance. The Bureau of Social Affairs followed up by blanketing the city with notices forbidding Nanjing residents to hold any sort of ceremony on the fifteenth, while the Bureau of Education launched a typical propaganda campaign of street lectures and wall posters (Zhongguo Di'er Lishi Dang'an Guan Cang 1929).

Beyond the simple desire for neat modern display, however, the ban on the Ghost Festival coincided with serious stresses on Nanjing's urban population. Residency in the city skyrocketed 38 percent between 1927 and 1928, and grew another 8.7 percent the year after. This growth rate far outstripped that of other large Chinese cities at the time, and was due not only to the arrival of a new administrative class but to a steady influx of poor farmers and refugees seeking opportunity in the Nationalist promise—not necessarily the new citizens that urban planners such as Liu Jiwen desired most (Wang Y. 2001:107–9; Lipkin 2006:82–85). The prospect of dealing with a homeless population and other problems of sudden growth surely increased the urgency of clamping down on unsupervised, serial public gatherings such as the events of the seventh lunar month, especially activities that "ignorant and gullible" persons from the countryside would be likely to seek out.

Furthermore, land reclamation and reorganization stood high on the list of urban management priorities in the capital, affecting the many liminal spaces in which Ghost Festival rituals were conducted. The capital government's numerous land surveys particularly focused on the widening of thoroughfares and the clearing of squatters, as well as on the rationalization of official property belonging to the former Qing government that had slipped into private hands (Nanjing Difangzhi Biangua Weiyuanhui, ed. 1996:112–17). Given that much of the local Ghost Festival activity took place not simply at Qingliangshan but along the very roadsides that the city was trying to clear of even permanent structures such as shops, or at former Qing property such as Huang Yisheng's naval yard, the conflict between administration ambitions and the festival becomes even clearer. Lastly, Mayor Liu aimed forces at the Qinhuai River itself—that is, at its famed entertainment districts and the pursuit of prostitution therein, which was officially prohibited in September 1928 (Lipkin 2006:178–86). Though the effort ultimately failed, it did have the effect of temporarily heightening police surveillance in certain riverside neighborhoods, and created an official discourse stigmatizing the "Qinhuai atmosphere." This further emphasized the illegitimacy of the public presence of the festival.

Whether the public took such messages to heart is another matter. By the mid-1930s, the concurrently enacted bans on ritual specialists and spirit money—key components of Ghost Festival observances—had petered out (Nedostup 2001:492–93, 515–16). In an amusing twist, officials carrying out a two-year joint effort of the Interior and Education Ministries to transpose select holidays of the lunar calendar to the national calendar actually conceded defeat in the case of the fifteenth day of the seventh lunar month (referred to as *Zhongyuan jie*). They admitted that it was impossible to eliminate *Zhongyuan jie*, though they nevertheless attempted to expunge its Buddhist and Daoist "corruption" by redefining it as a day devoted to ancestor worship (Neizheng Gongbao, June 1930, 3:5 [IIc:11–12]). The transplantation of the holiday failed to take root, however, so when the national party and government launched the New Life Movement in early 1934—centered on, among other virtues, the goals of making China "productivized, militarized, and aestheticized" (*shengchan hua, junshi hua, meishu hua*)—the Nanjing city government took it as an opportunity to revive the old prohibitions. Meanwhile, the central government's Ministry of Interior now decided to issue a nationwide call to eradicate the Ghost Festival once and for all, as a "disturbance to local peace and security" (*Zhongyang Ribao*, August 25, 1934, 2:3). This second ban appears to have been purely reactive: it was announced in the official press on the day after the fifteenth of the seventh lunar month.

Even if the new prohibition was hastily arranged, the party did manage to provide attendant propaganda. Two columns below the order, the GMD's *Central Daily News* printed the observations of a reporter who had spent several hours at the Dizang temple and other Qingliangshan shrines during the early hours of the fifteenth, where, he remarked, worshippers continued to arrive in great numbers. The article is most notable for its reflection of the persistent theme of temple festivals as primarily an (unproductive) economic pursuit. The most orderly aspect of the entire scene, the reporter finds, is the beggars lining the path up to the temple gate, "arrayed in ranks" and numbering more than one hundred. Querying the Dizang temple manager on finances, he discovers that the institution possesses fields in northern Jiangsu, and also typically received 1,000 (*yuan*) in donations during the "ghost month." Doing some quick calculations, he concludes that this is more than sufficient to pay for ritual items and the meals and salary for the hundred extra temple attendants that needed to be hired: "Because the government doesn't take taxes, the daily income from donations can nicely support [the temple]." Taking careful note of all places where worshippers deposit coins and other offerings, the writer concludes, "When going home, one must leave behind several sticks of 'returning incense,' as well as purchase Taipinggan, Lixianggao, Huabangchui, etc. [all famous types of tea], in order to get good luck" (*Zhongyang Ribao*, August 25, 1934, 2:3). In other words, the Ghost

Festival was at its heart a financial enterprise, one that operated to the detriment of the pockets of poor folk.

Yet the fascinating thing is that ample evidence exists for another reading of the Republican Ghost Festival, one leading to commemorations of the dead more generally and into the very ranks of the Nationalists themselves. In other words, my aim here is not simply to critique the GMD view of the Ghost Festival as a nonproductive, economically harmful, wasteful ritual, although that is easy enough to do on a number of grounds. Anthropological and historical literature has aptly contested the notion that ritual economies and market economies somehow lie in opposition, with particularly fruitful explorations coming from Mayfair Yang and Robert Weller (M. Yang 2000; Weller 1999, chap. 5; see also Dean 1998:221–25). In the larger work from which this material is drawn, I argue that the narrow view that many Nationalist officials adopted of religion deprived them of key inroads into local power, whereas local stakeholders were able to use both ritual networks and new political connections and discourses to argue for their rights according to the new political "script." Thus it is not difficult to considerably complicate the GMD's picture of the religious "affective regime."

OR GHOSTS SAVING THE NATION?

The 1930s were such a politically and socially charged moment, however, that we can see a considerably greater degree of instability and layering of meaning in the modernizing political "affective regime" as well. Preexisting social and political elites adapted Nationalist symbols and slogans into hybrid Ghost Festival–nationalist commemorations. Moreover, some GMD leaders themselves struggled to find appropriate rites of salvation and unity as the country fell deeper into political turmoil and faced the threat of foreign invasion. Some of the most overt instances of ritual revival and hybridity emerged outside the capital. For instance, Poon Shuk Wah describes how in Guangzhou elements associated with the Ghost Festival—an altar to local ghosts and, above all, the presence of an effigy figure of a "filial son"—appeared at a November 1932 service commemorating the heroism of the Nineteenth Route Army earlier in the year (Poon 2004:216–21). The powerful local charity the Fangbian Hospital sponsored a seven-day *wanrenyuanhui* (萬人願會, prayer service for the dead) under the auspices of honoring national martyrs, which, Poon argues, attracted local residents eager to fulfill the religious purpose of the banned Ghost Festival, albeit some four months later. She makes the case that this and other fascinating instances of hybrid or disguised festivals reveal not only the penetration of national symbols into religion but the persistence of local religion in the face of nationalizing anti-superstition projects.

This is an important point. In fact, once one peers a little farther past the totalizing rhetoric of the anti-superstition campaign, cases of the melding of nationalism and religion appear throughout China during this period, and at various levels of power. In particular, they emerge in the realm of observations for the dead that cross the lines separating "private," "public," and "government," and also "religious" and "secular." In much the same way that the merchants supporting the powerful Fangbian Hospital refused to excise ritual activity from their definition of civic engagement, we find, for example, that the educated elite, businessmen, and diverse others belonging to the new eclectic religious society called the Daoyuan (School of the Way) argued for the group's morality and patriotism in the face of a GMD ban (Nedostup 2001:148–50; Duara 2003:110). Though the Nationalist government only ceded legitimacy to the group's charitable arm, the Hongwanzihui (Red Swastika Society), archives show that not only did the Daoyuan continue to thrive but several of its women's auxiliaries in the lower Yangzi and north China regions continued to observe the Ghost Festival during the 1930s by holding sutra readings and burning Dharma boats (Zhongguo Di'er Lishi Dang'an Guan Cang 1936).

Indeed, it seems that the events of the 1930s gave people more (rather than fewer) reasons to hold commemorations of the dead and to seek peace for, or appeasement of, lonely or unruly ghosts. In addition to honoring the Nineteenth Route martyrs, who became vastly popular national heroes for fighting the Japanese when Jiang Jieshi would not, the Fangbian Hospital rites pacified the spirits of the numerous victims of that year's natural disasters. Between 1931 and 1937, Nanjing and the lower Yangzi fell prey to flood, disease, war, and a resulting refugee crisis. As the sense of the nation's peril and the government's impotence grew, officials began sponsoring religious services that sought the country's well-being, and held them on government grounds. In August 1935—two months after the first perilous appeasement agreement with Japan—the Beiping (now Beijing) branch military council held a large-scale *Yulanpen* service, inviting monks to recite sutras for fallen soldiers and officers (Zhang & Bian 1993:243). Much closer to the center of Nationalist power, from the early 1930s on the party leader Dai Jitao sponsored Buddhist ceremonies (*puli fahui*) praying for both lives lost and the future of the country (Yao 1936:136, 178–79; Tuttle 2005:178).

Nonetheless, we should take some care to distinguish these ritual instances from one another, as their sponsors did themselves. Dai Jitao scrupled to present himself as an opponent of superstition—not an incompatible stance from the point of view of numerous Buddhist reformers and practitioners of his era. Dai proposed no divine role for his country's leadership, but rather saw Buddhism as a vehicle of ethics and national unity. The ceremonies he sponsored were not events for the broad public, linked to local social networks and manifesting a ritual variety in the way that the happenings along the Qinhuai River and at Qingliangshan were—or even those at the Fangbian Hospital. As Dai clearly enunciated in his invocation, "[We] pray that the Buddhist multitudes . . . do not become mired in ghosts and spirits, and desert living things" (Dai 1972a [1931]).[11] This was by no means a revival of the Ghost Festival in all its multiplicities and meanings.

Dai belonged to a group of conservative GMD leaders who also greeted the crises of the 1930s by advocating sanitized commemorations of "national heroes" (*minzu yingxiong*) such as Yue Fei (a Song-dynasty general who exemplified loyalty) and Guandi (the God of War), and a "National Tomb-Sweeping Day" (Minzu Saomu Jie) that brought officials together at the burial places of select dynastic founders and restorers, including Ming Taizu, Han Wudi, and figures from myth-history such as the Yellow Emperor (Nedostup 2008). Such ceremonies followed the same basic format as Sun Zhongshan remembrances, memorials for revolutionary martyrs, and even reformed funerary ritual drawn up by the Ministry of Interior's Department of Rites and Customs. Speeches and the singing of the national anthem bookended the key ceremonial moments, in which representatives presented circumspect offerings of wreaths or flowers to a portrait, and the assembly bowed three times. Even though such efforts to seek strength from an invented Chinese past drew on a vague gesture toward ancestor worship, they functioned in an entirely different way from the rites of the imperial state, eschewing both blood sacrifice and cosmological reference in favor of didactic messages about the nationalist significance of the central symbol. They also failed to draw the attention of the public at large, even in the capital.[12]

What the coincidence of the tomb-sweeping ceremonies, Dai Jitao's Dharma meetings, and the Fangbian Hospital's *wanrenyuanhui* rites shows, however, is that the growing sense of national crisis and spiritual malaise of the 1930s brought ritual competition to new heights. Of course, ritual should not be seen only as a "response" to stimulus. Observances such as the Ghost Festival are regularly occurring events, not reactions to specific trauma, even if a given instance may take on significance in trauma's wake. But the sudden efflorescence of Nationalist commemorative ritual in the mid-1930s can be traced directly both to the personal anguish of their Nationalist sponsors and to the provocative presence of street protesters demanding that the government act against Japan. Even more specifically, the revival of "culture heroes" and visits to the tombs of barbarian-defeating dynastic ancestors represented an effort to constitute and mobilize a Chinese collective against the Japanese ritual deployment in Manchukuo of some of these same personages under the mantle of *wangdao* (王道, the "kingly way" of the ethical monarch).

Why, then, did the local rites continue and adapt while the new civic ritual failed? One possible answer returns to the redefinition of religion as the realm of belief, and to the fixation on ritual as deriving meaning from its symbolic and didactic content. It also brings us back to the question of the calendar.

BODIES IN MOTION

In *How Societies Remember*, Paul Connerton remarks on the modern inclination "to focus attention on the content rather than on the *form* of ritual" (1989:52). This was certainly the case for the Nationalist reformers concerned with problems of eradicating superstition and fostering faith in the party: to them, form and content converged into a single rationalizing process. Yet the evidence hints that it was precisely this privileging of content over form that hampered their efforts in ritual competition.

Nationalist ritual by nature confined form and meaning. Connerton argues that modern invented rites are "marked out by their inflexibility" because their extensive sets of regulations are meant to mask the sharp break with the bodily remembered past that capitalism brings (1989:60–62). In the GMD situation, the key break seems attributable less to capitalism alone than to the revolutionary and intellectual context described earlier as well. Civic ceremonial of the Nationalist era centered on two basic forms: the "collective offering" (公祭, *gongji*), and the parade or rally. The denuded, didactic nature of the *gongji* has already been described with respect to public commemorations, "national tomb-sweeping," and their ilk. Officials also strove to contain the format and meaning of parades and rallies. Perhaps the most surprising, and telling, manifestation came at the celebration of the January 1 New Year.

Minister of Interior Xue Dubi, among others, had pinpointed the successful transposition of "all the vibrant entertainment of the entire month" surrounding the lunar New Year to the national calendar as the key element in promoting the changeover (*Neizheng Gongbao*, June 1, 1928, 1:2 [VII:1]). In the city of Nanjing, this at first generated a climate of fear, since police decided the best means to effect such a transformation was to eliminate the old celebrations first. In one of her keen essays on life behind the scenes of power in Nanjing, Yao Ying describes the effects:

> Prior to the year before last [1933], because the movement to promote the national calendar was at its height, each house had to open its doors on the lunar New Year. If you didn't comply, the police would come and pound and pound on your gate; once you opened, they would ask about any little noise inside, so as for any firecracker or noisemaker, you simply daren't set it off! (Yao 1936:41)

As it turned out, though, so many people violated the firecracker ban that the Nanjing police couldn't arrest them all. After a year or two, officials simply threw up their hands. As a result, Yao Ying wrote, in 1935 Nanjing was enjoying its "second year of liberation, so things are especially exciting!" (Yao 1936:41). Meanwhile, chronic absenteeism on the old holiday posed a continuing problem, even in government offices. After the major push to make 1930 the "year of the national calendar," newspapers such as *Shenbao, Shishi Xinbao* (*The China Times*), *Dagong Bao* (*L'Impartial*), and the party's own *Zhongyang Ribao* (*Central Daily News*) show a resurgence in both reports about the celebration of the lunar New Year in cities around China and special advertising placed according to the old as well as the new calendar. The "abolished calendar" (廢曆, *feili*) changed from a description of a goal to be reached or a remembrance of an artifact of the past to a strange paradox in the present: a thing whose very name meant that it wasn't *supposed* to exist, but whose every further mention proved that it was indeed alive and kicking. Local newspapers ran stories with helpful suggestions for readers on how to prepare their households for *feili* New Year's, thereby simultaneously naming and defying the calendar's abolition (*Da Guang Bao*, January 25, 1929, 2b).

Things never seemed to get terribly exciting on January 1, however. By far the most popular feature of the day appeared to be the free or half-price tickets that urban and town movie theaters and other entertainment venues offered (*Shishi Xinbao*, January 1, 1931, 3:3 and 4:1; *Nanjing Wanbao*, January 1, 1937, 2). Otherwise, major communal activities of the day consisted of "group New Year's ceremonies" (*xinnian tuanti baili*) and street parades. Resembling political rallies rather than New Year's visitations or banquets, ceremonies followed the usual pattern set out by the party-state, and were attended by government and party officials, as was fitting for the holiday's dual nature as the beginning of the new year and the anniversary of the founding of the Republic (representative descriptions can be found in *Zhongyang Ribao*, January 1, 1930, 3:3; *Da Guang Bao*, January 1, 1930, 3:11; *Nanjing Wanbao*, January 1, 1935, 2). The slogans shouted at the 1935 New Year's meeting in Nanjing, for instance, simply reflected current politics:

> Reverently carry out the teachings of the Premier!
> Keep our martyrs' spirit of struggle alive!
> Complete the construction of tutelary government!
> Purge the red bandits and pacify society!
> Strive to reclaim the lost land of Manchuria!
> (*Zhongyang Ribao*, January 1, 1935, 2:2)

The parades, meanwhile, were meant to incorporate representatives of the various social sectors (*jie*), usually represented in press reports by the phrase "every type of organ, school, group, and the masses."

A 1937 description of one such parade in Nanjing is illustrative. Spectators watched, in order, the following pass by: a mounted unit, the Nanjing mayor, the National Government military band, the party and national flags, and congressional floats; floats from the naval band and the Boy Scouts; the Chinese musical troupe of the municipal government; the floats of various groups; and the representatives of a further three types of government or civic organizations. It was not until the very tail end that they finally saw the more typical festive lanterns (*Nanjing Wanbao*, January 1, 1937, 2). The tightly organized parade, heavily featuring government officials and stage-managed representatives of social "sectors," recalled New Life Movement rallies of the same period. There, too, the party had taken an action that was originally energetic, participatory, and variously organized—in this case, the political rally and protest march—and transformed it into a demonstration of authority and state power (Anonymous 1935). Though the newspaper account argued that the 1937 New Year's parade was good for local businesses, it was nonetheless an event that most city residents could take part in only as passive spectators. If the new holiday could not incorporate the communal and family celebrations of the lunar New Year, then the two occasions would remain separate—and unequal. One year earlier, a tart account had appeared in the *Nanjing Evening News* describing the once-again flourishing trade in special foods, firecrackers, and all the accoutrements of the lunar holiday. The headline summed up the situation: "You Celebrate Your New New Year, I'll Celebrate My Old One" (*Nanjing Wanbao*, January 18, 1936, 4).

CONCLUSION: "FUN," HYBRID RITUAL, AND DUAL TIME

Focusing on the Nationalist capital of Nanjing—a circumscribed space and time—has allowed us to see how ritual competition develops. Clearly this is not the whole story of even the Nationalist period, though one small example from the world of contesting affective regimes in the countryside offers a suggestive piece of evidence that leads us toward a broader conclusion. In 1936, two researchers published the results of a survey of cultural attitudes among 916 male and female farmers from around the country, which included a set of questions about the calendar. A little more than half of the respondents (54 percent) said that they preferred using the old calendar to the new (tellingly, the researchers failed to provide the option of choosing both old and new). When respondents who preferred the old reckoning were asked why they did so, many cited agricultural necessity and the responsibilities of ancestor worship. The third most popular reason, however, is in many ways the most intriguing: the old calendar, the farmers said, was *renao*—"fun," or "hot and exciting" (Chen & Chen 1936:84–86).

Did the new calendar lack fun? The historian, ethnographer, and frequent critic of the GMD Gu Jiegang certainly thought so. "In the past and right now," he wrote in 1932, "the government has barely paid attention to mass education, yet hollowly proclaims, 'Destroy superstition.'" It was bad enough, he noted, that the string of national crises had "almost caused people to forget entirely" the holidays he remembered so vividly from his childhood. But then the government, banning the celebration of festivals according to the old calendar, had failed to create adequate replacements. As a result, "It is almost as if we were allowed no holidays at all." Gu was convinced that the majority of people, even in well-developed large cities such as Beijing, lacked reasonable alternatives to traditional forms of entertainment. New-style public parks charged admission, required near-formal modes of dress and deportment, and banned artisans and merchants on the premises. No wonder Beijingers preferred to visit the Temple of the Eastern Peak at New Year's, he concluded. Arguments that such temples should be closed to eradicate superstition failed to move him: "Please go [to these temples] and make a count: are there more people who are there to burn incense, or more who are there to sightsee and have a good time?" (Gu Y. 1932). In his own way Gu here betrays a different sort of modernist categorization of religious practice, separating "entertainment" or "leisure" from "religion." But his analysis of the Nationalists' failure is spot on: the new ritual regime remained socially and culturally detached from people outside the immediate circles of party and government.

This might not have happened had the Nationalist worldview, and the powerful rewriting of the meaning of Chinese religion that affected it so strongly, not necessitated ritual competition on the level it did. The denial of authorship and participation on the local level, the insistence on wresting symbols from their ritual contexts and attempts at historical erasure, and the conviction that meaning overrode action—all these set up the fight. They also undercut the Nationalists' chances of winning it. Thus do monolithic claims of modern state authority undermine themselves from the very beginning.

The hybrid commemorations of the dead in the 1930s suggest directions that a more fluid approach could have accommodated. Indeed, in both Ozouf's study of French Revolutionary festivals and Lane's analysis of Soviet rites, it is funerals and rites of war memory that are the most successful, for they are a clear way to link the suffering of individuals and families with that of the nation as a whole, and even to expiate—if only for a brief, tense moment—the traumatic violence of the revolution itself. The Nationalist Party, too, had such events in its experience. The first National Day commemoration of the Nanjing government, for instance, honored the cult of revolutionary martyrs in a detailed and heartfelt fashion. The ritual featured spirit tablets of the deceased, photos of soldiers who had been killed in action, and a eulogy composed in the classical style that invoked the image of "thousands, tens of thousands of miles of sprays of gushing blood (*xuehua*)" (Zhongguo Guomindang Xuanchuanbu 1928:12). As the years went on, such vivid recognition of the sacrifice of war was replaced by moral exhortations to honor party and nation, while the individual photos and tablets gave way to Sun Zhongshan portraits and invocations of resurrected heroes from China's past, arrayed for a select audience. Very little is still known about how the violence and dislocation of the 1920s and 1930s may have been greeted in Chinese ritual life, either from within political and military forces or without.[13] Yet even the limited examples described here show a public hunger for recognition of their suffering, as well as a prolonged struggle within the party-state to develop a ritual regime that accurately reflected the gravity of the times.

Many Republican citizens in fact shared the end goals for which the GMD thought they were battling superstition and constructing their own affective regime—cohesiveness, economic survival, a battle for sovereignty against Japan, and a quest for China's rightful place in the world. Yet many also saw the ban on the lunar calendar and temple festivals as detracting from those goals, not building toward them. The redefinition of the relationship of religion, politics, and society forced them into a competition not of their own choosing. As Asad writes, "Given that the modern nation-state seeks to regulate all aspects of individual life—even the most intimate, such as birth and death—no one, religious or otherwise, can avoid encountering its ambitious powers" (Asad 1999:191). Yet by defying government bans on temple festivals and holidays of the lunar calendar, by eschewing superficial new civic rituals, and by giving meaning to nationalism by combining new symbols, scripts, and personal and social events with preexisting forms, social actors demonstrated that it was indeed possible to live under two "regimes" at once.

4 Heretical Doctrines, Reactionary Secret Societies, Evil Cults

*Labeling Heterodoxy in
Twentieth-Century China*

David A. Palmer 宗樹人

Since the repression of Falungong (法輪功, Practice of the Wheel of the Law) in 1999, the question of "cults" has become a critical issue in the Chinese religious field, leading Chinese scholars and ideologues to elaborate a new discourse on the category of "evil cults" (邪教, *xiejiao*). This was a term from imperial times that had fallen into disuse but was now reactivated to replace the concept of "reactionary secret societies" (反動會道門, *fandong huidaomen*), which had been used in the 1950s in the campaigns to exterminate unorthodox religious groups such as the Yiguandao (一貫道, Way of Pervading Unity).[1] This discourse draws equally on references to a genealogy of sectarian rebellions going back to the second century C.E. and on Western sources on "cults" associated with Christian apologetics and the academic discipline of the sociology of religions. This chapter attempts to trace the contours of the evolution of discourse on stigmatized religious groups in twentieth-century China—a discourse that has reinvented itself twice, defining itself first within the context of revolutionary struggle, and then as part of the contemporary worldwide anti-cult movement. Although it was the Falungong case that stimulated the production of the contemporary general anti-*xiejiao* discourse discussed in this chapter, this discourse is distinct from the specifically anti-Falungong propaganda deployed during the repression campaign, which is not considered here.[2]

Unlike the introduction of other modern paradigms such as the science-religion-superstition dialectic, which led to the tearing apart of China's traditional cultural fabric and to the reshaping of its politico-religious landscape, the use of modern categories to label "cults" appears to have only served to mask the redeployment of the classical Chinese paradigm of the conflict between the State and the Sect. But the current recourse to universalist discourses of the social sciences could, in the long term, have unpredictable consequences for the Chinese state's legitimizing of its anti-cult campaigns.

The field of Chinese "cults," or "sects," is a mined one, in which it is difficult to draw a clear line between a category deployed by the Chinese state's ideology and propaganda, be it imperial or communist (which has always had little relationship with the reality on the ground) and what appears to be a specific and widespread form of Chinese religion (which, lacking a name of its own, has always been situated outside of traditional China's ritual and orthodox order). To the problem of categorization that already exists in the Chinese language is added a further element of confusion when Western terms such as "cult," "sect," "sectarian tradition," "sectarian milieu," or even "new religious movements" are used to designate these groups, despite all the caveats and well-argued sociological justifications used by scholars, including the author of these lines (Jordan & Overmyer 1986; Seiwert 2003; Palmer 2002; 2005:421–29; 2006; 2007:285–90). Indeed, their translation and their use in China have led to a new form of "translingual practice"—the invention of new categories based on Western concepts that take on a new meaning in the Chinese context (L. Liu 1995; Asad 1986).

In the case that interests us here, the Western family of terms "sect," "cult," and "new religious movement," which make possible a constant and ambiguous oscillation between anti-cult polemics and a neutral scientific idiom, lends itself perfectly to the needs of the Chinese authorities who, through the elaboration of a discourse circulating between ideologues, scholars, and officials, seek both to provide an a posteriori justification for the harsh repression of some groups and to develop a more objective understanding of the religious phenomenon in order to better manage it in the future.

Discourse is not merely a reflection or representation of the reality being talked about: by defining and producing the objects of our knowledge, it shapes and orients our interactions with the world; it is thus inseparable from the exercise and circulation of power (Foucault 1980). The case of *xiejiao* described here can be seen in two ways. On the one hand, we see how the Chinese state has used the production of discourse to control the religious field, adapting to changes in ideology and political regime by using different idioms (cosmological, revolutionary, social scientific) to elaborate and legitimize an unchanging dichotomy between groups that reinforce or submit to the political and ideological order, and those that undermine it or cannot fit into it. Thus we can trace the discursive shifts that follow the transitions from one regime to another: (1) *the late imperial (to 1911)*, with its pretension to integrate the civilized world within a grand cosmic order revolving around the emperor, Son of Heaven, who promoted and demoted the gods within the celestial bureaucracy, and under whose protection a plurality of gods and teachings could flourish, but in which rival universal cosmologies could not be tolerated; (2) *the Republican (1911–49)*, marked by a concern for reinventing China into a modern nation as the solution to foreign encroachment and internal instability, and during which the nation's backwardness and weakness were blamed on tradition and superstition; (3) *the revolutionary (1949–79)*, during which all groups not falling under Chinese Communist Party (CCP) control were to be exterminated; and (4) *the reformed socialist (1979–present)*, in which the CCP attempted to reassert its power and authority while leading China toward greater integration with the international community.

On the other hand, the picture is not one of neat and tidy correspondences between discourses and historical phases. Discourses linger from one era to another, new twists and interpretations arise, elements from seemingly incompatible sources are combined, and unexpected affinities come to light, such as Maoist historians inscribing White Lotus rebels in revolutionary genealogies or the contemporary CCP, in its battle against evil cults, identifying itself with the Qing dynasty and Christian orthodoxy. As discourses are constantly adjusted and revised to match political and social realities, we also see that they have a life of their own, sometimes contributing to unintended reconfigurations. Thus, in the case of the contemporary *xiejiao* discourse, they open an unresolved tension between social scientific relativism, which undermines the anti-*xiejiao* campaigns, and the upholding of Religion as a normative standard, which undermines the secular foundations of the socialist State.

THE SECTARIAN REBELLION PARADIGM
AND THE PROBLEM OF THE WHITE LOTUS

In traditional Chinese thought, the proper "upright" order (正, *zheng*) embodied by the state (and its Confucian orthodoxy) is opposed by the evil, "crooked" forces of chaos (邪, *xie*). The notion of heresy (*yiduan*) appears for the first time in the *Analects* of Confucius, which argues that heterodox ideas must be resisted to reduce their menace to society. Confucius's disciple Mencius used the term in his attack on the egalitarian ideas of Mozi, claiming that in periods of decline, when the orthodox way is weakened, "heretical sayings" (*xieshuo*) proliferate and destroy the authority of sovereigns and fathers.

But it was during the Eastern Han (25–220 C.E.) that a discourse specifically stigmatizing politically heterodox religious groups appeared for the first time, following the millenarian movement of the Taipingdao (太平道, Way of Supreme Peace), whose leader, the charismatic healer Zhang Jue, launched the Yellow Turban Rebellion in 184 C.E., which mobilized tens of thousands of fighters and, though crushed after bloody battles, durably weakened the reigning dynasty, which collapsed a few decades later (Stein 1963; Seidel 1969–70; Seiwert 2003:23–80). This revolt inaugurated the paradigm of the conflict between the state and the sectarian rebellion, whose master has the ambition of becoming emperor, destroys social order, and threatens the survival of the dynasty: since then, the Chinese state has always had its sectarian rebels, and the struggle against them is constitutive of its self-definition and legitimacy.

For the entire subsequent history of imperial China, and once again today, the Yellow Turbans have been and are invariably invoked to justify the suppression of religious groups judged to be heterodox. Later, the rebellions of Faqing (515), Han Shantong (1351), Xu Hongru (1622), Wang Lun (1774), the White Lotus (1796), the Eight Trigrams (1813), and the Taipings (1851–64), which were all associated with religious movements, successively enriched the discourse on the danger of "heretical doctrines," or *xiejiao*.

Starting in the fourteenth century, the name Bailianjiao (白蓮教, White Lotus Teachings) was often used to designate this type of heretical group, to the point that Chinese and Western historiography have long believed in the existence of a "White Lotus sect," an error exposed in Barend ter Haar's study of the history of the White Lotus (ter Haar 1992). Ter Haar shows that a lay Buddhist movement that called itself the Bailianhui (White Lotus Society), which existed in the Song (960–1279) and expanded rapidly during the Yuan (1271–1368), was the target of a petition submitted to the imperial throne accusing the society of "meeting at night and dispersing at dawn," "indiscriminately mixing men and women," and "practicing vegetarianism and worshipping demons." This petition led to the banning of the White Lotus by Emperor Wuzong in 1308, though the movement was respected by the elites and the edict revoked five years later (ter Haar 1992:74). In 1397, however, Zhu Yuanzhang, who had founded the Ming dynasty in 1386 with the remaining forces of the Maitreyanist rebellion of Han Shantong, and was thus acutely aware from his own experience of the potential power of religious movements, banned almost all forms of popular religious activity—the "heterodox ways," or *zuodao*—with the exception of seasonal sacrifices and a few Buddhist and Daoist monasteries. This law, which can be seen as the model and foundation of all subsequent legislation and policy on religion in imperial China, and to a great extent the People's Republic as well, specifically bans four named groups: the White Lotus Society, the White Cloud Society, Maitreyanism, and Manicheism (de Groot 1976 [1901]:137–48). As ter Haar has shown, from then on the "White Lotus" name would become a label that was used indiscriminately to stigmatize lay Buddhist associations and, eventually, any unorthodox group. *Xiejiao* and "White Lotus" became virtually synonymous terms, and no group dared identify itself as affiliated to a "White Lotus" tradition: the history of the "White Lotus sect" since the Ming is in reality the history of the usage of the White lotus label and its associated stereotypes to denounce and persecute certain groups.

THE END OF THE EMPIRE AND OF THE DISCOURSE ON HERETICAL DOCTRINES

With the fall of the Qing in 1911 and the founding of the Republican regime, the anti-*xiejiao* and "White Lotus" discourse seems to have petered out, eclipsed by debates about the new categories of "religion" and "superstition" (Goossaert 2003; Nedostup 2001), and on the place of "secret societies" in the Chinese revolution. In the midst of the confusion around these concepts, and of the general political instability, several groups and networks that would have been banned and persecuted as "White Lotus" or *xiejiao* under the Qing emerged from obscurity or formed themselves anew, openly expanding and even dominating the religious landscape in some cities and regions. Around the same time that the first generation of religious associations was born in 1912, as described by Vincent Goossaert in his chapter of this volume, several of these groups also founded national modern-style associations that registered with the state as religious, philanthropic, or public interest associations, with a head office, a national organization with provincial and municipal branches, and a doctrine that attempted to modernize the Chinese syncretic tradition with the aid of a more modern, academic language and by incorporating Christianity and Islam to the traditional Union of the Three Teachings (*sanjiao heyi*). Thus the Zailijiao (Teaching of the Abiding Principle) incorporated itself in 1913 as the All-China Association for Promoting Abstention from Opium and Alcohol (Zhonghua Quanguo Lishan Quanjie Yanjiu Zonghui)—followed by the Society for the Study of Morality (Daode Xueshe) in 1916; the

Fellowship of Goodness (Tongshanshe) in 1917; the Universal Morality Society (Wanguo Daodehui) in 1918; the School of the Way (Daoyuan) in 1921; the Association of the Sagely Way of China's Three Teachings (Zhongguo Sanjiao Shengdao Zonghui) in 1924; the Association of the New Teachings for World Salvation (Jiushi Xinjiaohui) in 1925; the School of the Way of the Return to Oneness (Guiyi Daoyuan) in 1927; the Society for the Study of Religious Philosophy (Zongjiao Zhexue Yanjiushe) in 1930; and so forth (Shao 1997:165–94). These associations, which often had their own scriptures, philosophical system, simplified ritual, congregational mode of participation, and hierarchical national organization, actually conformed as much, if not more, to the model of the Christian church, which had become the new paradigm of "religion" in China, than to that of the ancient Buddhist, Daoist, or Confucian institutions: it is not surprising, then, that several of them obtained the status of religious associations in the first years of the Republic, and appear not to have been specific targets of the first waves of polemics against superstition.

The Guomindang Nationalist government, established in Nanjing in 1927, was much less favorably disposed toward these groups than the Beiyang regime, and the largest organizations, notably the Wushanshe, Tongshanshe, and Daoyuan, tainted by their close ties with the leaders of the deposed warlord regime, were, in the edict "On Banning *Xiejiao*," officially outlawed as "superstitious organizations" (*mixin jiguan*), accused both of being tools of warlords and local gentry to increase their influence under the cover of religious and philanthropic activities, and of spreading superstition and retarding progress (Lu Z. 2002:173–74; She 1997:227; Lin B. 1990:325; Wang J. 1995). Rarely applied, the ban seems to have had little effect; many groups counted high-level political and military officials among their members. Some groups continued to operate legally under the front of their charitable branch, such as the Daoyuan's Red Swastika Society (Hongwanzihui), which drew inspiration from the International Red Cross Society (Nedostup 2001:145–53). The relationships between these groups and the Guomindang regime have not yet been studied in detail, but the use of the *xiejiao* label does not seem to have been systematic or supported by an elaborate discourse; rather, criticism of the groups was couched in the more general terms of the struggle against superstition and against obstacles to progress (Duara 2003:109).

In any case, the Japanese invasion made it virtually impossible to enforce the suppression of these groups. The Nationalist regime now gladly approved their charitable works; in fact, it began a policy to systematically reorganize, infiltrate, and control them as tools for anti-Japanese resistance. In Shandong, for instance, each branch in a given area was to be renamed as the "self-defense association against the enemy of the XXX society of XXX county, Shandong province," to accept instructions in anti-Japanese defense from government agents assigned to work with each group, and to receive regular military training. This policy was attempted on the Red Swastika Society and was quite thorough in case of the Zailijiao (Lu Z. 2002:213–16; 234–35).

Although some Japanese in the areas under Japanese control saw in these associations an expression of authentic religion and a means by which Asian spiritual values common to Japan and China could be promoted to resist Western materialism, the puppet regime in Manchuria was suspicious of the "superstitious" character of these associations. Instead of banning them, however, it attempted to coopt them and make them instruments of its social policy: they thus enjoyed unprecedented growth in Manchukuo and, later, in the occupied parts of China (Duara 2003:103–22).

After the Japanese defeat, as the Guomindang tried to reestablish its control over the country, it began to move to suppress Yiguandao, a network of salvationist congregations whose worship of the Unborn Mother and apocalyptic eschatology of the three kalpas continued a tradition that had been persecuted as "White Lotus doctrine" under the Ming and Qing. The Yiguandao lineage had been founded in Shandong at the end of the nineteenth century, but it was only in the early 1930s, under the leadership of Zhang Guangbi (1889–1947),[3] that Yiguandao congregations began to multiply throughout China, especially in the areas under Japanese occupation; the Minister of Foreign Affairs of the puppet Chinese regime was himself an initiate (Jordan 1982:435–62). After the end of the Sino-Japanese War, between 1945 and 1949, the Yiguandao continued to experience spectacular growth, with a presence—according to a study of mentions of the group in local gazetteers—in 81 percent of China's prefectures at the beginning of the 1950s (Fu 1999:47). According to police reports in the early 1950s, the number of members had reached 178,000 in Beijing and 140,000 in Tianjin, and even the majority of the residents of a large number of villages (Shao 1997:470; DuBois 2005:134). A detailed estimation of the number of Yiguandao members in China remains to be done, but if we remember that this growth occurred during a period of only fifteen years, in conditions of extremely difficult communication during the Sino-Japanese and then civil war, the exponential expansion of Yiguandao can be compared to that of Falungong in the 1990s. This growth appeared to go unchecked at a moment when the

GMD and the CCP had were struggling to establish a tenuous hold on the nation.

In Tianjin, where the police acted against the Yiguandao and other groups, tracts were distributed labeling the group as a *xiejiao* and stressing that it descended from the White Lotus and the Boxers (Li S. 1975[1948]:34). The CCP conquest of the Mainland occurred before the GMD could do much against the Yiguandao, however (a change that, as described below, would offer little respite to the movement), but the hostile policy would continue in Taiwan. The imperial-era *xiejiao* discourse was explicitly used to justify the continued banning of Yiguandao on the island, with the White Lotus connection repeatedly evoked to warn against Yiguandao as a politically subversive group possibly infiltrated by Communist agents. This rhetoric was amplified by Buddhist polemics against the Yiguandao as a heterodox *xiejiao*, which had begun as early as 1935 and which were reiterated in several tracts through the 1970s (Lin B. 1990:335).

ALLIANCES BETWEEN REVOLUTIONARIES AND "SECRET SOCIETIES"

If the Japanese had wanted to coopt these "redemptive societies," to use Duara's term, it was partly to prevent them from going underground and becoming, as in the Guomindang-controlled areas, harder to control (Duara 2003:116). Indeed, while the imperial-era anti-*xiejiao* discourse was only sporadically employed during the Republican period, the redemptive groups were increasingly seen as belonging to the ambiguous category of "secret societies" (秘密社會, *mimi shehui*).

The discourse on Chinese secret societies goes back to the legislation against sworn brotherhoods enacted in the seventeenth century, during the first decades of the Qing dynasty. The term used for these groups in legal documents of the time, *jiebai dixiong*, implies the creation of inverted relationships between elder and younger brothers, which was contrary to Confucian notions of hierarchy (Antony 1993:192–93, 206). In the eighteenth century, mutual aid societies based on fictive kinship, which David Ownby calls "brotherhood associations," proliferated in Southern China in a context of social dislocations and weak state authority in the region, evolved a complex form of organization with initiation rituals and a secret language, and gave themselves names such as "Father and Mother Society" and "Peach Garden Society" (Ownby 1993:15). During this period, official discourse increasingly linked these brotherhoods to banditry and the threat of rebellion, and the law became increasingly harsh toward them. Following the rebellion of Lin Shuangwen, the first occurrence of the "Heaven and Earth Society" (天地會, Tiandihui)—the notorious Triads—in official reports of the 1780s, treats the group as a *xiejiao*. But according to research by Robert Antony, officials subsequently stopped identifying South Chinese secret societies as *xiejiao*. Thus it seems that what texts called "creating associations and forming cliques" (*jiehui shudang*) constituted, in the eyes of the Qing, a category distinct from that of the "heretical doctrines" (Antony 1993:197, 206). The only thing the two categories had in common was the fact that they were seen as threats to social order and as potential sources of rebellion.[4]

Around the end of the Qing regime, both these types of groups began to be called "secret societies" (*mimi shehui, mimi jieshe*), borrowing the term used by British colonial administrators in Malaysia. Indeed, in the late Qing both the brotherhood associations and the salvationist societies were illegal, had been driven underground, and were perceived as rebellious and opposed to the Qing. We know that Sun Zhongshan (Sun Yat-sen), founder of the Chinese Republic and himself a leader of the Tongmenghui (同盟會, United Alliance Society), cultivated relationships with the secret societies of the overseas Chinese, and that China's first revolutionaries heavily relied on them to provide troops and mobilize the people. Among some of these associations, a "nationalist" ideology circulated that called for the overthrow of the Qing (Manchu) dynasty and restoration of the Ming (Chinese); the radical intellectuals' task with these groups was to convince them to modernize their thinking and support the establishment of a Republican regime. Thus a new discourse on "secret societies" emerged, which described them as protorevolutionary associations that had existed since the early Qing to oppose the imperial regime (Ownby 1993:6; Borokh 1972).

During the civil war between the Guomingdang and the CCP, and also during the Sino-Japanese War, the three sides tried to enlist the "secret societies." The Communists continued to elaborate a discourse on their popular nature and revolutionary potential, which was not without ambiguity. On the one hand, in 1921, Chen Duxiu, Marxist intellectual and founding secretary-general of the CCP, had written of the Fellowship for Goodness (Tongshanshe) that the working and student masses did not believe in these heresies, which recalled the humiliation of the Boxers and the political oppression and social decadence of China (Nedostup 2001:97). But despite this critique of the backward nature of this type of association, superstition was not to be an obstacle for tactical alliances: elsewhere, Chen Duxiu wrote of the Red Spears (紅槍會, Hongqianghui)—a form of self-defence militia which practiced magical invulnerability rites similar to those of the Boxers, and which had millions of practitioners in North China (Perry 1982; Tai 1985)—that despite the superstitious coloration of peasant thinking, the barbarian and destructive nature of their struggle against the ruling classes should not be opposed (Li S. 1996:198). Zhu De, one of the Red Army's top generals, was also a member of the Gelaohui, or Elders' Society (Schram 1966:6; Smedley 1956:88–89), and Mao Zedong (Mao Tse-tung)'s own thinking was not without a certain romanticism for the bandit heroes and wandering knights of the popular novel *The Water Margin,* whose mythology was maintained in the brotherhood associations. In 1926, Mao described the secret societies—of which he enumerated a list which made no distinction between brotherhood associations, armed militias, and redemptive societies (Triads, Elders' Society, Big Swords, Morality Society, Green Gang, etc.)—as mutual help associations of floating populations in their economic and political struggle (Schram 1966:4). The CCP's second enlarged congress (1926) specifically discussed the question of the Red Spears, and passed a resolution stating that "the Red Spears are one of the most important forces in the national revolutionary movement," which proposed giving them the means to organize and unify themselves in a systematic fashion, and stressed that "we should not oppose the superstitious beliefs of the Red Spears. They are the basis on which the association organizes and fights. Although they are only relics of ideas which the peasants cannot abandon, we must ensure that these superstitious activities are beneficial for the revolution" (quoted in Tai H. 1985:106). Ten years later, Mao published an "Appeal from the Central Soviet Government" to the "Brothers of the Elders' Society," in which he warmly praised its anti-Qing tradition and called on them to join the anti-Japanese front (Schram 1966:11–13; Munro, ed. 1989:99–101.)

But the CCP's embrace of secret societies was purely opportunistic; the ultimate goal was to coopt their leaders and make them useless by creating grassroots revolutionary associations that could better meet the needs of the people. CCP cadres did not hesitate to establish secret society shrines which were but fronts for Party cells (Chen Y. 1986:488–92). Secret society associations defended purely local interests and could just as well be manipulated by the Guomindang and the Japanese: there were clear limits to their revolutionary potential. In the Wuxi area, for instance, the Way of Anterior Heaven (Xiantiandao) was infiltrated by both the CCP and Japanese—whose praise for the "religious faith" of the believers turned into denunciation of the group as a *xiejiao* deluding the masses once the

CCP had managed to spur several of its lodges into violent anti-Japanese action (Shao 1997:378–79). Furthermore, groups like the Fellowship for Goodness, the Elders' Society, and the Red Spears were very different in terms of their membership, their structure, their beliefs, their rituals, and their objectives. A thorough study of discourses on these groups during the Republican era remains to be done, but it seems, based on the sources available, that no fixed category existed: many terms, such as *banghui, huimen, jiaomen, daomen,* and *daohui,* were used without systematically distinguishing among them, but usually with connotations of shady underground or secret associations. This indetermination was the result of the absence of an effective central state during this period, and of an unstable dynamic in which these groups could impose themselves sometimes as potential allies, sometimes as enemies, thus eluding unilateral objectification.

SECRET SOCIETIES BECOME "REACTIONARY SECTS"

Everything changed with the founding of the People's Republic of China (PRC) in 1949, and even before that in some areas already controlled by the CCP. On January 4, 1949, the People's Government of North China banned secret societies—the *huimen* and the *daomen*—stressing that these organizations were not only feudal and superstitious but also "instruments of the counterrevolutionaries" and "enemy spies" who "propagate rumors," "agitate popular sentiment," "organize armed revolts," and "disturb social order." The leaders of these organizations were summoned to turn themselves in to the authorities and to repent if they wanted to avoid a harsh punishment. Meanwhile, the ordinary followers, who had been "fooled" by the reactionary societies, were ordered to withdraw from these associations and cease any activity if they wanted to avoid being prosecuted, and were promised a reward if they provided information on these associations and their acts of "sabotage" (Shao 1997:405–6).

Other regional governments did the same later in 1949. Official discourse crystallized: the groups in question became "reactionary secret societies" (反動會道門, *fandong huidaomen*), this term being a conflation of the terms huimen and daomen; they were to be ruthlessly exterminated in the national campaign against counterrevolutionary activities launched at the end of 1950, which called for the death sentence or life imprisonment for those who used "feudal secret societies" (*fengjian huidaomeni*) to engage in counterrevolutionary activities. The campaign against these groups reached its climax in 1953 and 1954, during which, according to police reports, 820,000 leaders and organizers, and 13 million followers, were implicated (Shao 1997:452, 455).

By far the largest of these societies, and hence the principal target of the campaign, was the Yiguandao, which thus found itself at the center of the struggle against reactionary forces. All forms of propaganda were deployed against it, from editorials and speeches by Mao published in the *People's Daily* and the rest of the press to posters, comics, exhibits, denunciation assemblies, and even theatrical performances. The name "Yiguandao" became a synonym for a counterrevolutionary sect and even a favored insult used by children in schoolyards (Shao 1997:465; DuBois 2005b:148). One wonders to what extent "Yiguandao," like "White Lotus" centuries earlier, became a stigmatizing label used to demonize any suspect individual or group during the revolutionary fervor, even with no real link to the Yiguandao itself. Indeed, according to a Daoist monk I interviewed in July 2004 at a temple in Chengdu, the anti-Yiguandao campaign was a pretext for arresting most of that city's Daoists in the early 1950s, thereby circumventing the "freedom of religion" which was supposed to protect Daoism as an official religion. According to newspapers at the time, 30 percent of Sichuan's population were members of the Yiguandao—a fantastical figure that allowed one to see the Yiguandao danger everywhere (Deliusin 1972:232).

The campaign against the *huidaomen* and Yiguandao appears to have been largely successful: in the region of Hebei studied by Thomas Dubois, the Yiguandao was already little more than a memory by the end of the 1950s (DuBois 2005b:148–51). But the "threat" resurfaced after the Cultural Revolution, as many societies took advantage of the freer political climate to reconstitute themselves. The number of *huidaomen* cases dealt with by the police, most of which concerned the Yiguandao, was reported to have increased by 79 percent in 1981, 31 percent in 1982, and 30 percent in 1983 (Gong'anbu, ed. 1985:60). The anti-*huidaomen* discourse was reactivated in the press in the first half of the 1980's. Reports emphasized that the groups were organized and recruited followers; they "fabricated apocalyptic rumors," "sabotaged the Four Modernizations," "proclaimed themselves emperor," and "had the ambition to change dynasties"; they "abused superstition" to "swindle their followers out of their money"; they "put lives in danger" by "prescribing superstitious remedies," they "seduced and raped women," "printed reactionary tracts," "diffused superstition and heresy," "constantly changed activities and methods," and were "infiltrated" by "foreign forces," including the Taiwan Guomindang regime's spy network (Gong'anbu, ed. 1985:67–80). In a phrase that could have been taken directly from Ming imprecations against White Lotus followers who "congregated at night and dispersed at daybreak," *huidaomen* leaders were said to "keep a low profile in the daytime, going out only to call meetings at night" (Gong'anbu, ed. 1985:78). In his study of the Way of the Temple of the Heavenly Immortals (Tianxian Miaodao), which was repressed in the 1950s but resurfaced in the 1980s, David Ownby notes that police documents reveal an obsession with those group teachings and slogans that could be interpreted as signs of an ambition to found a new imperial dynasty, although such allusions, while present in the groups' literature, are relatively rare and can be interpreted in different ways depending on the context (Ownby 2001:84–85).

Paradoxically, although the anti-*huidaomen* propaganda repeated many of the same themes as the old discourse against the White Lotus, White Lotus rebellions were described in generally positive terms in the new Communist historiography, as part of the revolutionary genealogy of peasant revolts against feudal authority and even against foreign imperialist churches (see, for example, Cai 1996 [1990]: 203–68). The Yellow Turbans similarly became a paradigmatic case of a peasant rebellion inspired by religious egalitarianism. Sun Zuomin, a leading historian of peasant rebellions in the 1950s, argued that heretical sects expressed the interests and desires of the lower classes, and opposed the upper-class religion which sought to delude the people. Sun considered that such religious groups provided peasants with the only effective form of organizational and ideological framework to unite the peasantry in the absence of political parties; empowered peasants by giving them a sense of mystical invincibility; and, after rebellions were defeated, provided peasants with the means for the secret transmission of the ideas and resources of resistance—the latter factor being especially evident in the case of the White Lotus, with its repeated uprisings emerging from underground splinter groups (Sun Z. 1956).[5] The role of religion in peasant rebellions was the subject of heated academic debates in the PRC in the 1960s and early 1980s, but overall, the "White Lotus" sects of the Yuan, Ming, and Qing were depicted as having played a beneficial role of resistance against feudal domination.

It thus became necessary to distinguish White Lotus sects from the "*huidaomen*" societies of the Republican era, which, in the revolutionary discourse, had only one objective: to defend feudalism and restore the empire (Lu Z. 2002:7). At the same time, it became necessary to reconcile the proletarian and protorevolutionary origins of the *huidaomen* as described in the socialist historiography, with their current counterrevolutionary nature. Thus an internal document published by the ministry of Public Security places the *huidaomen* in direct affiliation to the White Lotus, stating that such societies first appeared at the end of the Yuan dynasty; then,

> In the initial period of the emergence of the secret societies, they played a clearly progressive role in the struggle against imperialist invasion and the corrupt Qing-dynasty regime. For example, the famous Boxer movement at the end of the Qing was launched with the "White Lotus sect" and the "Red Yang sect" as its organizational core. Later, the secret societies were gradually coopted and controlled by the reactionary ruling classes, to become counterrevolutionary political groups protecting the dominant class at different periods. (Gong'anbu, ed. 1985:1)

THE RETURN OF *XIEJIAO* VIA CHRISTIANITY AND THE WEST

With the deepening of economic reforms in the post-Mao era, the state gradually distanced itself from revolutionary ideology, going so far as to abandon the theory of class struggle. In this context, as the "reactionary secret society" label began to seem anachronistic and limited to the counterrevolutionary groups of the early years of the People's Republic, the label *xiejiao*—previously used in the Ming and Qing dynasties—resurfaced and entered popular discourse in the mid 1990s, but this time to translate the term "cult" in Chinese press coverage of the tragedies of the Branch Davidians (U.S.A., 1993), the Order of the Solar Temple (Switzerland, Quebec, and France, 1994 and 1995), and Aum Shinrikyo (Japan, 1995). In 1995, the State Council and the CCP Central Committee issued a circular banning several groups designated as *xiejiao*, most of which had been denounced as heretical by the official Christian associations: the Shouters (Huhanpai), the Complete Domain Church (Quan Fanwei Jiaohui), the New Testament Church (Xinyue Jiaohui), the Oriental Lightning (Dongfang Shandian), the Assembly of Disciples (Mentuhui), and the Church of Spirits (Linglinghui), as well as a Buddhist-inspired group headquartered in Taiwan, the Guanyin Dharma Gate (Guanyin Famen). The contemporary reappearance of the *xiejiao* label is thus associated with Christian and foreign groups, and translates Western categories of the "cult" disseminated by the anti-cult movement which, in North America, is dominated by Christian interests.

At the same time, journalists and scientists who, in 1995, were in a heated polemic against the "superstitious" and "pseudo-scientific" deviations of the *qigong* movement noted the similarities between foreign *xiejiao* and some *qigong* organizations, and called for an immediate purge of such groups before they became Aum Shinrikyo–style cults and caused large-scale deaths (Palmer 2007:170–72). Following this polemic, the political support that had contributed so much to the spread of the *qigong* movement dissipated, and the state attempted to regulate the thousands of *qigong* associations and networks. In 1998, several Buddhist magazines specifically attacked Falungong, which had become the most popular *qigong* form, as a *xiejiao* that drew lay Buddhists away from orthodoxy, and inscribed Falungong in a genealogy which linked it to the Yiguandao and the White Lotus (Palmer 2007:262–63; Chen X. 1998). Thus, through the combination of scientistic polemics and Christian and Buddhist apologetics, a new Chinese discourse on "cults" emerged, which resuscitated the old imperial model of *xiejiao* and the White Lotus and combined it with fears of the collective suicides and mass murders of Western and Japanese cults. Ironically, this reappearance of the *xiejiao* discourse on the Mainland occurred just after it had faded in Taiwan, with the end of martial law and the legalization of Yiguandao in 1987.

The PRC's ministry of public security, which in 1997 had begun an investigation on Falungong as an "illegal religion" (*feifa zongjiao*), lauched a new investigation in 1998, this time designating it as a *xiejiao* (Palmer 2007:265). Starting on July 22, 1999, when the CCP decreed the total suppression of Falungong, the *xiejiao* label, which had now become a mark of political demonization, was repeated ad nauseam in the propaganda campaign that saturated the media for several months. Translated in documents published for foreign audiences, *xiejiao* became "evil cult" or "destructive cult" in English and, in French, "*secte*" or "*secte insane.*"[6] Scholars and religious leaders were summoned to conferences in which the category of *xiejiao* was defined on the basis of Western cases, applied to Falungong, and distinguished from orthodox religion (Chen & Dai, eds. 1999). On October 30 of the same year, the state retroactively gave itself the legal instrument of repression when the highest legislative body passed a resolution banning *xiejiao*, "which act under the cover of religion, *qigong*, or other illicit forms," and stipulated the punishment of those who "manipulate the members of *xiejiao* organizations to break the laws and decrees of the state, organize mass gatherings to disturb the social order and deceive the public, cause deaths, rape women, and swindle people of their goods and money, or commit other crimes of superstition or heresy" (Standing Committee of the Ninth National People's Congress 1999).

THE NEW CHINESE DISCOURSE ON *XIEJIAO*

A legal framework having been set up, and a flurry of anti-Falungong books and propaganda materials having been released, it was now necessary to produce a more sophisticated discourse to legitimate the repression and to elaborate a general policy to counter evil cults, of which Falungong was seen to be but one case of a general phenomenon. An anti-cult association of ideologues, scholars, and journalists was founded on November 13, 2000; international conferences of Chinese and foreign "experts" on cults were organized; and a large number of works was published from 2000 onward. In contrast to the imperial discourse against "heretical doctrines" and the Communist discourse against "reactionary" societies, in which groups were condemned according to explicitly political criteria defined arbitrarily by the state itself, the new discourse aimed to be objective and scientific, defining *xiejiao* as a universal category in time and space, dangerous for society and humanity in general rather than for the present political regime in particular. Hence many articles drew on the Western sociological and Christian literature to enumerate the characteristics of a *xiejiao*. In the book *Lun xiejiao* (*On Evil Cults*), which collected the proceedings of the first "International Symposium on Destructive Cults" held in Beijing in November 2000, the first chapter is the contribution, translated into Chinese, of an American anti-cult activist who defines a "cult" as a group whose doctrine contradicts that of its mother religion: for example, it does not admit the doctrines of the Trinity, the bodily resurrection of Christ, salvation by grace, and so on. A cult uses methods of psychological pressure, forms a totalitarian community, and its founder is self-proclaimed, dogmatic, messianic, and charismatic, and considers that the ends justify the means to make money and recruit followers. The author continues by listing the sociological characteristics of the cult—authoritarianism, psychological manipulation, psychopathology, breaking of family ties, communal living, distortion of sexuality, deprivation, fraud, and deception—and gives psychological explanations for joining a cult: the need for love and encouragement, idealism, poverty, intellectual satisfaction, health, and so forth (Pearson 2002).

These criteria, which are a basic summary of the Western anti-cult discourse that combines elements of Christianity, sociology, and psychology, were widely referred to, discussed, and debated by Chinese authors, often with quotations from the Bible and references to the history of Christianity, in the new literature on *xiejiao*, and even in university textbooks and reference works on the theory of religious studies or of the sociology of religions (Lu C. 2001; Chen & Chen, eds. 2003; Sun S. 2001). Other works use psychological methods to analyze the "mental control" that Falungong uses on its victims, and to evaluate the techniques used to reconvert (轉化, *zhuanhua*) them (Zhongguo Kexueyuan, eds. 2002). Western terminology is studied and its Chinese equivalents discussed at length: articles are often riddled with English, German, French, Latin, and Greek terms—"*kult*," "*cultus*," "*sekten*," "crazed," "destructive," "heresy," "*airesis*," "*secare*," "*sequi*," "denomination," "charisma," and so forth (see Guo, ed. 2003:8–13). Indeed, this literature shows a great interest in the foreign experience with cults. The work *Xiejiao zhenxiang* (*The True Face of Evil Cults*, Chen & Zhang, eds. 2001), for example, devotes its first volume to cults abroad (Aum Shinrikyo, Branch Davidians, Order of the Solar Temple, etc.) and the second volume to the Chinese cases (Yiguandao, Shouters, Assembly of Disciples, Falungong, etc.), as if to insist that the Chinese experience is but the local expression of a world phenomenon. Indeed, the introduction to *On Evil Cults* argues that the trend of cult activities is one of internationalization, so that "it is impossible for a single country to stop cultic expansion alone. It is thus necessary to reinforce international anti-cultic cooperation" (Shehui Wenti, ed. 2002:2). Entire books are devoted to anti-cult movements around the world, giving special attention to the American and French cases and presenting the anti-cult policies of countries as varied as Belgium, the Philippines, and the Democratic Republic of Congo (Guo, ed. 2003:292–342; Luo W. 2002).

One of the problems the authors of this literature face is how to clarify the relationships between the current usage of *xiejiao*, the imperial meaning of *xiejiao*, the *huidaomen* of the Republican and Maoist eras, the "new religions" (新興宗教, *xinxing zongjiao*), which also entered the Chinese academic lexicon in the 1990s, and, of course, the concept of "religion" (*zongjiao*) itself. In their introduction to a series on Chinese "secret societies," Qin Baoqi and Tan Songlin note that the term *xiejiao* was used by the Ming and Qing dynastic authorities but should not be used today to label groups from that period because that would imply ignoring their contribution to popular resistance to imperial dictatorship. Qin and Tan therefore prefer giving these groups the more neutral term *jiaomen*, or "teaching lineage." But they then add that since the beneficial actions of these groups ended during the Republican period, using a neutral term is no longer justified, and the pejorative label of *huidaomen* should be used to name groups active during that period. Further on, Qin and Tan note several commonalities between *huidaomen* and foreign *xiejiao*— the political ambition and self-deification of the master, the apocalyptic doctrines, the corrupt life of the master compared to the ascetic denial imposed on followers. But to avoid "conceptual confusion," they insist on the importance of maintaining a distinction between the *huidaomen* as groups active in China in the first half of the twentieth century and the *xiejiao* as contemporary foreign cults and Chinese groups that "raise the banner of Christianity to carry out anti-social activities" (Qin & Tan 2002:2–3, 113–21).

Overall, however, even though some historians stress the different social conditions prevailing at different periods, the new discourse burdens itself less and less with such intellectual acrobatics to separate the various generations of groups that existed under different political regimes. Rather, *xiejiao* becomes a universal category encompassing all evil cults at all periods of Chinese history and in all parts of the world. The discourse on the "beneficial" contribution of these groups to peasant resistance against feudal dynasties is entirely revised: *xiejiao* masters used their organization and their charisma to coopt and exploit popular revolts in order to further their personal ambition to establish a new feudal theocracy; they thus diverted the imperial authorities from gaining an accurate understanding of the true causes of popular discontent and provoked all kinds of calamities for common people (Liu X. 2002:332–34; Liu P. 2002; Zhao Z. 2002; Zhang L. 2002). At the same time, there is an interest in the methods deployed by the imperial state to exterminate *xiejiao*—not in order to condemn the feudal oppression of peasant rebellions, but to glean lessons from the past and, in one study, to take inspiration from the successful policy of the Jiaqing emperor (1796–1821) against the White Lotus and Eight Trigram revolts (Zheng & Ouyang 2001; Zheng Y. 2003; Dong & Zhou 1999).

Several articles on the etymology, usage, and history of *xiejiao* in imperial China have been published since 1999 in Chinese newspapers and journals. In a synthesis of these studies, Guo An concludes that in Chinese history, it was the government and the orthodox religions that defined which groups were *xiejiao* on the basis of their "anti-social and anti-orthodox" nature—namely, on the grounds that they "opposed the interests of the governing group (*tongzhi jituan*) or "turned their backs on orthodox religion" (Guo, ed. 2003:7). Although Guo tries to deny making links with the current situation in China, it is clear that the same criteria are in operation today, under an alliance between political and religious orthodoxy. Indeed, the new discourse on *xiejiao* gives particular attention to drawing a clear boundary between *xiejiao* and "religion," and even between *xiejiao* and "new religious movements," to such an extent that both "traditional" and "new" religions are depicted in a good light for their contributions to social stability. The demarcation line between "orthodox religion" (*zhengjiao*) and *xiejiao* is not based on heresy in relation to the doctrines and practices of particular established religions, but on general notions of moral and social order, almost identical to ancient Chinese notions of politico-religious orthodoxy, but this time extended to the whole world with the aid of a universalist discourse derived from the social sciences.

Comparing religion and *xiejiao*, Guo An lists several differences. On the object of devotion, religion worships a transcendental divinity toward which the clergy are mere servants, whereas *xiejiao* demand the absolute veneration of a man who himself claims to be god. Concerning eschatology, religions do have doctrines on the "end of the world" but without a clear date or seen as occurring in a distant future, and busy themselves with bringing spiritual encouragement to practical life, so that "traditional religion contributes to social stability," whereas *xiejiao* predict the imminent end of days and try to terrorize their followers with their prophecies. When it comes to behavior, religions propagate "ethical and moral values recognized and accumulated by humanity for millennia," whereas *xiejiao* force their followers to sacrifice all their possessions and even their families in order to put themselves under the protection of their master. Concerning organization, traditional religions have an open and "relatively democratic" organization that does not contravene the constitution or the law, and the clergy do not intervene in the life of believers, whereas *xiejiao* "establish secret organizations and underground kingdoms, exert a dictatorial control on their adepts, practice forced brainwashing." Finally, in relation to their social and political role, the main religions of secularized countries "take the initiative" to harmonize their relations with the government and "do not have an anti-governmental potential"—all the more so in countries which do not separate the state and religion, where the national religion plays "a crucial role" as a "supporting force" for the government, whereas the "evil nature" of *xiejiao* is to "destroy social stability, slow down economic development and overthrow the government" (Guo, ed. 2003:36–42).

Though some Chinese authors, following Western categories, consider that *xiejiao* are a form of religion (Dai K. 1999:311–15), the consensus—imposed by the CCP's policy, which guarantees the freedom of religion but forbids *xiejiao*—sees "religion" and *xiejiao* as two diametrically opposed categories:

> A demon who wears the mask of a beautiful girl is not a beautiful girl; a wolf wearing a sheepskin is a wolf, not a sheep. *Xiejiao* organizations that drape themselves in religious language cannot become religions and can only be *xiejiao* gangs of social criminals. In dealing with the

evil forces and social garbage of *xiejiao*, they must absolutely not be
considered as religions, nor be given a legal social status: they can only
be swept into the rubbish heap of history with the iron broom of the
law. . . . Eliminating *xiejiao* has no impact on the rigorous application
of the policy of religious freedom; on the contrary, given that the
xiejiao stain the reputation of religion and distort religious concepts,
inverting black and white and sowing confusion in public opinion, to
eliminate *xiejiao* signifies respecting and protecting religion. (Feng
2001:24–25)

At the same time, a clear distinction is also made between *xiejiao* and
"new religious movements" or "new religions" (*xinxing zongjiao*), which
became known to Chinese scholars and religious affairs officials beginning about 1997 or so, both through acquaintance with Western academic
works on this subject and through the introduction to China, following
China's greater opening up to foreign contacts, of certain "new religions"
from abroad. Guo An thus insists that although several *xiejiao* were originally new religious movements, one cannot consider all new religions to
be *xiejiao*. On the contrary, he affirms that most new religions remain
within the realm of "orthodox" religion and have "an internal structure
which governs their organization and the relationships between believers
and the society" which, though different from that of traditional religion,
"remains within the bounds of social norms and morals." As products of
"religious secularization," new religions propose a "vision of the future
and a worldview adapted to social development, whose objective is to
enable a given religion to better conform itself to a dramatically changing
social reality and respond to the spiritual needs of those who are perplexed
by this reality," whereas *xiejiao* claim that "one merely needs to join their
organization for all one's troubles to be immediately solved" with the sole
objective of increasing the number of recruits in order to control their
minds, their property, and even their bodies, which followers "completely
and unconditionally sacrifice to satisfy the selfish and unspeakable desires
of the master." While new religions "practice their teachings by exhorting
to do good and by bringing benefits to the world, and are constantly developing community applications which are beneficial to society in order to
gain the understanding and support of society," *xiejiao* turn their backs
on social morality and the law, oppose the government, culture, and even
material life, disdain the existing social order and collective ethics, and
constantly attempt to use various means to destroy state institutions and
threaten the life of the people and the security of public property" (Guo,
ed. 2003:51–52).

CONCLUSION: THE END OF MODERN IDEOLOGY AND THE ELEVATION OF RELIGION

In December 2007, an "International symposium on cultic studies" was organized by the Chinese Academy of Social Sciences in Shenzhen to discuss the sociological concept of the "cult"—translated as *mobai tuanti* (膜拜團體) rather than as *xiejiao*. This reflected a shift in scholarly discourse toward a more neutral, sociological understanding of the term. Indeed, the production of books and articles on *xiejiao* by academics seemed to be petering out: perhaps this conference signaled the end of mainstream Chinese academia's active participation in the anti-*xiejiao* discourse. While some of the scholars present advocated finding terms more appropriate to the Chinese cultural background, there was a clear attempt to use more value-neutral terms and to avoid the term *xiejiao*, which was said to have become a purely political concept, to be used in the realm of political propaganda and judiciary proceedings but not in academic research.

Indeed, the importing of two modern paradigms—the revolutionary model in the mid-twentieth century, and the social science of religions paradigm fifty years later—appears at first glance to have only provided new ideological clothing for a category that never changed in its essence, that of *xiejiao*, which became *huidaomen* in the Maoist period and reverted to the *xiejiao* appellation under Jiang Zemin. But the application of modern paradigms reflects an attempt to inscribe the struggle against evil cults into a universal framework: the worldwide struggle against imperialism and feudal oppression in the case of the *huidaomen*, and the struggle against the international menace of destructive cults in the case of contemporary *xiejiao*. In the latter case, however, the recourse to academic institutions to produce social scientific discourses, when these institutions are increasingly integrated into international research circuits, is a change from earlier situations in which the anti-cult discourse was elaborated entirely in relation to the ideological framework of Confucianism or Marxism.

The new Chinese discourse on *xiejiao* combines traditional notions of heretical doctrines with Western elements derived from Christian apologetics, psychology, and the social sciences. The result is a *xiejiao* category that borrows from imperial Chinese ideology a concept of orthodoxy based on notions of order and social harmony (of which the state is the prime protector, with the assistance of religion as an instrument of moral education, or *jiaohua*), and that borrows from Western discourse a universalist approach (which defines "social order," "religion," and so forth in general and abstract terms, citing examples from the whole world without giving a special role of arbiter to the Chinese state or to specific religions recognized as orthodox in China). Whereas anti-*huidaomen* propaganda of the 1950s and 1980s defined these groups almost exclusively as a function of their feudal and counterrevolutionary nature, without giving much consideration to the relationship between such groups and religion, the new discourse places a strong emphasis on the relationship between *xiejiao* and religion, practically defining *xiejiao* as an anti-religion. In striking contrast to the central role of scientism and anti-superstition campaigns that oriented religious policy in the first half of the twentieth century,[7] and that structured the polemic around *qigong* until the end of the 1990s, "science" as an absolute value is rarely called on to discredit *xiejiao*, and "superstition" is not the principal charge made against these groups. Rather, their cardinal sin is their "anti-social" and "anti-human" nature—namely, their ambition to destabilize the socio-political order. Indeed, the discourse of the struggle against superstition and "pseudoscience," which was the chief weapon of the first polemists to attack *qigong* and Falungong in the mid-1990s (Palmer 2007:122–26; 160–62; 170–77), seems to have become less salient since the *xiejiao* label was officially fixed on Falungong in 1999.

A general and universal concept of "religion" has thus become the defining standard. We are far from the doctrine of religion as the opium of the masses, from the Marxist and modernist idea of religion as a relic of the past destined to naturally and gradually disappear, and even from the recent admission in official pronouncements that religion will still last for a long time. What is significant here is the unambiguously benign evaluation of "religion," whose "orthodox" nature is understood quite broadly, rarely specifically mentioning China's five official religions and even embracing new religions.

We can now begin to discern the possible long-term structural consequences of the Falungong affair on China's politico-religious dynamic. Although the Falungong suppression campaign uses all the classical instruments of propaganda and repression of a communist regime, the discourse on *xiejiao* that has emerged from it marks a complete rupture from fifty years of socialist and secularist ideology, a return to the traditional paradigm of the state as protector of the orthodox Order against the heretical and demonic forces of Chaos, and the entrance of Religion onto the stage as a supportive force for protecting social order and the moral and ethical heritage of society.

5   Animal Spirits, Karmic Retribution, Falungong, and the State

Benjamin Penny 裴 凝

On April 25, 1999, between ten and fifteen thousand Falungong (法輪功, Practice of the Wheel of the Law) practitioners gathered outside Zhongnanhai in central Beijing, the compound that houses the most senior officers of the Chinese government and the Communist Party. This was the moment when the name "Falungong" became familiar to the wider world, even if that audience had little idea at the time as to what constituted the movement. It was also the moment when China's leaders became concerned about the profound threat they perceived Falungong to pose. Press reports at the time indicated that practitioners hoped to appeal to the government for official recognition when they gathered outside Zhongnanhai (Zong 2001:49). About three months later the government responded by banning Falungong and launching a savage suppression. Thus, for both the Chinese authorities and movement itself, the relationship between Falungong and the Chinese state was crucial: on the one side, Falungong evidently saw the leadership of the country as a final authority from whom to seek justice and recognition; on the other, Falungong's demonstration was a disturbing eruption of unsanctioned protest and potential subversion. Why both sides held to these positions requires explanation and adumbration, but it is what Falungong expected of the state that is the topic of this chapter. To understand the Falungong position, however, requires taking a step back and asking how they perceived what constituted—or better, what properly constituted—the state, and how their relationship to it should be understood.

The suppression of Falungong has seen some hundreds of adherents sent to jail for terms of up to eighteen years, and some thousands placed in administrative detention in "Re-education through Labor" camps. Millions have severed their connections with the movement, at least publicly, and a considerable number of practitioners has died in custody, although exact figures are hard to obtain. This formidable assault came as a great blow to Falungong, which had gone from strength to strength since it was launched in 1992. What had been since its inception (explicitly, at least) a nonpolitical movement interested in the transformation of practitioners through cultivation of body and mind was forced into taking a stand against an aggressive state apparatus.

Falungong and the Chinese authorities have not always had an antagonistic relationship. From 1992 until the beginning of 1996, Falungong was a registered member of the government's *qigong* (氣功) regulatory authority, the Chinese Association for Scientific Research into Qigong (Zhongguo Qigong Kexue Yanjiu Hui). At this stage of its evolution, as evidenced in the textual corpus, there was little in Falungong that could be seen as obviously political, in a simple, direct sense, let alone as antigovernment. If anything, the scriptures promote an acquiescent and law-abiding polity whose concerns should be with the individual person's own bio-spiritual cultivation rather than with affairs of state.

However, the actions of the government in suppressing Falungong aroused in it a response that changed this stance. The Falungong reaction has broadly taken three forms. First, it has attempted to transform itself into an activist organization, adopting the discourses of human rights familiar to its now largely Western audience, but much less so to its original Chinese followers, in order to argue its case to the world. Falungong's continuing campaign has, therefore, been directed at publicizing the plight of those imprisoned and killed—in recent times their chief allegation has been that practitioners have been killed in order to "harvest" their organs for transplantation—condemning the Chinese authorities, and seeking the assistance of sympathetic governments, nongovernmental organizations (NGOs), and individuals to press their claims.

Second, since the end of 2004 Falungong has supported—some would say sponsored, or even instigated—a campaign attacking the Communist Party itself as an institution. This campaign has been promulgated under the auspices of the newspaper the *Epoch Times* (*Dajiyuan*), which apparently has intimate links with Falungong.[1] Specifically, the attack on the Party has centered on a long document called "Nine Commentaries on the Communist Party" (*Jiuping gongchandang*) available widely in print and on the web, and an associated campaign that urges members of the Communist Party to resign from it and all related organizations.[2]

Third, one of the tasks that has been assigned to Falungong practitioners since 2001 is to "send forth righteous thoughts." The purpose of "sending forth righteous thoughts" is to "clear away the evil dark minions and rotten demons, and eradicate the Communist evil specter and all of the evil factors of the Communist Party in other dimensions."[3] In practice, adherents silently recite two verses written by Li Hongzhi (李洪志, 1951–), the founder and leader of Falungong, for "five to ten minutes" at 6:00 A.M., midday, 6:00 P.M., and midnight (Beijing time), preferably while sitting in meditation and using one of two prescribed hand gestures.[4] The verses must be recited in Chinese—pronunciation guides are provided for non-Chinese speakers. These verses read (in the official translation):

> The Fa rectifies the Cosmos, the Evil is completely eliminated
> (*fa zheng qian kun, xie e quan mie*).
>
> The Fa rectifies Heaven and Earth, immediate retribution in this
> lifetime
> (*fa zheng tian di, xian shi xian bao*).

After reciting the verses inwardly, the practitioner should "focus powerful thoughts in saying the word *Mie* ['to destroy,' 'to extinguish,' 'to exterminate']. The *Mie* word needs to be so strong that it's as large as the cosmic body, encompassing everything and leaving out nothing in any dimension."

It is clear from these campaigns that since the suppression of Falungong, opposition to the Chinese governing authorities has become central to the concerns of the movement, and that practitioners have changed from being acquiescent to the Chinese state to becoming activists against it. We should note, though, that the actions the movement undertakes in relation to the authorities range across registers from the standard political activism we might expect from an orthodox political pressure group to a kind of attempted metaphysical intervention. Since practitioners believe that their actions—political as well as metaphysical—have efficacy, the breadth of activities they engage in implies that, for Falungong, the Chinese state is not simply a creature of mundane politics but is susceptible to action directed against it in the realm of the spiritual.

Underpinning the motivations of practitioners who pursue action against the Chinese state are certain conceptions of the state itself. To understand these conceptions we must take cognizance of Falungong's teachings as they are explained in the authorized writings of the movement.[5] However, the nature of the state does not arise as a distinct topic in the scriptures, so their ideas must be inferred from other parts of the doctrine. This chapter concentrates on two aspects of Falungong's teachings. The first comprises ideas surrounding the belief in the possibility of humans being possessed by the spirits of foxes, weasels, and snakes. These teachings come from early strata in Falungong writings—specifically, the primary scripture of Falungong, *Zhuan Falun* (轉法輪, *Rotating the Wheel of the Law*), which appeared in December 1994, and which comprises edited versions of the nine introductory lectures given to new practitioners by Li Hongzhi. The second set of ideas that I will explore concerns the analysis in Falungong writings of natural disasters that have recently occurred in China and personal tragedies suffered by specific people who have "persecuted" Falungong practitioners. The latter ideas became current only after the suppression and are found on Falungong's websites, notably but not exclusively Minghui.org and its English-language counterpart, Clearwisdom. org. However, before proceeding to these topics, it is necessary to explore some of the ideas about how the Chinese state and the religions of the Chinese people have interacted over time, especially as they relate to the categories of the orthodox and the heterodox.

HETERODOXY AND ORTHODOXY, "EVIL CULTS" AND "RELIGION"

Since the suppression, the Chinese authorities have branded Falungong a *xiejiao* (邪教)—literally, a "heterodox teaching," but consistently translated in official documents as an "evil cult." *Xie,* "heterodox," was opposed in premodern China to *zheng* (正), "true" or "correct," or, in this case most appropriately, "orthodox." The distinction between a *xiejiao* and a *zhengjiao* rested on whether or not the teachings concerned were authorized by the state and its functionaries at a local level, and this authorization was in turn based on the perception of whether or not such teachings were likely to lead to social disruption. A classic early iteration of this view is found in the *Mencius* (late fourth century B.C.E.), where Mencius is discussing the rival philosophers Mozi and Yang Zhu:

> The teachings current in the Empire are those of either the school of Yang or the school of Mo. . . . If the way of Yang and Mo does not subside and the way of Confucius is not proclaimed, the people will be deceived by heterodoxies (*xieshuo,* 邪說) and the path of morality will be blocked. When the path of morality is blocked, then we show animals the way to devour men, and sooner or later it will come to men devouring men. (Mencius 1970:114)[6]

This passage encapsulates the logical trajectory of the argument: if heterodox doctrines are permitted to circulate among the people, they will be deceived by them and will change their behavior in undesirable ways—

Mencius says that Yang Zhu "advocates everyone for himself, which amounts to a denial of one's prince; Mo advocates love without discrimination which amounts to a denial of one's father." Such shifts away from the normative relationships will inevitably lead to disorder and the destruction of human society. A declaration, therefore, that something was heterodox was an invitation to suppression. This is not to say, of course, that the definition of what exactly constituted heterodoxy was consistent over time or space, but simply that, for the state (and people who had cause to appeal to its authorized officers), the ability to label something "heterodox" was always an available weapon in their armory, and that once the label had been approved, certain punitive action was incumbent on the organs of government.

As Christian Jochim has pointed out, by way of comparison with the Roman Catholic Church in medieval Europe, "Only the state in China had the kind of organization and power that could effect religious controls" (Jochim 1986:77). Generally speaking, however, it did not choose to implement those controls as consistently or as harshly as it might have. Indeed, as Hubert Seiwert has argued:

> The issue of orthodoxy and heterodoxy was essentially a political one, since the standards of what was acceptable were defined primarily by political and not by clerical authorities. Certainly, there were internal differences and rivalries between the recognized religions, but as long as the state did not take sides these were not matters of orthodoxy and heterodoxy. The question of whether a certain teaching, ritual practice or deity accorded with Buddhist or Daoist traditions usually did not concern the state. What mattered was the social impact of religious groups. (Seiwert 2003:163)

It is important to stress in this context that a religious teaching branded as "heterodox" did not necessarily see itself in this way: in fact, sometimes the adherents of such teachings regarded themselves either as the real orthodoxy—implying, of course, that those accorded the status of the orthodox in their time were in some way false—or simply as not crossing any boundary of religion, politics, or ethics. For those groups that saw themselves as the true upholders of righteousness and propriety, the hope and aspiration to be accepted as the new orthodoxy (or at least allowed into that class of tolerated beliefs and practices) remained a tenable position even (perhaps, especially) in the face of official condemnation. Susan Naquin also reminds us that within any one broad category of religious groups—in her case, what she calls White Lotus sectarianism—heterodoxy was often a matter of degree and was subject to change: "Just as some

sects were more heterodox that others, so it was possible for a sect to transform itself slowly or rapidly in either direction. Whereas one group might
deliberately make itself more acceptable, another might be persuaded by
a daring leader to adopt a more radical style" (Naquin 1985:290). In any
case, the state's own definitions were also mutable: "Even the definition
of heterodoxy (as set by the state) was very fluid. The Ming and Qing
governments drew the line in different places at different times. A sect
ignored one year as no more than a group of innocent Buddhists might be
prosecuted later as a seditious society" (Naquin 1985:290).[7]

The explicit criminalization of certain religious behaviors and beliefs
appears to date from a Tang edict of 715 targeting people with "white
dress and long hair who falsely claim that Maitreya has descended and
been reborn" (Seiwert 2003:151). Subsequently, the Song prohibited
Manichaeans in 1120, but making laws against certain religions was a
piecemeal activity until the Ming victory, when various independent
regulations were brought together in the new legal code toward the end
of the fourteenth century.[8] The specific use of the term *xiejiao* in such
laws dates from 1642, coming into effect under the Manchu regime just
before the beginning of the Qing dynasty. The term did not enter the
Chinese legal code until the turn of the eighteenth century under the
Kangxi emperor (Liu & Shek:484).[9] In the contemporary Chinese context,
"organizing or utilizing" an organization based on a *xiejiao* in order "to
undermine the implementation of national laws and administrative regulations, . . . to cheat other people thereby causing death to a person . . . or
to have sexual relations with a woman or to swindle property" are all
explicitly outlawed in the 1997 Chinese Criminal Code (Lo 1998:161,
285).[10] In October 1999, when the suppression of Falungong was in full
swing, the National People's Congress adopted a much broader "Anti-Cult
Law" explicitly banning what it termed *xiejiao,* and issued accompany-
ing judicial explanations. Such organizations, it says, "shall be resolutely
banned according to law and all of their criminal activities shall be dealt
with severely. . . . Operating under the guise of religion, *Qigong* or other
illicit forms, which disturb social order and jeopardise people's life and
property, must be banned according to law and punished resolutely."[11]

Thus, when the Chinese government branded Falungong with the designation *xiejiao,* it was walking the well-trodden path of using the accusation
of heterodoxy to demand the group's eradication. It is, therefore, pertinent
that instead of using one of the standard renderings of *xiejiao* into English,
the government chose to deploy the term "evil cult" in its publications for
those markets. For an English-language readership, "evil cult" brings to

mind, I would argue, the pejorative discourse used by the so-called anti-cult movement, with its accusations of "brainwashing" and attempts to "deprogram" unfortunate young people who have fallen under the spell of charismatic monsters. Classifying Falungong as an "evil cult" also places it alongside recent violent and sometimes apocalyptic religious groups in the West and Japan such as the People's Temple, Heaven's Gate, the Branch Davidians, and Aum Shinrikyo—a connection the Chinese authorities have encouraged in their publications. This rhetoric acts as an invitation to denounce Falungong in a way that "heterodox teaching" would not: in the West, where these texts are read, the beneficial and harmful valuations given to orthodoxy and heterodoxy, respectively, are not as clear as they once were. "Teachings" are always good, of course, and if they are "heterodox," perhaps—for a contemporary Western reader—that simply means they are transgressive and interesting.

Although the Chinese state now labels Falungong an "evil cult," it had originally accepted its membership in the national organization in charge of *qigong*, as noted above. *Qigong* is a modern umbrella term used to describe a variety of systems, usually involving some form of exercise or meditation or both, best described as "bio-spiritual cultivation." All forms of *qigong* (as its name implies) have to do with the cultivation and manipulation of *qi* (氣), a word that originally referred to breath, or vapor. In the 1980s and 1990s China experienced a boom in *qigong* practice, with probably hundreds of millions of people actively engaged in one form of cultivation or another.[12] This enthusiasm was so pronounced that it acquired in Chinese the name "*qigong* fever" (*qigong re*). This fever produced several journals, two newspapers, many hundreds of new *qigong* forms, thousands of books, celebrity masters, television specials, controversies, *qigong* sanatoriums, mass public displays, trade fairs, and psychoses—diseases caused by "*qigong* deviation" now appear in China's psychiatric manuals (N. Chen 2003b:77–106). Falungong emerged into this hive of activity in 1992, at first as just one of many *qigong* forms. But its popularity grew through the 1990s until, by the time of the Zhongnanhai demonstration and subsequent suppression, it claimed supremacy. Like most of the *qigong* groups that emerged in the 1980s and early 1990s, Falungong was a creature of its times. For all the resonances that can be found with Chinese religious thought and practice from earlier periods in Li Hongzhi's writings, his is a movement that could only have appeared in the late twentieth century. His writings are infused, for instance, with an all-pervasive scientistic rhetoric reflecting the obsessive concern with laboratory testing and empirical measurement of *qi* in the 1980s. In addition, born in the infancy of the People's Republic and experiencing the Cultural Revolution as a teenager, Li appears constantly aware of the political context in which he is operating—even in the essay entitled "No Politics" (Li H. 2001).[13] He also makes use of the imagery of the Communist Party in some of his own visual representations, as I have shown elsewhere (Penny 2002), and Falungong is described in a biography from 1993 in these terms:

> Falun Dafa founded by Mr Li Hongzhi is like a red sun rising from the east, whose radiance with unlimited vitality will illuminate every corner of the earth, nourish all the living things, warm the whole world and play an unparalleled role in the realisation of an ideal and perfect human society on this planet.[14]

Despite Falungong's formal affiliation to *qigong*, it is, according to Li Hongzhi, a superior form offering nothing less than "salvation to humankind" (Li H. 1994:1.1).[15] This is a grand claim by any measure, and part of his justification for it is that, unlike other forms of *qigong*, Falungong does not, in fact, cultivate *qi*. Practitioners of Falungong are, apparently, transported beyond mere *qi* cultivation by Li Hongzhi when they first become adherents. Thus beginners in Falungong have already moved (or been moved) beyond the goal of standard *qigong*. Practitioners are aiming at what is known in Falungong texts as "consummation" (*yuanman*)—one of many Falungong terms borrowed from Buddhism—which Li explained in his 1998 lecture delivered in Geneva as the culmination of cultivation, equivalent to Buddhist nirvana or Daoist "corpse-liberation" (Li H. 1998:60). Falungong is therefore a system that claims to offer universal salvation, it has a master who can intervene metaphysically in his followers' bodies, and its practitioners aim at consummation. In addition, Li Hongzhi's books have the status of scriptures among his followers, and practitioners have regular, prescribed individual and group practice; Li teaches the existence of deities in the form of what he calls "Buddhas, Daos, and Gods," and that the world of our existence is but one of many dimensions in which we live simultaneously in different forms. In other words, although its original affiliation was with *qigong*, Falungong appears to have acquired many of the traits we could expect of a religion.

However, Li Hongzhi has always explicitly and consistently rejected the category "religion" to describe Falungong, distinguishing, in particular, between outward manifestations of religiosity and inward practice, or "cultivation." In his discussion of Buddhism (against which Falungong often defines itself), Li maintains that what Sakyamuni taught, as well as "Tiantai, Huayan, Zen Buddhism, Pure Land, Tantrism, etc.," includes forms of cultivation, but the cultivation component is not the same as the religious component and can be distinguished from it. Here, as I have argued elsewhere, Li follows a line of interpretation of religion favored in the People's Republic, where religious phenomena can be separated into what is seen as essential—usually texts, philosophy, and meditation—and what is seen as inessential—namely, ritual, institutions, and popular practices like fortune-telling (Penny 2005). But there are also bureaucratic and pragmatic reasons for Falungong to reject the label of religion.

As far as the Chinese government is concerned, "religion" is primarily an administrative category, and in these official terms China has only five religions—Buddhism, Daoism, Islam, Protestant Christianity, and Roman Catholic Christianity—each of which has its own state-run association that administers its places of worship, its clerics, its publications, and so on. Other religious or spiritual activities fall outside the government's category of "religion" and are consigned to the categories of "superstition" (typically "feudal superstition") or "heterodox teachings" (or "evil cults"); as much as we might imagine that "cults," even evil ones, would fall within the analytical category of "religion," under the Chinese administrative arrangements they do not. Organizations or activities that are categorized as "superstitious" or labeled "heterodox teachings" immediately engender suspicion and condemnation. Thus, for the Chinese government Falungong was not a religion simply because it was not one of the authorized five. And for Falungong to have claimed the status of "religion" while not associating itself with one of the five authorized religions would have been to invite negative government action as soon as it was launched.

ANIMAL SPIRITS AND FALUNGONG'S CONCEPTION OF THE STATE

If Falungong's view of ultimate reality does not stop with humans in their ordinary lives, the society in which they live, and the processes that govern them, it is reasonable to assume that, as we have seen in the discussion above of "sending forth righteous thoughts," their conception of the state itself is not limited to the mundane concerns of how to construct an institution that will best manage a society and an economy. Although Li Hongzhi is never explicit in his writings on the subject of how the state is constituted and what its relationship to religion ought to be, there are specific notions about these themes implicit in his teachings that echo earlier conceptions of the nature of the state. These conceptions, in particular, relate to the idea that the state is properly the determinant of orthodox religion, that the religion so honored is a national (rather than local or regional) phenomenon, and that the role of this national religion is to support the state by, among others things, promoting social cohesion and cleansing the country of pernicious entities. During the Tang dynasty, when Daoism held sway in the religious world—partly as a source of legitimation for the ruling house, by virtue of their sharing the family name Li with Laozi (in the traditional accounts of his life)—Daoist leaders "were not only summoned to render religious advice, but were even viewed as protectors of the realm, whose engagement with superhuman forces enabled them to thwart nefarious plots and avert all manner of disasters," as Russell Kirkland (2004:146) has observed. Both the Western tradition of research on Chinese political history and the indigenous Chinese Confucian traditions of scholarship on the nature of Chinese government have tended to obscure, for different reasons, the religious underpinnings of the Chinese imperial institution and the system of government that derived from it. Throughout premodern China the state arrogated to itself the right to determine the limits of acceptable religiosity, whether that meant promoting some religions or banning others; yet almost without exception, China's ruling houses also claimed their legitimate right to rule from the unseen powers of the cosmos, regularly sacrificed to them, and sought the assistance of intermediaries in the form of one or another kind of religious specialist to maintain their relationship in good condition. We see some of these ideas on the nature of the state lurking behind Li's teachings on the possibility of humans being possessed by the spirits of foxes, weasels, and snakes, and it is necessary to digress briefly into that lore before returning to the main argument.

When Falungong first appeared in 1992, it was one of many varieties of *qigong* available; in a 1993 compendium of *qigong*, it appears as only one of several hundred forms described (Wu 1993). To gain a toehold in this crowded *qigong* marketplace, Falungong first had to differentiate itself from its competitors. One way it did this was to blacken the reputation of those varieties of *qigong* currently in circulation. Thus a recurrent theme throughout *Zhuan Falun* is the corruption of what were known as "*qigong* circles" in the China of the early 1990s. It was a potentially dangerous world for the aspiring cultivator: "Nowadays," Li said, "sham *qigong*, phony *qigong*, and those people possessed by spirits have all made up something at will to deceive people, and their number exceeds that of genuine *qigong* practices by many times" (Li H. 1994:1.4). Li wrote about some fake *qigong* masters in this way:

> Some sham *qigong* masters can be identified from their speeches and
> conduct, or by what they say and what they are after. All those *qigong*

masters making such statements usually have spirit or animal possession. Just look at the way a *qigong* master possessed by a fox eats a chicken. When this person gobbles it up, he is not even willing to spit out the bones. (Li H. 1994:7.1)

In this passage, evidence for Li's assertion that fake *qigong* masters are possessed by fox spirits is found in their assumption of the character of the animal spirit that has possessed them—in this case, eating chicken as a fox would. I should note at this point that the word Li uses that is translated as "possession" (附體, *futi*) has the literal meaning of "attaching to the body": in Li's text, "people who are possessed" are literally "people who have something attaching to their body." But these spirits can also attach themselves to other things. When Li speaks of the process of consecrating a statue of the Buddha, he notes that it is a great mistake to ask a fake *qigong* master to provide this service because "a fox or a weasel will sneak onto the Buddha statue," turning the righteous practice of making offerings to the Buddha into a perverse and dangerous one (Li H. 1994:5.7). These ideas are still current—Thomas DuBois reports that a contemporary healer in Tianjin diagnosed the cause of some strange occurrences in a particular house to be "that the Guanyin statue in the front room was possessed by a fox spirit" (2005b:69). *Qigong* masters who are possessed by animal spirits can also spread this contagion through the circulation of their books. Li tells us that their publications are full of snakes, foxes, and weasels that will leap out at you from the words on the page while you are reading them.

Li's teachings about how people become possessed by animal spirits are linked closely with his ideas about cultivation and the acquisition of what he calls "supernormal powers"—things like the ability to see into other dimensions, the ability to heal, and so on. As he understands it, these powers are gained as a byproduct of the righteous cultivation he teaches, underpinned as it is by a strict moral code and a disciplined approach to practice. This road is not easy: practitioners inevitably encounter tribulations that they must overcome in order to purify their bodies and progress up the ladder of cultivation. As one gains spiritual power, supernormal abilities appear naturally, but in an echo of much older Chinese teachings across all the major religious traditions, these powers are not to be displayed. Healing others is explicitly banned.

Master Li, of course, has the ability to rid people of any animal spirit that has attached itself to them. He did this routinely as part of the bodily purification he performed as people listened to the introductory series of nine lectures he gave in the early days of Falungong between 1992 and

1994. This purification happened to people unawares as they listened to his words and was necessary for them to begin cultivation. Apparently, since that time, he has been performing this cleansing of "those who truly practice cultivation on their own" on a case-by-case basis wherever they may be. Intriguingly, along with this bodily purification he insists on practitioners "throwing away the spirit tablet for the fox or weasel that [they] previously enshrined" (Li H. 1994:3.8).

These teachings relate to a long-standing question in Chinese history. The question can be summarized in this way: For what purposes and by what means can and should excessive and improper cults (淫祀, *yinsi*) be eradicated?[16] While this question places religion at its core, we see that it bears significantly on the ways Falungong views the nature and role of the state.

When Daoism as an organized religion began in 142 C.E., with the revelation from Lord Lao, the Most High, to Zhang Ling of a new compact between Heaven and Man, a new imprimatur was given to a struggle that had been waged sporadically, even then, for centuries. The message that was revealed was not limited to Zhang, or his clan, or his locality. It encompassed the whole of the known world, and the new doctrine that became known as the "Way of the Celestial Masters" was intended to change the religious landscape of China. As Michel Strickmann observed, "Chang Tao-ling and his immediate followers clearly effected a religious revolution. They inaugurated a new dispensation that defined itself, then as now, not in relation to Buddhism or 'Confucianism,' but rather in antithesis to the false gods whom the benighted populace worshipped with blood offerings" (1979:165). Indeed, one of the defining characteristics of Daoism, according to Strickmann, was the worship of "the pure emanations of the Tao rather than the vulgar gods of the people at large." More recently he wrote: "The chief rival of early Taoism was not Buddhism, and not the so-called Confucian state. Rather it was the despised and neglected 'nameless religion' of the people, the scores of local deities and the hundreds of practitioners who invoked and embodied them" (Strickmann 2002:4). The textual record of Daoist history since that time is replete with examples of true Daoists overcoming locally powerful, exploitative, arrogant gods who keep their neighbourhoods in fear and ignorance. Powerful Daoists typically subjugate the defeated minor deity and bind it to serve in the forces of the Dao thereafter. The same cleansing dynamic occurs in Buddhist stories, of course, but in those the denouement comes not with subjugation but with the defeated deity accepting the Triple Gem and honoring the teachings of the Buddha.

Essentially, the crusades of both individual Daoists and Buddhists as they roamed the countryside were, they believed, efficacious because of the greater power of their deities and doctrines compared with that of the tyrannical local gods. It is not that these bully gods were false for their Daoist and Buddhist detractors, in the sense that they did not have the powers they claimed—the opposite was the case; rather, it was the nature of the worship they demanded that rendered them excessive and improper. It is important to stress that it was taken as a given that the local gods did actually have spiritual power when people spoke and wrote of them in premodern China. The analysis of these authors concerning what was acceptable and what was excessive and improper was based on the notions of codified versus chaotic, pure versus blood-soaked, and orthodox versus heterodox—the *zheng* and *xie* that we have seen earlier.

Clearly the goal of both Daoists and Buddhists, in medieval times and later, was the imposition of a new orthodoxy over China, a project that, of course, required whatever government happened to be in power to acquiesce to their desires. Indeed, the highest goal was to gain a degree of symbiosis with the state itself, in the form of a declared or undeclared theocracy, a situation that existed at times for long periods in Chinese history. And although relations between Buddhism and Daoism were sometimes antagonistic—at times they competed directly for the attentions of the emperor—both saw the emanations of local religion as prime targets for eradication. Promoting and enforcing any new orthodoxy required both government action in the terrestrial realm as well religious action—including the eradication of improper spiritual powers and their servants on earth—in the metaphysical realm.

A dynamic very like this, it seems to me, is at work in Li Hongzhi's discussions of animal possession. His claim is that he offers a new revelation, a cultivation practice that will grant salvation to humankind. Not only is it, therefore, superior to all other forms of *qigong*, but many of the Masters associated with those other forms are powerful only because they are possessed. Li's powers, based as they are on righteousness, inevitably triumph over the trifling spirits of the foxes, weasels, or snakes with their insatiable demands from the benighted folk who have succumbed to their wiles. Li tells a story about one of his triumphs in *Zhuan Falun*. It begins several centuries ago:

> Back in the Ming Dynasty there was a cultivator who got possessed by a snake when he was cultivating. He never managed to finish his cultivation. He died, and the snake took over his body and eventually cultivated a human form.

When Li Hongzhi first went Guizhou province to teach, he tells us, a person came to one of his classes saying his grand master wanted to see Li. Li refused, claiming he didn't have the time. The grand master—actually the snake spirit from the Ming—apparently became upset and transformed back into the snake he truly was in order to challenge him. Li says that he "caught it in my hand and used an extremely powerful energy called Dissolving Energy to melt its lower body into water. Its upper body slithered back to where it came from." Later,

> a young follower of his contacted the Assistant in charge of the Guizhou Assistance Center, and told her that his grandmaster wanted to see her. . . . She entered a pitch black cave and couldn't see anything, except for a shadow that was sitting there, with its eyes emitting green light. When the eyes opened, the cave lit up and when the eyes closed, the cave went dark. The shadow said in a local dialect, "Li Hongzhi is coming again. This time none of us will misbehave. I was wrong. Li Hongzhi is here to save people." His follower asked him, "Grandmaster, please stand up. What's wrong with your legs?" He replied, "I can't stand anymore. My legs were injured." After he was asked how they got injured, he began to talk about how he made trouble. But then in 1993 . . . he messed with me again. He was always doing terrible things and tried to ruin my transmission of the Great Law, so I completely destroyed him. (Li H. 1994:5.7)

This story is strongly redolent of the cleansing stories from premodern times discussed above. Li appears here as a new Master with a national dispensation who meets with a locally powerful deity on his grand tour. The arrogant and untrustworthy local bully challenges the interloper, only to find that he is ruthlessly and easily overpowered. The new Law gains a victory, a new patch of territory is cleansed, and the unfortunate populace of the area can now turn to the righteous path and seek salvation.

The claim that lies behind this story and the whole complex surrounding animal possession and false *qigong* masters in Falungong is that Li's new dispensation is the new orthodoxy. He arrogates to himself the role of national savior, offering a way forward for individuals and for the country. It is important in this context to note that until only one month prior to the announcement of the suppression of Falungong by the government in July 1999—by which time it was obvious to all observers that Falungong was going to be banned—Li had never made any statements criticizing the Party or the Chinese system of government. Indeed, far from encouraging subversion, he urged his practitioners to be model patriotic citizens. In this context we should take seriously what Falungong practitioners themselves said when they gathered outside Zhongnanhai in April 1999—that they were appealing to the government for official recognition, that Falungong was not the anti-social, superstitious, retrogressive cult it was accused of being, and also that it had the right to exist as a state-sanctioned activity.[17] Implicitly there was also the maximalist hope that it would be recognized as the new doctrine of salvation for the nation by the state itself.

Thus, lurking behind Li's teachings on animal spirits is a conception of the state as the organ that determines religious orthodoxy, that recognizes that one role of a national religion is to cleanse the country of pernicious spiritual entities (as the state itself does for pernicious terrestrial ones), and that elevates such a national religion to the status of savior of the nation. This, of course, echoes earlier Chinese conceptions of the symbiotic relationship of the state and the national religious orthodoxy; it also, importantly, places the sage in a position of counselor to the emperor, a model of governmental authority that Anna Seidel (1983) magnificently analyzed for the early medieval period, and characterizes the imperial house as a quasi-religious institution. The religious character of the state is also seen in the second set of teachings I will discuss, namely, those that refer to natural disasters that have recently occurred in China and personal tragedies suffered by people who have "persecuted" Falungong practitioners.

THE STATE IN FALUNGONG'S TEACHINGS
ON KARMIC RETRIBUTION

Beginning in May 2001, almost two years after the suppression began, Falungong websites regularly began to post articles that came to be grouped under the heading "Good Is Rewarded, Evil Provokes Retribution."[18] These postings have continued to the present and take two forms. The first and most numerous concerns individuals in China who have either gone out of their way to help Falungong practitioners or have actively participated in the suppression of Falungong. In these stories the people who perform these perceived good or bad deeds are rewarded or punished by good or bad things happening in their lives. The second set of postings takes a broader regional or city focus, interpreting freak weather events as "warnings" to desist from persecuting Falungong practitioners.

There are literally hundreds of stories of personal retribution on the Falungong websites, and almost all follow the same pattern; in postings from a sample period between August and October 2005, "persecutors" of Falungong apparently met with the following grisly catalogue of disasters:

they have died or been severely injured in car accidents, have been blinded by rocks flying into their eyes, been struck down with femoral necrosis, have developed pancreatitis or have acquired lung, liver, intestinal, oesophageal, or colon cancer. They have had brain hemorrhages, kidney failure, stroke, heart attacks, and have been diagnosed with AIDS. They have committed suicide by poisoning, have drowned, suffered unexplained paralysis, have been killed while making firecrackers, and have been chased by lightning. One child of a "persecutor" has developed "psychosis," while the buildings on the family's farm all collapsed and the roof flew off their chicken coop.

Disasters on a community scale are less frequently noted. Nonetheless, over the last few years catastrophes in several localities have been blamed on the activities of court officers, police, prison guards, and others who have taken part in the suppression of Falungong and who live and work in those districts. Min County in Gansu, for instance, encountered "the flood of the century," with 30 dead, 16 missing, and 17 injured, plus thousands of *mu* of crops, tens of kilometers of roads and embankments, and some bridges destroyed. This is blamed on activities in the "Pingantan [i.e., Ping'antan] Labor Camp" in the same province.[19] More bizarrely, due to activities of several city officials "actively following orders from Jiang [Zemin] and his political gang," on the morning of the Qingming festival in 2002, in Shuangcheng in Heilongjiang,

> It began to rain . . . [and the next morning] the sky suddenly turned dark. Yellow sand fell from the sky. Then at noon, muddy rain started to fall, mixed with some snow. Yellow dirt covered the cars, houses, stairs, and windows on every street. Somebody asked, "It rained for a whole day yesterday, and there was no wind. Where did the sand come from?" The temperature continued to drop on the morning of April 8, and heavy snow began to fall. The phenomenon of sudden hot weather, followed by sudden cold weather, sand falling from the sky and unusual snowy weather after Ching Ming Day is completely abnormal. It is a warning to the people from Heaven.[20]

Among other reports, in 2001, high temperatures, drought, and a plague of locusts hit Xilin'guole in Inner Mongolia,[21] and an earthquake of magnitude 8.1 occurred in Qinghai.[22] In 2002, "repeated sandstorms inundated Beijing,"[23] and storms and gale force winds struck Hubei.[24] In 2003, six provinces suffered severe flooding.[25] In 2005, a rare autumn drought occurred in Jiangsu.[26]

The general understanding of why people or communities suffer the consequences of their actions comes from an interpretation of the operation of karma (the law of cause and effect), specifically, the idea that karmic retribution can occur in this lifetime.[27] This more expanded discussion comes from April 2002:

> In the end, good will always be rewarded with good, and evil will meet with evil. Throughout Chinese history, any dictator who tyrannized his people inevitably met his own destruction. Innumerable facts from history have proven that any persecution of cultivators would enrage Heaven and Earth and bring endless disasters to the people and the country. The persecution of Falun Dafa by Jiang [Zemin]'s gang of political hooligans has put hundreds of millions of Chinese people in a very dangerous situation. Since 1999, when the persecution of Falun Dafa started, Mainland China has repeatedly and constantly encountered natural and man-made disasters. Those are the mercy warnings from Heaven. The Gods are warning those in authority to stop their atrocities. Through these disasters they warn the world to see the truth of the persecution of Falun Dafa and not be deceived by the lies or do things against heavenly principles and their conscience; otherwise, if the warnings are disregarded, people will harm not only others but themselves as well.[28]

This passage deserves close scrutiny. The idea that good acts are rewarded and bad acts punished is standard and uncontroversial Buddhism. However, the idea that a ruler would be punished for his misrule and that the "the people and the country" would suffer because "Heaven and Earth" were enraged departs from any standard Buddhist reading of the operation of karma. To add to this, that these actions are intended as "mercy warnings" (慈悲警示, *cibei jingshi*) from Heaven is to move into the realms of quite other Chinese philosophical traditions entirely.

Early in China's textual tradition, the mutual interlinking of Heaven, Earth, and humankind was understood in terms of "sympathetic resonance" (感應, *ganying*). Based on the notion that things of like substances resonate with each other over a distance—such as when one stringed instrument literally resonates when another in the same room is plucked—this idea formed the basis of action under the complex and elaborate system of correlative cosmology. In this scheme, which reached its height in Han writings, natural disasters were often interpreted as consequences of the actions of the sovereign. Robert Sharf summarizes the "Hongfan" chapter of the *Shangshu* (the *Classic of History*, or *Book of Documents*), an ancient text dating to before the second century B.C.E., to the effect that

> excessive rain results from an emperor's wildness, excessive drought from arrogance, heat from indolence, cold from hasty judgment, and winds from stupidity. The view that anomalies in the heavens, disturbances on earth, earthquakes, avalanches, sightings of unusual birds or

animals, and other such wonders were a reflection of the behavior of
the king has been termed "phenomenalism" by Western sinologists.
(Sharf 2002:88)

The introduction of Buddhism into China integrated this "phenomenalism" as an additional layer into the doctrine of karma, which brought its
own version of a natural law of response and retribution. The complicated and uneven ways that elements of Buddhism were understood or
misunderstood, or accepted, rejected, or changed by preexisting native
Chinese systems of thought, were all discussed among Chinese Buddhists.
Similarly, the compatibility of the traditional Chinese understandings of
reward and punishment based on sympathetic resonance and the new law
of karmic retribution was sometimes commented on by authors sympathetic to Buddhism.[29]

At the same time, during the Six Dynasties period a subgenre of more
popular *zhiguai* stories, or "Records of the Strange," appeared that was
concerned with ideas of retribution in Buddhist and non-Buddhist contexts. As Sharf comments:

Such stories emphasized the need for moral reform through graphic
and often entertaining descriptions of the rewards and punishments
that await one in one's future life. The punishments suffered by sinners
are often horrific, but the tales illustrate that it is never too late to
mend one's ways, as one can expunge one's prior transgressions
through meritorious acts. (Sharf 2002:94)

Later in the Song, the genre of *shanshu* (善書, morality books) made extensive use of the idea of divine retribution. Its most well-known and widespread
representative, the 1165 *Taishang ganying pian* (*Treatise of the Most High
on Action and Retribution*), listed the various punishments— typically the
reduction of a person's lifespan by a certain number of days—for any given
transgression (Brokaw 1991:36–43). Importantly, by this time and in this
milieu, there are agents in Heaven that perform the retribution, that is to
say, Heaven is seen to be a conscious entity that reacts to human action
rather than an impersonal automatic operator in a system of natural law.

Thus the view of Heaven (or "Heaven and Earth") that is present in
Falungong's reading of the etiology of natural disasters and personal tragedy finds antecedents deep in Chinese religious history. While Falungong
possesses a strong understanding of personal punishment for personal sin,
it also, I would argue, preserves an ancient model of large-scale heavenly
response to the transgressions of the central authorities of the state. Hence
when Falungong articles speak of "mercy warnings from Heaven" they

are echoing a cosmological ideology that reaches back deep into Chinese governmental thought. Under this ideology, the actions of the state are not simply a matter for judgment and action by the citizenry but have implications for the cosmos as a whole. The state, therefore, is a metaphysical entity, the middle term between Heaven and humankind, and when the state misbehaves, a reaction is necessarily induced from Heaven.

This understanding of the state is, in many ways, compatible with that implied in the discussion of animal spirit possession. For Falungong, the state is by its nature an intermediary between Heaven and humankind that is cosmically enjoined to act in a correct way, including the proper authorization of a religious orthodoxy, consisting, in this case, of the teachings of Li Hongzhi. For practitioners, the suppression of Falungong since 1999 is not just an issue of human rights—indeed, it may not at base be an issue of human rights at all—but a contravention of the law of the cosmos. The basic moral teachings of Falungong, the triumvirate of "truthfulness, compassion, and forbearance" (*zhen, shan, ren*), are, according to Li Hongzhi, "the most fundamental characteristic of this universe" and are "in the microscopic particles of air, rock, wood, soil, iron and steel, the human body, as well as in all matter" (Li H. 1994:1.3). To deny the righteousness of Falungong and to persecute its practitioners is, therefore, to go against the course of the universe.

Under these circumstances, it is no wonder that practitioners are enjoined to "send forth righteous thoughts" in order "to eliminate the evil." Nor is it surprising that the Communist Party is thought to have "evil factors . . . in other dimensions." The battle between Falungong and the CCP is a truly cosmic one. These ideas are reflected in the "Nine Commentaries on the Chinese Communist Party" mentioned at the beginning of this chapter. The title of the fourth commentary refers to the Party as an "anti-universe force" and declares that,

> in the last hundred years, the sudden invasion by the communist specter has created a force against nature and humanity, causing limitless agony and tragedy. It has also pushed civilization to the brink of destruction. Having committed all sorts of atrocities that violate the Tao and oppose heaven and the earth, it has become an extremely malevolent force against the universe . . . the communist movement is destined to fail since it violates the law of the universe and runs counter to heaven. Such an anti-universe force will surely be punished by the heaven's will and divine spirits.[30]

Falungong emerged into a China where the memory of the exercise of force by the state against its own people—the massacres in Beijing of

1989—was only three years old. The previous generation of leaders of the same regime had exerted brutal, often fatal, force against followers of various religions in earlier decades. The suppression of Falungong in 1999 can be seen, therefore, as simply the most recent iteration of a pattern of the uncompromising display of power by the Chinese state directed against recalcitrant religious groups. Falungong appeared in 1992, and Li Hongzhi's teachings necessarily reflect that context, reveling in the discourses of the present. Yet we can observe the lineaments of a particular model of the Chinese state in them—one that promotes its role as the arbiter of proper religion, as it did in imperial times. However, for Falungong the state also represents the middle term between Heaven and humankind in the great cosmic performance of governance. In viewing the state in this light, Falungong echoes doctrines about the nature of rulership, the behavior of sovereigns, and the fundamental relationships between the people, the state, and the cosmos that are rooted deep in Chinese history.

6 Christianity and "Adaptation to Socialism"

Ryan Dunch 唐日安

The Chinese Communist Party (CCP) is uncomfortable with religion. Religious adherence in Chinese society is growing extremely rapidly. Two simple and incontestable statements, yet in the contradictions between them lie tensions with profound implications for Chinese society. Those tensions, particularly as they pertain to Protestant Christianity, are the subject of this chapter.

When "freedom of religious belief" was reinstated in 1978, Chinese Communist Party leaders expected that only a small remnant of elderly religious believers remained, and that the disappearance of religion from socialist China was only a matter of time. Permitting open religious activities was, therefore, initially seen as a pragmatic and temporary concession to a small social minority, a concession that could have only relatively minor harmful consequences. That expectation was challenged and displaced as religious activities of all sorts gathered influence and adherents, including among the young. This chapter traces how the policy of limited religious toleration opened up an implicit pluralism that religious believers sought to claim and expand upon, and that the state sought to manage and circumscribe. The upshot has been an uneasy equilibrium in which Christianity and other religions highlight the pluralism that exists in Chinese society but that remains only implicit in party-state ideology, while the state's effort to ensure that religious activities and teachings "adapt to" socialist society, and to the national agenda as the party-state defines it, influences the theological and organizational expressions of Protestantism in China (including those outside of the officially recognized aegis).

The interaction between religion and the state in the People's Republic of China is often cast as one of state control and religious resistance to that control, particularly in the cases of Christians, Tibetan Buddhists, and sectarian movements. However, the control-and-resistance paradigm is insufficient to convey the complexity of these interactions (Goossaert 2006a; Cao 2006). It is certainly true that the balance of power rests overwhelmingly with the state, which frames the policies and regulations that govern religion in China and exercises the coercive measures that enforce them. Nevertheless, state policy is not simply imposed, and religious organizations and individuals have participated in constructing and modifying official ideological positions on religion and the policies and regulations governing religion. Indeed, in requiring the formation of nationwide "patriotic religious organizations" (愛國宗教組織, *aiguo zongjiao zuzhi*) for each of the five religions recognized by the state (Buddhism, Daoism, Islam, and Catholic and Protestant Christianity), Party policy actually endorsed those bodies as participants in a dialogue with the state, albeit on unequal terms.

The alternative model presented in this chapter is that Protestant Christians have been participants in a "long conversation" with the state (borrowing from Comaroff & Comaroff 1991) that has led to modifications on both sides about the place of Christianity in China's "socialist modernity." On the state side, the persistence and growth of religion in China since 1978, confounding official expectations, has induced adjustments in state ideology to allow for the incorporation of religious believers as legitimate participants in the nation. As we will see, religious leaders, with Protestants prominent among them, played an important role through intellectual and political advocacy in bringing these adjustments about. They may have been less than content with the result, however—namely, an increasing state reliance on regulation to clarify the duties and limits of religious believers and institutions. Just as importantly, the state has translated its theoretical *concession* that religion can be compatible with socialism into a *prescription* about the kinds of religious ideology and activity that ought to be regarded as compatible with socialism, and it has required religions to adapt themselves accordingly, under the rubric of "adaptation to socialism" (與社會主意社會相適應, *yu shehui zhuyi shehui xiangshiying*), a slogan first coined in 1993 that has become a staple of official rhetoric since 2000. Here again, however, Protestants have played a more active role than a model of control and resistance would allow, because the prescription that religion must adapt to socialism has fueled a movement for "theological reconstruction" (神學建設, *shenxue jianshe*) that has been embraced by some church leaders to sanction theological positions they see as desirable. Moreover, although not treated in depth here, intellectuals outside church circles have seized upon Christian theologizing as an intellectual and cultural project that has become institutionally embedded as "Sino-Christian theology" in academic institutions and scholarly networks within and beyond the People's Republic (Li Q. 2007). In short, what we see in the case of Protestant Christianity and the state in post-Mao China is a dynamic relationship in which each side influences the other within the field of discourse marked out by the terms "religion," "modernity," and "the nation."

CONTESTING CHRISTIANITY'S PLACE IN THE MODERN NATION BEFORE 1949

The question of the place of Christians in the nation has beset Chinese Christianity throughout its modern history. Protestant missionaries in the nineteenth century tried to position Protestant Christianity as the uniquely modern religion, fully compatible with science, progress, universal education, and constitutional government, and, indeed, *necessary* to them. In the early Republican period, global missionary evangelists such as Sherwood Eddy presented Christianity as the one "universal" religion left standing and growing while other beliefs fell by the wayside in the course of historical progress, while Chinese Protestants welcomed the opportunities the new politics afforded them to take prominent roles on the national stage, as did some Catholics as well (Dunch 2001a, chap. 5; Hayhoe 1996). Chinese Christians thus entered public life individually and collectively, and founded new national publications and organizations— most notably both the large national denominations merging different missionary churches from the same traditions and the National Christian Council, formed in 1922 under Chinese rather than missionary leadership (Latourette 1973:794–801).

Developments in the 1920s made the position of Christians in the nation much less secure. The more strident anti-imperialist nationalism of that era made the Protestant discourse of progress far less persuasive, and both Protestants and Catholics were placed on the defensive in the face of accusations of hidden agendas and complicity with imperialist exploitation. At the same time, the emergence of sectarian Protestant movements and of related theological controversies among missionaries and Chinese Protestants undermined what had been a relative consensus about the Protestant role in the nation (Bays 1996). Add to that the political uncertainty of the warlord period and the new politics of the revolutionary party-state, and it is small wonder that we can trace a relative shift in

Protestant circles toward revivalist religion emphasizing individual spiritual experience, on the one hand, and focused efforts at social amelioration in particular areas at the margins of state capacity, on the other (Dunch 2001a, chap. 6).

As other chapters in this volume explore, over the same decades, successive Chinese states were attempting to formulate the place of religions within the modern Chinese nation. A fundamental step in that process was the adoption of the term *zongjiao* ("religion") as a global comparative category, which then served simultaneously as an organizing and an exclusionary device in juxtaposition to both modernity and the state (and to science and superstition). In contrast to Japan, where elements of popular religion were incorporated into the new national religion of Shinto (Hardacre 1989), in China the ritual practices of the Chinese empire—the focus of a whole wing of the imperial bureaucracy—became the non-religion "Confucianism," while popular religion became "superstition," the rhetorical foil to religion and an *impediment* to the construction of national modernity. In the absence of either official ritual or popular religion, the modern Chinese nation-state took shape in a default secularity that had at its core what one scholar has called "the culture of the barracks"—namely, an authoritarian statist nationalism shorn of agreed-upon cultural content (Cohen 1995).

In treating religion, modernity, and the state in China, therefore, we are discussing two completely new terms plus one older one, "the state," infused with substantially new content. All three took on their novel meanings over the late nineteenth and early twentieth centuries within a developing discourse that was both global/comparative in spatial terms and progressive/historical in temporal terms. The preamble to the benchmark "Standards for Retaining or Abolishing Deity Temples" (神祠存廢標準, *Shenci cunfei biaozhun*) of 1928 illustrates both dimensions in its statement that "in this age of cultural renewal and scientific enlightenment," failing to eliminate superstition "will bring ridicule to the nation." The "Standards" went on to define the particular acts to which the "freedom of religious belief" granted in the 1912 Constitution would apply. Permitted observances fell under two categories: (1) those honoring a highly select list of worthy exemplars from Chinese history, purged of supernatural overtones and rites, and (2) those deemed "religious," which were defined as being organized along church-like lines and cleansed of what the compilers considered to be "noncanonical" (不經, *bu jing*) accretions, thus mirroring the typically Christian concern with historical and textual purity. To be abolished outright was a much longer list of "ancient gods" allegedly invalidated by modern science, and also "licentious shrines" (淫祠, *yinci*; Anonymous 1933b; Duara 1991).

Evident in these regulations was the tendency Vincent Goossaert identifies in his chapter in this volume for both state actors and religious leaders to favor "church-like" national structures as the characteristic that set "religion" apart from "superstition." It is therefore ironic—and vital for what happened after 1949—that the most dynamic growth in Chinese Protestantism from the 1920s on occurred in the indigenous sectarian movements, which were usually anti-foreign, anti-mission, suspicious of the alignment between the established mission churches and modernity (especially modernist theology), and in many cases virulently opposed to typical church structures, such as ecclesiastical hierarchy and an educated professional clergy (Bays 1996). That is to say, at the same time that key figures in other religions in China were setting out to emulate an imagined Christian model of a modern religion, Protestants themselves, in large and growing numbers, were rejecting this model as foreign and theologically suspect. The importance of these developments was not fully reflected within the national institutional forms of Chinese Protestantism before 1949, but by 1949 the mission-aligned churches that made up the National Christian Council, though still representing a majority of Chinese Protestants, omitted very important and growing sectors of Protestant life in China.

THE CHINESE COMMUNIST PARTY AND RELIGION

The status of Christianity in relation to other Chinese religions was ambiguous in the Republican period. Christianity was not (usually) classed, like superstition, as belonging absolutely to the past; rather, it was attacked for its links to imperialism, most heatedly during the 1920s. Nevertheless, Christians were able to lay claim to a legitimate place within the modern Chinese nation, albeit an uneasy one at times. The international status of Christianity and the attempts to present it as "modern," along with the treaty protections for it and its influence within the Guomindang leadership, all played a role in this.

No such ambiguity afflicted the Chinese Communist Party's view of Christianity. The CCP accepted the distinction between religion and superstition, but regarded both in Marxist terms as having their roots in humanity's "oppression by the forces of nature and society," to be rectified by scientific education and the elimination of class exploitation (Bush 1970:16). For the Communists, Christianity's association with Western

imperialism was a further basis for critique, *in addition to* the critique of
false consciousness that applied to any religion.

The Communist Party's initial approach to religious believers reflected
its expectation that religion would disappear in relatively short order in
the course of reconstituting China as a socialist society. Like successive
Republican regimes going back to 1912, the CCP adopted the minimal
constitutional guarantee of "freedom of religious belief" (宗教信仰自由,
zongjiao xinyang ziyou), understood as one of the rights ascribed to the
individual citizen, with indeterminate application to collective bodies such
as religious congregations, associations, and institutions. Toward the latter, administrative measures like registration, cooption, regulation, and
circumscription were applied, as they had been under the Guomindang,
but now with far greater vigor and effectiveness. The Party recognized
the existence of five "religions" in China—Daoism, Buddhism, Islam, and
Protestant and Catholic Christianity—and required that all five adopt
structures—the "patriotic religious organizations"—that would bring
them under unified and accountable management and free them from class
exploitation and foreign influence. Falling outside this limited sphere of
toleration were noncooperating elements within those religions; "reactionary" Chinese sectarian movements and secret societies; and the diffused
rites and sites associated with Chinese popular religion, now designated
"feudal superstition." Even that limited sphere of toleration was gradually curtailed through the 1950s and 1960s, as Chinese politics moved to
the left, and it was abrogated altogether during the Cultural Revolution
of 1966–76, in favor of an all-encompassing vision of the unified masses
of "new socialist" men and women, without distinctions of class, race, or
creed (Bush 1970; MacInnis 1972; Welch 1972). Unlike in Communist-
era Romania, in which the party-state incorporated Romanian Orthodox
elements into its national ideology and the personality cult of Ceausescu
(Tanasescu 2005), in China religion remained external to the party-state's
construction of the nation, and measures to accommodate religious minorities were seen as pragmatic and temporary concessions.

POST-MAO RELIGIOUS POLICY: RELAXATION OR BETTER MANAGEMENT?

The restoration of the policy of freedom of religious belief began with a
national religious work conference attended by more than eight hundred
cadres and religious leaders in Shanghai in January 1979. The conference
criticized the undermining of religious policy by the "Gang of Four,"

and announced both the rehabilitation of key religious leaders and the Party's intention once again to permit "normal religious activities" (B. Whyte 1988:344). The revived religious policy was formulated by government leaders and newly reinstated Religious Affairs Bureau cadres in discussion with prominent religious leaders over the ensuing months (Martinson 1980:84), culminating in the publication of the first post-Mao policy statement on religion in the *People's Daily* on March 15, 1979 (in MacInnis 1989:32–34). Implicitly picking up on a polemical exchange in the mid-1960s on the difference between religion and feudal superstition (see MacInnis 1972:35–89), the article asserted a distinction between them, stating that "religion"—meaning "principally" the world religions of Christianity, Islam, and Buddhism—is a special category of superstition with "scriptures, doctrines, religious rituals, and organizations." Since the disappearance of these religions is a "long-term matter" depending on "the disappearance of classes and on the popularization and development of culture and science," they should be allowed to function under religious organizations supervised by the state. "Feudal superstitions," however, must be resolutely suppressed. These points were elaborated in a series of articles in Party organs over the next two years (MacInnis 1989:26–41), culminating in March 1982 with the release of Central Committee Document 19 on religion (in MacInnis 1989:8–26), which laid down the core doctrine that the disappearance of religion is a long-term goal that cannot be forced, and which also defined the aim of the Party's religious work as "unit[ing] all the people . . . in order that all may strive to construct a modern, powerful socialist state."

It is important to realize that the change in policy was not simply a reversion to the pre-1966 situation (Duan 2001). Where there had been no agreement in Party circles before 1966 that religion would exist in socialist China for a long time, that became the starting point for religious policy from Document 19 on. The new policy sought to correct "leftist errors" going back to the early 1950s, including, importantly, those on tangible matters like real property. In 1980, the State Council issued a circular requiring all religious property that had been confiscated since 1949—not just churches and temples and not just those few that had still been operational in 1966—to be returned to the appropriate religious organizations, and compensation to be paid for the years of occupation (Zhonghua Renmin Gongheguo Guowuyuan 1980). Another signal of the new approach was the new criminal code adopted in July 1979, which added a clause (Article 147) making state personnel liable to prosecution for depriving citizens of their religious freedom (A. Hsiao 1979:134).

Protestant leaders welcomed these steps with enthusiasm, and matched them with statements of their own distancing themselves from the more politically charged Three-Self Patriotic Movement (TSPM, 三自愛國運動, Sanzi Aiguo Yundong) reforms of the 1950s, which had alienated many grassroots believers from the church leadership. In step with the general climate of critiquing "leftist errors" that marked the early Deng Xiaoping era, church leaders expressed regret over the politicization of the churches from the late 1950s, and gave assurances that the pulpit was henceforth to be used only for religious purposes (Deng Z. 1979:146; Chao & van Houten 1988:175). In addition, in 1980 the Protestants founded a new national body, the China Christian Council (CCC), to serve as the umbrella for the Protestant churches across China, parallel to but separate from the TSPM, which was widely perceived to have been more political than religious, and was in addition an organization of individuals rather than churches. In practice the two structures have had considerable overlap in function and personnel, but it was still a symbolically important signal of the new reality for Christianity in China.

The mere fact that other excesses of the leftist era were also being reversed does not in itself explain why the reimplementation of the religious policy was so complete. Pragmatic considerations surely played a role: Chinese leaders recognized that allowing religious life to resurface would ease China's full reentry into the world of diplomacy, and a more tolerant approach to religion could aid national unity by enlisting the support of as many social groups as possible in the new economic endeavor. Judging from the documents of the time, however, the most important factor was that the spread of religious activities had *already* become a cause of concern to the state. For instance, a national forum on atheism in late 1978 noted that "the power of religious faith and feudal superstition still prevails in the country" because of Lin Biao and the Gang of Four, who were accused of "restoring feudal fascism" and even of "reviving religious superstitions."[1] In a similar vein, the *People's Daily* article of March 15, 1979, in commenting on "superstitious" practices, stated:

After Liberation, this kind of activity gradually lost its strategic
position among the broad masses. However, in the past few years,
due to the vicious destructiveness of Lin Biao and the Gang of Four,
these things have raised their heads again in villages where "disasters"
have struck heavily. In a few areas, they have even grown to the extent
of influencing normal production and the life of the masses, and have
harmed the financial, physical and mental health of some of the working
people. (MacInnis 1989:32–34)

Other documents of the era included similar statements, and Document 19 stated that the anti-religious violence of the radicals had "forced religious movements underground," leading to the rise of illegal practices and counterrevolutionary groups (MacInnis 1989:19). In other words, the lifting of state restrictions on religion was intended not so much to restore a lost freedom as to restore effective state supervision over a social area that had flourished outside of state control during the radical period. From this perspective, the return to a policy of freedom of religious belief was a statist restoration clothed in the language of retracting the state's reach (cf. Shue 1988:6). Allowing a sphere of toleration for religions viewed as legitimate, under the management of "patriotic religious personages" of proven loyalty, would enable the state to distinguish "genuine" religious believers from those engaged in superstitious or counterrevolutionary activities, who could then more easily be suppressed.

PROTESTANT CHRISTIANITY IN DIALOGUE
WITH THE POST-MAO STATE

In short, then, China's religious policy as laid down in Document 19 aimed to unite all the believers in each religion under one umbrella and bring them into the open, thus ensuring that religious groups stayed loyal to the regime and that religious activities remained within acceptable limits, with no foreign involvement. These aims were to be achieved through the cooption of the institutional religious leadership under the auspices of the patriotic religious organizations, which were to function under the administrative leadership of the state. At the same time, as Document 19 also noted, the logic of the religious policy required that the leadership of the state over the patriotic religious organizations not be heavy-handed, lest the effectiveness of the organizations as a bridge between the party-state and religious believers be undermined. Thus the religious associations occupied an ambiguous space from the outset, as autonomous voluntary associations representing their religious constituencies, on the one hand, and as organizational structures for religious life sanctioned by the state and accountable to it, on the other.

To put it another way, the CCP's religious policy distinguished religious believers from the nation proper, thus protecting the secularity of the nation and reaffirming the state's role as the arbiter of which social elements belonged in the nation, and on what terms. At the same time, however, by allowing that religious minorities did have a legitimate status for the foreseeable future, the religious policy inevitably reopened the question of how to define the role of religious minorities within the nation, for Protestants as for other religious groups, and also created a domain for the discussion of that question in the form of the national associations and the seminaries, churches, and media organs under their control. What resulted in the Protestant case was an ongoing conversation between two unequal participants, the state and the national Protestant associations, conducted within parameters defined by the state yet involving give-and-take and mutual concessions within those parameters.

On a general level, the place of Protestants in the nation since then has turned on the compatibility between Protestant adherence and Chinese patriotism. The struggle of Chinese Protestants to win acceptance of their patriotism had been an enduring theme since the 1920s. In the 1950s, demonstrating patriotism became interwoven with the party-state's requirement to cut off ties with and denounce the "imperialist" legacy of missionary Christianity, and its litmus test was the requirement that all churches be "self-governing, self-supporting, and self-propagating"—the "three selfs" of the Three-Self Patriotic Movement (Bush 1970; Wickeri 1988). In the post-Mao period, the basic requirement that Protestants must be patriotic has been expressed in the core slogan "Love one's country, love one's religion/church" (愛國愛教, *aiguo aijiao*), in that order. Essentially, this slogan is an affirmation of Protestant good citizenship, and it often comes up in accounts of charitable work or good character demonstrated by Protestants in society. It is also a way of signaling which forms and expressions of Protestantism (or other faiths) are appropriate and which are not: examples of the latter would include being so devoted to one's faith that one does not care much about the country, stressing withdrawal from the mundane world, or stressing international linkages (whether Christian, Islamic, or Buddhist) across national boundaries. The insistence on "mutual non-interference" in the interactions between the Chinese Protestant associations and churches outside China, and the regular condemnations of "religious infiltration" are also bound up with this "patriotic" dimension of the place of Protestants in the nation.

More particularly, questioning the place of Protestants in the nation has implied debating their role in China as a specifically socialist nation under the leadership of the Chinese Communist Party. This complex and interesting discussion, under way since 1980, has involved core questions of Marxist theory and social analysis, on which Protestant leaders, intellectuals of various convictions, Party theorists, and the top echelon of China's leaders have all weighed in. The net result has been a gradual redefinition of the Communist Party's ideology on religion to allow for the possibility that some forms of religion can be compatible with socialist society (rather than a regrettable and temporary accommodation of backward elements), and a corresponding effort at "theological reconstruction" in Protestant circles to define a Chinese Protestant theology that is compatible with socialism. More to the point—since, as we have noted, this is a conversation between unequal partners—the Party's recognition that religion can be compatible with socialism was soon translated into a *requirement* that the recognized religions take forms that are compatible with socialism, and a new system of categorization for differentiating between acceptable and unacceptable forms of religion. "Theological reconstruction" was, then, a Protestant response to what was both an *opportunity* for fresh thinking and a *demand* for it.

INTELLECTUAL SKIRMISHES IN THE 1980S: THE "THIRD OPIUM WAR" AND RELIGION UNDER SOCIALISM

It is not necessary here to trace in detail the stages of theoretical debate that led to the new definitional paradigm, but it is worth noting some of the key stages. It began very soon after the restoration of the "freedom of religious belief" policy, when Protestant leaders began using the internal-circulation journal *Zongjiao* (*Religion*), published from 1979 by the Religious Studies Institute of Nanjing University, to press for a more flexible interpretation of the Marxist theory of religion. Although attached to Nanjing University, the institute was actually staffed by the teaching faculty of the Nanjing Union Theological Seminary, and they were frequent contributors to the journal (D. Yu 1990:170). In 1980, *Zongjiao* published a collation of statements by Marx, Engels, Lenin, Stalin, Mao, and Zhou Enlai on religion, neatly putting the single statement "Religion is the opium of the people" into a more complex interpretive context (Anonymous 1980). Another article in the same issue argued that the description of religion as an opiate "refers only to one aspect of the attributes of religion, and is, moreover, a metaphorical expression" (Qian 1980:13). Articles in *Zongjiao* through the 1980s continued to discuss Marx's views on religion and argue for a more nuanced view than that implied by the "religion is opium" dictum.

Naturally, this discussion was not purely theoretical. On the contrary, the "Third Opium War," as it came to be dubbed (Ting & Wang 1988:4), was a debate with direct policy ramifications between the liberal "Southern School" of religious studies, centered in Nanjing and Shanghai, and the "Northern School" of more doctrinaire Marxist theorists associated with the Institute of World Religions in the Chinese Academy of Social

Sciences, or CASS (D. Yu 1990: 172; van Houten 1986). The debate came out of internal-circulation journals and into the open in 1985, when Zhao Fusan used the yearly session of the Chinese People's Political Consultative Conference (CPPCC) as a forum to press for a more liberal attitude toward religion (Zhao F. 1985). Zhao, a vice president of the national TSPM committee, was the most prominent Protestant intellectual in China, being at the time a deputy secretary-general in CASS. He pointed out the intimate links between religion and culture in all civilizations, and argued that simply labeling religion "a political tool of the reactionary classes" or "opium" was unscientific and incomplete as a representation of the objective reality of religion in society. His speech reportedly received a standing ovation (Brown 1986:193).

Zhao followed up this effort with a major academic article entitled "A Reconsideration of Religion" (Zhao F. 1986). Starting with the insistence that Marxism is an open system, not a set dogma, Zhao historicized the statement that "religion is the opium of the people" through a careful exegesis of Marx's use of it and its intellectual context. He then argued that the essence of religion is different under socialism than under capitalism, and that the dogmatic assertion that "religion is an opiate" can only obscure the complexity of religion and harm the cause of uniting religious believers with the rest of the people to work for socialist modernization.

Official mediation of the opium debate came in the form of an article in the authoritative theoretical journal *Hongqi* (*Red Flag*) by Jiang Ping, deputy head of the central United Front Work Department (Jiang P. 1986). On the basis that class struggle still exists under socialism and that religion is essentially a superstructural remnant of the presocialist economic base, Jiang reaffirmed the applicability of the opiate view of religion in socialist society, while also acknowledging that some writers had applied the concept too simplistically. In a rebuke to the attempts of religious believers like Zhao and the *Zongjiao* writers to enter the Marxist theoretical debate on religion on Marxist terrain, he wrote,

> Although some people apply Marxism to the study of religion, they adapt Marxism haphazardly to the religious belief of their religious followers in order to satisfy their demands. Some people use religious points of view to explain Marxism. . . . Academic circles should respect the ideological beliefs of religious circles, whereas religious circles should also respect academic circles' Marxist study of religious theory and propaganda activities. (Jiang P. 1986:36)

Although Zhao Fusan and those who wrote for *Zongjiao* did not succeed in getting "religion is opium" written out of the official party line on religion in the 1980s, they did contribute to the concept's fading from prominence in Chinese academic circles. They also had some success in arguing that religion could play a beneficial role in the construction of "socialist spiritual civilization." This question also pitted doctrinaire Marxists against scholars more sympathetic to religion. The position that religion was a residue of the old society naturally begged the question of whether religious believers could ever play a positive role in socialist spiritual as well as material construction (Ting & Wang 1988). Conservative theorists insisted that religion and "socialist spiritual civilization" were diametrically opposed, and stressed the need to balance freedom of religion with the propagation of atheism (Lei 1985; MacInnis 1989:38–41).

This viewpoint was challenged by Protestant and other thinkers who sought to emphasize the fundamental changes in China's religions under the conditions of socialism, which had stripped religions of their role in class exploitation and purged them of imperialist connections and feudal elements. They asserted that, with the exception of superstitious activities and of "counter-revolutionaries acting under the cloak of religion," religion could now be seen as fully compatible with socialism (Ting & Wang 1988). As with the opium question, *Zongjiao* provided a forum for this discussion. One piece by the Protestant scholar Xu Rulei even argued that religion is part of the superstructure of socialism, not merely a remnant of the previous social order (Xu R. 1985). Making similar arguments beyond the Protestant aegis was the important book *The Religious Question in China in the Socialist Period* (*Zhongguo shehui zhuyi shiqi de zongjiao wenti*), published in 1987. Compiled by scholars at the Shanghai Academy of Social Sciences led by Luo Zhufeng, a veteran Party cadre who had headed the Religious Affairs Bureau for East China in the early 1950s, this volume broke new ground both in its theoretical commitment to the long-term persistence of religion under socialism and in its empirically based field studies of religious life in contemporary China (Luo Z., ed. 1987; translated as Luo 1991).

Although the CCP did not go as far as to agree that religion was part of the superstructure of socialism itself, by 1986 it had endorsed the idea that positive elements compatible with socialism were predominant in China's religions, and Politburo member Xi Zhongxun told a meeting of Chinese Protestants that "it is wrong to think of promoting [socialist spiritual] civilization as conflicting with citizens' believing in religion" (B. Whyte 1988:358–67, quote from 367; Wickeri 1988:89–92). Other Party sources that year acknowledged that religion could be a beneficial force in society, and that religious morality could "play an auxiliary role" in the construction of "socialist spiritual civilization."[2]

These developments in the theoretical understanding of religion were part of an overall shift in Chinese academic circles in the mid-1980s away from reductionistic Marxism and toward empirical research (Brugger & Kelly 1990). They also probably contributed to the more favorable kind of attention that Christianity began to receive from Chinese thinkers outside of religious circles in the late 1980s. As discussion of China's cultural legacy blossomed in intellectual circles from around 1987 on, a number of young thinkers began to study Christianity as the basis of Western civilization. Liu Xiaofeng (1989), then a professor of comparative literature at Shenzhen University, published a series of articles on the thought of modern theologians in the popular monthly *Dushu* (*Reading*) in 1988–89. The iconoclastic critic Liu Xiaobo (1991) also took an interest in Christianity, particularly in the doctrines of transcendence and repentance (Barmé 1991). Christianity to these thinkers was of interest less as a personal belief system than as a perspective from which to critique Chinese culture, but it was indicative of a profound intellectual shift that Christianity was being discussed favorably by non-Christian Chinese intellectuals, really for the first time since the early years of the May Fourth era (Leung 1991). In the 1990s that trend continued and developed, and the term "cultural Christians" was coined to describe Chinese intellectuals who wrote positively about Christianity without accepting Christian faith personally (Zhuo 2001).

RELIGIOUS GROWTH AND STATE REGULATION SINCE 1990

The political upheavals of 1989 meant that this intellectual questioning did not result in an immediate policy shift. As far as religious studies was concerned, although academic opinion had swung firmly behind the empirical approach of Nanjing and Shanghai by 1988 (Zhang X. 1989; Ting & Wang 1988), endorsement by the Party of their more liberal theoretical line was limited. Influential voices within the bureaucracy and among prominent Beijing theorists with links to policy-makers continued to press the opiate view of religion, the need to strengthen atheist propaganda, and the incompatibility of religion with socialism, while Zhao Fusan, the highest-profile Protestant intellectual in the country, defected to France after the military suppression of the student movement in 1989.

Over the 1990s, however, the more doctrinaire theoretical voices became less influential, and the Communist Party continued to moderate its theoretical view of religion and accept the long-term persistence of religion in socialist China. The Institute of World Religions within CASS, once a bastion of the hard-line Marxist "science of religion," became much more adventurous and began pursuing links with overseas scholars and institutions, including religious ones (Gong 1994). The Party's growing acceptance of the long-term persistence of religion in socialist China was undoubtedly due in part to its having to come to terms with the rapid growth of religious participation in China. Whereas in 1985 the official line had been that there were "more than 20 million" believers in the five religions, by 1988 the Religious Affairs Bureau was giving the number as more than 100 million, a figure that did not include members of sectarian groups or new religious movements, members of unregistered Protestant and Catholic churches, or the untold millions more engaged in popular religious practices.[3] That overall number remained unchanged in official sources until early 2007, when researchers at East China Normal University raised eyebrows with a much higher estimate of 300 million religious adherents, or around 25 percent of the total Chinese population (Wu 2007).

With regard to Protestant Christianity specifically, the number of open churches and meeting points affiliated with the Three-Self Patriotic Movement/China Christian Council (hereafter TSPM/CCC) increased from 1,600 in 1984 to 6,375 churches (2,683 of which were new buildings, not old premises returned) and 16,000 meeting points by the end of 1988, and more than 12,000 churches and 25,000 meeting points, served by some 18,000 clergy (i.e., about one person per two locations) by 1997. According to official estimates, the number of Protestants affiliated with the TSPM/CCC was around 3 million in 1986, over 4.5 million in 1988, and around 17 million by 2003.[4] In 1949 there were no more than 1 million Protestants of all stripes in China, so by any measure the growth has been remarkable, especially when one recalls that there are also many Protestants not under TSPM/CCC auspices.[5]

This growth was the context in 1993 when Jiang Zemin, then general secretary of the CCP, made a major statement on religion that has formed the foundation of Party policy since then. This policy, sometimes referred to as the "Three Sentences," was not a policy shift so much as an elaboration of the policy implications of the long-term persistence of religion in socialist China, and its direction had already been foreshadowed by a major Central Committee document released in early 1991 (Document 6 of 1991, in Spiegel & Tong 2000:56–63). The "three sentences" prescribed (1) that the policy of religious freedom must be "completely and correctly" implemented; (2) that the Party must strengthen the administration of religious affairs in accordance with (and by means of) law; and (3) that it must "actively guide" the religions in China to adapt themselves to socialist society (X. Ye 1996; see also Amity News Service 2003).

On one level, Jiang's speech signaled that the Party intended to rely increasingly on legal measures to define the rights, role, and limits of religion in Chinese society (the best analysis in English of the formation of this legislative regime is Ying 2007). This was a continuation of a trend that had begun in the later 1980s with the promulgation of municipal and provincial regulations in Guangdong and discussion of a national law on religion (Dunch 1991:44–48, 82–87; Madsen & Tong 2000). A key point of contention at that time had been whether the patriotic religious organizations would be responsible for overseeing the registration of places of worship. Religious leaders including Ding Guangxun (K. H. Ting) of the Protestants and Zhao Puchu of the Buddhists had balked at this, arguing that it would make the religious organizations function as administrative organs of the state, contravening the separation of religion and the state (Ding 1988; MacInnis 1989:76). The registration requirement raised particular difficulties for Protestants, who were beginning to acknowledge openly that many Protestant groups in China remained unconnected to the TSPM/CCC. In response to the registration measures, Ding and some other national Protestant leaders argued that independent Protestant congregations ought to be permitted to register without reference to the TSPM/CCC, and urged that the government publicize the criteria by which applications to register as a religious venue would be accepted or rejected (Amity News Service 1993, 1994).

Within a few months of Jiang's "Three Sentences" speech in late 1993, the first two national-level regulations on religion were released. These regulations, one regulating the venues for religious activity and the other concerning the participation of foreign nationals in religious activities within China, were more limited in scope than had been mooted in the 1980s, and reflected the concerns of religious leaders to the extent that they refrained from making the national religious organizations responsible for administering the registration of religious venues. Other regulations followed at national and lower levels of government (Fu X. 2003), culminating in the promulgation in March 2005 of the most comprehensive legal document to date, the "Regulations on Religious Affairs" (*Guojia Zongjiaoju* 2004). This document, in 48 articles, represented the first comprehensive effort to define the legal rights of and restrictions on religious sites, clergy, and religious bodies and their property.

As Ying Fuk Tsang has recently pointed out, neither this nor any of the other centrally issued regulations to date have been "laws" in the strict sense, which in China must be discussed and passed by the National People's Congress (NPC). Instead, they are administrative regulations (行政法规/規章, *xingzheng fagui/guizhang*), issued by the State Council under powers vested in it to regulate particular areas of Chinese life, ostensibly on a trial basis to allow time for the NPC to draft and pass legislation proper. However, Ying notes that administrative regulations of this nature have greatly exceeded actual laws passed in China (Ying 2007:15).

The "Regulations on Religious Affairs" in some respects opened up more space for religion in Chinese society. For instance, their complete lack of reference to the patriotic religious organizations is striking, implying a broader definition of a "religious body" under law than that enshrined in Document 19 (e.g., a body not connected to the national religious organizations—such as an independent Protestant congregation, or a community temple—might be encompassed by the wording). They also recognized that some religious observances require a large-scale public gathering that cannot be contained within a church, temple, or mosque, and laid down legal procedures for securing government approval for such events. The greater specificity in the regulations had the potential to reduce the arbitrariness and abuses in the implementation of religious policy, the first of Jiang Zemin's "Three Sentences" and a recurrent issue for all religions going back to 1978 (Hamrin 2005). Overall, however, the regulations were the latest stage in the quest to regularize and strengthen the state's management of religious life in China by means of law, a quest given greater urgency by the dramatic rise in sectarian activity since the late 1990s, discussed by David Palmer and Benjamin Penny in this volume (see also Human Rights Watch 1997). Their standing as State Council administrative regulations rather than law also underlines the fact that their underlying impulse is to strengthen state prerogatives rather than religious citizens' rights.

ADAPTATION TO SOCIALISM AND THEOLOGICAL RECONSTRUCTION

The other main policy initiative in Jiang Zemin's 1993 speech was the insistence that religion must "adapt to socialist society" under the "active guidance" of the Communist Party. This was the logical corollary of the recognition in theory that religion would persist under socialist conditions, and reflected the Marxist assumption that changes in the base will produce corresponding changes in the superstructure. It also provided an expedient way to distinguish the permitted from the sectarian and other religious elements so worrisome to the Party, which were *ipso facto* unadapted to socialism. As we have noted, the prescriptive expectation that religions must "adapt to socialism" has been repeated frequently and forcefully since then, and it has been embraced by the national leaders of the TSPM/ CCC. What "adapting religion to socialism" is supposed to mean in practice has been left fairly general, although occasional statements have emerged about what it is (and what it is not—e.g., no rapprochement between idealism and materialism or between theism and atheism is contemplated). The most authoritative clarification came, again, from Jiang Zemin, who reportedly described it as follows during an important work meeting on religious affairs convened jointly by the CCP Central Committee and the State Council in December 2001:

> The adaptation of religion to socialist society does not require religious believers to give up their faith but demands that they love their motherland, embrace the socialist system and the leadership of the Party, respect state laws, regulations and central policies, and serve the people and the nation through their religious activities. (Amity News Service 2002)

Even this statement, however, was couched in terms of religious believers as individual citizens, and its implications for religions as organized entities were not specified.

Like all such policy pronouncements, "adaptation to socialism" functions as both code and cover: code for a set of officially sanctioned expectations, and cover for a broad range of intellectual and theological agendas invoking it as legitimation. As with the post-Mao religious policy more broadly, its generality allows it to be deployed by different groups to different ends. For example, the head of the Religious Affairs Bureau in Shanghai stated quite baldly in 2000 that the "adaptation of religion to socialist society, according to the rule of law" benefited both the Communist Party and religious groups, the former by having a "clear and well-defined framework within which to relate to religious groups," the latter by "being *compelled* to structure and manage themselves in a more organized fashion" (Amity News Service 2000b, my emphasis). A more circumspect phrasing that may be little different in practice is the statement in the national government's White Paper on Religion that China has "established a politico-religious relationship that conforms to China's national conditions" (State Council 1997).

By contrast, national Protestant leaders have usually placed the term within a theological rather than an organizational context, and the movement for "theological reconstruction" has become a major focus in the seminaries and publications of the TSPM/CCC since 2001. As with other dimensions of the Protestant experience in China, it is too simple to view this as a state imposition on the church. On one level, it is a continuation of the long-standing effort since the early twentieth century (and arguably earlier) to articulate an indigenous Chinese Christian theology (Dunch 2001b:204–7). It also reflects anxiety about the direction of the Chinese church once the older leaders have passed from the scene. Most young church workers in China today are junior high school graduates with a two-year Bible college diploma, so their level of theological education is not high, and theological reconstruction is often linked to another slogan that reflects underlying concern about the future of the church in a time of generational transition, namely, "running the church well." Some older church leaders have expressed worry that the new generation, with no personal experience either of the missionary era or of the suffering of pastors during the political campaigns of the Maoist decades, will modify the direction of the church in damaging ways, for example, by abandoning the "three-self" principle or being too ready to accept unregistered or anti-TSPM Protestant groups (Qin S. 1990), and "theological reconstruction" ties in to these anxieties.

Given the mixture of impulses behind it, it is not surprising that the range of work published under the rubric of "theological reconstruction" is quite broad. As with "adaptation to socialism" itself, "theological reconstruction" is simultaneously code for a set of officially sanctioned expectations and cover for a broad range of intellectual and theological agendas. Some writers invoking "theological reconstruction" have engaged in a sophisticated way with Chinese culture, the contemporary socialist context in China, and theological and philosophical trends abroad (W. Wang 1997; T. Ji 1997; A. Wang 2002). Others have picked up on the implication in the party line that the "adaptation" of religion and socialism "to each other" might in fact be mutual (the mutuality never seems to be stressed in Party documents), suggesting that the Chinese church should mature into "the social conscience of Chinese society" (A. Wang 2003; see also Amity News Service 2003).

Some of this work has dovetailed with the Sino-Christian theology movement, which has developed out of the "cultural Christian" element in Chinese intellectual life since the early 1990s. The leading figures in this movement—Liu Xiaofeng, Yang Huilin, He Guanghu, and others—

are academics in some of China's leading universities and research institutions. The participants in this movement have aimed to incorporate
Christian theology into Chinese-language humanistic scholarship, to the
enrichment of both, without necessarily adopting a standpoint of belief,
but at the same time actually engaging in theological inquiry, not simply
taking Chinese Christianity as an object of study (Defoort 2004; Q. Li
2007; Yang & Yeung 2006). This movement has remained institutionally
distinct from the churches and seminaries, but there has been a certain
degree of cross-fertilization between it and the efforts at "theological
reconstruction" within them (H. Yang 2004:25ff).

Conversely, however, it would be mistaken to claim that the "theological reconstruction" movement is unrelated to state religious policy.
It flows from the long-standing Protestant concern to articulate a role
for Christianity within the nation, but particularly within the "China"
of official discourse, a unified socialist nation undergoing modernization under the leadership of the Chinese Communist Party, a leadership
embraced by the masses. In the words of one Protestant leader, theological
reconstruction takes as its "central task" Jiang's injunction to "actively
guide the adaptation of religion to socialist society" (A. Wang 2001). It
rules out viewing religion as nothing more than an opiate, but also rules
out viewing religion as a dissident force or a pluralist element that would
call the Party's political leadership into question (Amity News Service
2003).

One of the major emphases in the theological reconstruction effort has
been to take the concept of "reconciliation" as a core tenet, paralleling
the reconciliation of humanity to God in Christ with social reconciliation
between Christians and non-Christians in China. This is a key element
in the theology of Bishop Ding Guangxun (K.H. Ting), the most important TSPM/CCC leader in the post-Mao era, who has linked a theology of
reconciliation to "affirming the reasonableness of socialist society, thus
enabling Christianity to adapt to socialist society" (Y. Chen 2003). The
relationship between theological reconstruction and adaptation to socialism is clear in this case, although as we have noted, Bishop Ding has also
been an insistent and resourceful advocate for fuller autonomy for the
churches (Wickeri 2007 is essential reading on the life and thought of this
seminal and complex figure). Other writers have juxtaposed a theology of
reconciliation to more traditional Protestant emphases on "justification by
faith" or on the distinction between the church and the world (G. Wang
2005). The political implications are often just below the surface in these
discussions. At other times they are entirely evident, as in this quotation

from another prominent Protestant leader, which also recalls the mutual entanglement of religion, modernity, and the state with which this volume is concerned:

> To reconcile with the Chinese revolution is a recognition of the rightness and legality of the leadership of the Chinese Communist Party. To reconcile with the Chinese people is to cast off the label of foreign religion so that Three-Self may be well done. To reconcile with Chinese modernization is theological reconstruction—to respond to the challenges of modernization. (A. Wang 2005)

THE STATE, THE NATIONAL ASSOCIATIONS, AND THE RELIGIOUS MASSES

We have seen how state policy on religion has unfolded over the decades since 1978, initially struggling to forge a working consensus in the aftermath of the Cultural Revolution, and then solidifying the tenet that religion will continue to exist in China for a long time, relying increasingly on administrative regulations to manage it, and stipulating the expectation that religions will adapt to socialism. Input and advocacy from religious leaders have contributed to the shaping of these policies, as we have seen. Moreover, the "adaptation" policy can be regarded as the outcome of a conversation between the state and the religious associations around the core issue of the place of religion in a China that is imagined as a modernizing socialist nation. The shift in Party ideology and theory over the Reform era toward a more positive assessment of the role of religious believers in the nation, allowing for the compatibility of certain forms of religion with Chinese socialist modernity, was due to the changing religious reality on the ground, but it also reflected the participation of Protestant and other religious leaders and scholars in theoretical debates, and their efforts to secure greater autonomy for the religions they represented, over the 1980s and 1990s. The resulting consensus is a significant modification both of the Communist Party's understanding of the Marxist view of religion and of the longer-standing default secularity of Chinese state nationalism.

As for the religions themselves, clearly the state's agenda has shaped the parameters within which religious believers operate, in institutional terms and intellectual ones. Here again, though, the metaphor of a "conversation" between the state and the national Protestant associations, in which each side expresses its own views within a frame of reference defined by the state, gives us a better picture of the process than a model of state domination and Protestant response (or one that treats the Protestants as fully autonomous). The "theological reconstruction" effort illustrates this, for it has been simultaneously a response to the political context of the Chinese Protestant church, as defined by the Communist Party's religious policy, and a theological movement flowing out of intellectual and practical concerns about the role and future of the Protestant church in post-Mao China.

Thus far we have focused on the "conversation" between the national Protestant associations and the state. Missing from this portrayal, clearly, are the tens of millions of ordinary Protestants who are not on seminary faculties or in the leading circles of the TSPM/CCC, many of whom distrust those leaders and their motivations and insist on remaining unaffiliated with the organization. In principle, these millions are "represented" by the national associations and their leaders. At the same time, they are the *object* of the prescriptive side of both state policy and theological reconstruction. The basic reality is that most Chinese Protestants—within and outside the TSPM/CCC churches—hold a literal view of the Bible and are more oriented to personal spirituality than academic theology (Dunch 2001b:203–4). There have been periodic complaints in the national Protestant press about the conservative theology and straightforward view of the Bible that prevails among Chinese Protestants. Similarly, Ye Xiaowen, head of the national Religious Affairs Bureau, told church leaders in 2001 that "adaptation to socialism" meant altering the conservative theological orientation of Chinese Protestants, and he connected "theological reconstruction" explicitly to that agenda. His views were summarized as follows in the church magazine *Tian Feng* (*Heavenly Wind*):

> Despite the achievements of the past fifty years, there were still
> numerous problems affecting Chinese Protestant Christianity,
> Ye conceded. He mentioned conservative currents of theology still
> popular with many Chinese Protestants. Such theological remnants
> of the past could impede social development and prove problematic for
> the adaptation to socialist society, Ye warned. Therefore, the ongoing
> movement for building theology was of great importance for Chinese
> Protestantism, Ye maintained. The criterion for its success was whether
> it promoted Protestantism's adaptation to socialist society. Ye expressed
> his hope for broad participation in the movement for building theology
> and promised the Party's encouragement and support. (Amity News
> Service 2000a)

Such overt state pressure on the internal content of religious belief is rarely expressed as openly as this, but it illustrates the fundamental dilemma of religion, modernity, and the state in contemporary China. In political terms, most Protestants, whether or not they are affiliated with the TSPM/CCC, see themselves as loyal and patriotic citizens who accept the "love-one's-nation, love-one's-religion" principle and the need for religious believers to participate beneficially in society. However, on the more particular question of the "nation" as defined in official discourse, Protestants are likely to accept Communist Party rule as ordained by God (following Romans 13) but to view the church and the state as separate, and to be more reserved than their ecclesiastical leaders about the theological implications of socialist modernization. In fact, one bitter irony of the religious situation in China is that those Protestants who refuse either to register with the state or to cooperate with the TSPM/CCC are generally the most determinedly apolitical in their religious outlook, because the characteristic reason for such resistance is the perception that the TSPM and CCC are political entities and that the church must remain totally separate from the political sphere (Dunch 2001b:209ff.). These Protestants argue that they are patriotic citizens who are engaging in normal religious activities that do not subvert the state or violate the rights of others.[6] However, the state has generally regarded their refusal to register or to affiliate with the TSPM/CCC as a political act, and has routinely employed its coercive power against them, with penalties running from short-term detention or fines to prison sentences of fifteen years or more (Human Rights Watch 1993). It remains to be seen whether the regulations of 2005 will signal a relaxation of that dynamic (for early indications to the contrary, see Fielder 2007). In the meantime, ironically, Party policy has kept the relationship of church to state a more fundamental preoccupation and source of conflict within Chinese Protestant Christianity than it has usually been for Christians in other social and historical settings.

The TSPM/CCC has had some success, therefore, in pressing for broader toleration of religion and its role in society. However, the flip side in the Protestant case has been entering a conversation with the state on ground already defined for it, as exemplified in the movement for "theological reconstruction." Not only are the definitional categories and boundaries set by the state, but the legitimacy of the state's power to set those parameters is accepted and perpetuated by participation in the conversation on the terms given.

Moreover, participation in the conversation tends to widen the gulf between the top echelon of church leaders and the majority of Protestant believers. Viewed from within, the theological reconstruction movement addresses a vital issue in the history and present reality of Chinese Christianity, namely, the place of Protestants within the Chinese nation.

However, it has produced readings of Christian theology that are out of step with the faith held by most Chinese Protestants, and is thus open to the criticisms of being too liberal, too political, too accommodationist. Prescriptive statements by party-state leaders, like that of Ye Xiaowen just quoted, heighten this risk by drawing attention to the prescriptive dimension that is intertwined with the theological endeavor. If allowed to open too wide, such a gulf can undermine the effectiveness of the TSPM/CCC in its core task under the state's religious policy, which consists of uniting believers to participate in socialist modernization under the leadership of the Communist Party. In the case of the Protestant groups that resist affiliation with the TSPM/CCC, it has long since done so.

The Protestant case shows that the mutual construction of religion and nation applies even in China since 1978, notwithstanding the great disparity in power between the state and religious believers. The state for its part has had to accept the long-term persistence and growth of religion and adjust its ideology to allow religious believers to be legitimate participants in Chinese socialist modernity. It has responded by turning to legal measures to clarify the role and limits of religion in Chinese society, and to reduce the ambiguities and arbitrariness in the administration of its religious policy. It has also translated the conclusion that religion can be compatible with socialism into a prescription about the kinds of religious ideology and activity that ought to be regarded as compatible with socialism, and has required religions to adapt themselves accordingly. On the Protestant side, this prescription has been expressed in the movement for theological reconstruction, which has been intellectually invigorating on one level, but which also has the potential to alienate the church leadership from ordinary Protestants. In short, what prevails today is an uneasy equilibrium that is unlikely to be permanent, but that reveals some of the tensions that exist at the interface between state and society in discourse and reality in contemporary China.

7 Islam and Modernity in China

Secularization or Separatism?

Dru C. Gladney 杜磊

China's Muslims are now facing their second millennium under Chinese rule. Many of the challenges they confront remain the same as they have for the last thirteen hundred years of continuous interaction with Chinese society, but many others are a result of China's transformed and increasingly globalized society. Muslims in China live as minority communities amid a sea of people who, in their view, are largely pork-eating, polytheist, secularist, and "heathen" (*kafir*). Nevertheless, many of their small and isolated communities have survived in rather inhospitable circumstances for nearly two millennia.

Though small in population percentage (about 2 percent in China, 1 percent in Japan, and less than 1 percent in Korea), the Muslim populations of East Asia are nevertheless large in comparison with those of many Muslim states. There are more Muslims living in China today than there are in Malaysia—and more than in every Middle Eastern Muslim nation except Iran, Turkey, and Egypt (and about the same number as in Iraq). As Muslims in Asia, they are part of the largest Islamic populations in the world.

This chapter examines Islamic religiosity and identity in China, with special attention to the Hui and Uyghur. I argue here that successful Muslim accommodation to minority status in China is a measure of the extent to which Muslim groups allow the reconciliation of the dictates of Islam to the contexts of their particular socio-historical settings. This goes against the opposite view that can be found in the writings of analysts of Islam in China such as Raphael Israeli and Michael Dillon, who have consistently argued that Islam in the region is almost unavoidably rebellious and that Muslims in general are inherently problematic to a non-Muslim state (Israeli 1981, 2002; Dillon 1997, 2004). For these analysts, Muslims in

China, whether Uyghur, Hui, or otherwise, are Muslims first and citizens last—their loyalty is to Islam, and that will always be a threat to a secularizing state that seeks to nationalize religion in the name of modernity.

One of the defining moments of secularization for China's Muslims involved the redefinition of their very identification. From the beginning, the people now known as the Hui have been liminal, the perpetual immigrants in China, or, as Jonathan Lipman (1998) calls them in the title of his Hui history, *Familiar Strangers*. Not only do they have an entirely different culture than their host culture of China, but despite more than thirteen hundred years of intermarriage and integration, they are still regarded as a separate race. In China, "Race . . . would create nationhood," according to Frank Dikötter's thesis (1992:71) and it had much to do with Han Chinese representations of Hui otherness. Even their name, "Hui" (回), in Chinese can mean "to return," as if they were never at home in China and destined to leave. Descended from Persian, Arab, Mongolian, and Turkish Muslim merchants, soldiers, and officials who settled in China from the seventh to fourteenth centuries and married Han women, and living largely in isolated communities, the only thing that some (though not all) had in common was a belief in Islam. Until the 1950s in China, Islam was simply known as "the Hui religion" (回教, *Hui jiao*): believers in Islam were Huijiao believers, and anyone who was a believer in Islam was a "Hui religion disciple" (回教徒, *Huijiao tu*).

The term "Hui" narrowed in the late nineteenth and early twentieth century from a generic term including all Muslims, no matter what their ethno-linguistic background, to a word denoting mostly Chinese-speaking Muslims who were caught up in the nationalist movements of twentieth-century China. Djamal al-Din Bai Shouyi, the famous Hui Marxist historian, was the first to argue persuasively that "Islam" should be glossed in Chinese as *Yisilan jiao* (伊斯蘭教), not as *Hui jiao* (Bai 1951). In a chapter entitled "The Huihui People and the Huihui Religion," Bai argued that even though the Hui are descendants of Muslims and have inherited certain Muslim cultural traditions such as abstaining from eating pork, they do not all necessarily believe in Islam. A "Muslim" is different from a "Hui person" (*Hui min*), and one should not use the term *Hui jiao* ("Hui religion") but the term *Yisilan jiao* ("Islam"). He argued that the Hui believed not in their own religion but in the world religion of Islam, and that they therefore are Muslims in faith, while in ethnic terms they are the Hui people, not "Hui religion disciples." In Marxist terms, he identified a process of the indigenization of a world religion—in this case, Islam—to a local context, which for the communities now known as the Hui had been going on for twelve hundred years. Muslim groups, identified by Chinese linguists with what was supposedly their own language, derived their ethnonym from their language family; in this way the Uyghur, Kazakh, Tajik, Uzbek, Kyrgyz, and Tatar were identified. In this, the Chinese were heavily influenced by the 1920s Soviet identification of these peoples in Soviet Central Asia (Connor 1984:53ff.).[1] Bai Shouyi went on to identify the Muslim peoples not distinguished by language or locality as a catchall residual group known as *Hui min*, not *Hui jiao*. Thus the official category of the Hui was legitimated and, one might even say, invented, as far as the legal definition of who is considered Hui is concerned.

ISLAM IN CHINA TODAY

According to the reasonably accurate 2000 national census of China, the total Muslim population is 20.3 million, including: Hui (9,816,805); Uyghur (8,399,393); Kazakh (1,250,458); Dongxiang (513,805); Kyrgyz (160,823); Salar (104,503); Tajik (41,028); Uzbek (14,502); Bonan (16,505); and Tatar (4,890).[2] The Hui speak mainly Sino-Tibetan languages; Turkic-language speakers include the Uyghur, Kazakh, Kyrgyz, Uzbek, Salar, and Tatar; combined Turkic-Mongolian speakers include the Dongxiang and Bonan, concentrated in Gansu's mountainous Hexi corridor; and the Tajik speak a variety of Indo-Persian dialects. However, the Chinese census registered people by nationality, not religious affiliation, so the actual number of Muslims is still unknown, and all population figures are clearly influenced by politics in their use and interpretation. Nevertheless, there are few Han converts to Islam, and perhaps even fewer members of the ten nationalities listed above who would dare to say they are not Muslim, at least in front of their parents. As I have argued elsewhere (Gladney 1996:112–18), Muslim identity in China can best be described as ethno-religious, in that history, ethnicity, and state nationality policy have left an indelible mark on contemporary Muslim identity and it is almost impossible to discuss Islam without reference to ethnic and national identity.

Archaeological discoveries of large collections of Islamic artifacts and epigraphy on the southeast coast suggest that the earliest Muslim communities in China were descended from Arab, Persian, Central Asian, and Mongolian Muslim merchants, militia, and officials who settled first along China's southeast coast from the seventh through the tenth centuries. Later, larger migrations to the north from Central Asia under the Mongol-Yuan dynasty in the thirteenth and fourteenth centuries added to these Muslim populations by gradually intermarrying with the local Chinese populations and raising their children as Muslims. Practicing Sunni, Hanafi Islam and residing in independent small groups clustered around a central mosque, these communities were characterized by relatively isolated, independent Islamic villages and urban enclaves whose residents related with one another via trading networks and later became known as the "Gedimu" (from the Arabic *qadim*, for "ancient"), or traditionalist Hui Muslims. Nevertheless, these scattered Islamic settlements shared a common feeling of belonging to the wider Islamic community (*umma*), which was validated by origin myths and folktales and continually reinforced by traveling Muslim teachers known locally as *ahong* (*imams*).[3]

HUI MUSLIMS AND ISLAMIC ACCOMMODATION TO CHINESE SOCIETY

Over the last thirteen hundred years, Islam in China has primarily been propagated among the people now known as Hui, but many of the problems confronting them are relevant to the Turkic and Indo-European Muslims on China's Inner Asian frontier as well. Though Hui speak a number of non-Chinese languages, most Hui are closer to Han Chinese than to other Muslim nationalities in terms of demographic proximity and cultural accommodation. The attempt to adapt many of their Muslim practices to the Han way of life has led to criticism from some Muslim reformers. In the wake of modern Islamic reform movements that have swept across China, a wide spectrum of Islamic belief and practice can now be found among those Muslims in China referred to as the Hui.

The Hui have been labeled "Chinese-speaking Muslims," "Chinese Muslims," and most recently, "Sino-Muslims."[4] However, this terminology is misleading because by law all Muslims living in China are "Chinese" by citizenship, and there are large Hui communities who speak primarily the non-Chinese languages dominant in the areas where they live. To paraphrase Aihwa Ong, in this case citizenship, like religious membership, has been rather inflexible in China since the end of the last dynasty (1999:23).[5] This is the case, for example, with the Tibetan, Mongolian, Thai (*Dai zu*), and Hainan Muslims of China, who are also classified by the state as Hui. These "Hui" Muslims speak Tibetan, Mongolian, and Thai as their first languages, learn Han Chinese at school, and in some cases study Arabic and Persian at the mosque.[6] The Tajiks are the only Shi'ite Muslims in China, adhering to Ismaili Shi'ism and quite distinct from the majority Sunni Tajiks in neighboring Tajikistan.

Nevertheless, most Hui are closer to the Han Chinese in terms of

Figure 7.1. Hui (Chinese Muslim) restaurant in Urumqi,
Xinjiang Province. Photo by Dru Gladney.

demographic proximity and cultural accommodation than are the other
Muslim nationalities in China, adapting many of their Islamic practices to
Han ways of life. This type of cultural accommodation can be the target
of sharp criticism from some Muslim reformers. In the past, this was not
as great a problem for the Turkic, Mongolian, and Tajik groups because
they were traditionally more isolated from the Han and their identities
not as threatened, though this has begun to change in the last forty years.
As a result of the state-sponsored nationality identification campaigns
launched in the 1950s, these groups began to think of themselves more
as ethnic nationalities, as something more than just "Muslims." The Hui
are unique among the 55 identified nationalities in China, and are the
only nationality for whom religion (Islam) is the only unifying category

of identity, even though many members of the Hui nationality may not actively practice Islam. Indeed, in Yang Shengmin's (2002:35) ethnography of China, the Hui are included with the Han in the section dedicted to "Han-language nationalities" (Hanyu minzu).

The Guomindang's (GMD) "nationality" (minzu) policy identified five peoples of China, dominated by the Han. The Nationalists included Uyghurs under the general rubric of "Hui Muslims," which referred to all Muslim groups in China at that time. The Communists continued this policy and eventually recognized 56 nationalities. Uyghurs and eight other Muslim groups were split out from the general category "Hui" (which henceforth was used only with reference to Muslims who primarily spoke Chinese or did not have a separate language of their own). As a policy of ethnic control, this owed much to practices that the Soviet state had applied earlier to Central Asia. It proved to be an effective means by which the Chinese Communists could integrate the religion into China.

The institution most responsible for regulating and monitoring Islamic practices in China is the China Islamic Affairs Association (Zhongguo Yisilanjiao Xiehui). This association—founded in 1953 at the same time China formed the Three-Self Patriotic Movement (Sanzi Aiguo Yundong), which is responsible for monitoring all Christian (Catholic and Protestant) activities—makes the final recommendations to the government about the establishment of new mosques, formation of Islamic schools, and general policy on the legality of certain Islamic practices (such as outlawing headscarves in public schools), and plays an increasingly important role in China's Middle Eastern international affairs, as well as particularly supporting Islamic schools among the Hui.

In the Northwest, in addition to allowing from two to four students (halifat) to train privately in each mosque, the government approved and funded several Islamic schools (yixueyuan) throughout the region. In 1988 the state provided funding to establish a large Islamic seminary and mosque complex outside the West Gate of Yinchuan near Luo Village. Similarly, in Urumqi the Islamic college was established in 1985, and other regional and provincial government schools have followed suit. This indicates a "regionalization" of state-sponsored Islamic education, which until the 1980s had been officially concentrated at the China Islamic Affairs Commission in Beijing, located near the Oxen Street Mosque in the Xuanwu District in southwest Beijing (see Fuller & Lipman 2004:325–30).

The increased promotion of exchange with foreign Muslim countries is exposing more urban Hui to international aspects of their Islamic heritage. Though in the past coverage of the Palestinian-Israeli conflict was rather

minimal, increased coverage of the first Gulf War raised Muslim awareness of political and religious conflicts in the region. Widespread coverage of the wars in Iraq and Afghanistan on China's border have exposed
Muslims in China as never before to the many tensions in the Middle East.
Islamic knowledge tends to be higher among urban Hui than among those
who live in rural areas, perhaps because of increased educational levels and
more media exposure. Unlike the vast majority of Hui in rural areas, many
urban Hui whom I interviewed keep up on international affairs, and they
often read *China's Muslims* (*Zhongguo Musilin*), the magazine published
by the China Islamic Affairs Association. Few were aware of or interested
in the sectarian disputes in the earlier Iran-Iraq conflict, but most knew of
Shiism, and most were keenly interested in the U.S.-led war in Iraq.

Institutions engaged in managing China's Muslims, and the Muslims
themselves, have all been strongly affected by Middle Eastern affairs over
the last two decades. As one of five permanent voting members of the
U.N. Security Council and a significant exporter of military hardware to
the Middle East, the People's Republic has become a recognized player in
Middle Eastern affairs. After the temporary but precipitous decline in trade
with many Western nations after the Tiananmen massacre in June 1989,
the importance of China's Middle Eastern trading partners (most of them
Muslim, since China did not recognize Israel until 1992) rose considerably.
This may account for the fact that China established diplomatic relations
with Saudi Arabia in August 1990, initiating the first direct Sino-Saudi
exchanges since 1949 (Saudi Arabia canceled its long-standing diplomatic
relationship with Taiwan and withdrew its ambassador, despite a lucrative trade history). In the face of a long-term friendship with Iraq, China
went along with most of the U.N. resolutions in the first Gulf War against
Iraq. But it abstained from Resolution 678, on supporting the ground war,
and did not endorse the U.S.-led coalition war against Saddam Hussein
in 2003—and thus continues to enjoy a fairly "teflon"-like reputation in
the Middle East as a source of low-grade weaponry and cheap, reliable
labor (see Harris 1993; Shichor 1984). In the words of the late Hajji Shi
Kunbing, former lead imam of the famous Oxen Street Mosque in Beijing,
whom I interviewed during Ramadan in 1985: "With so much now at stake
in the Middle East, the government cannot risk antagonizing its Muslim
minorities."

Interestingly, although China's government did not endorse the U.S.-
led coalition war against Iraq, and only voiced "strong concern" about
the possible collateral injury of civilians, urging a peaceful resolution, its
Muslim population publicly condemning the U.S.-led war. A statement

issued on March 23, 2003 by Chen Guangyan, vice president of the China Islamic Affairs Association, included the following:

> We strongly condemn the United States and its allies for attacking Iraq and not turning to diplomacy to resolve this conflict. . . . We side with the war protesters in the US and elsewhere around the world. We strongly urge the US to stop its campaign and to return to the negotiating tables to resolve this issue. War is wrong.[7]

The next day, Hajji Muhammad Nusr Ma Liangji, lead imam of the Great Mosque in Xi'an, which boasts 70,000 members, made the following statement: "Though we don't go to the Middle East that often, we are all part of the same brotherhood. . . . Mr. Bush's invasion of Iraq is an incursion of Iraq's sovereignty. Islam is a religion of peace and the U.S. shouldn't do this. No one in the world agrees with this and we in the Muslim community in China absolutely object to this."[8] I was able to visit the headquarters of the China Islamic Affairs Association in the Niujie district of Beijing shortly after these statements were made, and Hajji Yu Zhengui, president of the China Islamic Association, confirmed that Muslims across China were deeply angered by the U.S.-led war and had been asking the government for permission to engage in public street protest. As of late March 2003, permission had not been granted, though there were rumors of small Muslim protests in Changzhi (Shanxi), Tianjin, Nanjing, Beijing, and Shandong. The Chinese did give permission for some limited protests by foreigners and students in late March and early April, but perhaps out of fear that a Muslim protest might get out of hand, possibly disturbing social stability or, even worse, disrupting improving Sino–U.S. relations, the Muslims were never allowed to protest the war on Iraq. These examples illustrate the increasing international role of institutions engaged in managing China's Muslims and their Islamic expression. These institutions have helped the Hui negotiate between the vicissitudes of Islamic religiosity and state secularization.

HUI ISLAMIC ORDERS AND CHINESE CULTURE

Sufism began to make a substantial impact on China proper in the late seventeenth century, arriving mainly along the Central Asian trade routes with saintly *shaykhs* (sheiks), both Chinese and foreign, who brought new teachings from the pilgrimage cities. These charismatic teachers and tradesmen established widespread networks and brotherhood associations, including most prominently the Naqshbandiyya, Qadariyya, and Kubrawiyya. Islamic preachers in China, including Ma Laichi, Ma Mingxin, Qi Jingyi, and Ma Qixi, spent most of their time trying to convert other traditionalist Gedimu Muslims to their religious order, leading to disputes that had a great impact on twentieth-century Islam in China. Nevertheless, Islam in China has for the most part grown biologically, through birth and intermarriage. Historical records do not yield evidence of large conversions of non-Muslims to Islam in China, except through birth, adoption, and intermarriage. The later mode of Sufist Islam was perhaps popular among traditionalist Gedimu because it offered immediate experiential access to God without formal mosque training in Arabic or in Islamic theology, as well as patron-client protection of Hui adherents during the declining social order of the late Qing dynasty.

The hierarchical organization of Sufi networks helped mobilize large numbers of Hui during economic and political crises of the seventeenth through nineteenth centuries, assisting widespread Muslim-led rebellions and resistance movements against late Ming and Qing imperial rule in Yunnan, Shaanxi, Gansu, and Xinjiang. In the late nineteenth and early twentieth century, Wahhabi-inspired reform movements, known as the Yihewani, rose to popularity under Nationalist and warlord sponsorship. These movements were noted for their critical stance toward traditionalist Gedimu Islam, which they viewed as being overly acculturated to non-Muslim Chinese practices, and also toward forms of popular Sufism such as saint and tomb veneration.

The Chinese state also launched its own criticisms of certain Islamic orders among the Hui. The stakes in such debates were often economic as well as ideological. For example, during the Land Reform campaigns of the 1950s, the state appropriated mosque and *waqf* (Islamic endowment) holdings from traditional Muslim religious institutions. These measures met with great resistance from the Sufi *menhuan* (religious lineages of Islamic authority), which had accumulated a great deal of wealth due to their hierarchical centralized leadership. As I have suggested elsewhere (Gladney 2004:121–38), the earlier movements of Islamic peoples and ideas into China can be divided into (1) the initial diasporic mode of traditionalist Gedimu Islam, and (2) the later mode of interconnected alliances of Sufi patron-client networks. A third mode—or, to use Fletcher's (1995) term, tide—of Islam in China was caught up in the same nationalist conflicts that gave rise to World War I.

THE RISE OF SECULARIST/MODERNIST ISLAM IN CHINA: THE YIHEWANI BROTHERHOOD

An important new Islamic modality swept China's Muslims at the end of the nineteenth century, perhaps as a response to nationalism and secularization rising in popularity, due to nationalist reformers seeking to modernize China and overthrow the ancient imperial regime. This new tide began among Muslims at the end of the Qing dynasty, a period of increased interaction between China and the outside world, when many Muslims began traveling to and returning from the Middle East. In the early decades of the twentieth century, China was exposed to many new foreign ideas and, in the face of Japanese and Western imperialist encroachment, sought a Chinese approach to governance.

Influenced by Wahhabi ideals in the Arabian peninsula, returning Hui reformers introduced the Yihewani (Chinese for Ikhwan al-Muslimin, or the Ikhwan Muslim Brotherhood) to China—a religio-political movement that in some cases supported China's nationalist concerns and in other cases championed warlord politics. Although the Ikhwan Muslim Brotherhood elsewhere in the Islamic world has been depicted as antimodernist and recidivist, this was not true in China. In fact, the Yihewani in China eventually diverged so far from its beginnings that it is misleading to even refer to it as "Ikhwan," or as a single movement or order. It has now become merely another "mode" of Islamic practice, an alternative to traditional Gedimu Islam and Sufism in China.

The beginnings of the Yihewani movement in China can be traced to Ma Wanfu (1849–1934), who returned from the *hajj* in 1892 to teach in the Hezhou area. The initial reformers who eventually became known in China as the Yihewani were primarily concerned with scripturalist orthodoxy—so much so that they are still known as "the faction that venerate the scriptures" (*zunjing pai*). Though the reformers had goals beyond merely "correcting" what they regarded as unorthodox practice, like earlier reforms in China, it was at the practical and ritual level that they initiated their critique. Seeking, perhaps, to replace "Islamic theater" with scripture, they proscribed the veneration of saints, their tombs and shrines, and sought to stem the growing influence of well-known individual *ahong* (*imams*) and Sufi *menhuan* (religious lineage) leaders. Stressing orthodox practice by advocating a purified, "non-Chinese" Islam, they criticized such cultural accretions as the wearing of white mourning dress (*dai xiao*) and the decoration of mosques with Chinese or Arabic texts. At one point, Ma Wanfu even proposed the exclusive use of Arabic and Persian in all education instead of Chinese.

Following strict Wahhabi practice, Yihewani mosques are distinguished by their almost complete lack of adornment on the inside, with white walls and no inscriptions, as well as a preference for Arabian-style mosque architecture. This contrasts sharply with more Chinese-style mosques in

China, typical of the "old" Gedimu, whose architecture resembles that of Confucian temples in their sweeping roofs and symmetrical courtyards (the Xi'an Huajue Great Mosque being the best example). The Yihewani also proscribed the adornment of their mosques with Arabic or Chinese Qur'anic texts and banners, whereas this is the most striking iconographic marker of Sufi mosques and worship centers in the Northwest, whose walls and tombs are often layered with Arabic and Chinese texts on silk and cloth banners in the distinctive Hui-style art that fluidly combines Arabic and Chinese calligraphy.

The Yihewani flourished in Northwest China under the patronage of several Muslim warlords during the Nationalist period, most notably Ma Bufang. Arguing that the Yihewani supported education, a rationalized, less mystical religious expression, and a strong Chinese nation, Ma Bufang supported the expansion of the Yihewani throughout Northwest China. He must also have been aware that wherever the Yihewani went, the hierarchical authority of the Sufi *shaykhs* and the solidarity of their *menhuan* were contested, thus protecting Ma from other organized religious institutions that might orchestrate an effective resistance to his expansion.

This could not have been lost on the early Communists, either, who traveled through Ma Bufang's territory and the Northwest on their Long March, which ended in Yan'an, near Ningxia, a heavily populated Muslim area dominated at the time by Ma Hongkui, a cousin of Ma Bufang who also supported the Yihewani. After the founding of the People's Republic, the state quickly suppressed all Sufi *menhuan* as feudalistic and gave tacit support to the Yihewani. Though Ma Bufang and Ma Hongkui both fled with the Nationalists to Taiwan, their policy of opposing Sufi organizations was left behind with the Communists. The China Islamic Affairs Association, established in 1953, was heavily dominated by the Yihewani, and was supportive of the 1957–58 public criticisms and show-trials of the Naqshbandi Shaykh Ma Zhenwu, and of Sufism in general, as feudalist and exploitative of the masses. After the purges of the Cultural Revolution, in which all Islamic orders were eventually affected, the Yihewani was the first Muslim group to receive renewed state patronage. Most of the large mosques that were rebuilt with state funds throughout China, as compensation for damages and destruction caused by the Red Guards during the now-repudiated Cultural Revolution, happened to be Yihewani mosques, though all orders were equally criticized during the radical period.

Although no Chinese official will admit that the Yihewani receives special treatment, this is cause for some resentment among Muslims. The great South Gate Mosque in Yinchuan city, the capital of the Ningxia Hui Autonomous Region, was one of the first mosques rebuilt in Ningxia with state funds; it just happened to be staffed by Yihewani imams, though the state said it was a "nonsectarian" mosque. After the state spent more than 50,000 *yuan* to rebuild the mosque in 1982, the local Muslims, most of whom were Gedimu and Khufiyya, refused to attend. The building sat almost empty for the first few years. The state attempted to recoup its losses by turning the large Arab-styled architectural structure into a tourist attraction, selling tickets at the entrance. This, of course, only confirmed the mosque's lack of religious legitimacy among many local Hui Muslims, especially the Gedimu and Sufis. In 1985, a visiting Kuwaiti delegation to the mosque became aware of the situation and instead of donating money to the South Gate Mosque, as originally planned, they gave $10,000 USD (about 80,000 *yuan*) toward refurbishing the much smaller traditional Central Mosque, which was a Gedimu mosque popular among the locals.

The Yihewani continue to be a powerful Islamic group throughout China. Like the Gedimu, the Yihewani emphasize leadership through training and education rather than inheritance and succession. The Yihewani differ from the Gedimu primarily in ritual matters and in their stress on reform through Chinese education and modernism. Unlike the Gedimu, they do not chant the scriptures collectively, do not visit tombs, do not celebrate the death days of their ancestors, and do not gather for Islamic festivals in remembrance of saints. Because of their emphasis on nationalist concerns, education, modernization, and decentralized leadership, the movement has attracted urban intellectual Muslims. This is why the Yihewani in China cannot be regarded as a tightly founded "order," as the Muslim Brotherhood is often portrayed in the Middle East; rather, the Yihewani is a mode of Islamic reform and orientation in China that educated and often urban Muslims find more attractive than the traditional Gedimu or the Sufis.

The Yihewani's nationalistic ideals, and its cooptation by the earlier Republic Nationalists and the CCP, led many of its more religious members to become disillusioned with the order, which they saw as no longer a fundamentalistic agent of reform but as an institutionalized organ of the state for systematizing and monitoring Islamic practice. Though still influential politically, the Yihewani has lost its dynamic appeal for many of the most conservative Muslims in China. For the vast majority of urban Hui Muslims, and even many rural Muslims in the small towns of the northern plains, however, it is merely the mosque that they belong to by virtue of birth or marriage, and few could tell me the difference between Yihewani and Gedimu, let alone between the myriad orders of Sufis. One Hui worker in Hangzhou once told me that the basic difference between the Gedimu (he used the term *laojiao*, "old teachings") and, in this case, the Yihewani (*xinjiao*, "new teachings") was that the Yihewani did not eat crab and the Gedimu did—the reason that Yihewani did not eat crab being that "crabs walk sideways."

The isolation of the early Gedimu communities was mitigated somewhat during the collectivization campaigns in the 1950s, when Han and Hui villages were often administered as clusters by a single commune. They have also been brought closer together through national telecommunications and transportation networks established by the state, including such umbrella organizations as the China Islamic Affairs Association, which seeks to coordinate religious affairs among all Muslim groups. With the dismantling of the commune in China, however, these homogeneous Hui communities are once again becoming more segregated. Although these disparate communities among the Gedimu were generally linked only by trade and a sense of a common religious heritage—an attachment to the basic Islamic beliefs as handed down to them by their ancestors—it was the entrée of the Sufi brotherhoods into China that eventually began to link many of these isolated communities together through extensive socio-religious networks.

The total population of the various Islamic associations in China has not been published, but one Muslim Chinese scholar, Yang Huaizhong (1991:58), estimates that of the 2,132 mosques in Ningxia Hui Autonomous Region in 1990, 560 belonged to the Yihewani, 560 to the Khufiyya, 464 to the Jahriyya, 415 to the traditional Gedimu, and 133 to Qadiriyya religious worship sites (some of which include mosques). The most comprehensive estimate given so far for Hui membership in Islamic orders throughout China is by the Hui historian Ma Tong. Of an estimated total of 6,781,500 Hui Muslims in 1988, Ma Tong (1983:115) recorded that 58.2 percent were Gedimu, 21 percent Yihewani, 10.9 percent Jahriyya, 7.2 percent Khufiyya, 1.4 percent Qadiriyya, and 0.7 percent Kubrawiyya.

THE RISE OF THE SALAFIYYA: A FOURTH MODE OF FUNDAMENTALIST ISLAM?

The recent rise in popularity of the Salafiyya in Northwest China is difficult to assess because there are no published figures of its membership or number of mosques, and few discussions of the movement in the voluminous literature on Islam in China. However, having lived in China for three years in the mid-1980s, and returned every year to Muslim areas since 1985, I have been frequently impressed by the many Muslims I have met who were formerly associated with the Yihewani or Gedimu but who said they had either recently joined the Salafiyya or were considering doing so. Perhaps discontent with the official patronage of the Yihewani by the political warlords and official organs of power in China, the Salafiyya originally arose out of the Yihewani in the mid-1930s and quickly spread throughout the Northwest. Since the early 1980s reforms, when religious expression was again officially allowed in China, the Salafiyya has flourished perhaps more than any other Islamic movement among the Hui. One Chinese scholar calls it "the faction that is most faithful to the original teaching of Islam" (Da 1988:157). Its adherents take the Qur'an as the very words of Allah (in the terms of American fundamentalism, as the verbally inspired word of God). As Dale Eickelman found among the Salafiyya in Morocco:

> Like their counterparts who emerged in the eastern Arab world in the late nineteenth century, Salafi Muslims argued that the Quran and the traditions of the Prophet were the only true bases of Islam, thus sharply distinguishing what they considered "true" Islam from the popular Sufism of urban religious brotherhoods and of maraboutism. (Eickelman 1976:227)

Unlike the Yihewani leadership in China, the Salafiyya stressed a nonpoliticized fundamentalistic return to Wahhabi scripturalist ideals. Arguing that the Yihewani had been corrupted by Chinese cultural accretions—such as the loss of its original founder's ideal to pursue pure Islamic education in Arabic and Persian—as well as coopted by the state, the Salafiyya represents one of the most recent versions of reform movements in China. While its scripturalist debates with the Yihewani did not lead to a "battle for the Qur'an" in China, the struggle for legitimacy of both Yihewani and Salafiyya took place in a discourse of Qur'anic textualism.

Like earlier Islamic reform movements, the Salafiyya was transmitted (and translated) to China through the agency of a returned Hajji from the Islamic heartland who began spreading his "new teaching" in China's own Muslim heartland, Hezhou. In 1934, a small group of Hui members of the Yihewani left Hezhou on the *hajj* from the heavily Muslim-populated Guanghe County's Bai ("White") Village. Led by Ma Debao, the group included Ma Yinu, Ma Zhenliu, and Ma Ling; together, these men later became known as "the four Ma's."[9] While on the pilgrimage, Ma Debao came under the influence of a Salafiyya named in Chinese sources Huzhandi, who was reported to be from the Soviet Union. It is not known whether or not this Huzhandi was a direct disciple of Muhammad ᶜAbdu, the founder of the Salafiyya and a disciple of al-Afghani, but many Hui Salafiyya believe this to be the case. Many of China's Muslims were educated at the al-Azhar in Egypt, where Muhammad ᶜAbdu was himself schooled, so it is not unlikely that there were some connections. In addition to bringing back to China his new interpretations of the Qur'an and the original teachings of the Prophet, Ma Debao brought two Salafi manuals, listed in Chinese sources as the *Buerhenu Satuier* (*Glorious Explanation*) and the *Xianyoushe Islamu* (*Army of Islam*). After returning to China, he trained further under a visiting foreign Salafiyya teacher, Jialei Buhali, reportedly an Arab from Bukhara (Da 1988:158–59).

As a result, Ma Debao began to suspect that Islam in China had been too influenced by Confucian, Buddhist, and Daoist ideas. He wished to return to a more purified, Arabian Islam, free from Chinese cultural and ideological syncretic adaptations. Thus Ma Debao was confronted with a challenge similar to the one that had faced by the founder of his order, only from a different direction. As Ira Lapidus notes, "for ᶜAbduh the central problem was not political but religious: how, when Muslims were adopting Western ways and Western values, could they maintain the vitality of Islam in the modern world?" (Lapidus 1988:621). For Hui Muslims in 1930s China, caught between the fall of the last Chinese dynasty, the imperial aggrandizements of the Western colonial powers, and the civil war between Nationalists and Communists, their concerns were certainly political *and* religious. However, Ma Debao and his followers thought that only through a fundamentalist return to the precepts of the Qur'an and the teachings of the Prophet would Muslims be able to survive this stormy period and help renew their nation, as opposed to the Yihewani, whom Ma saw as seeking the patronage of one political faction over another. Similar to ᶜAbd al-Hamid b. Badis, the leader of the Islah reform among the Young Tunisians, who also took his inspiration from the Salafiyya, it was the Qur'an and the *hadith* (narratives attributed to Muhammad) that were to serve as the rallying point of the Salafiyya in China.

Since Ma Debao and his followers were critical of the Yihewani for moving away from their earlier Wahhabi ideals, they held several open debates with famous Yihewani scholars, particularly disputing the authority of the four schools of jurisprudence. In 1937 the Salafiyya in China formally split from the Yihewani. The Yihewani was under the patronage at that time of the Nationalist warlord Ma Bufang, so the Salafiyya were severely restricted in their movements, persecuted as "heterodox" (*xiejiao*) and followers of "foreign teachings" (*waidao*), and unable to propagate their order except in secret. It was only after the founding of the People's Republic in 1949 that they began to come out into the open. By 1950, of the twelve Yihewani mosques in Hezhou's Bafang Muslim district, there were two mosques, the New Fifth Mosque and the Qi Mosque, which belonged to the Salafiyya, along with seven imams. This period of open propagation was short-lived, however, because in 1958 the state initiated a series of radical "Religious Reform Campaigns" that viewed almost all religious practices as feudal, forcing the Salafiyya to go underground again. Public approval did not come until twenty years later, under the economic and social reforms of Deng Xiaoping, who in 1978 allowed more open religious expression. It was only in 1982, however, that most Muslims in the Northwest began to rebuild their mosques and practice Islam openly. The central mosque for the Salafiyya in Hezhou is now the Qianhezhe Mosque, in the Bafang district (Linxia 1986:77). The Salafiyya also claims to have mosques and followers throughout the Northwest, including Qinghai, Ningxia, and Xinjiang, particularly in market and urban centers such as Linxia, Lanzhou, Weixian, Wuwei, Tianshui, Zhangjiachuan, Pingliang, Yinchuan, and Xi'an.

Due to its suppressed and rather secretive beginnings, the Salafiyya became known by various names. Since Ma Debao was from Bai ("White") Village, outside of Hezhou, and the movement gained quick acceptance there, it became known as the Bai, or White, Teaching. Since the Salafiyya emphasize that *salaf* in Arabic means "ancestral," or "the previous generations," its members say that their order reveres the first three generations of Islam. They signify their adherence to these first three generations by raising their hands three times, with palms extended upward, during namaz (obligatory Islamic prayers). Among outsiders, they have therefore been derided as the Santaijiao (Teaching of the Three Salutations), because most Muslims in China raise their hands only once during prayer (see Qiu 1992:819). Instead, they prefer to be known as either the Salafiyya or, in Chinese, the Shengxun Pai (Faction of the Prophet's Teaching).

Following the Yihewani, the Salafiyya promote a scripturalist Islam that is rationalist and anti-experiential. Like the late Rashid Rida (1865–1935), their fellow Salafi leader in Syria, they emphasize opposition to Sufism and cultural syncretism, rather than modernism (Lapidus 1988:666–67). Perhaps as a result of the drift of the Yihewani toward secularism and nationalism, the Salafiyya in China put more stress on scripturalism and orthodox practice. Again publicly repudiating other Islamic expression in China at the level of practice, they emphasize divine unity and criticize the Sufis and Gedimu alike for their patronage of tombs, saints, and the miraculous. They will not accept alms during readings but offer to use the money to buy scriptures instead. They regard the burning of incense during worship, still practiced by the Gedimu and Yihewani, as the syncretistic influence of Buddhism and Daoism. They also reject the commemoration ceremonies on the fourth, seventh, and fortieth days and on the one-year and three-year memorial death days, as frequently practiced by Gedimu, Sufis, and some Yihewani. They also oppose the collection of fees for performing engagement and marriage ceremonies, as is common among the Yihewani. Like the Yihewani, the insides of their mosques are unadorned by Islamic insignia or scriptures, although the outside may have one Arabic verse, in contrast to the Chinese frequently seen on the outside of Gedimu and even some Yihewani mosques, and the ornate Arabic and Chinese banners throughout Sufi mosques and tombs.

Like their founder Muhammad ʿAbdu, the Salafiyya see renewal as a result of educational, legal, and spiritual reform. But for them these reforms are all based on the Qur'an, whereas the Yihewani allowed secular and even Marxist educational training. Just as the discrediting of the Sufis and urban Muslim intellectuals by the French in Morocco helped promote the cause of the Salafiyya (Eickelman 1976:227–8; Lapidus 1988: 707), so the domination of the intellectual elite among the Yihewani and other Islamic orders by the Communist Party in China may well have contributed to the Salafiyya movement's call for a purified, nonaccommodationist, largely nonpolitical Islam. The further discreditation and decentralization of the Communist Party in most of the world, if not eventually China, may also give credence to the Salafiyya's cause. The Salafiyya is one of the few Islamic movements in China that can claim to have resisted both Chinese cultural assimilation *and* collaboration with the state. This may account for its dramatic rise in popularity since 1980, and may augur well for its place at the forefront of a new tide of Islamic reform in China. The Salafiyya is one of the few Islamic movements to coalesce after and flourish after the founding of the People's Republic, when China's diplomatic relations with Middle Eastern Muslim relations took several critical twists and unexpected turns.

Hui Muslims have been negotiating their accommodation to Chinese rule since the late Tang dynasty, when their numerical and political importance increased with the rise of the overland and maritime trade routes. The many Islamic relics in Quanzhou and Canton are evidence of the continuity of traditionalist Hui Muslims communities since the early period of Tang and Song trade with the Middle East via the silk roads and spice routes. It is also important to note that the legitimizing practices developed by these early Hui Muslims to adapt early Islam to Chinese culture and contexts found their greatest expression in the late Ming and early Qing (fourteenth-fifteenth centuries), when literati Muslims such as Liu Zhi, Ma Zhu, and Lan Xu sought to express the tenets of Islam in terms of Confucian understandings. Although this extraordinary academic effort did not greatly transform the traditionalist mode and practices of Islam as outlined above, as Zvi Ben-Dor Benite (2005) so eloquently describes, it did set the stage for Hui engagement with Chinese culture at the highest intellectual and moral levels.

However, as David Atwill (2005) acutely notes, the eruption of Hui rebellions in all corners of the fading empire (such as Yunnan) in the late nineteenth century suggests that Hui intellectual attempts to harmonize Islam with Chinese culture could hold little sway in the face of poor governance, social upheaval, and widespread prejudice against China's "familiar strangers." Like the Sufis described above, Hui Confucian scholars intellectualized Islam to such an extent that they became convinced that the very nature of the Chinese cosmos, as expressed by the nature of the Dao, was encapsulated as well in the basic tenets of Islam as outlined in the Holy Qur'an (Benite 2005:100–6). The transformation of a world religion, Islam (known earliest as "the Pure and True Teaching," or *Qing zhen jiao,* 清真教), into the religion of the Hui (*Hui jiao*) was followed much later by the transition from being called "Hui religion disciples" (*Huijiao tu*) to being officially the Hui "nationality" (*minzu,* 民族). This socio-political designation of *minzu* allowed the Hui to negotiate an accommodation to Chinese rule that continues to be relevant today.

ISLAM AND CHINESE NATIONALISM

In the twentieth century, many Muslims supported the earliest Communist call for economic equality, autonomy, freedom of religion, and recognized nationality status, and were active in the early establishment of the People's Republic of China (PRC). However, many of them later became disenchanted by growing critiques of religious practice during several periods in the PRC beginning in 1957. During the Cultural Revolution (1966–76), Muslims became the focus of both anti-religious and anti-ethnic nationalist critiques, leading to widespread persecutions, mosque closings, and at least one large massacre of one thousand Hui, following a 1975 uprising in Yunnan Province. Since Deng Xiaoping's post-1978 reforms, Muslims have sought to take advantage of liberalized economic and religious policies while keeping a watchful eye on the ever-swinging pendulum of Chinese radical politics. There are now more mosques open in China than there were prior to 1949, and Muslims are allowed to go on the *hajj* to Mecca, as well as to engage in cross-border trade with coreligionists in Central Asia, the Middle East, and, increasingly, Southeast Asia.

With the dramatic increase in the number of Muslims traveling back and forth to the Middle East have come new waves of Islamic reformist thought, including criticism of local Muslim practices in China. Through similar channels, other Chinese Muslims have also been exposed to various types of new, often politically radical Islamic ideologies. These developments have fueled Islamic factional struggles that have continued to further China's Muslims internal divisions. For example, in February 1994 four Naqshbandi Sufi leaders were sentenced to long-term imprisonment for their support of internal factional disputes in the southern Ningxia Region that had led to at least sixty deaths on both sides and to People's Liberation Army intervention.

Increasing Muslim political activism on a national scale and rapid state responses to such developments indicate the growing importance Beijing attaches to Muslim-related issues. In 1986 Uyghurs in Xinjiang marched through the streets of Urumqi protesting a wide range of problems, including the environmental degradation of the Zungharian plain, nuclear testing in the Taklamakan district, increased Han immigration to Xinjiang, and ethnic insults at Xinjiang University. Muslims throughout China protested the publication of a Chinese book entitled *Sexual Customs* in May 1989, and a children's book in October 1993 that portrayed Muslims, and particularly their restriction against eating pork, in a derogatory fashion. In each case the government responded quickly, meeting most of the Muslims' demands, condemning the publications and arresting the authors, and closing down the printing houses (see Gladney 1996:1–22).

These developments have influenced all Muslim nationalities in China today. However, they have found their most overtly political expressions among those Hui who are most faced with the task of accommodating new Islamic movements within Chinese culture. The Uyghurs, in contrast, due to their more recent integration into Chinese society (as a result of Mongolian and Manchu expansion into Central Asia), have been forced to reach different degrees of social and political accommodations that have challenged their identity. The Uyghurs are perhaps the Muslim group least integrated into Chinese society, while the Hui are, due to several historical and social factors, at the other end of the spectrum.

Increased Muslim activism in China might be thought of as "nationalistic," but it is a nationalism that often transcends the boundaries of the contemporary nation-state via mass communications, increased travel, and more recently, the internet. Earlier Islamic movements in China were precipitated by China's opening to the outside world. No matter what conservative leaders in the government might wish, China's Muslim politics have now reached a new stage of openness. If China wants to further participate in the international political sphere of nation-states, this is unavoidable. With the opening to the West in recent years, travel to and from the Islamic heartlands has dramatically increased in China.

UYGHURS, MUSLIMS, AND CHINESE CITIZENSHIP

In 1997, bombs exploded in a city park in Beijing (on May 13, killing one person); on two buses (on March 7, killing two); and on in the northwestern border city of Urumqi, the capital of Xinjiang Uyghur Autonomous Region (on February 25, killing nine). Sporadically reported since the early 1980s, such incidents have been increasingly common since 1997 and are documented in several scathing reports on Chinese government policy in the region by Amnesty International (1999, 2002, 2003).

Most Uyghurs firmly believe that their ancestors were the indigenous people of the Tarim basin, which did not become officially known in Chinese as Xinjiang until 1884. It was only in 1760 that the Manchu Qing dynasty exerted full and formal control over the region, establishing it as their "new borderland/dominions/territories" (*xinjiang*). This administration lasted for a century before it fell to the Yakub Beg Rebellion (1864–77) and expanding Russian influence (see Kim 2003). With the resumption of Manchu Qing rule in the region, the area became known for the first time as Xinjiang (Millward 1998). The end of the Qing dynasty in 1912 and the rise of Great Game rivalries between China, Russia, and Britain saw the region torn by competing loyalties and marked by two short-lived and drastically different attempts at independence: the establishment of an "East Turkestan Republic" in Kashgar in 1933, and another in Yining in 1944, led largely by secular nationalist Uyghurs influenced by Soviet-style bolshevism (Benson 1990; D. Wang 1999). As Andrew Forbes (1986) has noted, these rebellions and attempts at self-rule did little to bridge competing political, religious, and regional differences among the Turkic people who had only become known as the Uyghurs in 1921 under the Nationalist governor Sheng Shicai, who was catering to Soviet "divide-and-rule" strategies of recognizing groups such as the Uyghur, Uzbek, and Kazakh as separate Turkic nationalities

(Forbes 1986: 29). Furthermore, Justin Rudelson's (1997) research suggests persistent regional diversity along three, or perhaps four, macro-regions of Uyghuristan: the northwestern Zungaria plateau, the southern Tarim basin, the southwest Pamir region, and the eastern Kumul-Turpan-Hami corridor.

UYGHUR INDIGENEITY AND THE CHALLENGE TO CHINESE SOVEREIGNTY

The Chinese Nationalists' Soviet-influenced *minzu* (nationality) policy identified five peoples of China, with the Han in the majority. The recognition of the Uyghurs as an official Chinese *minzu* contributed to the widespread acceptance today of (1) the idea of their continuity with the ancient Uyghur kingdom, and (2) the gradual "ethno-genesis" of the concept of "Uyghur" as a bona fide nationality. This policy was continued under the Communists, who eventually recognized 56 nationalities, with the Han occupying a 91 percent majority in 1990. The "peaceful liberation" of Xinjiang by the Chinese Communists in 1949, and its subsequent establishment as the Xinjiang Uyghur Autonomous Region on October 1, 1955, perpetuated the Nationalist policy of recognizing the Uyghurs as a minority nationality under Chinese rule (Shahidi 1984). Designation of the Uyghurs as a "nationality" nevertheless masks tremendous regional and linguistic diversity because the term also includes groups such as the Loplyk and the Dolans, which have very little in common with the oasis-based Turkic Muslims who had come to be known as the Uyghurs. At the same time, contemporary Uyghur separatists look back to the brief periods of independent self-rule under Yakub Beg and the Eastern Turkestan Republics, in addition to the earlier glories of the Uyghur kingdoms in Turpan and Karabalghasan, as evidence of their rightful claims to the region.

Today a number of Uyghur separatist organizations exist, based mainly in foreign cities such as Istanbul, Ankara, Almaty, Munich, Amsterdam, Melbourne, and Washington, D.C. Though they may differ on their political goals and strategies for the region, they all share a common belief in the validity of a unilinear Uyghur claim on the region that has been disrupted by Chinese and Soviet intervention. The independence of the former Soviet Central Asian Republics in 1991 has done much to encourage these Uyghur organizations in their hopes for an independent "East Turkestan," despite the fact that the new, mainly Muslim Central Asian governments all signed protocols with China in the spring of 1996 stating that they would not harbor or support separatists groups.

Within the region, though many portray the Uyghurs as united around separatist or Islamist causes, they continue to be divided from within by religious conflicts (competing Sufi and non-Sufi factions), territorial loyalties (whether they be oases or places of origin), linguistic discrepancies, commoner-elite alienation, and competing political loyalties. These divided loyalties where evidenced by the attack in May 1996 on the imam of the Idgah Mosque in Kashgar by other Uyghurs, as well as the assassination of at least six Uyghur officials in September 2001.

It is also important to note that, historically, Islam was only one of several unifying markers of Uyghur identity, which depend on who the Uyghurs were cooperating with at a given time. For example, to the Hui Muslim Chinese, the Uyghurs distinguish themselves as the legitimate autochthonous minority, since both groups share a belief in Sunni Islam; in contrast to the nomadic Muslim peoples (Kazakh or Kyrgyz), the Uyghurs might stress their attachment to the land and oases of origin; and in opposition to the Han Chinese, the Uyghurs will generally emphasize their long history in the region. It is this contested understanding of history that continues to influence much of the current debate over separatist and Chinese claims to the region. The multiple emphases involved in defining Uyghur identity have also served to mitigate the appeal that Islamic fundamentalist groups (often glossed as "Wahhabiyya" in the region), such as the Taliban in Afghanistan, have had among the Uyghur.

During the war in Afghanistan, U.S. forces arrested as many as 22 Uyghurs fighting with the Taliban, who are still incarcerated in Guantánamo Bay, Cuba.[10] Amnesty International has claimed that Chinese government roundups of so-called terrorists and separatists have led to hurried public trials and immediate, summary executions of possibly thousands of locals. At the Fiftieth Anniversary celebrations of the establishment of the Xinjiang Uyghur Autonomous Region in October 2005, Party Secretary Wang Lequan, promoted in 2004 to membership in the Politburo due to his effective suppression of Uyghur separatism in the region, stated that the threat had not subsided and there would a ramping up of the Strike Hard Campaign.[11]

International campaigns for Uyghur rights and possible independence have become increasingly vocal and well organized, especially on the internet. Repeated public appeals have been made to Abdulahat Abdurixit, the Uyghur People's Government Chairman of Xinjiang in Urumqi. Notably, the elected chair of the Unrepresented Nations and People's Organization

Figure 7.2. Uyghur mosque in Urumqi, Xinjiang Province.
Photo by Dru Gladney.

(UNPO) based in the Hague is an Uyghur, Erkin Alptekin, son of the separatist leader Isa Yusuf Alptekin, who is buried in Istanbul, where there
is a park dedicated to his memory. In the spring of 2004, Erkin Alptekin
was elected by several international Uyghur organizations as the head of a
newly formed World Uyghur Congress. The growing influence of "cyber-
separatism" and the international popularization of the Uyghur cause concern Chinese authorities, who hope to convince the world that the Uyghurs
do pose a real domestic and international terrorist threat.

China's Uyghur separatists are small in number, poorly equipped,
loosely linked, and vastly outgunned by the People's Liberation Army

and People's Police. Moreover, though sometimes disgruntled about some rights abuses and mistreatment issues, China's nine other official Muslim minorities do not in general support Uyghur separatism (Becquelin 2001:15). There is continued enmity between Uyghur and Hui (often known as "Dungan" in Xinjiang and Central Asia; see Bellér-Hann 2001b). Few Hui support an independent Xinjiang, and the one million Kazakh in Xinjiang would have very little say in an independent "Uyghuristan." Local support for separatist activities, particularly in Xinjiang and other border regions, is ambivalent and ambiguous at best, given the economic disparity between these regions and their foreign neighbors, including Tadjikistan, Kygyzstan, Pakistan, and especially Afghanistan. Memories in the region are strong of mass starvation and widespread destruction during the Sino-Japanese and civil wars in the first half of the twentieth century, including bloody intra-Muslim and Muslim-Chinese conflicts, not to mention the chaotic horrors of the Cultural Revolution. Many local activists are not calling for complete separatism or real independence but expressing general concerns over environmental degradation, anti-nuclear testing, religious freedom, overtaxation, and recently imposed limits on childbearing. Many ethnic leaders are simply calling for "real" autonomy, according to Chinese law, for the five Autonomous Regions, all of which are led by First Party Secretaries who are Han Chinese controlled by Beijing. Freedom of religion, protected by China's constitution, does not seem to be a key issue, as mosques are full in the region and pilgrimages to Mecca are often allowed for Uyghurs and other Muslims (though some visitors to the region report an increase in restrictions against mosque attendance by youth, students, and government officials). In addition, Islamic extremism does not as yet appear to have widespread appeal, especially among urban, educated Uyghurs.

However, the government has consistently rounded up any Uyghur suspected of being "too religious" (see Fuller & Lipman 2004:329), especially those identified as Sufis or the so-called Wahabbis (a euphemism in the region for a strict Muslim, not an organized Islamic school). Also, in contrast to most strict Wahhabi practices, it is clear that Uyghur Islam continues to celebrate the mystical, enjoying tomb veneration and saint patronage as well as Uyghur cultural practices such as raucous singing and dancing (see Bellér-Hann 2001a). These periodic roundups, detentions, and public condemnations of terrorism and separatism have not erased the problem; rather, they have forced it underground, or at least out of the public's eye, and increased the possibility of alienating Uyghur Muslims even further from mainstream Chinese society.

CONCLUSIONS

The history of Chinese-Muslim relations in Xinjiang has been one of relative peace and quiet, broken by enormous social and political disruptions
that have been fostered by both internal and external crises. The relative
quiet of the last several years does not indicate that the ongoing problems
of the region have been resolved or opposition dissolved. Interestingly, a
recent *neibu* (internal-circulation only) collection of articles discussing "the
Xinjiang problem" and the challenges of separatism and terrorism (with
the terms often conflated) recognizes that there have been no incidents
since the year 2000, and blames the tensions between Han and Uyghurs
in the region on the "internationalization" (*guoji hua*) of the issue.[12] That
the Hui have either been largely silent or stridently opposed to separatist
and terrorist events in Xinjiang suggests that they wish to preserve the
accommodation to Chinese rule dictated by their early twentieth-century
resolution to the *Hui jiao* versus *Hui min* debate. Though sympathetic to
the plight of Muslims in Iraq, Palestine, and even Chechnya, the Hui's
hesitancy to become engaged in "the Xinjiang problem" suggests the
rather delicate nature of the balance that this accommodation achieved.
The Hui do not wish to be accused of supporting Uyghur separatism for
either nationalist or religious reasons. However, the events in the Middle
East since September 11, 2001 have begun to force even Hui Muslims to
rethink their position vis-à-vis the state and Islam. In the same interview
quoted earlier, in which Hajji Ma Liangji, the head imam of the Great
Xi'an Mosque, perhaps the largest in China, emphasized that Islam was a
religion of peace, he also suggested that Hui Muslims were being forced
to choose between Osama bin Laden's message and the U.S.-led war on
terrorism, which is supported by China:

> Osama bin Laden is a terrorist, but you see he really has nothing to do
> with Islam, which preaches peace and love. . . . But it is Mr Bush who
> is forcing those of us who otherwise didn't have a strong feeling about
> Osama one way or another to side resolutely against the US. September
> 11 was wrong, but Mr Bush's use of violence . . . is absolutely wrong.[13]

The late Joseph Fletcher (1995:90) has argued that despite their conquer-
ing Xinjiang in 1754 and driving out the Zungar Mongolian overlords of
the Turkish peoples, the Qing did not begin to attempt to incorporate the
region into the Han Chinese realm until 1821, when massive migration of
Han Chinese was encouraged. Additionally, according to Kim Hodong's
(2003:8) definitive study of nineteenth-century Xinjiang, it was only dur-

ing this early period that the Qing maintained any secure hold on the region (Millward 1998:72). The Yakub Beg Rebellion that established the thirteen-year Kashgar Emirate (1864–77) crystallized Uyghur resistance against what they perceived to be a cultural as well as political Chinese threat to their identity. Although the Uyghurs involved in this rebellion were divided into the local, ideological, and socio-economic factions that usually disunited them—which Kim (2003:74) argues contributed to their downfall—the uprising nevertheless played an important role in setting all Uyghurs apart from the Chinese state. It could be argued that this period of rebellion in the late nineteenth century forged an ethno-religious identity that not only led to the largely secularist nationalist establishment of short-lived East Turkestani states in the early twentieth century (see Benson 1990; D. Wang 1999) but that has also kept many Uyghurs from going in the other direction, toward support of jihadist Islam. It remains to be seen whether recent Chinese policies will push them in one direction or another.

The opposition to Chinese rule in Xinjiang has not reached the level of the conflict in Chechnya or the Intifada in Israel. Like the opposition of Basque separatists of the Euskadi Ta Askatasuna (ETA, "Basque Homeland and Freedom") movement in Spain, or former Irish Republican Army (IRA) members in Ireland and England, however, it is opposition that may erupt in limited, violent moments of terror and resistance (see Bovingdon 2002:40–41). And just as these oppositional movements have not been resolved in Europe, so the Uyghur problem in Xinjiang does not appear to be one that will readily go away. The admitted problem of Uyghur terrorism and dissent, even in the diaspora, is thus problematic for a government that wants to encourage integration and development in a region where the majority population are not only ethnically different but also devoutly Muslim. How does a government integrate a strongly religious minority (be it Muslim, Tibetan, Christian, or Buddhist) into a Marxist-capitalist system? China's policy of economic stimulus combined with intolerance toward dissent has not seemed to resolve this issue.

It is clear that Muslims in China are deeply divided in their responses to Chinese state policy toward Islamic religiosity. The resolution achieved by Hui Muslims between their *Hui jiao* (Hui religion) and *Hui min* (Hui person) identities in the last century—perhaps grounded in the earlier neo-Confucian synthesis of the fourteenth and fifteenth centuries—continues to enable them to negotiate their identity rather peacefully, and often prosperously, in the secularist-modernist-socialist-capitalist Chinese state. The Uyghurs have not been so successful. This is not surprising given the relatively recent integration of the region into China proper and its continued integration today. Should Uyghurs in China and in the diaspora respond to the Chinese religious policy as either jihadists or secularist nationalists, the results will most likely be the same: increasingly harsh, forced integration to Chinese rule, which may have disastrous implications for the region and its neighbors. Finding a middle ground may not be so easy in an increasingly decentered Middle Kingdom.

PART III

The Reinvention and Control of Religious Institutions

8 Republican Church Engineering

The National Religious Associations in 1912 China

Vincent Goossaert 高萬桑

Western paradigms of the political management of religion have been clearly and explicitly influential in China since the early twentieth century. These paradigms are quite varied, from the U.S. "wall of separation" to French *laïcité* and northern Europe's national churches, but they all have in common a post-Enlightenment definition of religion as a church-like institution separate from society, and processes of negotiation between church and state for privileges and uses of the public sphere.

The effect on the Chinese world of these paradigms began at the turn of the twentieth century, when the Western categories that underpin these paradigms were first introduced in China and then used by the dying empire (–1911) and by the Republic of China (1912–) to elaborate new religious policies. The bottom line of these policies was the recognition and limited support for those "religions" that could prove they fit a certain definition of this alien category, along with active suppression of anything else, categorized as "superstition" (Goossaert 2003, 2006a). It is in this framework that the successive Chinese regimes have conducted a policy branded as secular, even though, as many of the chapters in this volume show, this secularism should be considered a claim rather than a fact. The new religious policies of the Republican regime entailed the abandonment by the state of the imperial regime's religious prerogatives and the creation of a realm where "religions" could manage their own affairs within a framework of control and regulation set up by the "secular" state. Creating such a realm proved to be more complex than initially imagined by Republican leaders.

From an institutional perspective, one of the major aspects of state secularization worldwide has been the negotiation, or tension, between state and religion in defining their respective realms and the scope of their relationships. Such a process of negotiation was first experienced in the Christian West, where religion was equated with the church, which had authoritative representatives able to negotiate with the state. In places long Christianized, such as Latin America, this model of the state versus religion-as-church fit naturally. But China, like many other countries in Asia and elsewhere, did not fit such a model: to negotiate the institutional processes of secularization, the modern Chinese state first had to engineer, or help engineer, the building of church-like institutions so as to have a legitimate religious counterpart to deal with. This process was a top-down initiative in which both political and religious leaders saw the need for a new kind of religious institution for a variety of reasons, including aligning Chinese practice with the Christian model, playing the new game of political representation, exerting effective control from the center, unifying the nation, and reforming society.

This is the context in which we can understand the sudden appearance, as early as the first months of 1912 (the Republic proclaimed by revolutionary insurgents having become the legitimate state with the emperor's abdication on February 12), of nationwide associations claiming to represent the various traditions seeking state recognition and protection under the new category of "religions." These associations were both rushed attempts to face immediate threats (temple confiscation, in particular) and attempts to reinvent traditional religions as Christian-like churches.

By comparing the creation of national Daoist, Buddhist, Confucian, and Muslim associations in 1912—we will see that Christians are a case apart—I would like to document and analyze the first stage of these church-building efforts, the effects of which have dominated the relationships between Chinese states (in the PRC and in Taiwan) and religions for almost a hundred years. In spite of disappointing early results, this church-building enterprise met with increasing success, notably during the Communist period. In Taiwan until 1986, and to a large extent in the PRC to this day, the national religious associations were the only legal and formal framework for practicing religion and for conducting negotiations between state agents and religious leaders.[1] This situation is now being contested, both by groups at the margin of legality and by increasing formal possibilities of conducting religious activities outside of these associations. And even though these century-long efforts at reinventing Chinese religions in the framework of the national associations have mostly (with the possible exception of Islam) failed to live up to the expectations of the associations' leaders, they have nonetheless deeply changed the way Chinese religions are organized, both in relation to the state and internally.

A NEW PARADIGM: RELIGION AND SUPERSTITION

A press article published in 1901 by the famed essayist Liang Qichao (1873–1929) introduced to the Chinese language the term *zongjiao* (宗教), destined to translate the Western notion of "religion," and this word was from the start paired with its opposite, *mixin* (迷信, "superstition"). Both were taken over from Japanese, in which they had been coined some years before (Bastid 1998; Chen X. 2002). These neologisms were part of a larger set of imported categories used to reclassify the whole of knowledge and social and political practices, including such words as "science" and "philosophy." Chinese intellectuals first debated the meaning of these notions, so foreign to the late imperial Chinese world where religious life and social organization were deeply intertwined. During the first years of the century, *zongjiao* was almost synonymous with Christianity, but soon also included Islam, which was logical because it translated Western models of "religion." *Zongjiao* only gradually came to include Daoism and Buddhism, and heated arguments for and against the inclusion of Confucianism in this category raged for many years before the opponents gained the upper hand by the 1920s. Most of Chinese religion (or Chinese popular religion, as it is often labeled) remained excluded and was categorized as "customs," "folklore," or "superstition," even though this is now changing with the formation of new official categories such as "popular faith."

The notion of "religion" brought a theoretical justification to a vast project conducted by various sections of the late imperial and Republican political elites, aiming at reconfiguring the religious field and drastically reducing the realm of legitimate religion. This realm shrank from the rather encompassing category of orthodoxy defined by the imperial regime to just a few "religions" on a Christian-based model. One of the consequences of this drastic reduction was the confiscation and destruction of a very large number of local temples, formerly orthodox but now labeled superstitious. This destruction was conducted in the name of anti-superstition, but also in order to appropriate the material and symbolic resources of local religious institutions toward state-building. I have attempted in another publication (Goossaert 2006b) to sketch the emergence of this project around 1898 and the key figure of Kang Youwei (1858–1927).

The provisional constitution of the Republic of China, proclaimed on March 11, 1912, stipulated the "freedom of religious belief" (信教自由, *xinjiao ziyou*). This text did not guarantee protection against destruction and violence in temples, but it encouraged legislators and thinkers to elaborate on the difference between legitimate "religion" and "superstition."

This approach to religious policies was carried over and formalized by the Nationalist regime after 1927. As Rebecca Nedostup (2001) has shown, after having rejected early temptations to declare an outright ban on religions, the regime decided to work with recognized, institutional religions along a corporatist model, while launching an all-out fight against "superstitions."

Such is the intellectual context in which the early Republican government elaborated a new official doctrine for religious policies. Religious affairs were entrusted to a bureau under the Ministry of Education—itself a telling fact in a context where tens if not hundreds of thousands of temples were being forcibly converted into schools. In June 1912, this bureau published a blueprint in which it declared that it aimed at reforming (*gailiang*) existing religions so that they might contribute to social progress.[2] This document did not in itself constitute the solid foundation of a long-standing policy because it was published in a time of political chaos, when leaders and ideas came and went in rapid succession. Yet it deserves attention inasmuch as it was part of the immediate context in which the first national religious associations were created. Furthermore, it established quite clearly, and very early on, the modern Chinese state's fundamental positions in matters of religious policies, and these positions have remained more or less the same ever since: the state was ready to recognize "religions" as doctrinal, spiritual, and ethical systems with a social organization, but only if they got rid of "superstition" (including most of their ritual). The document plans to "respect each religion's basic doctrines while rectifying its later derivations such as rituals and customs" (依據宗教之本義而糾正其末流之儀式及習慣, *yiju zongjiao zhi benyi er jiuzheng qi moliu zhi yishi ji xiguan*).

The document left the list of such "religions" open, but it included Buddhism (if cleansed of its ritual practices) a priori, while excluding Confucianism (the debate on this point would rage through the 1910s) as well as Daoism. Only on the last point would later policies depart significantly from the June 1912 blueprint, since Daoism—or, rather, a very purist, streamlined interpretation of "Daoism"—was included among the religions recognized by the Beiyang, Nationalist, and Communist states.

The criteria by which the modern Chinese state decided whether or not to include a religious tradition on its list of recognized "religions" have mostly remained hazy, with few explicit guidelines. Other countries, notably in Asia, have experienced comparable processes of selecting recognized "religions," but they usually had clearer and more precise criteria that religions-to-be had to conform to.[3] The Chinese state's attitude has been quite pragmatic: a religion was recognized if it could prove it was "pure" (spiritual and ethical in nature), well organized (hence the national associations), and useful (patriotic and contributing to social welfare and progress). Therefore, the official list of recognized religions was never closed but encompassed those for which a national religious association was officially registered by the state; requests for such registration were always treated on a case-by-case basis (Nedostup 2001:82–90). In practice, the current list of five recognized religions (Catholicism, Protestantism, Islam, Buddhism, Daoism) appeared as early as 1912, but at various points in Republican history some other traditions, including the new religious groups known in recent scholarship as redemptive societies, were added to the list when their association was officially recognized.

One of the earliest of these was the Zailijiao (Teaching of the Abiding Principle), which set up the Republic of China General Association for the Prevention of Alcohol and Tobacco according to Li Virtuous Teachings (中華全國理善勸戒煙酒總會, *Zhonghua Quanguo Lishan Quanjie Yanjiu Zonghui*) that was recognized by the Yuan Shikai government in June 1913. The Zailijiao chose to officially take the form of a charity, but other redemptive societies adopted a more clearly religious status, such as the Tongshanshe (同善社, Fellowship of Goodness), which set up its own nationwide association recognized by the Peking government in 1917; more redemptive societies were to follow the same path during the 1920s. Because I focus here on the national associations created in 1912, I must keep the redemptive societies largely out of the discussion, while remembering that they actually played a central role in the religious institutional engineering of the Republican period.

THE CHRISTIAN NORMATIVE MODEL

The religious policy paradigm at work in 1912 was based on the prestige and influence among political elites of a Christian normative model of religion. This influence was partly due to the role of Chinese Christians. The first and ephemeral president, Sun Yat-sen, had been baptized in 1884, at age 18, after having been trained in Christian colleges in Hawai'i and Hong Kong (Bergère 1994:28–30). Among the 274 members elected (indirectly, through assemblies of local elites) between December 1912 and January 1913 to the first national parliament, 60 were Christians. This proportion was totally out of measure when we consider that Christians accounted for much less than 1 percent of the population. It was not as Christians that these MPs were elected, though, but because Christians accounted for a large proportion of the new classes of urban elites and political activists that fully supported the Republican enterprise, notably professionals (doctors, lawyers, engineers, custom officers).

One key factor in Christianity's influence over the new elites was its control over higher education. Many professionals and urban elites had been trained in Western colleges in China or abroad. Among the universities and technical training institutes founded since the last years of the nineteenth century, a good half were church-run (either Catholic or Protestant), and some private universities had been founded by Christian Chinese philanthropists. The only (but important) exception to Christian influence was military academies. In addition, the press, which was still in part inspired by Western interests, although to a lesser extent than during the last decades of the Qing, played a major role in the diffusion of Christian ideals about the building of a new China.

As a result, fair numbers of non-Christian political activists were, until the 1920s, happy to work with and to support the political and civic initiatives of Chinese Christians. Institutions such as the YMCA united Christian and non-Christian local leaders in projects to promote education or hygiene. Such non-Christian acceptance of Christian elites sprang from their sharing a political vision of a new, modern, democratic China that both espoused Western political ideals, most notably the U.S. model, and were ready to stand up and criticize Western powers for any encroachment on Chinese sovereignty (Dunch 2001a). Chinese Christians served as intermediaries in the transfer from the West of ideas and practices of a modern nation-state, such as civic rituals around the flag and the national anthem. Furthermore, Christians provided the notion that a good believer—that is, a public-minded, thrifty, honest, sober, decent person—was de facto a good citizen. The involvement of many Chinese Christians in public life, civic projects, and campaigns against opium, foot-binding, and other "social ills" convinced many urban Chinese of the practical benefits of religion, and these became sympathizers or even converted.

More than the number of converts, then, the Christian normative model of religion proved to be influential by its impact on Confucian, Buddhist, and Daoist leaders. Not only was Christianity thus the model for "religion," but throughout the twentieth century, Chinese political, intellectual, and religious leaders have been extremely sensitive to Western judgments and analyses of Chinese religion.[4] A particularly telling case of such sensitivity is Kang Youwei's utterance: "Foreigners come in our temples, take photographs of the idols, show these photographs to each other, and laugh."[5] This sentence was later copied verbatim in the introduction of the most important and famous anti-superstition law of the Nationalist government, the 1928 "Standards for Retaining or Abolishing Deity Temples" (*Shenci cunfei biaozhun;* Anonymous 1933b). This example and many similar statements show that under Western, mostly Protestant, influence, worship and ritual (the sensory forms of religion) were most often categorized as superstition.

THE 1912 INVENTION OF CHURCH-LIKE RELIGIONS

In the new context of 1912, in which a "religion" had to conform to a Western, Christian-based model to be recognized by the state and protected by law, Chinese religious traditions, notably Buddhism and Daoism, had to reinvent and redefine themselves. They were to represent themselves as religious institutions separate from "lay" society and without any connection to the local cults of village society ("superstition"). They had to create national associations capable of representing them and of negotiating with the state. This was the first time that Buddhism, Daoism, Confucianism, and Chinese Islam had organized themselves in a hierarchical manner. Such a reinvention was no easy enterprise, not only because it generated internal conflicts and confusion but because Buddhism and Daoism both actually operated as clerical, elitist traditions in the service of local cults and lay communities, providing them with salvation techniques, liturgies, and religious specialists trained to take over all sorts of clerical work (rituals, temple management, fund-raising, writing history and other kinds of texts, etc.). The task was particularly difficult for Daoism, which was intimately interlocked with local cults.

Before 1911, there were no Daoist, Buddhist, Confucian, or Muslim organizations coordinating all clerics at the national level, even though in some areas clerical specialists, like many other professions, had set up guilds. The late Qing years had also seen the birth of some local religious associations, mainly with educational goals. But the only kind of China-wide organization was the state, which controlled Confucians through the school system, and, more distantly, Buddhists and Daoists through the clerical branches of the bureaucracy, the Taoist Clerical Administration (Daolu Si) and the Buddhist Clerical Administration (Senglu Si). These two institutions, however, were weak and even nonexistent in many districts; they mostly worked as intermediaries between the state and clerics and did not play any role in helping Buddhists or Daoists get together and make collective decisions to further their common interests.[6] In any case, the imperial state was opposed to any such organization and collective action. For their part, Muslims were subjected to no such institution of control, and the "sectarian" traditions (out of which the redemptive societies emerged) were outright illegal.

The birth of new religious policies after 1898 and the advent of the Republic in 1912 dramatically changed this situation. First, the Daolu Si and Senglu Si, as well as the imperial code and the special status it granted to clerics, were all gone. Second, the ideology of the new regime, inspired by Western and Japanese political models, was to allow social groups to organize and represent their lawful interests to the state. Third, the assorted reformers and revolutionaries who staffed the various local and national governments of the Republican period shared a common program of assaulting traditional religion and expropriating temples. Being in a legal limbo and fearing, with cause, for their temples and monasteries, Buddhists and Daoists alike felt the urgent need to muster any kind of organized defense they could. Although less directly threatened, Confucians and Muslims also had to redefine their place in the new political and social order.

Faced with both the fresh possibility and the urgent need to form associations to unite and act on the political scene, Confucians, Buddhists, Daoists, and Muslims (terms by which I mean both religious specialists and engaged laypersons) reacted with energy as well as predictable confusion. Many of them had ideas about how to adapt their religion to the new context, and all proceeded to create their own national associations. Some were mostly apologetic, while others had more radical plans for a religious modernization. During the 1912–27 period, such associations mushroomed. Most had only an ephemeral existence, with tiny memberships and grand projects that never made the transition from paper to reality. Naturally, such competition among the numerous associations all claiming to represent the whole of their religion contradicted their common project of China-wide unification. The only associations that managed to build a China-wide membership, to obtain government recognition, and to score some success in the legislative battles against radical anti-religious projects were those presided over by prestigious leaders, usually charismatic clerics, and commanding widespread respect among lay sympathizers.

Buddhist Associations

The Buddhists were the first to organize during the early months of 1912, and they did so in a very disorderly fashion. Modernists, notably the radical monk Taixu (1890–1947) and the anti-clerical layman Ouyang Jian (1870–1943), proposed a complete overhaul of clerical training and management of monastic property. Both men created an association that managed to get some degree of support from the nascent Republican government. In March 1912, Ouyang Jian established in Nanjing the Buddhist Association (佛教會, Fojiao Hui), which was granted recognition by Sun Yat-sen's government.[7] This prompted a reaction by the monastic establishment, which set up on April 1, 1912 in Shanghai a broad-based national organization, the General Buddhist Association of China (中華佛教總會, Zhonghua Fojiao Zonghui), under the direction of the celebrated ascetic Abbot Bazhi (Bazhi Toutuo, or Jing'an, 1852–1912).[8] It was the latter association that became the official representative of Buddhism, but it was disbanded in 1918, when its requests displeased the Republican government. Up to 1949, the same story of various Buddhist associations, jostling for supremacy, continued along the lines of a division between radical reformers and the monastic establishment.[9]

The charter of the General Buddhist Association (Shanghai) emphasized the role of the association in the diffusion of Buddhism. It envisioned the founding of schools (thereby institutionalizing various local initiatives toward Buddhist schools since the early 1900s), in addition to confessional universities along the Japanese model. It also planned to establish a corps of missionaries (who would be sent among the military, into prisons and hospitals, and abroad), presses and journals, research institutes, and various welfare programs.

At the same time, the association granted itself the authority to control the behavior of its members (in particular monks and nuns) and the power to prevent a master from taking a disciple who would not be fit for a clerical career. The following article in the association's charter, for instance, flies in the face of two thousand years of Chinese Buddhist practice, in which each temple and monastery was totally independent:

> The current messy situation of the clergy is due to the lack of control over the selection of novices. From now on, any temple or monastery where [a monk/nun] wishes to take a novice must first submit a report to the local branch of the association, which will in turn enquire about the candidate's background and his/her motivation for entering the clergy. Only with the association's formal authorization will the candidate be admitted. (Zhongguo Di'er Lishi Dang'an Guan 1998:708)

Historians of modern Chinese Buddhism have emphasized the revolutionary aspects of the associations set up by Taixu, Ouyang Jian, and other reformers who wanted to gain control of religious landholdings and other resources (which were traditionally managed autonomously by each monastery or temple). Yet the innovations—notably those exerting control over clerics and centralized discipline—that were brought up, at least on paper, even by the more "conservative" and "consensual" General Buddhist Association (Shanghai) are quite remarkable. They suggest the extent to which, in the context of 1912, even conservative leaders envisioned a radical and far-reaching reinvention of the way their religion worked.

Daoist Associations

The Daoists followed the Buddhist example in trying to establish an organization capable of acting on the political stage, and also in exhibiting divisiveness, although along different lines. They were mostly divided between the two major clerical orders, the monastic Quanzhen order and the Zhengyi order of priests, under the liturgical authority of the Zhang Heavenly Master (Zhang Tianshi). The first national Daoist organization, the Daojiao Hui (道教會, Daoist Association), was formed in March 1912 at the initiative of Chen Mingbin (1854–1936), the abbot of the White Cloud Monastery (Baiyunguan), a very prestigious Quanzhen monastery in Peking (Qing X., ed. 1995:291).[10] It published a manifesto, as well as an open letter to the National Assembly, and on April 8, 1912, it obtained government approval and recognition (Anonymous 1994a, 1994b). This association clearly wanted to entrust the future of Daoism to the small group of abbots of the major Quanzhen monasteries in Northern China. The manifesto was signed by eighteen Quanzhen dignitaries: the main leaders, along with Chen Mingbin, were Ge Mingxin (1854–1934), the abbot of the Taiqinggong in Shenyang; Zhao Zhizhong, the abbot of the Baiyunguan in Shanghai; and Wang Lijun, the abbot of the Wuliangguan on Qianshan, a major Quanzhen center in Manchuria.

The manifesto insisted that Daoism was the most ancient indigenous religion in China, and thus best placed to become the national religion (國教, guojiao; Anonymous 1994a:1). Yet to conform to the new notion of "religion," Daoism also claimed to be universal and planned for branches to be set up in every country. It offered a political vision of Daoism as the moral and spiritual arm of the Chinese state, and criticized those who saw Daoism solely as an individual pursuit of transcendence. According to the authors of the manifesto, only by coopting indigenous Daoism could the Republic gain the support of the people and expect compliance with its laws. More than two thousand years before, they wrote, Laozi had already set out a blueprint for democracy and freedom, nationalism and social progress. Practically speaking, the association proposed to organize the study of inner alchemy (neidan) and Quanzhen discipline for clerics, and the management of charity and morality programs for the laity. The association's organization, laid out in great detail on paper, was very hier-archical, with the Baiyunguan abbot as ex officio president. Membership was open to clerics and "believers"; the association's charter made it an obligation for all members to congregate on Sundays for joining a Daoist service (Anonymous 1994b:10).

This document is a surprising, sometimes uneasy mixture of three different concerns: (1) the ambition of Quanzhen dignitaries to become effective leaders of Daoism as a whole, in which they saw themselves as the natural elite; (2) a hurried reaction to the pressing political needs of getting Daoism recognized and protected by the new regime (which, as we saw, was not self-evident at all) and of securing its monasteries and temples from seizures; and (3) an awkward attempt to recast Daoism as a "religion" with a national hierarchy, Sunday services, an organized laity, and other Christian-like features. It is not clear to what extent this attempt to reinvent Daoism was just a ploy to help gain Daoism government recog-nition as a "religion," and to what extent the abbots really meant to intro-duce Sunday prayers and other features of a church organization. Nothing resembling Daoist Sunday prayers or hierarchical congregations was ever implemented in actual fact, either in 1912 or at any later time.

Apparently, the Daoist Association (Peking) was dormant outside of these times of urgency, when it mobilized its political friends and net-works of support. However, branches were created in various provinces, notably in Sichuan, where they seem to have been active throughout the Republican period (Qing X., ed. 1995:430–33). At any rate, this associa-tion dominated by Quanzhen leaders did not meet with universal approval among Daoists, and, immediately after its foundation, a rival association, the General Daoist Association (中華民國道教總會, Zhonghua Minguo Daojiao Zonghui), was established in Shanghai by the Sixty-Second Heavenly Master, Zhang Yuanxu (?–1924, Heavenly Master in 1904).[11] This association, however, failed to develop outside of the Shanghai area (Chen Y. 1992:428–34); although many Daoists were traditionally loosely affiliated with the Heavenly Master administration, they declined to translate such affiliation into membership in an institution that vowed to control them.

Confucian Associations

Reinventing Confucianism proved even more difficult than reinventing Buddhism and Daoism. In 1912, Confucianism had just lost its status as the official doctrine of the defunct imperial regime. Intellectuals identifying themselves as Confucians did not necessarily regret this change because it offered the possibility of renewal. Since the last decades of the imperial period, some reformers had been thinking that the strength and cohesiveness of Western countries were due to their (supposedly) having a single national religion. During the 1890s, Kang Youwei had formulated a project of national religion (*guojiao*) based on a hybridization of Confucianism and Christianity. He envisioned the transformation of all Chinese temples into Confucius temples, operating as the centers of parishes, where the local population would gather every Sunday to hear Confucian priests read Confucian scriptures and preach. Although Kang's extreme views and personality repelled most of his contemporaries, many of his ideas were widely shared by intellectual and political leaders. In particular, the movement to protect Confucianism (*baojiao*, "protecting the teachings") by adopting Christianity's own weapons met with great success. Quite a few of Kang's contemporaries, including some of his declared opponents, developed projects similar to his, aimed at transforming Confucianism by imitating the Christian model of proselytizing, missionary activity (quite a few of them were dreaming of converting the West), and social engagement.

As Chen Xiyuan (Hsi-yuan) has brilliantly shown, this widespread but informal intellectual movement organized and institutionalized itself in 1912 (H. Chen 1999). A number of self-declared Confucians, many of whom were direct or indirect disciples of Kang Youwei, established Confucian associations with the aim of having Confucianism declared as national religion. The most influential of these associations, with more than 130 local branches, was the Kongjiao Hui (孔教會, Confucian Association), established in October 1912 and presided over by Chen Huanzhang (1881–1933).

Like its Buddhist and Daoist counterparts, the Confucian Association's project failed, at least as far as its immediate explicit aims were concerned. After several public debates in Parliament, the proposal it had introduced for instituting Confucianism as a national religion was voted down, first in 1913 and again in 1916. For many members of Parliament, the notion of national religion contradicted the freedom of religious belief enshrined in the 1913 provisional constitution. The Japanese model, which distinguished between a national cult, Shinto (Hardacre 1989), and *religions*, was not adopted or imitated. The radical break with the imperial regime necessitated, in the opinion of many members of Parliament, the abrogation of all kinds of state ritual and doctrine (Gan C. 2005). Incidentally, this decision was not perceived by all Chinese observers as reflecting a deep commitment to an equal treatment of all religions, but rather as a desire to replace Confucianism with Christianity. The strong influence of Christians among the revolutionary elites (beginning with Sun Yat-sen) caused quite a few Chinese to consider the Republic to be a Christian regime.

Notwithstanding the failure of its national religion project, the Confucian Association deserves as much attention as the other national religious associations, with whom it shares some common features. Like the Buddhist and Daoist associations, it developed a project of religious reform and reinvention. Chen Huanzhang and the other leaders of the association set out to radically reinvent Confucianism—notably by making the cult of Confucius universal (until 1911 it was the privilege of the gentry, that is, those who had passed the first level of the examination system) in every Chinese home and village, and by totally suppressing the cults of all the other Confucian saints (such as Guandi, Wenchang, etc.). The association launched a confessional journal (*Kongjiao hui zazhi*) and institutionalized a Confucian proselytizing program (Chen himself was preaching on Sundays in New York's Chinatown when he was a student at Columbia in 1904). By means of an audacious reading of the Confucian classics, Chen justified the seven-day week and Sunday worship, and strove to prove that Confucianism is a religion because, like Christianity, it has uniforms, a canon, rules, a liturgy, a theology featuring a single god, belief in the immortality of the soul, a doctrine on retribution, schools, temples, and holy sites (H. Chen 1999:127–29).[12] Local Confucian Association activists established halls for studying and distributing the Confucian classics, modeled on Christian Bible-reading groups (Fang 2004:62).

Muslim Associations

Islam had in late imperial China a rather particular place, as an officially recognized religion (despite occasional bouts of intolerance by officials) but without any official organization of control. In 1912, Chinese-speaking Muslims established several associations, the largest and most influential of which was the Muslim Association for Mutual Progress (中國回教俱進會, Zhongguo Huijiao Jujin Hui), founded in Peking in July 1912 (Zhang J. 1997/98). The president was Ma Linyi (a Ministry of Education official); among the other leaders, three were particularly important: Wang Yousan, Wang Haoran, and Zhang Ziwen. All three were reformist *ahong* (imams), employed in various Peking mosques and with experience traveling in the Middle East. Zhang Ziwen was also active in the business of publishing Islamic books and journals.

During the months following the establishment of the association, these leaders wrote to and visited a large number of Chinese Muslim communities throughout the country to elicit the creation of local branches. The association's aims, as detailed in its charter (Zhang J. 1997/98:16–18), included the publication of journals and translations into Chinese of Islamic texts, the foundation of schools and vocational training programs, the completion of surveys on the social conditions of the Chinese Muslims, and the promotion of frugality, hygiene, and nationalism. The Muslim Association for Mutual Progress was distinctive in that it combined a reinvention of religion (in this case, in the perspective of Muslim reformism) with an ethnic representation of the Chinese Muslims as a "people" or "race" (*Huizu*)—a notion that had appeared during the nineteenth century and recently been made official by Sun Yat-sen's notion of the Republic of China as comprised of five people (Han, Tibetans, Manchus, Mongols, and Hui). However, many of its aims and tools (journals, school, research) bear comparison with those of the Buddhist, Daoist, and Confucian associations.

The nationalist commitment of the founders and later leaders of the Muslim Association for Mutual Progress proved to be a strong influence on Chinese Islam. The most influential Muslim leader of the Republican period, Ma Wanfu (1853–1934), studied in Arabia between 1888 and 1892, and on his return decided introduce to China a text-based, reformed Islam, opposed to particularistic and localist Sufi affiliations. His disciples advocated uniting the divided Muslim Chinese community, and—after one of Ma's disciples, Hu Songshan (1880–1956), had felt humiliated as an ethnic Chinese during the Mecca pilgrimage—contributing thereby to the building of a strong Chinese state.

Thus the introduction of reformist ideas—which coalesced into the Ikhwan movement, directly inspired by the Muslim Brotherhood, and now dominant in institutional Chinese Islam—was intimately linked to nationalist ideas, and both the reformist and the nationalist strand promoted the invention of the ideal of a Muslim citizen. Although here the Western paradigm and its Christian normative model were much less at work than in the cases of Buddhism, Daoism, and Confucianism, we still observe a situation where religious leaders infused ideas of a nation-state into religious reform, and vice versa.

The Case of Christianity

Since the Western, Christian-based ideals of "religion" formed the primary basis for the reinvention projects of the various Buddhist, Daoist, and Confucian associations established in 1912 (the Muslim case being distinct but parallel), it might come as a surprise that no national Catholic or Protestant association was established that year. Indeed, the national Chinese Christian associations were only created later. The first plenary council of the Catholic Church convened in 1924 in Shanghai; for the Protestants, the National Christian Conference met in 1922 to launch the Church of Christ in China, which several Protestant organizations (but not Anglicans, Lutherans, or the new indigenous fundamentalist movements) joined. Not before the Communist period did inclusive national Catholic and Protestant associations form on the model already adopted by the Buddhist, Daoist, and Muslim associations. Thus we have here a process more complex and interesting than a pure adoption by "native" religions of Western paradigms, since the Western-influenced modern institutions crafted by local religions shaped in their turn the evolution of Western religions in China.

The reasons Chinese Christians did not adopt the model of the national religious association are many, including foreign leadership (missionaries); a specific relationship to the state different from that of the Buddhists, Daoists, and Muslims (Christian interests being already protected by the Western powers); and the existence among Chinese Christians of other, transdenominational organizations that played some of the roles taken on by the national religious associations among Buddhists, Daoists, Confucians, and Muslims. For instance, education, propaganda, and lobbying were carried out by institutions such as the YMCA and the Catholic Action groups.[13]

THE NATIONAL RELIGIOUS ASSOCIATIONS: CHURCHES IN THE MAKING?

The historiography of the various national religious associations created in 1912, and those that followed in their footsteps, has most often focused on the conflicts and competition within each of the various confessions. Indeed, these associations have often been used as vehicles for personal ambitions and competing ideas. Yet they cannot be reduced to that aspect of their historical development: I rather think that these associations make most historical sense when considered together, as aspects of a single process of religious institution-building, since even associations that were locked in conflict with one another shared many ideas as to what a national religious association should be. Behind their real differences, they all shared a common model—the national religious association—which was a new phenomenon in the history of state-religion relationships in China, and which had far-reaching implications in and of itself.

Therefore, it may be illuminating to examine the various 1912 associations as a whole and to consider them as projects, independently of their actual realizations. Even though these projects may not have gained the active support of very many people, and may very well have had hidden agendas quite different from their apparent intentions, they were nevertheless the forerunners of the associations that later played a crucial role in the evolution of institutional religion in Nationalist and Communist China.

The first thing that strikes the reader who compares the various texts produced by the 1912 associations is a strong formal resemblance in the vocabulary, the charts, and the general rhetoric of the associations' projects. Their leaders envisioned on paper (we will never know how much they themselves believed in such projects) vast bureaucratic organizations, with bureaus for propaganda, doctrine, research, missions, and discipline, subdivided into numerous offices. What paradigm was at work here? The reorganization of the bureaucratic state, with a staggering expansion of the number of state agents, ongoing since the last years of the Qing, certainly formed the background for this organizational culture. Indeed, the religious traditions were not the only quarter of society that engaged in such institution-building: the year 1912 saw the proliferation of national associations for all sorts of professions (Xu X. 2001) and interest and opinion groups, including many religious groups smaller than those discussed here. All were based on a Western liberal model of social representation.

Mary B. Rankin has discussed the role of civic organizations (chambers of commerce, educational associations) that had already formed during the 1901–11 decade, as well as new private associations in the early Republican state-building process (Rankin 1997:272–73). These associations shared with Republican officials the goals of modernity and national progress, even though they might in some circumstances oppose the government. Rankin mentions the YMCA and the Red Cross as prominent examples, particularly relevant since they combined the Western liberal model of representation with the Christian model of religion (the two being in fact closely linked in their historical development in the West). Very early on, the combination of these two models by Christians in China was emulated by native religious associations, such as the Buddhist, Daoist, Muslim, and Confucian associations discussed here as well as the redemptive societies. The various ways the Christian associations established a presence in the public sphere, such as the confessional press (Löwenthal 1978), were adopted by all the national religious associations. The General Buddhist Association (Shanghai), the Muslim Association for Mutual Progress, and the Confucian Association each published a journal; the Daoist associations did not, but the various journals of the redemptive societies did carry a lot of Daoist contents.

Another feature shared by all the national religious associations in 1912 was that they sought to redefine their relationship to the state. All of them insisted that the Republic had proclaimed the separation of state from religion, yet they also claimed for themselves a special relationship to the state. The Buddhist and Daoist associations presented themselves as the natural ally and moral arm of the secular state; the Muslim Association for Mutual Progress aimed to contribute to the process of state-building; and both the Daoist Association (Peking) and the Confucian Association claimed the status of "national religion." As the authors of the Daoist Association wrote:

> The Daoist Association requests formal recognition from the Republican government so as to ensure the equal standing and mutual cooperation of political and religious powers (*zhengquan, jiaoquan*). State officials and religious leaders must help each other and build a magnificent, perfect nation, so that men will be able to expand Truth and our coreligionists' hopes will be fulfilled. (Anonymous 1994a:4b)

In addition, the various associations all insisted on the weakness of their current situation and the necessity for unity. The rhetoric of unification pervades all their texts, beginning with the statement of purpose. For instance:

> [The Muslim Association for Mutual Progress] aims at bringing together all Muslims within the country and extolling their cohesion, furthering their unification and contributing to their common progress, in order to strengthen the nation and expand the Islamic doctrines. (Zhang J. 1997/98:16)

> [The General Buddhist Association (Shanghai)] aims at unifying Buddhism and developing Buddhist teachings so as to help the moral progress of the masses and the prosperity of the nation. (Zhongguo Di'er Lishi Dang'an Guan, ed. 1998:707)

This rhetorical focus on unification is clearly related to a sea change in the official religious policies between 1898 and the early Republican period, that is, the new and strong desire among the political elites to unite the people behind a single unitary national project and ideology. This desire was seen as contradictory to the Chinese belonging to multiple autonomous communities, each with its own cults and religious practices. From this perspective, the state and its nationalist project appeared to ally themselves with some religious leaders who also formulated the ambition to unite and standardize their religion through the suppression of the autonomy of local temples, communities, and traditions of practice.

As a consequence, all the 1912 associations also envisioned the enforcement of internal discipline. This certainly reflects a frustration, which must have been much older than 1912, among religious leaders unable to control fellow clerics and practitioners. Such leaders saw in the national religious association a means to gain at last the power to impose discipline—a power they had utterly lacked in late imperial times.

We should note, too, that even though the anti-superstition discourse was not yet very apparent in the 1912 texts (it would be more in evidence among the national associations of the Nationalist period), some of the religious reform goals of the state (or of some state agents, such as those who published the June 1912 blueprint) were endorsed by the religious associations. For instance, liturgy and ritual services to the population are markedly absent from the texts produced by the various associations.

These similarities between the discourses produced by the various new national religious associations were all derived from a common political and ideological context. Yet the associations also reacted to this context with different strategies. One important aspect of these differences is the nature of the leadership. Some associations gave authority and power to existing leaders who had already played a leadership role in the late imperial order of things,[14] such as the Heavenly Master and the Baiyunguan abbot, who were *ex officio* presidents of the two competing Daoist associations, and the prestigious abbot of a Chan monastery who presided over the General Buddhist Association (Shanghai).

In contrast, other associations promoted to leadership positions persons who could not claim any religious authority on the national scene before 1912, such as the Confucian Chen Huanzhang, the Buddhists Ouyang Jian and Taixu, and, to a certain degree, the Muslims Wang Yousan, Wang Haoran, and Zhang Ziwen. This second type of leader, who gained access to leadership and authority thanks to the new associations, tended quite logically to propose more radical reinventions of "religion" than the first type.

From this perspective, the case of Daoism is atypical. Whereas among Buddhist, Confucian, and Muslim leaders, some were earnest, zealous reformers who conducted real (albeit limited) field experiments at changing their communities' practices and implementing a reinvention of religion, there was no such figure among Daoist leaders, who remained clerics invested with traditional modes of authority. This was not due to a general backward-looking attitude among early twentieth-century Daoists—far from it; in fact, various Daoist masters emerged who engaged with the modern media in order to create new networks and institutions for the transmission of their practice (Goossaert 2007, chap. 7). For instance, Chen Yingning (1880–1969) established seminaries and journals in Shanghai (Liu X. 2001). Although much less assertive and aggressive than radical Buddhist reformers such as Taixu, Chen Yingning did share some ideas with the famed Buddhist reformer. Chen and Taixu both developed a vision of a scientific religion that was rid of its liturgical tradition, concentrating on self-cultivation, and available to the masses through a systematic curriculum. Chen drew up plans for a modern, nonsuperstitious Daoism with a larger role for laypeople. But, remarkably, neither Chen nor any of the other new Daoist masters was interested in using the medium of the national association to further his own project and vision, at least before the late 1930s. For this reason, the adoption of anti-superstition ideas (and subsequent ruptures with the liturgical structures of Chinese religion) was much more limited among Daoist associations than among their Buddhist or Confucian counterparts.

Another problem linked to the question of leadership is the definition of the religious community. If such a definition is fairly straightforward in the case of Islam, it becomes rather tricky among the "three religions" of Buddhism, Daoism, and Confucianism. The issue is still not solved to this day precisely because Chinese religion was and is a pluralist religious system in which it is mostly clerics who declare themselves "Buddhists," "Daoists," or "Confucians," while most other people pay respect to and use the services of all three traditions. In such a context the definition of the lay community, even though it might seem easy in theory (e.g., the Three Refuges identify a "Buddhist"), remains very hazy in actual social practice. Most of the 1912 associations' charters—including that of the General Buddhist Association (Shanghai), the Daoist Association (Peking), and the Confucian Association—refrain from positing a precise definition of their lay membership, even though they make great use of a few prominent, politically connected lay supporters. As a matter of fact, throughout the twentieth century, the Buddhist and Daoist associations have remained clerical associations by and large .

The 1912 associations developed a rhetoric of a unification of the religious community, but without any apparent clear idea about how to proceed. The very notion of a unified, China-wide Buddhist or Daoist community was quite far from sight in 1912, and the first institutional leaders can be excused for being at a loss as to how to conjure up that modern dream. Their subsequent failure can be contrasted with the situation of the Muslim community, which, through its associations and their print media, managed as early as the 1930s to mobilize large numbers of militants to stage protests against perceived insults or threats (Allès 2002). Another point of contrast is the redemptive societies, which had much clearer rules for joining and did maintain membership lists. For instance, the charter of the Tongshanshe (Fellowship of Goodness, established in 1917), in many other respects very similar to that of the other national religious associations, delineated more precisely how members were to be recruited and what their participation should be (Wang J. 1995:72–81), causing the Tongshanshe to be closer than the Buddhist and Daoist associations to the Christian model of a religion.

Whatever the success of such endeavors, uniting members in a hierarchical association was widely felt to be a crucial part of inventing "religion" and surviving in the modern context. Similarly, when nationalist leaders attempted to create Shinto as the national cult in Meiji Japan (1868–1912), their creation really began to take on a life of its own when all Shinto priests, heretofore organized in thousands of totally independent local lineages, formed a national association and a journal, and began to act on the political and religious scene as an organized body (Hardacre 1989:36–37).

THE LEGACY OF THE 1912 PROJECTS

The various national religious associations, formed in 1912 with both enthusiasm and a sense of panic, developed projects that mostly failed to become reality; their most notable achievement was official recognition by the state and the limited (though not negligible) protection that this entailed. The grand plans to create hierarchical churches with countless bureaus for research and propaganda, and branches in every part of China and the world, were never realized. Moreover, the reinvention of religion that these associations intended to carry out (exit superstition, ritual, and autonomous local groups, enter China-wide corps of ethical militants) did not overly impress their contemporaries. For instance, local gazetteers (*difangzhi*) of the 1910s and 1920s on the whole maintained the late imperial categories (official sacrifices, local cults, monasteries) to describe the religious situation in the field, and did not refer to either the associations or their vision of what "religion" was.

The associations themselves seem to have been locked in the national political arena, focusing their efforts, up to the late 1920s, on lobbying the president of the Republic and the Parliament to the exclusion of other possible fields of action. The Confucian Association is an extreme case because it identified itself so much with its project of a national religion that it became a marginal institution once this project was voted down by the Parliament. The real growth in relevance for the remaining national religious associations came only later, under the Nationalist regime, thanks to two factors: (1) the official recognition of the Buddhist and Daoist associations' role in the management of temples and monasteries in the Temple Management Act (December 1929), and (2) the creation in many districts of local branches of these associations. These local branches often managed to include the various orientations or clerical factions among the local clergy and to work quite efficiently, not pressing for any grand reform plan but striving, more modestly, to protect and help local temples and clerics through negotiations with local authorities.[15] Thereby, the Buddhist and Daoist associations found a new raison d'être by taking over the role played under the imperial regime by the Daolu Si and Senglu Si.

Thus the national religious associations of the 1930s were different in nature from their 1912 predecessors. However, even though each change of regime entailed a re-foundation of the national religious associations, so that these associations could share the history and temporality of the political regime with which they were allied (hence the wave of new associations set up after 1928 and after 1949), closer examination shows that the associations were also characterized by a marked continuity in ideology and leadership. Therefore, in spite of their initial failure, the associations established in 1912 formed the first stage in a long process of religious institutionalization under state control. Indeed, reading the 1912 texts with later developments in mind, one finds in them many of the themes more usually associated with the Nationalist and Communist periods: bureaucratic control of religion, assimilation of political ideology into the religious discourse, anti-ritual rhetoric, national unification. From this perspective, then, the role of the 1912 associations in the religious history of modern China may not be so negligible after all.

A major part of the historiography of modern Chinese religions (including Daoism, Buddhism, Islam, and Christianity) was built around the process of institutionalization (Jones 1999; Goossaert 2006a). Such political histories, as well as the biographies of institutional leaders, are of course necessary and welcome, yet they should not avoid questioning assumptions taken for granted in the discourse held by institutional leaders— particularly the idea, shared by all the associations, that their efforts at institutionalization, unification, and modernization actually ushered in a renewal of their religion. For instance, Buddhist, Daoist, and Muslim leaders often consider that before the twentieth century, their religion was very poorly organized and therefore declining and weak: efforts at institutionalization and modernization through the national religious associations are therefore described as revivals in the face of decline.

This theme, found as early as 1912 and still common today in both confessional and scholarly discourse, needs to be critically examined. We should question what kind of "weakness" and "decline" late imperial Buddhism and Daoism were in, and whether institutionalization was not destructive of certain practices and ideas (notably, local variety in practices and answers to the population's expectations) at the same time that it was a political road to survival and adaptation. Such an approach would certainly help us better understand the failures and difficulties encountered by the religious associations from 1912 to the present day, such as the refusal of certain clerics to join, heated debates about who is qualified to join,[16] competition between rival associations, and, of course, tense negotiations between religious institutional leaders and local state agents.

In the political and ideological context of modern China, the legitimacy that a national association can confer on a religious tradition, both directly (through state recognition) and indirectly (through social prestige), nevertheless remains a very strong incentive for building up such associations. Recently, certain religious specialists, such as spirit mediums and diviners, who are not organized as clergies (that is, who have no national ordination and training institutions or unified textual traditions and rules), have taken the initiative to establish associations on the Buddhist and Daoist model. For instance, during the 1980s a fraction of Taiwanese spirit mediums organized a national association with training and licensing programs in order to gain state and social recognition (Paper 1996; Tsai Y. 2002).

CONCLUSION: OTHER MODERNITIES, OTHER SECULARIZATIONS

The history of the early Republican national religious associations (and of their successors up to the present day) could be used to make a case for postcolonial theories. These associations are clearly the result of the impact of Western paradigms of religion and political management of religion, adopted and zealously implemented by Chinese nationalist leaders, both religious and political. Postcolonial research tends to emphasize either the problems created by non-Western adoption of Western models or the agency of local cultural brokers who transform such models for their own ends. In our case, both aspects are in evidence. Indeed, the early

Republican associations exhibit both rank suppression of native models (as shown by the associations' rejection of varieties of local ritual practices) and interesting attempts at creating hybrid creatures. The Daoist and Confucian Sunday prayers and the Buddhist bureaucratic selection of monks were ultimately unlike anything else in either China or the West. Hence, rather than simply going along with postcolonial theories, I would like to emphasize the mixed possibilities opened up by the national association model in the Chinese religious field. The associations attempted to unify and/or destroy certain practices, but mostly failed; at the same time, as eloquently shown by Ji Zhe's chapter in this volume, they did invent a space for religion in modern China's public sphere. They did so by following a secularizing path quite different from the one anticipated by classic secularization theory.

Many of the major cases of separation of the state from religion during the twentieth century, such as those in Russia, Mexico, and Turkey, pitted a nascent nation-state against a religion that was organized more or less as a church. In such cases, the secular state labeled as superstitious the religion that it was separating itself from; no clear distinction was made between religion and superstition. In early Republican China, however, an important part of the political elite actually favored church-like institutions and "religions" in order to fight superstitions. For this reason, the Chinese state from 1912 to this day has not opposed the church-building projects of the new national religious associations, but rather favored and tutored them.

From this perspective, my analysis of the Chinese national religious associations, particularly during their earliest stage in 1912, concurs with Peter van der Veer's work on colonial India. Van der Veer (2001) finds a simultaneous production of "religion," secularism, and modernity. The separation of religions from the state creates religion under a new national form, and actually provokes its expansion into the public sphere. If the context (imperialist rather than colonial) and the particular institutions that are used to express the invention of religion (the national religious associations rather than new hybrid religions) are quite different in China than in India, the processes at work in both places are nonetheless comparable. In China as in India, the new "religions" also extended into the public sphere (the national religious associations published journals and actively engaged in political lobbying) in ways unimaginable in the late imperial context; and they defined themselves in ways that were intimately linked to the nation-state and its secular ideals.

Such an analysis has the potential to show that current paradigms about secularization, which emphasize the "privatization" and "deconstruction" of established religions in favor of individual choices, may neglect opposite trends whereby modern states favor the creation of religious institutions with which they share many ideological options: national unification, self-definition in terms of national/global issues, exclusive ideological affiliation. These new religious institutions produced by modernity are much more centralized and institutionalized than the traditions that they claim to continue. In other words, the extremely complex construction of nation-state and nationalism as it unfolded in the interplay between state and religion in China actually created a modernity and a secularization quite different from those exemplified and exported by Western countries.

9   Secularization as Religious Restructuring

Statist Institutionalization of Chinese Buddhism and Its Paradoxes

Ji Zhe 汲喆

This chapter undertakes to analyze the statist institutionalization of Buddhism in modern China and suggests that there are some paradoxes in the process of secularization, and in the relationship between the state and religion. I would like to show that secularization in China, understood as a state policy to restrain religion, may also produce what is, in essence, contrary to its aim: that is to say, some constructive consequences for religion. In fact, secularization could be understood to be a process of social restructuring, rather than a unidirectional decline of religion or religious institutions.

In the sociology of religion, "secularization" is a highly contentious concept with its specific historical roots in Christian Europe. Therefore, I first propose an approach to secularization that focuses on the power relations between religion and the state, so as to be able to clarify the specific political and religious contexts of secularization in modern China. Next, coupling sociological interpretation with a historical perspective, I illustrate how Buddhism was institutionalized, and therefore secularized by the Communist state. Finally, I analyze the paradoxical effects produced in this secularization process when the social conditions of the state-religion interaction changed in the post-Mao era.

RETHINKING SECULARIZATION IN A CHINESE CONTEXT
Toward a Theory of Secularization as Religio-Political Struggle

Following the resurgence of new religious movements and the revival of traditional religions in many parts of the world since the 1970s, the classical theory of secularization that argued for the decline of religion in modernization has been openly questioned. More recently, in the last twenty years, a number of scholars have suggested some interesting adjustments to secularization theory. These have included Karel Dobbelaere's (1981) multidimensional concept of secularization, which proposes that we must distinguish between different levels of secularization—the societal level, the church level, and the individual level—and José Casanova's (1994) approach to secularization as a set of three independent propositions: the differentiation of the secular sphere from religious norms and institutions, the decline of beliefs and practices, and the relegation of religion to the private sphere. Other scholars have supported the "deinstitutionalized" paradigm of secularization, which argues that the deep differentiation of social structures in modernity and the increase in individual autonomy have led to the marginalization of religious institutions and the privatization of religion in modern society (Luckmann 1967). This understanding of secularization refers not only to the loss of the power of once-dominant religious institutions over the whole society (Martin 1978; Dobbelaere 1987), but also to an overlapping of two tendencies: the "institutional deregulation" of historical religions on the one side, and the proliferation of new social expressions of religion on the other (sects, the New Age movement, personal "bricolage" of beliefs, etc.) as the means by which modern individuals constitute their beliefs (Hervieu-Léger 1993, 1999).

To a certain degree, these revisions do alleviate the often glaring discrepancies between classical secularization theory and the actual religious landscape around the globe. However, it would seem that they still cannot resolve an essential problem in existing secularization theory, namely, its entrenched Eurocentrism. Like the classical theory of secularization, which is principally based on the experiences of European Christianity since the Enlightenment, these new secularization theories are fundamentally conceived in and for the Christian West. That is to say, they remain essentially concerned with Western models of religious change, such as the separation between church and state, the distinction between public and the private spheres, and the tension between religious institutions and individualism. They do not account for situations where there is no "church" to speak of or no received separation between public and private, nor do they address the possibility that, in some places in the world, modernity and secularization might produce a new kind of *institutionalization*, rather than deinstitutionalization or privatization of religion.

It would seem that any promising theory of secularization must be able to undergo the trial of a global challenge, and be more open to diverse social configurations and sensitive to particular histories of different religious traditions. First, we need to escape the Eurocentric trap from the very beginning. Thus the notion of secularization should be dissociated from a particular set of assumptions and expectations grounded in specific Western religious and social structures. Second, we can no longer work with a definition of religion that is implicitly based on the features of Christianity and its social integration. The religious situation to which secularization refers must be subjected to concrete and historical interpretations by inserting particular historical religious facts into their proper relations with other social facts. With these considerations, I would like to suggest that one possible strategic choice is to return to the original juridical meaning of secularization, and take it as the starting point of this research about the modern change of Chinese Buddhism.

In its original juridical meaning, the term "secularization" referred to the appropriation of religious properties by the secular state power. That is to say, it described the process and effect of the confrontation between state and religious forces: the former is relatively dominant; it takes and uses the properties, material or symbolic, of the latter. Here "religious forces" not only refers to the dominant "churches" but encompasses a variety of social aggregates of religion, including sects, communal cults, and diverse religious movements. The first advantage of this definition is that it reminds us of the interaction between religion and the state—two key social forces, or collective agents, in modernity's process of secularization. Thus the focus of our observation should be the power relations between religion and the state, rather than a macro-social and macro-structural trend that "affects the totality of cultural life and of ideation" (Berger 1969:107) in modernization. Conceived as an ongoing process of struggle between these two social forces, secularization cannot be taken as either unilateral or irreversible. In most cases, it can only be a complex process full of setbacks and twists and turns. Hence the main task of any sociological study of secularization is no longer to explain a unidirectional linear and teleological change based on Christian Western experiences, but to reconstitute the history and examine the logic of the concrete struggles between two specific historical agents: the state and religion—their conflicts, negotiations, and complicities.[1]

Another advantage of this approach to secularization is that a special connection between secularization and modernity is brought into bold relief. One of the most significant consequences of modernity is the emergence of the modern state. With legitimated violence and rationalized governance, the modern state can now exercise power over social realms that the premodern state could never have penetrated so deeply (Giddens 1985;

Foucault 1976a). In virtually all modern nation-states, religious believers are first identified as citizens, and religious groups as associations, just like other secular ones. Both individual religious followers and religious organizations must be submitted to state regulation. Moreover, as Pierre Bourdieu (1993) has shown, being a powerful military, political, and economic entity, the modern state claims, explicitly or not, a monopoly on symbolic power. Above all, this symbolic power is gained and applied by the production and usage of a legitimate language or discourse (Bourdieu 1982). Hence the modern state, especially in the first phase of its establishment, tends to produce a set of discourses about good and evil, right and wrong, true and false, progressive and backward that is in competition with traditional religious values, and then seeks to recompose and even replace the latter. This struggle for symbolic power is not carried out only in a symbolic way; in fact, it is often accompanied by the extension of state administrative exercises into the domain traditionally controlled by religious authorities (Loveman 2005). By penetrating the management of religious properties and the affairs of religious personnel, the state can more easily and efficiently assert its superiority over religious authorities. Therefore, conflicts between the modern state and religious forces are more or less unavoidable, and can be both material and symbolic, both organizational and discursive. In this sense, though the process of secularization is not totally modern, its modern form is unparalleled in history due to the distinctive expansionary features of the modern state.

Contexualizing the Secularization of Chinese Buddhism

In China, the contemporary fate of Buddhism is deeply imbricated with the formation of the modern state. Especially after the People's Republic of China (PRC) was founded in 1949, the nationalization of the Buddhist and the other religious material and symbolic properties was an explicit and basic state policy. Before analyzing the means by which the Communist state sought to secularize Buddhism and how Buddhist clerics and laypeople reacted when faced with this secularization, we should take into consideration both the political context and the Buddhist specificities in China. In particular, this concerns Communist ideological claims and governance patterns, and the role of Buddhism in the Chinese religious field.[2]

As a compelling social change for answering the foreign diplomatic, military, and economic impacts in nineteenth-century China, modernization was an urgent reform that was forced on Chinese society by threats "from without," rather than being an endogenous historical process. Hence from the very beginning it implied a voluntary break with Chinese traditions, including the religious ones. During the Republican period (1912–49), Chinese religious beliefs had already been considered by numerous political and intellectual elites as spiritual obstacles to modernization. Thus to an extent the anti-religious policy of modern China had its historical origin here, rather than with the Chinese Communist Party (CCP). But when the CCP came into power, the political hostility toward traditional beliefs was strengthened much further and extended to all religions by the ideology of class struggle and historical materialism. Religion was then essentially considered a domination tool of the reactionary ruling classes and an evil legacy of the presocialist societies. Accordingly, the constriction and even suppression of religion became a state policy. Worse still, this policy was put into effect along with the establishment of a totalitarian regime. Through the successive violent social restructurings in the 1950s, the Communist state successfully penetrated the whole social fabric, from associations, local communities, and families to one's personal and private life. For more than the next twenty years, even though religious liberty was allowed in theory according to the Chinese Constitution, religious belief and practice could not be freely manifested, either in the public or the private sphere. To be more precise, the public-private boundary was canceled in reality. All social fields were subjected to the party-state hegemony. Both collective and individual religious life were exposed to governmental surveillance and control. Strictly speaking, the privatization of religion, which characterizes secularization in the West, did not exist in the PRC until the 1980s, when the CCP began the reform in favor of the de-étatization of society.

Neither the privatization thesis nor the separation-of-church-and-state thesis is appropriate for an understanding of Chinese Buddhism and modernity. In secularization theories based on the Christian experiences of Western societies, "legitimation" is a central theme for studying state-religion relations. That is to say, any modern state organized in a rational way ceases to be legitimated by religion, and is therefore no longer the enforcement agency of the religious institution (Berger 1969:130–31; B. Wilson 1982:153–59). Thus secularization is often conceived of in the West as the separation between church and state. In a Chinese context, this separation formulation would only have had heuristic value for understanding the secularization of Confucianism, which was essential to the ideological, bureaucratic, and educational systems of imperial China, had Confucianism been allowed to continue intact in modernity. It is relatively barren for the study of politically nondeterminant religions such as

Buddhism, Daoism, and other religious bodies in China that have never legitimated the state but have exerted an important social influence.

In contrast to the Christian monopoly of the West, China was and still is characterized by its religious pluralism. Without mentioning Islam and Christianity, the three "great traditions" (Confucianism, Buddhism and Daoism) and many kinds of popular cults coexisted there. These religious expressions were often mutually imbricated and merged with one another. In many situations, laypeople could believe and practice the available religions in a pluralistic way: they did not have a clear-cut and exclusive religious identity according to the Western criteria. However, these religions were also in competition with one another. Their positions in the religious field and their relations with political power were very different. Generally speaking, Confucianism had been the main "state religion" since the second century B.C.E., while Buddhism and Daoism were rather subordinated, being appreciated or restrained by emperors at different times. The popular cults and sectarian societies were often in tension with the state, and they sometimes functioned as the instigators of political revolt.

In the modern era, their secularization experiences were also quite different. Compared with Confucianism, Buddhism managed to remain more intact when the monarchy was abolished. As soon as it was founded in 1912, the Republican government devoted itself to building a secular state by eliminating the religious aspects of Confucianism from its political institutions and national education. Then, in the May Fourth Movement (1919) for a "new culture," Confucianism became the principal target of attack by anti-traditionalist intellectuals and was gravely desecrated. Moreover, with the downfall of the empire, Confucianism lost its institutional framework, which had been indistinguishable from the imperial ritual, bureaucratic, and scholastic architectures (Gan 2003).[3] Buddhism, due to its differentiation and institutional separation from traditional politics, seemed to have a better chance of surviving the first phase of Chinese modernization, even appearing to thrive in the Republican period. And in contrast to the popular cults, which were considered not rational or organized enough, and which were ruthlessly decimated by modern Chinese states as "superstitions" during the twentieth century,[4] Buddhism, with its sophisticated theology, monastic institution, and international influence, was recognized as a "religion" par excellence by both the Nationalist (1927–49) and the CCP government.

The situation of Chinese Buddhism in the PRC can therefore be summarized as follows. On the one hand, under the totalitarian regime, Buddhism had to endure absolute political control by the state, with no real private sphere to protect and shelter it. On the other hand, as a given organized religion that could be differentiated from the politics of empire and that was influential in various communities in- and outside of China, Buddhism was recognized by the CCP as one of only five legal religions, along with Daoism, Islam, Catholicism, and Protestantism. In general, the CCP adopted a policy of constricting, remolding, and using Buddhism rather than either leaving it in the private sphere or suppressing it.

Thus, unlike European Catholicism, which is separated from the state and privatized, for Buddhism in Communist China, secularization essentially meant étatization or politicization. That is to say, the human, material, and spiritual resources of Buddhism were controlled, appropriated, and used by the secular party-state according to its ideology and for its own political purposes. This leads to the question of how this secularization process was carried out. To answer to this, the key issue we must tackle is the statist institutionalization of Buddhist religious organization.

Institutionalization as a Pattern of Secularization

As mentioned above, in the recent theoretical development of secularization, "deinstitutionalization" is a central notion. As a kind of substitute for the idea of the decline of religion, deinstitutionalization means an individual detachment from the church—and, more widely, the process by which religious practice and representation are removed from the domination of religious institutions and submitted to personal or new communal religiosities. In this chapter, the term "institutionalization" is not used at the same level. In fact, the deinstitutionalization thesis focuses on the general relation between social structure and individual believers. In this respect institutionalization signifies the socialization effects of (Christian) institutional identity and norms on the individual, which decline in Western modernity.

However, what I am interested in is the relation between the larger social structure and religious organizations. Here, on the one hand, institutionalization involves the structuring model of power relations and the degree of rationalization in the regulations within an organization. Compared with voluntary associations, an "institutionalized" social grouping means that its members are submitted, at least partially, to some established and rationalized rules in a hierarchical structure (Weber 1965:384–98, 1971:49–60). On the other hand, and more importantly for us, institutionalization refers to the effects of the external institutional conditions on organizations. According to Anthony Giddens (1979, 1984), at the social structure level, an "institution" could be conceived of as the general manner of the reproduction of rules and resources. If an organization is reconfigured by the encompassing external institutional arrangement, so that its structure and its rules about the reproduction and distribution of resources tend to be identical with its institutional environment, then it can be seen as an "institutionalized" organization. Thus we must recognize that the institutionalization of a social organization includes two aspects: one is internal and the other is external. The internal institutionalization of an organization can be influenced by its larger institutional environment to different degrees, whereas the external institutionalization cannot be accomplished without the internal institutionalization.

In a society like Communist China, where state power is strong and the society is weak, political interference in social organizations is extremely significant. Before the policy of "reform and opening up" appeared, the state as a legitimate coercive force, without restraints from market and civil society, formulated the fundamental institutional conditions of all social organizations in China, including the religious ones. The Chinese Communist state affected not only the structure and performance of Buddhist organizations but the interrelations between them. The modern Chinese state also engendered an official monopolistic Buddhist institution through which it penetrated the Buddhist field, in order to control and transform Buddhism. In this sense, the process of statist institutionalization can be seen as one of the main secularization patterns of Chinese Buddhism.

THE INSTITUTIONALIZATION OF BUDDHIST ORGANIZATIONS: AN ASSOCIATIVITY SHAPED BY SECULARIZATION

With its own theological system, unique rituals, and independent, specialized organization of personnel, Chinese Buddhism is a typical institutional religion.[5] However, Buddhism in China never constructed a centralized priesthood or a national religious structure (Yang 1961:307–40), even though the internal rules of the *sangha* (monastic clergy) were highly rationalized. Generally speaking, Buddhist monks were organized in an introverted monastic order whose orientation was other-worldly. On the one hand, monastic life was regulated by *sīla* (precepts) and other religious disciplines, at a considerable distance from the secular norm.[6] On the other hand, Buddhism was also influenced by kinship institutions and restricted by communally based social structures, so that Buddhists formed very loosely organized associations attached to religious lineages or local communities. Each Buddhist monastery was a relatively independent social body. Buddhism, like Daoism, never developed an autonomous, empirewide organization, nor did it ever have a centralized and integrated hierarchical structure like the Christian church. But this situation began to change in the twentieth century. With the formation of the modern state and society in China, a strong desire emerged for a new organizational integration beyond the old system of lineages and localities in Buddhism.

Organizational Integration of Chinese Buddhism before 1949: A Resistance to Secularization

The first attempt to form an association of Buddhist monasteries was a reaction to the policy of "building schools with temple property" (廟產興學, *miaochan xingxue*) in the last years of the Qing dynasty. In 1898, Zhang Zhidong (張之洞, 1837–1909), one of the leaders of the conservative reformist politicians, proposed in his famous *Exhortation to Learning* (勸學篇, *Quanxuepian*) that the government confiscate a majority of the property of Buddhist, Daoist, and other popular temples for establishing new schools. This proposal was adopted by the Qing court as part of a larger project to strengthen the empire with Western sciences and technologies, and was put into practice in 1901. Confronted with such a crisis of secularization, from 1907 through 1910 a number of Buddhist leaders founded in succession the Associations for Sangha Education (僧教育會, Seng Jiaoyu Hui) with local gentry in some parts of the country. By taking the initiative in establishing Buddhist or civil schools, the related monasteries tried to legally conserve their property. Although these associations functioned only at the local level, what is historically significant is that, for the first time, they had gone beyond the old system of Buddhist monasteries and lineages (Chen & Deng 2000:35–36; Deng 1994:105–12).

After the Republic was founded in 1912, the secularization drama of "building schools with temple property" was staged once more. Consequently, the movement to protect property remained the main dynamic of Buddhists' organizational unification (Wang L. 1994). Indeed, a collective action framework was an effective way for Buddhism to negotiate with the state and the other social forces. Moreover, at that time, the emerging notion of the nation-state offered an extended scope to Buddhist united organization. Inspired by the new models of modern political parties and associations, Buddhist reformers hoped to realize their ambition through the new organizations outside the old monastic structure (He J. 1992). However, as Vincent Goossaert points out in his chapter in this book, taking Christianity as the model of an authentic religion, the new Republican government preferred organized religions that could establish church-like national associations. For these reasons, in Buddhism, Daoism, and some other Chinese traditional cults, people actively invented national associations in order to gain political recognition and contend for the redistributed religious power. From 1912 to 1929, at least eighteen separate so-called national Buddhist associations were launched in China (Welch 1968:26). Among them, the two that had any real national influence were the General Association of Chinese Buddhists (中華佛教總會, Zhonghua Fojiao Zonghui, 1912–18), based on the early Associations for Sangha Education, and the Chinese Buddhist Association (中國佛教會, Zhongguo Fojiao Hui), founded in 1929. The latter was officially recognized by the Nationalist government and was the most important Buddhist association in China until 1949.

Even though these new Buddhist organizations represented diverse ambitions of the different reformist and conservative factions and suffered some political constraints, they achieved some remarkable successes in protecting the rights and monastic properties of Buddhists. For example, due to the efforts of the Chinese Buddhist Association, the "Rules for Regulating Temples," considered unfavorable to Buddhism, was repealed by the Nationalist government in 1929, less than a year after this law had come into effect. In 1931, the same association, led by the famous Buddhist monk-reformer Taixu (太虛, 1889–1947), even made the government issue an order protecting monastic property. Under the Republican regime, Buddhist associations had been relatively autonomous, though the Nationalist government seemed in favor of the Buddhist reformers. The state only intervened more than usual in the Anti-Japanese War (1937–45), in order to reconcile the reformists and the conservatives, the monks and the lay Buddhists so as to mobilize all Buddhists during wartime (Chen & Deng 2000:45–55).

Secularization under the Communist Regime: Socialist Transformation by Participatory Mobilization

The prolonged wartime era of the 1930s hindered the Chinese Buddhist Association in fully playing its desired role. However, when peace finally arrived in 1949, the situation of Buddhist organizations did not become any better. In reality, another revolution began. As soon as the CCP came into power, it carried out the total socialist transformation of politics, economy, culture, and social relations. A state of unprecedented strength in Chinese history came into being. With the thorough change in state-society relations in the country, the Buddhists were reorganized, monastic property was appropriated, and Buddhist symbolic resources were utilized by the new political power. As in other domains, the socialist transformation of Buddhism was accomplished through the participatory mobilization of Buddhists themselves.[7]

In September 1949, soon after the occupation of North China by the CCP, a progressive monk named Juzan (巨贊, 1908–84) organized the first pro-Communist Buddhist group in Beijing for "political study," and then transferred it into a more structured "study group" (學習班, *xuexiban*). Very quickly Juzan's study group became a widely followed model. From 1950 to 1960, study groups were organized by Buddhist groups all over the country, especially in the major cities (Welch 1972:89–97). This ideological mobilization became a preparation for the general reorganization of Buddhists. In fact, the reform of the local branches of the old Chinese Buddhist Association and the establishment of the new local Buddhist organizations were frequently initiated by political study groups.

The basic activities in the study groups were practices of discourse. According to the requirements of actual political campaigns, the monks and lay Buddhists gathered together to read the works of Chairman Mao, the texts of Marxism-Leninism, Party documents, official newspapers, and so forth. At the same time, they had to show that their "level of awareness" was raised thanks to such a study. Thus they had to be active in the discussions; they were encouraged, if not pushed, to put up wall posters, draft "patriotic compacts," compose big-character posters, and write confessions (Welch 1972:90–91). The study groups appeared to be voluntarily organized by Buddhists themselves, but they were always conducted by supervisors in charge of religious affairs or by progressive Buddhists close to the CCP. In reality, collective study was a technique of power through which the authority of official discourse could be established by ritually respectful reading and explanation. In group discussions, everyone had to make known his or her political "position." Under this collective pressure, consensus could be realized to a certain degree and the "activists"—those who played the drama well, in conformity with official rules, or who had really interiorized the given values and norms—could be distinguished from the "backward elements." Hence the study group was not only a political ritual device for remolding Buddhists' minds but also a means by which Buddhist associations absorbed the party-state and its power mechanism into their own institutions.

What was more fatal for Buddhism was the socialist reform of the ownership system of the means of production. In 1950, Land Reform was launched. In this process, most of the monasteries' land was expropriated and only a small proportion was set aside for the monks' basic subsistence, according to criteria set at the local level. The consequence was crucial: the monks lost the farm rents that had been their main source of income for more than a thousand years (Welch 1972:42–83). Moreover, the significance of this land redistribution was not merely economic. Land reform was in fact an important step for the new state to take in order to mobilize the peasants, extend the space of its administrative exercise, and implant its power in rural social life (Man 2005). Accordingly, like the lay peasants, the Buddhists were mobilized to participate in the obligatory collective activities, such as criticism and denouncement meetings. The newly founded local Buddhist organizations were all in the service of the local governments, providing them with statistics of Buddhist personnel and land as a kind of "knowledge of the state." Furthermore, with the forced redistribution of monastic property, the power inside Buddhist circles was also redistributed. A few monks and lay Buddhists ready to collaborate with the government were appointed representatives of the religious population. According to the new political norm and productive model, they assisted the government in reallocating Buddhist human and material resources, such as the division of the monasteries and monks into groups for organized labor and the management of the monks' residential registrations. The "conservative" monks were marginalized, especially some of the older and more highly ranked ones. In the worst cases they were even executed as "monk-lords of feudalism" (封建僧閥, fengjian sengfa). In the process of the secularization of Buddhism, the internal struggle for power among the monks and the reorganization of Buddhist monasteries and organizations were correlative processes.

Another remarkable change in state-Buddhist relations concerned the way the state used Buddhist symbolic resources. It is true that both the Chinese imperial state and the Communist one were interested in using Buddhism. However, the former shared a religious logic with the Buddhists, for it respected both a higher transcendental realm above earthly powers and the symbolic resources needed to access such higher powers. When Buddhism served the state in imperial times, the distinction between the sacred and profane defined by Buddhism was affirmed, the primacy of other-worldly salvation in relation to worldly affairs was respected, and ritual practice was generally controlled and performed by the monks themselves. The imperial state's utilization of Buddhism was not detrimental to Buddhist symbolic capital, and sometimes even strengthened the symbolic power of the monks. However, under the Communists, the political utilization of Buddhism was totally incorporated into the state-monopolized secular ruling structure. In general, the Buddhists were merely mobilized in a secular way for secular objectives, like any other social group subjected to state power. Thus the participation of Buddhists in state activities only signified an alienation of Buddhist symbolic power and authority, and a recognition of and deference to a new earthly ruling structure. For example, in the early 1950s, Buddhism, which historically had been held in high esteem because of its pacifism, was steered by the state toward influencing public opinion to justify the PRC's military engagement in the Korean War. Through the newly established organizations, Buddhists were mobilized to make statements and publish written protests against the United States, organize anti-American demonstrations, criticize American imperialism in international exchanges, and even donate money for weapons to be used by the Chinese troops (Welch 1972:101–8). By using Buddhism in such a secular way, the state diverted the Buddhists' interests from religious life, further undermined the autonomy of Buddhist associations, and nationalized Buddhist symbolic resources and power.

Formation of the Buddhist Association of China: Rendering State Rule Routine

This official reorganization of Buddhists remained at a local level from 1949 to 1953. In May 1953, as a new "channel of government control" (Welch 1972:17), the official Buddhist Association of China (BAC, 中國 佛教協會, Zhongguo Fojiao Xiehui) came into being. This meant that the state organizational mobilization of Buddhists had entered the national level and become something routine.

As Holmes Welch has pointed out, since 1949 progressive Buddhists had tried more than once to set up a national association. To begin with, these attempts were not approved by the Communist government. According to Welch, at that time the CCP had not yet decided how to use Buddhism in a constructive way, and how much scope Buddhists should be given. But in September 1952, when the "Peace Conference of Asia and the Pacific Regions" was held in Beijing (attended by Buddhists from eight different countries), the CCP had been persuaded to support a national association, to make Chinese Buddhists speak "with a single voice" (Welch 1972:17–18). In this same year, Land Reform and the stabilization of the urban economy were accomplished; the new state power system was established all over the country, including Tibet. Having stabilized the new nation, the CCP could give more priority to diplomatic affairs and ethnic integration work. Buddhism appeared useful to the government because of its influence in Tibet, Inner Mongolia, other non-Han Chinese regions, and certain Asian countries. Since ethnic and diplomatic affairs could not simply be dealt with at a local level, a national Buddhist apparatus in conformity with the central government became necessary.

Therefore, from the very beginning, the BAC was designed to serve the government in national unification and international exchanges. Thus, in each session of the BAC councils, there were several Tibetans and Mongolians who held the posts of chair or vice chair. Even though these titles were rather honorary, the multiethnic representation in the BAC became a symbol of Chinese national unity. In terms of the international exchange, the BAC played the role of a state diplomatic reception and propaganda organ, receiving foreign Buddhist dignitaries. According to the statistics of Welch (1972:185–201), from 1952 through 1966, at least thirty-six foreign Buddhist delegations visited China, and eleven Chinese Buddhist delegations went abroad. During the same period, twenty-five or more individuals were invited to China as Buddhists. In most cases, it was the BAC who was in charge of these meetings.

Another reason for the Chinese government to encourage a national Buddhist association could be understood as a strategy to limit the number of players with which it had to negotiate in the Buddhist field. In the economy of authoritarian domination, the fewer the collective actors, the more easily the state ensures its control. The ideal result is the monopoly of the state-owned enterprise in each sector. Thus, on the one hand, the BAC absorbed step by step the previously founded local Buddhist organizations with state support. On the other hand, the government eliminated the other relatively independent and competitive Buddhist groups, such as the Shanghai Buddhist Youth Society and the famous lay Buddhists' group, the Beijing Sunshi Society, by accusing them of being counterrevolutionary or superstitious. Thus by the mid-1960s the BAC was the only representative organization of Chinese Buddhists. This reconfiguration of the Chinese Buddhist field greatly reduced the complexities in the traditional Buddhist power structure. Gradually, the emphasis of the state secularization policy turned from appropriation and redistribution of Buddhist property to stable control and routine use of Buddhism through the BAC.

The Nature of the Buddhist Association of China: An Institutionalized Organization in a State-Corporatist Structure

The BAC was neither a clerical body, like the Christian church, nor an institution representative of the Buddhists' interests, like the old Chinese Buddhist Association of the Republican era. Rather, it was a heteronomous organization, an intermediary of the state in its control of the Buddhists.

Holmes Welch has also pointed out this characteristic aspect of the BAC. According to him, as a servant of government, the BAC was similar to the *sangha* officials system of the Ming and Qing dynasties and different from the Chinese Buddhist Association of the Republican era, which had worked for the Buddhist community (Welch 1972:25). This is correct, although it seems that the resemblance between the BAC and the ancient *sangha* officials system is only superficial. First created in the fifth century, the *sangha* officials system was reformed many times in different dynasties (Xie & Bai 1990), but its essential feature remained the incorporation of highly ranked monks into the imperial bureaucracy. With the assistance of these monks, the state attempted to supervise the qualification of religious personnel and the building of temples. However, this control system was only a marginal articulation of imperial bureaucracy. State power never really dominated monastic life. Inside the *sangha*, the monk-officials followed the internal Buddhist disciplines, just as they had always done. Their responsibility to the government was essentially formal and procedural.

Under the Communist regime, in contrast, although the BAC was not directly a part of the state bureaucracy, its internal rules and objectives were adjusted according to the deep penetration of state power into the whole of society. As we have seen, the organizational model of the BAC was perfectly in tune with the ruling structure and power techniques of the state. The task assumed by the BAC was more political than administrative. Its main functions were not licensing the priesthood and controlling the number of temples, as in the old *sangha* officials system, but the mobilization of Buddhist clergy and laypeople to contribute Buddhist resources to the cause of state-building. As the BAC's 1953 constitution put it, the association's goals were

> to unite all the country's Buddhists so that they will participate,
> under the leadership of the People's Government, in movements
> for the welfare of the Motherland and the defense of world peace;
> to help the People's Government fully carry out its policy of freedom
> of religious belief; to link up Buddhists from different parts of the
> country; and to exemplify the best traditions of Buddhism. (translated
> by Welch 1972:20)

Since the objective, the discourse, the action model, and the inner power relationship of the BAC were all assimilated to those of its institutional environment—namely, the Communist regime—we could say that the BAC was an "institutionalized organization," like the secular "work-units" (單位, *danwei*) that organized the working lives of city dwellers in the PRC.[8]

Certainly, the BAC was different from ordinary work-units. In theory, it had the autonomy of an independent association. As the single legitimate "mass organization" for all Chinese Buddhists, it was in line with the "united front" strategy of the CCP.[9] Viewed from this angle, the BAC could be considered a concrete embodiment of state corporatism under the Communist regime. According to Philippe Schmitt:

> Corporatism can be defined as a system of interest representation in which the constituent units are organized into a limited number of singular, compulsory, noncompetitive, hierarchically ordered and functionally differentiated categories, recognized or licensed (if not created) by the state and granted a deliberate representational monopoly within their respective categories in exchange for observing certain controls on their selection of leaders and articulation of demands and supports. (Schmitt 1974:93–94)

Schmitt distinguished two types of corporatism: societal and state (Schmitt 1974:103–5, 1977; Gu & Wang 2005). Societal corporatism can be found in a democratic political system. It is the multilayerd or deeply differentiated societal structure that engenders corporations. For each social category, there can be multiple corporations whose relative positions are determined through an open competition. By contrast, state corporatism is usually associated with a strong centralized, hierarchical political system. At the national level, the state licenses or creates only one organization as the sole legal representative of a functionally differentiated category. By intervening in the leadership and the structure of this organization, the state constructs an unequal partnership with the organization and uses it as an instrument of social regulation.

For some scholars (Unger & Chan 1995), China already possessed a corporatist structure in Mao's era, albeit a sort of "proto-corporatism." Corporations such as the National Labor Union could not function very well under the Party's control, and some of them were short-lived. Thus these scholars suggest that real corporatism did not exist in the PRC until the 1990s, when many commercial, professional, and sporting associations came into being at both national and local levels. These arguments are reasonable to a certain extent. However, applying the notion of "state corporatism" proposed by Schmitt helps us make sense of some strategies of governance even in Mao's China (with the possible exception of the period of the Cultural Revolution from 1966 to 1976). Schmitt has suggested that in any country where state corporatism is found, the party system tends to be dominated or monopolized by a single weak party. Yet even in a totalitarian regime with a single strong party, it is impossible for the party-state to exercise its social control without an intermediary, especially in the religious field. Unlike categories based on objective criteria such as age, sex, class, ethnicity, profession, and region, the identity of religious believers is essentially subjective and internal. It is relatively difficult for the state to identify the religious believers in the population, notably the lay converts, and keep them under surveillance. Thus the institutional arrangement of state corporatism can be a channel through which state power more effectively reaches religious believers. That is why the official, monopolistic national-association structure is found in all five recognized religions in the PRC, of which the BAC is only one.

Of course, we are dealing here with a state corporatism in which state interference is extremely active and strong. In China, the BAC was explicitly submitted to the state, as indicated in its founding charter. Its leadership served the Religious Affairs Bureau (RAB) of the government and the United Front Work Department of the CCP. Normally, the leaders of the BAC were associated with the political system through the Chinese People's Political Consultative Conference (CPPCC, a political advisory body) and the National People's Congress (NPC, the highest state body and only legislative house in the PRC). Their positions within these political institutions corresponded to their places in the hierarchy of the BAC. The state also directly controlled the leadership of the BAC. For example, I was informed by a number of Buddhists that Zhao Puchu (趙朴初, 1907–2000), the key figure in charge of the substantive work of the BAC as a lay Buddhist, was in fact a Communist Party member, even though this was never publicly acknowledged. Soon after Shanghai was occupied by the CCP, he was engaged in the Communist political system. From 1950 on, he was successively appointed deputy director of the Civil Affairs Branch and deputy director of the Personnel Branch of the Military and Political Commission of East China, then deputy director of the Political and Juridical Commission of the Shanghai People's Government, until June 1953, when he became vice chair and secretary-general of the newly founded BAC. Since the very beginning, he wielded the real power of the BAC; the other chairs and vice chairs were only figureheads, such as Buddhist leaders of minority groups and some venerable Han Chinese monks. Zhao held the post of chair of the BAC from 1980 until his death in 2000. One of Zhao's assistants before the Cultural Revolution, Guo Peng (郭朋, 1920–2004), vice secretary-general from 1953 to 1962, was even *officially* recognized as a Party member.

UNINTENDED CONSEQUENCES OF STATIST
INSTITUTIONALIZATION: THREE PARADOXES

By means of the state-corporatist model, the CCP tended to control all the religious fields through officially institutionalized religious organizations. However, no power relation can be settled conclusively, and the domination of the state over religious groups is no exception. Once state regulation becomes less effective, once the religious corporations are empowered by new resources, or once the religious field is reconfigured, the relationship between the state and the religious corporations would be renewed. This has been exactly the case in China since the 1980s, as communist totalitarianism has been progressively replaced by authoritarianism.

The Ambivalent Role of the Buddhist Association of China: Between State Agency and Church

Thanks to the policy of "reform and opening up," state constraints on social life are relatively relaxed today in China. The economic, cultural, and social exchanges of Chinese people are becoming more enriched and diversified. The private sphere and civil society are beginning to be liberated from state hegemony. In this context, some significant changes can be found in the performance of the BAC. Above all, its main function has been adjusted from social mobilization to clerical management; its first goal has been revised from serving state-building to protecting the Buddhists' rights and interests.

In 1983, at the second conference of the fourth council of the BAC, the "Resolution on the Problems of the Tonsure and the Initiation into Monkhood or Nunhood in Han Chinese Buddhist Monasteries" was adopted. Its final version was published in April 1984. According to this resolution, the initiation ritual for monkhood must be organized by the provincial branches of the BAC; the certificate of monkhood should be designed uniquely by the BAC and distributed by its provincial branches. This resolution marked the beginning of the centralization of the clerical power from the monasteries to the BAC. From then on, the BAC progressively became a church-like organization. Its constitution, modified at the sixth national congress in 1993, confirmed this transformation. Since then, the official definition of the BAC is no longer simply "an association of Chinese Buddhists of all ethnicities" but "a patriotic group and an organization in charge of the clerical affairs" of Chinese Buddhists. At the same congress, a series of monastic regulations were adopted, such as the "Administrative Regulations of Han Buddhist Monasteries," "General

Rules of Collective Life in Han Buddhist Monasteries" and "Method for Buddhist Monasteries in Han Chinese Regions to Fund the BAC for Buddhist Undertakings." In his report entitled "Forty Years of the BAC," BAC chair Zhao Puchu appealed to Buddhists to "shift their focus and work emphasis to the construction of Buddhism itself and the improvement of the quality of the monks and lay Buddhists." In the following years, the BAC also established the "Regulations for the Great Commandments of the Three Altars for Han Buddhist Monasteries,"[10] "Regulations for the Appointment and Removal of the Abbots in Han Buddhist Monasteries," and "Method for Putting into Practice the Monkhood License System in Han Buddhist Monasteries." It is evident here that secular-political issues have lost their central position in the BAC's agenda. Remarkably, the BAC has begun to transform itself from a state agency into a Buddhist "church."

Furthermore, the BAC has embarked on a defense of the "legal rights and interests" of Buddhists. First of all, the BAC has contributed considerably to the revival of Buddhism after the Cultural Revolution (Xu Y. 1997). Since the 1980s, it has played a key role in demanding that the government reopen the closed monasteries and return appropriated Buddhist property. It has also offered a trans-monasterial framework for promoting the Buddhist reconstructive enterprises on a regional or national scale, such as the edition and publication of Buddhist literature, the reestablishment of Buddhist institutes, and the coordination of grand ceremonies. In addition, as the sole institutional intermediary between Buddhists and the state, and pushed by Buddhists elsewhere who enjoy more freedom, the BAC has begun to negotiate with political authorities for Buddhist community on the legal and policy level. For example, at the beginning of the 1990s, it set forth amendment plans for certain articles concerning religions in the Chinese Constitution, in criminal law, and in the civil code. It even succeeded in persuading the CCP to add an article to the penal code to punish those state agents who "illegally deprive the citizens of their rights to religious belief or infringe on the customs and habits of the ethnic groups." At the annual meeting of the Chinese People's Political Consultative Conference in 2003, the monk Shenghui, the current vice chair of the BAC, demanded revision of the chapter on the "Social Effects of Religion" in the "Political Idea" textbook for senior secondary schools. According to him, this official textbook has distorted the facts about religions.

The modifications of the BAC constitution also reflect the evolution of the role of this quasi-state organization. In its 1953 version, the constitu-

Figure 9.1. Two Buddhist monks entering the Great Hall of the People in
Beijing for the Tenth National Committee of the Chinese People's Political
Consultative Conference, March 8, 2003. Photo by Liu Weibing.

tion only mentioned that the BAC should "help the People's Government
fully carry out its policy of freedom of religious belief," without any mention of the protection of Buddhists' rights or their interests. In the 1980
version, the phrase "defend the Buddhists' freedom of belief" was added as
one task of the BAC, but this modest claim was still put after the item "to
unite all the Buddhists and promote their participation in various works
to serve the people." In 1987, the order of the two tasks was significantly

reversed. Finally, in 1993, this key phrase was enriched and became more detailed so that the constitution stated that the BAC should

> defend Buddhists' rights for freedom of belief; defend the legal interests of Buddhist groups, of Buddhist sites of activity, of Buddhist educational institutions, and of Buddhist self-supporting service institutions; maintain close contacts with Buddhists of different ethnicities, make thorough investigations and studies to give expression to Buddhists' wishes; [and] put forward suggestions on the problems in laws and policies [to the state]. (*Fayin*, no. 12, 1993:26)

Admittedly, the BAC is still under the control of the state; it is still a servant of the CCP, especially in international exchanges, relations with Taiwan, and anti-sect movements. Each year, the BAC and its branches have to report to the Religious Affairs Bureau with information about their personnel, activities, and finances. Nevertheless, the BAC is the first real unified national Buddhist organization in Chinese history. For better or worse, with its monopolistic framework, it is capable of balancing the contending forces inside Buddhism at a national level and negotiating with the state and other social groups. Today, the BAC is still far from being independent of the state, but it enjoys more and more autonomy, along with the increasing social and religious liberty in China, and it has begun to work for the interests of the Buddhist clergy and the general promotion of Buddhism.

Hence a paradox in the relations between the state and Buddhism has appeared: it was the state's attempt to control Buddhism that initially gave rise to a monopolistic Buddhist national organization without parallel in Chinese history. Now this state institutionalization has laid the foundation for a strong church-like institution and an integrated representative of the Buddhist community that has begun to negotiate with the state on its own terms. Thus, just as Michel Foucault pointed out, power is not simply repressive but, rather, endlessly productive (1976b, 1994a, 1994b).

This-Worldly Buddhism: From Secularized Theology to Legitimating Discourse

The productive effect of state power over Chinese Buddhism was not only organizational but also discursive. In fact, a new state means a new regime of discourse. Soon after 1949, when the PRC was founded, the discourse of proletarian revolution and socialist construction became overwhelmingly dominant. There was a flood of terms, such as "revolution," "New China," "the people," and "socialism," in the Chinese public's expressions. Finally, the official ideology was accepted as the only sound reference point of reasoning. In this situation, to gain a more favorable position in the "new society," Buddhists began to reinterpret Buddhist doctrine in politically correct rhetoric (Welch 1972:267–97) to show that the values and vision of history imposed by the new regime were all compatible with Buddhist orthodoxy. Thus, if monks lost their monastic property and had to be engaged in "productive labor," it was a return to the tradition of "combining Chan with agricultural work" (農禪幷重, *nong chan bingzhong*). If Buddhists were forced to participate in political campaigns, it was for "practicing the Bodhisattva Way" and "repaying the debt of gratitude to the Motherland." If Buddhists had to support the PRC's engagement in the Korean War, it was a concrete manifestation of the Buddhist spirit of "Great Compassion" (大悲, *dabei*) and "dauntlessness" (無畏, *wuwei*). In some cases, even killing (counterrevolutionaries and the imperialist enemy) was justified. Generally speaking, Buddhist doctrine was reoriented from other-worldly to this-worldly, even politico-centric concerns. Henceforth, Buddhists had to seek their salvation nowhere but in "patriotic movements," working to serve the people and building a "Pure Land in this world" in socialist China.

Despite its creative discursive adaptations to the new Communist world, Buddhism did not escape the tragic fate of destruction during the Cultural Revolution. However, compared with other religions, Chinese Buddhists manifested an extraordinary capacity to engage in the tactics of discourse. After the Cultural Revolution, under the command of the BAC, they have begun to deploy the dominant official discourse as a resource in arguing for the legitimate revival and existence of Buddhism.

In his report to a conference for the BAC in 1983, Zhao Puchu once again employed the slogan of "this-worldly Buddhism" (人間佛教, *renjian fojiao*), which had originally been voiced by the reformist monk Taixu in the 1920s,[11] and reinterpreted by Juzan and other progressive Buddhists when the PRC was founded. This time, it was summarized by Zhao as the "three excellent traditions of Chinese Buddhism," seemingly focusing on secular causes: "combining Chan with agricultural work," "intellectual study" (學術研究, *xueshu yanjiu*), and "international friendly exchange" (國際友好交流, *guoji youhao jiaoliu*). At first appearance, the first two were repetitions of two slogans—"shift to production" (生產化, *shengchanhua*) and "shift to scholarship" (學術化, *xueshuhua*)—launched by Juzan in 1949, and the third was only a description of the task assumed by the BAC since its inauguration. However, neither the objectives nor the effects of these seemingly similar discourses were actually the same. During the first phase of the establishment of the Communist regime, the end of "shifting to production" was to separate Buddhism from the "feudal economic system," while "shifting to scholarship" was a method for eliminating the "superstitious" element from Buddhism. After the Cultural Revolution, when Buddhism had almost been destroyed, the idea of "combining Chan with agricultural work," as a way of "participating actively in building the socialist material civilization," was actually understood as a practical strategy to help Buddhists to revive their religious practices through economic self-reliance. The slogan of "combining Chan with agricultural work" now no longer legitimized the appropriation of monastic properties by the state, as in Mao's era, but was meant to encourage Buddhists to rebuild their monastic life by working on the land returned by the state in the process of decollectivization (Ji Z. 2004). In the same manner, the discourse of "shifting to scholarship" was reinterpreted as a way of "participating actively in building the socialist spiritual civilization," which now served to renew the education of young monks and the propagation of Buddhist culture after a rupture of nearly twenty years. Even the discourse of "international friendly exchange," which had implied that Buddhism should render service to the state, was reinterpreted to emphasize the importance of reopening and rebuilding monasteries for the purpose of receiving foreign Buddhists, especially Japanese and overseas Chinese Buddhists who brought financial aid to Buddhists.

In fact, as Foucault revealed, discourse should be considered a series of discontinuous segments whose tactical function is neither uniform nor stable (1976b:132–35). Discourse does not support or oppose power in an unchanging way. Different discourses can be used for the same strategy, and the same discourse can serve different and even opposed objectives. The effects of a discourse depend on who uses it, the user's power position, and the location of the user in a particular institutional context. Therefore, discourse can become a "starting point for an opposing strategy" when the ways and the historical conditions in which it is used change. That is why the vectors of politically correct discourses quoted and produced by Buddhists in the 1980s were different from those of the period before the Cultural Revolution.

Thus we see another paradox in Chinese state-Buddhism relations. Under political pressure, Buddhist discourses and missions were officially fixed in a this-worldly-oriented theology and secular cause. However, this secularization of discourse granted Buddhism a necessary and legitimate space for its reconstruction and development in a society where religion was officially thought of as harmful. Indeed, the discourse of power is not only the instrument of the dominant. It can also be used by the dominated as a tactic for empowering itself, so as to produce consequences that the dominant had not intended.

The Dilemma of State Regulation of Religion: State Corporatism in a Reopened Field

For the Chinese state, another serious, unintended consequence of its statist institutionalization policy has been a crisis in its regulation of religious affairs on the whole. As is well known, in principle only five historical and organized religions, including Buddhism, are officially recognized in China. All other religious forms and popular cults are considered "feudal superstitions" to be abolished. By supervising the officially institutionalized and monopolistic associations of these five religions, the state aims to control all the religious life of its people. However, for this strategy to be valid, one has to assume the closed structure of the religious field in question. That is to say, no new religious group enters the field of play, as was the case in Mao's era. But today in China, the religious field has been reopened. On one side, Chinese people have more freedom to express their increasing religious needs. On the other side, restrained by strict political control, the official religious institutions cannot fully satisfy the religious demands of the people. Seizing this chance, many nonofficial religious enterprises are now either emerging, beginning to enter, or reentering the religious market.

In the Buddhist field, orthodox Buddhism and its official association, the BAC, find the task of absolute monopoly increasingly difficult. For the last two decades, more and more spiritual groups have entered into rivalry with official Buddhism for power in the management of Buddhist "salvation goods." First, at the end of the 1980s, several Buddhist sects originating in Taiwan, Hong Kong, or other overseas Chinese communities (such as the "Guanyin Famen" [Guanyin Dharma Gate] and the "Zhenfozong" [True Buddha School]) arrived in China. The leaders of these sects often claimed to be a "living buddha" (活佛, huofo) or bodhisattva. By promoting some para-Buddhist ethics and methods, they rapidly gained a large following in the PRC, from workers to artists, in both urban and rural areas. Despite governmental suppression, these sects have never been entirely eliminated.

Second, the new native religious groups in China began to strategically dodge political control by presenting themselves in alternative forms. For example, in the name of qigong—a collection of bodily skills for controlling one's spirit, breath, and behavior to achieve a state of physical and mental well-being—some organizations became vehicles of new Buddhist sects.[12] By borrowing Buddhist symbols and terms and equating *qigong* masters with Buddhist saints, these groups promised their members spiritual and physical health, miraculous capacities, and even salvation, or enlightenment. Sometimes they appropriated Buddhist labels in naming themselves, such as Damogong (Practice of Bodhidharma), Huiliangong (Practice of the Lotus of Wisdom), Putigong (Practice of the Bodhisattva), and Falungong (Practice of the Wheel of the Law; Fori 1999). Carefully presenting themselves as sports or leisure groups for therapeutic education and exercises, they were allowed to develop freely for a relatively long time in the PRC, until 1999, when the Falungong movement and some other *qigong* organizations were cruelly suppressed.[13]

Third, in addition to the organized sects, there are numerous lay "great masters" of para-Buddhism who offer individual religious services outside the official Buddhist framework. They usually style themselves the foremost exponents of certain secret Buddhist schools. Around these figures some informal groups may also exist.

The relationship between official Buddhism and the new Buddhist faiths is an ambiguous and ambivalent one. On the one hand, their memberships are not completely exclusive. A believer can belong to two or more groups at the same time and move from one to the other. It is not rare for people to first become interested in Buddhism in a para-Buddhist sect and later convert to official Buddhism. At the same time, the tension between official Buddhism and the new Buddhist groups is obvious and even irresolvable: the latter threaten the monopolistic authority of the former. Generally speaking, the virtues and titles claimed by the sectarian leaders (who are nearly all laypeople) cannot be recognized by the monastic authorities. The legitimacy of their teachings is often doubted and criticized by both monks and lay Buddhists who belong to official Buddhism. The attitude of the BAC to Falungong clearly illustrates this tension. In fact, three yeas before governmental suppression, the Buddhists in the BAC system had begun to berate Falungong in their publications.[14] In 1999, the BAC played an active role in criticizing Falungong as an "evil cult."[15] The active participation of the BAC in the anti-Falungong campaign cannot be reduced simply to its need to display loyalty to the CCP under political pressure, but must also be seen as the reaction of a "church" to competition from a new "sect."

Nor are the new religious faiths limited to the Buddhist field. As is well known, certain recomposed communal beliefs and popular cults have returned to Chinese society with amazing vitality, and the underground

Christian churches are more and more influential. Though the official religious institutions are maintaining their relatively dominant position, the offerings of the religious marketplace have become much more diversified. Thus Chinese religious policy is caught in a dilemma. On the one hand, the state's rigid restraint of institutional religions actually pushes people to seek fulfillment in underground, communitarian, sectarian, individual, or alternative forms of religion (Ji Z. 2006). Therefore, the more rigorous the state control over the five legal religious institutions, the more nonofficial religiosities flourish, and the more difficult it is for the state to manage religious affairs as a whole. On the other hand, the state can no longer simply close the religious field, as it did during its totalitarian period. If the state wishes to support the monopoly of the official religious institutions in the religious marketplace, it has to give them more autonomy so as to make them more competitive. However, this inevitably entails the weakening of state control over the five legal religions.

Thus there arises yet another paradoxical result of the state-corporatist policy: regardless of whether the state strengthens or weakens its control over the official religious institutions, a partial deregulation of the religious life of the people is unavoidable. In effect, the violent repression of Falungong in 1999 revealed the failure of Chinese religious policy. The state had to resort to a highly expensive resolution, and its excessive reaction failed to change any of the structural causes of the proliferation of the new religious enterprises.

CONCLUSION: SECULARIZATION AS RESTRUCTURING PROCESS

By returning to the original juridical meaning of secularization, which is centrally concerned with the power relations between political and religious forces, I have tried to dissociate the theory of secularization from Christian European and North American experiences of modernization, thus opening it up to the multiplicity of modernities and the variety of religions and their institutions in the world. Focusing on concrete state-religion interactions, this approach suggests a multivariate, dynamic, and contextualized case study. In fact, secularization processes and consequences differ widely according to political regime, the role of each religion in the religious field, the means through which the state and religion interact with each other, and the changing social conditions of the interaction between the state and religions.

The case of Chinese Buddhism shows that once the study of secularization is linked with the nondominant historical religions in non-Western countries, the classical arguments of secularization have to be revised. For Chinese Buddhism, church-state separation and privatization are no longer the key issues of its secularization. Instead, in the context of the étatization of society in China, Buddhism's secularization was marked by the politicization of religion and by statist institutionalization. Through collective political study, Land Reform, the rearrangement of monastic property, and forced participation in political campaigns and civic activities, the Chinese Communist state not only redistributed Buddhist resources and power but reorganized the Buddhist clergy. Finally, according to the logic of state corporatism, the CCP created a national monopolistic Buddhist association, the BAC, as the routine intermediary through which (1) Buddhists were put under the total and continuous surveillance of the government, and (2) Buddhist resources were used for political ends.

With the relative liberalization of society since the 1980s, the statist institutionalization policy gave rise to a number of consequences contrary to its original aim. As I have shown, the official BAC, as a secularization product and instrument, has tended to be transformed into a more autonomous church-like institution for the promotion of Buddhism. The official discourse that has secularized Buddhist doctrine is also used by Buddhists as a legitimate resource for the reconstruction and development of Buddhism. The rigid control of the institutional religions stimulates the thriving of nonofficial religious expressions, based on the possibilities created by current social change, so that the state regulation policy of religion becomes embroiled in a crisis.

In summary, a study of secularization as religio-political struggles must address the sociology of domination. From this perspective, secularization is related to the characteristics of the power relation in general, in which repressions and resistances, conflicts and negotiations, strategic plans and unintended consequences may occur. Certainly, religion is dominated by the state in secularization, so that religious properties would be expropriated by the state and religion itself would be remodeled in its organizational, discursive, and practical aspects. However, even if state power becomes overwhelming in a certain phase, we can hardly say that the oppressed religion will definitively decline. At another historical conjuncture, the same tactics and instruments of the state in secularization might be used by the religion itself as factors favorable for its revival. In fact, all power relations manifest autonomy and dependence in a reciprocal way (Giddens 1979:141–50). That is why they are essentially paradoxical:

the dominant has to depend on the dominated; the constraints may be transformed into resources; dissolving factors may become constructive; the mode of control produces new problems that could disable the controller itself. Historically speaking, secularization in this sense, as an effect of the power relations between religious and state forces, is a dialectical process for deconstructing and reconstructing religion.

10 State Control of Tibetan Buddhist Monasticism in the People's Republic of China

José Ignacio Cabezón

On March 10, 1959, after a popular Tibetan uprising against Chinese troops stationed in Lhasa, the Fourteenth Dalai Lama fled Tibet and received political asylum in India.[1] Approximately a hundred thousand Tibetans followed him into exile. The vast majority of Tibetans—both those living in exile and those still in Tibet—consider this date to mark the beginning of Chinese colonial occupation of their homeland, an occupation that brought with it the most widespread destruction of Buddhism ever witnessed in Tibetan history. From the point of view of the Chinese government, 1959 marks the final stage in the "peaceful liberation" of the Tibetan people from the yoke of the feudal oppression they had suffered at the hands of the Tibetan aristocracy and religious elites. Whatever one's political viewpoint on what has come to be known as "the Tibet question," one thing is clear: the face of Tibetan religion has changed radically in the wake of Chinese control of Tibet. From 1959 to the end of the Cultural Revolution in 1976, thousands of monasteries and nunneries were destroyed, tens of thousands of monks and nuns were forcibly laicized, scores of high-ranking monastic officials were imprisoned or executed, and a large portion of Tibet's religious-artistic patrimony was confiscated, destroyed, or sold on the international antiquities market.

Tibetans are a devout people. Religion is at the very heart of Tibetan ethnic identity,[2] and monastic institutions are one of the hallmarks of Tibetan religion. According to the most conservative estimates, monks made up 10–12 percent of the total male population (Samuels 1993:309 and appendix I) in central agricultural regions (the percentages for nuns being somewhat lower). Most Tibetans had close family members—children, siblings, aunts or uncles—who were monks or nuns. Monasteries served as a focal point for many lay religious practices. They were places that people visited to worship, to circumambulate, and to make offerings. Monasteries were also the site of important villagewide or regional festivals and pilgrimages. Because of the importance of monasteries to Tibetan religious and cultural life, it is not surprising that Tibetans should view the Chinese government's systematic dismantling of Tibetan monasticism from 1959 to 1976 as part of a multipronged strategy to destroy Tibetan cultural identity.

Like religious institutions in the rest of China, Tibetan monasteries benefited from the more liberal policies toward religion that the CCP set into motion in the late 1970s and early 1980s. Over the past two decades, many of Tibet's monastic institutions have been rebuilt and repopulated by monks and nuns (though never to pre-1959 levels). The reestablishment of monasticism in Tibet was, of course, welcomed by Tibetans. Like the Han Chinese majority, Tibetans in general (and Tibetan clergy in particular) began to test the limits of their newly found freedoms, exploring, for example, whether the liberalization extended to other areas of life beyond religion. Beginning in the mid-1980s, monks and nuns played a prominent role in organizing a series of pro-independence protests in Lhasa. The government's response was quick and severe, leaving no question that such actions went beyond what it was willing to tolerate. Lhasa was put under martial law, the monks and nuns who had participated in the protests were jailed, and new policies were instituted in an attempt to tighten control over the monastic population, which, from this point forward, was seen as the most potentially destabilizing internal force[3] threatening the government's control of Tibet.[4]

I lived among exiled Tibetan Buddhist monks in India from 1980 to 1985, and have been visiting the Tibetan Autonomous Region (TAR) for research purposes since the late 1980s. This chapter is based on various studies of Tibetan monasticism in post-Mao China (Goldstein & Kapstein 1998; Swartz 1994; International Campaign for Tibet [ICT] 1996, n.d.), and on my own fieldwork in India and Lhasa over the past fifteen years. It focuses especially on the three largest monasteries in Lhasa, the so-called *densas*, or "seats of learning," the elite monastic universities of the Geluk school that before 1959 were the largest monasteries in the world. My goal is to examine some of the policies and strategies used by the Chinese government to control Tibetan Buddhist monasticism. What bureaucratic apparatus has been created to implement policy? What types of controls have been put into place? What is the perceived purpose and goal of these policies? How are they viewed by Tibetans, and especially by monks? How effective have these policies been in achieving their desired goals? Are there more effective policy options? To understand current

Chinese government policy, monks' responses to it, and the nature of the disagreements between the two groups, it is necessary to understand the very different worldviews out of which the two parties operate. We begin by trying to get some sense of the different *Weltanschauung* out of which the CCP and the monasteries operate.

COMPETING WORLDVIEWS

A debate has raged in the field of Tibetan studies about the nomenclature that should be used to characterize the political economy of pre-1959 Tibetan society, with much of the controversy focusing on the appropriateness of the use of terms like "feudal" and "serf." Far less controversial is the claim that Tibet was a premodern society, a society that not only never made the transition to modernity but self-consciously *resisted* making that transition. Of the forces that worked to prevent Tibet's transition to modernity, few were as powerful as the *densas* (*gdan sa*)—Drepung, Sera, and Ganden—the mammoth monasteries of the Dalai Lama's Geluk school that, from their founding in the fifteenth century up to 1959 (and especially after the Fifth Dalai Lama's consolidation of power in 1642), played an increasingly prominent role in Tibetan politics (Goldstein 1989:815f.).

Many examples of the conservatism of the *densas*, and of their role in resisting the encroachment of modernity, could be cited. I shall discuss just one. Fearing that it would bring about the destruction of Buddhism, the *densas* actively lobbied against the introduction of modern education into Tibet. In 1944, for example, Sera and Drepung in particular presented a united front against the Tibetan government's attempt to found a modern school for young Tibetan aristocrats at Gyangtse (rGyal rtse)—a school that was to include in its curriculum the study of English language, science, and mathematics (Goldstein 1989:419ff.; Cabezón 2003:41–42). As Goldstein writes:

> The abbots, and other conservative monk officials believed . . . that educating young and impressionable boys in the English style of thinking would change their attitude toward Buddhism and the Tibetan way of life. They feared that such boys would no longer be strong patrons of the monastic order and that the income of the monasteries would eventually be severely damaged. The monks also feared that as these young boys became ranking officials, they would want to give predominance to the temporal segment of the Tibetan government, thus potentially endangering the dominance of Tibet's religious form of government. (Goldstein 1989:424)

The *densas'* fears were not utterly baseless. The attempt to modernize another institution, the military, two decades earlier appears to have led to a plot to deprive the Thirteenth Dalai Lama "of temporal power and to leave only religious affairs in his hands" (Goldstein 1989:132). Monks' equation of modernization with a weakening of the institution of the Dalai Lama and of the *densas'* power within the government was therefore not unjustified. That the separation of church and state would of necessity also have brought about the demise of Buddhism in Tibet is, of course, an altogether different claim. It is true that before 1959 the monks of the *densas* generally did believe that the survival of the religion depended on keeping the forces of modernity at bay. This led them not only to oppose the various modernist movements that arose from within Tibetan society, but also to argue for very limited contact with the West. The latter was one of the major factors contributing to a more general isolationist policy in the first half of the twentieth century—which, among other things, made it impossible for Tibet to convincingly argue for its status as a sovereign nation-state before the international community in 1959.

The events of 1959, the destruction of religion that took place in the subsequent two decades, and the more recent revival of religion have all affected monks' views. *Densa* monks have for the most part come to realize that it was a mistake to oppose modernization and endorse isolationism. They have also come to see that Buddhism is capable of withstanding even the most radical and violent of modernist secularizing processes (such as the Cultural Revolution). In short, monks have come to realize that religion is not as fragile as they once thought, and that it can exist and even flourish in a modern secular society. Most monks in Tibet today have adapted to living in an atheistic "Communist" state. More than simply accepting the inevitable, however, monks have come to a critical self-consciousness of the problems of the "old society" (*spyi tshogs rnying pa*) and of the need for a polity different from what was in place in Tibet before 1959.[5] Although most monks continue to believe in the desirability of a political system that at some level "combines Dharma and government" (*chos srid zung 'brel*), very few monks see a return to a premodern, feudal theocracy as either possible or desirable.[6] Thus the views of *densa* monks have changed, at least politically. But none of this implies that monks have jumped whole hog onto the modernist bandwagon. True, they have a new perspective on modernity—in part arrived at critically and voluntarily, in part imposed on them as the result of historical events—but this new relationship to modernity is not an unqualified acceptance of modernity with all its trappings.

Monks' opposition to modernity today is different from what it was before 1959. The contemporary critique of modernity has several aspects. The more general critique is one that is shared with many other religions: namely, that modernist ideologies are incapable of addressing the most fundamental problems of human existence, and that science and technology—while not inherent evils, and, indeed, while generally improving our material lot in life—have too often steered us away from the most basic existential questions, diverting our attention in the direction of the trivial and banal. The price to be paid for material progress—the harmful effects this has had on the environment, society, families, and individuals—has in many instances been too high.

Monks, however, also have more idiosyncratic reasons for opposing modernist ideologies and institutions. The wholesale destruction of Tibetan culture, they point out, took place in the name of material and scientific progress—in the name of modernity. Monks also say that history has shown them that modern nation-states, their derivative institutions (such as the United Nations), and the ideologies that undergird them are either impotent or too self-serving to remedy the plight of the powerless. Modern political institutions, after all, failed Tibetans in their greatest moment of need. Finally, modernist secularism and skepticism—the denial of karma and reincarnation, of deities and spirits—undermine ethics and create obstacles to maintaining a proper relationship between the human and the nonhuman realms, something that is necessary for human flourishing.[7] As monks have adopted more modernist *political* views, therefore, they have also begun to elaborate a critique of modernism along *philosophical* and *"theological"* lines.

In the eyes of monks it is, of course, Buddhism that is the most effective response to modernism. As an institution, Tibetan Buddhism has weathered the most violent modernist attacks upon it. It has served Tibetans as a tool for individual survival in the face of the most abusive policies,[8] and it has managed to attract the attention of the world in ways that the Tibetan political cause (at least until very recently) has not. *Densa* monks believe that it is their role to preserve their specific brand of Buddhism by reestablishing the traditional educational and ritual life of their monasteries. Their goal is to re-create a modified version of the monasticism that existed prior to 1959, a version that, while jettisoning corrupt premodern practices and institutions—like the "punk monk," or *dobdob* (*ldob ldob*), fraternities and the monastic estate (*mchod gzhis*) system[9]—nonetheless preserves the core values of their monastic way of life.

The version of Buddhism that *densa* monks seek to reestablish is a form of conservative, scholastic Buddhism that is concerned with the keeping of vows, the study of classical texts, and the enactment of prayer and ritual cycles that increase spiritual capital (i.e., merit) and establish a proper relationship between the world of men and that of the gods. This worldview presumes the existence of deities and other planes of existence, the efficacy of magic, the existence of past and future lives, and the possibility of human perfection. Socially, the traditional organization of *densa* monastic life was hierarchical.[10] A monk's alliegance was to his teacher (*dge rgan*), regional house (*khang tshan*), college (*grwa tshang*), monastery (*dgon pa*), and sect or school (*chos lugs*), usually in that order. To re-create and preserve these types of institutions today, Tibetan monks believe that they must have internal autonomy: the freedom to establish their own policies, manage their own affairs, and not to be subject to ideological pressures or other forms of interference from the state. In Tibet today, it is precisely the issue of autonomy—the freedom to opt for a Buddhist way of life and to establish such a way of life institutionally—that is the greatest source of conflict with the Chinese state.

Since this is an important point, let me reiterate that *densa* monks do not want to re-create the political economy of pre-1959 Tibet either at the macro-national or at the micro-institutional level. Put another way, monks are disposed to accept political modernism. They are willing to inhabit the modern nation-state as long as they are given the freedom to maintain their traditional way of life. Their project is not only to recuperate traditional forms of religious learning and practices, but to reconstruct a way of life that they see as more conducive to human flourishing than the materialism (both communist and capitalist) that surrounds them. Viewed from this perspective, the question of Chinese policy vis-à-vis the *densas* is "the Tibet question" writ small. How much autonomy is necessary to make monks (Tibetans) happy? How much is the Chinese government willing to give them? Can a compromise be reached?[11]

In contrast to the *densas*, the CCP is an institution whose identity is in large part constructed on the basis of a modernist ideology: that of the nation-state as the principal locus of allegiance; of progress defined in material terms; and of the triumph of the secular over the sacred, of science over "superstition," and, more recently, of the free market over religion. For example, Wang Lixiong, one of the most important PRC intellectuals writing on Tibet today, states that

> a market economy has certainly helped to clear up the religion problem, particularly among the urban Tibetans who have gotten more deeply involved in market actions, where the religious mindset is being

steadily downplayed, and the people are starting to take an interest in worldly enjoyment. A trip to Lhasa today leaves the strong impression that the once "sacred city" is being "secularized" . . . [that] urban religion is being undermined by materialism. (L. Wang 1999)[12]

The rhetoric of modernism is ubiquitous in CCP policy statements and educational/propaganda literature.[13] We shall focus here on a single document, a 2002 booklet used for "patriotic education" of monks and nuns in the TAR. *Book No. 4*, as I will refer to this work, makes it clear, for example, that science will triumph over superstition,[14] but that to bring this about the Party must "employ methods of education and guidance with respect to superstitious activities among the masses, and diffuse scientific knowledge to raise the level of their understanding and dispel superstitious views" (Anonymous 2002b:112).

The praise of progress and its equation with material productivity are also found throughout *Book No. 4*. As Ryan Dunch's chapter in this volume also makes clear, material progress is the responsibility not only of the state but also of religious organizations, which should

> endeavor under the direction and oversight of government, to increase virtuous and generally beneficial activities conducive to social progress and thus help to improve the economic growth and lifestyle of ordinary believers, so that in making more effort toward a happier existence in the present life, the masses of ordinary believers set their minds to economic construction. (Anonymous 2002b:120)

In Tibet in particular, it is necessary for "Tibetan Buddhist personalities to preach the goals of social progress *as an essential religious duty*" (Anonymous 2002b:120; my emphasis). From the CCP's viewpoint, the chief value of Tibetan Buddhism is its ability to instill a sense of ethical uprightness in the common people, so that it will be possible to "gradually eliminate the grounds which are unhelpful to the Socialist system and unhelpful to the productivity, livelihood and physical well-being of the masses" (Anonymous 2002b:121). Religion must therefore contribute to the goal of progress, which is to be measured in economic and material terms—namely, productivity, livelihood, and physical well-being "in this life."

Although religion will, as a matter of historical necessity, eventually die out according to Marxist theory, until this happens, true religion,[15] with proper state "guidance," can contribute to the modernist enterprise. "The fundamental duty of religious work," *Book No. 4* tells us, is "to build modernity and bring about the sacrosanct progress of Chinese minorities"

(Anonymous 2002b:108). However, not all religions are presently capable of contributing to the construction of modern socialism:

> Some religions . . . at present appear to be in various levels of disarray, and since the backward views and etiquette of the bygone era are apparent in varying degrees in some religions, they exert a deleterious residual influence on the livelihood, productivity and ideological outlook of ordinary believers. (Anonymous 2002b:119)

It is the duty of the various organs of the CCP to intervene when religions find themselves in this state of "disarray," bringing them into conformity with modern socialism by "neutralizing and reforming backward ideological views and antiquated forms of etiquette" so that they can then be made to contribute to modern socialism (Anonymous 2002b:119.[16] In particular, "the practice of Tibetan Buddhism must be harmonized with the objectives of building modern Socialism . . . Socialism with Chinese characteristics." Tibetan Buddhism must therefore adapt to socialism, "rather than Socialist society adapting to Tibetan Buddhism or other religions and sects, and there is no question of any mutual support on equal terms" (Anonymous 2002b:119). Religion exists to support socialism (here seen as identical with the Chinese state), not vice versa. To the extent that religion can be "adapted"—that is, "modernized" and made to contribute to the goals of a modern socialist society—it can be tolerated and even allowed to flourish. When religion does *not* adapt, it must be corrected. The mechanism for making religion adapt to socialism in Tibet, as elsewhere in China, is "management according to law"—the "regulation" and "regularization" of religious activity.

Although the Chinese government recognizes the state to be composed of different "nationalities," or ethnic groups, the nation-state is nonetheless fundamentally unitary: the unified Motherland. That unity, however, is seen as being under constant threat from "splittist" elements and foreign powers that resort to "infiltration" and false propaganda to accomplish their aims of "westernizing" and "fragmenting" China. In propaganda documents like *Book No. 4*, resistance to Chinese government policies is almost always portrayed as being instigated by extra-national forces—for example, by "the Dalai clique or 'East Turkestan' terror groups"—and hardly ever as the free-will choice of members of these various ethnic groups. Protestors are therefore portrayed as dupes, and never as free agents,[17] or else as "heretics or downright criminals carrying the banner of religion" (Anonymous 2002b:111). True religion and truly religious people can never, as a matter of definition, oppose the state, for whenever the government is criticized on religious grounds, both the "grounds" and the individual engaging in the critique cease to be religious.

To cite a concrete example of this, when Tenzin Delek, a Tibetan lama living in Sichuan, was sentenced to death in 2002 for allegedly engaging in "separatist and terrorist activities," the provincial-level United Front Work Department issued a press release containing statements from local religious leaders supporting the court's decision. Provincial People's Congress Vice Chairman Jiadeng Luorang, for example, is quoted as stating that

> religion must respect the laws of the country. At the same time religion has rules. Zhaxi's [i.e., Tenzin Delek's] behavior not only went against the laws of the country, but also against the rules of religion. If religion hurts people, then it is plainly not religion.[18]

In this logic, (1) the state is infallible when it comes to determining what is best for the people; (2) when a religious figure opposes the government, he or she must therefore be acting against welfare of the people; (3) religion, by definition, cannot oppose the welfare of the people; and therefore (4) opposition to the government cannot be religious, and must therefore be "heresy." A religious criticism (and even a religious person's criticism) of the government is a logical impossibility.

All of this is to say that religion must at all times be subservient to the state and its interests. *Book No. 4* makes this very point when it states:

> Freedom of religious belief does not mean that there is no limitation whatsoever on the conduct of religious activity. Since religious people and ordinary believers are *first and foremost* PRC citizens, they must put the interests of the nation and the people first, and accept responsibility for observing constitutional law, legal code and official policy. (Anonymous 2002b:111; my emphasis)

Allegiance to the nation-state trumps all other allegiances. In Tibet, where the state competes with a variety of other potential sources of allegiance, "the basic requirement for adaptation of religion . . . is 'Patriotism and obeying the law'" (Anonymous 2002b:119). To the extent that Tibetan Buddhists have allegiances that supersede allegiance to the nation, they are not "patriotic"; they have failed to make religion adapt to modern socialism, and they therefore require correction through "patriotic education" and through "the law."

The conflict between Tibetans and Chinese over the status of Tibet is complex and multifaceted, involving issues of race/ethnicity, economics, politics, education, and religion, to name just a few. But whatever else it may be, it is also clearly a conflict between a traditional, conservative, religious worldview and a modernist, secular-materialist one. If our goal is to ponder the issue of religion, modernity, and the state in China (which is the purpose of this volume), it is hard to imagine a better way to explore this in the Tibetan case than by turning our attention to the policies instituted by the Chinese government to control Tibetan Buddhist monasticism.

STATE-MONASTIC RELATIONS IN TIBET BEFORE 1959

It is naïve to think that the *densas'* transition from a traditional culture to modernity represents a simple transition from being controlling agents to being controlled objects. True, before 1959 these monasteries were a powerful political force. Throughout the centuries the *densas* and the Tibetan government had negotiated a relationship that granted the monasteries a tremendous amount of internal autonomy and a great deal of say in government policy. The *densas* were wielders of power. For example, they had a major voice in the Tibetan National Assembly. But the *densas* were also the *objects* of power: they were regulated by the Tibetan government.

It is sometimes thought that because the Dalai Lama was a member of the Geluk school and the *densas* were Geluk institutions, the *densas* therefore were the government, but this is not the case. The Tibetan government—the so-called Ganden Potrang (Dga' ldan pho brang) or Palace of Ganden—was a complex, multitiered institution headed by the Dalai Lama (or, in his minority, by his regent). Although monastic officials held positions in the government, the most powerful positions below that of the Dalai Lama and his regent were held not by monks but by the Tibetan aristocracy. While the *densas* were powerful, they were also responsible and answerable to the government, and in some areas it was the Ganden Potrang that had the final say. The *densas* did, however, have the right to enforce their own rules and regulations internally. For example, most minor violations of the law by monks—fighting, petty theft, and so forth— were usually dealt with internally. However, if a monk violated the law by committing a major crime (such as murder or grand larceny), he was first disciplined internally by the monastery (usually beaten and defrocked) and then turned over to the civil authorities for trial and punishment. In a symbolic act that performatively reinscribed the jurisdictional pact between the monasteries and the government, the defrocked monk would be brought to the gate of the monastery (the symbolic boundary), where police officers would take him, now no longer a monk, into custody.

Sometimes internal factionalism in the *densas* led to a collapse of the internal order of the monasteries, and in a few cases monks actually took up arms against the government. When this happened, the government crossed the jurisdictional line and entered the monasteries to put down revolt, take errant monks into custody, and restore order. This suggests that although the *densas* were self-regulating institutions with something like a quasi-autonomous legal system of their own, they were also responsible to civil authorities—that is, to the Tibetan government. While the great monasteries had a great deal of power, they did not have absolute power.

The Tibetan government also had a great deal of say about the governance of the *densas*. For example, the Dalai Lama (or his regent) had the right to appoint the *densas'* abbots. The government also regulated certain aspects of the finances of these monasteries. It could grant or deprive these institutions (and individual lamas) of the estates—farm lands, grazing pastures, and herds of animals—that were their most important sources of income. The Ganden Potrang also determined the internal ranking of monks within a monastery by deciding which reincarnate lamas were given which ranks. It decided what shares of offerings went to the different ranks of lamas and administrators. If disputes between different factions of the monastery could not be adjudicated internally, the government stepped in to issue final judgments.[19] Finally, the Tibetan government routinely issued permits and policies on a variety of minor issues, from the construction of ornamental banners on buildings to the seating order of high lamas at state functions.

All of this is to say that Tibetan monasteries in general, and the *densas* in particular, have always been the object of regulation and control. We should not think, therefore, that monasteries went from being free, unregulated, all-powerful institutions before 1959 to being controlled by the Chinese government thereafter. The issue, therefore, is not *the fact* of control but *the agent* and *the nature* of control before and after 1959. Perhaps the most important element that made Tibetan government control of the *densas* possible before 1959 was the fact that the Ganden Potrang was a government under the leadership of the Dalai Lama, a monk whose incarnation lineage could be traced back to the very origins of the *densas'* Geluk school, and who was universally recognized by *densa* monks (and by most Tibetans) as being a manifestation of Avalokiteśvara, the Buddha of Compassion.[20] Without this metaphysical capital, it is unlikely that the Ganden Potrang could have intervened successfully in the affairs of the *densas*.

Densa monks, needless to say, do not recognize the Chinese state as having the metaphysical capital that would legitimize it as a source of religious authority.[21] Even apart from this, however, Chinese government policies regulating the internal affairs of the monasteries are seen by monks as a violation of the *densas'* traditional right to self-governance—a right that the monasteries had negotiated over the centuries with the Tibetan government. To sum up, the Tibetan government controlled the *densas;* these monasteries nonetheless had a considerable amount of internal autonomy; and the Ganden Potrang's control of the *densas* was based in large part on its metaphysical status as a government of and by an enlightened being (the Dalai Lama). With this by way of background, the discussion that follows will be easier to understand.

CHINESE GOVERNMENT CONTROL OF THE *DENSAS*

CCP policy toward Tibetan monasticism must undoubtedly be seen as the historical legacy of Chinese (and perhaps, more generally, East Asian) polities to (micro)manage institutions at all levels of the culture—in other words, to bring them under the bureaucratic control of the state.[22] Ji Zhe's chapter in this book gives some of the historical background for this. Among the various types of institutions, religious institutions have been seen as a perennial and special object of concern, in part because of the extent to which they penetrate all levels of the society, and in part because of their potential to challenge the power of the state.[23]

The Bureaucracy of Control

Shortly after assuming power in Tibet, the Chinese government created the same bureaucratic structure for controlling monasteries in Tibetan areas as it had in the rest of the country. Broadly speaking, this structure has two parts: (1) the superstructural bureaucracy that regulates monasteries from above, and (2) the infrastructural apparatus embedded within monasteries that controls them from below. Monasteries are therefore situated within a broader state-regulatory system, and in turn contain an internal regulatory apparatus that implements state policy from within.

It is the Chinese Communist Party's highest officials and bodies (such as the Standing Committee of the Politburo) that issue major policy decisions about religion and religious institutions.[24] Major policies are then implemented through dual parallel bureaucracies—one under the "government," and the other under the CCP. Occupying the next highest tier under the CCP's top leadership are two agencies: the Religious Affairs Bureau (RAB),[25] a government agency administratively located under the State Council; and the United Front Work Department, an organ of the CCP responsible for creating and maintaining relationships with non-party elements in the society—including religious organizations, ethnic groups, and intellectuals. The Buddhist Association of China (BAC), a body answerable to the RAB and to the United Front Work Department, functions more as an advisory body. In the Tibetan context it appears to have less power than it does in other regions of China, even with respect to a fairly circumscribed area like "clerical management" (on which see Ji Zhe's chapter in this volume). Although the BAC has no substantial policy-making role in Tibet, like all "patriotic religious organizations," it helps to "manage the relationship between church and state," and as such functions "as additional instruments of control" (Spiegel 2002). Each of these offices—the RAB, the United Front, and the BAC—exists at both the national and regional level.

Tibetan monasteries fall most directly under the Religious Affairs Bureau (Tib. Chos don u yon lhan khang) of their local county or municipality. High-profile institutions like the *densas*, however, in part because they are perceived as a threat, are also supervised by various bodies within the Tibetan Autonomous Region, such as the regional RAB and the regional Commission on Nationality Affairs. They are also supervised by the Lhasa Municipality itself, and by the Lhasa and TAR Public Security Bureaus (PSB; Tib. Spyi bde las khungs).[26]

At the level of infrastructure, it is principally the Democratic Management Committee (DMC; Tib. Mang gtso bdag gnyer u yon lhan khang) that serves as the conduit for the "downward" implementation of policies and as the vehicle for the "upward" movement of information to the government's policy-making bodies. At Sera Monastery, to take one example about which we have written documentation,[27] the DMC is a committee of eleven monks and three nonmonastic Tibetan officials, with one position always left vacant. The DMC has two parts: (1) the directorate (*kru'u ring/ran*), with five members, and (2) the council (*u yon*), with eight members. The directorate is composed of the two operational directors (*rgyun las kru'u ring*)—one of them a monk and the other a nonmonastic, mid-level Party bureaucrat—and three junior directors (*kru'u ring gzhon pa*), all monks.[28] The council of eight is composed of one officer from the local police station (*mngag gtong khang*),[29] one cadre appointed by the Religious Affairs Bureau, and six monks. There are no fixed terms of office. Council members move into the directorate by virtue of seniority, loyalty to the government, and administrative ability. When there is a vacancy for a monk on the council, the directorate nominates someone from the ranks of the monks and submits his name to the Religious Affairs Bureau for approval. The RAB does a background check on the monk to make sure that he has no record of political dissent.

The DMC has five working boards, or subcommittees (*yan lag khang*):

1. The *governing board* (*gzhung las khang*), composed of the two operational directors and two junior directors, is the most powerful subcommittee, responsible for making major policy recommendations to the RAB for its approval.

2. The *religious affairs board* (*chos don khang*), composed of the disciplinarian, the chant leader, one of the junior directors, and two nonmonastic cadres, is responsible for curriculum implementation and scheduling of religious rituals.

3. The *propaganda subcommittee* (*dril bsgrags khang*), composed of two junior directors and two nonmonastic cadres appointed by the RAB, is responsible for communicating government policy to the monks.

4. The *security subcommittee* (*bde 'jags khang*), composed of the police officer who sits on the DMC, two monks from the council, and five monks from the general monastic population, is responsible for maintaining order within the monastery.

5. The *financial affairs subcommittee* (*nor don khang*), composed of three monks from the general monastic population, is chiefly responsible for twice-yearly audits, though it has little power to make financial decisions, all of which are made by the governing board.

The abbot (*mkhan po*) of the monastery is nominated by the DMC as a whole but must be approved by the RAB. The disciplinarian (*dge bkod*) and chant leader (*dbu mdzad*) are voted into office by the monastery as a whole, but they, too, require approval by the RAB. In short, the government has veto power over any monk who occupies any kind of administrative position within the monastery. The abbotship is today largely ceremonial and has no real power. True decision-making power lies with the governing board, but even then, any major decision must be approved by the RAB before it can be implemented.

Types of Control

The various offices just mentioned—both intra- and extra-institutional—are involved in different types of decision-making and policy that control various aspects of monks' individual and institutional lives:

- *Issuing or denying formal registration to monasteries.* Monasteries that operate without being formally registered are considered renegade institutions. This is not a problem for well-established monasteries like the *densas,* whose formal status has long been recognized by the government, but it is a problem for many small monasteries in the TAR and in other Tibetan regions of China. Recent policy directives have called for shutting down unregistered monasteries, although to date this does not appear to have taken place on a large scale.[30]

- *Who may or may not become and/or remain a monk or nun.* For example, "children under eighteen" and people who are (or whose parents have been) classified as having politically problematic views are prohibited from entering the monastic life.[31] Once admitted, the RAB or PSB can question, expel, and/or arrest monks who are believed to be disloyal to the state or who are seen as a threat to the social order. Punishments can be extremely severe and lack uniformity. For example, in the past few years a monk in Qinghai Province was given a three-year prison sentence for distributing pro-independence materials, whereas a monk in Sichuan was given an eleven-year sentence for raising the Tibetan flag in public. Former monk and nun prisoners now living in exile have reported that torture is widespread in prisons and PSB detention centers.

- *Who will or will not be granted "official status" in a monastery and be issued an official identity card.* Large monasteries in the TAR often have an "unofficial" monastic population that can be up to half of the official number of resident monks. These unofficial monks and nuns have little status and no real privileges in the monastery. (For example, they are not allowed to receive a share of monetary contributions made to the monastery for distribution in assemblies.) Whereas monks and nuns used to be the ones to decide who would be granted official status when an official monk left, retired, or died, this decision is increasingly made by government bodies.

- *The number of monks or nuns allowed to live within a monastery.* This is discussed in greater detail below.

- *The identification of reincarnate lamas or tulkus (sprul sku), called "living buddhas" (huofo) by Han Chinese.* Although Tibetans consider the identification of *tulkus* to be a religious matter, the Chinese government has increasingly sought to control the process of identifying high-ranking *tulkus*. It is now considered illegal for monks to identify *tulkus* without the approval of government authorities.[32]

- *What types of religious images can be displayed, and what types of rituals can be enacted.* For example, since 1996, pictures of the Fourteenth Dalai Lama have been officially banned in public places (Barnett 2001). The policy is not as strictly enforced in eastern Tibetan ethnic regions as it is in the TAR. Prayers and rituals for the Dalai Lama are also prohibited. In 2002, at least seven Tibetans in the Kardze region of Sichuan were given prison terms for their participation in such ceremonies (ICT n.d.:77–78).

- *What radio transmissions monks may listen to, and what internet sites they access.*[33] For example, monks are prohibited from listening to the Tibetan-language broadcasts of Voice of America and Radio Free Asia, and are subject to interrogation and punishment if caught.

- *Who monks may and may not associate with.* Monks' and nuns' association with foreigners is closely watched,[34] and monasteries are prohibited from establishing ties to foreign organizations.

- *The type of instruction that monks and nuns receive, the type of Buddhism that may be practiced, and the types of religious degrees awarded.* For example, the government sees itself as having the right to implement "patriotic re-education" campaigns of ideological indoctrination whenever this is seen as necessary (see below). What is more, only a specific form of Buddhism should, in principle, be taught and practiced in monasteries. Practices traditionally found within monasteries—like divination and oracles—are classified as "superstitions" and are proscribed.[35] In recent years the government has also forced monks of the *densas* to once again begin awarding the traditional Geshe (*dge bshes*) degree, mostly against their will.[36]

- *The monastic calendar.* For example, government agencies control the hours during which monasteries can remain open to the public, and can order their sudden closure if they perceive a security problem. They also control whether, when, and how festivals and public teachings and rituals may be convened.[37] For example, in August 2004, Lhasa city authorities changed the date of the Drepung Zhotön ('*Bras spungs zho ston*) festival, which traditionally varies according to the Tibetan lunar calendar, in order to promote tourism.

- *The types of renovation that can be carried out.* In recent years such permits have been routinely denied (Ackerly 1991:137–38).

- *Finances.* The RAB monitors the finances of the *densas* through the DMC, and has the power to determine how some of the monasteries' funds will be spent. Ackerly writes, for example, that "entrance fees to monasteries go into an account controlled by the Chinese authorities which are then spent according to Chinese wishes—not as Tibetans would spend them . . . [for example, for] beautification projects to make the monastery more photogenic, instead of projects that would improve the quality of life and education of the monks" (Ackerly 1991:143).[38]

Of the various policies implemented by Chinese governmental agencies in recent years, I focus here only on the three that I see to be the greatest sources of friction between the monks and the government: (1) the decision to limit the number of monks in a monastery, (2) minimum age requirements for monks and nuns, and restrictions on relocation, and (3) "patriotic re-education."

The Decision to Limit the Number of Monks in a Monastery   If there is a single policy that has radically changed the face of Tibetan monasticism from what it was before 1959, this is probably it. In the "old society," monasteries operated under a policy of "open admissions." This led to the phenomenon that some have called "mass monasticism." The three *densas* were the largest monasteries in the world. Drepung had a monastic population of somewhere between 10,000 and 13,000 monks, Sera Monastery had close to 10,000 monks on its roles, and Ganden, close to 5,000. The *densas* encouraged large monastic enrollments for various reasons, but two seem to me to be the most important:

1.   Monks believed that the production of great scholar-saints was one of the chief functions of the *densas*. Many monks would even say that it was their *telos*. The law of averages requires that to produce a few great men, one must admit many—hence the Tibetan monasteries' policy of open admissions.[39]

2. The large monasteries of the Geluk school saw themselves as bastions of Buddhist orthodoxy, and as the protectors of the faith. Before 1959, as we have seen, they saw themselves as responsible for preserving traditional Buddhist values in the face of an encroaching modernity. They also realized that this conservative position could not be maintained without clout. Mass monasticism was, among other things, this clout. The large monastic populations of the *densas* made these institutions (at least potentially) quasi-military establishments whose power always loomed large, assuring the lamas, abbots, and administrators a voice in government policy-making.[40]

These two reasons are undoubtedly seen by Chinese policy-makers as reason enough to *limit* the size of monasteries. Vis-à-vis the first reason, a new generation of charismatic scholar-saints, monk-leaders around whom a cult of the person can form, is perceived as a threat to the government: (1) it is considered ideologically anathema, since it belies the official rhetoric that religion is on the decline; (2) it creates a cult of the lama that is seen as competing with the cult of the Chinese "sovereign"; (3) it is potentially destabilizing, since it invests the charismatic religious leader with a certain level of power; and (4) if the authorities must intervene against the leader and his followers,[41] it creates martyrs, potentially putting the government in the position of being portrayed as violating human rights.

The second reason, however, is arguably more important as grounds for limiting the size of the *densas*. Huge Tibetan monasteries are seen as a potential security threat to the state.[42] Many Tibetan monks and nuns living in exile in India have publicly stated that, being unencumbered by the responsibilities that come with having a spouse and children, they consider themselves freer than their lay brethren to engage in political action.[43] Many monks and nuns who participated in the 1980s protests have stated this to be one of the principal reasons they considered it incumbent upon them to engage in political protests. If imprisoned or killed, they have said, they had no dependents who would suffer as a result of their actions (R. Schwartz 1994:71).

The RAB has enforced strict limits on the size of monasteries ever since they were reopened. Before 1959, as we have said, Sera Monastery had an enrollment of close to 10,000 monks, although the "mythical" size of the monastic population—a figure that had been in circulation for decades (and perhaps for centuries)—was just 5,500. The RAB, it appears, simply removed one zero from the classical Sera monastic population and set the limit for the new Sera at 550 official monks, where it has remained to this day.

In his important 1998 article on the revival of monastic life in another of the *densas,* Drepung Monastery, Melvyn Goldstein gives the impression that the monks of these monasteries came to see the logic of limiting monastic enrollment and agreed with the limits imposed by the government.[44] I have come to the opposite conclusion. Although most monks today undoubtedly do not wish to return to the huge, pre-1959 monastic populations and deplore the excesses of the "mass monasticism of the old society," they object to the current size limits imposed on them by the RAB. They see this quite literal decimation of the monasteries as a violation of the rights of young Tibetan men to enter the religious life, an infringement on monasteries' right to internal self-governance, and an obstacle to achieving their educational objectives. Before 1959, the *densas* were divided into colleges, or *dratsang* (*grwa tshang*). The various philosophical colleges used different textbooks, or *yigcha* (*yig cha*), and they maintained many unique traditions of ritual, chanting, and music. These differences were the basis of a sense of "college-identity" and the source of a healthy competition among the colleges that invigorated their intellectual life (Dreyfus 2003). Because the monastic enrollment of these institutions is so low today, the college system has had to be abandoned. Monks for the most part study a single set of textbooks and engage in a single set of ritual practices. Apart from the loss of entire traditions of textual learning and liturgy, the collapse of the college system has eliminated the opportunity for the types of intellectual exchange among monks of different colleges that existed prior to 1959, along with the spirit of college-based competition that so enlivened *densa* life. This has been just one of the effects of low limits on monastic enrollments.

The government's policy of limiting monastic enrollments to their current low levels is also considered to be a form of *economic exploitation.* Monks believe that the government's strategy is to allow just enough of a monastic presence in the monasteries to ensure their physical maintenance—that is, to ensure that they can be physically preserved as "cultural relics" (*mi rigs kyi rig rdzas*) and maintained at a level sufficient for their exploitation as tourist venues. Maintaining these huge institutions is an enormous labor, leaving monks insufficient time for religious activities, which is, after all, their reason for being monks. Although the policy of having smaller monasteries serves the purposes of the government, it does so at the expense of the monks' own goals. Moreover, since the number of official monks in a monastery is fixed, new monks can be admitted into the official ranks (*skyid sdug*) of the monastery only after another monk leaves, retires, or dies. Rather than admitting scholar-monks, however, government bureaucrats, who have the final say on whether or not a given monk will be admitted, are increasingly opting for middle-aged worker-monks who, being past the ideal age for beginning rigorous scholastic training, are understandably more interested in working than in studying. This means that the population of serious scholarly monks in the *densas* is gradually on the decline, something that is obviously contributing to a decline in the intellectual life of the monasteries.

Finally, monks point out that they are increasingly treated as actors on the tourist stage. For example, the daily debate sessions in the monasteries, one of the most important venues of monastic learning, must be convened at a time that is convenient for the local tourist industry. During the peak of the tourist season, busloads of tourists descend on the monasteries in the early afternoon, cameras in hand. It is not uncommon for tourists to outnumber monks in the debate courtyards of the *densas* during this time. This is obviously disruptive, making a spectacle out of a serious educational pursuit.[45]

Monastic response to the CCP's policy of limiting monastic enrollments is at least in part the result of a clash between the secular, materialist, security-concerned worldview of the Chinese state and the religious, traditional, Tibetocentric worldview of monks. By restricting the monastic population to a number just large enough to run the monasteries and provide "costumed natives" for the tourist industry, Chinese government policy-makers are privileging values like political stability, the physical preservation of monastic institutions as historical/cultural relics, and the tangible economic gains derived from treating these institutions as tourist venues. When monks object to such a policy, they are privileging another set of values: (1) that the *densas* are living educational institutions whose chief purpose is to create disciplined, well-trained scholars, (2) that obtaining such training is the right of all Tibetans, (3) that it is the monks themselves who know the conditions best suited to achieving their goal, and therefore (4) that they should be the ones to regulate the size of the monastic population in the *densas*. Monks do not want to return to the "mass monasticism" that existed before 1959, but they do want larger monasteries than are permitted under present policy.

Minimum Age Requirements for Monks and Nuns, and Restrictions on Relocation In addition to limiting the absolute numbers of monks within monasteries, the RAB has moved to change the internal demographics of monasteries through two significant policy decisions. The first of these, *the decision not to allow persons under the age of eighteen to enter the densas,* has had a major effect on Tibetan monastic life. In the first year of its enforcement in the early 1990s, more than six hundred young monks and nuns were expelled from Tibetan monastic institutions.

Before 1959, the official minimum age for young boys wishing to enter the *densas* was approximately seven years of age, but this was not always adhered to, and it was not unusual to find boys as young as five in Tibetan monasteries. Parents sent boys to the *densas* as an act of religious piety. They also believed that their children stood to gain a good classical education that could serve them well both in the religious and in the secular sphere. After the liberalization of the early 1980s, Tibetans once again started sending their children to the monasteries.[46]

In response to this, the CCP created laws that prohibit the ordination of anyone under eighteen. *Book No. 4's* discussion of the issue reads as follows:

> Children under 18 may not be instructed in religious doctrine, children in normal schools may not be exposed to religious propaganda, religious studies classes are not permitted in schools apart from religious studies institutes, monasteries and places of worship, and no one at all may cite religious reasons to prevent the education of children in Marxism-Leninism, Mao Zedong thought, the theories of Deng Xiaoping or scientific knowledge. (Anonymous 2002b:115)

Several factors play into the CCP's decision to enforce the prohibition against the ordination of youth:

1. *The view that religious education of children is tantamount to forced religious indoctrination.*[47] "Children are still growing up and their outlook on the world is not fully formed, and since they do not have experience of scientific knowledge and social life, to instruct underage youngsters in religious doctrines . . . is the same as forcing them into religious belief" (Anonymous 2002b:115).

2. *The view that children educated in monasteries are imbued with a conservative Buddhist worldview* that remains with them for their entire lives, even if they later leave the monastery (which many of them do). During their years as monks and nuns, young men and women may come to experience firsthand the policies of the government in the monasteries, which can, in turn, engender in them a view of the government as creating obstacles to religious expression.

3. *The view that some adolescents who harbor such views may impetuously "act out"*—for example, organizing or participating in public protests.

4. Finally, *the view that children are relatively nonproductive as far as an institution's physical maintenance is concerned,* making their presence in monasteries and nunneries a waste of resources.

Factors like these all play a greater or lesser role in the RAB's decision to enforce the policy that prohibits anyone under eighteen from taking ordination.

Monks, in contrast, have traditionally held that the best monks are those who enter the monastery at a very young age, and they believe this for several reasons:

1. Monks who enter as children are acculturated into monastic life and habits more easily than monks who enter later in life. For example, monks believe that young boys, since they will not have yet had sexual experiences, can more easily maintain the discipline of celibacy later in life.

2. The childhood years are also considered the best years for acquiring the study habits required to succeed in a monastic education. This is especially true of memorization. If a young boy is not taught to memorize from a very young age, he will find it very difficult to do so later in life.

3. Aside from learning *how* to memorize, childhood is believed to be the best time for amassing large *quantities* of memorized text, since the mind is still very flexible and capable of assimilating large quantities of memorized data during these early years.

For these various reasons, monks see the RAB minimum-age policy as undercutting monastic religious and educational goals.

As with the regulation that limits the absolute numbers of monks in the *densas*, the policy that prohibits anyone under eighteen from being enrolled as a monk represents a clash of worldviews. The government position privileges one set of values: the creation of a secularized, socialist citizenry whose primary loyalty is not to "antiquated" religious ideologies but to scientific materialism and to the modern nation-state. It also privileges immediate, tangible economic productivity over the acquisition of intangible religious/spiritual capital, whose benefits to the state—indeed, whose very existence—it is loath to acknowledge. Monks privilege a set of values that emphasizes the importance of the formation of religious persons over the formation of loyal citizens. The monastic worldview also sees childhood as a period to be utilized principally for the acquisition of learning skills (memorization of religious texts) and religious character-building. It eschews the notion that lack of ability to be materially productive is a criterion for denying anyone the right to live in monasteries.

The imposition of limits on monastic enrollments, and the creation of a minimum age requirement for monks are not the only sources of conflict between Tibetan clergy and the CCP. Up to the end of the Cultural Revolution, the movement of Tibetans in ethnic Tibetan regions of the PRC was tightly controlled through the use of the "residential permit" system (Tib. *them tho*, Ch. *hukou*). Although the system exists throughout China, Tibetans have generally had a more difficult time getting permission to change residences than have Han Chinese (ICT 1996:75–77). And although the influence of the *hukou* system as a way of regulating where people may live is on the decline, it is still used as a basis for *controlling the movement of monks*. For example, monks from the eastern ethnic Tibetan areas of Kham (Khams) and Amdo (A mdo)—presently part of Sichuan, Yunnan, Qinghai, and Gansu provinces—are routinely prohibited from traveling to the *densas* in the TAR for higher studies, something that was very common before 1959, given that the quality of education in the *densas* was higher than at any other Geluk institution in Tibet. Even when allowed to travel to the TAR for study, monks are not given permission to officially change their residence to Lhasa, making it impossible for them ever to become official *densas* monks and enjoy the privileges that come from this status. In addition to changing the age demographics of the monasteries, the government has also, therefore, changed the regional diversity that once existed in the *densas*. Arguably more importantly, it has effectively prohibited all but monks from a limited area of the country from ever being official *densa* monks. All this has gone a long way toward transforming the *densas* from diverse, intellectually lively institutions whose *telos* was the production of scholarly monks into more homogeneous, museum-like centers for the preservation of physical culture. It has transformed monks from custodians of knowledge into custodians of buildings. *Densa* monks still manage to keep the traditional education system alive, but day by day it becomes more difficult to do so.

"Patriotic Re-education"   In the last decade, even more radical mechanisms of control have been implemented in Tibetan monasteries. In 1996, the CCP launched the so-called Strike Hard Campaign (Tib. *rdung rdeg*

tsha nan, Ch. *yanda*) in Tibet.[48] Although principally an anti-crime campaign in other areas of China, in the Tibet Autonomous Region it brought
teams of Party members into monastic institutions to "disseminate patriotic educational reform within the monasteries" (*dgon sde'i nang rgyal
bces ring lugs glugs kyi slob gso spel ba*).[49] The ostensible purpose of
"patriotic re-education" was to (re)train monks in Party ideology. In actual
fact, the campaign was aimed at identifying monks and nuns who were
deemed "unpatriotic," to expel and/or imprison them, and to extract loyalty pledges from those remaining (Tibet Center for Human Rights and
Democracy [TCHRD] n.d.:29). The ultimate goal was to root out "splittist"
elements in the monasteries and purge these institutions of "Dalai clique
sympathizers." According to one report, in one year alone the Strike Hard
Campaign

> resulted in 2,827 expulsions, 165 arrests, nine deaths and 35 [individuals]
> voluntarily leaving their monasteries and nunneries. . . . A five-point
> political pledge requires monks to oppose the idea of an independent
> Tibet, to denounce the Dalai Lama and to recognise the Chinese-
> appointed Panchen Lama. (Tibetan Government in Exile n.d.)[50]

The "work teams" (Tib. *las don ru khag*, Ch. *gongzuo dui*) of the campaign are composed of Tibetan members of the CCP from various offices
(including the PSB). They spend weeks, and sometimes months, in monasteries delivering lectures to the assembled monks, who have no choice but
to attend. Soldiers are frequently stationed in the monasteries while the
reeducation teams are at work. No resistance or challenge is tolerated. For
example, two monks at Drepung who challenged the work team to provide
evidence for the claims they were making during a reeducation session
were each given a three-year prison term (TCHRD n.d.:29).

Since the mid-1990s, the three *densas* have had a combined monastic
population of slightly less than 2,500 monks (including unofficial monks).
After just one year of the Strike Hard Campaign, more than 500 *densa*
monks—or roughly 20 percent of the total monastic population of these
three institutions—had been expelled.[51] Less than a decade after the
Strike Hard Campaign was initiated in Tibet, by some estimates, more
than 11,000 monks and nuns had been expelled from monastic institutions in the TAR. Most were expelled for either refusing to undergo
patriotic reeducation[52] or for refusing to sign the pledge that denounces
the Dalai Lama.[53] Although the first phase of the reeducation campaign
has officially drawn to a close, reeducation work teams are still sent into
monasteries.[54]

As this chapter was first being written in October 2005, a new work team was being dispatched to Drepung Monastery (the largest of the three *densas*) to implement another round of reeducation. Five monks, including the abbot, refused to sign the statement denouncing the Dalai Lama. They were arrested by the PSB. Two days later, 400 Drepung monks engaged in what was probably (in terms of sheer numbers, at least) the largest act of resistance the monastery had seen to that date. They marched into the courtyard of their main assembly hall and sat in silence. The PSB and People's Armed Police quickly entered the monastery. Monks were forced into their rooms. The monastery was then closed for two days, and armed soldiers were stationed at strategic points.[55] The arrested monks were released, but several of them were also expelled from the monastery. A year later the issue was still not resolved, with the Drepung monks refusing to accept the conditions of the reeducation program until the recently expelled monks had been reinstated. This unresolved issue between monks and the government was one of the causes of the most recent (March 2008) round of monk protests in Lhasa, protests that led to violent riots and to the tragic deaths of dozens of Tibetans and Han Chinese. The Lhasa riots subsequently gave way to a wave of anti-government protests at dozens of sites in different Tibetan ethnic regions of China. These protests, and the massive government crackdown that has ensued, are events that are still unfurling as this volume is going to press. While this latest round of Tibetan protests cannot be reduced to the actions of monks, there is no question that monks' disillusionment is one of the many sparks that led to the most recent conflagration.

Has the Strike Hard Campaign in its Tibetan manifestation been successful (either as a way of changing Tibetans' attitudes toward the Party or as a method of purging dissidents)? Given that the drama of "patriotic re-education" must be reenacted over and over, isn't this an indication that something is amiss? As Whyte (1974:233) and Schwartz (1994:55) have maintained, such programs are simply ineffective at changing people's attitudes. What happens, moreover, to monks and nuns who have been purged? Some of them go back to their home regions in Tibet, where they eventually reintegrate into their local communities, carrying with them their narratives of persecution. Others, however, flee to India to continue their education. Having completed their studies, some will go abroad to become teachers at Buddhist centers in various corners of the globe. Is the government any better off with disenfranchised Tibetan clergy living and working at religious institutions around the world? Is the CCP better off losing these young people to the Tibetan diaspora? In the end, does this policy make the CCP any less vulnerable, or the TAR any more secure? Finally, what reason is there to think that the monks and nuns who *do* sign the loyalty pledge are doing so out of a sense of loyalty to the CCP? For a decade or more, the Dalai Lama has made public announcements urging monks and nuns in Tibet *to denounce him*, if that is what it takes to get Chinese government bureaucrats to allow them to practice their religion in peace. Words, in the end, are just words. They do not necessarily reflect people's true sentiments or loyalties.

In the rhetoric of the Strike Hard Campaign, one often sees reference to "severing of the serpent's head," a metaphor for eradicating "splittism," the ostensible root cause of all problems in the TAR. But perhaps a better mascot for the campaign would be the Hydra, a mythical monster that grows two heads for every one that is cut off.

CONCLUSION

> Tibet is more prosperous now than ever before in its history.
> However, this has not gained the PRC the allegiance of the
> Tibetans, more and more of whom have become attached to
> the Dalai Lama, who has never given them a penny. There have
> been no recent street riots, and things look peaceful on the sur-
> face. But there is no difficulty in sensing where their feelings lie.
> Virtually all Tibetans have the Dalai in their hearts. . . . It would
> be wrong to regard the present situation as more stable than in
> 1987 [when the Lhasa protests first occurred]. At that time, it was
> mainly monks and disoriented youth who led the riots. Nowadays,
> opposition lurks among cadres, intellectuals, state employees. In
> the words of one retired official: "The current stabilization is only
> on the surface. One day people will riot in much greater numbers
> than in the late eighties." . . . Today, the person who controls the
> two banners [of religion and nationality] in Tibet is none other
> than the Dalai Lama, who enjoys the status both of the highest
> spiritual leader and the internationally recognized symbol of
> Tibetan nationhood.
>
> WANG LIXIONG, "The People's Republic of China's
> 21st Century Underbelly"

How prescient these words seem to us today. Despite continued Chinese government rhetoric about its successes in Tibet, these remarkably candid remarks from one of China's most important writers on Tibetan issues demonstrate that Chinese intellectuals are all too aware of the failures of the present policy. When opposition lurks even among cadres, what need is there to say that it is very much alive among monks and nuns?

While it is true that protests decreased in number from the late 1980s until March 2008, we can see today how fragile the situation in the Tibetan world truly is. Tactics like the Strike Hard Campaign have been unable to effectuate any real shift in monks' attitudes toward the government, or at least any shift of the kind hoped for by the CCP. On the contrary, the micromanagement of monasteries and schemes like the Strike Hard Campaign have created a great deal of resentment. They have shown monks and nuns the extent of the compromises required of them if they are to inhabit the modern Chinese state. Many Tibetans continue, albeit reluctantly, to make those compromises, but many others refuse to do so. Many of those who refuse then make the trip to India, where they enter institutions like the diaspora *densas*—institutions where these same compromises do not have to be made. In the early 1980s, Sera Monastery in India, one of the *densas* in exile, had a monastic population of less than 1,000 monks. Today it has more than 4,000—a 300 percent increase. The additional monks are almost all recent arrivals from Tibet. They are, moreover, mostly monks who hail from eastern Tibet—precisely from those areas where monks have met with the greatest obstacles to obtaining permission to travel to the TAR for higher studies. Placing low limits on monastic enrollments in the TAR *densas*, creating barriers to eastern Tibetans being able to study at monasteries in central Tibet, and political reeducation campaigns have resulted only in resentment, monastic flight, and (most recently) another round of protests.

The CCP prides itself on its willingness to confront reality head on, on its ability to "adhere to the objective nature of things as the basis for accomplishing its agenda" (Anonymous 2002b:108). This being so, the Chinese leadership needs to ask itself whether the present policies are, objectively speaking, working, or whether, in fact, Tibetan devotion to the Dalai Lama, as a form of religious expression, might not be as difficult to eradicate as religion itself.[56] As Wang Lixiong says, "Virtually all Tibetans have the Dalai in their heart." No amount of political reeducation appears to be changing this. And in light of the Tibetan belief that the Dalai Lama will be reborn, there is no reason to think that Tibetans' devotion to him will cease once the present Dalai Lama dies.

Given that micromanagerial, strong-arm tactics and political indoctrination schemes have failed, the obvious question now is whether there are alternative policies that might better serve both the government and the monasteries. Someday it may be possible for Tibetan Buddhist intellectuals to engage in open and critical conversations with CCP intellectuals about the big issues (as Ryan Dunch describes Protestant theologians doing in his chapter in this book). Someday Buddhist scholars and CCP intellectuals may even be able to sit with each other as equals and debate the really big issues: the truth of Buddhism and Marxism, the question of whether there are universal human rights, the acceptable human costs of security, and the meaning of autonomy.

The day for such debates is not yet here. That does not mean, however, that more modest issues cannot be tackled. Given that present policies are not working, what are the alternatives? Let me conclude with some suggestions. My goal here is very pragmatic—to suggest steps that might be incrementally taken to make life more livable for all parties. Without denying that there are fundamental areas of disagreement, are there nonetheless practicable small steps that can be taken to ameliorate the situation? I believe there are.

1. *Reform of the governance system of monasteries.* Because the CCP bureaucracy effectively controls the DMCs in large monasteries like the *densas,* this form of governance has little credibility with monks.[57] DMCs therefore need to be reformed. They should be replaced by *governance boards composed exclusively of monks and nuns who are members of the community and who are elected by their peers* (with no interference or veto power from the government). This, in any case, is consistent with Article 4 of the 2004 decree of the PRC State Council, the "Regulations on Religious Affairs," which states that "all religions shall adhere to the principles of independence and self-governance."[58] That same document calls for the government "at various levels to solicit the views of religious bodies." Given the strained relations that exist between the monasteries and the Party, one wonders whether *a monastic affairs board, consisting of clergy from different Tibetan ethnic regions, and provincial- or regional-level officials of the RAB*, might not be helpful. Such a board, if established, should go beyond the pro-forma, photo-op ceremonialism that has heretofore characterized so many encounters between Tibetan clergy and CCP officials. Members should have the trust of their respective institutional bodies and be truly representative of their respective constituencies. The Party officials involved should have real policy-making power. Monk and nun members should be elected by their local institutions (subject to no veto power by the Party). The

purpose of the forum should be to devise more effective policy, and not simply to implement policy handed down from above. As a first step, this pan-regional board might tackle the pressing problem of renegotiating enrollment limits and minimum age requirements so that monasteries and nunneries can fulfill *both* of their traditional functions of (1) maintaining the artistic and architectural heritage bequeathed to them, and (2) realizing their religious and educational goals. As part of this discussion, the board should consider whether it is feasible, as a first step, to simply grant official status to all unofficial monks and nuns already residing in these institutions. Finally, *a formal grievance board, consisting of representatives of both the government and the monasteries*, should be established, and formal procedures for addressing grievances—from either monasteries or the government—should be instituted.

2. *Moving toward greater autonomy for monastic institutions.* Government policy should move in the direction of giving monks and nuns greater control over religious and educational programming (both content and scheduling), as well as full control over finances. It is not unreasonable, however, for clergy to provide financial statements to the government. The elected governance boards of monasteries should have complete say about which monks and nuns are admitted when slots become available. They should also be charged with maintaining order within the monasteries.

3. *Moving toward greater individual freedoms for monks and nuns.* Tibetan monks and nuns enjoy a relatively limited degree of freedom compared to PRC citizens in other regions of China. The government should begin moving in the direction of normalizing this situation, so as to bring Tibetan clergy in line with the level of individual autonomy enjoyed by Han Chinese in other parts of the country. This means doing away with surveillance, abandoning restrictions on accessing foreign media, and ending mobility restrictions that discriminate on the basis of ethnic identity or clerical status.

4. *Moving to freer exchanges between Tibetan monasteries in Tibet and their sister institutions in India.* Although only mentioned in passing here, the level of training of monks in the diaspora monasteries is much higher than that in their sister institutions in the TAR.[59] Most of the senior Geshes of the *densas*, for example, have fled to India, and many of the more serious and gifted young

monks in Tibet continue to travel to India for studies. This amounts to a brain-drain out of Tibet and into the diaspora. To remedy this situation, monks returning to Tibet (and some *do* return) should not, as a matter of policy, be treated with suspicion, nor should they encounter reprisals, be subjected to harassment, or be the subject of targeted surveillance, as is often the case today. In addition, the government should not create impediments to senior teachers returning to Tibet for limited periods of time to teach. On the contrary, it should encourage and facilitate such exchanges.

5. *Abandoning the failed policy of "patriotic re-education."* Whatever apparent "stabilization" this policy has brought is, as one official has said, "only on the surface." Rather than accomplishing any of the government's goals, the Strike Hard Campaign in its Tibetan manifestation has simply brought into question China's commitment to freedom of religion and human rights. Rather than reforming the views of Tibetan monks and nuns, it has simply driven dissent underground and created martyrs out of those who resist. Rather than purging the TAR of separatist elements, it has simply generated greater overall resentment.

There is no question that these suggestions require a shift in CCP policy. They presume, on the part of the Chinese administration, a willingness to try out new strategies: for example, to shift from a top-down, hierarchical model of policy creation and implementation to a more local, representational, and consensual model—from a reactionary model of policy-making (one that acts in response to crises that have already happened) to a preventative model that addresses the causes of potential crises and attempts to do away with them (before crises happen). Even if implementing these suggestions does not require that "Socialist society adapt to Tibetan Buddhism" or that socialism and Buddhism exist "on equal terms," it does require the government to go beyond its present perception of Tibetan monastic institutions as the archaic vestiges of a backward culture, as the means for placating the masses, and as revenue-producing tourist venues. Positively, it requires the government to acknowledge that monasteries have been and continue to be an important and valued aspect of Tibetan cultural life, that they are the repositories of valuable traditional knowledge, and that this aspect of Tibetan civilization, which is not reducible to its materiality, is something that is worth preserving.

Chinese policy-makers have repeatedly asked an important question when addressing the larger political issue of Tibet: "What does China have to gain from kowtowing to international pressure to make Tibet more autonomous?" The same question can, of course, be asked about Tibetan monasteries: "What does China have to gain from making these institutions more autonomous?" Until March 2008, it might have been argued that the political situation was under control, that there had been no major monk-led protests, that monasteries were serving the tourist industry well, and that there was sufficient religious freedom in monasteries that neither the Tibetan masses nor foreigners could credibly complain that the CCP was violating people's right to worship. But as this volume is going to press—with all three *densas* surrounded by army troops, with all of Tibet forcibly closed and inaccessible to the outside world, and with a worldwide outcry against Chinese policy in Tibet—we can see precisely what the Chinese government has to lose unless it is willing to rethink its policy toward Tibetan religious institutions.

Rather than preventing instability, it is the policy itself that today is *the very cause* of instability. Unless Chinese policy-makers acknowledge monks' dissatisfaction—for example, their frustration over low monastic enrollments and forced "patriotic re-education"—and unless they reach a negotiated settlement with Tibet's clergy, it is only a matter of time before we see a new round of monk-led protests. "The grim potential dangers" mentioned by Wang Lixiong (L. Wang 1999) are no longer "potential." They are real. Dealing with monks' and nuns' grievances will not solve the Tibetan issue, but there is no resolving of the broader issue without adequately responding to the clergy's grievances.

Mao Zedong once said that the Chinese Communist Party should always work "to accept what is useful and healthy, and to discard what is not." Let these words serve as a guide for the Chinese leaders tackling the issue of Tibetan religion in the twenty-first century.

PART IV

Taiwan and Transnational Chinese Religiosity

11 Religious Renaissance and Taiwan's Modern Middle Classes

Richard Madsen 趙文詞

A remarkable religious renaissance has been taking place in Taiwan from the mid-1980s down to the present (Madsen 2007)—a time period that, not coincidentally, corresponds to Taiwan's transition to economic prosperity and political democracy (Gold 1987; Rigger 1999).[1] Taiwan has always been an island full of folk religion. The months of the lunar calendar are punctuated with many festivals. All phases of the life cycle are marked by colorful rituals. But until recently, popular Taiwanese religious practices have mostly represented the parochial, particularistic, habit-driven aspects of traditional Taiwanese life rather than the cosmopolitan, rationalized, reflexive aspirations of its modernizers (Weller 1987).

The Daoist (and sometimes Buddhist—because Taiwanese folk religion is often syncretistic) deities, housed in spectacularly cluttered local temples, were local gods who took care of their own. Though the temples carried out works of charity, these were usually confined to their particular communities. Deeply embedded in the social and political life of their communities, such temples were a nexus of those informal, particularistic, clientalistic relationships that political reformers usually label "corruption." To this day, such temples are not infrequently accused of being conduits for money laundering and political patronage. Popular religious activities have been focused on rituals for bringing personal good fortune and a happy afterlife, not on organized efforts to improve one's moral life and change society (Weller 1987:84–88).

The past two decades, however, have witnessed the rapid rise of new forms of religious practice with broad appeal to Taiwan's emerging middle classes (H. Hsiao, ed. 1993). These are based on "this-worldly" (renjian) efforts to reconcile traditional beliefs with modern science and technology, to provide answers to the moral dilemmas presented by mobile, urban lifestyles, and to provide solutions to the social problems faced by a dynami-cally industrializing society. These new forms of religious practice are propagated by sophisticated organizations, employing the latest advances in information technology and reaching out into the Taiwanese diaspora around the world.

It has been a renaissance mostly of Buddhism and Daoism. Despite the considerable efforts of foreign missionaries, the combined presence of Catholics and Protestants in Taiwan never amounted to more than about 7 percent of the population; and although some denominations continue to grow, the aggregate numbers of practicing Christians have been declining (Qu 1998). This is an ironic development because many Protestants and Catholics in the 1950s, 1960s, and 1970s saw themselves, with some degree of accuracy, as Taiwan's modernizers. When Taiwan was still largely a rural society, they established major universities (the Protestant Donghai [Tunghai] and the Catholic Furen [Fu Jen] universities), built hospitals, and organized a wide array of professionalized social services—all in contrast to Buddhism and Daoism, which were mostly identified with traditional, rural folk religious practice. However, by the time Taiwan really did become modernized, it was Buddhist temples, and some Daoist ones, that emerged as the major vehicles for the moral aspirations of the new urban middle classes. As we shall see, this has made important contributions to the development of a democratic state in Taiwan.

That there has been such a religious renaissance in Taiwan is surpris-ing and calls out for explanation. No less a sociologist than Max Weber deemed Buddhism and Daoism incapable of sustaining the rational, inner-worldly asceticism necessary for the transition to modernity (Weber 1964). Moreover, until the late 1970s, Taiwan's Guomindang (GMD) govern-ment did whatever it could to discourage the modernization of Taiwanese Buddhism and Daoism. While working to coopt local religious leaders and to use local temples as conduits for the "black gold" of corrupt politics, the GMD aimed to legitimize itself as a secular, modernizing govern-ment. While promoting classic Confucian moral virtues (interpreted so as to justify obedience to authoritarian government), the GMD's public education attempted to make students critical of traditional "supersti-tions." Meanwhile, the government made it difficult for religious leaders to develop more sophisticated understandings of their practices or to use modern forms of organization to expand their influence. A partial excep-tion was the GMD's policy toward Christian missionaries. Because of its need to maintain favor with the United States, the GMD government was somewhat more tolerant toward Protestant and Catholic missionaries than toward its indigenous religions. For example, it allowed Protestants and Catholics to establish universities while denying this right to Buddhists and Daoists.

Under these circumstances, one might have expected that as the Taiwanese economy shifted away from agriculture to an increasingly knowledge-intensive high-tech industry, its mobile, cosmopolitan, well-educated urban middle classes would replace their traditional folk religious practices either with Christianity or with nothing. The surprising renaissance in "this-worldly" Buddhism, and in what I call "reform" Daoism, pushes us to reconsider commonly held assumptions about the relationship between religion and modernity. For example, a superficial reading of the sociological theories derived from Max Weber (often found in the work of the "modernization theorists" of the 1950s and 1960s, and recently in Samuel Huntington's [1993] writings on the "clash of civilizations") might suggest that the only cultural matrices conducive to advanced industrial society are based either on Protestant Christianity or on complete secularism. The ethnography presented in this chapter thoroughly refutes that assumption. Taiwanese Buddhism and Daoism are providing remarkably strong support for a dynamic, high-tech-based economy and, indeed, for a vital democracy.

The ethnography, however, supports other aspects of Weber's sociology of religion. Weber argued that the urban "middle class, by virtue of its distinctive pattern of economic life, inclines in the direction of a rational-ethical religion, wherever conditions are present for the emergence of a rational-ethical religion" (Weber 1964:97). For Weber, a "rational-ethical religion" downplays mysterious doctrines and elaborate rituals so as to focus the believer on responsibilities within this world, and it tends to reduce religion to ethics. As we shall see, the Taiwanese urban middle classes are indeed embracing such forms of "rational-ethical" religiosity.

At the same time, the middle classes of an advanced industrial society like Taiwan are more complicated than those studied by Weber in his historical research. This chapter attempts to give some sense of that complexity. It shows how different segments of the Taiwanese urban middle classes tend to adopt forms of Buddhism and Daoism with varying degrees of rational-ethicality; and in each case they retain important elements of mystery and ritual. As Weber might suggest, this chapter partially links these different patterns of religious practice to "distinctive patterns of economic life." In line with poststructuralist theories like those of Pierre Bourdieu, it also shows how these patterns of religious practice are shaped by the efforts of different middle-class segments to distinguish themselves from one another. Finally, in ways that the Weberian tradition, with its tendency to define religions in terms of ideal types that are sharply contrasted with one another, has difficulty grasping, this chapter shows how Taiwanese religious culture is shaped by the globalization of culture. Far from representing a clash of civilizations, it points to the possibilities of a confluence of civilizations.

I develop my argument by comparing the histories of four Taiwanese religious organizations whose similarities represent important general trends and whose differences give us clues about the complicated origins and direction of these trends. The first three are forms of "this-worldly Buddhism" (Birnbaum 2003; Wang S. 1994); the fourth is a "reformed" version of Daoism. The information on these groups comes mostly from my own ethnographic and archival research.

EXAMPLES OF RELIGIOUS RENAISSANCE IN TAIWAN

The Buddhist Compassionate Relief Association (慈濟功德會, Ciji Gongdehui)

We begin with Ciji (Tzu Chi), the popular name for the "Buddhist Compassionate Relief Association," which is probably the best known and most influential of all these organizations. Ciji was founded by the Buddhist nun Zhengyan Fashi (證嚴法師; Dharma Master Zhengyan, 1937–) in 1966. The daughter of a prosperous Taiwanese family in Taichung, Zhengyan decided to "leave the family" (chujia) and become a nun in the early 1960s. By 1966 she had established a small community of nuns in Hualian. Influenced—so the legend goes—by a conversation with some Catholic nuns who had asked her why Buddhists devoted all their efforts to seeking other-worldly satisfaction rather than trying to improve this world through good works, Zhengyan organized a small group of Buddhist laywomen to help care for the poor and sick. This group grew steadily but slowly during the 1970s. In early 1979, Zhengyan decided that Hualian—in a relatively remote, poor area populated heavily by aborigines—needed a modern hospital, and she "vowed" to build it. With support from President Jiang Jingguo and other government leaders, she was eventually given government land for the hospital. Meanwhile, with the help of her lay volunteers, she embarked on a major effort to raise 20 million dollars to fund it. Against all expectations, she succeeded, and this feat won her renown throughout Taiwan. The hospital was opened in 1986. Her lay organization then exploded in size and influence after 1987, when martial law was lifted in Taiwan. (Her nunnery—"The Abode of Still Thoughts"—in Hualian only has a membership of about 100 nuns.) Ciji now has over four million members, defined by their willingness to pledge a regular amount of money to the organization each month. Moreover, the small group of lay volunteers (originally all women) has grown from about 500 in 1987 to about 15,000 today (about a third of them men). Wearing distinctive navy-blue uniforms, these "commissioners" attend regular meetings and dedicate an enormous amount of time and energy to the work of Ciji. The commissioners are the center of concentric circles of devoted but less fully committed lay volunteers, who are available to be mobilized for Ciji projects, such as rebuilding houses after the September 21, 1999 earthquake (Jones 1999; Huang & Weller 1998; Laliberté 2004).

Beginning around 1990, Ciji made a major effort to become international. Branches were set up not only throughout Asia but throughout the United States, Europe, Latin America, and Africa. Local branches are encouraged to take initiative but are subject to supervision from the headquarters in Hualian. Membership is open to all, but in practice most members are Chinese (and, in the United States, immigrants from Taiwan rather than from the PRC). Ciji now receives direct contributions of about 150 million dollars annually (Ciji 2001). Over time, it has accumulated significant assets, such as its hospital and other property, which some estimates have valued as high as 9 billion dollars.

Ciji uses its money, the energy of its volunteers, and its enormous network of connections to carry out a variety of charitable and educational works. Each local branch raises its own money, which it uses to care for people in need within its area. (Branches in the United States, for example, raised money and organized volunteers to help victims of the September 11 attacks and Hurricane Katrina.) The central headquarters in Hualian dispatches teams of professional relief workers to help direct and coordinate the efforts of local branches. Ciji also dispatches teams of professionals and volunteers to disaster sites where there are no branches. Such teams have provided disaster relief on many occasions to Mainland China and North Korea, Turkey, Kosovo, Bangladesh, Rwanda, Somalia, Hondurus, El Salvador—and even, after the American invasion, Iraq.[2]

A more routine form of Ciji work is medical. To the Ciji hospital in Hualian have been added two other hospitals in Taiwan (in Jiayi and Taipei). These hospitals attempt to combine high-quality scientific medicine with compassionate care for their patients, facilitated by mobilizing volunteers to provide comfort and care for the sick. Inspired by a Buddhist sense of the continuity between life and death, they have also been pioneers in hospice care and in long-term care for the elderly. Outside of Taiwan, they have established an array of clinics to serve the poor (including a free clinic in the Los Angeles area). Finally, Ciji has established Asia's largest (third largest in the world) bone marrow registry.

On the culture and education front, Ciji has created a series of textbooks and classroom materials, based on Master Zhengyan's writings, to give "values education" in primary and secondary schools. (These materials, which use highly interactive teaching methods rather than the rote learning that was common in earlier moral education, are one of the options teachers can use to replace Sun Yatsen's "Three Principles" doctrine in Taiwan's schools.) Ciji teacher trainers have been invited to present these materials in schools in Fujian Province (where they were followed nervously by Public Security agents), as well as in Chinese schools throughout the diaspora, including the United States. Ciji also has a medical and a nursing school and a comprehensive university in Hualian, as well as handsome private primary and secondary schools in Hualian and several other places in Taiwan.

Finally, Ciji employs a sophisticated array of media to convey its message. In addition to publishing books and magazines, it owns its own cable television station (whose programs are available throughout the world) and maintains multilingual websites.

Throughout the networks established by this array of activities, there flow broad streams of people and ideas. Visitors are constantly coming from around the world to the Abode of Still Thoughts in Hualian for meetings, retreats, training sessions, and inspirational visits, and Ciji volunteers are circulating from Taiwan throughout the Chinese diaspora.[3]

Buddha's Light Mountain (佛光山, *Foguangshan*)

Based near Gaoxiong, in southern Taiwan, Buddha's Light Mountain (Foguangshan) is comparable to Ciji in visibility and influence and has an even greater claim to be the foundation for humanistic Buddhism in Taiwan (Chandler 2004). Its founder is Dharma Master Xingyun (星雲法師, 1927–), who came as a young monk from the Mainland in 1949 and built a reputation as an inspiring Buddhist teacher in the 1950s and 1960s. An excellent speaker and enterprising organizer, he was one of the first monks to use regular radio and television programs to spread his message. He aroused some suspicion from the authorities when he refused to join the government-controlled Buddhist Association of the Republic of China (BAROC). Nonetheless, he eventually managed to cultivate good enough contacts in political and religious circles to begin building the massive temple and monastery complex of Foguangshan in 1968 (Hsing Y. 2001).

On five hills within the complex are five temples, each devoted to one of the five major lineages within Chinese Buddhism (and representing Xingyun's aspiration of integrating those lineages). Although Buddha's Light Mountain was well established by the 1980s, it took off to new levels of membership and influence after the ending of martial law. At its site near Gaoxiong, the monastery now houses about 1,300 monks and nuns. In addition to branch temples scattered throughout Taiwan, it has constructed temples throughout East Asia and, in the early 1990s, the Hsi (Xi) Lai Temple near Los Angeles—the biggest Buddhist temple in the United States.

In 1992, Buddha's Light Mountain established its own lay organization, the Buddha's Light International Association (BLIA), which has tens of thousands of members throughout Asia and around the world. About 1.5 million people have formally "taken refuge" (the basic Buddhist rite of initiation) at Buddha's Light Mountain. In addition to helping to organize various Buddhist rituals, the BLIA volunteers participate in a wide array of social welfare and educational activities.[4]

Unlike Zhengyan, who, claiming poor health, never leaves Taiwan, the founder of Buddha's Light Mountain, Xingyun, travels constantly to spread his message and build his organization. Tens of thousands of people fill stadiums and auditoriums from Taipei to Singapore to listen to his "Dharma talks," a familiar American analogy of which might be Billy Graham's rallies. These events are typically staged in spectacular fashion, with multimedia light and sound effects. Xingyun visits regularly with world leaders like the Pope and heads of state, and, amidst some controversy a few years ago, with then Vice President Al Gore at the Hsi Lai Temple (Jones 1999; Chandler 2004).

There are Buddhist universities both at the Foguangshan site and at the Hsi Lai Temple in Los Angeles. Like Ciji, Buddha's Light Mountain publishes an extensive array of books and magazines (translated into many languages), produces television programs, and maintains sophisticated multilingual websites. Buddha's Light Mountain also has extensive assets, in the range of 5 billion dollars (C. Fu 1996).

Dharma Drum Mountain (法鼓山, Fagushan)

Though not as large as Ciji or Buddha's Light Mountain, the Dharma Drum Mountain organization—known in Taiwan as "Fagushan"—has a considerable following among influential intellectuals and professionals. Its head is Dharma Master Shengyan (聖嚴法師, 1930–), who, like Xingyun, originally became a monk (at age 13) in Mainland China and came to Taiwan in 1949. Unlike Xingyun, he had to leave the monastic life behind and join the army to get to Taiwan. After retiring from the army at the age of 30, he was reordained as a monk. He then underwent a six-year period of spiritual cultivation as a hermit on a remote mountain. After this, he studied at a Buddhist university in Japan, where he earned a Ph.D. Unable to find a satisfactory niche in Taiwan, he accepted an invitation to work in a Chan (Zen) Buddhist center in New York City. After the grand master of the Nongchan Temple in Taipei died, Shengyan returned to take over as its leader (Shengyen & Stevenson 2001).

The Nongchan Temple is a simple structure built on land that was not zoned for religious buildings. To get around the regulations, the temple has been constructed with sliding doors all around its sides and with partitions that can be used to block off its altar from the rest of the building, so that it can be classified as a shed. Surrounding this building are rather ramshackle residences and offices for more than a hundred monks and nuns. As the city of Taipei has expanded to encompass the formerly semi-rural district where the temple is located, its land has become too valuable for officials to ignore the zoning laws. Thus Shengyan has recently built a large Buddhist center on a mountain north of Taipei. Besides a large temple and monastery, this place, now named Dharma Drum Mountain, includes a Buddhist university. It was formally dedicated in October 2005.

Like Ciji and Buddha's Light Mountain, the Dharma Drum Mountain organization exploded in size and complexity in the 1990s. In 1990, Shengyan established the Institute of Buddhist Studies, an educational and research institute that has become the core of Dharma Drum Mountain University. The institute runs a number of extension courses for laypeople who want to learn more about Buddhism. Following the example of Ciji and Buddha's Light Mountain, Shengyan also established an organization of laypeople who carry out tasks ranging from teaching to charity work to hospitality. There are more than three hundred computers in use in the offices of Dharma Drum Mountain, to keep track of donors and volunteers as well as to prepare manuscripts for the organization's publishing house. The temple has a regular television show.

Like Xingyun, Shengyan travels widely, spending almost half the year away from Taiwan, either in New York or traveling to Buddhist meetings around the world. When he is in Taiwan, he gives a Dharma talk (a sermon commenting on sutras) almost every Sunday, to a packed temple. Many of his congregants have themselves traveled widely, and an unusual number of the monks and nuns have studied abroad. There are constant retreats, classes, and ceremonies not only at the main temple in Taipei but across Taiwan. Every year there are at least three ceremonies at which a thousand people take refuge in the Buddha at Dharma Drum Mountain.

Each of the three organizations described above claims to be developing a tradition of "this-worldly Buddhism" (*renjian fojiao*). This is a tradition inspired by the reformist monk Taixu, whose work was begun in Shanghai in the 1910s, but because of disruption by war and revolution did not reach fruition during his lifetime. A prime tenant of this tradition is that one must "enter the world in order to leave the world" (*ru shi wei chu shi*). One finds salvation not by retreating into a monastery but by bringing Buddhist compassion into the midst of ordinary life. One must also adapt the Dharma to the conditions of modern life (Birnbaum 2003; Pittman 2001).

Enacting Heaven's Business Temple (行天宮, Xingtiangong)

Although this-worldly Buddhist organizations are the most visible examples of the religious renaissance that has swept through Taiwan's middle classes since 1987, some Daoists have made similar contributions. The best-known example is the Enacting Heaven's Business Temple—Xingtiangong—in the heart of Taipei (Chen H. 1990).

The temple has most of the features of a typical Taiwanese Daoist temple: a large bronze incense burner; huge, dark-faced statues of Chinese folk deities—the main deity in this case being Enzhu Gong (Merciful Lord, another name for Guan Gong, or "Lord Guan"); long tables for offering gifts of food and flowers to the gods; and a system for divining one's fortune by throwing crescent-shaped blocks of wood in front of the gods. But, its leaders claim, its inner spirit is different. The temple was established in the early 1960s by Xuan Kong (玄空, 1911–), a wealthy coal-mine owner who, according to the official story, at the age of 39 "gave up relations with his wife and began a path of spiritual cultivation."[5] He developed the Xingtiangong by taking over an older temple. Xuan Kong purged this temple of its "superstition" (*mixin*). This meant getting rid of practices that were typical of most Taiwan temples, such as burning paper money to the gods, consulting spirit mediums, and offering sacrifices of meat to the gods. Xuan Kong instead emphasized a this-worldly, morality-based form of religious practice. The temple has established two branch temples, one in the Taipei suburb of Beitou, the other in Sanxia.

In the discourse of temple leaders, "superstitious" rituals were those that automatically brought supernatural help without regard to one's moral intentions. A typical sermon delivered at the temple goes as follows:

> We worship god, not men. So we don't burn paper money. Worship should begin with a good heart. . . . Every day we say a good word, every day we pick up a bag of garbage [the temple urges followers to help clean up the environment], we continue the spirit of our temple. We hope we can renew the spirit of our society. We hope our society can do good things together. Happiness comes from [a morally good] heart. (transcribed and translated by the author)

In literature published by the temple, "faith is the only emphasis of the ritual" performed in the temple. The deities represented by the statues are exemplars of moral virtue, but they do not exist as active agents in the world. The rituals are symbols of a person's intention to practice the virtues exemplified by the gods, not techniques for eliciting the gods' favor.

The virtues are those of the Confucian tradition, which is interpreted so as to stress not the duties of subordinates (sons, wives, subjects) to accept the authority of their superiors (fathers, husbands, rulers) but the mutual obligations of people engaged in interdependent roles. Publications issued by the temple not only tell stories of classical moral exemplars (especially from the *Romance of the Three Kingdoms*) but offer sophisticated accounts of how modern philosophers are interpreting these virtues for the present day.

The temple is organized to attract mobile urban middle classes. At any time of the day, it is busy with well-dressed people of all ages (about two-thirds women) who, by their appearance, seem to be office workers, store clerks, and students, as well as small business owners and housewives. But the people do not necessarily reside near the temple (which is conveniently located near major bus and subway lines) and have not necessarily grown up with religious practice. Unlike most temples in Taiwan, there is a chart on the wall near the entrance explaining how to offer incense and carry out the various rituals. The temple is considered a very popular place for carrying out the *shenjing* ritual (especially popular in the aftermath of the September 21 earthquake), in which incense sticks are passed over the body to pull out bad energy residing within, because at Xingtiangong the procedure is done very efficiently and does not require that one have any personal relationship with the temple priests.

Like the Buddhist groups described above, the Xingtiangong has made new use of laypeople. Its rituals are assisted by a group of elderly women "helpers" (*xiaolaosheng*) dressed in pale blue smocks. Such women help in other temples, but on a much less formal basis than in Xingtiangong, where they are trained and put on regular schedules. The temple also mobilizes laypeople to assist in professionally organized social services.

Through a foundation controlled by the directors of the temple, Xingtiangong has built a handsome public library and a modern hospital. It publishes an attractive magazine, and sponsors a range of educational and cultural activities, from concerts (both Western and Chinese classical music) to classes on managing interpersonal relationships. These activities are managed by well-educated, professionally trained staff, but they also call upon the assistance of volunteers, for instance, to assist with patient care in the hospital. The foundation also has plans to build a university. Such professionalized social outreach activities have been organized only since the late 1980s.

COMMON PATTERNS OF RELIGIOUS EVOLUTION

Despite important differences that will be discussed below, all four of these groups share features that come from a common wrestling with the dilemmas of Taiwan's modernization. First, all of them have at least partially demythologized traditional beliefs. That is, instead of taking these beliefs as a solid, literal representation of a world beyond the one of ordinary experience, they see the beliefs as symbolic expressions of the challenges of common human life. Reminiscent of the quest of the Protestant theologian Dietrich Bonhoeffer (1971) for a "religionless Christianity," some of the members of these Taiwanese organizations describe their faith as "religionless." As a nun at Foguangshan put it, "This is our cultural tradition, it isn't a religion." A nun at the Ciji monastery spoke of her commitment as a "way to express the culture of my race." Members of Dharma Drum Mountain described their practice as more philosophy than religion, and, as we have seen, the leaders of Xingtiangong talk of their deities as symbols of moral principles within their cultural tradition.

When they say things like this, however, they are not advocating an uncritical acceptance of their inherited culture. As Xingyun, the founder of Buddha's Light Mountain, writes:

> Professor John Dewey, the American philosopher, educator, and teacher of Dr. Hu Shih [Hu Shi], once said, "We must reappraise the meaning of value." His remark has had a tremendous impact on my thinking and my method of reappraisal and reorientation when dealing with issues of Buddhism, life, and society. . . . I do not unconditionally follow tradition. I do not toy with the idea of emptiness and talk in

vain about abstruse things. I do not consciously accept the opinion of the majority. Instead, I constantly review our tradition, observe, and think about the future of Buddhism. I keep on reappraising values as I grow. (Hsing 2000:76)

Members of Ciji sometimes refer to this process as "adaptation to life" (*shenghuohua*), adapting the best of their cultural values to the changing conditions of life in modern Taiwan. The other two groups we have described also support earnest efforts to get back to the basic premises of their traditions and extend them to modern conditions.

In all the groups, there is indeed much talk about "cultivating practice" (修行, *xiuxing*), a term well known from books on Confucian philosophy, but one that I had never heard used much in ordinary conversation until I became engaged with these Taiwanese religious groups. The term refers to the process of spiritual development that enables one to understand how to apply them in the broadest possible contexts. The many multimedia publications of all of the groups aim to facilitate this understanding.

The norms of filial piety, for instance, have to be adapted to a world of high-tech occupations in which, to be successful, children have to learn to think critically for themselves and may eventually have to move far away from their parents. The religious groups that I have studied all say that one should still hold on to the principle of filial piety under these circumstances, but that one must understand it in a deeper way and exercise it through new methods. To be truly filial, one must not blindly obey one's parents but thoughtfully assimilate the lessons they have taught and carry on their legacy in a cosmopolitan world that they may not be able to comprehend.[6] The collective work of these religious groups is an example of how to do this. They devote themselves to reworking the lessons that parents in Taiwan typically impart to their children. They encourage followers to help strangers in need as if they were one's own parents. If one is living far away from home, then, one can help one's parents by generously caring for someone else's parents—and in the process one can gain confidence that other members of one's religious community will be on hand to take good care of one's own parents. Self-cultivation, then, is not just improvement of one's individual self (using neo-Confucian language, publications of these groups refer to a "small self"—*xiao wo*) but a broadening of vision that generates affiliations to a wider community (a "big self"—*da wo*).

Another common characteristic of the groups studied here is a devaluation of ritual. Although all of them still regularly practice rituals, they all claim to subordinate external ritual practice to internalized morality. As one Ciji commissioner put it, before she followed Master Zhengyan, "I had the habits of Buddhism but not the heart. I used to offer sacrifices twice a month. But when I accepted the right Path of becoming a member of Ciji, I realized that what is important is not just to worship a lot of Buddhist images. It is changing the heart. . . . Instead of offering two sacrifices every month, cultivate yourself."

Along with a devaluation of ritual comes a dilution of hierarchy. In their formal structure, these groups remain authoritarian, not democratic. The Dharma Master in the Buddhist organizations is a supreme leader whose decisions are final. The priests of the Xingtiangong have unchallenged authority in interpretations of ritual and practice. But if rituals led by Buddhist monks or nuns or by Daoist priests are no longer as important as the good intentions harbored in a well-cultivated heart, then laypeople can be just as important as ordained masters. All the organizations studied here have created dynamic associations of lay followers, which have rapidly expanded and which carry out much of the public work of the organization. One secret of the success of these lay associations is that their members are encouraged to take initiative. Even though formal hierarchy remains, therefore, its power is diluted by, as well as disseminated through, the active initiatives of the lay associations.

A final common characteristic of all these groups is the rationalization of their organizations. When one passes through the gate of the Foguangshan monastery from the noisy, cluttered, busy streets of its neighboring towns, the effect can be shocking. Inside the monastery grounds, all is orderly and serene. Although there is an enormous amount of activity always going on at the monastery, there is a place for everything and everything in its place. Events in all of the Buddhist organizations run on extremely precise schedules. Even the Xingtiangong seems more orderly than most Daoist temples; and its foundation offices, with their neatly attired professional staff working at banks of computers, seem the very model of rational efficiency.

Yet the organizations are not bureaucratic. "We are not an organizational apparatus (*jigou*)," says a Ciji commissioner. "People don't come to work every day. So everybody has to know what has to be done and how to fit in." Authority is not passed down from top to bottom through layers of specialized offices. Since these organizations depend so much on volunteers, they have to elicit their goodwill, not enact their obedience, and rely on their general skills rather than any specialized training. The religious organizations do this by putting great effort into educating their key volunteers to understand the vision of the organization and to articulate this to one another. A key part of the vision is that work should be carried out in a self-conscious, disciplined, efficient way, and that members should constantly discuss this with one another and encourage one another to act accordingly.

The above-listed characteristics fit Max Weber's description of a "rational-ethical religion." Using terminology developed by the anthropologist Mary Douglas to analyze this style of religion, these Taiwanese developments could be characterized as movement from what Douglas calls "restricted speech codes" to what she calls "elaborated speech codes" (Douglas 1973:44–58). A restricted code offers the speaker a limited range of alternatives for describing natural and social reality. It is the language of myth or unquestioning faith, of sacred stories that claim a monopoly on truth. While limiting the speaker's ability to articulate alternatives, the restricted code carries great emotional resonance and moral power—so powerful that, in the very act of being expressed in sacraments and magic, it can bring about what it symbolizes. An elaborated code enables the speaker to elucidate abstract, general principles that allow for many fine distinctions, can lead to many different conclusions, and can legitimate many different personal choices. Sociologically, the restricted code has a solidarity-maintaining function. In the restricted code, "utterances have a double purpose: they convey information, yes, but they also express the social structure, embellish and reinforce it" (Douglas 1973:44). The elaborated code, in contrast, maximizes the individual's autonomy and becomes a "specialized tool for decision making" (Douglas 1973:51).

For Douglas, the different speech codes are connected to different forms of society:

> It is essential to realize that the elaborated code is a product of the division of labor. The more highly differentiated the social system, the more specialized the decision-making roles—then the more the pressure for explicit channels of communication concerning a wide range of policies and their consequences. The demands of the industrial system are pressing hard now upon education to produce more and more verbally articulate people who will be promoted to entrepreneurial roles. By inference, the restricted code will be found where these pressures are weakest [that is, among people whose jobs are routine and require little verbal facility]. (Douglas 1973:44–45)

Taiwan's high-tech industrial economy is dependent on middle-class professionals who have mastered the elaborated code. If Douglas is correct, it is likely that if they maintain any religious practice at all, they will want one that has been translated into such a code. The effects of such a translation, Mary Douglas tells us, will be a devaluation of ritual, an increased emphasis on interior religious experience, and a move to "humanist philanthropy."

Relative to traditional Taiwanese religious practices, the Buddhist and Daoist organizations we have described here are making precisely this transition to a rational-ethical form of religious practice. They have made it to different degrees, however; and as Douglas might have predicted, those organizations that are most closely identified with the new middle classes of educated professionals have made the most extensive transitions.

DIFFERENT FORMS OF MIDDLE-CLASS MODERNITY

None of our four groups introduced above has completely discarded the powerful, "condensed" symbols of the restricted code, nor have they completely replaced ritual with a cult of inner experience and with "humanist philanthropy." (As Mary Douglas [1973] notes, a complete abandonment of condensed symbols and ritual would be terribly alienating and dehumanizing.) We can, however, array them on a continuum.

The Daoist Xingtiangong remains the most closely bound to the restricted code and to ritual. Its analogue in the American Christian landscape might be an inner-city Catholic church whose priests give sermons about pursuing social justice in the modern world while congregants are busy lighting candles and performing devotions to Mary and the saints. It reflects the wonderfully jagged development of Taipei itself, where sleek, modernist office buildings and innumerable McDonalds and Starbucks restaurants line the main thoroughfares, while a vibrant world of artisans, peddlers, folk healers, and traditional Taiwanese food sellers clogs the side alleys. The religious functionaries at the temple are constantly preaching that moral cultivation is more important than ritual offerings, the temple does not sell food or flowers to offer to the gods, and the glossy magazine it publishes shows no pictures of such sacrificial offerings. But crowding against the sidewalk adjacent to the temple are dozens of peddlers (mostly women in typical farmers' garb) selling materials for such offerings. The temple officially disavows the peddlers. There is a red line painted along the edge of the sidewalk, and any peddlers who cross it are driven away by the temple's security guards. The peddlers stand in the street just across the line. This, however, violates city laws. Every few hours, city police drive up on motorcycles and force the peddlers to retreat to the other side of the street. But after about ten minutes, the police leave and the peddlers return. Business is brisk. Worshippers mostly buy bouquets of flowers or bags of fruit, which they place on special wooden plates on long tables in front of the statues of the deities. But offerings can include anything edible, except for meat. One often sees large boxes of instant noodles and cases of Coca-Cola.

The temple sponsors many different rituals to help people discern their fate and seek good fortune. The main rituals, redolent with the allusive, condensed symbolism of the restricted code, are divided into two parts; in between the two, worshippers must listen to a sermon (broadcast throughout the temple) about how moral cultivation is more important than external ritual. Some people listen attentively, but others doze off, talk on their cell phones, or chat with one another while waiting for the efficacious part of the ritual to continue.

As mentioned above, the temple, through its foundation, has built a hospital and a library, and it sponsors cultural events. This "humanist philanthropy" is managed by sophisticated professionals. But these professional managers do not necessarily have much to do with the temple. As one of the top administrators of the hospital told me, the temple is a good part of Taiwanese folk culture, but it does not appeal much to him.

Buddha's Light Mountain is more than a few steps ahead on the path toward a religion based on an elaborated code. If Xingtiangong is like an inner-city American Catholic church in a mixed neighborhood of recent immigrants, Buddha's Light Mountain is like a suburban American Catholic church where most congregants join in common prayer and singing rather than practicing private devotions during Mass—but where the church's nooks and crannies still hold images of Mary and the saints that sustain quasi-magical private devotions. Compared with the bustle of Xingtiangong, the atmosphere at the Buddha's Light Mountain temple complex is remarkably controlled and orderly. There are none of the jarring contradictions between officially approved sermons stressing inner morality over external ritual on the one hand, and unofficial peddlers purveying the accoutrements of ritual on the other. There is none of the syncretism. Buddha's Light Mountain has attempted to purify Buddhism, consistent with its foundational texts and traditional practices. Nonetheless, the Buddhism here is presented in all its historical and sociological diversity, without any effort to subordinate the parts to a consistent organizing principle. My first impression upon entering the temple complex was of a vast clutter of buddhas—thousands and thousands of buddha-statues of all sizes and styles, from the huge welcoming buddha (one of the largest in Asia) on a hill near the entrance to the thousand small buddhas that cover the inner marble walls of the cavernous central temple; from the exquisite ancient buddha in Foguangshan's Buddhist museum to the kitschy statues in the "buddhaland" cave (like a somewhat cheap imitation of a Disneyland exhibit). Buddha's Light Mountain does indeed achieve its founder's ambition to be a Buddhist "supermarket or a filling station," with something for everybody.[7] If Xingtiangong is like a Taiwanese night market, with its jumble of independent merchants peddling their different wares, Foguangshan is like a modern supermarket, selling many different products with sometimes contradictory uses, but in an orderly way under a single management.

The many programs of Buddha's Light Mountain seem aimed to ensure, however, that the different products of this supermarket will lead to an internal moral transformation. Its books and videos familiarize the public with the meaning of Buddhist customs and teachings, so that people can practice in an informed, thoughtful way. Also, Buddha's Light Mountain constantly hosts retreats and courses that train its followers in prayer, meditation, and practice. Finally, Xingyun and the other leaders of Foguangshan try to make distinctions between internal principle and outer practice, to make Buddhism more "user friendly" to busy modern people in a diverse society.

The internal moral integration promoted by Buddha's Light Mountain, however, can be fully accomplished only within the walls of the monastery. In keeping with classic Buddhist practice, Buddha's Light Mountain puts great emphasis on recruiting and training monks and nuns—and as can be seen from the 1,300 monastics at Foguangshan, it is has been very successful in doing so. Retreats for lay followers are billed as opportunities to experience a monastic way of life. People come to the monastery to regenerate their spirits after being buffeted by the contradictions of secular life.

Ciji, in contrast, tries to instill in its lay followers a level of personal moral discipline sufficient to change the way they carry out their professions in the secular world. It greatly simplifies the clutter of folk Buddhist rituals, encouraging its followers to think in terms of basic Buddhist principles while expressing their inner goodness through efficiently organized works of philanthropy. If Buddha's Light Mountain reminds an American of a suburban Catholic church, the Ciji headquarters in Hualian reminds one of a classic New England Congregational church, magnificent in its simplicity. The heart of Ciji is its convent in Hualian, the Abode of Still Thoughts, where Master Zhengyan lives with about a hundred nuns. There are also guest dormitories (not individual rooms, as at Foguangshan, but large common rooms for men and for women) where several hundred lay followers can sleep when they come to listen to and work for the Master. At the front of the Abode is a chapel (*fotan*) made of dark hardwood (not marble, like the temples on Foguangshan), with a single elegantly carved wooden statue of the Bodhisattva Guanyin (the Bodhisattva of Compassion) in front. The statue is flanked not with huge vases of flowers and mounds of fruit, as at Buddha's Light Mountain, but with several orchids arranged in elegant simplicity. This chapel is used for morning and evening chanting, but the rest of the day it serves as a meeting room. Often a large movie screen is pulled down in front of the Guanyin statue for video projections. After breakfast, Master Zhengyan holds a morning conference here. This is more like a talk on current events than a talk on Buddhist sutras. Her talk illustrated (and perfectly coordinated) with video images, the Master discusses the various disasters in the recent news and reports what Ciji volunteers are doing to meet the needs of people afflicted by them.

The same patterns of architecture and practice are repeated on a grander scale in the newly built Hall of Still Thoughts, located several miles away from the Abode of Still Thoughts, next to the Ciji General Hospital. It is a massive new building that houses administrative offices, meeting rooms, and a large worship space. The wood-paneled main hall, about the same size as the main temple at Foguangshan, has no buddha-statues—only a blank wall on which a buddha-image can be projected during worship. At other times the hall serves as a general meeting room.

If Buddha's Light Mountain tries to create a modern way of being Buddhist, Ciji tries to fashion a Buddhist way of being modern. Buddha's Light Mountain uses modern construction techniques to build temples according to traditional designs—like using modern techniques to reproduce Gothic cathedrals in Europe. Ciji's Hall of Still Thoughts, however, is basically a modernist building, with a sleek form aimed to carry out practical functions, but with a sweeping curved roof that evokes Tang-dynasty temple style without reproducing it. The same motif is carried out in Ciji's branch offices, hospitals, and schools. The differences in architecture between Buddha's Light Mountain and Ciji represent differences in their general approach toward embedding Buddhism in modern life.

Most of Ciji's work is focused on humanistic philanthropies of charity, medicine, education, and culture. There is far more emphasis on these works of mercy than on traditional Buddhist meditation and prayer ceremonies. If at Buddha's Light Mountain prayer before statues of the Buddha is supposed to lead to a compassionate heart that will perform works of charity, at Ciji it is the ritualized performance of philanthropy that leads to meaningful prayer.

At Ciji, works of mercy are seen as having an educational purpose. The Ciji motto is "Help the poor and educate the rich." The giver, not the recipient, is to be grateful for acts of kindness, because it helps the giver learn about his or her essential buddhahood. (As they say in Ciji, "Give with gratitude, receive with joy.") Helping others becomes an end in itself, a fundamental religious act.

Though Ciji's good works are seen to benefit the giver even more than the receiver (echoing the Protestant dictum that "it is more blessed to give than to receive"), the works are, of course, also supposed to have a beneficial effect not only on direct recipients but on society as a whole. Having adapted Buddhism to the professional delivery of modern services, Ciji aims to transform the spirit of professional practices. Consider, for example, the way Ciji operates its hospitals and medical school. In its mission to provide the most modern forms of Western medicine, it has to compromise the basic Buddhist precept forbidding killing of any sentient beings. At the Abode of Still Thoughts, both nuns and lay visitors make assiduous efforts not to kill even mosquitoes or ants. But the Ciji hospital and medical schools conduct scientific research that involves killing animals—and Master Zhengyan permits this if it is "done for a good purpose and if the animals are not made to suffer unnecessarily."[8] At the same time, Ciji seeks creative ways to inject Buddhist values into modern medical practice. For example, the Ciji medical school has a distinctive way of conducting its anatomy class. Before students dissect the human cadavers used in the class, they pray for the souls of the deceased. On the walls of the classroom, they post biographies of the cadavers they are working on, and students write essays expressing their gratitude to the person who donated his or her body. When the bodies are cremated at the conclusion of the class, half the ashes are returned to the deceased person's family, and the other half are kept in an urn in a chapel next to the anatomy classroom, where students can meditate and express gratitude for the lives of the people who have helped them in their education. The aim is to instill in young doctors a respect for the human beings who will be their patients, and to imbue them with the Ciji commitment to "compassionate care."

Unlike the Xingtiangong, which, after paying for its hospital, does not interfere with the hospital's professional administrators, Ciji exercises a deep if sometimes subtle control over the work of its hospital. This is not a matter of interfering with the professional autonomy of physicians. For instance, although Ciji Buddhists believe that abortion is wrong and the hospital does not encourage it, the administration's policy is not to second guess the clinical decision of a physician to perform a therapeutic abortion. Rather, Ciji influence is focused on making the hospital a place where patients feel especially well loved, respected, and cared for as they undergo their medical procedures. It hopes by this to provide an example that will benefit the medical profession throughout Taiwan.

Finally, Dharma Drum Mountain marks the largest step on our continuum from restricted to elaborated code. Unlike Foguangshan, Dharma Drum Mountain does not offer a supermarket of Buddhist products. It subordinates all other forms of Buddhist devotion to one—Chan (Zen) Buddhist practice. Unlike Ciji, which aims to cultivate an integrated, ethical life through ritualized practice of good works, Dharma Drum Mountain places Chan meditation first, and aims through this to produce the inner mindfulness that will engender meaningful work to transform the world. Besides the pure forms of Chan sitting meditation, Dharma Drum Mountain infuses a Chan spirit into other devotional practices.

By no means does it reject ritual; but its rituals are focused, even more than those of Ciji, on creating a deep inner experience. For example, I took part in an afternoon-long ceremony centered on recitation of the name of Amitabha Buddha (阿彌陀佛, Omituo Fo). Dressed in black robes in a large simple room lit only by dim natural light, about two hundred of us stood, then prostrated ourselves a hundred times while reciting the name. (It was like doing calisthenics.) Then a procession began in which we walked two by two back and forth within the room, while continuing to recite the Buddha's name. We began at a normal walking pace, but gradually the person leading the procession began to slow down, until finally we were walking at a snail's pace. The mind, though wishing to race forward, was gradually focused on the present. The procession finally ended with everyone back at his or her original place. Sitting in the lotus position in near darkness, we gradually chanted faster and faster. The effect was hypnotic. Everything melded together, and we seemed to become one extended self.

It was a powerful lesson on Buddhist emptiness—the individual self as an illusion, the true reality of the world subsisting in our interconnection. At the same time, such practices lead a person's consciousness to become intensely focused. It is, perhaps, a consciousness particularly suited to the demands of modern middle-class life in Taiwan's knowledge-intensive industries, where people have to take initiative for thinking through problems while remaining acutely aware that they are part of a collective enterprise.

Up to a point, therefore, Mary Douglas's socio-linguistic theory about the transition from a restricted to an elaborated code helps to explain the patterns of religious evolution that have taken place among the Taiwanese middle classes. But it does not explain why so many middle-classTaiwanese have gravitated toward religion at all, or why they seem to prefer Buddhism and Daoism to Christianity. Nor does Douglas's theory help us discern the social and political consequences of these religious developments. To address such questions, we must look more closely at the social constitution of Taiwan's middle classes and the political development of Taiwan. We need to pay more attention to the contingencies of Taiwan's history.

RELIGION AND STATUS DISTINCTIONS

As suggested by the work of Pierre Bourdieu (1984), individual middle-class Taiwanese tend to utilize the distinctions in reputation of the different religious groups as a map of relative social status, and then try to celebrate or enhance their own status by moving between different religious groups. Religious affiliations intersect with and reinforce the status distinctions created by consumer advertising. *Rhythms,* Ciji's general-interest magazine on culture, contains advertisements for automobiles like BMWs. Presumably, the advertisers have found that people who are attracted to Ciji see themselves as the kind of people who can, or would someday like to, purchase such high-status automobiles while compassionately helping the poor.

Besides providing a map of different statuses stemming from occupation and education, the distinctions commonly made between the different religious groups also provide a map of the ethnic divisions that intersect class divisions in Taiwan. Xingtiangong is thoroughly Taiwanese. Its ceremonies and sermons are all in the Taiwanese language; its practices remain rooted in the folk customs of Taiwanese village life. Ciji is also Taiwanese—its founder is Taiwanese, the language most commonly used in its ceremonies is Taiwanese, and many of its followers take great pride is saying that Ciji represents the best in Taiwanese culture—a more refined and cosmopolitan Taiwanese identity than that associated with Xingtiangong. Buddha's Light Mountain is Mainlander.[9] Its founder was from the Mainland, and he has been associated with Mainlander political factions in the GMD. Dharma Drum Mountain is also Mainlander.

With the exception of Xingtiangong, whose membership is almost entirely Taiwanese, however, the religious groups have become quite mixed ethnically. Although neither Buddha's Light Mountain's Xingyun nor

Dharma Drum Mountain's Shengyan speaks in Taiwanese, many of their associates do. Their Dharma talks are often given half in Mandarin, half in Taiwanese. Participants in their rituals are a mixture of Taiwanese and Mainlander in rough proportion to their mixture in the general population (with perhaps a slight overrepresentation of Mainlanders). Ciji's Master Zhengyan speaks both Taiwanese and Mandarin (some interviewees told me that her Mandarin has improved significantly in recent years), and in recent years there have been increasing numbers of Mainlanders participating in the organization, some in high positions.

This gap between what our four organizations *represent* and what they *are* is of great importance sociologically and politically. Taiwan's rapid economic development has produced a middle class full of conflicts. Meanwhile, the island's delicate geopolitical position and conflicted history set up potentially devastating conflicts between Mainlanders and native Taiwanese. The differences between popular religious organizations could provide a frame of reference for thinking about such social and political divisions. When this happens in other societies, religious groups can become the agents of violent social polarization. But this has not happened in Taiwan. The groups that I have described have encouraged the blending of different segments of the population and facilitated reconciliation between potentially warring factions. This undoubtedly has helped Taiwan make a relatively peaceful transition to democracy since the end of martial law in 1987 (Rigger 1999:128–93).

To understand how this has happened, we need to consider how the historical development of these organizations has intersected with the particular history of state-building in Taiwan and with the general forces of globalization.

RELIGIOUS RENAISSANCE AND THE TAIWANESE STATE

Although they are now successful with the Taiwan middle classes, these four organizations were not popular when they first began. Their religious practices were not fashioned with a view to achieving popularity, but to fulfill the founders' religious ambitions and to respond to needs immediately at hand. One characteristic shared by all the founders was that they were nonconformists. Xingyun refused to take part in BAROC and for years was regarded with suspicion by the Buddhist establishment and the political establishment. In 1962, Zhengyan took the very untraditional step of shaving her own head to become a Buddhist nun. When she applied for formal ordination in 1963, she was at first rejected because she had not received her tonsure at the hands of a recognized authority. Shengyan had to largely fund his own education in Japan (by chanting sutras for the dead) and, when finished, could not find a monastery to lead in Taiwan. Despite his wealth, even Xuan Kong had to overcome many obstacles before he could take over the Xingtiangong.

In the 1970s, these groups gradually grew and developed their distinctive approaches to Buddhism and Daoism, but even as economic development began to produce a sizable middle class, their followings remained relatively small. A major obstacle was political. Religious organizations had to contend with government suspicion of any large groups not under government control. Xingyun of Buddha's Light Mountain overcame some of this suspicion by cultivating favor with GMD politicians (Fu C. 1996:244–53; Chandler 2004). The other groups simply remained too small to pose a threat to the government. It might be tempting to see the explosion in popularity of such groups in 1987 as driven by citizens' desire to participate in organizations that were not controlled by the state. In fact, however, it was the government itself that helped these groups gain an important social role in the late 1970s and early 1980s, a role that prepared them for takeoff in 1987. Subsequently, the relationship of these organizations to the government has mainly been one of cooperation rather than rivalry. The people who become involved with these groups do so from a variety of motives, but these do not include a desire to oppose the Taiwanese state.

In 1976, the Taiwan provincial government instructed all temples to carry out charity work (Anonymous 1997). This fit a general strategy (common to East Asian newly industrializing countries) of keeping government social welfare expenditures low by relying on the private sector to take care of the poor, sick, and weak. In earlier stages of development, this had meant relying on extended families to take care of their own. Due to the increasing complexity and mobility of Taiwanese society, however, families could no longer meet such needs. Christian churches had carried out many types of welfare work since the 1950s. But the Christian community remained tiny. If the government was to rely heavily on religious groups to provide welfare, these would have to be Buddhist and Daoist.

The difference between the current proposals in the U.S. to promote "faith-based charities" and this Taiwanese approach was that the government commanded rather than encouraged, and it gave special support to groups it deemed to have followed its commands most effectively. Ciji won an award for being the best provider of welfare services—an important milestone in its rise to prominence. In the early 1980s, it was the Taiwan provincial government that played a major role in the building of the Ciji General Hospital. The initiative—the vow—to build the hospital came from Master Zhengyan. But when she made her vow, she had no resources to carry it out. In particular, she had no land upon which to build a hospital. In October 1980, Taiwan Provincial Governor Lin Yangkang—and, a few days later, Taiwan's President Jiang Jingguo—visited the Abode of Still Thoughts and offered to help Ciji obtain the land. The hospital was eventually built on public land donated by the Hualian County government. Prominent political leaders Li Denghui (who by this time was provincial governor, and who would become president after the death of Jiang Jingguo) and Lin Yangkang (at this time minister of the interior) attended groundbreaking ceremonies (Anonymous 1997).

In the late 1970s and early 1980s Foguangshan similarly benefited from government support in obtaining land for its temples and for other ventures.[10] The Nongchan Temple (the foundation of Dharma Drum Mountain) benefited from government willingness to let it stay on illegal land, even as that land was becoming extremely valuable. Favorable connections with the government enabled Xingtiangong to benefit from its land deals. Thus even though the government may have initially been ambivalent about supporting such Buddhist and Daoist religious organizations and may have slowed their early growth, it actually helped build a solid foundation for their later expansion. These religious organizations do not fit the image of a "civil society" that grows up independently of the state.

The years following the end of martial law, when most restrictions on free association were swept away, were truly a springtime for Taiwan's civil society. People flocked to all manner of associations representing an extraordinarily wide range of causes, from politics to social reform, community improvement, and philanthropy (H. Hsiao 1994:38). Many of these groups remained small; others grew quickly and died. The religious groups studied here grew quickly and steadily precisely because they had had good, if somewhat detached, relations with the government before 1987. Participating in them was a respectable and safe way of taking initiative to help address Taiwan's social problems. Such organizations were by no means "transmission belts" from the government to the people, but perhaps they were like belt buckles joining private and public sectors.

Though there is some necessary tension in this union, it is considerably more cooperative than any relationship between church and state currently possible in the United States. Although Ciji and other Buddhist organizations embarrassed the government in 1999 by responding more quickly and efficiently to the Taiwanese earthquake than the government itself did, some of Ciji's most important reconstruction efforts have actually been aimed at rebuilding government schools. Ciji has been building fifty new public schools to replace the ones destroyed in the earthquake. Though Ciji raises money for the schools, designs them (with special concern that they be earthquake proof and environmentally friendly), supervises their construction, and mobilizes volunteers to help landscape and decorate them, the schools are to be government-run public schools, with curricula and teachers furnished by the government. Unlike "faith-based" organizations in the U.S., which currently want public money to do their private work, Ciji raises private money to do public work.

The other organizations we have described have similar cooperative relations with the government. Their contribution to Taiwan's political culture is thus a conservative, stabilizing one. Since they see the state as a necessary, beneficial force, they are not tempted to mobilize particular constituencies against it. Even though they may naturally attract different segments of the middle class, they have no interest in fomenting class conflict. On the contrary, since they wish to expand, they have every interest in reaching out to as broad a cross section of the population as possible. This is justified, especially for the Buddhist groups, by a religious commitment to "great compassion for all." As they expanded during the 1990s, therefore, they have in practice served to soften class and ethnic divisions, even though by reputation they represent different segments of the middle class. Their reputations are based on their position within the Taiwanese cultural landscape at the moment when they emerged from the restrictions of martial law and began the process of seeking more members. Their ecumenical practices are based on their commitment to expand in a nonconflictual way with a basic attitude of respect for the state.

Even though their leaders and most committed members see these organizations as religious rather than political enterprises, such religious organizations have unintended, beneficial civic consequences. They help take some of the rough edges out of the conflicts between native Taiwanese and Mainlanders, and between the relatively successful and relatively poor. They nurture a spirit of engagement with public affairs and encourage a cooperative (but not uncritical) attitude toward the government. By no means do I argue that such religious organizations (as some of their members, particularly those in Ciji, might say) are the solution to Taiwan's social and political problems. Taiwanese political culture continues to have many rough edges and sometimes teeters on the brink of chaos. The fact that—despite a history of atrocities committed by Mainlanders against Taiwanese, the legacy of a harshly authoritarian regime, a "Confucian" cultural tradition that many experts have considered incompatible with democratic values, all its tensions with Mainland China, *and* its lack of political recognition by the international community—Taiwan has avoided chaos and made a successful if still shaky transition to a stable democracy is, perhaps, the true "Taiwan miracle." The fact that some of Taiwan's most influential religious organizations have moderated conflict rather than added to it is an important part of this miracle.

GLOBALIZATION AND RELIGIOUS RENAISSANCE

Besides being influenced by particular currents in Taiwanese history, the middle-class religious renaissance is affected by broader trends in cultural globalization. The homogenization of popular cultural symbols—the "McDonaldization" of the world—seems, paradoxically, to evoke a resurgence of particular identities, expressed through local cultural practices, around the world (Barber 1995). Thus, in offering Coca-Cola to the gods, Xingtiangong practitioners affirm their participation in a world of multinational consumer goods but affirm a particular Taiwanese identity as well. On a more upscale level, Ciji members do the same when they accept BMW ads for their magazine. However, unlike societies where the assertion of particular religious identities leads to hostility toward the rest of the world—as Benjamin Barber puts it in *Jihad vs. McWorld* (1995)—the assertion of Buddhist and Daoist identities in Taiwan has produced ecumenical cooperation.

Perhaps this is because of their history of borrowing from different cultural and religious traditions. Although based on Chinese religious traditions, the organizations I have described in Taiwan have absorbed many influences from Japan and the West to create their new forms of religious practice. The most important influence has been from Japan, both from the Japanese colonial period (1895–1945) and from the more recent past (Jiang C. 2001). Japanese Buddhism has been more focused on worldly service than has traditional Chinese Buddhism. Master Zhengyan's first Buddhist teacher, Master Xiudao, had gone to school in Japan, and helped introduce to Zhengyan the notion that monasteries should work in the world.[11] Japanese Buddhism also pioneered the organization of educated laywomen for community service. However, Japanese Buddhists had moved away from the strict practices of Chinese Buddhism—for instance, Japanese monks could get married. While adopting the social concerns of the Japanese Buddhists, Taiwanese Buddhists retained the purity of Chinese monastic life, and thus helped maintain a distinctive cultural identity.

Taiwanese religions also borrowed from West, sometimes in order to compete with it. Administrators at the Xingtiangong Foundation said that the idea of organizing volunteers to help the community was brought to Taiwan by the service clubs formed by American military wives. And as already mentioned, according to Ciji's official history, Master Zhengyan was inspired to take up social service work after being visited by three Catholic nuns who tried to show her that Catholicism was superior to Buddhism because it performed so many works of social service. Whatever the accuracy of this story, it suggests that competition with Christians was one force driving Ciji's religious evolution. The theme of competition becomes even stronger with Buddha's Light Mountain. Master Xingyun saw the encroachment of Christianity on Taiwan as problematic. He thought that he had to adopt some of the effective religious marketing used by Western Christian organizations if he was to maintain Buddhism's place in Taiwan.[12] Other Buddhist groups, as well as reformed Daoist organizations like the Xingtiangong, adopted his methods. By now, all the religious organizations described in this chapter have more sophisticated magazines, television programs, and websites than most Christian organizations in Taiwan.

These religious movements are thus like the rest of Taiwan's emerging national culture—a distinctive reconfiguration of Chinese cultural traditions under the stimulus of influences from Japan and the United States, a unique blend of East and West that is "made in Taiwan." With their visibility and global outreach, these Taiwanese religious organizations can become vehicles for the collective representation of national identity, a role that looms especially large in Taiwan's peculiar geopolitical circumstances.

How much Buddhism and Daoism is lost in such translation into the language and logic of a globalized network society? There are debates within Taiwan's religious circles about this. Ciji is sometimes criticized for being "insufficiently dharmic" (*bu ru fa*). Yet even as they adopt some of the idioms of globalized media culture, these organizations criticize important parts of the content of that culture. All of them warn against consumerism and stress that true happiness comes from cultivating the heart, not acquiring things. They all warn against self-indulgence and encourage generosity. All of them—but Ciji most effectively—urge people to achieve harmony with the natural environment. Are their efforts destined to be defeated by the seductive pressures of global consumer culture, or can they actually help to transform that culture?

CONCLUSION

It would be foolish to try to predict whether or not these possibilities will be realized. What I have tried to demonstrate in this chapter is only that Taiwan's emerging middle classes have generated forms of religious imagination and religious association that are playing a beneficial role in building a moderate, responsible, civic culture. Contrary to simplistic interpretations of the Weberian tradition in the sociology of religion, the Taiwan case shows that Buddhism and Daoism have the capacity both to adapt to modernity and to humanize the modern world. It further shows that globalization can encourage a kind of religious renaissance that leads to dialogue among civilizations rather than clashes between them. Buddhists might say that the emergence of such religious resources was the result of "good karma." But from a sociological point of view, it was by no means preordained. I have tried to show how the growth of these organizations was the result of a fortuitous confluence of separate processes, as well as of the wisdom that enabled certain spiritual leaders to make the best use of the "causes and conditions" in which they found themselves.

12 Goddess across the Taiwan Strait

Matrifocal Ritual Space, Nation-State, and Satellite Television Footprints

Mayfair Mei-hui Yang 楊美惠

The said "return of the religious" . . . is not a simple *return*, for its globality and its figures (tele-techno-media-scientific, capitalistic and politico-economic) remain original and unprecendented.

JACQUES DERRIDA, "Faith and Knowledge"

This chapter examines the complex interactions among the forces of nation-state, popular religion, media capitalism, and gendered territorialization as these are inflected across the Taiwan Strait.[1] Relations across the Strait have been fraught with political tension and military preparations over the question of whether Taiwan is part of China or an independent state. Since the 2000 presidential elections in Taiwan, the new government there has been more vociferous about Taiwan independence, and Mainland China's Communist Party has responded with more vigorous claims on Taiwan, which had earlier included the launching of a warning missile over the island in 1996. Under these conditions, it is all the more remarkable that in recent years there has been an increasing number of religious pilgrimages and exchanges across the Strait, and that in 2000, one such pilgrimage by Taiwanese worshippers of the maritime goddess Mazu (媽祖) to her natal home in Fujian Province was broadcast live from China back to Taiwan via satellite television.

I conducted fieldwork on popular religion and media development in Taiwan for four months in 2000 and 2001, and traveled with Dongsen Television News Station (東森電視台, ETTV News) from Taiwan to Mainland China in July 2000, observing their reporters and technicians deliver live satellite television coverage of the historic religious pilgrimage.[2] In contemporary Taiwan, Mazu has the largest deity cult, her temples are the most numerous of all, and popular estimates are that 70–80 percent of Taiwanese worship her in some form. The pilgrimage of 2000 was orga-

nized by one of Taiwan's most prominent Mazu temples, Zhenlangong (
鎮瀾宮, Zhenlan Temple), in the central Taiwanese town of Dajia. This
mediatized pilgrimage to a female deity propelled about two thousand
worshippers—an unprecedented number, consisting mostly of women
of the lower middle or rural classes—from Taiwan across the politically
tense Taiwan Strait to the sacred ritual center of the Mazu goddess cult on
Meizhou Island (湄洲島), Fujian Province. It was indeed a historic "media-
event" (Dayan & Katz 1992), in which the forces of popular religion
deployed the largest contingent of Taiwanese media crews ever to cover
such a phenomenon (Zhenlangong even paid the expenses of more than
eighty media personnel), in order to solidify their national position and
engage with the grassroots religious revival in China.

This mutual deployment of religion and media took place against the
larger historical backdrop of the emergence of the modern nation-state
in China and Taiwan. It has often been observed that modern states are
predicated on territoriality, the fixing and monitoring of the population,
and patrol of state borders (Anderson 1991).[3] Anthony Giddens draws a
useful distinction between "frontiers" and "borders" when he writes that
the frontiers of archaic empires or premodern states were marginal areas
at the periphery where "the political authority of the centre [was] diffuse or thinly spread," or were occupied by tribal communities not fully
colonized by archaic states. Borders, however, are found only with modern
nation-states and the global state system. They are sharply and clearly
demarcated, and despite their location at the edges of the nation-state, they
convey a state presence (through border patrols, customs checkpoints, and
media messages) equal to that of the political capital (Giddens 1987:50).[4]
Modern state territorialities in both Taiwan and China have developed
ways of excluding, containing, or rechanneling de-territorializing forces
such as capitalism (Deleuze & Guattari 1987), migration (Scott 1998), the
transnational media, and, more recently, religious pilgrimage.

Television's power to promote cultural integration (Ang 1996:5) has
not been lost on nation-states, which have established or guided national
broadcast systems and which control media access, media importation,
and programming to varying degrees. Whereas nineteenth- and early
twentieth-century nationalisms relied on newspapers, nation-states now
actively deploy television to construct what Benedict Anderson (1991) calls
the flattened homogenized monolingual and simultaneous space-time of
the national imaginary. In the U.S., we see the role of the state in the
ironic use of the First Amendment to establish an internal cultural space of
national identity in the media, by blocking local governments from creat-

Map 12.1.   Route of the pilgrimage of the maritime goddess Mazu from Dajia, Taiwan, to Meizhou Island, Fujian Province, July 2000. Map by Choonghwan Park and Han Xiaojuan.

ing regional media audiences and by limiting foreign media access to U.S. airwaves (Price 1994). The lack of cosmopolitanism in American television and other media served the Bush administration well in building popular support for the invasion of Iraq in 2003.

The advent of satellite and cable television and the internet has disrupted the correspondence between state geographies and electronic communities (Morley & Robins 1995). Not only can satellite television disaggregate established audiences, it can also create new ones across and within national boundaries. Euro-American transnational media began using satellite broadcasts in the 1960s, and these media are still dominant today in terms of their global reach, services, and programming (Parks 2002). But in the twenty-first century, we also see the emergence of new regional satellite services that transcend nation-states and challenge the hegemony of Western global media. Increasingly, as Michael Curtin (2001) suggests, transnational cultural-civilizational media communities drive the regional production of media and challenge the dominance of Hollywood, the one production center that now has truly global reach. One example of an influential regional television station is the Al Jazeera satellite news station operating out of Qatar and serving 35 million Arabic speakers in 22 nations (Ajami 2001; Salamon 2002).

In Asia, a conjunction of economic liberalization, transnational capital, and cable and satellite technologies (China News Digest 2000) has also begun to reconfigure the space of nation-states and their terrestrial broadcast systems. As in Europe, both supranational and subnational electronic communities are emerging in Asia as alternative sites of allegiance (Morley & Robins 1995:2, 34, 43–44; M. Yang 1997). Japan's Direct Broadcasting Satellite, BS-2A, launched in 1984, "first broke the link between the terrestrial broadcasting systems and national borders" as its footprint extended over countries like South Korea, Taiwan, and Malaysia, whose governments responded by banning satellite-receiving hardware (Chin 1997:86–89). Seven years later, in 1991, Star TV began to broadcast in Asia. Owned by Australian media mogul Rupert Murdoch, along with Hong Kong and Chinese companies, Star TV became Asia's dominant satellite broadcaster, with 300 million viewers in 53 countries (J. Chan 1997). In the past decade, additional Chinese-language supranational and subnational satellite electronic communities have also emerged in the region, with the potential to produce alternative units of culture and identity to nation-states, and this chapter examines such developments in Taiwan media (J. Chan 2003; Long 2000; Chen Q. 1996; C. Lee 1999; M. Yang 1997). However, the outcome of this process around the globe is not yet in sight as nation-states mount different strategies to control access to satellite orbital slots above the equator (Price 1999), counter the creation of regional and local electronic communities of identity, and seek to implant state values in transnational media culture even as they cross political boundaries (Price 2002).

The relationship between modern nationalisms and religious traditions is a complex and multifaceted one. The secular foundation of modern Western liberal societies relied on the very category of "religion," which reduces religion from a way of life that cuts across social institutions to a matter of personal belief (Asad 1993, 1999). Around the world, postcolonial nationalist imaginaries have followed the Western model of shrinking and neutralizing the religious sphere—and, through enforced modernization, police action, and public education, have banned or curtailed many religious practices from both public and private life. These represent explicitly modernist departures from sacred temporalities of the-eternal-past-in-the-present, from mythological deities and founding ancestors. As Dipesh Chakrabarty (2000b) and Prasenjit Duara (1995b) have shown, modern nationalisms are inseparable from History, especially a secular, linear, teleological history that sacralizes modernization, futurity, and national strength. Where nationalisms override and displace "religion" with their own origin narratives, pantheons of national martyrs, and secular state rituals, there may be virtually no domain of religion left even in the private sphere, as in Revolutionary China, or religion may be relegated to marginal rural communities and/or to the domestic sphere, as in Guomindang-controlled Taiwan.

Critiques of economic, political, and colonial domination have too often been deaf to the language through which subaltern classes and cultures in Asia establish counterpublics through religion (Chakrabarty 2000b). We need to pay more attention to how subaltern or other forces express themselves through religious practice and discourse in confronting the nation-state. Those perspectives which do recognize the inextricability of religion, polity, and media focus on the dominant Judeo-Christian-Islamic traditions (De Vries 2000; Derrida 1998; Lefort 1988), whose monotheism and patriarchy lend themselves to the needs of nation-state. This chapter explores the political significance of a very different tradition, the cult of the goddess Mazu, in a polytheistic Chinese religious tradition that, despite its patriarchy, has a strong thread of matrifocal logic.

In the age of mediatization, any culture or subculture that does not receive media attention—especially from the electronic media, with their enormous powers of attraction and geographical encompassment—operates at a severe disadvantage. But in national media systems, minority groups, religious communities, indigenous peoples, and oppositional groups are usually excluded from the mediatized public sphere (Ginsburg 1999). Even as China today allows a huge infusion of popular consumer culture from Asia and the U.S. into its media, it has not welcomed the broadcast of popular religion. By contrast, the insistent voices and images of popular religion have gained entry to Taiwanese televisual space, albeit amid a deluge of entertainment and consumerist messages and an endless parade of pop stars, politicians, and television personalities.

PILGRIMAGE TO MEIZHOU ISLAND: DIRECT SEALINKS, AIRPLANE TRANSFERS, AND SATELLITE UPLINKS

The political hostility between China and Taiwan has long posed an obstacle for Taiwan's religious movements seeking to reconnect with their ritual origins in Mainland China. Since there is no official agreement governing the "three direct links" (三通, *santong*) of communication, transportation, and trade between Mainland China and Taiwan, all religious pilgrimages from Taiwan to Fujian have had to take an indirect route by airplane via a third point of transfer, such as Hong Kong or Tokyo. This roundabout journey was costly and arduous for pilgrims, who stood to save considerable money and effort by a *direct* sealink across the 70-mile Strait from Taizhong (Taichung) Port.

In May 2000, after the inauguration of newly elected President Chen Shuibian (陳水扁) in Taiwan, the chubby chairman of the Mazu temple Zhenlangong, Yan Qingbiao (顏清標), whose betel-nut chewing and heavy Taiwanese accent marked him as a man of the common people, challenged the new government. He reminded the new administration of their campaign promise to open up cross-Strait transportation and communication, and criticized their slowness in forging a "direct religious sealink" (宗教直航, *zongjiao zhihang*) between Taiwan and Fujian. He invited the media to broadcast his public consultation of Mazu by throwing wooden divination crescents (擲筊, *buabui*) to establish the departure date for Zhenlangong's pilgrimage to Meizhou that year. Mazu picked the date of Sunday, July 16, which had the effect of setting a timeline for the Chen Shuibian government and its Mainland Affairs Committee to approve the first direct sealink. Meanwhile, Zhenlangong negotiated with a Moroccan shipping company to charter four large ferries to carry pilgrims to Meizhou and become the first direct legal pilgrimage by sea. The media playfully enlarged on the tensions between Zhenlangong and the government Mainland Affairs Committee, headed by Cai Yingwen, and on the religion versus the state angle of this story, with newspaper headlines like, "Is Mazu Bigger or the Mainland Affairs Committee? Human and Deity Battle It Out" (Wang M. 1999:2), and "Cai Yingwen Does Not Get Outsmarted by Mazu" (Li H. 1999:22).

The Mazu cult poses thorny problems for the state in both Taiwan and China. I was told that many of Zhenlangong's core constituency, who are neither wealthy nor educated, voted in 2000 for President Chen and his Democratic Progressive Party (DPP; 民進黨, Minjindang), which was known for its support of Taiwan independence from China. However, the Mazu cult's origins in China, and the fact that its followers felt compelled to make pilgrimages to a religious center on the Mainland, made it more difficult for the DPP to appropriate the powerful Mazu cult as the ground for a new Taiwanese nationalism. The pilgrims' desire to cross the fraught political borders between Taiwan and the Mainland revealed the incon-

Figure 12.1. "Cai Yingwen, of the Mainland Affairs Committee in Taiwan, dragging her feet and being dragged to Meizhou by an impatient pilgrimage ferry." Cartoon by Coco, in the *Lian He Evening Paper*, June 16, 2000.

gruities between ritual territoriality and state territoriality. Conversely, while the Mainland government officially welcomed these pilgrimages in order to promote national unification, it was also nervous about dissemination of popular grassroots religious organization among local people, and it aggressively limited and monitored the movements of Taiwan pilgrims. Mainland official discourse conveniently forgot that what the Taiwan pilgrims were really returning to was not the nationalist imaginary of China, "the Motherland" (*zuguo*), but Meizhou Island, the sacred origin of the goddess Mazu. Rather than the political "unification" (*tongyi*) of China and Taiwan, it would seem that cross-Strait Mazu pilgrimages were in the process of creating a regional ritual space and religious community of Chinese coastal peoples and cultures that did not conform to existing political borders.

Failing to gain government approval for a direct sealink, Zhenlangong persisted with an indirect pilgrimage by airplane via Hong Kong and Macao in 2000.[5] The members of the temple's board of directors accompanied five Mazu images (which were seated in the First Class cabin) from Taiwan to Hong Kong, then to Xiamen in Fujian, then north by bus to Putian City and by ferry to Meizhou Island. More than two thousand Mazu worshippers from across Taiwan also made the airplane pilgrimage, some bringing the goddess-images from their small local Mazu temples. In Fujian, they were hosted by the large Mazu ancestral temple on Meizhou Island (which is controlled by Beijing), as well as by smaller, local-government-controlled and even grassroots Mazu temples in Putian and Quanzhou City. Zhenlangong also invited nine Taiwan television news stations and several newspapers to cover the six-day event. What was most significant (as mentioned above) was that it paid the airfares and hotel accommodations of more than eighty media personnel. This elaborate journey-cum-"media-event" was a testament to the transnational organizational powers of Zhenlangong, which exercises considerable influence with government powers and media organizations on both sides of the Strait.

Three cable television news stations in Taiwan—Dongsen, Sanli, and Zhongtian—and one network station, Minshi, were able to blanket the Taiwan news media in the summer of 2000 with on-site live satellite reporting of the pilgrimage. Their competitors, TVBS (a subsidiary of Television Broadcasts Limited of Hong Kong) and the three Taiwan government news stations, had to physically run their tapes to the Xiamen or Fuzhou television stations, which then relayed microwave signals to Beijing's Chinese Central TV, which sent them up to satellite before pickup in Hong Kong and transmission back to Taiwan a full day or two later. Those stations with live coverage made use of new Electronic News Gathering and on-location Electronic Field Production (ENG/EFP) technologies that have become standard practice in global news reporting since the late 1980s (MacGregor 1997). They uplinked to one of the three Dongsen-contracted satellites overhead—Asiasat, Apstar, or SuperBird (Long 2000). The Taiwan news crews brought their own Betacam videocameras, portable editing decks, and lighting and sound equipment to Fujian, but they could not ship their Satellite News Gathering (SNG) vans to China because China did not allow any broadcast equipment to be brought into the country. They thus needed to rent SNG trucks in China, but given the strict state controls on satellite uplinking in China, this proved a difficult task.

The details of how Dongsen Television News achieved a direct satellite uplink on the Mainland make up a fascinating tale of how two previously isolated and territorially sealed-off electronic communities were connected. Originally, Dongsen's Taipei office was negotiating via telephone with Beijing's Central Chinese TV station and Shanghai TV to rent their SNG vans, but things were not going well. Four days before Zhenlan Temple's entourage was due to arrive at Xiamen Airport, neither of the

Mainland stations had started sending out the vans. Dongsen's producers were very worried.

When Chen Jianxiang, the technical manager of Dongsen's satellite broadcasting division, got to Fujian, he found that the reason neither Beijing nor Shanghai TV had sent out their SNGs was that they could not get official permission for the satellite transmissions, despite the fact that the Taiwan Affairs Bureau in Beijing had already agreed that the Taiwanese media could transmit live coverage. In China, satellite uplinks need a special seal of approval from an administrative office, which assumes responsibility should anything go wrong (such as broadcasts of counterrevolutionary messages or state secrets). According to Chen, although much of the communication industry has now been privatized in China (e.g., microwave, or *weibo*, ground signals), it is much harder for satellite broadcasting to break away from the state and military and enter the commercial world.

Chen immediately set about securing approval for the transmission. He went to several different government offices, to no avail. No official wanted to take responsibility for an unprecedented six-day direct satellite transmission that was full of political risks. Finally, after waiting in an air-conditioned McDonald's for the long and hot Mainland summer lunch break to end at 3:00 P.M., he went to the Fujian Provincial Taiwan Affairs Office. They first tried to kick the matter upstairs, saying that this was up to the National Taiwan Affairs Office, but Chen patiently explained that the national office had already given permission and delegated authority to the provincial officials. Chen's years of experience dealing with a similar bureaucracy in Guomingdang Taiwan paid off, and he got the seal of approval.

In the end, Dongsen rented two SNG vans and sixteen technicians from a Fujian bureau that was a branch of the same military establishment that was also on alert for war with Taiwan. This was the first time the bureau had engaged in a direct commercial transaction with an overseas media company, and its administrators were very pleased with the income it generated. Much like the Zhenlan Temple forging a ritual community across the Strait, this transaction brought together the media of two politically sealed-off entities and was a step toward the reconfiguration of Taiwanese and Mainland media spaces.

Back in Taipei, I asked Wu Enwen, manager of Dongsen TV News, whether his company, like Zhenlan Temple, supported the "three direct links" with Mainland China. "That is correct," he said. "The Mainland is where our future market is, and all TV stations in Taiwan who wish to grow must do this." Dongsen broadcasted via satellite to Southeast Asia, but merely as a nonprofit service for overseas Chinese; it received subscriber fees, but no advertising revenue, since overseas Chinese there are too dispersed to attract advertisers (the main source of profits for broadcasters). "Since our product is in the Chinese language, we have no hope of exporting it to the U.S., like other Taiwan products. So our biggest market is China, but there are all these political obstacles."[6] Thus, in the television media community in Taiwan and on the Mainland, there was a growing desire to overcome political isolationist borders and achieve direct communication links. In 2000, Dongsen already had two reporters stationed in Beijing and two in Shanghai, who were rotated once a month due to Chinese visa restrictions. They were also developing a working relationship with Phoenix TV, the only foreign-owned Chinese-language television channel operating in China, to help them access the Mainland media space. Here we see an odd partnership between two transnational forces: popular religion carving out its own ritual space, and media capitalism expanding its market share—both operating against the grain of state territoriality. To understand the significance of this parallel movement across the Strait, we need to examine the historical vicissitudes of these two forces.

NATION, MEDIA, AND RELIGION IN TAIWAN AND CHINA

From the 1950s to 1980s, despite their ideological differences, the two media systems of China and Taiwan resembled each other in their state ownership and control; their centralized, homogeneous, and monolingual media culture; and the exclusion of religious, ethnic, or political opposition in favor of secular nationalism. The Guomindang media in Taiwan deployed a state Confucian discourse of family, hierarchy, and education to promote developmentalist state goals (Chun 1994; Chin 1997). The Minnan dialect spoken by the Taiwanese majority was barred from all broadcast media and public schools in favor of Mandarin, called the "national language" (*guoyu*). The Communist media celebrated the revolutionary spirit of peasants, workers, women, and the Party, all in Mandarin, or the "universal language" (*putonghua*), while suppressing commercial entertainment and eradicating religion, both on and off the media. The Enlightenment legacy of the May Fourth Movement in China, and its modernist attacks on "tradition" in the name of national strengthening, meant that, unlike the televised religious nationalism of India (Mankekar 1999), religious discourse was virtually absent from television in China and Taiwan.

Within China, capitalist forces have gradually transformed the media since the 1980s, so that television stations in 2000 were funded more through advertising than by government allocations, and propaganda value had been replaced by the entertainment value of consumer culture. The predictable government news coverage of solemn Party meetings and production outputs of the early 1980s had largely given way to gripping historical costume dramas, emotional soap operas, racy popular-music stage performances, stock market analyses, tourist travelogues, and socially conscious documentaries (M. Yang 1997). Although government censorship remained in place, the introduction of satellite and cable linkages had also started to reconfigure the Chinese mediascape. Upstart provincial satellite stations,, such as Hunan TV and the transnational, Hong Kong–based Phoenix Station, had broken free of state administrative boundaries and were challenging the monopoly of Beijing's Central Chinese Television (CCTV) for the national audience (J. Chan 2003). Yet despite the growing cosmopolitanism and diversity of Mainland television, the forces of popular religion had not gained entry, except as exotic objects representing the past for a touristic gaze. Certainly there was no religious organization strong enough in China to overcome the state prohibitions and financial hurdles to purchasing its own time on television or paying television news crews to report on its activities. Since the Chinese domestic television market is so vast, we have yet to see signs of television movement out from China, toward transnational broadcasting (except for CCTV-4, the voice of the central government).

The lifting of martial law in Taiwan in 1987 reduced state media censorship, and the passing of the Cable Television Law of 1993 legalized vast underground networks (both literally and figuratively) of cable television, producing far-reaching changes. Since then, Taiwan's commercial television market has become the most intense in Asia, and its news stations have become ever more sensationalist to compete with one another for the small audience of 22 million viewers. The exuberant growth of cable and satellite stations in the mid-1990s made Taiwan the biggest cable television center in Asia (C. Lee 1999; S. Chin 1997; Chen B. 1999). In 2000, there were more than 90 cable stations, and 77 percent of households subscribed to cable television (Ruo 2000:6). The increasing popularity of cable threatened the viability of the three government broadcast stations. Taiwanese cable television was more cosmopolitan than American television because it received transnational satellite broadcast from multiple American, Japanese, Hong Kong, and even Mainland stations. Following the general flow of Taiwanese capital, technology, and professional talent toward Mainland China (Gao 2000), Taiwanese television was also trying to establish a presence in China. According to Xie Mingjin, a manager at Dongsen News Station in Taichung City, several Taiwanese television companies were already forming their own satellite stations for broadcast to Chinese-speaking viewers in China, Southeast Asia, and North America in the early 2000s. They were competing against Hong Kong's Star TV and the Chinese state-run CCTV-4—the two Chinese-language satellite services with the most powerful global reach.

Thus the commercialization of the media began to de-territorialize the state monopoly media space. Deploying new satellite technology, Taiwanese media capitalism reached far beyond the stratosphere, to 22,000 miles above the territoriality of the nation-state. Satellites in geostationary orbit came to be owned jointly by several states, or by states and transnational capital. Through satellite transmission, the familiar boundaries between national cultures, between media ownership and content, and between state and capital began to be reconfigured. The terrestrial Chinese states on both sides of the Strait also embarked on programs to recapture and recode these flows.

In the martial law era before 1987, news in Taiwan was understood as the transmission of information about the government, economic production, foreign relations, local officials, and the like. According to Katie Fang of the nonprofit Broadcast Development Fund, television in the days of the three government stations was directed toward a middle-class audience and largely ignored the rural and working classes. After the lifting of martial law, many cable news stations found that these people were an important audience and market, and that reporting popular religious events as news boosted ratings. Thus popular religion rooted in the rural and working classes—deity cults, Daoist temples, city and earth gods, and spirit mediums—gained increasing exposure on TV news and on special programs marking local religious festivals.

After the 1990s, a cultural trend known as "indigenization" (本土化, *bentuhua*) swept the island. It was a movement to unlink national identity from the identity created by the Guomindang Party, which stressed continuity with a great Chinese Mainland civilization (*dazhonghua*). Indigenization sought to carve out a new Taiwanese identity by sifting through traditional Taiwanese rural cultures and religions, and the history of the early Minnan and Hakka settlers in the sixteenth to nineteenth centuries. The recent growth of the cult of Mazu (who is thought to have protected the early settlers who crossed the seas to Taiwan) is part of this nativization process. With the election of Chen Shuibian in 2000, indigenization increasingly became part of the construction of a new Taiwan national identity. At this historic moment, when Taiwan was caught between two national identities, we can see that the Mazu cult was not fully compatible with either national project, both because of its genealogy in a pre-nationalist past and because of the post-nationalist tendencies incident to its transnational organization (Appadurai 1996).

ONE GODDESS, MULTIPLE TEMPLES AND DESCENDANTS

Like all Chinese deities, the goddess Mazu was originally a human, born in 960 C.E. in the Northern Song dynasty in Xianlianggang, a fishing town in Putian County, Fujian Province. She led an exemplary life helping drowning sailors, died unmarried in 987, and ascended to Heaven on Meizhou Island. In the following centuries, as her reputation grew, several imperial courts bestowed official titles on the goddess, expanded her temple, and built other official Mazu temples. Mazu started as a minor local deity worshipped by poor fisherman, yet was transformed into one of the two most important female deities in the imperial religious pantheon overseen by the Board of Rites of the imperial state. Thousands of Mazu temples were built along the coast of China, from Manchuria in the north down to Guangdong Province, and waves of emigration brought Mazu to Taiwan, Southeast Asia, and Japan.[7] For the common people, Mazu stood for safety for seafarers, female fertility, and divine intervention in personal and familial adversity, while her cult was also standardized and appropriated by the imperial state as a symbol of a civilizing force and of the coastal state pacification of pirates, smugglers, and rebels (Watson 1985).

In Taiwan, Mazu worship was partially suppressed, first by the colonial government of Japan (1895–1947), which wanted to displace Taiwanese popular religion with State Shinto, and then by the incoming Guomindang government, whose modernizing elite viewed popular religion as a sign of the ignorance of the uneducated masses and also as a potential threat of ethnic nativism against the nationalism they themselves planned to impose. The resurgence of Mazu worship and other popular religion in the 1980s benefited from both the declining influence of the Guomingdang in Taiwan and the growing economic prosperity of the island (Weller 2000; Rubenstein 2001).

In China, the Mazu cult fell victim to the state eradication of religion until the 1980s, when the state changed its policies from prohibition to strict regulation of religious practice. Sadly, the centuries-old Meizhou temple complex in Fujian did not survive the destructive Cultural Revolution; in 1968, the local Revolutionary Committee tore down the

Figure 12.2. The Meizhou Mazu goddess hosting her Taiwan Mazu guests in her temple courtyard, Meizhou Island, Fujian Province, July 2000. Photo by Mayfair Yang.

entire hillside complex. It was in 1979 that a Taiwanese fisherman first snuck onto the island and started to worship at a small Mazu shrine the locals had secretly erected. The fishermen returned, bringing with them a metal incense burner, candleholders, and other ritual paraphernalia with which to pay homage to Mazu. Although the first two Meizhou temple halls were built in the 1980s with local donations, more recent structures were built with money provided by Mazu temples in Taiwan. Today the new ancestral temple has a website that welcomes tourists to the area and records the major donations of buildings and monuments from Taiwan temples. Countless official delegations from Beijing have visited the site and left their calligraphies promoting tourism and Taiwan's return to the Mainland. In a new movement of state appropriation, in Mainland state discourse Mazu now stands for reunification across the sea of Taiwan with China.

Many Taiwan Mazu temples sponsor annual festivals to celebrate the goddess's birthday on the twenty-sixth day of the third lunar month, and make pilgrimages to whichever senior Mazu temple they derive from. The most prominent Mazu temples compete for fame, political influence, worshippers, and lucrative donations, combing the historical archives to claim their close historical links with the ancestral temple in Meizhou. Many temples made pilgrimages across the dangerous Strait to the Meizhou temple before Japanese colonization ended such travel in 1895. This loss of ties with the Meizhou temple continued under the Guomindang government, which took over from the Japanese in 1947 and transformed the Strait into a tense militarized border. Nevertheless, Taiwan Mazu temples maintained a sense of their ancestral connections across the Strait. For example, in the visitors' hall of the Tianhou Temple in the coastal town of Lugang, there is a photograph of the rare "ritual across a long distance" (*yaoji*) conducted in 1984. Daoist priests presided over the ceremony, in which a three-hundred-year-old, incense-darkened statue of Mazu from Tianhou Temple was carried on a palanquin back and forth along the shore, so as to beckon to her Meizhou "mother" across the sea.

According to temple records, Zhenlan Temple in Taiwan was founded in 1730, when a native of Meizhou Island crossed the Strait bearing a statue of the Mazu goddess and started a temple in the Dajia area near Taizhong City. Since the 1970s, the temple has transformed itself from a rural and local territorial cult into an islandwide national religious force. Taiwan anthropologist Zhang Xun (2003) has carefully traced how Taiwan's new transportation networks, urbanization, population mobility, and media have helped Zhenlangong evolve from a small local temple to an influential, nationally recognized temple. I would emphasize that priority must be given to Zhenlangong's skillful harnessing of the Taiwan media, at a time when media forces were gaining increasing autonomy from the state.

In the 1980s, Zhenlangong managers figured out how to capture the national media's attention. Before each annual pilgrimage, the temple would buy television commercial time to announce the event. It purchased

Figure 12.3.   Zhenlan Temple chairman Yan Qingbao (center) and Zhenlan Temple pilgrims bearing the Taiwan Mazu goddess's palanquin in the Meizhou Mazu Temple courtyard, July 2000. Photo by Mayfair Yang.

expensive television time-slots to show off the temple's power to mobilize a hundred thousand pilgrims for the eight-day walk to Chaotian Temple in Beigang (北港朝天宮). "Zhenlangong knows how to accommodate the media," said Wu Enwen, mangager of Dongseng Television News. "For example, they know that weekends are the best times for the media to broadcast any news about them, since government offices are closed and our reporters are at a loss for news. So when they '*buabui*' [cast wooden divination crescents] to consult the deity for the best date for events, they only give Mazu two options to choose from: a Saturday or Sunday." A Taiwanese pilgrim woman I met in Meizhou said that television coverage helps to expand pilgrimage participation each year: "Before, many families did not want their elderly folk to go on pilgrimage, for fear they might collapse on the arduous journey, but after seeing other old people going on television, they start to feel it's OK." One resident of Dajia told me, "Before the media, our little town was only known for the straw hats and bed mats which are our native product, but now we are known for Zhenlan Temple."

    An important historical turn for Zhenlan Temple occurred in 1987. Increasingly dissatisfied with its lower ritual status implied by its annual pilgrimage to Chaotiangong, the Zhenlangong board hit upon the ingenious idea of a new pilgrimage straight to Mazu's ancestral temple on Meizhou Island in Fujian to celebrate the millennial anniversary of Mazu's ascension to Heaven.[8] At the time, this was a risky undertaking because of the Taiwan government ban on travel to China. Nevertheless, seventeen board members undertook the exciting historic airplane journey via Japan, taking with them one of the temple's statues of Mazu. There they were greeted warmly by local Mainland officials and the Meizhou temple committee. The sacred objects they brought back—a Meizhou Mazu statue, a carved stone seal and an embroidered altar skirt, an incense burner and incense ashes from the Meizhou temple (Guo J. 1993:95)—established Zhenlangong's new status as a temple that now had a clear and direct relationship of descent from the ancestor temple. The pilgrims' triumphant return to Taiwan created a media sensation, and worshippers from around Taiwan converged to see the Meizhou Mazu. This daring pilgrimage emboldened Zhenlangong to declare in 1988 that, since it was not an offshoot temple of Chaotian Temple, henceforth it would no longer direct its annual pilgrimage there but change its destination to Fengtiangong Temple in Xingang.

By the 1999 presidential election campaigns, Zhenlangong had already become a staple topic for the Taiwan media. Its large constituency of voting worshippers throughout the island made it an important stop on the campaign trail, and all three major presidential candidates, Chen Shuibian of the DPP Party, Lian Zhan of the Guomindang, and Song Chuyu of the Qingmindang, went to Zhenlangong to burn incense to Mazu and cultivate an image of dedication to the goddess. These visits, and temple Chairman of the Board Yan Qingbiao's public endorsement of Song Chuyu for president, were given extensive media coverage by all television news stations. However, this intense media exposure and involvement in national politics also had its drawbacks for the temple. The temple's challenging of the Chen Shuibian government over the direct sealink was not forgotten by the new administration, which also disapproved of the temple's close ties with Mainland authorities. There was much public speculation that mafia elements, attracted by the lucrative temple finances, had penetrated Zhenlan Temple's management, and this presented a perfect opportunity for the government to simultaneously uphold the law and deter a political adversary. Yan Qingbiao was arrested by the Chen government in 2001 and accused of connections to the mafia, resulting in a loss of donations to the temple. However, the government was unable to convict Yan, and he was even elected to serve as a local representative while in prison. In this struggle between the government and the Zhenlan Temple leadership we can see broader tensions between nation-state territoriality and identity on the one hand, and the transnational ritual spatiality of Chinese popular religion on the other.

Thus, what Derrida (1998) called the "return of the religious" is not in Taiwan a simple return. Religion has now harnessed the media—an indubitable sign that popular religion is engaged with modernity, albeit as a dissonant cultural voice against the secular professional elite. This means that popular religion can no longer be regarded as merely traditional folk culture that disappears with modernization. Rather, it is an expression of the rural, working, and lower middle classes, who voted for the progressive policies of a DPP that supported labor, feminism, social welfare, and multiethnic representation but demurred when it came to the DPP's secular nationalism and pro-independence state territoriality. Given the increasing interactions across the Taiwan Strait, this "return" *qua* new departure suggests that popular religion may also eventually come to harness the media on Mainland China.

RITUAL TRANSNATION AND THE FLUID LINES
OF MATRIFOCAL KINSHIP SPACE

Over the centuries, the Mazu ancestral temple on Meizhou spawned thousands of offspring temples along the China coast and Taiwan. In the ritual process of establishing descendant temples, called "dividing spirit" (分靈, *fenling*) or "dividing incense" (分香, *fenxiang*), ashes from incense in the mother temple are put into an incense urn and taken to a newly established temple (Schipper 1990; ter Haar 1990; Sangren 1993). This process of division is understood through an idiom of kinship. As Mazu scholar Zhou Jintan of Putian said to me, "Relations between Mazu temples are like kin relations between human beings," in which kinship distance and generational ranking are taken into account. He further described pilgrimages from offspring temples, such as those from temples in Taiwan back to the ancestral temple in Fujian, as a process of "coming back to recognize kin" (*huilai renqin*).

Given the Chinese patrilineal kinship system, the gender of the goddess and the kinship language employed about her temples are of tremendous significance. The journey of five Zhenlan Temple Mazu statues from Taiwan to the Meizhou ancestral temple in 2000 was described as the goddess "returning to her mother's home" (回娘家, *hui niangjia*). In a patrilineal culture with patrilocal marriage residence for women, this phrase adopts the subjectivity of women and evokes the warmth and security of a married woman going back to her familiar natal family for a visit with her mother. Due to the extended period when ties with the ancestor temple in Meizhou were broken off, a separate system of pilgrimage circuits developed in Taiwan, centering on the major Taiwan Mazu temples and their offspring temples. These pilgrimages were also described as "returning to mother's home," and temples descended from the same "mother" thought of themselves as "sister temples" (姊妹廟, *jiemei miao*).

In an important article on Chinese female deities, Steven Sangren asserts that the Mazu cult's system of branch temples emphasizes affinal over agnatic kinship (1983:9). As an expression of female affinal linkages, Mazu occupies the position of Chinese wives, who mobilize horizontal, affinal kinship connections across vertically constructed, self-contained patrilineal communities. With her temple divisions and pilgrimages, the goddess Mazu, like Chinese women in patrilineal kinship, is a figure of movement that contrasts with the rootedness and localization of male lineages and territorial cults whose icons, deities, and ancestors are usually male gods, their authority parallel to that of bureaucrats administering a region (Wolf 1974; Sangren 1983).

I would submit that, besides affinal kinship, what this female-centered language also suggests is a suppressed logic of matrilineal descent by which successive generations of Mazu temples trace their lineage to the ancestral mother temple. Mazu literally means "mother ancestor" or "mother's ancestor." The term *niang* (mother) in "returning to mother's home" (*hui niangjia*) has two meanings here. On the one hand, it refers to the patriline to which the mother belongs, with the implication that a woman's role is to promote affinal connections between two patrilines. On the other hand, when a wife returns to her natal home, the most important person she is going to see is her mother, so the mother-daughter relationship is what is foregrounded. Thus *niang* suggests something independent of the patriline: an ancestress whose descendants return to seek renewal through her. However, as the staff at Lugang's Tianhou Temple told me, despite the "matrilineal society" (母系社會, *muxi shehui*) features and potentials of temple relations, many Taiwanese temples refuse to recognize their line of descent past the third generation, especially as they get bigger, wealthier, and more influential. Sometimes they deny or alter their genealogy in order to claim direct descent from Meizhou in China. Lugang's Tianhou Temple claims to have been so bypassed by Beigang's Chaotian Temple, and Chaotian Temple has made similar complaints about Zhenlan Temple's switching its age-old pilgrimage to Fengtian Temple. These intertemple squabbles reflect the dominance of the patrilineal principle in Chinese kinship culture more generally. That is, matrilineal potentials tend to be culturally suppressed down to merely two or three generations, unlike patrilineal descent, which can be traced through thirty or more generations.

The gender- and kinship-inflected spatiality of relations among Mazu temples underscores the fact that Chinese rituals of territorial deities had evolved their own spatial logic long before the rigid lines of modern nation-state territoriality. Scholars of Chinese popular religion have recognized how popular ritual inscribes territory and geographical space, and have examined the substantive role of this ritual spatiality in constructions of collective identities. Many Chinese gods are local, presiding like local officials with jurisdiction over local areas and protecting the local community. Lin Meirong's classic distinction between "ritual circles" (*jisiquan*, the bounded space of a localized community's ritual activities) and "belief circles" (*xinyangquan*, the larger regional territory of cults devoted to a single deity) shows how places are ritually marked and how collective ritual produces both the community and its self-identity. Fiorella Allio (2003) discovered a ritual processional system in the Tainan area where villages come together in a ritual procession demarcating a higher-level ritual space. A similar ritual spatial system called "the seven territories" (*qijing*) in rural Fujian has been unearthed by Ken Dean (2000) and Zheng Zhenman (1995). Villages take their main gods on a ritual procession around the borders of its territory, and then several villages embark on a joint procession around the boundaries of their collective area—all blessed by a day-long Daoist *jiao* ritual. These studies show the importance of the spatial dimension of Chinese ritual life, and suggest that space is not a simple geographic or administrative given, but is invested with meaning and power through ritual demarcation and socially inscribed through collective footsteps. As Henri Lefebvre has noted, the archaic "absolute space" of the sacred is marked and produced by the body, whereas in modern planned "abstract space," the body has increasingly lost this ability (1991:174). While local ritual processions carve out the space of local communities, long-distance pilgrimages ritually draw the contours of a larger space of collective identity across a region, or (in modern contexts) national borders.

It has often been observed that Chinese popular religion replicates the imperial bureaucratic structure of officialdom (Wolf 1974; Feuchtwang 2001), so that the popular Chinese pantheon of territorial gods with their local ritual jurisdictions has been called a "celestial bureaucracy" or an "imperial metaphor." It must also be noted that the actual contours of local ritual territories presided over by the gods often did not coincide with imperial state administrative territories (Sangren 1987).[9] Thus we must pay attention to how ritual territorialities have their own internal mechanisms and their own definitions of boundaries and movements through space, which are not reducible to the political orders outside the ritual polity. Even after state overcoding, ritual space may still reclaim state space. Chinese anthropologist Wang Mingming shows this in his excellent study of the popular appropriation and subversion of Ming-dynasty urban administrative units in the city of Quanzhou (M. Wang 1995). The local residents of Quanzhou transformed spatial units designed by the state for control and surveillance into a system of territorial festivals and ritualized community-building. Thus we cannot assume an isomorphism between socio-political formations and the ritual order, for the latter creatively reworks the existing administrative and spatial structures of social life. This autonomy of ritual space can be identified in late imperial China and also across contemporary nation-state boundaries.

Besides patrilineal corporate groups, the female-centered kinship and ritual space of Mazu temple and deity relations engenders a difference from another sort of male community, that of the modern nation-state. The English translation "Motherland" for 祖國 (*zuguo*, literally, "ancestral country") is most inappropriate: from ancient times, the Chinese have privileged patrilineal ancestors, so the term *zuguo* should properly be translated as "Fatherland." Mazu's female kinship contrasts with the patriarchal nationalist discourses on both sides of the Strait: in China, Mao was referred to as a "father" and "savior star" of the Revolution (M. Yang 1994b:258), and in Guomindang Taiwan, Sun Yat-sen was called "father of the nation" (*guofu*). With the beginning of a new and enlarged pilgrimage circuit from Taiwan to Fujian in the late twentieth century, Mazu's female iconicity assumes new significance as a mediator and boundary crosser between two male-defined modern "political entities." In cross-Strait travel, the Mazu cult reworks the ritual relations and spatial boundaries of communities long separated from one another, delineating the contours of a new matrifocal, transnational ritual community.

RITUAL CYBERSPACE AND THE COEVALITY OF
A TRANSNATIONAL RITUAL TEMPORALITY

Margaret Morse (1998) has pointed out that television represents an intermediate phase between film and new information technologies that create more immersive and interactive virtual environments. Print and film constructed "fictions of *representation*" in which the temporalities of production, transmission, narrative content, and reception were distinct and separate, and the detached readers/audience *viewed* rather than *interacted* with the subjects represented. Television—with its direct address to the audience by reporters and anchor hosts (the use of "we" and "you" pronouns), exhortations to dial a phone number or log on to an internet address, and frequent deployment of the third dimension "z" axis where objects seemingly move out from the TV screen and into the space of viewers—produces "fictions of *presence*" (Morse 1998:14–21). This ability of television to tie together the world on television and the lived world of the viewer through simultaneous transmission and reception makes it a suitable medium for transmitting the power of religious and magical forces, especially in ritual performances. The "liveness" (現場直播, *xianchang zhibo*) of the simultaneous transmission and reception of the grand sacrifice ritual in Meizhou can be seen as a rare media-event in which ritual moments of sacred and divine presence were transmitted to viewers across vast geographical and political distances. However, this mediated coevality of religious imaginaries across the Strait involved a continuous struggle between popular religion and the state, and between religious and market forces.

For instance, Zhenlan Temple managers fought with the Meizhou temple planners over the liveness of the voice of the master of ceremonies. The Meizhou officials wanted a prerecorded voice played out over the loudspeaker, to insure against politically incorrect remarks. On Chinese state television, except for occasional sports broadcasts, there was always a five-second delay to catch any "errors." But for Zhenlan Temple, it was essential that the master of ceremony's voice be part of the action of the ritual: her voice must not only be in synchrony with the ongoing ritual, but also set its pace. The ritual had to have its own temporal integrity and cohesion; its parts had to share a common presence, unfragmented into different temporalities. In the end, a compromise was reached in which Zhenlan Temple submitted a prewritten script that was reviewed for problems the day before the ritual. A local Fujian woman was selected to read the prepared script live, but not spontaneously. In this struggle, Zhenlan Temple tried to preserve the integrity of ritual temporality from state attempts to fragment it. Ironically, this integrity had already been compromised by the market forces of the Taiwanese media, whose "live" broadcast of the ritual was punctuated by frequent TV commercials and cut-aways to other news items.

I was struck by the contrast between the Taiwanese media sending so many people for six days of nonstop coverage and the relative lack of interest shown by the Mainland media. Local Mainland television news stations, such as Fuzhou TV, Dongnan TV in Xiamen, and Putian TV, gave the event some coverage, but they focused on the political implications of the Strait crossing and ignored the religious dimension. There was no national coverage on the evening news of China Central TV in Beijing. It was only one month later that a 15-minute special on the pilgrimage was broadcast on CCTV-4, which is aimed at overseas Chinese. When asked why the Mainland media hardly broadcast this event, Fujian locals generally gave two explanations. The most common answer was that this was only an "event of the people" (*minjian huodong*), not a government activity, and therefore unimportant. In Mainland thinking, the job of the media is to publicize the activities of the government, since the state is seen to propel society—not the other way around. Media editors and programmers did not seem curious about the various social forces that provide new impetus for social change. The other answer given to me was that this was a "religious event" (*zongjiao huodong*), and would therefore not be reported in the Party media, since Party principles do not condone religion. The arrival of an army of Taiwanese reporters and cameramen to cover what many still regarded as "superstition" generated great curiosity among Mainland reporters. Members of the Taiwanese press were repeatedly asked why they had come. The fact that the high-tech, secular Taiwanese media saw no contradictions in covering a religious, "backward" practice was puzzling to them.

The satellite broadcast of this pilgrimage was a small but important step toward dislodging satellite technology from the Chinese military and expanding not only commercial but religious uses of satellite. Although the satellite transmission was primarily a media-event for Taiwan viewers back home, there was nevertheless some leakage into the Mainland audience. Despite the ban on satellite receiving dishes for ordinary Mainland citizens, many homes in urban and coastal areas have clandestine dishes that are produced in rural factories (Lynch 1999). In addition, any apartment or work-unit (*danwei*) connected to a legal satellite dish can receive Taiwan television. Coverage of popular religion on Mainland TV may take a long time to develop, but the budding cable television industry in China may exert pressures for more diversified and cosmopolitan programming, as it did in Taiwan in the 1980s. The initiation of live broadcasting across the Strait harbors the potential that viewing communities in China and Taiwan will one day come to share the same temporality in mediated ritual events.

CONCLUSION

Historically flowing out from Fujian to Taiwan and now moving back from Taiwan to Fujian, the Mazu goddess cult's genealogy predates both modern nationalism and global capitalism. Now intertwined with the movement of globalizing media across political borders, this renewed religious force is a ritual re-territorialization of the state. Although it may seem to conform to the Mainland's expansionist desire to reincorporate Taiwan, Mazu worship is a polytheistic regional cult that counters the Mainland's monological, secular, and centralized national imaginary. Its kinship-based logic of transnational connectedness between ritual communities contrasts with what Deleuze and Guattari (1987) have called the "rigid state segmentarity" and homogeneous identity-formation of nationalism. Its female iconicity and matrifocal logic diminish nation-state masculinity. In her female affinal role, Mazu bridges and transcends two masculine spaces, ritually constructing local spaces of identity around village or town temples and a transnational space of identity across coastal China, Taiwan, and Southeast Asia. Her cult creates alternative ritual centers (Meizhou, Dajia, Beigang) to national capitals, shrines to national heroes, and commercial hubs. At the same time, transnational media also de-territorialize the nation-state with the swath of space lying within a satellite footprint. In this process, the liveness of satellite television and the matrilineal logic of the goddess can elevate a shared ritual temporality and sacred geography over the secular national History and territory promoted by the governments on both sides of the Strait, which always threaten to erupt into masculine warfare. Composed of rural, working-class, and lower-middle-class worshippers, the Mazu cult strikes a dissonant chord against the dominant professional and elite classes, who have had a history of embracing secular nationalism.

In this religious pilgrimage transmitted via satellite television, we see a strange convergence between the ritual territoriality of Mazu pilgrimage and the transnational expansion of media space. Both are propelled by an inner compulsion to cross existing political boundaries. The Mazu cult seeks to transcend localities and integrate ever larger communities of worshippers, to renew kinship ties with sites of ancestral origin, and to cultivate matrilineal and sisterly relations with temples in far-off lands. For satellite television, there is both an economic and technological compulsion to traverse the Strait, despite the Taiwan government's efforts to restrain capital flow to China. Capital's profit motive in the television industry takes the form of an endless quest for new audiences, markets, and advertisers; in the saturated Taiwan television market, the only way out is to expand abroad. Furthermore, the tremendous costs of constructing and launching satellites and renting satellite transponders often require a large audience base to attract advertisers. However, satellite footprints do not conform to the boundaries of nation-states. If a nation-state like China, with its huge population lying under a footprint, does not allow its people to set up receiving dishes, there is a great loss of revenue for the satellite launchers and transponder users. Satellite technology works best with large transnational audiences to sustain the system, and this goes against the grain of the current system of nationally protected media spaces. Thus there will be continuous efforts by capitalist media to overcome nation-state territoriality, even as states actively ward off these challenges (Price 1994, 1999, 2002; J. Chan 1997).[10]

Popular religion hitches a ride on the capitalist media's "desiring-machine," which decodes the flows of desire toward the "despotic state" (Deleuze & Guattari 1983:224). As popular cults make more use of media, they must also contend with a commercialization of religion that threatens to submerge their spiritual core. The Mazu cult has found an ally in the capitalist media, which are more than willing to help it carry its messages to both sides of the Strait and which also seek to overcome the boundaries of the nation-state for their own reasons. However, with time, what may come to the fore are the contradictions between the profit motive of media capitalism and Mazu's example of simplicity, generosity, and sacrifice, and between the logic of capital accumulation and that of ritual expenditure and generosity as well (M. Yang 2000).

Notes

1. I wish to thank Prasenjit Duara, David Palmer, Peter van der Veer, and an anonymous reader for valuable comments on this Introduction.

2. The May Fourth Movement was triggered in 1919, when Chinese intellectuals, students, workers, and merchants protested the Versailles Treaty after World War I, which handed Shandong Province over to the Japanese. Throughout the 1920s and 1930s, in public demonstrations and boycotts of Japanese goods, and in journals, novels, plays, and newspapers, these groups raised their voices against traditional Chinese culture and values, especially Confucian culture and popular religions, for their "backwardness" and irrelevance to modernity.

3. There have been many proposals to modify and salvage the secularization thesis, such as arguments that religiosity becomes deinstitutionalized in modernity, or retreats from the public sphere. See Ji Zhe's chapter in this volume.

4. There have also been critiques of *secularism*, or the moral-political doctrine that secularization is socially necessary and politically desirable for modernization, such as William Connolly's argument that a secular and rational public sphere lacks the compelling "visceral register of inter-subjectivity in moral and political life" (Connolly 1999:27).

5. For example, Falungong's apocalyptic rhetoric describes the present era as the end of a *kalpa* (the Buddhist notion of an aeon), thus implying that post-Mao China does not represent progress, since the end of the world calls for the salvation of souls. Furthermore, Falungong members often staged mass public gatherings to protest criticisms of their claims by scientists and the media. The largest and most significant of these was in front of national Party headquarters at the Zhongnanhai in Beijing in April 1999 (David Palmer, personal communication, and 2007; N. Chen 2003a).

6. Anthony Yu shows that throughout much of imperial history, Buddhism

and Daoism flourished only with the consent and patronage of the imperial court, and, along with sectarian religious movements, periodically suffered severe state persecution (A. Yu 2005).

7. I thank Cathy Chiu, librarian of UCSB East Asian collections, for helping me in the digital search of the *Siku Quanshu* (*Complete Library in Four Branches of Literature*).

8. *Mi* was combined with other terms to make compound words such as *mihuo* (迷惑, "to be confused or deluded"), *mishi* (迷失, "to lose one's way"), and *miwang* (密惘, "to lose one's sanity").

9. See Hildred Geertz's review of Keith Thomas's book *Religion and the Decline of Magic,* which takes Thomas to task for implicitly seeing the decline of magic in Christianity not only as historical fact but as beneficial for religion in general (H. Geertz 1975).

10. It is significant that the first anti-superstition salvo, the edict of 1898, came from the highest level—the emperor himself—and from *within* the imperial state. Of course, the Empress Dowager Cixi and conservative court officials quickly blocked its implementation, and the edict was drafted by Kang Youwei, a prominent reformer (Spence 1990:224–230). Nevertheless, the fact remains that the earliest moves against religion in China were initiated first by the imperial state and then by the new nationalist state. The disastrous failure of the Boxer Rebellion of 1900 strengthened the anti-superstition sentiments of the elite and state campaigns against superstition.

11. Chen Duxiu used this doctrine of materialism, which privileges sensory perception, to disprove the existence of ghosts, spirits, and souls (Chen 1918a). Being a pragmatist, Hu Shi was less dogmatic and strident than Chen, and took a more constructive approach. In 1919, he published an article that sought to liberate the notion of "immortality" (*buxiu*) from its superstitious baggage of souls, spirits, and ghosts (Hu 1919). He proposed that the only true immortality was "social immortality," in which a society lives on due to the accumulated contributions and actions of each and every human member.

12. For a brief biography of Ernst Haeckel and his ideas, see the website of discussions of evolutionary theory, maintained by the Museum of Paleontology at the the University of California, Berkeley: http://www.ucmp.berkeley .edu/history/haeckel.html

13. Julian Steward (1955) proposed the notion of "multilinear evolution," giving due emphasis to the Boasian tradition of cultural relativism, diffusion, and historical particularism and contingency, and to the Darwinian notion of adaptation to the environment.

14. Beijing University anthropologist Wang Mingming remembers that as a college student studying anthropology at Xiamen University, he felt the suffocating weight of Morgan in all his coursework, and was quite surprised, when years later, he read the original in English and found many insights he had never seen before (Wang M. 2004).

15. The best monograph on the fate of religious life in the Maoist period is Holmes Welch's book *Buddhism under Mao* (1972). Its evenhanded and

detailed analysis of Chinese refugee witness accounts, foreign traveler reports, and Party documents and media offers an excellent account of the shifting state policies and their implementation in the People's Republic. There are two collections of official documents on state religious policies edited by Donald MacInnis, one on the Maoist period (MacInnis 1972), the other on the 1980s (MacInnis 1989). The volume *Religion in China Today* (2003) edited by Daniel Overmyer provides excellent overviews of various religious traditions from 1949 to the present.

16. Monographs on the post-Mao religious revival include: Adam Chau (2006) on deity temples and the role of local officials in rural Shaanxi; Richard Madsen (1998) and Eriberto Lozada (2001) on Catholicism; Jing Jun (1996) on lineage revival and collective memory in Gansu Province; Erik Mueggler (2001) on spirit possession and healing among the Lolo (Yi) minority of rural Yunnan; Wang Mingming (1997) on popular religion as local autonomy and social welfare in rural Fujian and Taiwan; Dru Gladney (1996) on the porous boundary between ethnic and religious identities for Chinese Muslims; and Ole Bruun (2003) on *fengshui* divination in rural Sichuan and Jiangsu. Excellent edited collections include: Daniel Overmyer (2003); Melvyn Goldstein and Matthew Kapstein's on Tibetan Buddhist revival (1998); and Guo Yuhua's (2000) collection on rituals and social change. Three historical treatments trace religious developments from the late imperial to the post-Mao period: Kenneth Dean (1993, 1998) on Daoist cults and rituals in rural Fujian Province, and Thomas DuBois (2005b) on popular religion and localism in north Chinese villages. See also Cao Nanlai (2007) on the spread of Christianity by Christian entrepreneurs from Wenzhou, a prosperous coastal area.

CHAPTER 1. RELIGION AND CITIZENSHIP

1. However, the interiorization of religion did not necessarily lead to a separation of church and state everywhere in Europe; this separation occurred more gradually.

2. According to Koselleck (1988), the French Revolution was an effort to reunite or find this moral authenticity—which ultimately led to terror.

3. The most comprehensive work to date is van der Veer and Lehmann (1999).

4. It is worth exploring to what extent the New Life Movement also represented an extension—or development—of the state cult. Between Yuan Shikai and the New Life there were various efforts to modernize the state cult by eliminating sacrifices to nature gods and memorializing semi-deified heroes (see C. Yang 1967:365). Certainly, the fact that the New Life was a statist top-down movement of mobilization caused it to resemble the state cult or the Shinto state rather more than a movement of interiorized moral reconstruction.

5. Denys Lombard and Claudine Salmon (1994) have shown that there was

historically a strong mixing of Chinese and local Muslim communities, both at the elite and popular levels, for hundreds of years. Although Dutch colonial policies segregating the communities tended to stabilize the creole culture discussed by Skinner, Lombard and Salmon detect a distinct movement toward integration with Indonesian culture, particularly in response to the *dakwah,* or Muslim proselytizing movements, right up to World War II.

6. Chang Tso Lin (Zhang Zuolin) was the warlord of Manchuria who was believed to have collaborated with the Japanese during the 1910s and 1920s.

CHAPTER 2. REDEPLOYING CONFUCIUS

1. Anderson's notion of "official nationalism" is especially pertinent in light of the recent focus on the Qing as a multiethnic empire. The early Qing state adopted a strategy of ruling the empire by compartmentalizing the realm into ethnically distinctive regions, and by presenting a multifaceted representation of its power and authority according to each region's particular political culture (Crossley 1999; Elliott 2001).

2. The word *li* can be translated in several ways. The etymology of the word suggests its original association with the vessels used in various sacrificial rites in ancient times. By the Eastern Zhou (770–221 B.C.E.), it had acquired a wide range of connotations, such as "rite," "etiquette," "decorum," and "propriety."

3. Another difference between ritual government and Geertz's theater state (1980) involves the moral significance and power that the former assigns to ritual.

4. The state cult was indeed a Confucian institution, in the sense that it depended on the expertise of the classicists and classical precedent for the design of rituals (see Zito 1997; Wilson 2002b). However, the system amalgamated many local and regional cults whose origins were by no means Confucian (see Taylor 1990). Barend ter Haar also warned against reading the state cult as a straight expression of Confucian values. According to him, the notion of the Mandate of Heaven, which justified the conduct of the state cult, informed the same paradigm of power invocation that the messianic traditions of folk Daoism drew on (ter Haar 1998:306–24).

5. For example, when the late Ming and early Qing literati staged ritualized public protests against government mistreatment by wailing and burning their Confucian attire, the choice of venue was often the Confucius temple (Chen 1992).

6. The earliest record of a private cult of Confucius is found in the *Shiji,* in which Sima Qian (ca. 145–86 B.C.E.) claims to have witnessed the rite at a Zhongni temple (*Zhongnimiao;* Wilson 2002a:73).

7. The equation between *guomin* and the Western notion of citizenship is far from exact. The late Qing reformers did not view *guomin* as individuals vested with a well-defined set of rights. Instead, they used *guomin* to suggest a social-political boundary between those who shared the "Chinese" cultural

values (defined by the Qing state) and those who did not. Although the term did imply legitimate membership in the Chinese political community (defined in cultural terms), it suggested only a minimal individual empowerment. The meaning of the term thus lay somewhere between full-fledged citizenship and "national subject." I thank an anonymous reviewer for raising this point.

8. *Ding* is the fourth stem day on the stem-branch system of counting. This system combines the sequences of ten stems and twelve branches into a cycle of sixty. It was the most common way of reckoning days and years in China before the twentieth century.

9. The secularization of ritual no doubt expressed a political secularism, which, as Rebecca Nedostup highlights in her chapter in this volume, is integral to the epistemology of modern nationalism. However, as an epistemological construct, secularism does not halt the operational traffic between the religious and the secular addressed by Prasenjit Duara in Chapter One. Rather, exactly because of outward adherence to secularism, nationalism's appropriation of the religious into its ritual symbolism has to be clandestine, an act of smuggling achieved through ritual hybridization. The new scheme of Confucius worship instantiated such a hybridity. Thus although the rite was composed of imperial symbols and ritual movements whose religious connotations were abundant, these were grafted onto a nationalist, and presumably secular, semiotic order.

10. Traditionally, the worship of Confucius on nonimperial occasions followed a more inclusive ritual protocol. At both government and nongovernment schools, every student and teacher was usually included. Students would often form the focal ritual body and perform the rites as a group. However, the rite would still require the designation of a primary worshipper, usually the head of the school, and thus was not a thoroughly collective and egalitarian event.

CHAPTER 3. RITUAL COMPETITION

1. Versions of this chapter have been presented at the Harvard-Yenching Institute and at the workshop "Affect, Emotion and Public Life in Modern East Asia" at the Fairbank Center and the Reischauer Institute, Harvard University, as well as at the workshop that led to this volume; my gratitude to the participants at all these events for their feedback, as well as to the students in the graduate colloquium "Nation, Religion and the Meaning of the Modern" at Boston College in spring 2006 and 2008, who helped me refine my ideas on several of the points discussed here. Special thanks to Mayfair Yang, Henrietta Harrison, and the reviewers of this volume for their detailed comments and to Ya-pei Kuo and Adam Yuet Chau for conversation around many key ideas.

2. Geertz writes, in "Centers, Kings, and Charisma: Reflections on the Symbolics of Power," that the resemblance of the "gravity of high politics" and "the solemnity of high worship" might be more obvious in monarchies

than in what he calls "political regimes," but "it is not any less true" (Geertz 1983:124).

3. It might be argued that in so doing the Republican regime did not escape associations of the old "reign name" (*nianhao*) system or the impression that this was merely a new dynasty. Yet regardless of the appearance to observers and users of the calendar, it is quite clear that the Nanjing-era Nationalists did not see it that way, claiming Sun's declaration of Year One of the Republic as an act of revolution and the decisive break from four thousand years of imperial rule, and thus effectively arguing for *Minguo* (Republican, connoting popular sovereignty) time not as the beginning of a new cycle but as the start of linear, progressive time (see Zhongguo Guomindang Zhongyang Xuanchuanbu 1930:6, 37).

4. For a detailed account of the debate over situating the capital in Nanjing, see Musgrove (2002, chap. 1). On early advocacy of the adoption of the Western calendar in *Shenbao*, by Liang Qichao, and elsewhere, see Lee (1999:44–46). In addition to the use of the old calendar that persisted even after the renewed bans of the Nanjing decade, enterprising scholars, merchants, and other officials and private citizens from around the country continued to submit their own plans for improved alternatives to the "national calendar." In 1931, for example, the General Branch of the Confucian Society (Kongdao Zonghui) advocated returning to the stem-and-branch system, on the principle that the seven-day week was a "Christian superstition" (Zhongguo Di'er Lishi Dang'an Guan Cang 1931; five other similar proposals dating between 1929 and 1933 are included in this file; see also Guo Shi Guan Cang 1928b).

5. Xue Dubi would repeat this language about "arousing the laughter of other countries" later that year with respect to superstition in general; see Guo Shi Guan Cang (1928a, reel 259, 1455–59).

6. For a succinct but evocative description of how "layered" calendars operated in the life of Shanxi gentry Liu Dapeng, see Harrison (2001:67–68).

7. *Lianhuanao* is probably a local rendering of *lianhualuo*, the type of narrative folksong often sung by beggars, or, in some locales, the subspecialty of blind beggars in particular. I owe this connection to the anonymous reviewer of this volume.

8. Susan Naquin (1992:333–77, 340, 343) describes the significant role played by tea at Miaofengshan near Beijing. Tea was not simply among the commodities on offer to pilgrims; the donation of tea was marked as a meritorious deed by local pious associations (*xianghui*).

9. *Shao bai xiang shao rou xiang* refers to two types of special offering during pilgrimage: (1) alternately walking and prostrating oneself (often with the aid of wooden pattens on the hands), and (2) hanging censers directly from the flesh. Thanks to the anonymous reviewer of this volume for sending me in the right direction here.

10. Liu Jiwen (1890–1957), who had once received special international training in urban administration at the behest of the Guangzhou GMD government, eagerly launched a variety of social reform campaigns in his

role of first Nationalist mayor of Nanjing, including but not limited to anti-superstition reforms (see Lipkin 2006:48–49, 257–58).

11. After the outbreak of war in 1937, Dai Jitao's ritual activity did become much more official: the Dharma assemblies grew considerably larger and more public, gaining openly acknowledged sponsorship from other Buddhists in politics, such as President Lin Sen (Tuttle 2005:215).

12. Most such ceremonies could only command a captive audience of government officials, military officers, and school representatives, usually numbering a few hundred in the capital.

13. Scholars are only just beginning to examine the broader cultural effects of the wars of the militarist and Nationalist eras. Lary (1985) was an early exception to this; McCord (2001) is a more recent example. Neither addresses religious or ritual aspects, however.

CHAPTER 4. LABELING HETERODOXY

1. My thanks to the *Antenne expérimentale franco-chinoise en sciences humaines et sociales*, the Sociology Department of the London School of Economics and Political Science, and the Institute of History and Philology of the Academia Sinica for financing trips to China and Taiwan during which some of the materials used for this paper were collected. I would also like to thank Mayfair Yang and an anonymous reviewer for their suggestions for improving an earlier draft of this chapter.

2. The latter is examined critically in Ownby (2008). For an example, see Chen & Dai, eds. (1999).

3. Zhang Guangbi (1889–1947) was known as Zhang Tianran by Yiguan-dao followers.

4. Picking up on this distinction, much of the historical scholarship has insisted on the difference between the "secular" nature of the former and the "religious" nature of the latter. For a refutation of this point of view, see Ownby (1995).

5. For detailed discussions of religion in the Mao-era historiography of peasant rebellions, see M. Leung (1989); J. Harrison (1970:140–89).

6. See, for example, the press releases posted on the website of the Chinese Embassy in France: http://web.amb-chine.fr/dossier/falungong/falungong0301 .htm; http://web.amb-chine.fr/dossier/falungong/falungong0220.htm; accessed October 5, 2005.

7. On scientism, see Kwok (1965); on the anti-superstition movement, see Nedostup (2001).

CHAPTER 5. FALUNGONG AND THE STATE

1. Some indication of the closeness of the *Epoch Times* and Falungong is indicated by the excerpt from an essay by Li Hongzhi placed prominently on the front page of their Chinese website (http://www.dajiyuan.com).

Many of their staff, including some who have been imprisoned in China, are listed as Falungong practitioners (see the stories linked from their page entitled "Epoch Times Reporters Jailed in China," http://english.epochtimes .com/211,102,,1.html) .

2. See http://declaration.epochtimes.com/9comment.htm for downloadable versions in many other languages, http://www.epochtimes.com/gb/4/12/13/ n746020.htm. At the time of writing, *Epoch Times* claimed that 19,393,515 people had so far left the CCP (http://www.epochtimes.com/). There is an unmistakable echo in the title "Nine Commentaries on the Communist Party" with the name given to nine articles criticizing the Soviet Party that appeared between September 1963 and July 1964 in the context of the Sino-Soviet split—the "Nine Commentaries on the Communist Party of the Soviet Union" (*Jiuping Sugong*). I thank Geremie Barmé for bringing this to my attention.

3. For details on the practice, see "The Essentials to Sending Forth Righteous Thoughts and the Schedule for Sending Forth Righteous Thoughts at Set Times Around the World (Update 2)," http://clearwisdom.net/emh/ articles/2005/3/12/58362.html.

4. See http://www.clearwisdom.net/emh/articles/2001/6/12/11429.html for pictures of Li Hongzhi demonstrating these gestures.

5. Scholarly works to date on Falungong have tended to interpret the movement in terms of sociology, politics, or law. My approach is, rather, historical and textual in nature—an approach that I hope takes seriously the beliefs and practices of adherents and attempts to place them in the context of Chinese religious history, particularly that of relations between the Chinese state and Chinese religious groups over time. This is not to say, of course, that I appeal to any transcendental, unchanging, essentialist model of either the state itself or of relations between the state and religion in China. When I refer to "models" of the state, I am referring to propositions made about what constitutes the state, and how it operates (or should operate) *vis-à-vis* particular audiences at particular times. However, it is part of my argument here that Li Hongzhi does implicitly refer to a particular view of the state and religion—and that at times he does appear to subscribe to an essentialist view of Chinese culture.

6. *Mencius* III B 9. Translated by D.C. Lau, whose "heresies" (*xieshuo*) I have changed to "heterodoxies." The same passage is cited in Liu Kwang-Ching (2004:478), where Liu prefers Legge's translation—he renders *xieshuo* as "perverse speakings."

7. On the White Lotus teachings in general and how various religious groups have been so labeled in China, see ter Haar (1999).

8. On the proscription of Manichaeism, see Seiwert (2003:189–90). By the Song, Manichaeists had been already present in China for hundreds of years; see Liu Ts'un-yan (1976) and Lieu (1992).

9. On the prohibition of the new Ming code, see ter Haar (1999:123–30).

10. Article 300, under "Crimes of Disturbing Public Order." The other two categories of behavior mentioned in Article 300 are organizing secret societies

(*huidaomen*) and taking advantage of superstitions (*mixin*). In the 1979 Criminal Code, the equivalent crime is categorized under "Counterrevolutionary Crimes" (Article 99) but only mentions *huidaomen* and feudal superstition (*fengjian mixin*)—the term *xiejiao* does not appear (Diwujie Quanguo Renmin Daibiao Dahui 1979).

11. See, "China Issued Anti-Cult Law (Nov. 2, 1999)," http://www.china embassycanada.org/eng/xw/xwgb/t38871.htm

12. On the *qigong* boom, see Palmer (2006), N. Chen (2003), Zhu & Penny 1994, and Barmé & Jaivin (1992:374–85).

13. See also subsequent discussions of Li Hongzhi's essay "No Politics" on Falungong websites, which have titles such as "Re-evaluating the meaning of "No Politics'" and "[hrs}'No Politics' and 'Nine Commentaries.'"

14. See Penny (2003:651).

15. Since there are many different editions of *Zhuan Falun* in circulation in print and on the web, and since these all have different pagination, references to *Zhuan Falun* are given in the form of "Li Hongzhi 1994:lecture:section." Thus "Li H. 1994:3.4" means section four of lecture three.

16. On this question, see Stein (1979) and Mollier (2006).

17. The Zhongnanhai demonstration was called in response to actions allegedly taken against Falungong practitioners protesting in Tianjin a few days before. The cause of the Tianjin demonstration was an article by the famous Chinese scientist He Zuoxiu that made such accusations against *qigong* in general but which named Falungong specifically. The protest was held outside the editorial office of the journal that published He's article. The most convenient way to consult He's article, entitled "I do not approve of teenagers practicing *qigong*," is the translation published in Xia & Hua (1999:95–98).

18. "Good is Rewarded, Evil Provokes Retribution," http://www.clear wisdom.net/emh/85/.

19. "If Humankind Ignores Wrong Doings, Heaven Will Intervene," http:// minghui.cc/mh/articles/2001/8/1/14128.html (Chinese), http://clearwisdom. net/emh/articles/2001/8/9/12803.html (English).

20. "Sand, Muddy Rain and Heavy Snow Are a Warning to the People of Shuangcheng Ciy [sic], Heilongjiang Province," http://minghui.ca/mh/ articles/2002/4/10/28216.html (Chinese), http://clearwisdom.net/emh/ articles/2002/4/18/21096.html (English).

21. "High Temperatures and Drought Over Prairies in Xilinguole, Inner Mongolia, Have Brought Forth a Plague of Locusts," http://minghui.cc/ mh/articles/2001/8/1/14099.html (Chinese), http://clearwisdom.net/emh/ articles/2001/8/7/12783p.html (English).

22. "Qinghai Province, China: The Viciousness of Qinghai Labor Camp Incurs Anger from Heaven—Severe Earthquake," http://www.minghui.ca/ mh/articles/2001/11/18/19857.html (Chinese), http://clearwisdom.net/emh/ articles/2001/11/19/15912.html (English).

23. "As the 'Human Rights Scoundrel' Persecutes Good People, Repeated Sandstorms Inundate Beijing," http://www.minghui.org/mh/articles/2002/

4/13/28403.html (Chinese), http://clearwisdom.net/emh/articles/2002/4/18/21092.html (English).

24. "More Storms in China," http://minghui.org/mh/articles/2002/4/19/28714.html (Chinese), http://clearwisdom.net/emh/articles/2002/5/5/21687.html (English).

25. "Six Provinces in China Hit by Severe Rainstorms and Flooding," http://www.minghui.org/mh/articles/2003/5/19/50688.html (Chinese), http://clearwisdom.net/emh/articles/2003/5/26/36182.html (English).

26. "When Kind and Innocent People are Persecuted, Natural and Man-Made Disasters Will Follow," http://minghui.ca/mh/articles/2001/11/2/18960.html (Chinese), http://clearwisdom.net/emh/articles/2001/11/13/15705p.html (English).

27. In this case, as with many Buddhist terms used by Li Hongzhi, the meaning ascribed to "karmic retribution" differs from the orthodox Buddhist position; see Penny (2005).

28. See "Human Rights Scoundrel," note 23 above.

29. See, for instance, Yan Zhitui (531–ca. 590) in the sixteenth chapter of his *Yanshi jiaxun*: "Good or evil acts bring disastrous or fortunate consequences. The Nine Schools and the Hundred Philosophers all agree upon this theory. Are the Buddhist scriptures alone to be held as untrue and unreliable?" (Teng 1968:145–46). For the original, see *Yanshi jiaxun*, Wang Liqi, ed. (Beijing: Zhonghua shuju, 1993), vol. 16, p. 385.

30. "Epoch Times Commentaries on the Communist Party—Part 4: On How the Communist Party Is an Anti-Universe Force," http://www.epochtimes.com/gb/4/11/25/n727814.htm (Chinese), http://english.epochtimes.com/news/4-12-14/24953.html (English). Intriguingly, in the first commentary, *The Nine Commentaries* also describes the nature of Chinese party government in terms that will be familiar from Falungong's ideas on possession, assayed earlier: "The Communist Party's organs themselves never participate in productive or creative activities. Once they grasp power, they attach themselves to the people, controlling and manipulating them. They extend their power down to the most basic unit of society for fear of losing control. They monopolize the resources of production and extract wealth from the society. . . . In China, the CCP extends everywhere and controls everything . . . the organization of the CCP, like a giant evil possessing spirit, attaches to every single unit and cell of the Chinese society as tightly as a shadow following an object. It penetrates deeply into every capillary and cell of the society with its finest blood-sucking vessels and thereby controls and manipulates society." http://english.epochtimes.com/news/4-12-9/24672.html.

CHAPTER 6. CHRISTIANITY AND "ADAPTATION TO SOCIALISM"

1. *Guangming Ribao*, January 6, 1979, translated in *Federal Bureau of Investigative Services: Daily Report—China*, 79–16, January 23, 1979.

2. See "China's Policy Towards Religion is a Long-term Policy," in *China*

Study Project Journal vol. 1, no. 3 (1986):26–28, translated from *Liaowang*, June 9, 1986.

3. "Religion in Hong Kong and Relations with the Vatican," *China Daily*, April 7, 1985, in *Religion in the People's Republic of China: Documentation* 17 (August 1985):3; "Religious Statistics," *Dagong Bao*, February 23, 1988, in *China Study Project Journal*, vol. 3, no. 3 (1988):39.

4. "Christianity in China Today," *Beijing Review*, vol. 27, no. 24 (June 11, 1984):22; *"Dalu Jidujiao zhi duoshao?"* (What do you know about Christianity on the Mainland?), *Qiao*, no. 25 (September-October 1987); *"Jidujiao quanguo lianghui zuixin tongji shuzi* (zhi 1988 niandi)" (Newest Statistics from the Two National Christian Bodies—to the end of 1988), *Qiao*, no. 38 (November-December 1989):3; Fiedler (2004).

5. Estimates of the total number of Protestants in China vary widely, from 25 to 100 million. A recent ballpark estimate of 80 million Protestants and Catholics combined is given in Aikman (2003: 6–8).

6. See the statement adopted by house church leaders in November 1998, in *China Study Journal*, vol. 13, no. 3 (1998):54–60.

CHAPTER 7. ISLAM AND MODERNITY

1. Connor (1984:53) quotes the following statement by Stalin in 1923, which reveals his early intention of passing on the Soviets' nationality policy to China: "We must here, in Russia, in our federation, solve the national problem in a correct, *a model way*, in order to set an example to the East, which represents the heavy reserves of our revolution" (emphasis in original).

2. For an analysis of the 2000 population statistics, see Yang Shengmin and Ding Hong (2002).

3. For a study of Muslim origin myths and their relevance for contemporary identity politics, see Gladney (2004:99–115).

4. For the debate over the definition of the Hui and reference to them as "Sino-Muslims," see Lipman (1997:xxiv); Gladney (1996:21–35).

5. Uyghurs waiting for an independent Uyghuristan find Chinese citizenship the least flexible, especially when threatened with extradition while in the diaspora, whereas Hui have rarely challenged Chinese citizenship. Similarly, membership in the Muslim community in China is legislated by birth, in the sense that once born a Hui, one is always a Hui, regardless of belief or even membership in the Communist Party.

6. Tajiks are the only official nationality who must learn in either Uyghur or Han Chinese in their own Tajik Autonomous Country of Tashkurgan, because they still lack a script for their native language (Tashkurgan County Chairman interview, August 25, 2001). Interestingly, since Tajik is not an official language in China, the Tajiks of Xinjiang (who speak a Darian branch language distantly related to old Persian, and quite different from the Tajik languages spoken in Tajikistan) can send their children to school in either Turkic Uyghur or Han Chinese. Yang Shengmin has indicated that Uyghur

cadres opposed granting a separate written language to the Tajiks (personal communication December 4, 2003); however, political concerns over links to Iran and Tajikistan through the promulgation of a Persian script are clearly an important factor.

7. Cited in Allen T. Cheng, "A surprise move by the mainland's Islamic community," *South China Morning Post*, March 25, 2003.

8. Ibid.

9. "Ma" (馬) is the most common surname among Hui Muslims in China, tracing its origins to the Ming dynasty, when many Muslims were required to take Chinese surnames and "Ma" most closely resembled the first syllable for "Muhammad." It is also the Chinese character for "horse," and since many Hui were engaged as caravaneers, it was a natural choice for a surname.

10. See Agence-France Press, August 1, 2005, "US keeps Uighurs at Guantanamo after found innocent: rights group." In March 2006, five Uyghurs were released to Albania; the fate of the remaining 17 is still undetermined.

11. See September 29, 2005, "China orders renewed crackdown in Muslim-populated Xinjiang" http://newsvote.bbc.co.uk/mpapps/pagetools/print/news.bbc.co.uk/2/hi/asia-pacific/4292466.stm.

12. See Ma Dazheng (2002:128): "Since the first half of the year 2000, the situation in Xinjiang has been peaceful (平靜), despite my earlier description of the seriousness of this issue, and should be accurately described as dramatically changed since the internationalization of the Xinjiang problem (新疆問題國際化)."

13. Cited in Allen T. Cheng, "A surprise move by the mainland's Islamic community," *South China Morning Post*, March 25, 2003.

CHAPTER 8. REPUBLICAN CHURCH ENGINEERING

1. For Taiwan, see Katz (2003) and Jones (1999); for the PRC, see Potter (2003).

2. "Guanli zongjiao zhi yijian shu," *Shenbao* (Shanghai), June 22, 1912.

3. On Indonesia's case, see Picard (2003).

4. On the missionary discourse about Chinese religion, see Reinders (2004).

5. This famous sentence was first published in a "fake" memorial (written by Kang Youwei but, contra Kang's later assertion, not sent to the emperor during the 1898 reforms): *Qing zun Kongsheng wei guojiao li jiaobu jiaohui yi Kongzi jinian er fei yinci zhe*, 請尊孔聖為國教立教部教會以孔子紀年而廢淫祠摺 (Huang Z. 1974:464–70).

6. On the Senglu Si and Daolu Si, see Goossaert (2007, chap. 1).

7. The charter of the Fojiao Hui and a letter to President Sun Yat-sen appeared in *Foxue congbao* (*Buddhist Miscellany*), no. 2, 1912.

8. The charter of the Zhonghua Fojiao Zonghui was published in *Foxue congbao*, no. 1, 1912, and Zhongguo Di'er Lishi Dang'an Guan, ed. (1998:705–14).

9. On the history of Buddhist associations, see Welch (1968:23–50), and Chen & Deng (2000:29–74).

10. On Chen Mingbin and the Baiyunguan, see Goossaert (2007, chap. 4).

11. On the Zhang Heavenly Masters, see Goossaert (2004).

12. For Chen Huanzhang's essay, together with the charter of the Confucian Association, see Chen Huanzhang (1913).

13. On the YMCA, see Dunch (2001).

14. On the question of religious authority in China, see Goossaert (2008).

15. Nedostup (2001, chap. 2). On the situation in Peking, see Goossaert (2007:77–80).

16. See the fascinating case of the Guangzhou Daoists during the 1930s in Li Zhitian (2002).

CHAPTER 9. SECULARIZATION AS RELIGIOUS RESTRUCTURING

1. At this point, our approach is different from the ideological understandings of secularization of the simplistic religio-secular conflict paradigm. The two interpretative models of the latter have been well summarized by Habermas (2003:104): "The replacement model suggests a progressivist interpretation in terms of disenchanted modernity, while the expropriation model leads to an interpretation in terms of a theory of decline, that is, unsheltered modernity." But both of them make the same mistake: "They construe secularization as a kind of zero-sum game between the capitalistically unbridled productivity of science and technology on the one hand, and the conservative force of religion and the church on the other hand."

2. Here "religious field" could be understood as the configuration of the interrelations among the given religious apparatuses that function respectively for producing, maintaining, and legitimating the power of a certain social group. For the theory of "religious field" and its critics, see Bourdieu (1971); Hervieu-Léger (1993:158–62).

3. Confucianism remains haunted to the present day by its lack of an institutional dimension and is not recognized as a religion in the PRC.

4. For the selective destruction of Chinese religions at the turn of the twentieth century, see Goossaert (2003); also compare Palmer's chapter in this volume on the evolution of the official anti-sect discourses in China.

5. Following the theory of Joachim Wach, Yang (1961) distinguished institutional religion and diffused religion in China. An institutional religion had its own system of theology, rites, and specialized organization of personnel, as represented by universal religions such as Buddhism. As for diffused religion, its theology, practice, and personnel were diffused in one or several secular social institutions. For example, the cult of ancestors was established in the family. Of course, these two sorts of religions were interdependent in reality.

6. These Buddhist disciplines could be considered a kind of folk law in

traditional China, which was relatively independent of state laws. See Liang (2003).

7. The following description of Buddhist history in contemporary China is mainly based on Welch's study (1972) and the reports published in *Xiandai foxue* (*Modern Buddhism*) and *Fayin* (*The Voice of Dharma*). The monthly *Xiandai foxue* was created by Juzan and some other progressive Buddhists in 1950. It became the official journal of the Buddhist Association of China (BAC, Zhongguo Fojiao Xiehui) founded in 1953. It ceased publication in 1964. Since 1981, *Fayin* has become the new official journal of the revived association.

8. The *danwei*, or work-unit, was a special form of work organization in the PRC, such as factories, schools, government offices, and hospitals. It was not only a workplace but a multifunctional organism for social control and social integration. The whole life of a member of the *danwei*—marriage, reproduction, immigration, and otherwise—was under the surveillance of the supervisors of the *danwei*. In turn, each *danwei* was subjected to supervision by higher levels of governmental authority. At the same time, the *danwei* was to ensure the social protection of its members, notably medical care, old-age pensions, and housing. As Li et al. (1996) have pointed out, the *danwei* did not work according to requirements of efficiency but on the principles of a larger institutional environment: a planned economy and socialist politics. It is interesting that since the 1950s, in an analogous way, progressive Buddhists began to call the Buddhist monasteries, or all of Buddhism represented by the BAC, "*danwei*."

9. In the CCP's discourse, the "united front" strategy means forming a temporary alliance with non-communist social groups, including some secondary enemies, to consolidate the Party's power and to split up, isolate, and weaken its main enemy. This "united front," together with "armed struggle" and "Party-building," constitute the "three treasures" of the CCP originally defined by Mao for revolution.

10. The Great Commandments of the Three Altars (三壇大戒, *santan dajie*) is one of the most important Chinese Buddhist institutional ceremonies, through which novices are ordained as *bhiksu* or *bhiksuni*, that is to say, full-fledged monks or nuns.

11. On Taixu and his theory and practice of the reform of Chinese Buddhism, see Hong (1995) and Pittman (2001).

12. For a deep analysis of *qigong* as a new religious phenomenon, see Palmer (2005).

13. In April 1999, the Falungong movement organized a demonstration in front of the Chinese central government offices in Beijing. Frightened by its force of social mobilization, the CCP began to define Falungong as an "evil cult" and to repress it violently. This policy also affected other *qigong* organizations.

14. In 1996, several articles against Falungong appeared in successively issues of *Taizhou Buddhism*, the monthly publication of the Buddhist Association of Zhejiang Province. This was the first attack of official Buddhism on

Falungong. At almost the same time, Chen Xingqiao, then working for the Buddhist Association of Harbin city, and later for the central office of the BAC in Beijing, began to publish his criticisms of Falungong. His writings on this subject have been collected in Chen X. (1999).

15. See the special issue of *Fayin*, no. 8, 1999.

CHAPTER 10. STATE CONTROL OF TIBETAN MONASTICISM

1. I would like to thank Professors Gray Tuttle, Mayfair Yang, and David Palmer for their valuable comments on earlier drafts of this paper, and Nathan McGovern for his editorial help.

2. CCP policy-makers and CCP propaganda documents published in Tibet try to make a case for the fact that religion, and especially Buddhism, is *not* so central to Tibetan cultural identity. For example, "A Reader for Advocating Science and Technology and Doing Away With Superstitions" (ICT n.d.:96) states, "If it is said that Tibetan nationality has had a culture only after the spreading of Buddhism, is it not to say that Tibetan nationality is a nationality that has no culture of its own?" An example of how CCP scholars have difficulty accepting Tibetan religiosity is Wang Lixiong's reduction of Tibetan piety to fear: "The roots of their [i.e., the Tibetans'] intense religiosity lie in the terrors of their natural environment—the explanation, surely, for the extraordinary proliferation of deities and monsters within Tibetan Buddhism, differentiating it from Indian and Chinese variants. . . . Fear formed the core of the Tibetans' spiritual world. Only by propitiating their terror, by offering sacrifices to it in complicated ceremonies, by worshipping and obeying it, could one feel safe and free, reassured by its vast dominion and tremendous power. . . . The Tibetans' submission to a religion that apparently runs contrary to their material interests becomes perfectly comprehensible in the context of their worship of fear. Faced with a choice between a short spell of suffering in this world followed by a blissful hereafter, or an eternity of torture, the peasants inevitably remained in thrall to the monks who held the keys to heaven" (L. Wang 2002: 91–92). Rather than commenting on Wang's views here, I point the reader to the response of Tsering Shakya (2002).

3. It is, of course, the supposed foreign-backed "Dalai clique" that the Chinese government considers the most disruptive and destabilizing *external* force threatening the "unity of the Motherland."

4. For varying accounts of the protests, and the Chinese government's response to them, see Schwartz 1994; Kelly, Bastian, & Aiello 1991:245–57, 355–58; Goldstein n.d.; and Goldstein 1998.

5. Dung dkar Blo bzang 'phrin las, a former monk of one of the *densas* who remained in Tibet after 1959, has written a sophisticated Marxist historical analysis of the politics of the "old society" (Dung dkar Blo bzang 'phrin las 1997:481–628; see Dung dkar Blo bzang 'phrin las 1991 for Chen Guangshen's rough English translation). Although most monks in Tibet today would question Dung dkar rin po che's conclusion that Tibet is better off under Chinese

Communist rule, they would probably accept much of his analysis of the conditions leading to the unification of the religious and political spheres, as well as much of his analysis of its attendant problems.

6. The Dalai Lama himself has argued for a democratically elected government to replace the institution of the Dalai Lama as head of state. The so-called Drepung Manifesto, a document written by Drepung monks and printed secretly in Lhasa in the summer of 1988, makes it clear that Tibetan monks are in general agreement with a reform and "modernization" of the pre-1959 political system: "Having completely eradicated the practices of the old society with all its faults, the future Tibet will not resemble our former condition and be a restoration of serfdom or be like the so-called 'old system' of rule by a succession of feudal masters and monastic estates. Understanding that a democratic government embodying both religious and secular principles is necessary, and for the purposes of demonstrating the future way forward for the Tibetan people, His Holiness the Dalai Lama has bestowed a national law for the future Tibet that accords with the general practice of the contemporary world" (translated in Schwartz 1994:232). The Drepung Manifesto invokes many of the key concepts of the modernist political project (the nation-state, the rule of law, democracy) without jettisoning the traditional notion of "government conjoined to religion" (*chos srid zung 'brel*). Dipesh Chakrabarty has described Indian opposition to the colonial project in similar terms: "Colonial Indian History is replete with instances in which Indians arrogated subjecthood to themselves precisely by mobilizing, within the context of modern institutions and sometimes on behalf of the modernizing project of nationalism, devices of collective memory that were both ahistorical and nonmodern" (Chakrabarty 2000b:40).

7. Although the Dalai Lama himself has been something of an apologist for modernity, he is not, as Dreyfus (2005) has recently and convincingly argued, an unqualified modernist. One of the most interesting and sophisticated discussions of modernist historicism's repudiation of what Dreyfus calls the "peasant" worldview—a way of "being-in-the-world" that insists that gods and spirits are agents in history—is to be found in Dipesh Chakrabarty's discussion of Ranajit Guha's contributions in *Provincializing Europe* (Chakrabarty 2000b:11–15 and epilogue).

8. Tibetans' narratives of their imprisonment during the Cultural Revolution often mention the role that Buddhist faith and practice played in their survival. See the comments of Ama Adhe and Tenpa Soepa in Patt (1992:84, 253–54), and of Dr. Choedrak in Avedon (1984:259–60).

9. The punk-monk fraternities were gang-like institutions of worker-monks. *Dobdobs*, as Goldstein (1989) has shown, engaged in a variety of practices—such as fighting, competetive sports, and certain forms of homosexual sex—that, though contrary to the spirit of Buddhist monastic discipline, were nonetheless largely tolerated up to 1959. The *dobdob* fraternities were abolished in some of the *densas'* colleges even before 1959. They no longer exist in exile. The monastic estates were large estates in different parts

of Tibet, under the control of the *densas,* that provided these monasteries with grain and animal products through "taxation" of the workers attached to the land. Most monks today would agree with Chinese government writings that at least some of the "ten feudal privileges of the monasteries"—for example, "monastic conscription," in which families were forced to give a male child to the local monastery when monastic populations dwindled—were indeed corrupt practices that needed to be reformed. For a list of these ten, see *Book No. 4* (Anonymous 2002b:120).

10. Monastic governance in the *densas* was mostly meritocratic, which is to say that leadership in the community was based on monks' qualifications. Abbots, upper-level administrators (like the disciplinarian and chant leader), and the senior scholars who ran the regional houses—together, the highest authorities in the monastery—held power chiefly based on their qualifications.

11. Viewed in this context, Dipesh Chakrabarty's discussion of how it "may be possible to hold together both secular-historicist and nonsecular and nonhistoricist takes on the world by engaging seriously the question of diverse ways of 'being-in-the-world'" is indeed interesting (Chakrabarty 2000a and 2000b:21 and epilogue).

12. Wang Lixiong goes on to say in the article that in rural areas, where market reforms have yet to take hold, religion is still strong (L. Wang 1999). Wang's conclusion that religion is on the decline in Tibetan urban areas will need to be backed up with good sociological data for it to be credible. His belief that it took free-market reforms and a disdain of religion for Tibetans to "take an interest in worldly enjoyment" may indicate that he does not know Tibetan culture all that well, for Tibetans have never seen religion as standing in the way of enjoying worldly pleasures.

13. The rhetoric of modernism is also found in less formal documents. Ma Lihua, head of the publishing unit of the China Tibetology Research Center in Beijing, is a good example of this: "We are helping Tibetans catch up with the west. . . . It is not 'Hanification,' but globalization. . . . You try living in a tent and burning wood for heat every day. It is not fun. . . . The faces of villagers just lit up when they saw TV for the first time. They really loved it. . . . Tibetans want to make money now. To do that, they realise there must be stability" ("Beijing helping Tibetans catch up with the west, says author," *South China Morning Post,* January 28, 2004, translated by World Tibet Network News, http://www.tibet.ca/en/wtnarchive/2004/1/30_4.html).

14. A far more extensive critique of the "superstitions" of religion—the existence of heavens and hells, reincarnation, karma/fate, gods and spirits, healing through magical substances, the efficacy of incantations, spells, and prayer—is found in "A Reader for Advocating Science and Technology and Doing Away With Superstitions" (ICT n.d.:98f.).

15. Here "religion" is understood in contradistinction to "superstitions" and "evil cults," for which, the Marxist state claims, there can be no tolerance, and which must be rooted out.

16. See also Ryan Dunch's remarks, in his chapter in this volume, about the forms of popular Protestantism that are considered problematic by the Chinese government.

17. *Book No. 4* (Anonymous 2002b:110–11) does state, however, that "in some areas, the special prerogatives of religious hierarchs which were eliminated in the past are returning from the grave, [and] quite a few instances of using religion to interfere in administration, law enforcement, education etc. have emerged." Here the guilt seems to lie with "hierarchs"—that is, with indigenous bourgeois elements.

18. This appeared in an article in the *Kardze Daily* on December 27, 2002; translated in Human Rights Watch 2004, appendix III:88).

19. For example, when two "regional houses" (*khang tshan*) of Sera argued over the affiliation of an important young lama, Tromo Geshe Rinpoche, before 1959, each claiming him as their own, the Ganden Potrang issued the final verdict by giving *both* houses the right to claim him (Tshe dbang rin chen 1995:172).

20. Another important factor giving the government a kind of metaphysical hold on the *densas* was the regency. It was not uncommon for the regents—those monks who ruled Tibet from the death of one Dalai Lama until the next Dalai Lama was old enough to take the throne—to be *densa* monks. While this obviously gave the *densas* (or the particular *densa* from which the regent hailed) an additional voice in the government, the rule of a *densa* regent was not the rule of the *densa* itself, since regents often had their own agendas different from those of their mother institution.

21. Most Tibetans—both monastic and lay—have refused to accept as legitimate many of the reincarnate lamas identified in CCP-controlled searches, an instance of the claim being made here that the government is not seen as having the metaphysical capital, and therefore the authority, to make such decisions. One of the greatest ironies of recent Chinese government policy involves the government decision to intervene in the process of identifying the reincarnations of high lamas, most notably the Tenth Panchen Rinpoche and the Seventh Reting Rinpoche. Despite its avowedly atheist stance, and its repudiation of reincarnation generally, the government insists, for example, on having identified the "true" reincarnation of the Panchen Lama. The vast majority of Tibetans, both in Tibet and in exile, have refused to accept the Chinese candidate, favoring instead the candidate identified by the Dalai Lama (ICT n.d.:29–45).

22. A similar point is made in Chan & Carlson (2005:vi).

23. As Chan and Carlson state, "In some countries . . . the law has been designed primarily to protect religion from state interference. In China, however, the opposite appears to be true, that is, the 'law' has been developed to protect the state from interference by religions" (Chan & Carlson 2005:1).

24. Chan and Carlson state, "Relatively little religiously-oriented legislation has been passed by the people's congresses on national or regional levels. The will of high Party and government officials often determine the final

outcome of regulations, legislation, and—in important cases—court rulings" (Chan & Carlson 2005:1).

25. Offices of the Religious Affairs Bureau (RAB) and the Tibetan Buddhist Association were opened in Lhasa even in the late 1950s. Ackerly states that these two offices were "staffed by some Tibetans appointed by His Holiness the Dalai Lama, although the Tibetans had little actual power" (Ackerly 1991:135). These and the other bureaucratic bodies responsible for religious affairs mostly ceased to function during the Cultural Revolution. They were reopened in the late 1970s, when CCP policy toward religion began to change.

26. On the role of the Public Security Bureaus (PSB) in monitoring and controlling religious institutions in China, see Magda Hornemann, "China: How the Public Security system controls religious affairs," *Forum18 News* (Oslo), September 29, 2004, http://www.forum18.org/Archive.php?article_id= 422.

27. See Dung dkar Blo bzang 'phrin las 1995:134, 181. The composition of the Democratic Management Committee (DMC) is somewhat different today from what it was at the time Dung dkar rin po che was writing. The DMC is today composed of fourteen members, with one position always left vacant. The lower committee (the *u yon*) is composed of eight members. Dung dkar rin po che states that it has seven members. He also states that the DMC is further divided into subcommittees on (1) "culture" (*rig gzung*), containing two directors and eight workers, (2) security (*bde 'jags*), also with two directors and eight workers, and (3) finances (*nor rdzas*), with two directors and one worker. This, too, has changed; see what follows.

28. The chant leader of the monastery (*dbu mdzad*) is always one of the junior directors.

29. Each of the *densas* has its own police station attached to it. They are located just outside the monasteries.

30. These unregistered monasteries are not denied permits by the government because they fall on the "superstitious" side of the religion-versus-superstition divide, but for other reasons, most notably that (1) they are unnecessary, since saturation has been reached, and (2) they drain resources from more productive endeavors. Whatever other problems they might face, the state has always acknowledged the "churchiness" (in Goosaert's sense of the term in his chapter in this volume) of Tibetan Buddhist monasteries.

31. Ackerly (1991:140) gives a list of nine criteria that candidates for admission to monasteries should, in principle, have. The candidate should (1) be at least eighteen, (2) love the country and the CCP, (3) have the permission of his or her parents, (4) have a good political background, as should the candidate's parents, (5) come from the appropriate region of the country, (6) have approval from the DMC, (7) have approval from the local authorities, (8) have approval from county and provincial authorities, and (9) have PSB clearance.

32. Ackerly (1991:141–42) gives four rules that govern the recognition of *tulkus:* (1) the search must be conducted under the guidance of the CCP; (2) the *tulku* must be found within Chinese territory; (3) the lamas recogniz-

ing the *tulku* must reside within China; and (4) the *tulku* cannot be found within the families of members of the CCP. See also *Decree no. 426* (State Council 2004).

33. In Tibet, monks do not have access to the internet in monasteries, as they so often do in monastic institutions in India. They do, however, sometimes visit internet cafes in major cities.

34. Associating with foreigners is seen as problematic for two reasons: (1) fear that monks will bad-mouth government policies, and (2) fear that monks will be influenced by the anti-Chinese views of some foreigners, who are often portrayed as provocateurs when a demonstration or some other public expression of political dissent takes place in the TAR.

35. It is interesting to see how "normative Buddhism"—the type of Buddhism that should be allowed to flourish—is constructed in CCP literature. Characteristics of this type of Buddhism, which ends up looking very Protestant and very modern, include an emphasis on (1) the study of classical philosophical/ethical texts, called generically "scripture" (which is contrasted with "superstitious practices" like divination, exorcism, etc.); (2) those doctrines and practices that, when preached to the laity, will "set their minds to economic construction and social progress"—specifically, the forms of discipline and proper conduct that "gradually eliminate the grounds which are unhelpful to the Socialist system"; (3) frugality and self-sufficiency, as opposed to reliance on the laity, whose excessive generosity to monks is seen as a waste of resources; and (4) equality in leadership, giving up traditional hierarchies and the "etiquette of a bygone era" (*Book No. 4*, Anonymous 2002b:114, 119–22).

36. "Geshe" is a title given to those who have successfully completed about twenty years of *densa* scholastic studies and have submitted to public examinations. From 1988 (the year that protests in Lhasa brought a permanent end to the Great Prayer Festival) up to 2004, the *densas* in Tibet had not awarded any Geshe degrees. The reasons for monks' refusal to award the degree are complex. It has partly to do with monks' sense of having no real control of their destinies. Before 1959, monks who received the title of Geshe had a variety of career options open to them. They could go for "postgraduate" study to one of the Tantric colleges, where they would study the esoteric tradition. In principle, they could then ascend through various administrative rungs of the Geluk hierarchy until reaching the school's highest position, the "Holder of the Ganden Throne" (dGa' ldan khri pa). Alternatively, Geshes could go back to their home monasteries and teach. Or they might decide to remain at the *densas*, or go into retreat in one or another isolated location. Monks awarded the Geshe degree in exile today have additional options open to them—such as to serve as the spiritual directors of "Dharma centers" in various parts of the world. Most of these options, however, are not available to *densa* monks in Tibet. The Tantric colleges, though still extant in Lhasa, have effectively ceased to function as postgraduate institutions for Geshes. There is no longer a functioning Geluk hierarchy in Tibet. Many of the outlying monasteries have ceased to function as educational institutions, and

restrictions on the movement of monks make it difficult to relocate to other areas of Tibet, much less to go abroad. It seems that for these various reasons monks saw little point in reinstituting the Geshe degree. Moroever, to obtain the highest rank of the degree, monks traditionally had to submit to public examinations in gatherings composed of monks of all three *densas* during the "Great Prayer Festival," or Mönlam Chenmo (Smon lam chen mo) in Lhasa. For security reasons the Chinese government has prohibited the convening of the Great Prayer Festival. (A protest broke out during one of these events in 1988.) However, in July 2004, the RAB issued a directive to the *densas* to begin granting the degree. Failure to comply, RAB officials stated, would have dire consequences. As a result, the monasteries submitted the names of six elder monks to the RAB. The latter then organized a three-hour "public examination" before news cameras in a closed-door meeting in the Central Cathedral (Jo khang) in Lhasa. The reestablishment of the Geshe degree was widely announced on nationwide television broadcasts and in newspapers the following day. See "Tibetan Buddhism resumes top-degree academic exams for Lamas," *People's Daily Online*, July 29, 2004, http://english.peopledaily .com.cn/200407/29/eng20040729_151225.html.

37. "Restrictions are placed on the substance of teachings, who can give them, who can receive them, the size of the crowd receiving them, and so forth. Often monasteries must receive official permission from local authorities before a certain type of teaching or ceremony is performed" (Dhundup 2006).

38. Ackerly's article, however, was written in 1991, and it appears that this may no longer be the case. See also the ambiguous language about financial control used in *Decree no. 426*, Article 34, which states that the monies collected by religious institutions when they engage in "public undertakings" should be used for "religious activities *or* public undertakings" (State Council 2004; my emphasis). Until recently, 5 RMB of the price of every tourist admission ticket into the *densas* had to go to the RAB. This is no longer the case. Today the entire amount goes into the monasteries' coffers.

39. Goldstein (1998:15) states that "size rather than quality became the objective measure of the success of monasticism (and Buddhism) in Tibet." This is simply not true. Even worker-monks believed that education, and not enrollment numbers, was what the *densas* were all about. For example, even uneducated monks took an interest in the results of the yearly Geshe rankings, and took great pride when a Geshe from their own college was ranked first. In many ways worker-monks created an identity for themselves as providers of the services that made the *true* work of the monastery—namely, education— possible. Goldstein further states that "monks' commitment to large-scale, rather than an elite, monasticism implicitly meant a decision to recruit and sustain many monks who, on the average, were of low quality" (Goldstein 1989:816). I would put it differently. Monks were committed to elite monasticism, but felt that mass monasticism was the means to this end. Whether or not they were correct in this belief is, of course, a different question.

40. In the history of Tibet, it has been rare for a *densa* to actually take up arms against the government. Yet as late as 1947, the Tibetan government had to send the army to squelch an uprising by Sera monks.

41. The Chinese government did intervene with Khenpo Jikmé Puntsok (Mkhan po 'Jigs med phun tshogs) and his community in A mdo La rung gar (eastern Tibet) in 2001. Philip Pan, "A Struggle for Spiritual Freedom," *Washington Post*, October 3, 2004: "The party . . . appeared worried about the khenpo's ability to attract devoted followers and funding from a broad cross section of Chinese society. . . . In the summer of 2001, police and other officials from across the region converged on Larung Gar, demolished about 2,400 homes and evicted several thousand residents. . . . Authorities focused first on evicting the estimated 1,000 Han students, sometimes climbing on roofs and listening down smokestacks for voices speaking Mandarin."

42. The first major protest since 1959 took place in Lhasa in September 1987, and on March 5, 1989, a demonstration orchestrated by twelve or so monks escalated into a mass protest and riots that lasted for three days. Martial law was imposed and remained in effect until April 1990. Interestingly, the limits on *densa* enrollments in the early 1980s could not prevent the wave of demonstrations that took place in Lhasa either in the last half of that decade or more recently, in March 2008, bringing into question the efficacy of the policy as a means of preventing the public expression of dissent.

43. See Ellen Bruno's documentary film "Satya: A Prayer for the Enemy."

44. One gets this impression from Goldstein (1998) because he never speaks in this article about monastic opposition to these limits, making it seem as though the limits were arrived at organically and as the result of the need to re-create Drepung as an institution that was economically self-sufficient. However, elsewhere in his writings ("Tibet, China, and the United States" n.d.) Goldstein does acknowledge that "continuing restrictions on the monasteries in the form of limits on the total number of monks" was a factor in the 1980s protests.

45. This practice would also appear to be a violation of the recently promulgated decree of the State Council concerning religion, namely, *Decree no. 426*, Article 26 (State Council 2004).

46. For almost a decade after the revival of the *densas* in the early 1980s, the prohibition against monks under eighteen years of age, although on the books, was not enforced.

47. Goldstein (1998:26) puts it this way: "Because religious freedom was part of the more basic freedom to believe or *not to believe*, the state sought to create a level playing field by prohibiting religious education and recruitment of individuals into the priesthood who were under the age of eighteen." Given that there is compulsory *socialist* education for children, it is unclear how, precisely, the playing field is "level."

48. The Strike Hard Campaign was originally launched in China in 1983

as a crackdown on crime. It called for "severe and speedy punishment." Many prisoners were executed during the campaign after brief, summary trials (Amnesty International 1996). In Tibet in 1996, it appears to have been largely a campaign of ideological education aimed at monks and nuns. At the Fourth Tibet Work Forum in 2001, Jiang Zemin called for Party members to "strengthen the administration of religious affairs, strike those who use religion to carry out splittist, criminal activities, and vigorously lead Tibetan Buddhism to adapt to Socialism" (*Xinhua*, June 30, 2001; cited in TCHRD n.d.:24). After September 11, 2001, the Chinese government relaunched the Strike Hard Campaign in various parts of China (e.g., in Xinjiang) as a "war on terror," borrowing the rhetoric of the Bush administration and carrying out a harsh campaign aimed at destroying all opposition to its policies there.

49. *Book No. 2* and *Book No. 4* (Anonymous 2002a, 2002b), cited earlier, are part of the materials distributed to monks and nuns as part of the "patriotic re-education" sessions that in Tibet are the hallmark of the Strike Hard Campaign.

50. "The five principles listed for assent during these sessions are: (1) opposition to separatism; (2) unity of Tibet and China; (3) recognition of the Chinese government appointed Panchen Lama as the true Panchen Lama; (4) denial that Tibet was or should be independent; and (5) agreement that the Dalai Lama is destroying the unity of the motherland" (Tibetan Government in Exile n.d.).

51. The Tibetan Government in Exile (n.d.) puts the figures at 59 expulsions from Sera, 162 from Ganden, and 300 from Drepung.

52. Other reasons for expulsion include challenging the work teams; previous travel to India; being under the age of eighteen; possessing pictures of the Dalai Lama; not being on the official rolls of the monastery/nunnery; and not holding a valid identification card.

53. Throughout the 1980s and into the early 1990s, the CCP was content to allow a distinction to be made between the "Dalai clique" (labeled "splittist") and the Dalai Lama himself (who, whatever his political views, was not denied his status as a religious leader). This changed after Chen Kuiyuan's tenure as CCP secretary of the TAR. From the mid-1990s on, the Dalai Lama's opposition to Chinese policies in Tibet was seen as nullifying his religious status. (See above on why religious opposition to the government is considered a logical impossibility.) Allegiance to the Dalai Lama as a religious leader was therefore proscribed, and it is from this point forward that we begin to see bans on pictures of the Dalai Lama and attempts to coerce monks into denouncing him. See Barnett (2001) and R. Schwartz (1994:54–55).

54. For example, in July 2005 a patriotic reeducation work team was sent to Sera Monastery before the celebrations marking the fortieth anniversary of the founding of the Tibet Autonomous Region (TCHRD 2005). More recently, in May 2006, Zhang Qingli, CCP secretary of the TAR, launched a new campaign called "Fight to the Death." The new initiative prohibits any government employee (even those who are retired) from participating in public reli-

gious activities, even entering a temple or monastery. Patriotic reeducation was also relaunched in the monasteries under the banner of the Fight to the Death Campaign.

55. "Tibetan Monks Arrested, Monastery Closed Amid Protests," *Radio Free Asia*, November 11, 2005, at http://www.rfa.org/english/news/breaking_news/2005/11/29/tibet_arrest/.

56. Wang Lixiong and others have argued that while *religious* devotion to the Dalai Lama is on the decline, this has been replaced by the rise of the Dalai Lama as a *political* figure, the locus of "splittist" sentiments. This is simply an incorrect assessment of the situation. Devotion to the Dalai Lama as a religious leader has never been stronger, and one sees nothing changing this in the foreseeable future.

58. R. Schwartz (1994: 61) writes, "The members of these committees are supposed to be elected by the monks, but the monks report that they have only a small degree of control over the selection process. Some of the members, who reside at the monasteries, are lay people. . . . The older members have been selected because of proven loyalty to the Chinese administration."

59. See *Decree no. 426*, Article 4 (Guojia Zongjiaoju 2004).

CHAPTER 11. TAIWAN'S MODERN MIDDLE CLASSES

1. This is arguably less true of monasteries in eastern Tibet, where a good deal of traditional education/practice has been preserved and is allowed to flourish with less interference from Chinese authorities. How the recent round of protests, many of which took place in eastern Tibet, will affect the monasteries in this region remains uncertain.

2. This chapter is a partial summary of my book, *Democracy's Dharma: Religious Renaissance and Political Development in Taiwan* (Berkeley: University of California Press, 2007). Unless otherwise noted, information is based on interviews with members (including leaders) of the various religious organizations studied and on participant-observation ethnography. Most of the research was carried out between September 1999 and January 2000, when I was a research fellow at the Academia Sinica in Taiwan. The Chiang Ching-kuo Foundation provided funding for this project. I gathered additional data during a two-week research trip in July 2001, funded by the Pacific Rim Program of the University of California Office of the President. Able research assistance was provided by He Huachin and Guo Yayu.

3. This information is from Ciji Yearbooks and its website: http://www.tzuchi.org.tw. Ciji was the first Taiwanese charity to enter Iraq after the 2003 war. Working in conjunction with the Hashemite Charity Organization of Jordan, it distributed food and medical supplies to the Al Fallujah General Hospital and to Palestinian refugees in Baghdad.

4. This information comes from the annual yearbooks published by Ciji and from fieldwork I carried out in Taiwan in 1999.

5. This information is from Foguangshan's yearbooks and from my field-work in Taiwan.

8. This information is from an undated pamphlet published by Xingtian-gong.

6. One can see examples of this spirit in *Rebirth: Transformations in Tzu-chi* (Taipei: Buddhist Compassion Relief Association, n.d.), a collection of testimonials about how Ciji members were converted to working in the organization.

7. Xingyun makes this statement in *Foguangshan,* a video produced by his organization.

8. Interview with the superintendent of the Ciji Hualian Hospital.

9. The Mainlanders are those Chinese, mostly associated with the GMD, who came to Taiwan in the late 1940s, when the GMD was defeated by the Communists in the Chinese civil war. The Mainlanders constitute about 10 percent of Taiwan's population and speak Mandarin Chinese. Most native Taiwanese speak the Hoklou dialect (called Taiwanese), and some speak Hakka. To consolidate its control over Taiwan, the GMD systematically killed or imprisoned the Taiwanese intellectual and political elite. During the "White Terror" that began after the crackdown on Taiwanese dissent in the "February 28" (1947) incident and continued throughout the 1950s, as many as 30,000 Taiwanese were killed and hundreds of thousands were imprisoned. In the past two decades, a strong cultural nationalism has developed among some Taiwanese, especially in southern Taiwan, and it fuels sentiment for Taiwanese independence from Mainland China.

10. According to Fu Chi-ying (1996:246–47), "The government had no part whatsoever in the growth of Fo Kuang Shan. Not even a single tree or a blade of grass. Except, maybe, for ten years delay in matters of official registration." But the enormous growth of Foguangshan temples, schools, and other ventures throughout Taiwan in the 1970s and 1980s has benefited from the cooperation of important government officials.

11. This information was graciously provided to me by Alise DiVido.

12. As Fu Chi-ying puts it, "The seed [for the idea of building Hsi Lai Temple in Los Angeles] was sown when Hsing Yun first came to America as a guest of its bicentennial celebrations. . . . The country's cultural diversity and receptiveness struck him irrevocably. Further, the need for a spiritual anchorage for the fast increasing number of immigrants of Chinese heritage was more than obvious. But most of all, Hsing Yun pondered, in contrast to the heavily armed and intrusive ways in which Christianity penetrated China in the last century, could Buddhism now be taught peacefully in the West?" (Fu 1996:345).

CHAPTER 12. GODDESS ACROSS THE TAIWAN STRAIT

1. I thank the Chiang Ching-kuo Foundation for funding this research; the Institute of Ethnology, Academia Sinica, for providing a research base in

Taiwan; Dongsen Television News for allowing me to accompany their crew to Fujian; and Dong Zhenxiong of Zhennan Temple and Zhang Xun for my interviews at the temple. I am grateful to Lin Mei-rong for inviting me to present this chapter as a paper at the "International Conference on Mazu Belief and Modern Society," at Chaotiangong Temple in Taiwan, May 2001, and to Chin Chuan Lee for an invitatin to present it at the China Times Conference, "Media, Nationalism, and Globalization: The Case of China," School of Journalism, University of Minnesota, Minneapolis, also in May 2001. This paper was also presented at the American Anthropological Association meetings in San Francisco, November 2000 (thanks to Jeff Himpele); at the Institute for Advanced Study, Princeton University, in December 2000; at the Department of Cinema Studies, New York University, February 2001 (thanks to Anna McCarthy); and at the Institute for Chinese Studies, Oxford University, May 2003 (thanks to Vivienne Shue). Many thanks also to Beth Povinelli, Jing Wang, Monroe Price, and Michael Curtin for their comments. Finally, thanks to the journal *Public Culture* for permission to reprint this article from its 2004 issue in slightly modified form.

2. The English word "pilgrimage" is used to translate the Chinese term *jinxiang* (進香, "presenting incense"). What this Chinese term implies is that pilgrims bring incense to burn and make contact with the deity in a distant temple that is above their home temple in the ritual hierarchy. See the book edited by Susan Naquin and Chun-fang Yu (1992) for an important introduction to the Chinese tradition of pilgrimage.

3. In the transition from archaic empires to modern nation-states, Benedict Anderson (1991) has noted a process of "flattening," in which the hierarchical sacred court center, fading to indistinct peripheries, gives way to a homogeneous space of egalitarian comradeship bounded by clear-cut national borders.

4. Anthony Giddens (1987) notes that even when walls were built by such empires as China and Rome, the walls did not divide a population and did not mark the end of one culture and the beginning of another, since people on both sides often continued to live well beyond the walls without having to change their identities.

5. Since these events of 2000, the Taiwan government has loosened its prohibition on direct ferry service from Taiwan to Fujian. In September 2006, Zhenlan Temple sponsored a pilgrimage via ferry from Taizhong Port to Xiamen City and Meizhou Island. In July 2008, the new Taiwan government of President Ma Ying-jeou allowed regular direct flights between Taiwan and Mainland China.

6. The political barriers are readily demonstrable. As one television technician told me, Taiwan's offshore island of Jinmen, which is 260 nautical kilometers away, is now connected to Taiwan proper by a telecommunications undersea cable. Thus, to connect up Taiwan to China, one needs only to lay cable across the *one* remaining nautical kilometer that separates Jinmen from the city of Xiamen in Fujian Province, but this cannot be done yet.

7. According to the Meizhou Temple website, late Qing-dynasty local gaze-

teer sources record 1,200 Mazu temples in China at the end of the nineteenth century; in 1987, there were 800 in Taiwan, 57 in Hong Kong and Macao, and 135 in Japan, Korea, Thailand, Vietnam, Cambodia, Burma, Singapore, Malaysia, Indonesia, India, Philippines, the U.S., France, Brazil and Argentina. http://www.mz-mazu.org.cn/htmls/mzzm1.htm.

8. A temple that makes a pilgrimage to another temple is always positioned lower than the destination temple in the ritual hierarchy of temples. Thus a direct pilgrimage to Meizhou implies that Zhenlan Temple is subordinate only to the Meizhou ancestral temple.

9. This disjuncture between Chinese popular ritual territorialization and state administrative spatialization accords with Deleuze and Guattari's distinction between "primitive supple segmentarity" and "rigid state segmentarity" (1987:209–13). For Deleuze and Guattari, primitive segmentary societies are the original territorial machines, marking their shifting social organizations in the earth. The archaic state machine comes along and de-territorializes them, "overcoding" its own spatial divisions onto them or absorbing their segments into its own concentric bureaucratic apparatus, where all segments "resonate" with the same center. The modern nation-state, with its mapping of latitudes and longitudes, further rigidifies the outer edges of state boundaries.

10. Monroe Price (1994, 1999, 2002) observes that, in the age of media globalization, states are finding it less effective to rely on the traditional methods of deflecting foreign media invasions of state media space, such as resorting to legal prohibitions or restrictions, technological mechanisms to shut out unwanted messages, and force. Instead, states are actively engaged in negotiations with both the transnational media corporations who send these messages and with the states who host these corporations and media producers to limit, alter, or stop their transmissions.

Bibliography

SOURCES IN CHINESE AND OTHER ASIAN LANGUAGES

Anonymous 無名著

1928　迷信的破除 (*The Destruction of Superstition*). Nanjing: Zhongyang daxuequli tongsu jiaoyuguan tuiguangbu.

1930　萬行節約運動案 ("Thoroughly Executing the Frugality Movement"), in 中央黨務月刊 (*Central Party Affair Monthly*), Special Issue for the third full meeting of the third plenum of the Central Executive Committee, March.

1933a　首都警察廳取締團體遊行規則 ("Capital Police Department Guidelines to Clean up Group Marches"), in 中華民國法規彙編 (*Collected Laws and Regulations of the Republic of China*), 第四卷. 上海: 商務印書館. Shanghai: Shangwu yinshuguan. (Orig. pub. 1931.)

1933b　神祠存廢標準 ("Standards for Retaining or Abolishing Gods and Shrines"), in 中華民國法規彙編 (*Collected Laws and Regulations of the Republic of China*), 第四卷, 807–14. 上海: 商務印書館. Shanghai: Shangwu yinshuguan. (Orig. pub. 1931.)

1935　籌開市民大會須知 ("Essential Knowledge for Planning and Holding an Urban Mass Rally"], in 新生活運動促進總會會刊 (*Journal of General Association for Promotion of the New Life Movement*), 第二十卷.

1970　石城山志 (1900–1917) ("Mountain Gazetteer of Stone City, 1900–1917"), in 金陵瑣志 (*Linked Gazetteers of Nanjing*). 陳作霖等編 Chen Zuolin et al., comp. 台北: 成文出版社. Taibei: Chengwen Publishing Co.

1980　革命導師有關如何對待宗教問題的部分論述 ("Some Expositions by Revolutionary Leaders on the Question of How to Handle Religion"), in 宗教 (*Religion*), 第一期.

1994a　道教會布告—宣言書 ("Proclamation of the Daoist Associa-
tion: Manifesto"), in 藏外道書 (*Daoist Books Outside the
Canon*), 第二十四卷. 成都: 巴蜀書社. Chengdu: Bashu shushe.
(Orig. pub. 1912.)

1994b　道教會布告—道教會大綱 ("Proclamation of the Daoist Asso-
ciation: A Blueprint"), in 藏外道書 (*Daoist Books Outside the
Canon*), 第二十四卷. 成都: 巴蜀書社. Chengdu: Bashu shushe.
(Orig. pub. 1912.)

2000　湄洲媽祖祖廟 ("Meizhou Mazu Temple Website"). http://
www.mz-mazu.org.cn.

2002　黑龍江省雙城市的沙塵、泥雨、大雪警示着世人, in 法輪大法
明慧網 "Sand, Muddy Rain and Heavy Snow Are a Warning
to the People of Shuangcheng City [sic], Heilongjiang Province." http://minghui.ca/mh/articles/2002/4/10/28216.html.

Bai Shouyi 白壽彝著

1951　回回民族的形成 ("The Nature of the Hui Nationality"), in 光
明日報(*Guangming Daily*), 二月十七日第二版.

Bastid-Bruguière, Marianne 巴斯蒂著

1998　梁啟超與宗教問題 ("Liang Qichao and the Question of Religion"), in 東方學報 (*Eastern Journal*), 第七十冊. 張廣達.
Zhang Guangda, trans.

Bureau of Information, Administrative Yuan, Taiwan, ed. 新聞局行政院編印

1997　有線電視法 ("Cable Television Law"), in 台灣地區眾傳播事
業概況 (*Survey of Taiwan Mass Media and Broadcasting
Industry*). 台北: 新聞局行政院編印. Taibei: Bureau of Information, Administrative Yuan.

Cai Shaoqing 蔡少卿著

1996　中國秘密社會 (*Chinese Secret Societies*). 台北: 南天書局. Taibei: SMC Publishing Inc. First published 1990 by 浙江人民出
版社 Zhejiang People's Publishing Co.

Cao Yuanzhong 曹元中著

1916　傳心殿禮議 ("On the Rite of the Hall of Esoteric Transmission") in 禮議 (*On li*), 第一卷. 四川: 劉氏求恕齋. Sichuan:
Liushi qiushuzhai.

Chen Bing and Deng Zimei 陳兵和鄧子美著

2000　二十世紀中國佛教 (*Buddhism in China in the Twentieth
Century*). 北京: 民族出版社. Beijing: The Ethnic Publishing
House.

Chen Binghong 陳炳宏著

1999　台灣有線電視產業集團化趨勢 研究——以和信與力霸企業集
團為例 ("The Conglomeration of Taiwan's Cable Television
Industry: A Case Study of the Koos Group and the Rebar
Group"), in 廣播與電視 (*Broadcasting and Television*), 第十
四期.

Chen Duxiu 陳獨秀著

1918a 有鬼論質疑 ("Skeptical Questions on the Existence of Ghosts"), in 新青年 (*New Youth*), 第四卷, 第五號.

1918b 偶像破壞論 ("On the Smashing of Idols"), in 新青年 (*New Youth*), 第五卷, 第二號.

Chen Guodong 陳國棟著

1992 哭廟與焚儒服——明末清初生員層的社會性動作 (Temple Wailing and Confucian Attire Burning: The Shengyuan Group's Social Act in the Late Ming and Early Qing), in 新史學 (*New History*) , 第三卷, 第一期.

Chen Guofu 陳果夫著

1951 蘇政回憶 (*Memoirs of Jiangsu Government*). 台北: 正中書局. Taibei: Chengchung Book.

1991 廟會序言 ("Prefatory Words on Temple Festivals"), in 陳果夫先生全集 (*Complete Works of Mr. Chen Guofu*), 第四卷. 台北: 近代中國出版社. Taibei: Jindai Zhongguo chubanshe.

Chen Hongxing and Dai Chenjing, eds. 陳紅星和戴晨京編

1999 "法輪功"與邪教 (*Falungong and Evil Cults*). 北京: 宗教文化出版社. Beijing: Zongjiao wenhua chubanshe.

Chen Huanzhang 陳焕章著

1913 孔教論 (*On Confucianism*). 上海: 商務印書館. Shanghai: Shangwu yinshuguan.

Chen Huiming 陳慧敏著

1990 途爾甘與衛柏: 宗教學說 之比較及其在台灣民間宗教 之引用—以台北行天宮為例 ("Durkheim and Weber: A Comparison of Religious Discourse and Their Deployment in Taiwan Popular Religion—a Case Study of the Temple of Enacting Heaven's Business"), 政治大學碩士論文. M.A. thesis, Zhengzhi University.

Chen Lifu 陳立夫著

1976 與民生史觀 ("New Life and the Minsheng Conception of History"), in 革命文獻 (*Revolutionary Documents*) 第六十八輯, 新生活運動史料 (*Historical Materials on New Life Movement*). 中國國民黨中央委員會黨史委員會主編 Committee on Party History, CC, Guomindang, ed. 台北: 中央文物供應社. Taibei: Zhongyang wenwu gongyinshe.

Chen Lijiang and Chen Youduan 陳禮江和陳友端著

1936 農民對於文化反應心裡之調查與研究 ("A Survey and Research of the Cultural Attitudes and Responses of Farmers"), in 教育與民眾 (*Education and Masses*), 第八卷, 第一期.

Chen Linshu and Chen Xia, eds. 陳麟書和陳霞編

2003 宗教學原理 (*Principles of Religious Studies*). 北京: 宗教文化出版社. Beijing: Zongjiao wenhua chubanshe.

Chen Naixun and Du Fukun 陳迺勳和杜福堃著

1932 新京備乘 (*Complete Records of the New Capital*). 南京: 北平清祕閣南京分店. Nanjing: Beiping Qingmige Nanjing fen dian.

Chen Qinghe 陳清河著

1996 衛星電視的本土化經營屬性之研究 ("Research on the Local Management of Satellite Television"), in 廣播與電視 (*Broadcast and Television*), 第二卷, 第三期.

Chen Rizhang 陳日章著

1932 京鎮蘇錫遊覽指南 (*Travel Guide to Nanjing, Zhenjiang, Suzhou and Wuxi*). 上海: 世界與地學社. Shanghai: Shijie yudi xueshe.

Chen Xiyuan (Chen Hsi-yuan) 陳熙遠著

2002 "宗教"——一個中國近代文化史上的關鍵詞 ("'Religion'—a Key Term in Modern Chinese History"), in 新史學 (*New History*), 十三卷, 第四期.

Chen Xingqiao 陳星橋著

1999 佛教《氣功》與法輪功 (*Buddhist "Qigong" and Falungong*). 北京: 宗教文化出版社. Beijing: Religious Culture Press.

Chen Yaoting 陳耀庭著

1992 上海道教史 ("History of Daoism in Shanghai"), in 上海宗教史 (*History of Religion in Shanghai*). 阮仁澤和高振農編 Ruan Renze and Gao Zhennong, eds. 上海: 上海人民出版社. Shanghai: Shanghai People Publishing Co.

Chen Yongsheng 陳永生著

1987 海峽兩岸宗教政策之比較 ("A Comparison of Relations between State and Religion across the Taiwan Strait"), in 中國近代政教關係國際學術研討會論文集 (*Proceedings of the First International Symposium on Church and State in China*. 李擷芳主編 Li Jifang, ed. 淡水大學歷史系 Tamsui University, History Department.

Chen Zhimin and Zhang Xiangqi, eds. 陳智敏和張翔麟編

2001 邪教真相 (*The True Face of Evil Cults*). 北京: 當代世界出版社. Beijing: Dangdai shijie chubanshe.

Da Guang Bao 大光報. Suzhou.

Da Yingyu 達應庾

1988 中國伊斯蘭教賽來菲耶派略 ("A Brief Narration of China's Islamic Salafiyya Order"), in 中國伊斯蘭教研究文集 (*Compendium of Chinese Islamic Research*). Chinese Islamic Research Committee, ed. 銀川: 寧夏人民出版社. Yinchuan: Ningxia People's Publishing Co.

Dai Jitao 戴季陶著

1972a 仁王護國法會發願文 ("Prayer of the Dharma Assembly to the Benevolent Kings Who Protect Their Countries"), in 戴季陶先生佛學論集 (*Collected Writings on Buddhism of Mr. Dai*

Jitao). 東初編 Dongchu, ed. 台北: 華嚴蓮社. Taibei: Huayan lianshe. (Orig. pub. 1931.)

1972b   戴季陶先生佛學論集 (*Collected Writings on Buddhism of Mr. Dai Jitao*). 東初編 Dongchu, ed. 台北: 華嚴蓮社. Taibei: Huayan lianshe.

Dai Kangsheng, ed. 戴康生著

1999   當代新興宗教 (*Contemporary New Religions*). 北京: 東方出版社. Beijing: Dongfang chubanshe.

Deng Zimei 鄧子美著

1994   傳統佛教與中國近代化 (*Traditional Buddhism and Modernization of China*). 上海: 華東師範大學出版社. Shanghai: East China Normal University Press.

Ding Guangxun 丁光訓著

1988   丁光訓反對廣東省宗教政策 ("Ding Guangxun Opposes Guangdong Province Religious Policy"), in 百姓 (*Baixing*), 第一八七期.

Diwujie Quanguo Renmin Daibiao Dahui 第五屆全國人民代表大會通過 (The Fifth National Congress, Chinese People's Congress, adopted)

1979   中華人民共和國刑法 (*Criminal Code of the People's Republic of China*). 北京: 人民出版社. Beijing: People's Publishing Co.

Dong Xiaohan and Zhou Yiwen 董霄漢和周怡文著

1999   明清民間宗教的基本特點及政府的處置措施 ("Basic Characteristics of Popular Religious Sects in the Ming and Qing, and Methods Used by the State to Control Them"), in "法輪功"與邪教 (*Falungong and Evil Cults*). 北京: 宗教文化出版社. Beijing: Zongjiao wenhua chubanshe.

Du Jingzhen 杜景珍著

1997   略論道院遭禁(1928)后的動向 ("Brief Discussion on the Tendency of the Daoyuan after Its Banning in 1928"), in 民間宗教 (*Popular Religion*) , 第三期.

Dung dkar Blo bzang 'phrin las

1995   "Se ra theg chen gling gi lo rgyus mdor bsdus" (A Brief History of Sera Monastery") in *Se ra theg chen gling (Sera Monastery)*. Tshe dbang rin chen ed. Beijing: Mi rigs dpe skrun khang.

1997   "Bod kyi chos srid zung 'brel skor bshad pa" ("An Explanation of the Unity of Tibetan Religion and the State"), in *Dung dkar blo bzang 'phrin las kyi gsung rtsom phyogs bsgrigs (Collected Works of Dung dkar Blo bzang 'phrin las)*. Skal bzang dar rgyas, ed. Mtsho sngon: Krung go'i bod kyi shes rig dpe skrun khang.

Fang Yanhua 方艳華著

2004   民初山東孔教會及其活動 ("The Confucian Association in Shandong during the Early Republican Period and Its Activities"), in 成都教育學院學報 (*Journal of the Chengdu College of Education*), 第十二卷.

Feng Jinyuan 馮今源著
2001   邪教不是宗教 ("Evil Cults Are Not Religions"), in 論邪教
        (On Evil Cults). 社會問題研究叢書委員會編 Shehui Wenti
        Yanjiu Congshu Weiyuanhui, ed. 南寧: 廣西人民出版社.
        Nanning: Guangxi People's Publishing Co.

Fori 佛日著
1999   批判寄附于佛教之外道 ("Criticisms of Heterodox Sects
        Attached to Buddhism"), in 禪 (Chan), 第三期.

Fu Zhong 孚中著
2000   一貫道發展史 (History of the Development of Yiguandao).
        台北: 正義善書出版社. Taibei: Zhengyi shanshu chubanshe.

Gan Chunsong 干春松著
2003   制度化儒家及其解體 (Institutional Confucianism and Its
        Collapse). 北京: 中國人民大學出版社. Beijing: China People's
        University Press.
2005   清末民初孔教會實踐與儒家現代轉化的困境 ("The Situation
        of the Confucian Association during the Late Qing and the
        Early Republican Period and the Difficult Modernization of
        Confucianism), in 齊魯學刊 (Shandong Scholarly Journal),
        第三卷.

Gong'anbu Yiju, ed. 公安部一局編
1985   反動會道門簡介 (Brief Introduction to Reactionary Secret
        Societies). 北京: 群衆出版社. Beijing: Qunzhong chubanshe.
        (Partial translation in Syncretic Sects and Secret Societies:
        Revival in the 1980s, Robin Munro, ed., Special Issue of Chi-
        nese Sociology and Anthropology, 1989, vol. 21, no. 4.)

Goossaert, Vincent 高萬桑著
2006a   近代中國的國家與宗教: 宗教政策與學術典範 ("State and
        Religion in Modern China: Religious Policies and Scholarly
        Paradigms"), in 中央研究院近代史研究所集刊 (Bulletin of
        the Institute of Modern History, Academica Sinica), 第五十
        四卷.
2006b   See under Sources in English and Other Western Languages.

Gu Jiegang 顧頡剛著
1932   論中國的舊曆新年 ("On China's Old-Calendar New Year"), in
        民間月刊 (Folk Monthly), 第二卷, 第一期.

Gu Xin and Wang Xu 顧昕和王旭著
2005   從國家主義到法團主義——中國市場轉型過程中國家與專業
        團體關係的演變 ("From Statism to Corporatism: Changes in
        the Relationship between the State and Professional Associa-
        tions in the Transition to Market Economics in China"), in 社
        會學研究 (Sociological Studies), 第二期.

Gu Yuzhen 顧玉振著
1931   蘇州風俗談 (A Discussion of Suzhou Customs). Suzhou:
        Wenxin.

Guo An, ed. 郭安編
2003   當代世界邪教與反邪教 (*Contemporary Cults and Anti-Cult Movements*). 北京: 人民出版社. Beijing: People's Publishing Co.

Guo Jinrun, ed. 郭金潤編
1993   大甲馬祖進香 (*The Dajia Mazu Pilgimage*). 台中市: 台中縣立文化中心. Taizhong: Taizhong County Cultural Center.

Guo Shi Guan Cang 國史館藏 (Archives of Academia Historica), Taibei 台北
1928a   內政部部長薛篤弼致國民政府函 ("Letter From the Minister of Interior Xue Dubi to the National Government"), in 國民政府檔案 (*Archives of the National Government*), Reel 259: 1455–59, October 20.
1928b   王亢元致國民政府程文 ("Petition from Wang Kangyuan to the National Government"), in 國民政府檔案 (*Archives of the National Government*), Reel 294:1146–65, August.

Guo Yuhua, ed. 郭于華編
2000   儀式與社會變遷 (*Ritual and Social Change*). 北京: 社會科學文獻出版社. Beijing: Social Science Materials Publishing Co.

Guojia Zongjiaoju, Guowuyuan Fazhi Bangongshi 國家宗教局, 國務院法制辦公室著 (National Bureau of Religion, State Council Legal Office)
2004   宗教事務條例 ("Regulations on Religious Affairs"). 國務院第426號令(*Decree No. 426*). 北京: 宗教文化出版社. Beijing: Religious Culture Publishing Co.

Haeckel, Ernst 赫克爾著
1919   靈異論 ("On Miracles"), in 新青年 (*New Youth*), 第六卷, 第二號.

Hattori Unokichi 服部宇之吉著
1926   孔子及孔子教 (*Confucius and Confucianism*). 東京: 京文社. Tokyo.

He Jianming 何建明著
1992   民初佛教革新運動述論 ("On the Reformist Movements of Buddhism in the Early Years of the Republic of China"), in 近代史研究 (*Modern Chinese History Studies*), 第四期.

Hong Jinlian 洪金蓮著
1995   太虛大師的佛教現代化之研究 (*Study on Master Taixu's Modernization of Buddhism*). 台北: 東初出版社. Taibei: Dongchu chubanshe.

Hu Hanmin 胡漢民著
1964   南洋與中國革命 ("Nanyang and the Chinese Revolution"), in 中華民國開國五十年文獻 (*Documents of the Republic of China Fifty Years Since Its Foundation*), 第一編, 第十一冊, vol. 1, no. 11.

Hu Pu'an 胡撲安著
1978   中華全國風俗志 (*Nationwide Gazetteer of Chinese Customs*).
台北: 東方文化書局. Taibei: Dongfang wenhua shuju. (Orig.
pub. 1933.)

Hu Shi 胡適著
1998   四十自述 ("Autobiography at Forty"), in 胡適文集 (*Collection of Hu Shi*), 第一卷. 歐陽哲生編 Ouyang Zhesheng, comp. 北京: 北京大學出版社. Beijing: Peking University Press. (Orig.
pub. 1933.)

Huang Jingxing 黃進興著
2003a   權力與信仰: 孔廟祭祀制度的形成 ("Power and Belief: The Shaping of a National Cult, Worship of the Confucian Temple in Imperial China"), in 優入聖域: 權力: 信仰與正當性 (*"Entering the Master's Sanctuary": Power, Belief, and Legitimacy in Traditional China*). 台北: 允晨出版社. Taibei: Yunchen chubanshe.
2003b   道統與治統之間: 從明嘉靖九年(1530)孔廟改制論皇權與祭祀禮儀 ("Between Orthodoxy and Legitimacy: Reflections from the Debates on Ritual Reforms of the Confucian Temple in 1530"), in 優入聖域: 權力: 信仰與正當性 (*"Entering the Master's Sanctuary": Power, Belief, and Legitimacy in Traditional China*). 台北: 允晨出版社. Taibei: Yunchen chubanshe.

Huang Meiying 黃美英著
1993a   馬祖香火與神威的建構 ("Mazu's Incense and the Construction of the Authority of the Spirits"), in 歷史月刊 (*Journal of History*), 第四卷, 第六十三期.
1993b   祈福與還愿: 進香過程的體驗 ("Praying for Blessings and Repaying Granted Wishes: The Experience of Pilgrimage"), in 歷史月刊 (*Journal of History*), 第四卷, 第六十三期.

Huang Zhangjian 黃彰健著
1974   康有為戊戌真奏議 (附康有為偽戊戌奏稿) (*Authentic Memorials by Kang Youwei in 1898. Appendix: Spurious Memorial Drafts*). 台北: 中央研究院歷史語言研究所. Taibei: Institute of History and Philosophy, Academia Sinica.

Jiang Canteng 江燦騰著
2001   台灣佛教文化發展史: 日據時期 (*The Development of Taiwanese Buddhist Culture during the Japanese Colonial Period: A History*). 台北: 南天書局. Taibei: Nantian shuju.

Jiang Jieshi (Chiang Kai-shek) 蔣介石著
1976   新生活運動七周年紀念訓詞 ("Exhortation Speech Commemorating the Seventh Anniversary of the New Life Movement"), in 革命文獻 (*Revolutionary Documents*), 第六十八輯, 新生活運動史料 (*Historical Materials on New Life Movement*). 中國國民黨中央委員會黨史委員會主編 Com-

mittee on Party History, CC, Guomindang, ed. 台北: 中央文物供應社. Taibei: Zhongyang wenwu gongyingshe.

Jin Yufu et al., comps. 金毓黻等編
1987　宣統政紀 (*Historical Chronicle of Emperor Xuantong*). 北京: 中華書局. Beijing: Zhonghua Book Co. (Orig. pub. 1934.)

Kungang et al. 崑岡等著
1995　欽定大清會典 ("Imperial-Commissioned Collection of Statutes of the Great Qing"), in 續修四庫全書 (*Sequel Compendium in Four Treasuries*), 第七百九十四卷. 上海: 古籍出版社. Shanghai: Guji chuban she. (Orig. pub. 1899.)

Li Haozhong 李濠仲著
1999　蔡英文没被媽祖比下去 ("Cai Yingwen Is Not Defeated by Mazu"), on TVBS (a subsidary of Television Broadcasts Limited of Hong Kong) 月刊, 第一百三十七期.

Li Hongzhi 李洪志著
1994　轉法輪 (*Zhuan Falun*, or *Rotating the Wheel of the Law*),at http://www.falundafa.org/book/chibig5/zfl.htm, translation at http://falundafa.org/book/eng/zfl_new.html.
1998　法輪佛法在瑞士法會上講法 ("Teaching the Fa at the Conference in Switzerland"), at http://www.falundafa.org/book/chigb/swiss.htm, translation at http://falundafa.org/book/eng/switzerland1998.htm.
2001　不政治 ("No Politics"), at http://www.falundafa.org/book/chigb/jjyz2_28.htm, English translation at http://www.falundafa.org/book/eng/jjyz2_29.htm

Li Meng, Zhou Feizhou, and Li Kang 李猛, 周飛舟和李康著
1996　單位: 制度化組織的內部機制 ("Work-Unit: Inner Mechanism of an Institutionalized Organization"), in 中國社會科學季刊 (*Chinese Social Sciences Quarterly*), 第十六卷.

Li Shiwei 李世偉著
1996　中共與民間文化 (1935–1948) (*The CCP and Popular Culture, 1935–1948*). 台北: 知書坊出版社. Taibei: Zhishufang chubanshe.

Li Shiyu 李世瑜著
1975　現在華北秘密宗教 (*Secret Religions in Contemporary North China*). 台北: 古亭書屋. Taibei: Guting shuwu. (Orig. pub. 1948.)

Li Shizhong 李世眾著
2005　清中葉的宗族, 政府與地方治理 ("Lineage, State, and Local Governance in the Mid-Qing Dynasty"), in 歷史教學問題 (*Problems in the Teaching of History*), 第六期.

Li Xiuzhu 李秀珠著
1996　衛星電視的節目規劃: 從文化接近性談起 ("The Planning of Satellite Television Programming: An Examination of Cul-

tural Proximity"), in 廣播與電視 (*Broadcasting and Television*), 第二卷, 第三期.

Li Zhitian 黎志添著

2002 民國時期廣州市南嘸道館的歷史考究 ("A Historical Study of the Vernacular Daoist Halls in Guangzhou during the Republican Period"), in 中央研究院近代史研究所集刊 (*Bulletin of the Institute of Modern History, Academia Sinica*), 第三十七卷.

Liang Qichao 梁啟超著

1981a 中國歷史研究法 ("Methodology for Studying Chinese History"), in 飲冰室全集 (*The Complete Collected Works of the Ice-Sipping Studio*). 台北: 文華圖書公司. Taibei: Cultural Library Co.

1981b 輪宗教家與哲學家之長短得失 ("On the Strengths and Weaknesses of Religionists and Philosophers"), in 飲冰室全集 (*The Complete Collected Works of the Ice-Sipping Studio*). 台北: 文華圖書公司. Taibei: Cultural Library Co.

Liang Zhiping 梁治平著

2003 中國法律史上的民間法——兼論中國古代法律的多元格局 ("Folk Laws in Chinese Legal History: The Pluralism of Law in Ancient China"), in 在邊緣處思考 (*Thinking at the Edge*). 北京: 法律出版社. Beijing: Law Press.

Lin Benxuan 林本炫著

1989 一貫道與政府之關係—從查禁到合法化 ("Yiguandao and the State: From Banning to Legalization"), in 宗教與文化 (*Religion and Culture*). 鄭志明編 Zheng Zhiming, ed. 台北: 台灣學生書局. Taibei: Taiwan xuesheng shuju.

Lin Hongren and Li Yonglie 林鴻仁和李永烈主編

2000 大甲媽祖遶境進香 (*Dajia Mazu's Pilgrimage Tour*). 台中市: 台中縣文化局. Taizhong: Taizhong County Bureau of Culture.

Lin Meirong 林美容著

1989 由祭祀圈到信仰圈: 台灣民間社會的地域構成與發展 ("From Ritual Circle to Circle of Belief: The Construction and Development of Folk Society in Taiwan"), in 人類學與台灣 (*Anthropology and Taiwan*). 台北: 稻鄉出版社. Taibei: Daoxiang chubanshe.

Lin Wenhao 林文豪著

1990 媽祖與中華文化 (*Mazu and Chinese Culture*). 福建湄州: 湄州日報社. Meizhou, Fujian: Meizhou ribao chubanshe.

Linxia Hui Autonomous Prefectural Basic Situation Committee, ed. 臨夏回族自治州編

1986 臨夏回族自治州概況 (*Linxia Hui Autonomous Prefectural Basic Situation*). 蘭州: 甘肅民族出版社. Lanzhou: Gausu minzu chubanshe.

Liu Huanyue 劉還月著
1991 政治控制何時休? 從宗教法的制定談台灣寺廟文化 ("When
Will Political Control Cease? A Discussion of the Culture of
Taiwan Temple Cults and the Promulgation of the Law on
Religion"), in 台灣的歲節祭祀 (*Religious Festivals and Sacri-
fices in Taiwan*). 台北: 自立晚報社. Taibei: Zili wanbaoshe.

Liu Jinzao 劉錦藻編
1935 清朝續文獻通考 (*The Qing Dynasty's Sequel to Comprehensive Survey of Literary Remains*). 上海: 商務印書館. Shanghai: Shangwu yinshuguan. (Orig. pub. 1915.)

Liu Kunyi 劉坤一著
1870 文廟上丁禮樂備考 (*Investigation into the Rites and Music at
the Temple of Civil Culture on the First Ding Days*). 香港: 乙
藜齋. Hongkong: Yili zhai.

Liu Ping 劉平著
2002 中國歷史上農民叛亂的文化動力 ("Cultural Forces behind
Peasant Insurrections in Chinese History"), in 論邪教 (*On
Evil Cults*). 南寧: 廣西人民出版社. Nanning: Guangxi People's Publishing Co.

Liu Xianchen 劉現成著
1999 台灣影視產業的概況 ("An Overview of the Taiwan Television
Industry"), in 亞太媒介圖誌: 無線/有線暨衛星電視的形構
(*Geographical Survey of Asia-Pacific Media: The Structural
Formation of Network, Cable, and Satellite Television*). 李天
擇, 劉現成編著. Li Tianze and Liu Xianchen, eds. 台北: 亞太
圖書公司. Taibei: Yatai tushu gongsi.

Liu Xiangyu 劉翔宇著
2002 也談明清時期秘密教門的反叛活動 ("On the Rebellions of
Secret Sects during the Ming and Qing Periods"), in 再論邪
教 (*More on Evil Cults*). 南寧: 廣西人民出版社. Nanning:
Guangxi People's Publishing Co.

Lu Chunben 陸純本著
2001 對邪教認定中涉及到的幾個問題的探討與淺析 ("Discussion
on a Few Issues Arising from the Identification of Evil
Cults"), in 論邪教 (*On Evil Cults*). 南寧: 廣西人民出版社.
Nanning: Guangxi People's Publishing Co.

Lu Zhongwei 陸仲偉著
2002 民國會道門 ("Sects and Secret Societies of the Republican
Era"), in 中國秘密社會 (*Secret Societies in China*), 第五卷. 福
州: 福建人民出版社. Fuzhou: Fujian People's Publishing Co.

Lü Boyou 呂伯攸著
1936 破除迷信 (*Destroying Superstition*). 上海: 中華書局. Shanghai: Zhonghua Book Co.

Luo Weihong 羅偉虹著

2002 世界邪教與反邪教研究 (*Studies on World Cults and Anti-Cult Movements*). 北京: 宗教文化出版社. Beijing: Zongjiao wenhua chubanshe.

Luo Zhufeng, ed. 羅竹風主編

1987 中國社會主義時期的宗教問題 (*The Religious Question in China in the Socialist Period*). 上海: 上海社會科學院. Shanghai: Shanghai Academy of Social Sciences.

2001 漢語大詞典 (第十卷) (*The Great Chinese Dictionary, Vol. 10*). 上海: 漢語大詞典出版社. Shanghai: Hanyu dacidian chubanshe.

Ma Dazheng 馬大正著

2003 國家利益高於一切: 新疆穩定問題的觀察與思考 (*The State Takes Precedence: Research and Analysis on the Xinjang Stability Problem*). 烏魯木齊: 新疆人民出版社. Urumqi: Xinjiang People's Publishing Co.

Ma Tong 馬通

1983 *Zhongguo Yisilan jiaopai yu Menhuan zhidu shilue* 中國伊斯蘭教派與門宦制度史略 (*A History of Muslim Factions and the Menhuan System in China*). Yinchuan: Ningxia People's Publishing Society.

Ma Xisha and Han Bingfang 馬西沙和韓秉方著

1992 中國民間宗教史 (*The History of Chinese Popular Sectarianism*). 上海: 上海人民出版社. Shanghai: Shanghai People's Publishing Co.

Man Yong 滿永著

2005 土地改革與建國初鄉村政權的合法化建構 ("Land Reform and the Legitimation of the Political Power in Rural Areas in the Early Years of the People's Republic of China"), in 二十一世紀(網絡版) (*Twenty-First Century, Online*), 第三十七期. http://www.cuhk.edu.hk/ics/21c/supplem/essay/0412013.htm.

Manzhouguo Morality Society Editorial Department 滿洲國道德會編輯科編

1936 第三屆滿洲國道德會道德講習語錄 (*Oral Records of Morality Seminars of the Third Manzhouguo Morality Society*). Xinjing: 滿洲國道德會編輯科. Xinjing: Manzhouguo Daodehui bianjike.

Mao Zedong (Mao Tse-tung) 毛澤東著

1965 湖南農民運動考察報告 ("Report on an Investigation of the Peasants' Movement in Hunan"), in 毛澤東選集 (*Selected Works of Mao Zedong*), 第一卷. 北京: 人民出版社. Beijing: People's Publishing Co. (Orig. pub. 1927.)

Minsheng bao 民生報. Nanjing.

Mori Noriko 森紀子著

2004 日本和中國近代化過程中國際問題 ("International Affairs in the Modernization of Japan and China"). Paper presented at

近代中國的知識建構, 1600–1949 ("Conference on Constructing Modern Knowledge in China, 1600–1949"), Academia Sinica, November 25–26.

Nanjing Difangzhi Biangua Weiyuanhui, ed. 南京市地方志编纂委员会编 (Nanjing Local Gazeteer Editorial Committee)

1996 南京房地產志 (*Nanjing Gazetteer of Land and Real Property*). 南京: 南京出版社. Nanjing: Nanjing Publishing House.

Nanjing Shizhengfu Mishuchu, ed. 南京市政府秘書處編

1933 新南京 (*New Nanjing*). 南京: 南京市政府秘書處. Nanjing: Secretariat of Nanjing Special Municipality.

Nanjing Tebie Shizhengfu Mishuchu Bianyi Gubian, ed. 南京特別市政府秘書處編譯股編

1930 南京特別市政府工作總報告 (*Work Report of the Nanjing Special Municipality Government*). 南京: 南京特別市秘書處. Nanjing: Secretariat of Nanjing Special Municipality.

Nanjing Wanbao 南京晚報. Nanjing.

Neizheng Gongbao 內政公報. 內政部. Neizhengbu (Ministry of Interior), Nanjing.

Ong Shijie 翁仕杰著

2000 媽祖非要回湄洲進香不可嗎? ("Is It Necessary for Mazu to Go back to Meizhou?"), in 中國時報 (*China Times*), 六月二十七日.

Pan Zongding 潘宗鼎著

1929 金陵歲時記 (*Record of Yearly Customs in Jinling*). Nanjing: n.p.

Pearson, Faye 裴斐著

2001 論邪教 ("On Evil Cults"), in 論邪教 (*On Evil Cults*). 南寧: 廣西人民出版社. Nanning: Guangxi People's Publishing Co.

Qian Xue, pseud. 謙學著

1980 從宗教與鴉片談起 ("A Discussion of Religion and Opium"), in 宗教 (*Religion*), 第一期.

Qin Baoqi and Tan Songlin 秦寶琦和譚松林著

2002 總論 (*General Discussion*). 中國秘密社會 (*Secret Societies in China*), 第一卷. 福州: 福建人民出版社. Fuzhou: Fujian People's Publishing Co.

Qing Xitai, ed. 卿希泰編

1995 中國道教史 (*A History of Chinese Daoism*), 第四卷. 成都: 四川人民出版社. Chengdu: Sichuan People's Publishing Co.

Qiu Shusen, ed. 邱樹森主編

1992 中國回族大詞典 (*Great Encyclopedia of China's Hui Nationality*). 南京: 江蘇古籍出版社. Nanjing: Jiangsu guji chubanshe.

Qu Haiyuan 瞿海源著

1997 台灣宗教變遷的社會政治分析 (*The Political and Social Analysis of Religious Transformation in Taiwan*). 台北: 桂冠圖書股份有限公司. Taibei: Guiguan tushu gufen youxian gongsi.

1998   台灣社會變遷基本調查: 第三期第三次調查執行報告 (*Taiwan Social Change Survey: Reports of the Survey of the Third Year of the Third Circle*). 台北: 中央研究院社會學研究所. Taibei: Academia Sinica, Institute of Sociology.

Qu Xingui and Tang Liangyan, comps. 璩鑫圭和唐良炎編

1990   中國近代教育史資料彙編 (*Collected Corpus of Documents in China's Recent History of Education*). 上海: 上海教育出版社. Shanghai: Shanghai Education Publishing House.

Ruo Yu 若渝著

2000   2000 年台灣地區電視收視行為大調查(上) ("The Great Survey of Taiwan Television Viewing Behavior in 2000," Part 1), in 廣電人月刊 (*The Broadcaster*), 第六十八期, no. 68.

Sawada, Mizuho 澤田瑞穗著

1982   清末の祀典問題 ("The Question of State Cult in the Late Qing"), in 中国の民間信仰 (*Chinese Folk Religion*). Tokyo: Kōsakusha Publishing Co.

Shahidi, Burhan 沙希迪 · 包爾汗著

1984   新疆五十年 (*Xinjiang: Fify Years*). 北京: 文史資料出版社. Beijing: Wenshi ziliao chubanshe.

Shao Yong 邵雍著

1997   中國會道門 (*Chinese Sects and Secret Societies*). 上海: 上海人民出版社. Shanghai: Shanghai People's Publishing Co.

Shehui Wenti Yanjiu Congshu Weiyuanhui, ed. 社會問題研究叢書委員會編 (Committee for the Series on Social Problems Research)

2001   論邪教 (*On Evil Cults*). 南寧: 廣西人民出版社. Nanning: Guangxi People's Publishing Co.

2002   再論邪教 (*More on Evil Cults*). 南寧: 廣西人民出版社. Nanning: Guangxi People's Publishing Co.

Shishi Xinbao 時事新報. Shanghai.

Shu Xincheng 舒新城著

1945   我和教育 (*Education and I*). 北京: 中華書局. Beijing: Zhonghua Book Co.

Suemitsu, Takayoshi 末光高義著

1932   支那の秘密結社と慈善結社 (*China's Secret Societies and Charitable Societies*). 大連: 滿州評論社. Dalian: Manshu hyoronsha.

Su'erna et al., comps. 素爾訥等編

1968   欽定學政全書 (*Imperial-Commissioned Compendium of School Administration*). 台北: 文海出版社. Taibei: Wenhai chubanshe. (Orig. pub. 1774.)

Sun Shangyang 孫尚揚著

2001   宗教社會學 (*The Sociology of Religion*). 北京: 北京大學出版社. Beijing: Peking University Press.

Sun Zuomin 孫祚民著

1956 中國農民戰爭問題探索 (*Investigations on China's Peasant Wars*). 上海: 新知識出版社. Shanghai: Xin zhishi chubanshe.

Takizawa Toshiro 瀧澤俊亮

1937 宗教調查史料第三卷, 民間信仰調查報告書 (*Materials from the Survey of Religions, Volume 3: Report on the Survey of Popular Beliefs*). 新京: 民生部社会司 Shinkyo: Minseibu Shakai-shi.

Tong Enzheng 童恩正著

1989 摩尔根的模式與中國的原始社會的研究 ("The Morgan Model and the Study of Primitive Chinese Society"), in 文化人類學 (*Cultural Anthropology*). 上海: 上海人民出版社. Shanghai: Shanghai People's Publishing Co.

Tshe dbang rin chen

1995 *Se ra theg chen gling (A Brief History of Sera Monastery)*. Lhasa: Mi rigs dpe skrun khang.

Wang Jianchuan 王見川著

1995 同善社早期歷史初探 (1912–1945) ("A Preliminary Survey of the Early History of the Tongshan she, 1912–1945"), in 民間宗教 (*Popular Religion*), 第一卷.

Wang Leiquan 王雷泉著

1994 對中國近代兩次廟產興學風潮的反思 ("Reflection on the Two Waves of the 'Building Schools with Temple Property' in Modern China"), in 法音 (*The Voice of Dharma*), 第十二期.

Wang Lixiong. *See under* Sources in English and Other Western Languages.

Wang Mingming 王銘銘著

1997 村落視野中的文化與權力: 閩台三村五論 (*Culture and Power through Village Lenses: Five Discussions on Three Villages in Fujian and Taiwan*). 北京: 三聯書店. Beijing: San Lian Publishing Co.

2004 裂縫間的橋: 解讀摩尔根 《古代社會》 (*The Bridge Across the Chasm: Deconstructing Morgan's "Ancient Society"*). 濟南: 山東人民出版社. Jinan: Shandong People's Publishing Co.

Wang Mingyi 王銘義著

1999 媽祖大? 還是主委大? 卜杯事件人神交戰 ("Is Mazu Bigger, or the Mainland Affairs Committee? Human and Deity Battle It Out in the *Buabui* Incident"), in 中國時報 (*China Times*), 六月九日.

Wang Shunmin 王順民著

1994 宗教福利服務指初步考察: 以佛光山, 法鼓山, 慈濟 為例 ("Preliminary Investigation of the Welfare Services of Religion: Case Studies of Foguangshan, Fagushan, and Ciji"), in 思與研 (*Thought and Investigation*), vol. 32, no. 3.

Wang Weifan 汪維藩著
1986　　近年來我國學術界宗教研究情況簡介 ("Introducing the Religious Studies Situation in China's Academic Circles in Recent Years"), in 宗教 (Religion), 第一期.

Wang Yunjun 王云駿著
2001　　民國南京城市社會管理 (Urban Social Management in Republican Nanjing). 南京: 江蘇古籍出版社. Nanjing: Jiangsu guji chubanshe.

Wu Hao, ed. 吳昊编
1993　　中國當代氣功全書 (Compendium of Qigong in Contemporary China). 北京: 人民體育出版社. Beijing: Renmin tiyu chubanshe.

Xie Chongguang and Bai Wengu 謝重光和白文固著
1990　　中國僧官制度史 (History of the Chinese Sangha Officials System). 西寧: 青海人民出版社. Xining: Qinghai People's Publishing Co.

Xu Rulei 徐如雷著
1985　　宗教是社會主義社會的上層建築——讀《宗教概論》有感 ("Religion Belongs to the Superstructure of Socialist Society—a Reaction to Introduction to Religion"), in 宗教 (Religion), 第二期.

Xu Shuhui 許淑惠著
2000　　來去! 陪媽祖Go To湄洲! 全台信徒進香總動員 ("Let's Go! Let's Go with Mazu to Meizhou! All of Taiwan's Faithful Mobilize to Go on Pilgrimage"), on TVBS (a subsidiary of Television Broadcasts Limited of Hong Kong) 月刊, 第一百三十七期.

Xu Yucheng 徐玉成著
1997　　宗教政策知識法規問答 (Questions and Answers on Religious Policies). 北京: 中國社會科學出版社. Beijing: China Social Science Press.

Xuebu 學部著 (Board of Learning)
1906a　　學部奏請宣示教育宗旨摺 ("Board of Learning's Request for Promulgating Educational Guidelines"), in 近代中國教育史資料: 清末篇 (Documents in the Recent History of Chinese Education: The Late Qing). 多賀秋五郎編 Taga Akigoro, comp. 台北: 文海出版社. Taibei: Wenhai chubanshe, 1976.
1906b　　本部章奏: 代奏刑部主事姚大榮呈請升孔廟為大祀摺 ("Memorials and Reports of the Board: On Behalf of Yao Darong, Major Clerk, Board of Punishment to Request the Elevation of Confucius Temple to the Grand Sacrifice"), in 學部官報 (Official Post of Board of Learning), 第十一卷. 台北: 故宮博物院. Taibei: Gugong bowuyuan, 1980.

Yang Shengmin and Ding Hong, eds. 楊聖敏和丁宏编
2002　　中國民族志 (The Ethnic Groups of China). 北京: 中央民族大學出版社. Beijing: The Central University for Nationalities Press.

Yao Ying 姚穎著
1936   京話 (*Nanjing Conversation*). 上海 : 人間書屋. Shanghai:
            Renjian shuwu.
Ye Chucang and Liu Yizheng, eds. 葉楚滄和柳詒徵編
1935   首都志 (*Gazetteer of the Capital*). Nanjing: Zhengzhong shuju;
            reprint, 南京: 南京市地方誌編纂委員會辦公室. Nanjing: Nan-
            jing shi difang zhi bianzuan weiyuanhui bangongshi, 1985.
Zhang Boxi, Rong Qing, and Zhang Zhidong 張百熙, 榮慶和張之洞著
1904a   學務綱要 ("Outline of Educational Principles"), in 近代中國教
            育史資料: 清末篇 (*Documents in the Recent History of Chi-
            nese Education: The Late Qing*). 多賀秋五郎編 Taga Akigorō,
            comp. 台北: 文海出版社. Taibei: Wenhai chubanshe, 1976.
1904b   奏定各學堂管理通則 (General Rules for School Administra-
            tion), in 近代中國教育史資料: 清末篇 (*Documents in the
            Recent History of Chinese Education: the Late Qing*). 多賀秋
            五郎編 Taga Akigorō, comp. 台北: 文海出版社. Taibei: Wen-
            hai chubanshe, 1976.
Zhang Jingru and Bian Xingying, eds. 張靜如和卞杏英編
1993   國民政府統治時期中國社會之變遷 (*Social Change in China
            under the Nationalist Government*). 北京: 中國人民大學出版
            社. Beijing: China Renmin University Press.
Zhang Juling 張巨齡著
1997/1998   中國回教俱進會初創記評 ("Notes on the Foundation of the
            Muslim Association for Mutual Progress"), in 回族研究 (*Hui
            Studies*), 第二十八卷至第三十卷.
Zhang Li 張莉著
2002   乾隆九年龍華會集體自殺案始末 ("The Case of the Collective
            Suicide of the Dragon Flower Assembly in the Ninth year of
            Emperor Qianlong's Reign"), in 再論邪教 (*More on Evil
            Cults*). 南寧: 廣西人民出版社. Nanning: Guangxi People's
            Publishing Co.
Zhang Weida and Dong Xiaohan 張偉達和董霄漢著
1999   邪教與宗教 ("Evil Cults and Religion"), in "法輪功"與邪教
            (*Falungong and Evil Cults*). 北京: 宗教文化出版社. Beijing:
            Zongjiao wenhua chubanshe.
Zhang Wen 張文著
2005   社區慈善: 兩宋民間慈善活動的空間結構 ("Community Cha-
            rities: The Structure of Spaces for Civic Charitable Activities
            in the Northern and Southern Song Dynasties"), in 中國社會
            經濟史研究 (*Studies in Chinese Social and Economic His-
            tory*), 第四期.
Zhang Xinying 張新鷹著
1989   中國宗教學學會第三次會議在北京舉行 ("Third Conference
            of the China Religious Studies Association Convened in Bei-
            jing"), in 世界宗教研究 (*Studies in World Religions*), 第二期.

Zhang Xun 張珣著

2003 儀式與社會: 大甲媽祖祭祀圈之擴展與變遷 ("Ritual and Society: The Expansion and Transformation of Dajia Mazu's Ritual Circle"), in 媽祖信仰的發展與變遷 (*The Development and Change of Mazu Religion*). 林美容, 張珣編 Lin Meirong and Chang Xun, eds. 台北: 台湾宗教协会. Taipei: Taiwan Association of Religious Studies.

Zhang Zhidong 張之洞著

1962 籌定學堂規模次第興辦摺 ("Memorial on Planning the Scale of Schools and Its Procedures"), in 張文襄公全集 (*Complete Works of Zhang Zhidong*). 第五十七卷. 台北: 文海出版社. Taibei: Wenhai chubanshe. (Orig. pub. 1902.)

Zhang Zhidong and Liu Kunyi 張之洞和劉坤一著

1962 變通政治人才為先遵旨籌議摺 ("Memorial on Human Talent as the First in Changing the Politics"), in 張文襄公全集 (*Complete Works of Zhang Zhidong*). 第五十二卷. 台北: 文海出版社. Taibei: Wenhai chubanshe. (Orig. pub. 1901.)

Zhao Fusan 趙復三著

1985 宗教, 精神文明, 民族團結 ("Religion, Spiritual Civilization, Ethnic Cooperation"), in 天風 (*Heavenly Wind*), 第七期.

1986 怎樣認識宗教的本質 ("A Reconsideration of Religion"), in 中國社會科學 (*Social Sciences in China*), 第三期. Translation in *China Study Project Journal*, vol. 2, no. 2, 1987.

Zhao Zhi 趙志著

2002 談談明清時期民間秘密教門的反社會行為 ("On the Anti-Social Behavior of Popular Secret Sects in the Ming and Qing periods"), in 再論邪教 (*More on Evil Cults*). 南寧: 廣西人民出版社. Nanning: Guangxi People's Publishing Co.

Zheng Yonghua 鄭永華著

2003 清代秘密教門治理 (*Government Handling of Secret Sects in the Qing Dynasty*). 福州: 福建人民出版社. Fuzhou: Fujian People's Publishing Co.

Zheng Yonghua and Ouyang Enliang 鄭永華和歐陽恩良著

2001 清嘉慶朝治理教門對策述略 ("Policy toward Sects of the Jia-qing Reign in the Qing Dynasty"), in 論邪教 (*On Evil Cults*). 社會問題研究叢書委員會編 Shehui Wenti Yanjiu Congshu Weiyuanhui, ed. 南寧: 廣西人民出版社. Nanning: Guangxi People's Publishing Co.

Zheng Zhenman 鄭振滿著

1995 神廟祭典與社區發展模式: 浦田江口平原的列証 ("Deity Temple Rituals and the Model of Community Development: The Case of the Jiangkou Plain in Putian, Fujian"), in 史林 (*Forest of History*), 第一期.

Zhongguo Di'er Lishi Dang'an Guan, ed. 中國第二歷史檔案館 (Second Historical Archives of China)

1998   中華民國史檔案資料匯編: 第三輯 (*Compendium of Historical Documents of Republic of China, Volume 3*). 南京: 江蘇古籍出版社 Nanjing: Jiangsu guji chubanshe.

Zhongguo Di'er Lishi Dang'an Guan Cang 中國第二歷史檔案館藏 (Second Historical Archives of China)

1929   南京市政府工作報告 ("Work Report of Nanjing Municipality Government") 行政院檔案 (*Archives of the Executive Yuan*), 2:137.

1931   孔道總會會長陳桂蓀等上行政院呈文 ("Petition from Chen Guisun of the Confucian Society General Branch, to the Executive Yuan"), in 行政院檔案 (*Archives of the Executive Yuan*), 2:1081, July 15.

1932a   江蘇省溧陽縣風俗調查表 ("Survey of Local Customs in Liyang County, Jiangsu Province"), in 內政部檔案 (*Archives of the Ministry of Interior*), 12(6):18262.

1932b   江蘇省南匯縣風俗調查表 ("Survey of Local Customs in Nanhui County, Jiangsu Province"), in 內政部檔案 (*Archives of the Ministry of Interior*), 12(6):18263.

1932c   江蘇省如皋縣風俗調查表 ("Survey of Local Customs in Rugao County, Jiangsu Province"), in 內政部檔案 (*Archives of the Ministry of Interior*), 12(6):18264.

1936   道院總院致女道德總社函 ("Communication to the Women's Morality Society of the Daoyuan"), in 世界紅卍字會檔案 (*Archives of the World Red Swastika Society*), 257:65, July.

Zhongguo Guomindang Xuanchuanbu 中國國民黨宣傳部

1928   首都各節慶祝國慶紀念暨全國同一大會特刊 (*Special Publication on the Mass Rally of All the Capital in Celebration of National Day and the Unification of the Country*). 南京: 中國國民黨宣傳部. Nanjing: Zhongguo Guomindang xuanchuanbu.

Zhongguo Guomindang Zhongyang Weiyuanhui Dangshi Weiyuanhui Cang 中國國民黨中央委員會黨史委員會藏 (Archives of the Historical Commission, Central Committee of the Chinese Nationalist Party [GMD], Taibei)

1930a   十八年度中央宣傳部部務一覽 ("Overview of Department Affairs, Central Department of Propaganda, 1929") 436:187.72. 中國國民黨中央執行委員會宣傳部編 Department of Propaganda, Central Executive Committee, Chinese Nationalist Party, ed.

1930b   中國國民黨中央委員會宣傳部十一月份工作報告 ("November Work Report of the Department of Propaganda, Central Executive Committee, Chinese Nationalist Party") 436:199.11. 中國國民黨中央執行委員會宣傳部編 Department of Propaganda, Central Executive Committee, Chinese Nationalist Party, ed.

Zhongguo Guomindang Zhongyang Xuanchuanbu 中國國民黨中央宣傳部
1930   實行國曆 ("Instituting the National Calendar"). 浙江: 中國國
        民黨江蘇省黨務整理委員會宣傳部. Zhejiang: Zhongguo
        Guomindang Jiangsusheng dangwu zhengli weiyuanhui
        xuanchuanbu.

Zhongguo Guomindang Zhongyang Zhixing Weiyuanhui Xuanchuanbu, ed.
中國國民黨中央執行委員會宣傳部編 (Department of Propaganda, Central Executive Committee, Chinese Nationalist Party)
1929   破除迷信宣傳大綱 (*Propaganda Outline for Destroying
        Superstition*). 南京: 中國國民黨中央執行委員會宣傳部. Nanjing: Zhongguo Guomindang zhongyang zhixing weiyuanhui
        xuanchuan bu.
1930   中國國民黨與中國農民 (*The Chinese Nationalist Party and
        the Chinese Farmer*). Nanjing: Zhongguo Guomindang
        zhongyang zhixing weiyuanhui xuanchuan bu.

Zhongguo Kexueyuan Xinli Yanjiuso he Fan Xiejiao Yanjiu Ketizu, eds. 中國
科學院心理研究所和"反邪教" 研究課題組編 (Institute of Psychology of
the Chinese Academy of Sciences and the "Anti-Cult" Research Group)
2002   "法輪功"現象的心理學分析 (*Psychological Analysis of the
        "Falungong" Phenomenon*). 北京: 科學出版社. Beijing: Kexue
        chubanshe.

Zhonghua Mingguo Neizhengbu Tongji Bangongshi 中華民國內政部統計辦
公室 (Republic of China Ministry of the Interior, Office of Statistics)
2008   民政1-03: 宗教務概況 ("Civil Affairs 1:03: Overview of Religious Affairs"), in 中華民國內政部統計年報 (*Statistical
        Yearbook of the Ministry of the Interior of the Republic of
        China*). http://www.moi.gov.tw/stat/ (accessed 5/14/08).

Zhonghua Renmin Gongheguo Guowuyuan中華人民共和國國務院
1980   關于落實宗教團體房產政策等問題的報告 ("Report on Implementing the Policy on the Property of Religious Organizations and Related Questions"), at www.sara.gov.cn/GB/zcfg/
        zc/65a06a2d-2658-11da-8858-93180aflbb1a.html (accessed
        April 15, 2008).

Zhongyang Ribao 中央日報. Nanjing.

Zhu Shoupeng, comp. 朱壽彭編
1958   光緒朝東華錄 (*Chronicle Records of the Guangxu Reign*). 北
        京: 中華書局. Beijing: Zhonghua Book Co. (Orig. pub. 1909.)

Zhu Xie 朱偰著
1935   金陵古蹟圖考 (*Illustrated Study of Nanjing's Historical Relics*). 上海: 商務印書館. Shanghai: Shangwu yinshuguan.

Zong Hairen 宗海仁
2001   朱鎔基在一九九九 (*Zhu Rongji in 1999*). Carle Place, NY:
        Mirror Books. English Translation in *Chinese Law and Government*, vol. 35, no. 1 (January/February 2002). Andrew J.
        Nathan ed., Dorothy King, trans.

SOURCES IN ENGLISH AND
OTHER WESTERN LANGUAGES

Abe, Hiroshi
1987   "Borrowing from Japan: China's First Modern Educational
            System," in *China's Education and the Industrialized World:
            Studies in Cultural Transfer.* Ruth Hayhoe and Marianne
            Bastid, eds. Armonk, NY: M. E. Sharpe, Inc.
Ackerly, John
1991   "Hu Yaobang to Hu Jintao: Persecution of Tibetan Buddhism
            in the 1980s," in *The Anguish of Tibet.* Petra K. Kelly et al.,
            eds. Berkeley: Parallax Press.
Aikman, David
2003   *Jesus in Beijing: How Christianity Is Transforming China
            and Changing the Global Balance of Power.* Washington, DC:
            Regnery Publishing.
Ajami, Fouad
2001   "What the Muslim World Is Watching," in *New York Times,*
            November 18.
Allès, Elisabeth
2002   "A propos de l'Islam en Chine: Provocations antireligieuses et
            attitudes anticléricales du xix^c siècle à nos jours," in *Extrême
            Orient Extrême Occident,* vol. 24.
Allio, Fiorella
2003   "Spatial Organization in a Ritual Context: A Preliminary
            Analysis of the *Koah-hiu* Processional System of the Tainan
            County Region and Its Social Significance." Taibei: Institute
            of Ethnology, Academia Sinica.
Amity News Service
1993   "Interview with Shen Yifan," in *China Study Journal,* vol. 8,
            no. 3.
1994   "Tian Feng Interviews Bishop K. H. Ting on the Registration
            Issue," in *China Study Journal,* vol. 9, no. 2.
2000a   "Head of National Religious Affairs Bureau Addresses CC/
            TSPM Plenum," Amity News Service release 2000.11/12.2.
            http://www.amitynewsservice.org/page.php?page=750,
            accessed October 21, 2005.
2000b   "Shanghai at the Forefront of Implementing Religious Pol-
            icy," Amity News Service release 2000.5/6.1. http://www.
            amitynewsservice.org/page.php?page=784, accessed October
            21, 2005.
2002   "Chinese Government Reassesses Religion," Amity News
            Service release 2002.1/2.1. http://www.amitynewsservice.org/
            page.php?page=684, accessed October 21, 2005.

2003 "The Adaptation of Religion To Socialist Society," Amity News Service release 2003.7/8.2. http://www.amitynewsservice .org/page.php?page=338&pageno=2, accessed October 19, 2005. Translated from *Tian Feng*, May 2003.

Amnesty International

1996 "At Least 1,000 People Executed in 'Strike Hard' Campaign against Crime," July. http://web.amnesty.org/802568F7005 C4453/0/EE80B1B0DFFE2C748025690000692CE5.

1999 "People's Republic of China. Gross Violations of Human Rights in the Xinjiang Uighur Autonomous Region" London: Amnesty International, April 1. http://web.amnesty.org/ library/index/ENGASA170181999.

2002 "People's Republic of China: China's Anti-Terrorism Legislation and Repression in the Xinjiang Uighur Autonomous Region" London: Amnesty International, March. http://web .amnesty.org/library/index/ENGASA170472002, accessed 1 December 1, 2003.

2003 "USA Uyghurs held in Guantánamo Bay," Urgent Action Bulletin 356/03, AMR 51/147/2003, December 4, at http://www .amnesty.org/en/library/asset/AMR51/147/2003/en/ dom-AMR 511472003en.pdf.

Anagnost, Ann

1994 "The Politics of Ritual Displacement," in *Asian Visions of Authority: Religion and the Modern States of East and Southeast Asia.* Charles Keyes, Laurell Kendall, and Helen Hardacre, eds. Honolulu: University of Hawai'i Press.

Anderson, Benedict

1991 *Imagined Communities: Reflections on the Origin and Spread of Nationalism.* London: Verso Press.

Ang, Ien

1996 *Living Room Wars: Rethinking Media Audiences for a Postmodern World.* London: Routledge.

Anonymous

1997 *Lotus Flower of the Heart: Thirty Years of Tzu-chi Photographs.* Taibei: Still Thoughts Cultural Mission.

2000 *Love Transcends Borders.* Taibei: Still Thoughts Cultural Mission.

2002a "TAR Patriotic Education for Monasteries Propaganda Book No. 2," in *When the Sky Fell to the Earth: The New Crackdown on Buddhism in Tibet.* Washington, DC: International Campaign for Tibet.

2002b "TAR Patriotic Education for Monasteries Propaganda Book No. 4," in *When the Sky Fell to the Earth: The New Crackdown on Buddhism in Tibet.* Washington, DC: International Campaign for Tibet.

2006   "Shaolin Temple, Version 2.0," in *China Focus*, no. 91, July.

N.d.   *Rebirth: Transformations in Tzu-chi*. Taibei: Buddhist Compassion Relief Association.

Antony, Robert J.

1993   "Brotherhoods, Secret Societies, and the Law in Qing-Dynasty China," in *"Secret Societies" Reconsidered: Perspectives on the Social History of Modern South China and Southeast Asia*. David Ownby and Mary Somers Heidhues, eds. Armonk, NY: M. E. Sharpe, Inc.

Appadurai, Arjun

1996   *Modernity at Large: Cultural Dimensions of Globalization*. Minneapolis: University of Minnesota Press.

Asad, Talal

1986   "The Concept of Cultural Translation in British Social Anthropology," in *Writing Culture*. James Clifford and George Marcus, eds. Berkeley: University of California Press.

1993   *Genealogies of Religion: Discipline and Reasons of Power in Christianity and Islam*. Baltimore: Johns Hopkins University Press.

1999   "Religion, Nation-State, Secularism," in *Nation and Religion: Perspectives on Europe and Asia*. Peter van der Veer and Hartmut Lehmann, eds. Princeton, NJ: Princeton University Press.

2003   *Formations of the Secular: Christianity, Islam, Modernity*. Stanford: Stanford University Press.

Atwill, David

2005   *The Chinese Sultanate: Islam, Violence, and the Panthay Rebellion, 1856–1873*. Stanford: Stanford University Press.

Avedon, John F.

1984   *In Exile from the Land of Snows*. New York: Vintage Books.

Babb, Lawrence A., and Susan S. Wadley, eds.

1995   *Media and the Transformation of Religion in South Asia*. Philadelphia: University of Pennsylvania Press.

Bailey, Paul

1990   *Reform the People: Changing Attitudes towards Popular Education in Early 20th Century China*. Edinburgh: Edinburgh University Press.

Barber, Benjamin R.

1995   *Jihad vs. McWorld*. New York: Ballantine Books.

Barfield, Thomas

1989   *The Perilous Frontier: Nomadic Empires and China*. Cambridge: Basil Blackwell.

Barmé, Geremie

1991   "Travelling Heavy: The Intellectual Baggage of the Chinese Diaspora," in *Problems of Communism*, vol. 40, no. 1–2.

Barmé, Geremie, and Linda Jaivin
1992   *New Ghosts, Old Dreams.* New York: Times Books.
Barnett, Robert
2001   "The Chinese Frontiersman and the Winter Worms: Chen
Kuiyuan in the T.A.R., 1992–2000." Paper presented at the
History of Tibet Seminar, St. Andrews University, Scotland,
August 2001. http://www.columbia.edu/itc/ealac/barnett/
pdfs/link29-chenpiece.pdf.
Bastid-Bruguière, Marianne
1988   *Educational Reform in Early Twentieth-Century China.* Paul
Bailey, trans. Ann Arbor: Center for Chinese Studies, Univer-
sity of Michigan.
1997   "Sacrifices d'État et Légitimité à la fin des Qing," in *T'oung
Pao,* vol. 83, no. 1–3.
Bataille, Georges
1989   *The Accursed Share,* vol. 1. Robert Hurley, trans. New York:
Zone Books.
Bays, Daniel H.
1996   "The Growth of Independent Christianity in China,
1900–1937," in *Christianity in China: From the Eighteenth
Century to the Present.* Daniel H. Bays, ed. Stanford: Stanford University Press.
Becquelin, Nicolas
2001   "Xinjiang in the Nineties," in *The China Journal,* no. 44.
Bellér-Hann, Ildíko
2001a   "Making the Oil Fragrant: Dealings with the Supernatural
Among the Uyghurs in Xinjiang," in *Asian Ethnicity,* vol. 2,
no. 1.
2001b   "Temperamental Neighbors: Uighur-Han Relations in Xinjiang, Northwest China," in *Imagined Difference: Hatred and
the Construction of Identity.* G. Schlee, ed. Munster, Ham-
burg, London: LIT Verlag.
Benite, Zvi Ben-Dor
2005   *The Dao of Muhammad: A Cultural History of Muslims in
Late Imperial China.* Harvard East Asian Monographs,
no. 248. Cambridge, MA: Harvard University Asia Center.
Benjamin, Walter
1969   "The Work of Art in the Age of Mechanical Reproduction," in
Illuminations. Harry Zohn, trans. New York: Schocken
Books. (Orig. pub. 1936.)
Benson, Linda
1990   *The Ili Rebellion: The Moslem Challenge to Chinese Authority in Xinjiang, 1944–1949.* Armonk, NY: M. E. Sharpe, Inc.

Berger, Peter L.
1969   *The Sacred Canopy: Elements of a Sociological Theory of Religion.* New York: Doubleday and Company.

Bergère, Marie-Claire
1994   *Sun Yat-sen.* Paris: Fayard.

Bhargava, Rajeev, ed.
1998   *Secularism and Its Critics.* New Delhi: Oxford University Press.

Birnbaum, Raoul
2003   "Buddhist China at the Century's Turn," in *Religion in China Today.* Daniel L. Overmeyer, ed. Cambridge: Cambridge University Press.

Black, Cyril E., Louis Dupree, Elizabeth Endicott-West, Danile C. Matuszewski, Eden Naby, and Arthur N. Waldron
1991   *The Modernization of Inner Asia.* Armonk, NY: M. E. Sharpe, Inc.

Bonhoeffer, Dietrich
1971   *Letters and Papers from Prison.* Eberhard Bethgem, ed. London: SCM Press. First published in English in 1953.

Borokh, Lilia
1972   "Notes on the Early Role of Secret Societies in Sun Yat-sen's Republican Movement," in *Popular Movements and Secret Societies in China, 1840–1950.* Jean Chesneaux, ed. Berkeley: University of California Press.

Borthwick, Sally
1983   *Education and Social Change in China: The Beginnings of the Modern Era.* Stanford: Hoover Institution Press, Stanford University.

Bosco, Joseph, and Puay-Peng Ho
1999   *Temples of the Empress of Heaven.* New Delhi: Oxford University Press.

Bourdieu, Pierre
1971   "Genèse et structure du champ religieux," in *Revue française de sociologie,* XII.
1977   *Outline of a Theory of Practice.* Richard Nice, trans. Cambridge: Cambridge University Press.
1982   *Ce que parler veut dire: L'économie des échanges linguistiques.* Paris: Fayard.
1984   *Distinction: A Social Critique of the Judgement of Taste.* Richard Nice, trans. Cambridge, MA: Harvard University Press.
1993   "Esprits d'État: Genèse et structure du champ bureaucratique," in *Actes de la recherche en sciences sociales,* no. 96–97.

Bovingdon, Gardner
2002   "The Not-So-Silent Majority: Uyghur Resistance to Han Rule in Xinjiang," in *Modern China*, vol. 28, no. 1.

Bretthauer, Berit
2001   "Televangelism: Local and Global Dimensions," in *Religions/ Globalizations*. Dwight N. Hopkins, Lois A. Lorentzen, Eduardo Mendieta, and David Batstone, eds. Durham, NC: Duke University Press.

Brokaw, Cynthia J.
1991   *The Ledgers of Merit and Demerit: Social Change and Moral Order in Late Imperial China*. Princeton, NJ: Princeton University Press.

Brook, Timothy
1993   *Praying for Power: Buddhism and the Formation of Gentry Society in Late-Ming China*. Cambridge, MA: Harvard University Press.

Brown, G. Thompson
1986   *Christianity in the People's Republic of China*. Atlanta: John Knox Press, revised edition.

Brugger, Bill, and David Kelly
1990   *Chinese Marxism in the Post-Mao Era*. Stanford: Stanford University Press.

Bruun, Ole
2003   *Fengshui in China: Geomantic Divination between State Orthodoxy and Popular Religion*. Honolulu: University of Hawai'i Press.

Bush, Richard C.
1970   *Religion in Communist China*. Nashville: Abingdon Press.

Cabezón, José Ignacio
2003   "Buddhism and Science: On the Nature of Dialogue," in *Buddhism and Science: Breaking New Ground*. B. Alan Wallace, ed. New York: Columbia University Press.

Cao, Nanlai
2007   "Christian Entrepreneurs and the Post-Mao State: An Ethnographic Account of Church-State Relations in China's Economic Transition," in *Sociology of Religion*, vol. 68, no. 1.

Carrasco, David
2000   *City of Sacrifice: Violence from the Aztec Empire to the Modern Americas*. Boston: Beacon Press.

Casanova, José
1994   *Public Religions in the Modern World*. Chicago: University of Chicago Press.

Chakrabarty, Dipesh

2000a   "Translating Life-Worlds into Labor and History," in *Provin-cializing Europe: Postcolonial Thought and Historical Differ-ence*. Princeton, NJ: Princeton University Press.

2000b   *Provincializing Europe: Postcolonial Thought and Historical Difference*. Princeton, NJ: Princeton University Press.

Chan, Joseph Man

1997   "National Responses and Accessibility to Star TV in Asia," in *Media in Global Context*. Annabelle Sreberny-Mohammadi, Dwayne Winseck, Jim McKenna, and Oliver Boyd-Barrett, eds. London: Arnold.

2003   "Administrative Boundaries and Media Marketization: A Comparative Study of the Newspaper, Televison and Internet Markets in China," in *Chinese Media, Global Context*. Chin-Chuan Lee, ed. London: Routledge.

Chan, Kim-Kwong

1987   *Towards a Contextual Ecclesiology: The Catholic Church in the PRC, Its Life and Theological Implications*. Hong Kong: Chinese Church Research Center.

Chan, Kin-kwong, and Eric R. Carlson

2005   *Religious Freedom in China: Policy, Administration, and Regulation*. Santa Barbara and Hong Kong: Institute for the Study of American Religion and Hong Kong Institute for Cul-ture, Commerce, and Religion.

Chan, Wing-tsit

1987   "Chu Hsi and the Academies," in *Chu Hsi: Life and Thought*. Hong Kong: Chinese University Press.

Chandler, Stuart

2004   *Establishing a Pure Land on Earth: The Foguang Buddhist Perspective on Modernization and Globalization*. Honolulu: University of Hawai'i Press.

Chang, Hao

1987   *Chinese Intellectuals in Crisis: Search for Order and Mean-ing (1890–1911)*. Berkeley: University of California Press.

Chang, K. C.

1983   *Art, Myth and Ritual: The Path to Political Authority in Ancient China*. Cambridge, MA: Harvard University Press.

Chao, Jonathan, and Richard van Houten, eds.

1988   *Wise as Serpents, Harmless as Doves: Christians in China Tell Their Story*. Pasadena and Hong Kong: Wiliam Carey Library and Chinese Church Research Center.

Chatterjee, Partha

1986   *Nationalist Thought and the Colonial World: A Derivative Discourse*. Minneapolis: University of Minnesota Press.

1993   *The Nation and Its Fragments: Colonial and Postcolonial Histories.* Princeton, NJ: Princeton University Press.

1998   "Secularism and Tolerance," in *Secularism and Its Critics.* Rajeev Bhargava, ed. Oxford: Oxford University Press.

Chau, Adam Yuet

2006   *Miraculous Response: Doing Popular Religion in Contemporary China.* Stanford: Stanford University Press.

Chen, Hsi-yuan (Chen Xiyuan)

1999   "Confucianism Encounters Religion: The Formation of Religious Discourse and the Confucian Movement in Modern China." Ph.D. dissertation, Harvard University.

2005   "At the Threshold of the Pantheon of Religions: Confucianism and the Emerging Religious Discourse at the Turn of the Twentieth Century." Paper presented at the International Conference on Religion, Modernity, and the State in China and Taiwan, University of California at Santa Barbara.

Chen, Nancy N.

2003a   "Healing Sects and Anti-Cult Campaigns," in *Religion in China Today.* Daniel L. Overmyer, ed. Cambridge: Cambridge University Press.

2003b   *Breathing Spaces: Qigong, Psychiatry and Healing in China.* New York: Columbia University Press.

Chen, Sheng Jen

1990   "Understanding the Buddhist Tzu-chi Association—a Cultural Approach." Ph.D. dissertation, University of Southern California.

Chen, Yilu

2003   "Approaches to Theological Reconstruction in the Chinese Church: A Reading of K. H. Ting's Love Never Ends," in *Chinese Theological Review,* no. 16.

Chen, Yung-fa

1986   *Making Revolution: The Communist Movement in Eastern and Central China, 1937–1945.* Berkeley: University of California Press.

Chesneaux, Jean, ed.

1972   *Popular Movements and Secret Societies in China, 1840–1950.* Stanford: Stanford University Press.

Chiang, Kai-shek , Madame (aka Song Meiling 宋美龄)

1935   *General Chiang Kai-shek and the Communist Crisis.* Shanghai: China Weekly Review Press.

Chin, Sheila

1997   "Broadcasting and New Media Policies in Taiwan," in *Media in Global Context.* Annabelle Sreberny-Mohammadi, Dwayne Winseck, Jim McKenna, and Oliver Boyd-Barrett, eds. London: Arnold.

China News Digest (CND)
2000   "Demand Surging for Communications Satellites in Asia," in
        China News Digest, December 5.
Chow, Kai-wing
1994   *The Rise of Confucian Ritualism in Late Imperial China:
        Ethics, Classics, and Lineage Discourse.* Stanford: Stanford
        University Press.
Chow, Tse-tsung
1960   *The May Fourth Movement: Intellectual Revolution in Mod-
        ern China.* Cambridge, MA: Harvard University Press.
Chun, Allen
1994   "From Nationalism to Nationalizing: Cultural Imagination
        and State Formation in Postwar Taiwan," in *Australian Jour-
        nal of Chinese Affairs*, no. 31.
Cohen, Myron L.
1993   "Cultural and Political Inventions in Modern China: The Case
        of the Chinese 'Peasant,'" in *Daedalus*, vol. 122, no. 2.
1995   "Being Chinese: The Peripheralization of Traditional Iden-
        tity," in *The Living Tree: The Changing Meaning of Being
        Chinese Today.* Tu Weiming, ed. Berkeley: University of Cali-
        fornia Press.
Comaroff, Jean, and John Comaroff
1991   *Of Revelation and Revolution, Volume 1: Christianity, Colo-
        nialism, and Consciousness in South Africa.* Chicago: Uni-
        versity of Chicago Press.
1997   *Of Revelation and Revolution, Volume 2: The Dialectics of
        Modernity on a South African Frontier.* Chicago: University
        of Chicago Press.
Connolly, William E.
1999   *Why I Am Not a Secularist.* Minneapolis: University of Min-
        nesota Press.
Connerton, Paul
1989   *How Societies Remember.* Cambridge: Cambridge University
        Press.
Connor, Walker
1984   *The National Question in Marxist-Leninist Theory and
        Strategy.* Princeton, NJ: Princeton University Press.
Crossley, Pamela K.
1999   *A Translucent Mirror: History and Identity in Qing Imperial
        Ideology.* Berkeley: University of California Press.
Curtin, Michael
2001   "Media Capitals: Cultural Geographies of Global TV," in *The
        Persistence of Television: Critical Approaches to Television
        Studies.* Durham, NC: Duke University Press.

Dayan, Daniel, and Elihu Katz
1992   Media Events: The Live Broadcasting of History. Cambridge,
            MA: Harvard University Press.
De Vries, Hent
2001   "In Media Res: Global Religion, Public Spheres, and the Task
            of Contemporary Comparative Religious Studies," in Religion
            and Media. Hent De Vries and Samuel Weber, eds. Stanford:
            Stanford University Press.
De Vries, Hent, and Samuel Weber, eds.
2001   Religion and Media. Stanford: Stanford University Press.
Dean, Kenneth
1993   Taoist Ritual and Popular Cults of Southeast China. Princ-
            eton, NJ: Princeton University Press.
1998   Lord of the Three in One: The Spread of a Cult in Southeast
            China. Princeton, NJ: Princeton University Press.
2000   "Lineage and Territorial Cults: Transformations and Interac-
            tions in the Irrigated Putian Plains." Unpublished paper pre-
            sented at the Third International Conference on Sinology, at
            Academia Sinica, Nankang, Taiwan, June 29–July 1.
Defoort, Carine
2004   "Editor's Introduction," in Contemporary Chinese Thought,
            vol. 36, no. 1.
Deleuze, Gilles, and Félix Guattari
1983   Anti-Oedipus: Capitalism and Schizophrenia. Minneapolis:
            University of Minnesota Press.
1987   A Thousand Plateaus. Brian Massumi, trans. Minneapolis:
            University of Minnesota Press.
Deliusin, Lev
1972   "The I-kuan Tao Society," in Popular Movements and Secret
            Societies in China, 1840–1950. Jean Chesneaux, ed. Berkeley:
            University of California Press.
Deng, Zhaoming
1979   "Further Meeting with Protestant Leaders in China," in
            Ching Feng, vol. 22, no. 3.
Derrida, Jacques
1998   "Faith and Knowledge: The Two Sources of 'Religion' at the
            Limits of Reason Alone," in Religion. Jacques Derrida and
            Gianni Vattimo, eds., Samuel Weber, trans. Stanford: Stan-
            ford University Press.
2002   "Above All, No Journalists!" in Religion and Media. Hent De
            Vries and Samuel Weber, eds. Stanford: Stanford University
            Press.
Desan, Suzanne
1990   Reclaiming the Sacred: Lay Religion and Popular Politics in
            Revolutionary France. Ithaca. NY: Cornell University Press.

Dhundup Gyalpo
    2006   "State of Buddhism in Tibet" in *Tibet Bulletin*, vol. 10, no. 1. http://www.tibet.net/en/tibbul/2006/0102/focus1.html.

Dikötter, Frank
    1992   *The Discourse of Race in Modern China.* Stanford: Stanford University Press.
    2002   *Crime, Punishment and the Prison in Modern China.* New York: Columbia University Press.

Dillon, Michael
    1997   *Hui Muslims in China.* London: Curzon Press.
    2003   *Xinjiang: China's Muslim Far Northwest.* London: Curzon and Routledge Press.

Dobbelaere, Karel
    1981   "Secularization: A Multi-dimensional Concept," in *Current Sociology*, vol. 29, no. 2.
    1987   "Some Trends in European Sociology of Religion: The Secularization Debate," in *Sociological Analysis*, no. 48.

Douglas, Mary
    1973   *Natural Symbols.* New York: Vintage Books.

Dreyfus, Georges
    2003   *The Sound of Two Hands Clapping: The Education of a Tibetan Buddhist Monk.* Berkeley: University of California Press.
    2005   "Are We Prisoners of Shangrila? Orientalism, Nationalism, and the Study of Tibet," in *Journal of the International Association of Tibetan Studies*, no. 1. http://www.thdl.org/collections/journal/jiats/index.php?doc=dreyfus01.xml.

Duan, Qiming
    2001   "Reforms and Changes in the History of the Religious Affairs Organisations in the Chinese Government," in *China Study Journal*, vol. 16, no. 1.

Duara, Prasenjit
    1988a   *Culture, Power, and the State: Rural North China, 1900–1942.* Stanford: Stanford University Press.
    1988b   "Superscribing Symbols: The Myth of Guandi, Chinese God of War," in *Journal of Asian Studies*, vol. 47, no. 4.
    1991   "Knowledge and Power in the Discourse of Modernity: The Campaigna against Popular Religion in Early Twentieth-Century China," in *Journal of Asian Studies*, vol. 50, no. 1.
    1995a   "Critics of Modernity in India and China," in *Rescuing History from the Nation: Questioning Narratives of Modern China.* Chicago: University of Chicago Press.
    1995b   *Rescuing History from the Nation: Questioning Narratives of Modern China.* Chicago: University of Chicago Press.
    2003   *Sovereignty and Authenticity: Manchukuo and the East Asian Modern.* Lanham, MD: Rowman & Littlefield.

DuBois, Thomas David

2005a "Hegemony, Imperialism, and the Construction of Religion in East and Southeast Asia," in *History and Theory*, vol. 44, no. 4.

2005b *The Sacred Village: Social Change and Religious Life in Rural North China.* Honoloulu: University of Hawai'i Press.

Dunch, Ryan

1991 "Protestants and the State in Post-Mao China." Unpublished M.A. thesis in history, University of British Columbia.

2001a *Fuzhou Protestants and the Making of a Modern China 1857–1927.* New Haven: Yale University Press.

2001b "Protestant Christianity in China Today: Fragile, Fragmented, Flourishing," in *China and Christianity: Burdened Past, Hopeful Future.* Stephen Uhalley, Jr., and Xiaoxin Wu, eds. Armonk, NY: M.E. Sharpe.

Dung dkar Blo bzang 'phrin las

1991 *The Merging of Religious and Secular Rule in Tibet.* Chen Guangsheng, trans. Beijing: Foreign Languages Press.

Durkheim, Emile

1995 *The Elementary Forms of Religious Life.* Karen Fields, trans. New York: The Free Press. (Orig. pub. 1912.)

Eickelman, Dale F.

1976 *Moroccan Islam.* Austin: University of Texas Press.

Elliott, Mark C.

2001 *The Manchu Way: The Eight Banners and Ethnic Identity in Late Imperial China.* Stanford: Stanford University Press,

Engels, Friedrich

1972 *The Origin of the Family, Private Property, and the State.* New York: International Publishers. (Orig. pub. 1884.)

Esposito, John, and Azzam Tamimi, eds.

2000 *Islam and Secularism in the Middle East.* New York: New York University Press.

Feuchtwang, Stephan

1977 "School-temple and City God," in *The City in Late Imperial China.* G. William Skinner, ed. Stanford: Stanford University Press.

2001 *Popular Religion in China: The Imperial Metaphor.* Richmond, Surrey: Curzon Press.

Feuchtwang, Stephan, and Wang Mingming

1991 "The Politics of Culture or a Contest of Histories: Representations of Chinese Popular Religion," in *Dialectical Anthropology*, no. 16.

Fiedler, Katrin

2004 "How Many Sheep Are There in the Chinese Flock?" Amity News Service release 2004.11/12.4. http://www.amitynews

service.org/page.php?page=529&pointer=, accessed October
16, 2005.

Fielder, Caroline
2007 "Real Change or Mere Rhetoric?—An Evaluation of the 2005
Regulations on Religious Affairs a Year On," in *China Study
Journal*, Spring/Summer.

Fitzgerald, John
1996 "The Nationless State: The Search for a Nation in Modern
Chinese Nationalism," in *Chinese Nationalism*. Jonathan
Unger, ed. Armonk, NY: M.E. Sharpe, Inc.

Fletcher, Joseph
1995 *Studies on Chinese and Islamic Inner Asia*. Beatrice Forbes
Manz, ed. Hampshire, England: Variorum Press.

Forbes, Andrew D. W.
1986 *Warlords and Muslims in Chinese Central Asia*. Cambridge:
Cambridge University Press.

Foucault, Michel
1976a *Il faut défendre la société. Cours au Collège de France*. Paris:
Gallimard-Seuil.
1976b *Histoire de la sexualité*, tome I. Paris: Gallimard.
1977 *Discipline and Punish: The Birth of the Prison*. Alan Sheri-
dan, trans. New York: Vintage Books.
1978 *The History of Sexuality*, vol. 1. Robert Hurley, trans. New
York: Random House.
1980 *Power-Knowledge, Selected Interviews and Other Writings*.
Colin Gordon, trans. and ed. New York: Pantheon Books.
1982 "The Subject and Power," in *Michel Foucault: Beyond Struc-
turalism and Hermeneutics*. Chicago: University of Chicago
Press.
1994a "Entretien avec M. Fontana," in *Dits et écrits*, tome III. Paris:
Gallimard.
1994b "Non au sexe roi," in *Dits et écrits*, tome III. Paris: Gallimard.

Franke, Herbert, and Denis Twitchett
1994 *Cambridge History of China, Volume 6: Alien Regimes and
Border States (907–1368)*. Cambridge: Cambridge University
Press.

French, Howard W.
2006 "China Adds Restrictions in Effort to Shake the Faith of Independent Congregations," in *New York Times*, August 18.

Fu, Chi-ying
1996 *Handing Down the Light: The Biography of Venerable Master Hsing Yun*. Amy Lui-ma, trans. Hacienda Heights, CA:
Hsi Lai University Press.

Fu, Xiqiu (Bob), ed.
2003 *Chinese Law and Government*, vol. 36, nos. 2 and 3.

Fuller, Graham E., and Jonathan N. Lipman
2004   "Islam in Xinjiang," in *Xinjiang: China's Muslim Border-
        land*. Frederick S. Starr, ed. Armonk, NY: M. E. Sharpe, Inc.
Furth, Charlotte
1998   "Intellectual Change: From the Reform Movement to the May
        Fourth Movement, 1895–1920," in *An Intellectual History of
        Modern China*. Merle Goldman and Leo Ou-fan Lee, eds.
        Cambridge: Cambridge University Press.
Gao, Pat
2000   "Buying into China," in *Taibei Review*, vol. 50, no. 8.
Garon, Sheldon
1997   *Molding Japanese Minds: The State in Everyday Life*. Prince-
        ton, NJ: Princeton University Press.
Geertz, Clifford
1980   *Negara: The Theatre State in Nineteenth Century Bali*.
        Princeton, NJ: Princeton University Press.
1983   "Centers, Kings, and Charisma: Reflections on the Symbolics
        of Power," in *Local Knowledge: Further Essays in Interpre-
        tive Anthropology*. New York: Basic Books.
Geertz, Hildred
1975   "An Anthropology of Religion and Magic, I," in *Journal of
        Interdisciplinary History*, vol. 6, no. 1.
Gentile, Emilio
1996   *The Sacralization of Politics in Fascist Italy*. Keith Botsford,
        trans. Cambridge, MA: Harvard University Press.
Giddens, Anthony
1979   *Central Problems in Social Theory: Action, Structure and
        Contradiction in Social Analysis*. London: Macmillan.
1984   *The Constitution of Society*. Cambridge: Polity Press.
1985   *The Nation-State and Violence*. Cambridge: Polity Press.
1987   *The Nation-State and Violence*. Berkeley: University of Cali-
        fornia Press.
Ginsburg, Faye
1999   "Shooting Back: From Ethnographic Film to Indigenous Pro-
        duction and the Anthropology of Media," in *A Companion to
        Film Theory*. Bob Stam and Toby Miller, eds. Oxford:
        Blackwell.
Gladney, Dru
1996   *Muslim Chinese: Ethnic Nationalism in the People's Republic*.
        Cambridge, MA: Harvard University Press. (Orig. pub. 1991.)
2004   *Dislocating China: Muslims, Minorities, and Other Subal-
        tern Subjects*. Chicago: University of Chicago Press.
Gold, Thomas B.
1987   *State and Society in the Taiwan Miracle*. Armonk, NY: M. E.
        Sharpe, Inc.

Goldstein, Melvyn C.

1989   *A History of Modern Tibet, 1913–1951: The Demise of the Lamaist State.* Berkeley: University of California Press.

1998   "The Revival of Monastic Life in Drepung," in *Buddhism in Contemporary Tibet: Religious Revival and Cultural Identity.* Melvyn Goldstein and Matthew Kapstein, eds. Berkeley: University of California Press.

N.d.   "Tibet, China, and the United States: Reflections on the Tibet Question," in *The Atlantic Council of the United States' Occasional Papers.* http://www.columbia.edu/itc/ealac/ barnett/pdfs/link4-goldstn.pdf, accessed October 2006.

Goldstein, Melvyn, and Matthew Kapstein, eds.

1998   *Buddhism in Contemporary Tibet: Religious Revival and Cultural Identity.* Berkeley: University of California Press.

Gole, Nilufer

1996   *The Forbidden Modern: Civilization and Veiling.* Ann Arbor: University of Michigan Press.

Gong, Xuezeng

1994   "Current Situation of Religious Research in China," in *China Study Journal,* vol. 10, no. 1. Translated from *Shijie zongjiao yanjiu,* no. 4 (1994).

Goonasekera, Anura

2000   "Freedom of Expression in the Information Age: Access to Information," in *Media Asia,* vol. 27, no. 2.

Goossaert, Vincent

2003   "Le destin de la religion chinoise au 20e siècle," in *Social Compass,* vol. 50, no. 4.

2004   "Bureaucratic Charisma: The Zhang Heavenly Master Institution and Court Taoists in Late Qing China," in *Asia Major,* vol. 17, no. 2.

2005a   "Les fausses séparations de l'État et de la religion en Chine, 1898–2004," in *De la séparation des Églises et de l'État à l'avenir de la laïcité.* Jean Baubérot and Michel Wieviorka, eds. Paris: L'aube.

2005b   "State and Religion in Modern China: Religious Policies and Scholarly Paradigms." Paper presented at "Rethinking Modern Chinese History: An International Conference to Celebrate the Fiftieth Anniversary of the Institute of Modern History," Academia Sinica, Taibei, Taiwan.

2006a   *See under* Sources in Chinese and Other Asian Languages.

2006b   "1898: The Beginning of the End for Chinese Religion?" in *Journal of Asian Studies,* vol. 65, no. 2.

2007   *The Taoists of Peking, 1800–1949: A Social History of Urban Clerics.* Cambridge, MA: Harvard University Asia Center.

2008   "Abbés et saints crasseux: Essai de définition des autorités
            religieuses en Chine (1400–1911)," in *Les autorités
            religieuses*. Denise Aigle, ed. Turnhout: Brepols.

Grant, Bruce
1995   *In the Soviet House of Culture: A Century of Perestroikas.*
            Princeton, NJ: Princeton University Press.

de Groot, J. J. M.
1976   *Sectarianism and Religious Persecution in China.* Taibei:
            Cheng Wen Publishing Co. (Orig. pub. 1901.)

Gunn, T. Jeremy
2003   "The Complexity of Religion and the Definition of 'Religion'
            in International Law," in *Harvard Human Rights Journal,*
            vol. 16 (Spring).

Guo, Qitao
2005   *Ritual Opera and Mercantile Lineage: The Confucian Trans-
            formation of Popular Culture in Late Imperial Huizhou.*
            Stanford: Stanford University Press.

Habermas, Jüergen
2003   "Faith and Knowledge," in *The Future of the Human Nature.*
            Hella Beister, trans. Cambridge: Polity Press.

Haeckel, Ernst
1905   *The Wonders of Life: A Popular Study of Biological Philoso-
            phy.* Joseph McCabe, trans. New York: Harper and Brothers
            Publishers.

Hamrin, Carol Lee
2005   "Testimony before the US Congressional-Executive Commis-
            sion on China," March 14. http://www.cecc.gov/pages/round
            tables/031405/index.php, accessed July 15, 2006.

Hardacre, Helen
1989   *Shinto and the State, 1868–1988.* Princeton, NJ: Princeton
            University Press.

Harris, Lillian
1993   *China Considers the Middle East.* London: I. B. Tauris & Co.

Harrison, Henrietta
2001   *The Making of the Republican Citizen: Political Ceremonies
            and Symbols in China, 1911–1929.* Oxford: Oxford Univer-
            sity Press.

Harrison, James P.
1970   *The Communists and Chinese Peasant Rebellions: A Study
            in the Rewriting of Chinese History.* London: Victor Gollancz
            Ltd.

Hayhoe, Ruth, and Lu Yongling, eds.
1996   *Ma Xiangbo and the Mind of Modern China, 1840–1939.*
            Armonk, NY: M. E. Sharpe, Inc.

Hervieu-Léger, Danièle
1993   *La religion pour mémoire.* Paris: Cerf.
1999   *La religion en miettes ou la question des sectes.* Paris: Calmann-Lévy.

Hopkirk, Peter
1994   *The Great Game: The Struggle for Empire in Central Asia.* New York and Tokyo: Kodansha International.

Hsiao, Andrew K. S.
1979   "The Reawakening of the Church in China," in *Ching Feng,* vol. 22, no. 3.

Hsiao, Hsin-Huang Michael
1993   *Discovery of the Middle Classes in East Asia.* Taibei: Institute of Ethnology, Academia Sinica.
1994   "The Development and Organization of Foundations in Taiwan: An Expression of Vigor in a Newly Born Society," in *Quiet Revolutions on Taiwan, Republic of China.* Jason C. Hu, ed. Taibei: Kwang-hwa Publishing Co.

Hsing Yun (Xingyun)
2000   *The Philosophy of Being Second.* Hacienda Heights, CA: Hsi Lai University Press.
2001   *Where There Is Dharma There Is a Way.* Taibei: Foguang Cultural Enterprise Co.

Huang, C. Julia
2005   "The Compassion Relief Diaspora," in *Buddhist Missionaries in the Era of Globalization.* Linda Learman, ed. Honolulu: University of Hawai'i Press.

Huang, C. Julia, and Robert P. Weller
1998   "Merit and Mothering: Women and Social Welfare in Taiwanese Buddhism," in *Journal of Asian Studies,* vol. 57, no. 2 (May).

Huang, Grace
2005   "Chiang Kai-shek's Uses of Shame: An Interpretive Study of Agency in Chinese Leadership." Ph.D. thesis, University of Chicago.

Human Rights Watch/Asia (HRW)
1993   *China: Continuing Religious Repression.* New York, London, Washington, Brussels: Human Rights Watch.
1997   *China: State Control of Religion.* New York, London, Washington, Brussels: Human Rights Watch.
2004   "The Trials of a Tibetan Monk" in *Human Rights Watch,* vol. 16, no. 1 (C), February. http://hrw.org/reports/2004/china0204/china0204.pdf.

Huntington, Samuel P.
1993   "The Clash of Civilizations?" in *Foreign Affairs,* vol. 72, no. 3 (Summer).

Husband, William B.

2000   *"Godless Communists": Atheism and Society in Soviet Russia*. DeKalb: Northern Illinois University Press.

International Campaign for Tibet (ICT)

1996   *A Season to Purge: Religious Repression in Tibet*. Washington: ICT.

N.d.   "A Reader for Advocating Science and Technology and Doing Away With Superstitions," in *When the Sky Fell to the Earth: The New Crackdown on Buddhism in Tibet*. Washington: ICT.

N.d.   *When the Sky Fell to the Earth: The New Crackdown on Buddhism in Tibet*. Washington: ICT.

Israeli, Raphael

1981   *Muslims in China: A Study in Cultural Confrontation*. Scandinavia Monographs in East Asian Studies, no. 29. New York: Prometheus Books.

2002   *Islam in China: Religion, Ethnicity, Culture and Politics*. Lanham, Boulder, New York: Rowman & Littlefield.

Jakobsen, Janet R., and Ann Pellegrini

2000   "World Secularisms at the Millennium: Introduction," in Special Issue of *Social Text* 64 vol. 18, no. 3 (Fall).

Ji, Tai

1997   "Gospel and Culture: Interpretation and Reinterpretation," in *China Study Journal*, vol. 12, no. 2.

Ji, Zhe

2004   "Buddhism and the State: A New Relationship," in *China Perspectives*, no. 55.

2006   "Non-institutional Religious Re-composition among the Chinese Youth," in *Social Compass*, vol. 53, no. 4.

Jiang, Ping

1986   "Study Conscientiously Marxist Theory on Religion and the Party Policy for Religion," in *China Study Project Journal*, vol. 1, no. 2. Translated from *Hongqi*, May 1, 1986.

Jing, Jun

1996   *The Temple of Memories: History, Power and Morality in a Chinese Village*. Stanford: Stanford University Press.

Jochim, Christian

1986   *Chinese Religions: A Cultural Perspective*. Englewood Cliffs, NJ: Prentice-Hall.

2003   "Carrying Confucianism into the Modern World: The Taiwan Case," in *Religion in Modern Taiwan: Tradition and Innovation in a Changing Society*. Philip Clart and Charles B. Jones, eds. Honolulu: University of Hawai'i Press.

Jones, Charles Brewer

1999   *Buddhism in Taiwan: Religion and the State, 1660–1990*. Honolulu: University of Hawai'i Press.

Jordan, David K.
1982   "The Recent History of the Celestial Way: A Chinese Pietistic Association," in *Modern China*, vol. 8, no. 4.

Katz, Paul
2003   "Religion and the State in Post-War Taiwan," in *Religion in China Today*, vol. 174. Daniel Overmyer, ed. Cambridge: Cambridge University Press.

Keane, Webb
2002   "Sincerity, 'Modernity,' and the Protestants," in *Cultural Anthropology*, vol. 17, no. 1.

Kelly, Petra K., Gert Bastian, and Pat Aiello
1991   *The Anguish of Tibet*. Berkeley: Parallax Press.

Ketelaar, James Edward
1990   *Of Heretics and Martyrs in Meiji Japan: Buddhism and Its Persecution*. Princeton, NJ: Princeton University Press.

Kim, Hodong
2003   *Holy War in China: The Muslim Rebellion and State in Chinese Central Asia, 1866–1877*. Stanford: Stanford University Press.

Kipnis, Andrew
2001   "The Flourishing of Religion in Post-Mao China and the Anthropological Category of Religion," in *Australian Journal of Anthropology*, vol. 12, no. 1.

Kirkland, Russell
2004   *Taoism: The Enduring Tradition*. London: Routledge.

Koselleck, Reinhart
1988   *Critique and Crisis: Enlightenment and the Pathogenesis of Modern Society*. Cambridge, MA: The MIT Press.

Kwee, Tek Hoay
1969   *The Origins of the Modern Chinese Movement in Indonesia*. Lea E. Williams, trans. and ed. Ithaca, NY: Modern Indonesia Project, Southeast Asia Program, Cornell University.
1997   "Misleading Clamour," in *Political Thinking of Indonesian Chinese, 1900–1995: A Sourcebook*. Leo Suryadinata, ed. Singapore: Singapore University Press.

Kwok, D. W. Y.
1965   *Scientism in Chinese Thought, 1900–1950*. New Haven: Yale University Press.

Laidlaw, James
1999   "On the Theatre and Theory: Reflections on Ritual in Imperial Chinese Politics," in *State and Court Ritual in China*. Joseph P. McDermott, ed. Cambridge: Cambridge University Press.

Laliberté, André
2004   *The Politics of Buddhist Organizations in Taiwan, 1989–2003*. London and New York: Routledge Curzon.

Lane, Christel
1981   *The Rites of Rulers: Ritual in Industrial Society—The Soviet Case*. Cambridge: Cambridge University Press.
Lapidus, Ira M.
1988   *A History of Islamic Societies*. Cambridge: Cambridge University Press.
Lary, Diana
1985   *Warlord Soldiers: Chinese Common Soldiers, 1911–1937*. Cambridge: Cambridge University Press.
Latourette, Kenneth Scott
1973   *A History of Christian Missions in China*. Taibei: Chengwen Publishing Co. (Orig. pub. 1929.)
Lee, Chin-chuan
1999   "State Control, Technology, and Cultural Concerns: the Politics of Cable Television in Taiwan," in *Studies of Broadcasting*, no. 34.
Lee, Fengmao
2009   "Transmission and Innovation: The Modernization of Elixir Daoism in Postwar Taiwan," in David A. Palmer and Liu Xun, eds., *Taoism in the Twentieth Century: Between Eternity and Modernity*. Berkeley: University of California Press.
Lee, Leo Ou-fan
1999   *Shanghai Modern: The Flowering of a New Urban Culture in China, 1930–1945*. Cambridge, MA: Harvard University Press.
Lefebvre, Henri
1991   *The Production of Space*. Donald Nicholson-Smith, trans. Oxford: Blackwell.
Lefort, Claude
1988   "The Permanence of the Theologico-Political?" in *Democracy and Political Theory*. David Macey, trans. Minneapolis: University of Minnesota Press.
Lei, Zhenchang
1985   "Correctly Understanding Religious Problems During the Socialist Period," in *Religion in the PRC: Documentation*, no. 18, December. Translated from *Guangming Daily*, February 18, 1985.
Leung, Angela Ki Che
1994   "Elementary Education in the Lower Yangtze Region in the Seventeenth and Eighteenth Centuries," in *Education and Society in late Imperial China*. Benjamin A. Elman and Alexander Woodside, eds. Berkeley: University of California Press.

Leung, Ka-leung
1991   "Reflections of Contemporary Chinese Intellectuals on Chris-
            tianity and the Future of China," in *China Graduate School
            of Theology Journal*, no. 10, January.
Leung, Man Kam
1989   "The Relations between Religions and Peasant Rebellions in
            China: A Review of the Interpretations by Chinese Histori-
            ans," in *The Turning of the Tide: Religion in China Today*.
            Julian Pas, ed. Hong Kong: Oxford University Press.
Levenson, Joseph R.
1965   *Confucian China and Its Modern Fate: A Trilogy*. Berkeley:
            University of California Press.
Li, Qiuling
2007   "Historical Reflections on 'Sino-Christian Theology," Alison
            Hardie, trans., in *China Study Journal*, Spring/Summer.
Lieu, Samuel N. C.
1992   *Manichaeism in the Later Roman Empire and Medieval
            China*. Tübingen: Mohr.
Lin, Yusheng
1979   *The Crisis of Chinese Consciousness: Radical Anti-
            traditionalism in the May Fourth Era*. Madison: University
            of Wisconsin Press.
Lipkin, Zwia
2006   *Useless to the State: "Social Problems" and Social Engineer-
            ing in Nationalist Nanjing, 1927–1937*. Cambridge, MA: Har-
            vard University Asia Center/Harvard University Press.
Liu, Kwang-Ching
2004   "A Note on the Usage of the Chinese Terms for Heterodoxy,"
            in *Heterodoxy in Late Imperial China*. Kwang-Ching Liu and
            Richard Shek, eds. Honolulu: University of Hawai'i Press.
Liu, Kwang-Ching, and Richard Shek, eds.
2004   *Heterodoxy in Late Imperial China*. Honolulu: University of
            Hawai'i Press.
Liu, Lydia
1995   *Translingual Practice: Literature, National Culture, and
            Translated Modernity, China 1900–1937*. Stanford: Stanford
            University Press.
Liu, Ts'un-yan
1976   "Traces of Zoroastrian and Manichaean Activities in Pre-
            T'ang China," in *Selected Papers from the Hall of Harmoni-
            ous Wind*. Leiden: E. J. Brill.
Liu, Xiaofeng
1989   "God is God: In Memory of Karl Barth," in *Chinese Theologi-
            cal Review*, vol. 5.

Liu, Xun
    2001   "In Search of Immortality: Daoist Inner Alchemy in Early Twentieth-Century China." Ph.D dissertation, University of Southern California.
    2006   "Scientizing the Body for the Nation: Chen Yingning and the Reinvention of Inner Alchemy in 1930's and 1940's." Paper presented at the Conference "Between Eternity and Modernity: Transformations and Reinvention of Daoism in Twentieth Century China," Fairbank Center, Harvard University, June 14–15, 2006.

Lo, Wei
    1998   *The 1997 Criminal Code of the People's Republic of China.* Buffalo: W. S. Hein & Co.

Lombard, Denys, and Claudine Salmon
    1994   "Islam and Chineseness," in *Indonesia,* vol. 57, April.

Long, Mark
    2000   "The APSTAR Satellite System." http://www.mlesat.com/apstars.html.

Loveman, Mara
    2005   "The Modern State and the Primitive Accumulation of Symbolic Power," in *American Journal of Sociology,* vol. 110, no. 6.

Löwenthal, Rudolf
    1978   *The Religious Periodical Press in China.* San Francisco: Chinese Materials Center. (Orig. pub. 1940.)

Lozada, Eriberto P., Jr.
    2000   *God Aboveground: Catholic Church, Postsocialist State, and Transnational Processes in a Chinese Village.* Stanford: Stanford University Press.

Luckmann, Thomas
    1967   *The Invisible Religion: The Problem of Religion in Modern Society.* New York: Macmillan.

Luo, Zhufeng
    1991   *Religion under Socialism in China.* Donald E. MacInnis and Zheng Xi'an, trans. Armonk, NY: M. E. Sharpe, Inc.

Lynch, Daniel
    1999   *After the Propaganda State: Media, Politics, and "Thought Work" in Reformed China.* Stanford: Stanford University Press.

MacGregor, Brent
    1997   *Live, Direct and Biased? Making Television News in the Satellite Age.* London: Arnold.

MacInnis, Donald E., ed.
    1972   *Religious Policy and Practice in Communist China.* New York: MacMillan.

1989   *Religion in China Today: Policy and Practice.* Maryknoll,
             NY: Orbis Books.
Mackie, J. A., and Charles A. Coppell
1976   "A Preliminary Survey," in *The Chinese in Indonesia.* The
             Australian Institute of International Affairs.
MacKinnon, Stephen R.
1975   "Police Reform in Late Ch'ing Chihli," in *Ch'ing-shih wen-t'i,*
             vol. 3, no.4.
1983   "A Late Qing–GMD–PRC Connection: Police as an Arm of
             Modern Chinese State." Selected Papers in
             Asian Studies N.S., paper no. 14.
Madsen, Richard
1998   *China's Catholics: Tragedy and Hope in an Emerging Civil
             Society.* Berkeley: University of California Press.
2003   "Catholic Revival during the Reform Era," in *Religion in
             China Today.* Daniel L. Overmyer, ed. Cambridge: Cambridge
             University Press.
2007   *Democracy's Dharma: Asian Religious Renaissance and
             Political Development in Taiwan.* Berkeley: University of
             California Press.
Madsen, Richard, and James Tong, eds.
2000   "Local Religious Policy in China, 1980–1997," in *Chinese
             Law and Government,* vol. 33, no. 3.
Mahle, C.
1998   "Space Communications Corporation (SCC)." http://itri.loyola
             .edu/satcom2/c_14.htm.
Mahmood, Saba
2005   *Politics of Piety: The Islamic Revival and the Feminist Sub-
             ject.* Berkeley: University of California Press.
Malinowski, Bronislaw
1992   *Magic, Science, and Religion.* Prospect Heights, IL: Waveland
             Press. (Orig. pub. 1925.)
Mankekar, Purnima
1999   *Screening Culture, Viewing Politics: An Ethnography of
             Television, Womanhood, and Nation in Postcolonial India.*
             Durham, NC: Duke University Press.
Martin, David
1978   *A General Theory of Secularization.* New York: Harper &
             Row.
Martinson, Paul V.
1980   "Musings on Church and State in China—1979 and after?" in
             Ching Feng, vol. 23, no. 2.
Marx, Karl
1970   "A Contribution to the Critique of Hegel's *Philosophy of
             Right,*" in *Critique of Hegel's Philosophy of Right.* Joseph

O'Malley, ed. Cambridge: Cambridge University Press. (Orig. pub.1844.)

Mbembe, Achille

2005   *On the Postcolony*. Berkeley: University of California Press.

McChesney, Robert W.

1998   "The Political Economy of Global Communication," in *Capitalism and the Information Age*. Robert W. McChesney, Ellen M. Wood, and John B. Foster, eds. New York: Monthly Review Press.

McCord, Edward A.

2001   "Burn, Kill, Rape and Rob: Military Atrocities, Warlordism, and Anti-Warlordism in Republican China," in *Scars of War*. Diana Lary, ed. Vancouver: University of British Columbia Press.

McDermott, Joseph P.

1999   "Emperor, Elites, and Commoners: The Community Pact Ritual of the Late Ming," in *State and Court Ritual in China*. Joseph P. McDermott, ed. Cambridge: Cambridge University Press.

McIntire, C. T.

2002   "The Shift from Church and State to Religions as Public Life in Modern Europe," in *Church History*, vol. 71, March.

Mencius

1970   *Mencius*. D. C. Lau, trans. and ed. Harmondsworth: Penguin Books.

Millward, James A.

1998   *Beyond the Pass: Economy, Ethnicity, and Empire in Qing Central Asia, 1759–1865*. Stanford: Stanford University Press.

Mitchell, Timothy

1991a   "The Limits of the State: Beyond Statist Approaches and Their Critics," in *American Political Science Review*, vol. 85, no. 1.

1991b   "Preface to the Paperback Edition," in *Colonising Egypt*. Berkeley: University of California Press.

Mollier, Christine

2006   "Visions of Evil: Demonology and Orthodoxy in Early Daoism," in *Daoism in History: Essays in Honour of Liu Ts'un-yan*. Benjamin Penny, ed. London: Routledge.

Morgan, Lewis Henry

1963   *Ancient Society, or Researches in the Lines of Human Progress from Savagery through Barbarism to Civilization*. Eleanor Burke Leacock, ed. Cleveland: Meridian Books. (Orig. pub. 1877.)

Morley, David, and Kevin Robins

1995   *Spaces of Identity: Global Media, Electronic Landscapes and Cultural Boundaries*. London: Routledge.

Morse, Margaret
1998 *Virtualities: Television, Media Art, and Cyberculture.*
Bloomington: Indiana University Press.

Mueggler, Eric
2001 *Age of Wild Ghosts: Memory, Violence, and Place in Southwest China.* Berkeley: University of California Press.

Munro, Robin, ed.
1989 *Syncretic Sects and Secret Societies: Revival in the 1980s.*
Special Issue of *Chinese Sociology and Anthropology,* vol. 21,
no. 4.

Musgrove, Charles D.
2002 "The Nation's Concrete Heart: Architecture, Planning and
Ritual in Nanjing, 1927–1937." Ph.D. dissertation, University
of California, San Diego.

Nandy, Ashis
1998 "The Politics of Secularism and the Recovery of Religious Tolerance," in *Secularism and Its Critics.* Rajeev Bhargava, ed.
New Delhi: Oxford University Press.

Naquin, Susan
1985 "The Transmission of White Lotus Sectarianism in Late
Imperial China," in *Popular Culture in Late Imperial China.*
David Johnson, Andrew J. Nathan, and Evelyn S. Rawski, eds.
Berkeley: University of California Press.
1992 "The Peking Pilgrimage to Miao-feng Shan: Religious Organizations and Sacred Site," in *Pilgrims and Sacred Sites in
China.* Susan Naquin and Chün-fang Yü, eds. Berkeley: University of California Press.

Naquin, Susan, and Chun-fang Yü
1992 "Introduction: Pilgrimage in China," in *Pilgrims and Sacred
Sites in China.* Susan Naquin and Chün-fang Yü, eds. Berkeley: University of California Press.

Nedostup, Rebecca
2001 "Religion, Superstition and Governing Society in Nationalist
China, 1927–1937." Ph.D. dissertation, Columbia University.
2008 "Two Tombs: Thoughts on Zhu Yuanzhang, the Kuomintang,
and the Meanings of National Heroes," in *Long Live the
Emperor! The Uses of the Ming Founder across Six Centuries
of East Asian History.* Sarah K. Schneewind, ed. Minneapolis: Ming Studies/Center for Early Modern History, University of Minnesota.

Norton, David, ed.
2005 *The New Cambridge Paragraph Bible.* King James Version.
Cambridge: Cambridge University Press.

Ong, Aihwa
1999   *Flexible Citizenship: The Cultural Logic of Transnationality.*
            Durham, NC: Duke University Press.
Overmyer, Daniel L., ed.
2003   *Religion in China Today.* Cambridge: Cambridge University
            Press.
Ownby, David
1993   "Secret Societies Reconsidered," in *"Secret Societies" Recon-*
            sidered: Perspectives on the Social History of Modern South
            China and Southeast Asia. David Ownby and Mary Somers
            Heidhues, eds. Armonk, NY: M. E. Sharpe, Inc.
1995   "The Heaven and Earth Society as Popular Religion," in *Jour-*
            nal of Asian Studies, vol. 54, no. 4.
2001   "Imperial Fantasies: The Chinese Communists and Peasant
            Rebellions," in *Comparative Studies in Society and History,*
            vol. 43, no. 1.
2003   "A History for Falun Gong: Popular Religion and the Chinese
            State since the Ming Dynasty," in *Nova Religio,* vol. 6, no. 2.
2008   *Falun Gong and the Future of China.* New York: Oxford Uni-
            versity Press.
Ozouf, Mona
1988   *Festivals and the French Revolution Festivals and the French*
            Revolution. Alan Sheridan, trans. Cambridge, MA: Harvard
            University Press.
Palmer, David A.
2003   "Le Qigong et la Tradition Sectaire Chinoise," in *Social Com-*
            pass, vol. 50, no. 4.
2005   *La fièvre du Qigong: Guérison, religion et politique en*
            Chine, 1949–1999. Paris: Editions de l'École des Hautes Études
            en Sciences Sociales.
2006   "L'État et le Sectarisme en Chine Contemporaine," in *Reli-*
            gion et Politique en Asie. John Lagerwey, ed. Paris: Les Indes
            Savantes.
2007   *Qigong Fever: Body, Science and Utopia in China,*
            1949–1999. London: Hurst & Co. New York: Columbia Uni-
            versity Press.
Paper, Jordan D.
1996   "Mediums and Modernity: The Institutionalization of Ecstatic
            Religious Functionaries in Taiwan," in *Jounal of Chinese*
            Religions, vol. 24.
Parks, Lisa
2002   "Our World, Satellite Visuality, and the Fantasy of Global
            Presence," in *Planet TV: A Global Television Reader.* Lisa
            Parks and Shanti Kumar, eds. New York: New York University
            Press.

Parsons, Patrick R., and Robert M. Frieden
    1998   *The Cable and Satellite Television Industries.* Boston: Allyn and Bacon.

Patt, David, ed.
    1992   *A Strange Liberation: Tibetan Lives in Chinese Hands.* Ithaca, NY: Snow Lion.

Penny, Benjamin
    2002   "The Body of Master Li," Charles Strong Memorial Trust Lecture. http://www.charlesstrongtrust.org.au.
    2003   "The Life and Times of Li Hongzhi," in *China Quarterly,* no. 175, September.
    2005   "Falun Gong, Buddhism and 'Buddhist Qigong,'" in *Asian Studies Review,* vol. 29, no.1.

Picard, Michel
    2003   "What's in a Name? Agama Hindu Bali in the Making," in *Hinduism in Modern Indonesia: A Minority Religion between Local, National and Global Interests.* Martin Ramstedt, ed. London and New York: Routledge Curzon–IIAS Asian Studies Series.

Pittman, Don Alvin
    2001   *Toward a Modern Chinese Buddhism: Taixu's Reforms.* Honolulu: University of Hawai'i Press.

Potter, Pitman B.
    2003   "Belief in Control: Regulation of Religion in China," in *Religion in China Today,* vol. 174. Daniel Overmyer, ed. Cambridge: Cambridge University Press.

Price, Monroe
    1994   "The Market for Loyalties: Electronic Media and the Global Competition for Allegiances," in *The Yale Law Journal,* vol. 104, no. 3.
    1999   "Satellite Broadcasting as Trade Routes in the Sky," in *Public Culture,* vol. 11, no. 2 (Spring).
    2002   *Media and Sovereignty: The Global Information Revolution and Its Challenge to State Power.* Cambridge: The MIT Press.

Qin, Shenglan
    1990   "Three-Self Education for Theological Students," in *China Study Journal,* vol. 5, no. 3.

Rankin, Mary Backus
    1997   "State and Society in Early Republican Politics, 1912–18," in *The China Quarterly,* vol. 150.

Rappaport, Roy A.
    1999   *Ritual and Religion in the Making of Humanity.* Cambridge: Cambridge University Press.

Reinders, Eric
2004   *Borrowed Gods and Foreign Bodies: Christian Missionaries Imagine Chinese Religion.* Berkeley: University of California Press.

Reynolds, Douglas R.
1993   *China, 1898–1912: The Xinzheng Revolution and Japan.* Cambridge, MA: Council on East Asian Studies, Harvard University.

Rigger, Shelley
1999   *Politics in Taiwan: Voting for Democracy.* London: Routledge.

Roberts, J. A. G.
1992   "Religion and Science" in *China Through Western Eyes: The Nineteenth Century.* Wolfeboro Falls, NH: Alan Sutton Publishing.

Rossabi, Morris
1981   *China and Inner Asia from 1368 to the Present Day.* London: Thames and Hudson.

Rubinstein, Murray
2001   "Cross-the-Strait Pilgrimage/Tourism and the Reinvention of the Taiwan-Fujian Popular Religious Matrix." Paper presented at the International Conference on Mazu Cult and Modern Society, Chaotian Temple, Beigang, Taiwan, May.

Rudelson, Justin Jon
1997   *Oasis Identities: Uyghur Nationalism along China's Silk Road.* New York: Columbia University Press.

Salamon, Julie
2002   "Television Review: Al Jazeera Looking Like CNN on the Surface Only," in *New York Times,* May 14.

Samuels, Geoffrey
1993   *Civilized Shamans: Buddhism in Tibetan Societies.* Washington, DC: Smithsonian Institution Press.

Sangren, Steven
1983   "Female Gender in Chinese Religious Symbols: Kuan Yin, Ma Tsu, and the 'Eternal Mother,'" in *Signs,* vol. 9, no.1.
1993   "Power and Transcendence in the Ma Tsu Pilgrimages of Taiwan," in *American Ethnologist,* vol. 20, no. 3.

Sapiets, Marite
1989   "Anti-Religious Propaganda and Education," in *Candle in the Wind: Religion in the Soviet Union.* Eugene B. Shirley and Michael Rowe, eds. Washington, DC: Ethics and Public Policy Center.

Schiller, Herbert, I.
1992   *Mass Communications and American Empire.* second edition. Boulder, CO: Westview Press.

Schipper, Kristofer
1990   "The Cult of Pao-Sheng Ta-Ti and its Spreading to Taiwan—a
        Case Study of *Fen-hsiang*," in *Development and Decline of
        Fukien Province in the 17th and 18th Century*. Eduard B. Ver-
        meer, ed. Leiden: E. J. Brill.
1993   *The Taoist Body*. Karen C. Duval, trans. Berkeley: University
        of California Press.
Schmitt, Philippe C.
1974   "Still a Century of Corporatism?" in *Review of Politics*,
        no. 36.
1977   "Modes of Interest Intermediation and Models of Societal
        Change in Western Europe," in *Comparative Political Stud-
        ies*, vol. 10, no. 1.
Schneewind, Sarah
2006   *Community Schools and the State in Ming China*. Stanford:
        Stanford University Press.
Schram, Stuart R.
1966   "Mao Tse-tung and Secret Societies," in *China Quarterly*,
        no. 27.
Schwarcz, Vera
1986   *The Chinese Enlightenment: Intellectuals and the Legacy of
        the May Fourth Movement of 1919*. Berkeley: University of
        California Press.
Schwartz, Benjamin I.
1975   "Transcendence in Ancient China," in *Daedalus* (Spring).
1985   *The World of Thought in Ancient China*. Cambridge, MA:
        Belknap Press of Harvard University Press.
Schwartz, Ronald D.
1994   *Circle of Protest: Political Ritual in the Tibetan Uprising*.
        New York: Columbia University Press.
Scott, James C.
1998   *Seeing Like a State: How Certain Schemes to Improve the
        Human Condition Have Failed*. New Haven: Yale University
        Press.
Seidel, Anna K.
1969–70 "The Image of the Perfect Ruler in Early Taoist Messianism:
        Lao-tzu and Li Hung," in *History of Religions*, vol. 9, no. 2–3.
1983   "Imperial Treasures and Taoist Sacraments: Taoist Roots in
        the Apocrypha," in *Tantric and Taoist Studies in Honour of
        R. A. Stein, Volume II*. Michel Strickmann, ed. *Mélanges Chi-
        noises et Bouddhiques* 21.
Seiwert, Hubert Michael
1999   *Popular Religious Movements and Heterodox Sects in Chi-
        nese History*. Leiden; Boston: E. J. Brill.

Seiwert, Hubert Michael, in collaboration with Ma Xisha
2003　Popular Religious Movements and Heterodox Sects in Chinese History. Leiden: E.J. Brill.
Sered, Susan Starr
1994　Priestess, Mother, Sacred Sister: Religions Dominated by Women. Oxford: Oxford University Press.
Sharf, Robert H.
2002　Coming to Terms with Chinese Buddhism: A Reading of the Treasure Store Treatise. Honolulu: University of Hawai'i Press.
Shengyen, Master (Shengyan)
1998　In the Spirit of Ch'an: An Introduction to Ch'an Buddhism. New York: Dharma Drum Publications.
Shengyen, Master, and Dan Stevenson
2001　Hoofprint of the Ox: Principles of the Chan Buddhist Path as Taught by a Modern Chan Master. New York: Oxford University Press.
Shichor, Yitzhak
1989　East Wind over Arabia: Origins and Implications of the Sino-Saudi Missile Deal. Berkeley: University of California Press.
Shimazono, Susumu
2004　From Salvation to Spirituality: Popular Religious Movements in Modern Japan. Melbourne: Trans-Pacific Press.
Shue, Vivienne
1988　The Reach of the State: Sketches of the Chinese Body Politic. Stanford: Stanford University Press.
Sinor, Denis, ed.
1990　The Cambridge History of Early Inner Asia. Cambridge: Cambridge University Press.
Skinner, G.W.
1996　"Creolized Chinese Societies in Southeast Asia," in Sojourners and Settlers: Histories of Southeast Asia and the Chinese. Anthony Reid, ed. Sydney: Allen and Unwin.
Smedley, Agnes
1956　The Great Road: The Life and Times of Chu Teh. New York: Monthly Review Press.
Smith, Joanna F. Handlin
1999　"Liberating Animals in Ming-Qing China: Buddhist Inspiration and Elite Imagination" in Journal of Asian Studies, vol. 58, no. 1.
Smith, Richard J.
1990　"Ritual in Ch'ing Culture," in Orthodoxy in Late Imperial China. Kwang-ching Liu, ed. Berkeley: University of California Press.

Smith, Wilfred Cantwell
    1962   *The Meaning and End of Religion*. New York: Macmillan.
Soothill, W. E.
    1923   *The Three Religions of China*, second edition. London: Oxford University Press. (Orig. pub. 1913.)
Sorokowski, Andrew
    1989   "Church and State 1917–64," in *Candle in the Wind: Religion in the Soviet Union*. Eugene B. Shirley and Michael Rowe, eds. Washington, DC: Ethics and Public Policy Center.
Spence, Jonathan D.
    1990   *The Search for Modern China*. New York: W. W. Norton.
Spiegel, Mickey
    2002   "China: Religion in the Service of the State," Statement before the U.S. Commission on International Religious Freedom. http://www.hrw.org/campaigns/geneva/china-religion-state .htm.
Spiegel, Mickey, and James Tong, eds.
    2000   "Documents on Religion in China, 1980–1997: Central Government Policy (I)," in *Chinese Law and Government*, vol. 33, no. 2.
Sreberny-Mohammadi, Annabelle, and Ali Mohammadi
    1994   *Small Media, Big Revolution: Communication, Culture, and the Iranian Revolution*. Minneapolis: University of Minnesota Press.
Stalin, Josef
    1972   "Dialectical and Historical Materialism," in *The Essential Stalin: Major Theoretical Writings, 1905–1952*. Bruce Franklin, ed. New York: Anchor Books.
Standing Committee of the Ninth National People's Congress (NPC)
    1999   "Decision of the Standing Committee of the National People's Congress on Banning Heretical Cult Organizations, Preventing and Punishing Cult Activities," in *Beijing Review*, vol. 42, no. 45, November 8.
State Council of the People's Republic of China (PRC)
    1997   *White Paper—Freedom of Religious Belief in China*. Beijing: Information Office, State Council of the People's Republic of China.
    2004   *Decree of the State Council of the People's Republic of China, no. 426*. Trans. at http://www.amitynewsservice.org/page. php?page=1289.
Stein, Rolf A.
    1963   "Remarques sur les Mouvements du Taoïsme Politico-religieux au IIe Siècle ap. J.-C.," in *T'oung Pao*, vol. 50.
    1979   "Religious Taoism and Popular Religion from the Second to Seventh Centuries," in *Facets of Taoism: Essays in Chinese*

Religion. Holmes Welch and Anna Seidel, eds. New Haven: Yale University Press.

Steward, Julian H.

1955   "Multilinear Evolution: Evolution and Process," in *Theory of Culture Change: The Methodology of Multilinear Evolution.* Champaign-Urbana: University of Illinois Press.

Strickmann, Michel

1979   "The Alchemy of T'ao Hung-ching," in *Facets of Taoism: Essays in Chinese Religion.* Holmes Welch and Anna Seidel, eds. New Haven: Yale University Press.

2002   *Chinese Magical Medicine.* Bernard Faure, ed. Stanford: Stanford University Press.

Suryadinata, Leo

1993a   "Kwee Tek Hoay: A Peranakan Writer and Proponent of Tri-dharma," in Leo Suryadinata, *Peranakan's Search for National Identity: Biographical Studies of Seven Indonesian Chinese.* Singapore: Times Academic Press.

1993b   "From Peranakan Chinese Literature to Indonesian Literature: A Preliminary Study," in Hsuan Keng, *Chinese Adaptation and Diversity: Essays on Society and Literature in Indonesia, Malaysia and Singapore.* Leo Suryadinata, ed. Singapore: Singapore University Press. Honolulu: University of Hawai'i Press.

Tai, Hsüan-chih

1985   *The Red Spears, 1916–1949.* Ronald Suleski, trans. Ann Arbor, MI: Center for Chinese Studies.

Tambiah, Stanley

1990   *Magic, Science and Religion, and the Scope of Rationality.* Cambridge: Cambridge University Press.

Tanasescu, Alina

2005   "Nationalism, Religion and Tourism in Postcommunist Romania: An Examination of Church-State Relations, Reinvigorated Orthodox Miracle Cults and Pilgrimage Amidst Global Flows." M.A. thesis in Anthropology, University of Alberta.

Taylor, Romeyn

1990   "Official and Popular Religion and the Political Organization of Chinese Society in the Ming," in *Orthodoxy in Late Imperial China.* Kwang-ching Liu, ed. Berkeley: University of California Press.

Teng, Ssu-yü

1968   *Family Instructions for the Yen Clan by Yen Chih-t'ui.* Leiden: E. J. Brill.

ter Haar, Barend J.
1990   "The Genesis and Spread of Temple Cults in Fukien," in *Development and Decline of Fukien Province in the 17th and 18th Century.* Eduard B. Vermeer, ed. Leiden: E. J. Brill.
1992   *The White Lotus Teachings in Chinese Religious History.* Leiden: E. J. Brill; reprint Honolulu: University of Hawai'i Press, 1999.
1998   *Ritual and Mythology of the Chinese Triads: Creating an Identity.* Leiden: E. J. Brill.

Thomas, Keith
1971   *Religion and the Decline of Magic: Studies in Popular Beliefs in Sixteenth and Seventeenth Century England.* London: Weidenfeld & Nicolson.

Thompson, Roger
1996   "Twilights of the Gods in the Chinese Countryside: Christians, Confucians, and the Modernizing State, 1861–1911," in *Christianity in China: From the Eighteenth Century to the Present.* Daniel H. Bays, ed. Stanford: Stanford University Press.

Tibet Center for Human Rights and Democracy (TCHRD)
2005   "China intensifies control in Lhasa during the 40th founding anniversary of the 'TAR,'" August. http://www.tchrd.org/ publications/hr_updates/2005/hr200508.html#intensifies.
N.d.   "'Strike Hard' Campaign: China's crackdown on political dissidence." http://www.tchrd.org/publications/topical_reports/ strike_hard-2004/strike_hard-2004.pdf, accessed October 2006.

Tibetan Government in Exile
N.d.   "Religious Persecution through Patriotic Re-education," A White Paper. http://www.tibet.com/Humanrights/Human Rights97/hr97–1.html, accessed October 2006.

Ting, K. H., and Wang Weifan
1988   "Recent Developments in the Study of Religion," in *Chinese Theological Review,* vol. 4.

Tsai, Yi-jia
2002   "The Reformative Visions of Mediumship in Contemporary Taiwan." Ph.D. dissertation, Rice University.

Tsering Shakya
1999   *The Dragon in the Land of Snows: A History of Modern Tibet Since 1947.* New York: Columbia University Press.
2002   "Blood in the Snows," in *New Left Review,* no.14.

Tuttle, Gray
2005   *Tibetan Buddhists in the Making of Modern China.* New York: Columbia University Press.

Unger, Jonathan, and Anita Chan
1995   "China, Corporatism, and the East Asian Model," in *The Australian Journal of Chinese Affairs*, no. 33.
van der Veer, Peter
1994   *Religious Nationalism: Hindus and Muslims in India.* Berkeley: University of California Press.
2000   "Introduction," in *Nation and Religion: Perspectives on Europe and Asia.* Peter Van der Veer and Hartemut Lehmann, eds. Princeton, NJ: Princeton University Press.
2001   *Imperial Encounters: Religion and Modernity in India and Britain.* Princeton, NJ: Princeton University Press.
van der Veer, Peter, and Hartmut Lehmann, eds.
1999   *Nation and Religion: Perspectives on Europe and Asia.* Princeton, NJ: Princeton University Press.
van Houten, Richard
1986   "Is Religion Opium?" in *China and the Church Today*, vol. 8, no. 1.
Verdery, Katherine
1994   "Beyond the Nation in Eastern Europe," in *Social Text*, no. 38.
Wah, Poon Shuk
2004   "Refashioning Festivals in Republican Guangzhou," in *Modern China*, vol. 30, no. 2 (April).
Wang, Aiming
2001   "The Nature and Purpose of Theological Reconstruction in the Chinese Church," in *Chinese Theological Review*, vol. 15.
2002   "Understanding Theological Reconstruction in the Chinese Church: A Hermeneutical Approach," in *Chinese Theological Review*, vol. 16.
2003   "The Chinese Church in Vision," Amity News Service release 2003.5/6.5. http://www.amitynewsservice.org/page.php?page=613&pointer=, accessed October 20, 2005.
2005   "From Incarnation to Divine Reconciliation," in *Chinese Theological Review*, vol. 18.
Wang, David D.
1999   *Under the Soviet Shadow: The Yining Incident: Ethnic Conflicts and International Rivalry in Xinjiang, 1944–1949.* Hong Kong: Chinese University Press.
Wang, Gungwu
1984   "The Chinese Urge to Civilize: Reflections of Change," in *Journal of Asian History*, vol. 18, no. 1.
Wang, Guanghui
2005   "De-Emphasis on Justification by Faith: An Instance of Theological Adaptation," in *Chinese Theological Review*, vol. 18.

Wang Lixiong
1993 "The Dispute Between the Tibetans and the Han: When Will
    it be Solved?" in *Resistance and Reform in Tibet.* Robert Bar-
    nett and Shirin Akiner, eds. Bloomington: Indiana University
    Press.
1999 "The People's Republic of China's 21st Century Underbelly,"
    in *Beijing Zhanlue Yu Guanli,* January 2. Trans. in *BBC
    Summary of World Broadcasts,* http://www.columbia.edu/itc/
    ealac/barnett/pdfs/link14-wang-lixiong.pdf.
2002 "Reflections on Tibet," in *New Left Review,* no. 14.
Wang, Mingming
1995 "Place, Administration, and Territorial Cults in Late Imperial
    China: A Case Study From South Fujian." in *Late Imperial
    China,* vol. 16, no. 1.
Wang, Weifan
1997 "Chinese Theology and its Cultural Sources." in *China Study
    Journal,* vol. 12, no. 2.
Watson, James L.
1985 "Standardizing the Gods: the Promotion of T'ien Hou
    ('Empress of Heaven') along the South China Coast,
    960–1960." in *Popular Culture in Late Imperial China.* David
    Johnson et al., eds. Berkeley: University of California Press.
Weber, Max
1964 *The Sociology of Religion.* Ephraim Fischoff, trans. Boston:
    Beacon Press.
1965 *Essais sur la théorie de la science.* Julien Freund, trans. Paris:
    Plon.
1971 *Economie et société.* Julien Freund et al., trans. Paris: Plon.
Welch, Holmes
1968 *The Buddhist Revival in China.* Cambridge, MA: Harvard
    University Press.
1972 *Buddhism under Mao.* Cambridge, MA: Harvard University
    Press.
Weller, Robert P.
1987 *Unities and Diversities in Chinese Religion.* Seattle: Univer-
    sity of Washington Press.
1994 *Resistance, Chaos and Control in China: Taiping Rebels, Tai-
    wanese Ghosts and Tiananmen.* Seattle: University of Wash-
    ington Press.
1999 *Alternate Civilities: Democracy and Culture in China and
    Taiwan.* Boulder, CO: Westview.
2000 "Living at the Edge: Religion, Capitalism, and the End of the
    Nation-State in Taiwan," in *Public Culture,* no. 12.

Whyte, Bob
  1988   Unfinished Encounter: China and Christianity. London:
               Collins.
Whyte, Martin King
  1974   Small Groups and Political Rituals in China. Berkeley: Uni-
               versity of California Press.
Wickeri, Philip L.
  1988   Seeking the Common Ground: Protestant Christianity, the
               Three-Self Movement, and China's United Front. Maryknoll,
               NY: Orbis Books.
  2007   Reconstructing Christianity in China: K. H. Ting and the
               Chinese Church. Maryknoll, NY: Orbis Books.
Williams, Mark
  1999   "History in a Flash: Notes on the Myth of TV 'Liveness,'" in
               Collecting Visible Evidence. Jane M. Gaines and Michael
               Renov, eds. Minneapolis: University of Minnesota Press.
Willmott, Donald E.
  1960   The Chinese of Semarang: A Changing Minority Commu-
               nity in Indonesia. Ithaca, NY: Cornell University Press.
Wilson, Bryan
  1982   Religion in Sociological Perspective. Oxford: Oxford Univer-
               sity Press.
Wilson, Thomas A.
  2002a   "Ritualizing Confucius/Kongzi: the Family and State Cults of
               the Sage of Culture in Imperial China," in On the Sacred
               Grounds: Culture, Society, Politics, and the Formation of the
               Cult of Confucius. Thomas A. Wilson, ed. Cambridge, MA:
               Harvard University Press.
  2002b   "Sacrifice and the Imperial Cult of Confucius," in History of
               Religions, vol. 41, no. 3.
Wolf, Arthur
  1974   "Gods, Ghosts, and Ancestors," in Religion and Ritual in Chi-
               nese Society. Arthur Wolf, ed. Stanford: Stanford University
               Press. Also in Studies in Chinese Society. Arthur Wolf, ed.
               Stanford: Stanford University Press, 1978.
Wright, David
  2001   "Yan Fu and the Tasks of the Translator," in New Terms for
               New Ideas: Western Knowledge and Lexical Change in Late
               Imperial China. Michael Lackner, Iwo Amelung, and Joachim
               Kurtz, eds. Leiden: E. J. Brill.
Wu, Jiao
  2007   "Religious Believers Thrice the Official Estimate: Poll," in
               China Daily, February 7.

Xia, Ming, and Shiping Hua, eds.
1999   "The Battle between the Chinese Government and Falun
            Gong," in *Chinese Law and Government*, vol. 32, no. 5
            (September/October).

Xu, Xiaoqun
2001   *Chinese Professionals and the Republican State: The Rise of
            Professional Associations in Shanghai, 1912–1927.* Cam-
            bridge: Cambridge University Press.

Xuan, Fang
2007   "Buddhism in Contemporary China." Lecture presented in
            the Departments of Religious Studies and East Asian Studies,
            University of California at Santa Barbara, April 6.

Yang, C. K.
1961   *Religion in Chinese Society.* Berkeley and Los Angeles: Uni-
            versity of California Press.

Yang, Huaizhong
1991   "Sufism among the Muslims in Gansu, Ningxia, and Qing-
            hai," in *Minority Nationalities of China: Language and
            Culture.* Charles Li and Dru Gladney, eds., Unpublished
            manuscript.

Yang, Huilin
2004   "Inculturation or Contextualization: Interpretation of Chris-
            tianity in the Context of Chinese Culture," in *Contemporary
            Chinese Thought*, vol. 36, no. 1 (Fall).

Yang, Huilin, and Daniel H. N. Yeung, eds.
2006   *Sino-Christian Studies in China.* Cambridge: Cambridge
            Scholars Press.

Yang, Mayfair Mei-hui
1994a   "A Sweep of Red: State Subjects and the Cult of Mao," in
            Mayfair Mei-hui Yang, *Gifts, Favors, and Banquets: The Art
            of Social Relationships in China.* Ithaca, NY: Cornell Univer-
            sity Press.
1994b   *Gifts, Favors, and Banquets: The Art of Social Relationship
            in China.* Ithaca, NY: Cornell University Press.
1996   "Tradition, Traveling Anthropology, and the Discourse of
            Modernity in China," in *The Future of Anthropological
            Knowledge.* Henrietta Moore, ed. New York: Routledge
            Curzon.
1997   "Mass Media and Transnational Subjectivity in Shanghai:
            Notes on (Re)cosmopolitanism in a Chinese Metropolis," in
            *Ungrounded Empires: The Cultural Politics of Modern Chi-
            nese Transnationalism.* Aihwa Ong and Donald Nonini, eds.
            New York: Routledge Curzon.

1999   "Introduction," in *Spaces of Their Own: Women's Public Sphere in Transnational China*. Mayfair Yang, ed. Minneapolis: University of Minnesota Press.

2000   "Putting Global Capitalism in its Place: Economic Hybridity, Bataille, and Ritual Expenditure," in *Current Anthropology*, vol. 41, no. 4.

2004   "Spatial Struggles: State Disenchantment and Popular Reappropriation of Space in Rural Southeast China," in *Journal of Asian Studies*, vol. 63, no. 3.

N.d.   "Re-enchanting Modernity: Sovereignty, Ritual Economy, and Indigenous Civil Order in Coastal China." Book manuscript in progress.

Ye, Xiaowen

1996   "On the Importance of Sincerely Implementing the 'Three Sentences' When Carrying Out Religious Work," in *China Study Journal*, vol. 11, no. 2. Translated from *Renmin ribao* March 14, 1996.

Ying, Fuk Tsang

2007   "New Wine in Old Wineskins—An Appraisal of China's Religious Legislation and the 'Regulations on Religious Affairs,'" in *China Study Journal* (Spring/Summer).

Yu, Anthony

2005   *State and Religion in China*. Chicago: Open Court Publishing.

Yu, David C.

1990   "Religious Studies in China at Crossroads," in *Journal of Chinese Religions*, vol. 18.

Zarrow, Peter

1997   "Introduction: Citizenship in China and the West," in *Imagining the People, Chinese Intellectuals and the Concept of Citizenship, 1890–1920*. Joshua A. Fogel and Peter G. Zarrow, eds. Armonk, NY: M. E. Sharpe, Inc.

Zheng, Yuan

2001   "The Status of Confucianism in Modern Chinese Education, 1901–49: A Curricular Study," in *Education, Culture, and Identity in Twentieth-Century China*. Glen Peterson, Ruth Hayhoe, and Yongling Lu, eds. Ann Arbor: University of Michigan Press.

Zhou, Kate Xiao

1996   *How the Farmers Changed China: Power of the People*. Boulder, CO: Westview Press.

Zhu, Xiaoyang, and Benjamin Penny, eds.

1994   "The Qigong Boom," in *Chinese Sociology and Anthropology*, vol. 27, no. 1 (Fall).

Zhuo, Xinping
  2001   "Discussion of Cultural Christians in China," in *China and
             Christianity: Burdened Past, Hopeful Future*. Stephen Uhalley,
             Jr., and Xiaoxin Wu, eds. Armonk, NY: M. E. Sharpe, Inc.

Zito, Angela
  1997   *Of Body and Brush: Grand Sacrifice as Text/Performance in
             Eighteenth-Century China*. Chicago: University of Chicago
             Press.

Glossary and Chinese Proper Names

aiguo aijiao 愛國愛教　"Love one's country, love one's religion"; a Communist Party slogan

Bailianhui 白蓮會　White Lotus Society

Bailianjiao 白蓮教　White Lotus Teachings/Sect

Baiyunguan 白雲觀　White Cloud Daoist Monastery in Beijing (Quanzhen Daoist Order); since the 1950s, it has been the national headquarters of the Daoist Association

banghui 幫會　underworld gang

baojiao 保教　protecting the (Confucian) teachings

Bazhi Toutuo 八指頭陀　Abbot Bazhi (Jing'an 敬安, 1852–1912), the Buddhist abbot who directed the General Association of Chinese Buddhists (Zhonghua Fojiao Zonghui)

bentuhua 本土化　indigenization; said of Taiwan's process of realigning national identity away from the history of Chinese civilization, and toward local Taiwanese history and culture

buabui 擲筊　to cast wooden divination crescents (Taiwanese pronunciation)

bujing 不經　noncanonical

burufa 不如法　insufficiently dharmic

Chen Duxiu 陳獨秀　(1879–1942) Marxist intellectual and a leader of the May Fourth New Culture Movement, founder of the journal New Youth, founding member of the Chinese Communist Party, and influential critic of religion and superstition

Chen Huanzhang 陳煥章　(1881–1933) leader of the Confucian Association (Kongjiao Hui, established 1912), an organization promoting Confucian teachings as national religion

Chen Mingbin 陳明霖　(1854–1936) a former abbot of the White Cloud Daoist Temple in Beijing

Chen Yingning 陳櫻寧 (1880–1969) early twentieth-century leader, writer, and reformer of modern Daoism

Chuan Xin Dian 傳心殿 Hall of Esoteric Transmission

chujia 出家 "leave the family"; said of those who become Buddhist monks

cibei jingshi 慈悲警示 "mercy warnings"; an example of Falungong's theme of divine retribution

Ciji Gongdehui 慈濟功德會 Ciji (Tzu Chi) Foundation; the Buddhist Compassionate Relief Association, based in Taiwan

dabei 大悲 Great Compassion, a Buddhist concept

Dajiyuan 大紀元 Epoch Times, a newspaper with links to Falungong

danwei 單位 work-unit; a multifunctional productive organism in China—in line with the planned economy and socialist politics, it functioned for both social control and social integration

daochang 道場 Daoist ritual or prayer service; the enclosed space set up for a Daoist ritual performance

Daode Xueshe 道德學社 Society for the Study of Morality

Daodehui 道德會 Morality Society, an early twentieth-century syncretistic redemptive society

daohui 道會 cultivation society; a term used by Chinese Communists to describe a secret religious society

Daojiao Hui 道教會 Daoist Association; the first national Daoist association, formed in 1912 at the initiative of Chen Mingbin (1854–1936)

Daojiao hui dagang 道教會大綱 Outline of the Daoist Society

Daolu Si 道錄司 Daoist Clerical Administration, in the Chinese imperial government

daomen 道門 "cultivation lineage"; a term used by Chinese Communists to describe a secret religious society

Daoyuan 道院 School of the Way, a nationally organized religious and philanthropic society founded in 1921

dasi 大祀 grand sacrifice; the highest level of imperial Chinese state sacrifices, where the emperor pays homage to Heaven (or Tian), Earth, Spirits of Land-and-Grain, and imperial ancestors

datong 大同 Great Unity; an ancient Confucian utopian ideal of the perfect society of good government, equal distribution, social nurturing of the needy, and peace and harmony

difangzhi 地方志 local gazetteer

Ding Guangxun 丁光訓 (K. H. Ting, 1915–) Chinese Protestant leader

Dongfang Shandian 東方閃電 Oriental Lightning, an underground Christian sect banned by the Chinese Communist Party

du jing 讀經 the study of the Confucian/Chinese classics

Fagushan 法鼓山 Dharma Drum Mountain, a Buddhist organization based outside Taibei, Taiwan

Falungong 法輪功 Practice of the Wheel of the Law; a religious organization promoting exercise and meditation founded in 1990s China and banned in China since 1999

fandong huidaomen 反動會道門 reactionary secret societies (see huidaomen, huimen)

Faqing 法慶 (515 c.e.) leader of a Buddhist-inspired rebellion against the Northern Wei dynasty

feifa zongjiao 非法宗教 illegal religion

feili 廢曆 abolished calendar

fengjian 封建 feudal

fengjian sengfa 封建僧閥 "monk-lords of feudalism"; the Chinese Communist label for a type of criminality imposed on Buddhist clergy

fengshui 風水 Chinese geomancy; an ancient spiritual technology based on harmonizing human physical constructions (tombs, temples, houses) with the flow of qi, or primal energies, through the landscape, bodies of water, and mountains

fenling 分靈 "dividing spirit"; to start up a new branch temple from an older temple

fenxiang 分香 "dividing incense"; to take incense ash from a mother temple to start up an offspring temple in a new location

fenzuo 分胙 to distribute sacrificial food among people after the rite of offerings

Foguangshan 佛光山 Buddha's Light Mountain, a Buddhist organization based outside the city of Gaoxiong, Taiwan

Fojiao Hui 佛教會 Buddhist Association, established in Nanjing in 1912 by Ouyang Jian (1870–1943)

futi 附體 "have something attached to one's body"; Falungong's notion of spirit possession

gailiang 改良 reform

ganying 感應 sympathetic resonance, an ancient Chinese concept

Ge Mingxin 葛明新 (1854–1934) early twentieth-century Daoist leader based at the Taiqing Daoist Temple in the city of Shenyang

Gelaohui 哥老會 Elders' Society, a secret society that started at end of the Qing dynasty and flourished in early twentieth-century China

gongji 公祭 collective offering or sacrifice

Guandi 關帝 the God of War

Guanli zongjiao zhi yijian shu 管理宗教之意見書 Recommendations for the Management of Religions

Guanyin Famen 觀音法門 Guanyin Dharma Gate, a Taiwan Buddhist organization banned by the Chinese Communist Party in China

Guiyi Daoyuan 歸一道院 School of the Way of the Return to Oneness

guoji youhao jiaoliu 國際友好交流 international friendly exchange; encouraged in Communist China for religions such as Buddhism and Islam to contribute to the state's foreign relations

guomin 國民 people of the nation, citizen, citizenry, national (J. kokumin)

guomin jiaoyu 國民教育 national education; elementary education (J. kokumin kyōiku)

Han Shantong 韓山童 (?–1351) leader of the Red Turbans Revolt at end of Yuan dynasty

Hongqianghui 紅槍會 Red Spears Society, an early twentieth-century voluntary self-defense organization

Hongwanzihui 紅卍字會 Red Swastika Society, an early twentieth-century redemptive society

Hu Songshan 虎嵩山 (1880–1956) Muslim disciple of the Chinese Muslim leader Ma Wanfu

Huhanpai 呼喊派 the Shouters, an underground Christian sect banned by the Chinese Communist Party

Hui jiao 回教 the Hui teaching; Islam in China (also referred to as Yisilanjiao 伊斯蘭教 "teachings of Islam")

hui niangjia 回娘家 "returning to her mother's home"; said of a married-out daughter returning to her natal home to visit her mother

huidaomen 會道門 popular religious societies (see fandong huidaomen, huimen)

Huijiaotu 回教徒 Hui religious disciple; Chinese Muslim

huilai renqin 回來認親 coming back to recognize or reconnect with one's kin

huimen 會門 secret society (see fandong huidaomen, huidaomen)

Huizu 回族 Chinese Muslims (regarded in China as both an ethnic minority as well as religious group) who are more assimilated into the dominant Han Chinese culture than other Muslim ethnic groups like the Uyghurs and Kazaks

huofo 活佛 "living buddha"; a reincarnated lama or Buddhist teacher

Huoshen 火神 the God of Fire

Jiang Zemin 江澤民 (1926–) General Secretary of the Chinese Communist Party, 1993–2003

jiao 教 teachings

jiaohua 教化 moral education

jiaomen 教門 teaching lineage

jiaoquan 教權　theocracy

Jiaqing 嘉慶　(1760–1820) Qing-dynasty emperor, or the name of his reign period (1796–1820)

jie 界　(social) sector; bounded space

jiebai dixiong 結拜弟兄　sworn brotherhood

jiehui shudang 結會豎黨　"creating associations and forming cliques"

jiemei miao 姊妹廟　sister temples, referring to temples who share the same ancestry: being branch temples of an older goddess temple

Jieyue Yundong 節約運動　Frugality Movement, launched by the Guomindang in late 1920s

jinhualun 進化論　evolutionism; theory of evolution, especially social evolution

jinxiang 進香　pilgrimage (literally, "presenting incense")

jisi 祭祀　sacrifices and rites

jisiquan 祭祀圈　ritual circles; the bounded space of a localized community's ritual activities; localized ritual territory or jurisdiction of local god(s)

jiushi 救世　to save the world, redemption

Jiushi Xinjiaohui 救世新教會　Association of the New Teachings for World Salvation

junyu 餕餘　to feast on sacrificial food after it has been offered to the deity

Juzan 巨贊　(1908–84) Buddhist clerical leader and scholar who worked with the Chinese Communist Party to reform Buddhism

Kang Youwei 康有為　(1858–1927) Confucian scholar, reformer, and utopian thinker; instrumental in the short-lived Hundred Days Reform (Wuxu Bianfa) at the end of the Qing dynasty

Kongjiao Hui/Kongjiaohui 孔教會　Confucius Association, established in October 1912 and presided over by Chen Huanzhang (1881–1933); and/or the movement to establish Confucianism as a national religion

Kongmiao 孔廟　Confucius Temple

Kwee Tek Hoay 郭德懷　(1886–1952) Peranakan writer, dramatist, reformer, and founder of the Sam Kauw Hwee in the Dutch Indies

li 禮　ritual, ritual vessels, rite, etiquette, decorum, propriety

Li Hongzhi 李洪志　(1951–) founder of Falungong, the banned religious group

li, yi, lian, chi 禮義廉恥　propriety, justice, honesty and shame/modesty—four Confucian virtues

lianhualao 蓮花落　a type of beggar song

lianhuanaozhe 蓮花鬧者　singing beggars who sang folksongs about ghosts in the early twentieth century

Liang Qichao 梁啟超   (1873–1929) scholar, journalist, and reformer who took part in the Hundred Days Reform (Wuxu Bianfa) at the end of the Qing dynasty

Libu 禮部   Board of Rites or Ministry of Ritual in imperial China

Lidai Diwang 歷代帝王   emperors of previous dynasties

Lin Shuangwen 林爽文   seventeenth-century rebel leader in Taiwan

ling 靈   efficacy, divine power

Linglinghui 靈靈會   Church of Spirits, an underground Christian sect banned by the Chinese Communist Party

Lixue Guan 禮學館   Bureau for Studying the Rites in imperial China

Longshen 龍神   the Dragon God

lunli 倫理   ethics

Ma Bufang 馬步芳   Chinese Muslim warlord and Islamic reformer in Northwest China in the early twentieth century

Ma Linyi 馬鄰翼   President of the Muslim Association for Mutual Progress in the early twentieth century

Ma Wanfu 馬萬福   (1853–1934) Chinese Muslim leader who studied in Arabia

Mazu 媽祖   literally, "ancestral mother"; a maritime goddess worshipped in southeastern China since the Song dynasty

Meizhou dao 湄洲島   Meizhou Island, located off Fujian Province; the home of the Mazu goddess

Mentuhui 門徒會   Assembly of Disciples, an underground Christian sect banned by the Chinese Communist Party

miaochan xingxue 廟產興學   "building schools with temple properties"; part of the 1898 Wuxu Bianfa (Hundred Days Reform) at the end of the Qing dynasty, in which the Qing court called for converting Buddhist and Daoist temples and monasteries, and lineage ancestor halls, into modern schools

mimi jieshe 秘密結社   secret association

mimi shehui 秘密社會   secret society

minjian huodong 民間活動   civil nongovernmental activity

Minzu Saomu Jie 民族掃墓節   National Tomb-Sweeping Day

mixin 迷信   superstition; term introduced from the West

neidan 內丹   "inner alchemy"; Daoist self- and body-cultivation techniques that focus on internal mind-body processes instead of the ingesting of plant and chemical substances, which is called "outer alchemy" (waidan)

nong chan bingzhong 農禪幷重   combining Chan (meditation, rituals, and other religious activities) with agricultural work

Nongchan Si 農禪寺　Chan Agricultural Temple

Omituo Fo 阿彌陀佛　Amitabha Buddha; the repeated chanting of Amitabha's name that is common practice in Pure Land Buddhism

Ouyang Jian 歐陽漸　founder of the Chinese Buddhist Society in 1912 in Nanjing

Puli fahui 普利法會　Buddhist prayer meeting

Qianshan Wuliangguan千山無量觀　Wuliang Daoist Monastery on Qian Mountain

qigong 氣功　literally, "breath training"; breath control for cosmic energy

Qingzhen jiao 清真教　Pure and True Teaching; Islam (see huijiao)

Quan Fanwei Jiaohui 全範圍教會　Complete Domain Church, an underground Christian sect banned by the Chinese Communist Party

Quanxuepian 勸學篇　Exhortation to Learning, written by Zhang Zhidong (1837–1909) in 1898, calling for the teaching of core Chinese values and learning as the essence, and Western learning as a means, or for mere utility

Quanzhen 全真　Quanzhen Daoist Order, founded in the twelfth century

qunsi 群祀　miscellaneous sacrifice; the lowest level of the state sacrifices in imperial China

rencai 人才　people of talent

renjian fojiao 人間佛教　this-worldly Buddhism; emphasizes civic participation, charitable activities, and good deeds in this world

rushi wei chushi 入世為出世　"entering the world in order to leave the world"

Sam Kauw Hwee (or Sanjiaohui) 三教會　Three-in-One Society; a syncretistic sect that combines Buddhist, Daoist, and Confucian teachings; also known as Tridharma in Southeast Asia

sangang wuchang 三綱五常　Three Cardinal Principles (the hierarchical relationships between emperor and subject, father and son, and husband and wife) and Five Constant Virtues (humaneness, rightness, propriety, wisdom, and fidelity)—the inviolable norms of human society according to Confucian thought

sangui jiukou 三跪九叩　"three kneelings and nine prostrations"; a gesture of highest respect or obeisance

sanjiao 三教　the three religions (Confucianism, Buddhism, Daoism)

santan dajie 三壇大戒　Great Commandments of the Three Altars, a Chinese Buddhist ceremony through which the novices are officially ordained as monks or nuns

santong 三通　the three direct links (between Mainland China and Taiwan) of communication, transportation, and trade

Sanzi Aiguo Yundong 三自愛國運動 Three-Self Patriotic Movement (TSPM)—namely, being "self-governing, self-supporting, and self-propagating"; an effort by the Chinese Communist Party to reform Christianity in China and detach it from dependence on the West

Seng Jiaoyu Hui 僧教育會 Associations for Sangha Education, founded 1907–10 by Buddhist leaders and local gentry in some parts of China

Senglu Si 僧錄司 Buddhist Clerical Administration, in the imperial Chinese government

Shangding 上丁 the first ding days of the second and eighth months of spring and autumn, the designated dates for the state cult of Confucius

shanshu 善書 morality books; popular moral teachings that flourished with the printing revolution of the Song dynasty

shaobaixiang shaorouxiang 燒拜香燒肉香 burning of incense and mortification of one's own flesh as incense offering in penitence

Sheji 社稷 Spirits of Land-and-Grain

Shenci cunfei biaozhun 神祠存廢標準 "Standards for Retaining or Abolishing Deity Temples," a policy statement issued by the Nationalist government in 1928; a Chinese-government publication that defines the acts to which the "freedom of religious belief" granted in the 1912 Constitution apply

shengchanhua 生產化 shift to production; make productive

shenghuohua 生活化 adaptation to (practical everyday) life

shengren 聖人 sage

Shengyan Fashi 聖嚴法師 (1930–) Dharma Master Shengyan, Buddhist monk who founded the Dharma Drum Mountain Buddhist organization in Taiwan

Shennong 神農 the God of Agriculture

shenxue jianshe 神學建設 theological reconstruction

Shiji 史記 Records of the Historian, written by Sima Qian (ca. 145–86 b.c.e.) of the Han dynasty

shuyuan 書院 academy; nonofficial schools for classical learning in imperial China

sixiang gaizao 思想改造 thought reform, especially in Communist China

Sun Zuomin 孫祚民 leading 1950s Chinese historian of peasant rebellions

Taipingdao 太平道 Way of Supreme Peace; the millenarian movement whose leader, Zhang Jue, launched the Yellow Turban Rebellion in 184 c.e

Taiqing Gong 太清宮 Taiqing Daoist Monastery

Taixu 太虛 (1890–1947) Buddhist monk-reformer of the early twentieth century who advocated "this-worldly Buddhism" (*renjian fojiao*), or doing good works for society in one's lifetime

Tian 天 Heaven; the supreme deity

Tiandihui 天地會 Heaven and Earth Society; religious secret society that dates back to the late eighteenth century, also known as the Triads

tianming 天命 the Mandate of Heaven

Tianxian Miaodao 天仙廟道 Way of the Temple of the Heavenly Immortals

tianzi 天子 the Son of Heaven; emperor

Tiong Hoa Hwe Koan (or THHK) 中華會館 Chinese Association in the Dutch Indies, early twentieth century; also known as Zhonghua Huiguan

Toapekong 大伯公 name for Chinese gods in Southeast Asia

Tongmenghui 同盟會 United Alliance Society; the nationalist revolutionary organization founded by Dr. Sun Zhongsan (Sun Yat-sen)

Tongshanshe 同善社 Fellowship of Goodness, established in 1917

tongsi 通祀 general worship or sacrifice

Tongxinshantang 同心善堂 Unified Heart Charitable Society

tongzhi jituan 統治集團 governing group or ruling class

tudi gaige 土地改革 Land Reform, 1950–53

Wang Haoran 王浩然 an early twentieth-century Chinese Muslim reformist ahong (imam), based in a Beijing mosque and with experience traveling in the Middle East

Wang Lijun 王理鈞 early twentieth-century Daoist abbot of Wuliang Daoist Monastery on Mount Qian in Manchuria

Wang Lun 王倫 (?–1774) leader of peasant rebellion in the Qing dynasty

Wang Yousan 王友三 an early twentieth-century Chinese Muslim reformist ahong (imam), based in a Beijing mosque and with experience traveling in the Middle East

wangdao 王道 the "kingly way" of the ethical monarch

wangguo 亡國 extinction of the country or nation

Wanguo Daodehui 萬國道德會 Universal Morality Society

wanrenyuanhui 萬人願會 prayer service for the dead

wansui longpai 萬歲龍牌 dragon tablet of longevity; a wooden plaque that bears the official title of the head of the imperial household, used in ritual to identify the recipient of sacrifice and obeisance

Wenchang 文昌 the God of Literature

wenmiao 文廟 temples of civil culture

wenming 文明 civilization

wu 巫 ancient Chinese shamanism or shamans

Wujiaoheyi 五教合一 Five-in-One Religions

wuwei 無畏 fearlessness; dauntlessness

Wuxu Bianfa 戊戌變法 Hundred Days Reform Movement at end of Qing dynasty, 1898

Wuzong 武宗 Emperor Wuzong of the Yuan dynasty, who banned the White Lotus Sect in 1308

Xiandi 先帝 imperial ancestors, or Spirits of Former Emperors

xianghui 香會 "incense society"; piety association or organization of worshippers of a common deity

Xiantiandao 先天道 Way of Anterior Heaven; a secret society operating around the Wuxi area in the 1930s

Xianyi 先醫 Spirits of Former Physicians

xiao 孝 filial piety

xie 邪 evil, heterodox

xiejiao 邪教 heterodoxy, heretical teaching, "evil cult"

xieshuo 邪說 heretical sayings

Xingtiangong 行天宮 Enacting Heaven's Business Temple, in Taiwan

Xingyun Fashi 星雲法師 (1927–) Dharma Master Xingyun, founder of Foguangshan Buddhist organization in Taiwan

xinjiao ziyou 信教自由 freedom of religious belief (see *zongjiao xinyang ziyou*)

xinxing zongjiao 新興宗教 new religion

xinyangquan 信仰圈 belief circles; larger regional cults devoted to a single deity

Xinyue jiaohui 新約教會 New Testament Church, an underground Christian sect banned by Chinese Communist Party

Xinzheng 新政 the New Policies of the late Qing dynasty; program of political reforms initiated in 1902

xiushen 修身 moral (and body) cultivation

xiuxing 修行 practices of self-cultivation

Xu Hongru 徐鴻儒 (?–1622) leader of religious rebellion at end of the Ming dynasty

Xuan Kong 玄空 (1911–) founder of Xingtiangong in Taiwan

Xuanyanshu 宣言書 Proclamation Letter

Xuebu 學部 Board of Learning, or Ministry of Education, in late imperial government

xuehua 血花 sprays of blood

xueshuhua 學術化 shift to scholarship; academicization

xuexiban 學習班 study group; a form of social mobilization in Communist China in which small groups are formed to study doctrinal texts for ideological inculcation

xunzheng 訓政　political tutelage

yanhui 宴會　banquet

yiduan 異端　heresy

Yiguandao 一貫道　Way of Pervasive Unity, a syncretistic religious organization

yinci 淫祠　licentious shrines, or illicit temples and cults; a phrase used in late imperial Chinese official discourse to describe illicit religious organizations that needed suppression

yinsi 淫祀　illicit or licentious cults, or temples (see xiejiao)

yixue 儀學　Chinese schools in the nineteenth- and early twentieth-century Dutch Indies

yu shehui zhuyi shehui xiangshiying 與社會主義社會相適應　"adaptation to socialist society"; required by the Chinese Communist Party of all religious traditions practicing in China

Yuan Shikai 袁世凱　(1859–1916) first president of the Republic of China

yuanman 圓滿　consummation, the ultimate state of liberation that Falungong practitioners hope to attain

Yulanbanghui 盂蘭牓會　Ghost Festival, see Yulanpenhui, Zhongyuanjie

Yulanpenhui 盂蘭盆會　Ghost Festival, see Yulanbanghui, Zhongyuanjie

Zailijiao 在理教　Teaching of the Abiding Principle

zan 贊　the ceremonial master who announces the movements of the primary worshipper during a rite

Zhang Guangbi 張光璧　(1889–1947) leader of the Yiguandao secret religious organization in the 1930s

Zhang Jue 張角　(184 c.e.) charismatic healer and leader of the Yellow Turban Rebellion in the Han dynasty

Zhang Tianshi 張天師　the Zhang Heavenly Master; hereditary Daoist religious leaders since Zhang Daoling in the Han dynasty

Zhang Yuanxu 張元旭　(?–1924) sixty-second generation of the Heavenly Master lineage of Daoism in 1904; founder of the General Daoist Association (Zhonghua Minguo Daojiao Zonghui) in early twentieth-century China

Zhang Zhidong 張之洞　(1837–1909) Qing-dynasty official and reformer associated with the Xinzheng (New Policies) reforms

Zhang Ziwen 張子文　an early twentieth-century Chinese Muslim reformist ahong (imam), based in a Beijing mosque and with experience traveling in the Middle East

Zhanglaohui 長老會　the Elders Society (Presbyterian Church)

Zhao Puchu 趙朴初　(1907–2000) lay Buddhist leader and former head of the Buddhist Association of China (BAC); worked with Chinese Communist Party to reform Chinese Buddhism

Zhao Zhizhong 趙至中 early twentieth-century Daoist abbot of the Baiyun Daoist Monastery in Shanghai

zhen, shan, ren 真善忍 "truthfulness, compassion, and forbearance"; teachings of Falungong

zheng 正 upright, orthodox

zhengjiao 正教 orthodox teaching

zhengquan 政權 a political regime; political power

Zhengyan Fashi 證嚴法師 (1937–) Taiwan Buddhist nun and founder of the Ciji Compassionate Relief Association

Zhengyi 正一 Zhengyi Daoist Order

Zhenkongjiao 真空教 True Emptiness Teaching

Zhenlangong 鎮瀾宮 one of Taiwan's most prominent Mazu temples; in central Taiwan

Zhongguo Fojiao Hui 中國佛教會 Chinese Buddhist Association, established in 1929, recognized by the Guomindang government, and the most important Buddhist association in China until 1949

Zhongguo Fojiao Xiehui 中國佛教協會 Buddhist Association of China (BAC), established in 1953 by Chinese Communist Party and Buddhist leaders in Beijing

Zhongguo Huijiao Jujin Hui 中國回教俱進會 Muslim Association for Mutual Progress, founded in Peking in July 1912

Zhongguo Qigong Kexue Yanjiu Hui 中國氣功科學研究會 Chinese Association for Scientific Research into Qigong

Zhongguo Sanjiao Shengdao Zonghui 中國三教聖道總會 Association of the Sagely Way of China's Three Teachings

Zhongguo Yisilanjiao Xiehui 中國伊斯蘭教協會 China Islamic Affairs Association, established in 1953

Zhonghua Fojiao Zonghui 中華佛教總會 General Association of Chinese Buddhists, founded in Shanghai in 1912, directed by Abbot Bazhi (1852–1912)

Zhonghua Huiguan 中華會館 Chinese Association in the Dutch Indies, early twentieth century; also known as Tiong Hoa Hwe Koan, or THHK

Zhonghua Minguo Daojiao Zonghui 中華民國道教總會 General Daoist Association, was established in Shanghai by the Sixty-Second Heavenly Master, Zhang Yuanxu (?–1924)

Zhongnanhai 中南海 literally, "Middle and North Lake"; headquarters of the Chinese Communist Party in Beijing and former residence of Chairman Mao Zedong

Zhongnimiao 仲尼廟 Confucius temple

zhongsi 中祀　middle sacrifice; the second highest level of the state sacrifices in imperial China

zhongxue wei ti, xixue wei yong 中學為體, 西學為用　"Chinese learning for the essence, Western learning for the application"; adhere to Chinese cultural values as the core, but employ Western technology as a means

Zhongyuan jie 中元節　the fifteenth day of the seventh lunar month; Ghost Festival, see Yulanbanghui, Yulanpenhui

Zhu De 朱德　(1886–1976) Chinese Communist general of the Red Army and military strategist

Zhu Yuanzhang 朱元璋　(1328–98) founder and first emperor of the Ming dynasty; his reign period (1368–98)

Zhuan Falun 轉法輪　Rotating the Wheel of the Law; key text of the organization Falungong, written by Li Hongzhi (1951–)

zhuanhua 轉化　to reconvert

zongjiao 宗教　literally, "teachings of a religious school or sect"; the Chinese term used to translate the modern Western notion of "religion"

zongjiao huodong 宗教活動　religious event or activity

zongjiao xinyang ziyou 宗教信仰自由　freedom of religious belief (see *xinjiao ziyou*)

Zongjiao Zhexue Yanjiushe 宗教哲學研究社　Society for the Study of Religious Philosophy

zongjiao zhihang 宗教直航　direct religious sealink (between Mainland China and Taiwan)

zunjing pai 尊經派　"faction that venerates the scriptures"; another name for the Yihewani, a Chinese Muslim sect

Contributors

JOSÉ IGNACIO CABEZÓN is the XIVth Dalai Lama Professor of Tibetan Buddhism at the University of California, Santa Barbara. He is the author of the online book collection *The Hermitages of Sera*, which includes essays, images, and interactive maps on the Tibetan monastery; *Freedom from Extremes: Gorampa's "Distinguishing the Views" and the Polemics of Emptiness* (2006); and *Buddhism and Language: A Study of Indo-Tibetan Scholasticism* (1994).

PRASENJIT DUARA 杜贊奇 is Professor of History at the University of Chicago. He is the author of *Culture, Power and the State: Rural North China, 1900–1942* (1988), *Rescuing History from the Nation* (1995), and *Sovereignty and Authenticity: Manchukuo and the East Asian Modern* (2003). In 2008 he joined the National University of Singapore as Director of Research in Humanities and Social Sciences.

RYAN DUNCH 唐日安 is Associate Professor in the Department of History and Classics and Chair of East Asian Studies at the University of Alberta in Edmonton, Canada. He is the author of *Fuzhou Protestants and the Making of a Modern China, 1857–1927* (2001), as well as articles and book reviews. His current research is on missionary publishing in Chinese before 1911. He also serves as one of the editors of the online Asian Studies scholarly network, H-ASIA.

DRU C. GLADNEY 杜磊 is President of the Pacific Basin Institute and Professor of Anthropology at Pomona College in Claremont, California. His books include *Muslim Chinese: Ethnic Nationalism in the People's Republic* (1991, 1996); *Ethnic Identity in China: The Making of a Muslim Minority Nationality* (1998); and *Dislocating China: Muslims, Minorities, and Other Sub-Altern Subjects* (2004).

VINCENT GOOSSAERT 高萬桑 is a research fellow at the Centre National de la Recherche Scientifique, Paris, and since 2004 has served as Deputy Director of the Societies-Religions-Secularisms Institute (GSRL, Paris). His most recent book is *The Taoists of Peking, 1800–1949: A Social History of Urban Clerics* (2007), and he is coauthor with David Palmer of the forthcoming *The Religious Question in Modern China*. He is directing an international research project (2007–2010) on "Taoists and Temples in modern Modern Chinese Cities" and writing monographs on the politics of religion in late Qing China and on Chinese religious specialists.

JI ZHE 汲喆 is a postdoctoral fellow at the Societies-Religions-Secularisms Institute (GSRL) at the Centre National de la Recherche Scientifique, Paris. He is interested in issues of religious recomposition in contemporary Chinese societies, such as the revitalization of Buddhism, the reinvention of Confucianism, and the increasing youth religiosity. His articles have appeared in *Perspectives Chinoises, Social Compass, Cahiers internationaux de sociologie,* and other journals.

YA-PEI KUO 郭亞珮 is Assistant Professor of History at Tufts University in Boston. She earned her doctorate from the Department of History, Univeristy of Wisconsin-Madison. Her forthcoming book is tentatively entitled *Culture, Identity, and History: Critical Review and Conservatism in Modern China.*

RICHARD MADSEN 趙文詞 is Distinguished Professor and Chair of the Sociology Department at the University of California, San Diego, and a coauthor (with Robert Bellah et al.) of *The Good Society* (1991) and the award-winning *Habits of the Heart* (1985). His books on China include *Morality and Power in a Chinese Village* (1984), for which he received the C. Wright Mills Award, and *Democracy's Dharma: Religious Renaissance and Political Development in Taiwan* (2007).

REBECCA NEDOSTUP 張倩雯 is Assistant Professor of Chinese history at Boston College. Her forthcoming book, tentatively entitled *Superstitious Regimes: Religion and the Politics of Chinese Modernity,* focuses on the Nationalist era. Her research has also appeared in the *International Review of Social History,* in Dennis Washburn and A. Kevin Reinart, eds., *Converting Cultures* (2007), and in Sarah Schneewind, ed., *Long Live the Emperor!* (2008).

DAVID A. PALMER 宗樹人 is Assistant Professor in the Department of Sociology at Hong Kong University. He received his Ph.D. from the École Pratique des Hautes Études (Sorbonne, Paris) in 2002. His book *Qigong Fever: Body, Science, and Utopia in China* was published in 2007, and he is completing book manuscripts on *The Religious Question in Modern China* (with Vincent Goossaert) and *Global Taoism: The Search for Authenticity* (with Elijah Siegler).

BENJAMIN PENNY 裴凝 is a research scholar at the Division of Pacific and Asian History, Australian National University, specializing in the study of medieval Daoism, religion and spiritual movements in modern and contemporary

China, and the religion of Chinese Australians. He is the editor of *Biography and Religion in China and Tibet* (2002) and *Daoism in History: Essays in Honour of Liu Ts'un-yan* (2006), as well as numerous journal articles and book chapters.

MAFAIR MEI-HUI YANG 楊美惠 is the author of *Gifts, Favors, and Banquets: The Art of Social Relationships in China* (1994), which won the American Ethnological Society book prize; the Chinese translation was published in Taiwan by Nantian Publishing Co., and is forthcoming in China from Jiangsu People's Press. She is also editor of *Spaces of Their Own: Women's Public Sphere in Transnational China* (1999). She has produced two video documentaries, *Through Chinese Women's Eyes* (distributed by Women Make Movies) and *Public and Private Realms in Rural Wenzhou, China* (1994), and is at work on a monograph entitled *Re-enchanting Modernity: Sovereignty, Ritual Economy, and Indigenous Civil Order in Coastal China.*

Index